Contents

KU-496-251

Color section   1–16

Introduction 4
What to see 5
When to go 10
Things not to miss 11

Basics   19–40

Getting there........................... 19
Arrival 23
Getting around........................ 25
Crime and personal safety 28
The media................................ 30
Tourist information 33
Travel essentials 36

The City   41–294

❶ The Harbor Islands 43
❷ The Financial District 50
❸ City Hall Park and the
   Brooklyn Bridge 65
❹ Tribeca and Soho 73
❺ Chinatown, Little Italy, and
   NoLita 82
❻ The Lower East Side 93
❼ The East Village 99
❽ The West Village 107
❾ Chelsea 115
❿ Union Square, Gramercy Park,
   and the Flatiron District 121
⓫ Midtown East 129
⓬ The Museum of Modern
   Art 147
⓭ Midtown West 152
⓮ Central Park 163
⓯ The Metropolitan Museum
   of Art 173
⓰ The Upper East Side 188
⓱ The Upper West Side and
   Morningside Heights 204
⓲ Harlem and above 220
⓳ Brooklyn 237
⓴ Queens 265

㉑ The Bronx 277
㉒ Staten Island 287

Listings   295–456

㉓ Accommodation 295
㉔ Cafés and light meals 314
㉕ Restaurants 329
㉖ Drinking 363
㉗ Nightlife 376
㉘ The performing arts
   and film............................ 383
㉙ Gay and lesbian
   New York 396
㉚ Commercial galleries........ 403
㉛ Shopping 408
㉜ Sports and outdoor
   activities 427
㉝ Parades and festivals........ 440
㉞ Kids' New York 447
㉟ Directory 454

Contexts   457–494

The historical framework........ 459
Books 471
New York on film 480
Glossary 491

Travel store   495–510

Small print & Index 511–528

New York Architecture
color section following
p.144

Ethnic New York color
section following p.336

Color maps following
p.528

3

◀◀ Cantor Roof Garden, Metropolitan Museum of Art ◀ Statue of Liberty

Introduction to

New York City

New York City is everything its supporters and critics claim: an adrenaline-charged, history-laden place that never sleeps, rarely apologizes, and works harder and longer hours than anywhere else. It's also a town of icons, both past and present – you'll find it hard to move about the city without encountering a view of something world-famous, from the lovely green sward of Central Park to the mammoth Brooklyn Bridge to the cathedral-like Grand Central Terminal. The city's boundless energy and spirit will suck you in and make you want to come back again and again.

New York buzzes round-the-clock: not only can you find, buy, or enjoy almost anything 24 hours a day, seven days a week, but there are also enough cultural attractions to fill months of sightseeing. That said, there are some key activities and sights that travelers simply should not miss. Take the city's patchwork of vastly different **neighborhoods**: a stroll from Chinatown through Soho and Tribeca to the West Village reveals the variety of life wedged together in downtown Manhattan. Then there's the city's astonishing **architecture** – you can walk past glorious Art Deco skyscrapers on one block and rows of genteel brownstones on the next – as well as its excellent **museums**, both the celebrated, like the Met and the American Museum of Natural History, and the less well-known but equally worthy, such as the Frick Collection and the Brooklyn Museum. As if the sights weren't enough, New York has an

The **Rough Guide** to

New York City

written and researched by

Martin Dunford

with additional contributions by

Ken Derry, Sean Harvey, and Zora O'Neill

NEW YORK · LONDON · DELHI

www.roughguides.com

exhaustive selection of **shops**, and world-class **restaurants** and **bars** that cater to any taste, budget, and schedule. It is justifiably famous for its diverse **theater scene**, with dozens of venues offering everything from high-gloss Broadway musicals to scruffy avant-garde performance pieces. And if it's **nightlife** you're after, look no further: the city's throbbing, jam-packed clubs are known for their cutting-edge parties and music. In other words, just plan on sleeping once you get home.

What to see

hough New York City officially comprises the central island of **Manhattan** and **four outer boroughs** – Brooklyn, Queens, the Bronx, and Staten Island – to many, Manhattan simply *is* New York. Certainly, whatever your interests, you'll likely spend most of your time here. Understanding the intricacies of Manhattan's layout, and above all getting some grasp on its subway and bus systems, should be your first priority. Most importantly, note that New York is very much a city of neighborhoods, and is therefore best explored on foot. For an overview of each district, plus what to see and do there, turn to the introduction of each chapter.

This guide starts at the southern tip of the island and moves north. **The Harbor Islands** – the Statue of Liberty and Ellis Island – were the first glimpses of New York (and indeed America) for many nineteenth-century immigrants; the latter's history is recalled in its excellent Museum of Immigration. The **Financial District** encompasses the skyscrapers and historic buildings of Manhattan's southern reaches, including Ground Zero, the former World Trade Center site. Immediately east of here is **City Hall**, New York's well-appointed municipal center, and the massive Gothic span of the **Brooklyn Bridge**, while to the west is swanky **Tribeca**, the hub of the city's art scene in the twentieth century but now more of an upscale, outdoor fashion mall; **Soho**,

▲ Hot dog vendor

Getting around in Manhattan

Manhattan can seem a wearyingly complicated place to get around: its **grid-pattern** arrangement looks so straightforward on the map, but can be confusing on foot, and its many subway lines never meet up where you think they should. Don't be intimidated, though – with a little know-how you'll find

the city's **streets** easy to navigate and its **subways and buses** efficient and fast. And if you're at all unsure, just ask – New Yorkers are accurate direction-givers and take a surprising interest in initiating visitors into the great mysteries of their city.

There are a few simple terms that are important to learn. Firstly, "downtown Manhattan," "midtown Manhattan," and "upper Manhattan": **downtown Manhattan** runs from the southern tip of the island to around 14th Street; **midtown Manhattan** stretches from about here to the south end of Central Park; and **upper Manhattan** contains the park itself, the neighborhoods on either side of it, and the whole area to the north. Whatever is north of where you're standing is **uptown** (in other words, uptown trains are northbound, even if you're in upper Manhattan); while whatever's south is **downtown** (downtown trains are southbound even from Soho). As for east and west, those directions are known as **crosstown** – hence "crosstown buses."

Downtown Manhattan is tricky to navigate because it was the first part of the city to be settled, and so streets here have names not numbers, and are somewhat randomly arranged. The most fiendishly confusing part of downtown is the **West Village**, where it's essential to have a map at all times – the illogical tangle of streets is quaint but infuriating; for instance, somehow West 4th and West 11th streets, which should run parallel, actually intersect here. Things are much easier above Houston Street on the East Side and 14th Street on the West: the streets are numbered and follow a strict grid pattern like most other American cities. **Fifth Avenue**, the greatest of the big north–south avenues, cuts through the center of Manhattan until it reaches Central Park, whereupon the avenue runs along its eastern flank; crosstown streets are flagged as East or West (eg W 42nd Street, E 42nd Street) from this dividing line, and building numbers also increase as you walk away from either side of Fifth Avenue.

Note that the island of Manhattan is about **thirteen miles long** from base to tip, and around **two miles wide** at its widest point: as a rule of thumb, allow five minutes to walk each east–west block between avenues, and one to two minutes for each north–south block between streets.

just to the north, also boasts a large number of shops, as well as some historic cast-iron buildings. East of here is **Chinatown**, Manhattan's most densely populated ethnic neighborhood and a vibrant locale great for Chinese food and shopping. Now more a haven for pasta and red sauce than Italians, **Little Italy** next door is slowly being swallowed by Chinatown's hungry expansion, while the **Lower East Side**, traditionally the city's gateway neighborhood for new immigrants – whether German, Jewish, or, more recently, Hispanic – is being gentrified by young urban professionals. The **East** and **West villages** are known for their bars, restaurants, and shops that cater to students, would-be bohemians, and, of course, tourists. **Chelsea** has displaced the West Village as the heart of Manhattan's gay scene, and scooped Soho for

▶ Fifth Avenue crowds

So much to see, so little time...

As noted in our "22 Things not to miss" section (p.11), you can't experience everything New York City has to offer on a single trip. Your best bet is to enjoy the city at your own pace, take in the attractions that interest you most, and remember that you can always come back. The following suggested itineraries are based on what's possible in a day. They're mainly designed around key sights and neighborhoods, and they include suggestions for where to have lunch. Don't be afraid to skip the major attractions, though – just wandering about can be an extremely fulfilling way to see the city.

Three days
- Ellis Island/Statue of Liberty; Financial District (lunch); South Street Seaport; Brooklyn Bridge; Brooklyn Heights.
- East Village; West Village (lunch); Empire State Building; Macy's; Times Square.
- Grand Central Terminal; Rockefeller Center (lunch); St Patrick's Cathedral; Museum of Modern Art; Fifth Avenue shops.

Five days
As above plus...
- Central Park; Metropolitan Museum of Art; Frick Collection; Upper East Side shops.
- Lower East Side; Tenement Museum; Chinatown (lunch); Soho shops.

Seven days
As above plus...
- Lincoln Center; Upper West Side (lunch); Museum of Natural History
- Cathedral of St John the Divine; Columbia University; Harlem; The Cloisters.

On New York's menu

Don't come to New York on a diet or you'll miss out on one of its greatest pleasures: **food**, and lots of it. There's barely a country in the world whose cuisine isn't ably represented somewhere in the city, so while you should do what you can to experiment with a little from everything, there are some types of cuisine in which New York particularly excels. There is **Jewish-American deli fare** on the Lower East Side, such as overstuffed brisket and pastrami sandwiches, smoked fish and bagels, latkes, knishes, and chopped liver. All over town (especially in midtown) you can find traditional **steak joints** serving massive porterhouses and tender sirloins. The city is littered with **pizza**

places serving pancake-flat pies moist with fresh tomatoes and heaped with homemade mozzarella. You'll find pearlescent **dim sum** in Chinatown and you can't throw a stick without hitting a new **sushi** restaurant. This doesn't even really scratch the surface of the cuisines on offer here, including Ethiopian, Brazilian, Jamaican, and Korean, to name but a few. For more details on our picks, see Chapter 25, "Restaurants."

exciting gallery spaces; the area around **Union Square** and **Gramercy Park** features some lovely skyscrapers, including the Flatiron Building, and some of the city's best restaurants. This is where the avenues begin their march north through the busy, regimented blocks of **midtown**, which is punctuated by some of the city's most impressive sights, including Times Square, the Empire State Building, and the **Museum of Modern Art**.

Beyond midtown, the character of the city changes quite rapidly. For more than a dozen blocks, the skyline is relentlessly high-rise, and home to some awe-inspiring architecture; this gives way to first-class museums and appealing stores as you work your way up Fifth Avenue as far as 59th Street. That's where the classic Manhattan vistas are broken by the broad expanse of **Central Park**, a supreme piece of nineteenth-century landscaping. Flanking the park, the **Upper East Side** is wealthier and more grandiose, with many of its nineteenth-century millionaires' mansions now transformed into a string of magnificent museums known as "Museum Mile"; the most prominent of these is the vast **Metropolitan Museum of Art**. The residential neighborhood here is staunchly patrician and boasts some of the swankiest addresses in Manhattan, as well as a nest of designer shops along Madison Avenue in the seventies. On the other side of the park, the largely residential young professional enclave of the **Upper West Side** is worth a visit, mostly for performing arts mecca Lincoln Center, the American Museum of Natural History, and Riverside Park along the Hudson River. Immediately north of Central Park, **Harlem**, the historic black city-within-a-city, has today a healthy sense of an improving community. Still farther north, past the student enclave of **Hamilton Heights**, home to Columbia University, and **Washington Heights**, a largely Hispanic neighborhood that few visitors ever venture to visit, stands Inwood at the tip of the island. It's here you'll find the Cloisters, a nineteenth-century mock-up of a medieval monastery, packed with great European Romanesque and Gothic art and (transplanted) architecture – in short, one of Manhattan's must-sees.

It's an unfortunate fact that few visitors, especially those with limited time, bother to venture off Manhattan Island to the outer boroughs. This is a pity, because each of them – **Brooklyn**, **Queens**, **the Bronx**, and **Staten Island** – has points of great interest, for both historical and contemporary reasons. More than anything, though, some of the city's most vibrant ethnic neighborhoods (and consequently best food) can be found in the outer boroughs: sample the Greek restaurants of the Astoria district in Queens, for example, or the Italian restaurants of the Bronx's Belmont section. If visitors do leave Manhattan, it's usually for Brooklyn, where you can hang out in hip Williamsburg, wander the brownstone-lined streets of Cobble Hill, ride a rickety roller coaster and soak up the old-world charm of Coney Island, or gorge on borscht in the Russian enclave of Brighton Beach.

▼ Times Square

When to go

New York's **climate** ranges from sticky, hot, and humid in mid-summer to chilling in January and February: be prepared to freeze or boil accordingly if you decide to visit during these periods. Spring is gentle, if unpredictable and often wet, while fall is perhaps the best season, with crisp, clear days and warmish nights – either season is a great time to schedule a visit. It goes without saying that whenever you're visiting, plan to dress in layers, as it's the only way to combat overheated buildings in winter and overactive, icy air-conditioning come summertime. As noted above, one of the joys of New York City's compact layout is the ease with which you can sightsee by foot, so make sure to pack a pair of comfortable, sturdy shoes, no matter the season.

Average monthly temperatures and rainfall

	Temp °F		Temp °C		Rainfall	
	Max	Min	Max	Min	Inches	mm
January	38	26	3	-3	3.5	89
February	40	27	4	-3	3.1	79
March	50	35	10	2	4.0	102
April	61	44	16	7	3.8	97
May	72	54	22	12	4.4	112
June	80	63	27	17	3.6	91
July	85	69	29	21	4.4	112
August	84	67	29	19	4.1	104
September	76	60	24	16	4.0	102
October	65	50	18	10	3.4	86
November	54	41	12	5	4.4	112
December	43	31	6	-1	3.8	97

things not to miss

It's not possible to see everything that New York has to offer in one trip, so what follows is a selective taste of the city's highlights: classic restaurants, engaging museums, stunning architecture, and more. They're arranged in color-coded categories, which you can browse through to find the best things to see and do. All entries have a page reference to take you straight into the Guide, where you can find out more.

01 Brooklyn Bridge Page **71** • Take the less-than-a-mile walk across the bridge to see beautiful views of the downtown skyline and the Harbor Islands.

02 Katz's Deli

Page **337** • A slice of the old Lower East Side, with overstuffed sandwiches served up by a wisecracking counterstaff.

05 Halloween Parade Page **445** • One of the more inventive and outrageous of New York's many annual parades.

03 Statue of Liberty Page **44**
• There's no greater symbol of the American dream than the magnificent statue that graces New York Harbor.

04 Museum of Modern Art
Page **147** • Better than ever following a lengthy renovation, this is the most comprehensive collection of modern art in the world.

06 Lower East Side Tenement Museum Page **95** • Excellent guided tours of preserved nineteenth-century tenements make this one of New York's most informative and moving museums.

07 Metropolitan Museum of Art Page **173** • You could easily spend a whole day at the Met, exploring everything from Egyptian artifacts to modern masters.

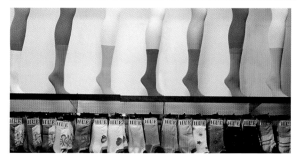

08 Macy's Page **154** • Whether or not it's actually the largest department store in the world, this midtown mammoth still retains something of its old-fashioned charm.

09 Radio City Music Hall
Page **161** • Taking a tour of this Art Deco gem is a midtown must.

10 St John the Divine Page **217**
• Definitely not your ordinary church, the dimensions and history of St John the Divine are remarkable.

11 The Cloisters Page **234** • At the northern tip of Manhattan, this is arguably the island's most peaceful and refined escape, full of gorgeous medieval artwork.

12 Zabar's Page **210** • An Upper West Side institution, and perhaps the ultimate New York gourmet store.

13 Empire State Building Page **129** • Still the most original and elegant skyscraper of them all.

14 **Peter Luger Steak House** Page **359** • This Brooklyn culinary time-warp serves possibly the best steak in the city, with a side order of gruff attitude.

15 **Brooklyn Esplanade** Page **244** • This park-like boardwalk serves as backyard to some of Brooklyn's finest apartment buildings, and provides stellar views of downtown Manhattan.

16 **Rockefeller Center** Page **135** • If anywhere can truly claim to be the center of New York, this elegant piece of twentieth-century urban planning is it.

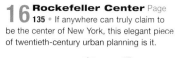

17 **Central Park** Page **163** • Practically everything about Central Park is fantastic, whether it's taking a boat ride, watching Shakespeare in the Park, or picnicking in the Conservatory Garden after a morning spent in a museum.

18 Coney Island Page **257** • Have a hot dog at *Nathan's* and take a ride on the Cyclone roller coaster – though not necessarily in that order.

20 Grand Central Terminal Page **140** • Take a free Wednesday lunchtime tour of this magnificent building to learn the history of the station's majestic concourse.

19 A night at the opera Page **209** • Put on your gladrags for a night out at New York's spectacular Metropolitan Opera at Lincoln Center.

21 The Frick Collection Page **191** • Though he may have been a ruthless coal baron, Henry Frick's discerning eye for art and the easy elegance of his collection's setting make this one of the city's best galleries.

22 Baseball at Yankee Stadium Page **279** • It would be a shame not to go to a ball game if you're here between April and October, and there's no more hallowed ground than the House that (Babe) Ruth Built.

Basics

Basics

Getting there 19

Arrival 23

Getting around 25

Crime and personal safety 28

The media 30

Tourist information 33

Travel essentials 36

Getting there

It's pretty easy to get to New York. The city is on every major airline's itinerary, and with three airports nearby, there is no shortage of incoming daily flights. New York is also a regional hub for train and bus travel and can be reached readily by both, if you don't mind your trip taking a little longer. Several expressways surround the city, making driving another viable option.

From North America

From most places in North America, **flying** is the most convenient way to reach New York. There are **three international airports** within close proximity of the city: **John F. Kennedy (JFK)** (☎718/244-4444), **LaGuardia (LGA)** (☎718/533-3400), and **Newark (EWR)** (☎973/961-6000). New York is, however, also very accessible by other modes of transportation.

By air

New York is a major hub for North American air traffic. All three airports provide daily **flights** to and from most major towns and cities on the continent, as well as a number of shuttles – flights used mainly by business-people during the week – between Boston and Washington DC.

Airfares to New York depend on the season and can fluctuate wildly. The highest prices are generally found between May and September; fares drop between March and April and again in October. You'll get the best prices during the low season, November through February (excluding late November through early January, the holiday season). The lowest **round-trip fares** from the West Coast tend to average around $350–400; from Chicago or Miami it's about $275. From Canada, reckon on paying Can$340–380 from Toronto or Montréal and Can$450 from Vancouver.

By train

New York is connected to the rest of the continent by several **Amtrak train lines** (☎1-800/USA-RAIL, ⊛www.amtrak.com). The most frequent services are along the Boston-to-Washington corridor – shuttle flights and the trains compete for commuters; there is also one daily train between Montréal, Toronto, and New York. Fares from Boston are about $125 round-trip, or $200 for the *Acela Express*, which saves 35 minutes. DC trains run about $145, considerably more on the *Metroliner* and *Acela Express*. Fares from Canada usually start around Can$165–195. Like planes, train fares are often based on availability; book as early as possible to get the cheapest rates.

Although it's possible to haul yourself long-distance from the West Coast, the Midwest, or the South, it's an exhausting trip (three days plus from California) and fares are expensive.

All Amtrak services arrive at Penn Station at 32nd St between Seventh and Eighth avenues; only local Metro-North commuter trains use Grand Central Terminal.

By bus

Going by **bus** is the most time-consuming and least comfortable mode of travel; because of the time factor, it is the most economical only for journeys of just a few hours. The only reason to take the bus any longer than that is if you're going to make a number of stops en route; if this is the case, you might check out **Greyhound**'s (☎1-800/231-2222, ⊛www .greyhound.com) **Discovery Pass**, which is good for unlimited travel within a set period of time.

Unlike most parts of the country, where Greyhound is the only game in town, in the busy northeast corridor there is fierce competition between bus operators, sending prices up and down within hours. One-way from either DC or Boston to New

York can go for as little as $30 on one of the major lines. **Bonanza** (☏1-800/556-3815, ⊛www.bonanzabus.com) has a $63 Boston–New York round-trip fare. The least expensive option by far is the **Fung Wah** bus (☏212/925-8889, ⊛www.fungwahbus.com), which runs nonstop between the Chinatowns of Boston and New York for $15 each way.

Buses arrive in New York at the Port Authority Bus Terminal, Eighth Avenue and 42nd Street.

From the UK and Ireland

Flying to New York from the UK takes about seven hours; flights tend to **leave Britain** in the morning or afternoon and arrive in New York in the afternoon or evening, though the odd flight does leave as late as 8pm. Coming back, most flights depart in the evening and arrive in Britain early next morning; flying time, due to the prevailing winds, is usually a little shorter.

As far as **scheduled flights** go, British Airways offers the most direct services each day from London's Heathrow to JFK, and also flies from Heathrow to Newark, and to JFK from Manchester. American Airlines, Virgin, Continental, and United also fly direct on a daily basis; there is not much difference in the prices on the different airlines. Round-trip **fares** generally tend to average £300–400.

The only nonstop scheduled services to New York from Ireland are provided by Aer Lingus.

From Australia and New Zealand

No direct flights serve New York **from Australia or New Zealand** – no surprise considering the great distance between the two end points. Most Aussies and Kiwis reach the eastern United States by way of the West Coast gateway cities of Los Angeles and San Francisco (flying time is approximately ten hours to the West Coast, with another six-hour flight to New York). You can buy an all-in ticket via LA or San Francisco or simply fly to LA and use one of the **domestic flight coupons**, or **air passes**, you can buy with your international ticket (these must be bought before you leave your home country).

These flight coupons cost around AUS$800/NZ$930 for three, which is the minimum amount you can purchase.

Fares from eastern Australian capitals are generally the same (airlines offer a free connecting service between these cities); fares from Perth and Darwin are about AUS$600/NZ$700 more. Return flights in high season start at around AUS$2100/NZ$2800 and go up from there; you might do better just by purchasing a direct ticket to either San Francisco or LA, then using the air passes to get to New York. The best connections through San Francisco and LA tend to be with United, Air New Zealand, and Qantas.

If you intend to take in New York as part of a world trip, a **round-the-world ticket** offers the best value for your money, working out just a little more than an all-in ticket. Check with the airlines listed on p.22 for the best options; it's quite possible you'd only spend a few hundred dollars more than on a normal return ticket.

Airlines, agents, and tour operators

Online booking

⊛**www.expedia.co.uk** (in UK)
⊛**www.expedia.com** (in US)
⊛**www.expedia.ca** (in Canada)
⊛**www.lastminute.com** (in UK)
⊛**www.opodo.co.uk** (in UK)
⊛**www.orbitz.com** (in US)
⊛**www.travelocity.co.uk** (in UK)
⊛**www.travelocity.com** (in US)
⊛**www.travelocity.ca** (in Canada)
⊛**www.zuji.com.au** (in Australia)
⊛**www.zuji.co.nz** (in New Zealand)

Airlines in the US and Canada

Air Canada ☏1-888/247-2262, ⊛www.aircanada.com.
Air Tran ☏1-800/247-8726, ⊛www.airtran.com.
American Airlines ☏1-800/433-7300, ⊛www.aa.com.
Continental Airlines ☏1-800/523-3273, ⊛www.continental.com.
Delta ☏1-800/221-1212, ⊛www.delta.com.
JetBlue ☏1-800/538-2583, ⊛www.jetblue.com.
Northwest/KLM ☏1-800/225-2525, ⊛www.nwa.com.

Fly less – stay longer! Travel and climate change

B

BASICS | Getting there

Climate change is a serious threat to the ecosystems that humans rely upon, and air travel is among the fastest-growing contributors to the problem. Rough Guides regard travel, overall, as a global benefit, and feel strongly that the advantages to developing economies are important, as is the opportunity of greater contact and awareness among peoples. But we all have a responsibility to limit our personal impact on global warming, and that means giving thought to how often we fly, and what we can do to redress the harm that our trips create.

Flying and climate change

Pretty much every form of motorized travel generates CO_2 – the main cause of human-induced climate change – but planes also generate climate-warming contrails and cirrus clouds and emit oxides of nitrogen, which create ozone (another greenhouse gas) at flight levels. Furthermore, flying simply allows us to travel much further than we otherwise would do. The figures are frightening: one person taking a return flight between Europe and California produces the equivalent impact of 2.5 tons of CO_2 – similar to the yearly output of the average UK car.

Fuel-cell and other less harmful types of plane may emerge eventually. But until then, there are really just two options for concerned travelers: to reduce the amount we travel by air (take fewer trips – stay for longer!), and to make the trips we do take "climate neutral" via a carbon offset scheme.

Carbon offset schemes

Offset schemes run by ⓦclimatecare.org, ⓦcarbonneutral.com and others allow you to make up for some or all of the greenhouse gases that you are responsible for releasing. To do this, they provide "carbon calculators" for working out the global-warming contribution of a specific flight (or even your entire existence), and then let you contribute an appropriate amount of money to fund offsetting measures. These include rainforest reforestation and initiatives to reduce future energy demand – often run in conjunction with sustainable development schemes.

Rough Guides, together with Lonely Planet and other concerned partners in the travel industry, are supporting a carbon offset scheme run by climatecare.org. Please take the time to view our website and see how you can help to make your trip climate neutral.

ⓦ**www.roughguides.com/climatechange**

Southwest Airlines ☎1-800/435-9792, ⓦwww .southwest.com.
United Airlines ☎1-800/241-6522, ⓦwww .united.com.
US Airways ☎1-800/428-4322, ⓦwww.usair .com.

Travel agents and tour operators in the US

Amtrak Vacations ☎1-800/654-5748, ⓦwww .amtrakvacations.com. Rail, accommodations, and sightseeing packages.
Contiki ☎1-888/CONTIKI, ⓦwww.contiki.com. 18- to 35-year-olds-only tour operator. Runs highly social sightseeing trips to New York that focus on major tourist attractions.

Delta Vacations ☎1-800/654-6559, ⓦwww .deltavacations.com. Offers packages to New York that include mid-range to upscale accommodations, plus optional sightseeing and airport transfers.
International Gay and Lesbian Travel Association ☎1-800/448-8550, ⓦwww.iglta.org. Trade group with lists of gay-owned or gay-friendly travel agents, accommodations and other travel businesses.
Maupintour ☎1-800/255-4266, ⓦwww .maupintour.com. Luxury tours. Runs Thanksgiving and Christmas trips to New York, with city tours, show tickets, and upscale meals.
New York City.com ☎1-888/VISITNY, ⓦwww .nyc.com. Touristy group packages, including show tickets.
New York City Vacation Packages ☎1-888/692-8701, ⓦwww.nycvp.com. All sorts of

short, reasonably priced New York vacations, from spa weekends to Broadway shows.

STA Travel US ☎ 1-800/781-4040, Canada ☎ 1-888/427-5639, 🌐 www.statravel.com. Specialists in independent travel; also student IDs, travel insurance, car rental, rail passes, and more. Good discounts for students and under-26s.

Viator 🌐 www.viator.com. Books piecemeal local tours and sightseeing trips within New York.

Airlines in the UK and Ireland

Aer Lingus UK ☎ 0870/876 5000, Republic of Ireland ☎ 0818/365 000, 🌐 www.aerlingus.ie.

American Airlines UK ☎ 0845/7789 789, Republic of Ireland ☎ 01/602 0550, 🌐 www .aa.com.

British Airways UK ☎ 0870/850 9850, Republic of Ireland ☎ 1890/626 747, 🌐 www.ba.com.

Delta UK ☎ 0845/600 0950, Republic of Ireland ☎ 1850/882 031 or 01/407 3165, 🌐 www.delta .com.

flyBE UK ☎ 0870/889 0908, Republic of Ireland ☎ 1890/925 532, 🌐 www.flybe.com. Low-cost flights from Belfast, Birmingham, Edinburgh, Glasgow, and Manchester to New York.

United Airlines UK ☎ 0845/844 4777, 🌐 www .unitedairlines.co.uk.

Virgin Atlantic UK ☎ 0870/380 2007, 🌐 www .virgin-atlantic.com.

Travel agents in the UK and Ireland

ebookers UK ☎ 0800/082-3000, Republic of Ireland ☎ 01/488-3507, 🌐 www.ebookers.com. Low fares on an extensive selection of scheduled flights and package deals.

North South Travel UK ☎ 01245/608 291, 🌐 www.northsouthtravel.co.uk. Friendly, competitive travel agency, offering discounted fares worldwide. Profits are used to support projects in the developing world, especially the promotion of sustainable tourism.

STA Travel UK ☎ 0870/1630-026, 🌐 www .statravel.com.

Trailfinders UK ☎ 0845/058 5858, Republic of Ireland ☎ 01/677 7888, 🌐 www.trailfinders.com. One of the best-informed and most efficient agents for independent travelers.

USIT Republic of Ireland ☎ 01/602 1904, 🌐 www .usit.ie. Student/youth travel specialists, offering discount flights to North America.

Airlines in Australia and New Zealand

Air New Zealand Australia ☎ 13 24 76, 🌐 www .airnz.com.au, New Zealand ☎ 0800/737 000, 🌐 www.airnewzealand.com.

American Airlines Australia ☎ 1300/130 757, New Zealand ☎ 0800/887 997, 🌐 www.aa.com.

British Airways Australia ☎ 1300/767 177, New Zealand ☎ 09/966 9777, 🌐 www.britishairways .com.

Continental Airlines Australia ☎ 2/9244 2242, New Zealand ☎ 09/308 3350, 🌐 www.continental .com.

Delta Australia ☎ 1300/302 849, New Zealand ☎ 09/379 3370, 🌐 www.delta.com.

Japan Airlines Australia ☎ 02/9272 1111, 🌐 www.au.jal.com/en; New Zealand ☎ 09/379 9906, 🌐 www.nz.jal.com/en.

Korean Air Australia ☎ 02/9262 6000, New Zealand ☎ 09/914 2000, 🌐 www.koreanair.com.

Lufthansa Australia ☎ 1300/655 727, New Zealand ☎ 09/303 1529, 🌐 www.lufthansa.com.

Qantas Australia ☎ 13 13 13, New Zealand ☎ 0800/808 767 or 09/357 8900, 🌐 www.qantas .com.

United Airlines Australia ☎ 13 17 77, 🌐 www .united.com.

Travel agents in Australia and New Zealand

STA Travel Australia ☎ 1300/733 035, New Zealand ☎ 0508/782 872, 🌐 www .statravel.com.

Trailfinders Australia ☎ 1300/780 212, 🌐 www .trailfinders.com.

Arrival

Most visitors to New York arrive at one of the three major international airports that serve the city: John F. Kennedy (JFK) (☏718/244-4444), LaGuardia (LGA) (☏718/533-3400), and Newark (EWR) (☏973/961-6000). All three share a website at ⓦwww.panynj.gov. You can find general information about getting to and from the airports on the website or by calling ☏1-800/AIR-RIDE. Amtrak trains arrive at Penn Station, and buses at the Port Authority Bus Terminal, both of which are in Midtown West.

By air

Whichever airport you arrive at, one of the most efficient ways into Manhattan is by **charter bus**. All airport buses use two bus terminals in Manhattan: **Grand Central Terminal** (at Park Ave and 42nd St) and the **Port Authority Bus Terminal** (Eighth Ave at 34th St, ☏212/564-8484). Grand Central, in the heart of midtown Manhattan, is more convenient for the east side of the island. The Port Authority Bus Terminal isn't as good a bet for Manhattan (you must carry luggage from bus to street level), though you'll find it handy if you're heading for the West Side of the city or out to New Jersey (by bus). Some airport buses also stop at **Penn Station** at 32nd St between Seventh and Eighth avenues, where you can catch the Long Island Railroad (LIRR), as well as Amtrak long-distance trains to other parts of America.

Taxis are the easiest transport option if you are traveling in a group or are arriving at an antisocial hour. Reckon on paying $20–30 from LaGuardia to Manhattan, a flat rate of $45 from JFK, and $35–55 from Newark; you'll also be responsible for the turnpike and tunnel tolls – an extra $5 or so – as well as a fifteen- to twenty-percent tip for the driver. Ignore the individual cabs vying for attention as you exit the baggage claim; these "gypsy cab" operators are notorious for ripping off tourists. Any airport official can direct you to the taxi stand, where you can get an official New York City yellow taxi. A few car services have direct phones near the exits; they're competitive in price with taxis (they charge set rates).

If you're not so pressed for time and want to save some money, it is also possible to take the **train**, commuter or subway, from Newark or JFK, connecting via the AirTrain system. Plan on it taking at least an hour to get to Manhattan and costing $7–12.

JFK

The **New York Airport Service** (☏212/875-8200, ⓦwww.nyairportservice.com) runs **buses** from JFK to Grand Central Terminal, Port Authority Bus Terminal, Penn Station, and midtown hotels every 15 to 20 minutes between 6.15am and 11.10pm. In the other direction, buses run from the same locations every 15 to 30 minutes between about 5am and 10pm. Journeys take 45 to 60 minutes, depending on time of day and traffic conditions. The fare is $15 one-way, $27 round-trip; discounts are available.

The **AirTrain** (ⓦwww.panynj.gov/airtrain) runs every few minutes, 24 hours daily, between JFK and the Jamaica LIRR, #E, #J, #Z, and Howard Beach #A stations. The cost is $5 on a MetroCard (see p.25).

There are a few options for **public transit** (☏718/330-1234, ⓦwww.mta.info). From the Jamaica and Howard Beach stations on the #A train, one **subway** fare ($2 on a MetroCard) takes you anywhere in the city. In the daytime or early evening this is a cheap, viable option, although at night it isn't the best choice – trains run infrequently and can be deserted. Travel time to Manhattan is usually a little under an hour from Howard Beach. The #B15 **bus** ($2, MetroCard, or exact change) runs to the last #3 train stop in Brooklyn, a convenient though somewhat seedy and desolate route.

LaGuardia

The **New York Airport Service** (☎212/875-8200, ⌨www.nyairportservice.com) runs **buses** from LaGuardia to Grand Central Station, Port Authority Bus Terminal, and Penn Station every 15 to 30 minutes between 7.20am and 11pm. In the other direction, buses run from Grand Central 5am to 8pm, from Port Authority 5.50am to 7.40pm, and from Penn Station 7.40am to 7.10pm. Journey time is 45 to 60 minutes, depending on traffic. The fare is $12 one-way, $21 round-trip.

You can also travel from the airport using **public transit**. The best (and least-known) bargain in New York airport transit is the #M60 **bus**, which for $2 (exact change or MetroCard) takes you into Manhattan, across 125th St and down Broadway to 106th St. Ask for a transfer (see p.26) when you get on the bus and you can get almost anywhere. Journey time from LaGuardia ranges from 20 minutes late at night to an hour in rush-hour traffic. Alternatively, you can take the #M60 bus to Astoria Boulevard. There you can transfer to the #N or #W **subway**, which runs through midtown Manhattan and south to Brooklyn.

Other public transit options include the #Q33 **bus** ($2) from LaGuardia to the Roosevelt Avenue subway stop in Jackson Heights, Queens, where you can get the #7, or a few minutes' walk away, the #E, #F, #G, #R, and #V, all of which go to midtown.

Newark

Newark Airport Express (☎877/863-9275, ⌨www.coachusa.com) runs **buses** to Grand Central Station, Port Authority Bus Terminal, and Penn Station every 20 to 30 minutes between 4am and 12.45am. In the other direction, buses run from the same locations just as frequently (about 5am to 1.30am); service to and from the Port Authority runs 24 hours per day. In either direction, the journey takes 30 to 45 minutes depending on the traffic. The fare is $14 one-way, $23 round-trip.

PATH Rapid Transit trains (☎1-800/234-7284, ⌨www.panynj.com) run to downtown Manhattan (and midtown with connections). Take the AirTrain to Newark's Penn Station, then transfer to the PATH train; the fare is $5 for AirTrain, $2 for the PATH train. The AirTrain runs from 5am to midnight. The PATH train runs 24 hours per day, but service is limited between midnight and 7am.

By train, bus, or car

Amtrak trains arrive at **Penn Station**, 32nd St between Seventh and Eighth avenues. If you come to New York by Greyhound or any other long-distance **bus** line (with the exception of the Chinatown buses, which arrive in Chinatown), you arrive at the **Port Authority Bus Terminal** at 42nd Street and Eighth Avenue.

If you're coming from the East Coast (or if you don't mind long journeys), **driving** is an option, but note that you probably won't need (or want) a car once you're in the city. Major **highways** come in from most directions (I-87 and 95 from the north; I-95 from the south; I-80 from the west), and you'll pay a **toll** for any number of bridges and/or tunnels to get into the city.

Getting around

Getting around the city is likely to take some getting used to; public transit here is very good, extremely cheap, and covers most conceivable corners of the city, whether by subway or bus. Don't be afraid to ask someone for help if you're confused. You'll no doubt find the need for a taxi from time to time, especially if you feel uncomfortable in an area at night; you will rarely have trouble tracking one down in Manhattan or on major Brooklyn avenues – the ubiquitous yellow cabs are always on the prowl for passengers. And don't forget your feet – Manhattanites walk everywhere.

By subway

The New York **subway** (☎718/330-1234, Ⓦwww.mta.info) is noisy and initially incomprehensible, but it's also the fastest and most efficient way to get from place to place in Manhattan and to the outer boroughs. Put aside your qualms: it's much safer and user-friendly than it once was, and it's definitely not as difficult to navigate as it seems.

It pays to familiarize yourself with the subway system before you set out. Study the map at the back of this book, or get a free map at any station or information kiosk. Though the subway runs 24 hours daily, some routes operate at certain times of day only; read your map and any service advisories carefully.

The basics

•The subway costs **$2 per ride**, including all subway and most bus transfers. In order to ride the subway, you must purchase a **MetroCard**, a card with an electronic strip, from a vending machine (in the subway station) or a subway teller. Vending machines accept credit and debit cards, although some machines may have a hard time reading foreign credit cards. Be sure to keep some fresh bills on hand in case you run into trouble with machines.

•The **MetroCard** is available in several forms. It can be purchased in denominations between $2 and $80; $10 gets you 6 rides for the cost of 5, $20 12 rides for the cost of 10, and so forth. Unlimited-ride cards – almost always the best deal if you intend to be on the go – allow unlimited travel for a certain period of time: a daily "Fun Pass" for $7, 7-day pass for $24, and 30-day pass for $76.

•Most train routes run uptown or downtown in Manhattan, following the great avenues. Crosstown routes are few.

•Trains and their routes are identified by a number or letter (not by their color).

•There are two types of train: the **express**, which stops only at major stations, and the

Safety on the subway

By day the whole train is safe, but don't go into empty cars if you can help it. Some trains have doors that connect between cars, but do not use them other than in an emergency, because this is dangerous and illegal. Keep an eye on bags at all times, especially when sitting or standing near the doors. With all the jostling in the crowds near the doors, this is a favorite spot for pickpockets.

At night, always try to use the center cars, because they tend to be more crowded. Yellow signs on the platform saying "During off hours train stops here" indicate where the conductor's car will stop. While you wait, keep where the token booth attendants can see you if possible. For more information on safety, see "Crime and personal safety," p.28.

local, stopping at every station. Listen to the conductor, who will usually announce the train's next stop.

•**Service changes** due to track repairs and other maintenance work are frequent (especially after midnight and on weekends) and confusing. Read the red-and-white Service Notice posters on bulletin boards throughout the system, and don't be afraid to ask other passengers what's going on. Listen closely to all announcements (though they can be hard to understand); occasionally, express trains run on local tracks.

•Don't hesitate to **ask directions** or **look at a map** on the train or in the station. If you travel late at night, know your route before you set out. Follow common-sense safety rules (see "Crime and personal safety," p.28).

•If you are **lost**, go to the subway teller or phone ☎718/330-1234. State your location and destination; the teller or operator will tell you the most direct route.

•In the interest of safety, some station entrances are open only during certain hours. An illuminated green globe outside the entrance identifies an open station; red means closed.

By bus

The **bus system** (☎718/330-1234, 🌐www .mta.info) is simpler than the subway, and you can see where you're going and hop off at anything interesting. The bus also features many more **crosstown** routes. The major disadvantage is that buses can be extremely slow due to traffic – in peak hours almost down to walking pace.

Anywhere in the city the fare is **$2**, payable on entry with a **MetroCard** (the most convenient way) or with the correct change – no bills.

Bus maps can be obtained at the main concourse of Grand Central Terminal or the Convention and Visitors Bureau at 53rd St and Seventh Ave, as well as in subway stations. There are routes on almost all the avenues and major streets. Most buses with an M designation before the route number travel exclusively in Manhattan; others may show a B for Brooklyn, Q for Queens, Bx for the Bronx, or S for Staten Island. The crosstown routes are most

useful, especially the ones through Central Park. Also good are the buses that take you to areas east of the park where subway coverage is sparse. Most crosstown buses take their route number from the street they traverse, so the #M14 will travel along 14th Street. Buses display their number, origin, and destination up front.

There are three types of bus: regular, which stop every two or three blocks at five- to ten-minute intervals; limited stop, which travel the same routes but stop at only about a quarter of the regular stops; and express, which cost extra and stop hardly anywhere, shuttling commuters in and out of the outer boroughs and suburbs.

Bus stops are marked by yellow curbstones and a blue, white, and red sign that often (but not always) indicates which buses stop there. Once you're on board, to signal that you want to get off a bus, press the yellow or black strip on the wall; the driver will stop at the next official bus stop. After midnight, you can ask to get off on any block along the route, whether or not it's a regular stop.

Transfers

If you're going to use buses a lot, it pays to understand the **transfer** system. A transfer allows a single fare to take you, one way, anywhere in Manhattan; they're given free on request when you pay your fare. Because few buses go up and down and across, you can transfer from any bus to almost any other that continues your trip. (You can't use transfers for return trips.) The top of the transfer tells you how much time you have in which to use it – usually around two hours. If unsure where to get off to transfer, consult the map on the panel behind the driver, or ask the driver for help. If you use a Metro-Card, you can automatically transfer for free within two hours from swiping the card.

By taxi

Taxis are always worth considering, especially if you're in a hurry or it's late at night.

There are two types of taxis: **medallion cabs**, recognizable by their yellow paintwork and medallion up top, and **gypsy cabs**, unlicensed, uninsured operators who tout for business wherever tourists arrive. Avoid gypsy cabs like the plague – they will rip you off. Their main hunting grounds are outside tourist arrival points like Grand Central.

Up to four people can travel in an ordinary medallion cab. Fares are $2.50 for the first fifth of a mile and 40¢ for each fifth of a mile thereafter or for each 90 seconds in stopped or slow traffic. The basic charge rises by 50¢ from 8pm to 6am, and when you take a cab outside the city limits you must agree on a flat fare with the driver before the trip begins (except trips to Newark Airport and Nassau County, for which there are previously determined fare rules). Trips outside Manhattan can incur toll fees (which the driver will pay through E-Z Pass and will be added to your fare); not all of the crossings cost money, however, and the driver should ask you which route you wish to take.

The **tip** should be fifteen to twenty percent of the fare; you'll get a dirty look if you offer less. Drivers don't like splitting anything bigger than a $10 bill, and are in their rights to refuse a bill over $20.

Before you hail a cab, work out exactly where you're going and if possible the quickest route there – a surprising number of cabbies are new to the job and speak little English. If you feel the driver doesn't seem to know your destination, point it out on a map. An illuminated sign atop the taxi indicates its availability. If the words "Off Duty" are lit, the driver won't pick you up.

Certain regulations govern taxi operators. A driver can ask your destination only when you're seated (this is often breached) – and must transport you (within the five boroughs), however undesirable your destination may be. You may face some problems, though, if it's late and you want to go to an outer borough. Also, if you request it, a driver must pick up or drop off other passengers, turn on the air-conditioning and turn the radio down or off. Many drivers use a cell phone while driving; this is common but prohibited, and while you can ask him or her to stop, don't expect compliance. If you have a problem with a driver, get the license number from the right-hand side of the dashboard, or medallion number from the rooftop sign or from the print-out receipt for the fare, and file a complaint at ⓦ www.nyc.gov/html/tlc/html/passenger/file_complaint.

By car

Don't drive in New York. Even if you're brave enough to try dodging demolition-derby cabbies and jaywalking pedestrians, car rental is expensive and parking lots almost laughably so. Legal street parking is nearly impossible to find.

If you really must drive, bear in mind these rules. Seatbelts are compulsory for everyone in front and for children in back. The city speed limit is 35mph. It's illegal to make a right turn at a red light. The use of hand-held cell phones is illegal while driving.

Read signs carefully to figure out **where to park** – if the sign says "No Standing," "No Stopping," or "Don't Even THINK of Parking Here" (yes, really), then don't. Watch for street-cleaning hours (when an entire side of a street will be off-limits), and don't park in a bus stop, in front of (or within several yards of) a fire hydrant, or anywhere with a yellow curb. Private parking is expensive, but it makes sense to leave your car somewhere legitimate. If you park illegally and are towed, you must liberate your vehicle from the impound lot over on the West Side Highway (☎212/971-0770) – expect to pay around $185 in cash ($20 for each additional day they store it for you) and waste your day.

Car theft and **vandalism** are more of a problem in less-traveled parts of the city, but no matter where you park, never leave valuables in your car.

For **foreign drivers**, any driver's license issued by their country is valid in the US – for more information check the state DMV's website (ⓦ www.nydmv.state.ny.us).

By bike

Cycling can be a viable, if somewhat dangerous, form of transportation. Wear all possible **safety equipment**: pads, a helmet (required by law), and goggles. When you park, double-chain and lock your bike (including wheels) to an immovable object if you'd like it to be there when you return.

Bike rental starts at about $7 per hour or $35 per day – which means opening to closing (9.30am to 6.30pm for instance). You need one or two pieces of ID (passport and credit card will be sufficient) and, in some cases, a deposit, though most firms will be satisfied with a credit-card imprint. Rates and deposits are generally more for racing models and mountain bikes. See Chapter 32, "Sports and outdoor activities," for more information on bicycle rental.

By foot

Few cities equal New York for street-level stimulation. Getting around on **foot** is often the most exciting – and tiring – method of exploring. However you plan your wanderings, you're still going to spend much of your time walking. Be aware of the people behind you, who will get impatient if you do not allow them to pass. Footwear is important (sneakers are good for summer; winter and spring often need something waterproof). So is safety: a lot more people are injured in New York carelessly crossing the street than are mugged. The city has a law against jaywalking, and some midtown intersections have cattle gates to prevent crossing at certain corners. Pedestrian crossings don't give you automatic right of way unless the WALK sign is on – and, even then, cars may be turning, so be prudent.

Crime and personal safety

In two words: don't worry. New York has come a long way in recent years. This doesn't mean you shouldn't be smart and play it safe while in the city, but no more so than you would in any metropolitan environment.

Staying out of trouble

While the city can sometimes feel dangerous, especially for first-time visitors unaccustomed to the volume of people and amount of noise, the reality is somewhat different. More than eight million people live in New York City, and as far as per capita crime rates go, Boston is more dangerous, as are Los Angeles, Chicago, Dallas, and Washington DC, and believe it or not, almost two hundred other US cities; in fact, New York is America's **safest city** with a population over one million.

This is not to say you should discount the possibility of danger altogether – just follow the lead of locals, and keep it in the back of your consciousness, not at the forefront. Walk with confidence. This guide outlines places where you should be careful and those few best avoided altogether, but really it's a case of using common sense; **be aware** of your surroundings at all times. While many neighborhoods may look astonishingly dirty, unkempt, and therefore frightening, only a few are really dangerous.

Contrary to popular belief, it's OK in New York City to let on you're a visitor – if you follow rules of paranoia and never look up, you'll miss a lot of the city's most interesting aspects. Just pay attention when you pause to look at your map. Carry bags closed and across your body, don't let cameras dangle, keep wallets in front – not back – pockets, and don't flash money around. Avoid crowds when possible, especially around rip-off merchants like street gamblers. Move away if you feel someone is standing too close to you.

Note that possession of any "controlled substance" is absolutely illegal. Should you be found in possession of a very small amount of marijuana, you probably won't go to jail – but you can expect a hefty fine and, for foreigners, the possibility of deportation.

Violent crime

There is still a great deal of crime in New York, and some of it is violent. While murders may make the big headlines, ninety percent of murder victims are known to their killers, which is to say that most killings are personal disputes rather than random attacks on strangers. **Mugging**, on the other hand, can and does happen. It's impossible to give hard-and-fast rules on what to do should you meet up with a mugger: whether to run or scream or fight depends on you and the situation. Most New Yorkers would hand over the money every time, and that's probably what you should do, too.

If the worst happens and your assailant is toting a gun or a knife, play it calmly. Keep still, don't make any sudden movements – and do what he says. When he has run off, hail a cab and ask to be taken to the nearest police station; taxis rarely charge for this, but if they do the police are supposed to pay. Standing around on the street in a shocked condition is inviting more trouble, though you'd be pleasantly surprised at the number of people who would sincerely come to your aid. At the station, you'll get sympathy and little else; file the theft and take the incident report to claim your insurance back home.

Women's safety

Women traveling in New York should know that they are much more likely to feel unsafe than actually be unsafe. A big part of visiting New York is to look as if you know what you're doing and where you're going. Maintain the facade and you should find that a lot of the aggravation fades away. If someone's bugging you, either turn away, leave, or let him know your feelings loudly and firmly. These tactics, while not much good in the event of extreme trouble, can lend you confidence, which in turn wards off creeps. Much more powerful are chemical repellents such as pepper sprays, available from sporting goods stores. If you do carry one of these, make sure you know how and when to use it, and what its effects will be. Avoid getting noticeably intoxicated unless you are with a trusted friend.

You're far, far less likely to be raped than mugged. Be wary about any display of wealth in the wrong place – think about where you're walking before setting out for the day. If you are being followed, turn around and look at the person following you, and step off the sidewalk and into the street; attackers hate the open. Never let yourself be pushed into an alley and never

turn off down an unlit, empty-looking street. Also, never, ever let yourself be pulled into a car or building by an attacker; it is much better to struggle, scream, and/or run and risk bodily harm. If you're unsure about the area where you're staying, ask other women's advice. They'll tell you when they walk and when they take a bus so as to avoid walking more than a block; which bars and parks they feel free to walk in with confidence; and what times they don't go anywhere without a cab. However, don't avoid parts of the city just through hearsay – you might miss out on what's most of interest – and learn to expect New Yorkers (Manhattanites in particular, many of whom feel incorrectly that anywhere outside of the borough shouldn't be risked) to sound alarmist; it's part of the culture.

Police

The New York City Police – the **NYPD**, aka "New York's Finest" – are for the most part approachable, helpful, and overworked. This means that asking directions gets a friendly response, while reporting a theft may bring a weary "Whaddaya want me to do about it?" – and any smile is appreciated. In this realm of New York life as in others, **race and gender** can play a part in the response you get. Wary of relations between police and minority communities (recent years have seen several young, unarmed black men die in conflicts with police), officers – even those from minority communities themselves – may be a little more reserved if your skin is any color but white. This is not to say that they'll refrain from helping you if you're in trouble, however.

Each area of New York has its own **police precinct**; to find the nearest station, call ☎646/610-5000 (during business hours

Victim services

If you are unlucky enough to be mugged, the Safe Horizon 24-hour hotline (☎212/577-7777) offers telephone advice and will direct anyone who has suffered a crime against their person to where they can receive one-to-one counseling.

only) or ☎311, or check the phone book. In emergencies, phone ☎911 or use one of the outdoor posts that give you a direct line to the emergency services. This information, plus crime stats, is available at ⓦwww .ci.nyc.ny.us/html/nypd/home.html.

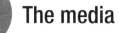

The media

Generally acknowledged as the media capital of the world, New York is the headquarters of just about all the country's major television news organizations and book and magazine publishers. This means that there is a newsstand on just about every corner selling a wonderful variety of newspapers and magazines, as well as frequent opportunities to take part in television-show tapings.

Newspapers and magazines

Although it's still the most vibrant news market in the US, New York is past the days when it could support twenty daily newspapers. Only four remain: the broadsheets the **New York Times** and the **New York Sun** and the tabloids the **Daily News** and the **New York Post**.

The *New York Times* ($1; ⓦwww.nytimes .com), an American institution, prides itself on being the "paper of record" – America's quality national paper. It has solid international coverage, and places much emphasis on its news analysis. The Sunday edition ($3.50) is a thumping bundle of newsprint divided into a number of supplements that take a full day to read.

It takes serious coordination to read the sizable *Times* on the subway, one reason many turn to the *Daily News* and the *Post*. Tabloids in format and style, these rivals concentrate on local news. The *Daily News* (50¢; ⓦwww.nydailynews.com) is a "picture newspaper" with many racy headlines.

The *New York Post* (25¢; ⓦwww.nypost .com), the city's oldest newspaper, started in 1801 by Alexander Hamilton, has been in decline for many years. Known for its solid city news and consistent conservative-slanted sermonizing, it also takes a fairly sensationalist approach to headlines.

The *New York Sun* (25¢; ⓦwww.nysun .com) is not widely read. Only published on weekdays, it's a broadsheet with a determinedly old-fashioned look and a stolid, conservative bent.

The other New York–based daily newspaper is the *Wall Street Journal* ($1; ⓦwww .wsj.com), in fact a national financial paper that also has strong, conservative national and international news coverage – despite an old-fashioned design that eschews the use of photographs.

The city offers many **free dailies**, as well, the most reputable among them being *AM New York* and *Metro New York*. These publications gloss over national events and local news, and are designed to be consumed by commuters between subway stops. Find these papers in dispensers on most street corners or handed out in early mornings near subway entrances.

The weeklies and monthlies

Of the **weekly** papers, the *Village Voice* (Tuesdays, free; ⓦwww.villagevoice.com) is the most widely read, mainly for its comprehensive arts coverage and investigative features. It offers opinionated stories that often focus on the media, gay issues, and civil rights. It's also one of the best pointers to what's on around town (including the most interesting, inexpensive cuisine and

TV-show tapings

If you want to experience the excitement, horror, boredom, and surprise of American TV up close, there are **free tickets** for various shows. While some of the more popular require written requests months in advance, almost all have standby lines where you can try your luck on a particular day. Not all shows tape year-round. For most shows you must be 16 and sometimes 18 to be in the audience; if you're underage or traveling with children, call ahead.

Morning shows

Good Morning America ☎212/580-5176, ⓦgma.abcnews.com. Show up at the Broadway entrance around 6am for a shot at a standby ticket.

Today There's no way to get advance tickets, just show up at 49th St, between 5th and 6th avenues, as early as possible. Unlike the rest of the morning shows, which run until 9am, *Today* ends at 10am.

Daytime shows

The Colbert Report ⓦwww.comedycentral.com/shows/the_colbert_report/index .jhtml. Standby tickets only. Arrive by 5pm at the studio on 54th Street, between 10th and 11th avenues.

Live with Regis and Kelly ☎212/456-1000. Send a postcard with your name, address, and telephone number to Live Tickets, PO Box 230777 Ansonia Station, New York, NY 10023-0777. Include your preferred date(s) and number of tickets (limit 4). For standby, go to ABC at 67th St and Columbus Ave as early as 7am Monday through Friday.

Total Request Live (TRL) ☎212/398-8549. You can also stand outside the studio at 44th and Broadway starting at 2pm. Live Monday through Thursday 4 to 5pm, Friday to 5.30pm.

Late-night shows

The Daily Show with Jon Stewart ☎212/586-2477, ⓔrequesttickets@thedailyshow .com. Email your full name, telephone number, and dates of interest. For standby, go to the studio at 733 11th Ave as early as you can; they tape Monday through Thursday at 5.45pm. Doors open at 5pm.

David Letterman ☎212/247-6497. Send a postcard (two-ticket limit per card) as far ahead as possible to Letterman Tickets, 1697 Broadway, New York, NY 10019. Shoots Monday through Thursday at 5.30pm, with an additional show Thursday at 8pm. Call at 11am on taping days to check for last-minute tickets.

Late Night with Conan O'Brien ☎212/664-3056. Write to NBC Tickets, "Late Night with Conan O'Brien," 30 Rockefeller Plaza, New York, NY 10112. For standby tickets go to the same place before 9am, Tuesday through Friday.

Saturday Night Live ☎212/664-4000. Send a postcard – which must arrive in August – with your name, address, and phone number to NBC Tickets, "Saturday Night Live," 30 Rockefeller Plaza, New York, NY 10112, and see what happens. They hand out standbys at the 49th St side of the GE Building at 30 Rockefeller Plaza at 9am any Saturday that there's a show (some Saturdays are reruns; call ahead).

shopping). Its main competitor, the *New York Press* (ⓦwww.nypress.com) is angrier, much more conservative, and not afraid to offend. The listings are quite good; look for its "Best of Manhattan" special edition, published each September.

Other leading weeklies include *New York* magazine ($3.99; ⓦwww.newyorkmetro.com),

which has reasonably good listings and is more of a society and entertainment journal, and *Time Out New York* ($2.99; ⓦwww .timeoutny.com) – a clone of its London original, combining the city's most comprehensive "what's on" listings with New York–slanted stories and features. The venerable *New Yorker* ($3.95; ⓦwww.newyorker.com) has good highbrow listings, and features poetry and short fiction alongside its much-loved cartoons. The wackiest, and perhaps best, alternative to the *Voice* is *PaperMag* ($3.50; ⓦwww.papermag.com), a monthly that carries witty and well-written rundowns on city nightlife and restaurants as well as current news and gossip. If you want a weekly with more of a political edge, there's the ironic *New York Observer* ($1; ⓦwww.observer .com) and the *Forward* ($1; ⓦwww.forward .com), a century-plus-old Jewish publication that's also published in Russian and Yiddish editions.

Many neighborhoods and ethnic communities have their own weeklies, led by the politically oriented African-American *Amsterdam News* (75¢; ⓦwww.amsterdamnews .org), and the *Brooklyn Papers* (free; ⓦwww .brooklynpapers.com).

International publications

British, European, Latin American, and Asian newspapers are widely available, usually a day after publication – except for the *Financial Times*, which is printed (via satellite) in the US and sold on most newsstands. If you want a specific paper or magazine, try any Universal News or Hudson News, sprinkled throughout the city. Barnes & Noble superstores (see p.411) stock magazines and international newspapers, which you can peruse for **free** over coffee (not free).

Television

Any American will find on TV in New York mostly what they find at home, plus several multilingual stations and some wacky public access channels. Channels 13 and 21 are given over to **PBS** (Public Broadcasting Service), which has earned the nickname "Purely British Station" for its fondness of British drama series, although it excels at documentaries and educational children's shows. The 70-plus stations available on **cable** in most hotel rooms may be a bit more fascinating for foreign travelers; most cable channels are no better than the major networks (**ABC**, **CBS**, **NBC**, and **Fox**), although a few of the specialized channels can be fairly interesting. **NY1** is the city's 24-hour local news channel, available exclusively on cable. Hopefully, you won't forget to see the New York sights altogether.

Radio

The FM dial is crammed with local stations of varying quality and content. Stations constantly open and close and change formats. While you'll find mostly music on FM, AM stations tend to be talk-oriented. The *New York Times* lists highlights daily; explore on your own, and you're sure to come across something interesting.

Incidentally, it's possible to tune in to the BBC World Service on the 49-meter short-wave band, or just the World Service news, broadcast on a number of the public radio stations. **BBC** (ⓦwww.bbc.co.uk/world-service), **Radio Canada** (ⓦwww.rcinet.ca), and **Voice of America** (ⓦwww.voa.gov) list all the World Service frequencies around the globe.

Tourist information

There is a veritable torrent of information available for visitors to New York City. Chances are, the answers to any questions you may have are readily accessible at a website or in a brochure.

General information

The best place for **information** is **NYC & Company** (the official visitors bureau), 810 Seventh Ave at 53rd St (Mon–Fri 8.30am–6pm, weekends and holidays 9am–5pm; ☎212/484-1200, ⓦwww.nycvisit.com). They have bus and subway maps, information on hotels and accommodations (including discounts), and up-to-date leaflets on what's going on in the arts and elsewhere. Their quarterly *Official NYC Guide* is good too, though the kind of information it gives – on restaurants, hotels, shopping, and sights – is also available in the various free tourist magazines and brochures in hotels and elsewhere.

You'll find other small **tourist information centers** and kiosks all over the city, starting with the airports, Grand Central and Penn stations, and Port Authority Bus Terminal. For a list of kiosks in other areas see the box below.

Maps

Other than our maps, the best **maps** of New York City are the free **bus maps** (ask any subway teller or librarian for one), as well as the huge, minutely detailed **neighborhood maps** found only on the wall near the teller booth of subway stations. **Professional maps**, like *The Rough Guide Map of New York City*, which is ripproof and waterproof, fill in the gaps. A great selection of New York City maps is available at ⓦwww.randmcnally.com. Street atlases of all five boroughs cost around $10–15; if you're after a map of one of the individual outer boroughs, try those produced by Geographia or Hagstrom, on sale online and in bookstores for about $4.

Tours

There are many different ways to take in the city. First-time visitors may be interested in taking a tour – they come in all kinds of lengths, themes, and modes of transportation.

Bus tours

Bus tours provide a good way to orient yourself with the city. Gray Line New York, Port Authority Terminal at 42nd St and Eighth Ave (☎800/669-0051 or 212/445-0848, ⓦwww.graylinenewyork.com), runs a large

Information centers and kiosks

Bloomingdale's International Visitors' Center Lexington Ave at 59th St ☎212/705-2098.

Brooklyn Tourism and Visitors Center Brooklyn Borough Hall, 209 Joralemon St ☎718/802-3846.

City Hall Park Visitor Information Kiosk Southern end of City Hall Park, Broadway at Park Row.

Harlem Visitors' Bureau 163 W 125th St ☎212/283-3315.

NYC Visitors Bureau ⓦwww.nycvisit.com. Official website of the New York Convention and Visitors Bureau.

Parks Department ⓦwww.nycparks.org. The official word on all of the obscure, famous, and thrilling events in the city's parks.

Times Square Visitor Information Center 1560 Broadway ☎212/869-1890.

Big Apple Greeter

If you're nervous about exploring New York, look into **Big Apple Greeter**, 1 Centre St, Suite 2035 (☎212/669-8159, ⓦwww.bigapplegreeter.org), one of the best – and certainly cheapest – ways to see the city. This not-for-profit organization matches visitors with their active corps of trained volunteer "greeters." Specify the part of the city you'd like to see, indicate an aspect of New York life you'd like to explore, or plead for general orientation – whatever your interests, chances are they will find someone to take you around. Visits have a friendly, informal feel, and generally last a few hours. The service is free. You can call once you're in New York, but it's better to contact the organization as far in advance as possible.

number of popular bus tours that range from two hours to two days. Discounts are available for children under 12. Call or look at the website for complete information and to book a tour.

Helicopter tours

A more exciting option is to look at the city by **helicopter**. This is expensive, but you won't easily forget the experience. **Liberty Helicopter Tours** (☎212/967-6464, ⓦwww.libertyhelicopters.com), at the Wall Street heliport at Pier 6, offers flights ranging from $69 per person (for five to seven minutes) to $186 (17 minutes). Reservations are required; times and locations vary on Sundays and holidays. Should you go by day or night? After doing one, you'll probably want to try the other.

Boat tours

A great way to see the island of Manhattan is a voyage on the **Circle Line ferry** (☎212/563-3200, ⓦwww.circleline42.com). Departing from Pier 83 at W 42nd St and Twelfth Ave, it circumnavigates Manhattan, taking in everything from the Statue of Liberty to Harlem, complete with a live commentary;

the three-hour tour runs year-round ($29, seniors $24, under-12s $16. The evening Harbor Lights Cruise (March–Nov; $24, seniors $20, under-12s $13) offers dramatic views of the skyline. If you're feeling really sporty, try *The Beast* (May–Oct $17, 12 and under $11), a speedboat painted to look like a shark that will throw you around for thirty minutes at a dashing 45 miles per hour.

Alternatively, check out tours offered by **NY Waterway** (☎800/533-3779, ⓦwww.nywaterway.com). Its 90-minute Harbor Cruises ($22, seniors $18, under-12s $12) leave the west end of Pier 78 at W 38th St several times daily, year-round.

None of these options beat the bargain of the free **Staten Island Ferry** (☎718/727-2508, ⓦwww.siferry.com), which leaves from its own terminal in Lower Manhattan's Battery Park and provides stunning views of New York Harbor around the clock. It's a commuter boat, so avoid crowded rush hours if you can. Departures are every 15 to 20 minutes during rush hours (7 to 9am and 5 to 7pm), every 30 minutes mid-day and evenings, and every 60 minutes late at night – weekends less frequently. Few visitors spend much time on Staten Island; it's easy to just turn around and get back on the ferry, although there's plenty to see if you stay. For info on visiting Staten Island, see p.287.

Walking tours

Options for walking tours of Manhattan or the outer boroughs are many and varied. You'll find fliers for some of them at the various visitor centers; for what's happening in the current week, check the weekly print edition of *Time Out New York*, or the weekly *Village Voice* (ⓦwww.villagevoice.com). **Columbia and NYU** run very frequent tours of their campuses, free of charge. Not all tour operators are open year-round, with the more esoteric running only a few outings annually. Phone ahead or check websites for the full schedules.

Tour companies

Art Entrée ☎718/391-0011, ⓦwww.artentree.com. Runs a range of art tours throughout the city, focusing on different art scenes, museums, galleries, neighborhoods, and genres like glass art and portraits. One tour series is geared toward collectors and potential collectors. Customized and group tours are their specialty.

Big Onion Walking Tours ☏212/439-1090, ⓦwww.bigonion.com. Guided by history grad students from local universities, venerable Big Onion specializes in tours with an ethnic and historical focus: pick one, or take the "Immigrant New York" tour and learn about everyone. Cost is $15, $12 for seniors, $10 for students; the food-included "Multi-Ethnic Eating Tour" costs $19. These last about two hours.

Brooklyn Center for the Urban Environment ☏718/788-8500, ⓦwww.bcue.org. This organization runs neighborhood and park tours on summer weekends, most of them in Brooklyn. All walking tours, such as "Bats in Brooklyn!", "The Yiddish Rialto," and "A Bed-Stuy Adventure," cost $11, students and seniors $8. Ask about the $35 ($30 for members, students and seniors) ecology boat tours around the Gowanus Canal.

City Hunt ☏877/HUNT-FUN, ⓦwww.cityhunt .org. Innovative scavenger hunts and urban "safaris" like the "Da Vinci Hunt," which begins at the Met, and private pub crawls. Prices range from $20 to $30.

Greenwich Village Literary Pub Crawl ☏212/613-5796. Actors from the New Ensemble Theater Company lead you to several of the most prominent bars in literary history and read from associated works. Tours meet at the White Horse Tavern, 567 Hudson St (see p.370). Reservations are required: $15, students and seniors $12.

Harlem Heritage Tours ☏212/280-7888, ⓦwww.harlemheritage.com. Thorough cultural tours of the historic neighborhood, ranging from "Spanish Harlem Salsa Walking Tour" to "Harlem Heritage Art Shuttle." The tours sometimes include food, a cultural performance, film clips, and/or bus service. Prices range from $20 to $65.

Harlem Spirituals Gospel and Jazz Tours ☏212/391-0900, ⓦwww.harlemspirituals .com/gospel.php. Professionally run, excellent-value tours ranging from Sunday-morning church services to soul food and jazz affairs taking in dinner and a club. $45–99 per person (discounts for children). Reservations required.

Municipal Arts Society ☏212/935-3960, ⓦwww.mas.org/Events/tours.cfm. Opinionated, incredibly detailed historical and architectural tours in Manhattan, Brooklyn, Queens, and the Bronx. Free ($10 donation suggested) tours of Grand Central Terminal start Wednesdays at 12.30pm from the information booth. Weekday walking tours cost $12; weekend combined walking/bus tours are $15.

New School Culinary Walking Tours ☏212/255-4141, ⓦwww.nsu.newschool.edu. Expert foodie tours of the Village, Harlem, Ninth Avenue, and more administered by the Culinary Arts program of New School University. Also conducts behind-the-scenes restaurant visits. Tours take place according to the New School academic calendar. $65, including food.

NoshWalks ☏212/222-2243, ⓦwww .noshnews.com. Weekend ethnic culinary tours of neighborhoods in Manhattan, Queens, Brooklyn, and the Bronx, incorporating local history and culture, by the author of two NYC food guidebooks. $30–33, plus food. Reservations recommended.

The Urban Park Rangers ☏311, ⓦwww .nycgovparks.org. Bona fide rangers with twelve stations in the parks of the five boroughs show you the tallest trees in Queens, the science of St Patrick's Day mythology in Central Park, and the history of Sunset Park. They also run hikes and overnight trips in the city. All programs are free.

Travel essentials

Costs

On a **moderate budget**, expect to spend about $150 per night on accommodation in a mid-range, centrally located hotel in high season, plus $15–20 per person for a moderate sit-down dinner each night and about $15–20 more per person per day for takeout and grocery meals. Getting around will cost $24 per person per week for unlimited public transportation, plus $10 each for the occasional cab ride. Sightseeing, drinking, clubbing, eating haute cuisine, and going to the theater have the potential to add exponentially to these costs. The New York City sales tax is 8.375 percent.

Disabled travelers

New York City has had **disabled access** regulations imposed on an aggressively disabled-unfriendly system. There are wide variations in accessibility, making navigation a tricky business. At the same time, you'll find New Yorkers surprisingly willing to go out of their way to help you. If you're having trouble and you feel that passersby are ignoring you, it's most likely out of respect for your privacy – never hesitate to ask for assistance.

For wheelchair users, getting around on the **subway** is next to impossible without someone to help you, and even then is extremely difficult at most stations. Several, but not all, lines are equipped with elevators, but this doesn't make much of a difference. The Transit Authority is working to make stations accessible, but at the rate they're going it won't happen soon. **Buses** are another story, and are the first choice of many disabled New Yorkers. All MTA buses are equipped with wheelchair lifts and locks. To get on a bus, wait at the bus stop to signal the driver you need to board; when he or she has seen you, move to the back door, where he or she will assist you. For travelers with other mobility difficulties, the driver will "kneel" the bus to allow you easier access. For a Braille subway map, call ☎718/694-4903; for more information about accessibility, call ☎718/596-8585.

Taxis are a viable option for visitors with visual and hearing impairments and minor mobility difficulties. For wheelchair users, taxis are less of a possibility unless you have a collapsible chair, in which case drivers are required to store it and assist you; the unfortunate reality is that most drivers won't stop if they see you waiting. If you're refused, try to get the cab's medallion number and report the driver to the Taxi and Limousine Commission at Ⓦwww.nyc.gov/html/tlc/html/passenger/file_complaint.

Services for disabled travelers

Big Apple Greeter 1 Centre St ☎212/669-3602, Ⓦwww.bigapplegreeter.org. Accepted by many as the main authority on New York accessibility. This free service matches you with a volunteer who spends a few hours showing you the city. Big Apple Greeter has also compiled a resource list for travelers with disabilities, which they will supply on request.

FEGS 315 Hudson St ☎212/366-8400, Ⓦwww.fegs.org. Formerly the New York Society for the Deaf, this is a good source of information on interpreter services, plus services for deaf individuals ranging from HIV-test counseling to kosher lunches.

The Lighthouse 111 E 59th St ☎212/821-9200, Ⓦwww.lighthouse.org. General services for the visually impaired.

The Mayor's Office for People with Disabilities 100 Gold St, 2nd fl ☎212/788-2830, TTY 788-2838, Ⓦwww.nyc.gov/html/mopd. General information and resources.

Electricity

US electricity is 110V AC, and most plugs are two-pronged. Unless they're dual-voltage, most foreign-bought appliances will need a voltage converter as well as a plug adapter. Be warned, some converters may not be able to handle certain high-wattage items, especially those with heated elements.

Entry requirements

Under the **Visa Waiver Program**, citizens of Australia, Ireland, New Zealand, and the UK do not require visas for visits to the US of ninety days or less. You will, however, need to present a machine-readable passport and a completed visa waiver form to Immigration upon arrival; the latter will be provided by your travel agent or by the airline. Canadians can travel in the US for an unlimited amount of time without a visa. For visa information, visit ⓦwww.travel.state.gov. For customs information, visit ⓦwww.customs.treas.gov.

Health

There are few health issues specific to New York City, short of the common cold. If you wash your hands frequently, especially after riding the subway or spending a day on the town, and don't eat off the sidewalk, you should be okay.

Minor ailments can be remedied at **drugstores**, which can more or less be found every few blocks. **Duane Reade** is the city's major chain. Foreign visitors should bear in mind that many pills available over the counter in other countries (for example, codeine-based painkillers) are only available

by prescription here and local brand names can be confusing. If you need advice, ask at the **pharmacy**, where prescription drugs are dispensed.

Should you find yourself requiring a **doctor**, look in the *Yellow Pages* under "Clinics" or "Physicians and Surgeons." Should you be in an **accident**, a medical service will pick you up and charge later. For minor accidents, **emergency rooms** are open 24 hours at these and other Manhattan hospitals: **St Vincent's**, Seventh Ave and W 11th St (☎212/604-7996); **New York Presbyterian (Cornell)**, E 70th St at York Ave (☎212/746-5050); and **Mount Sinai**, Madison Ave at 100th St (☎212/241-7171). Call ☎911 for an ambulance.

Insurance

You will want to invest in **travel insurance**. A typical travel-insurance policy usually provides cover for the loss of baggage, tickets, and – up to a certain limit – cash or checks, as well as cancellation or curtailment of your journey. Many policies can be chopped and changed to exclude coverage you don't need – for example, sickness and accident benefits can often be excluded or included at will. Before you take out a new policy, however, it's worth checking whether you are already covered: some all-risks home-insurance policies may cover your possessions when overseas, and many private medical schemes include cover when abroad.

Internet

Wireless Internet (WIFI) is widespread throughout New York City. Cafés like *Starbucks* have

---

Rough Guides travel insurance

Rough Guides has teamed up with Columbus Direct to offer you **travel insurance** that can be tailored to suit your needs. Products include a low-cost **backpacker** option for long stays; a **short break** option for city getaways; a typical **holiday package** option; and others. There are also annual **multi-trip** policies for those who travel regularly. Different sports and activities (trekking, skiing, etc) can be usually be covered if required.

See our website (ⓦwww.roughguidesinsurance.com) for eligibility and purchasing options. Alternatively, UK residents should call ☎0870/033 9988; US citizens should call ☎1-800/749-4922; Australians should call ☎1-300/669 999. All other nationalities should call ☎+44 870/890 2843.

free "hotspots," as do a good number of motels and hotels. If you're traveling without your own computer, there are any number of places to access the Internet. Try the *cybercafe*, 250 W 49th St (℡212/333-4109, Ⓦwww.cyber-cafe.com) or *alt.coffee*, 139 Ave A (℡212/529-2233, Ⓦwww.altdotcoffee.com), to name but a few. You can also visit one of the many Manhattan branches of Kinko's (Ⓦwww .kinkos.com), a commercial copy-service store. A great, free alternative is to stop by a branch of the **New York City Public Library**, where limited Internet access and printing are available. Each branch has its own rules; ask a librarian how to get online. Another option is **Bryant Park**, where free Internet access is also available.

Laundry

Hotels do it but charge a lot. You're much better off going to an ordinary laundromat or dry cleaner, of which you'll find plenty listed in the *Yellow Pages* under "Laundries." Most laundromats also offer a very affordable drop service, where, for about $1 per pound, you can have your laundry washed, dried, and tidily folded – often the same day. Some budget hotels, YMCAs, and hostels also have coin-operated washers and dryers.

Living and working in New York

It's not easy to live and work in New York, even for US residents. For anyone looking for short-term work, the typical urban employment options are available – temporary office work, waiting tables, babysitting, etc – as well as some quirkier opportunities, like artist's modeling in Soho or Tribeca. For ideas and positions, check the employment ads in the *New York Times*, *New York Press*, *Village Voice*, and the free neighborhood tabloids available throughout the city.

If you're a foreigner, you start at a disadvantage. For **extended legal stays** in the US you need someone who can sponsor you (relatives are best) or a firm offer of work from a US company. Armed with a letter stating this offer, you can apply for a special working visa from any American embassy or consulate abroad before you set off for New York. For further visa information, go to Ⓦwww.unitedstatesvisas.gov.

Finding a place to stay is tricky for everyone. A **studio apartment** – a single room with bathroom and kitchen – in a reasonably safe neighborhood can rent for upwards of $1200 per month. Many newcomers share studios and one-bedrooms among far too many people; it makes more sense to look in the outer boroughs or the nearby New Jersey towns of Jersey City and Hoboken. However, some of these neighborhoods are becoming expensive, and to find a real deal you must hunt hard and check out even the most unlikely possibilities. It frequently takes up to a month or two to find a place.

The best source for finding an apartment or room is **word of mouth**. Watch the **ads** in the *Village Voice*, the *New York Times*, and on Ⓦwww.newyork.craigslist.org (actually a great resource for all kinds of classified listings in New York). Try commercial and campus bulletin boards too, where you might secure a temporary apartment or sublet while the regular tenant is away.

Mail

Post offices in New York City are generally open Monday to Friday 9am to 5pm (though some open earlier), and Saturday from 9am to noon or later. There are also big blue **mailboxes** scattered throughout the city on various street corners. There are many post offices in the city; for the nearest one, search at Ⓦwww .usps.gov. You can buy **stamps** at post offices, as well as in some shops, supermarkets, and delis, although these may cost more than the face value. **Ordinary mail** within the US costs 39¢ for letters weighing up to an ounce, and 24¢ for postcards; addresses must include a **zip code** (postal code) and a return address in the upper left corner of the envelope. **Air mail** to anywhere else in the world costs 84¢ for a letter, 75¢ for a postcard.

You can have mail sent to you c/o **General Delivery** (known elsewhere as **poste restante**), New York City, NY 10116. Letters will end up at the main post office in midtown, 421 Eighth Ave, at W 33rd St (℡212/967-8585). It will be held there for thirty days before being returned to sender, so make sure the envelope has a return address.

Money

US currency comes in **bills** of $1, $5, $10, $20, $50, and $100, plus various larger (and rarer) denominations. The dollar is made up of 100 cents (¢) in coins of 1 cent (usually called a penny), 5 cents (a nickel), 10 cents (a dime), 25 cents (a quarter), 50 cents (a half-dollar), and one dollar. The $2 bill and the half-dollar and dollar coins are seldom seen. Change – especially quarters – is needed for buses, vending machines, and telephones, so always carry plenty.

Most people on vacation in New York withdraw **cash** as needed from automatic teller machines (**ATMs**), which can be found at any bank branch and at many convenience stores and delis in the city. If you're visiting from abroad, make sure you have a personal identification number (PIN) that's designed to work overseas. A **credit card** is a must; American Express, MasterCard, and Visa are widely accepted, and are almost always required for deposits at hotels. If you bring **travelers' checks**, its best to have them in US dollar denominations, as they can be changed in any bank and used as cash in many stores.

Banking hours are usually Monday–Friday 9am–4pm; some banks stay open later on Thursdays or Fridays, and have limited Saturday hours. Major banks – such as Citibank and Chase – will exchange travelers' checks and currency at a standard rate.

The relative value of the US dollar tends to vary considerably against other currencies. At press time, one dollar was worth 0.54 British pounds (£), 0.79 euros, 1.11 Canadian dollars (Can$), 1.36 Australian dollars (Aus$), and 1.61 New Zealand dollars (NZ$). For current exchange rates check ⓦwww.xe.com.

Opening hours and public holidays

The opening hours of specific attractions are given throughout the Guide. As a general rule, most **museums** are open Tuesday through Sunday, 10am to 5 or 6pm, though most have one night per week where they stay open at least a few hours later. Government **offices**, including post offices, are open during regular business hours, usually 9am

Public holidays

New Year's Day Jan 1
Martin Luther King, Jr's Birthday Third Mon in Jan
Presidents' Day Third Mon in Feb
Memorial Day Last Mon in May
Independence Day July 4
Labor Day First Mon in Sept
Columbus Day Second Mon in Oct
Veterans' Day Nov 11
Thanksgiving Day Fourth Thurs in Nov
Christmas Day Dec 25

to 5pm. Store hours vary widely, depending on the kind of store and what part of town you're in, though you can generally count on them being open Monday to Saturday from around 10am to 6pm, with limited Sunday hours. Many of the larger chain or department stores will stay open to 9pm or later, and you generally don't have to walk more than a few blocks anywhere in Manhattan to find a 24-hour deli. On national **public holidays** (see box), banks and offices are likely to be closed all day, and most shops will be closed or have reduced hours.

Phones

Public telephones are easily found on street corners and in hotel lobbies, bars, and restaurants, though functioning ones are becoming harder to find due to the popularity of mobile phones. The cost of a local call is 35¢. Long-distance rates are pricier, and you're better off using a **prepaid calling card**, which you can buy at most grocery stores and newsstands. If your pay phone won't accept your quarter, the change box is full.

There are three **area codes** in use in New York (☎212, ☎646, ☎718), four including the one used exclusively for cell phones (☎917). You must dial 1+ the area code, even if you're calling a number from a phone within the same area code. For directory assistance, call ☎411.

If you want to use your **mobile phone** from abroad, you'll need to check with your phone provider to make sure it will work,

Calling home from abroad

Note that the initial zero is omitted from the area code when dialing the UK, Ireland, Australia, and New Zealand from abroad.

US and Canada international access code + 1 + area code.

Australia international access code + 61 + city code.

New Zealand international access code + 64 + city code.

UK international access code + 44 + city code.

Republic of Ireland international access code + 353 + city code.

and what the call charges will be. Unless you have a tri-band phone, it is unlikely that a mobile bought for use outside the US will work inside the States.

Time

New York City is on **Eastern Standard Time** (EST), which is five hours behind Greenwich Mean Time (GMT).

Women travelers

Women traveling alone or with other women in New York City should attract no more attention than in any other urban destination in the US. For additional information on women's safety in New York, see p.29.

The City

The City

1 The Harbor Islands 43–49

2 The Financial District 50–64

3 City Hall Park and the Brooklyn Bridge 65–72

4 Tribeca and Soho 73–81

5 Chinatown, Little Italy, and NoLita 82–92

6 The Lower East Side 93–98

7 The East Village 99–106

8 The West Village 107–114

9 Chelsea 115–120

10 Union Square, Gramercy Park, and the
Flatiron District 121–128

11 Midtown East 129–146

12 The Museum of Modern Art 147–151

13 Midtown West 152–162

14 Central Park 163–172

15 The Metropolitan Museum of Art 173–187

16 The Upper East Side 188–203

17 The Upper West Side and Morningside Heights 204–219

18 Harlem and above 220–236

19 Brooklyn 237–264

20 Queens 265–276

21 The Bronx 277–286

22 Staten Island 287–294

The Harbor Islands

The southern tip of the island of Manhattan, together with the shores of neighboring New Jersey, Staten Island, and Brooklyn, encloses the broad expanse of **New York Harbor**. One of the finest natural harbors in the world, it covers 100 square miles in total and stretches as far as the Verrazano Narrows – the thin neck of water between Staten Island and Long Island. While it's possible to appreciate Manhattan simply by gazing back at it from the promenade in Battery Park City, to get a proper sense of New York's uniqueness and the best views of the celebrated skyline, you should really take to the water. You can do this by taking a boat ride out to **Liberty**, **Ellis**, or **Governors islands** – three highly compelling destinations – or, if you're feeling less purposeful, by catching the Staten Island Ferry, which traverses the harbor.

Visiting the islands: ferry logistics

The only way to get to any of the Harbor Islands is via **ferry**. Take the #1 train to South Ferry or the #4 or #5 trains to Bowling Green, then walk to the boat pier in Battery Park. From the pier, **Circle Line** ferries go to Liberty, then on to Ellis Island (daily, every 20–30min, 9am–4pm; round-trip $11.50, seniors $9.50, children 3–12 $4.50; tickets at Castle Clinton, in the park, or ☎866/782-8834 in advance (subject to booking fee); ☎212/269-5755, ⓦ www.circlelinedowntown.com, ⓦ www .statuereservations.com). Even if you book ferry tickets in advance, you'll still have to stand in line to pick them up and to get on the ferry, so allow plenty of time – lines can be long at any time of year, but they're especially bad in the summer (weekends in the summer are the worst). In terms of planning your visit, give yourself at least half a day to see both Liberty and Ellis islands, and more time if you don't want to be rushed. Liberty Island needs at least one hour (that's only if you're walking around the island, and not taking a tour of the inside), and Ellis requires at least two hours to do its museum justice. Start out as early as possible: keep in mind that if you take the last ferry of the day to Liberty Island, you won't be able to get over to Ellis.

Alternatively, the **Staten Island Ferry** (free; ☎212/639-9675, ⓦ www.siferry.com) departs every half an hour from Whitehall Terminal and shuttles some 20 million passengers between Manhattan and its namesake island every year. While it provides a beautiful panorama of the harbor and downtown skyline, it doesn't actually stop at any of the Harbor Islands. (See p.287 for more information on the Staten Island Ferry.)

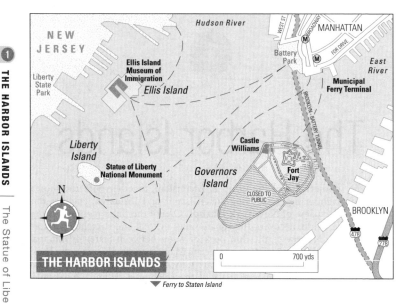

▼ Ferry to Staten Island

The Statue of Liberty

Of all America's symbols, none has proved more enduring than the **Statue of Liberty** (daily 9.30am–5pm; free; ☎212/363-3200, ⬤www.nps.gov/stli). Indeed, there is probably no more immediately recognizable profile in existence than that of Lady Liberty, who stands with torch in hand, clutching a stone tablet. Measuring some 305ft from base and pedestal, she has acted as the figurehead of the American Dream for more than a century. For Americans, the statue is a potent reminder of their country's heritage as a land of immigrants. When the first waves of European refugees arrived in the mid-nineteenth century, it was she who greeted them. As their ships entered New York Harbor through the Verrazano Narrows and rounded the bend of the bay, the crowded passengers were allowed a glimpse of "Liberty Enlightening the World" – the symbolic beginning of a new life.

These days an immigrant's first view of the US is more likely to be the customs check at JFK Airport, but the statue nevertheless remains a stirring sight. **Emma Lazarus**'s poem *The New Colossus*, inspired by the new immigrant experience and inscribed on a tablet on the bronze pedestal, is no less quotable now than when it was written in 1903:

> Not like the brazen giant of Greek fame,
> with conquering limbs astride from land to land;
> Here at our sea-washed, sunset gates shall stand
> a mighty woman with a torch
> whose flame is imprisoned lightning,
> and her name Mother of Exiles.
> From her beacon-hand glows
> world-wide welcome;
> her mild eyes command the air-bridged harbor

that twin cities frame.
"Keep ancient lands your storied pomp!"
cries she with silent lips.
"Give me your tired, your poor,
Your huddled masses yearning to breathe free,
The wretched refuse of your teeming shore.
Send these, the homeless, tempest-tost to me,
I lift my lamp beside the golden door!"

The statue itself, which depicts Liberty throwing off her shackles and holding a beacon to light the world, is the creation of French sculptor **Frédéric Auguste Bartholdi**, who crafted it a hundred years after the American Revolution, supposedly to commemorate the solidarity between France and America. (Actually, he originally intended the statue for Alexandria, Egypt.) Bartholdi built Liberty in Paris between 1874 and 1884, starting with a terracotta model and enlarging it through four successive versions to its present size of 151ft. The final product is a construction of thin copper sheets bolted together and supported by an iron framework designed by **Gustave Eiffel**. The arm carrying the torch was exhibited in Madison Square Park for seven years, but the rest of the statue remained in France until it was officially accepted on behalf of the American people in 1884.

Liberty had to be taken apart into hundreds of pieces in order to ship the statue to New York, where it was finally reassembled, although it was another two years before the figure could be properly unveiled. Money had to be collected to fund the construction of the statue's base, and for some reason Americans were unwilling to dip into their pockets. Only through the efforts of newspaper magnate Joseph Pulitzer, a keen supporter of the figure, did it all come together in the end. **Richard Morris Hunt** built a pedestal around the existing star-shaped Fort Wood, and Liberty was formally dedicated by President Cleveland on October 28, 1886, amid a patriotic outpouring that has never really stopped. Indeed, fifteen million people descended on Manhattan for the statue's centennial celebrations, and by 2001 some six million people were making the pilgrimage here each year.

In order to get inside the monument you have to take a tour. There are currently two options available, both of which require reservations in advance (free, apart from a $1.75 booking fee). The **Promenade** tour takes in the statue's entrance hall and an upstairs exhibition, and the **Observatory** tour includes all this plus the 192 steps to the top of the pedestal (due to security concerns, visitors are not allowed up to the crown). The downstairs lobby shows the original torch and flame, which was completed first and used to raise funds for the rest of the statue. The small exhibition upstairs tells the story of the statue with prints, photographs, posters, cuttings, and replicas of bits of the statue and the plaster casts used to build it. There are images of the statue from all kinds of sources – indicative of just how iconic an image it is. At the top of the pedestal you can look up into the center of the statue's skirts – make sure you get a glance of her riveted and bolted interior, and her fire-hazard staircase. After you've perused the statue's interior offerings, take a turn around the balcony outside – the views are predictably superb.

Ellis Island

Just across the water from Liberty Island, and fifteen minutes farther from Manhattan by ferry, sits **Ellis Island**, once the first stop for over twelve million immigrants to the US. Originally called Gibbet Island by the English (who used it for punishing captured pirates), the island became an immigration station in 1892, a processing point made necessary by the massive influx of mostly southern and eastern European immigrants to America in the late nineteenth century. It remained open until 1954, when it was abandoned and left to fall into atmospheric ruin. The main complex was eventually renovated and in 1990 reopened as the impressive, free **Ellis Island Museum of Immigration**.

The immigration process

Up until the 1850s, there was no official **immigration process** in New York. It was at this point that a surge of Irish, German, and Scandinavian immigrants, the former seeking to escape famine and the latter failed revolutions, forced authorities to open an immigration center at Castle Clinton in Battery Park. By the 1880s, the situation in Europe was even worse, with widespread hardship in eastern and southern Europe, pogroms in Russia, and massive economic failure in southern Italy. Ellis Island opened in 1892, just as America was coming out of its own depression and beginning to assert itself as a world power. News spread through Europe of the opportunities in the New World, and millions of desperate people soon left their homelands in search of a new life in America.

The immigrants who arrived at Ellis Island were all steerage-class passengers; richer immigrants were processed at their leisure on-board ship. The scenes on the island were horribly confused: most families arrived hungry, filthy, and penniless. Rarely were they able to speak English, and invariably were they awed by the beckoning metropolis of Manhattan. Immigrants were numbered and forced to wait for up to a day while Ellis Island officials frantically tried to process them. Though the processing center had been designed to accommodate 500,000 immigrants per year, double that number arrived during the early part of the twentieth century, and the island had to be enlarged by landfill so additional structures could be built. As many as 11,747 immigrants passed through the center on a single day in 1907.

Inside the center, con men were frighteningly numerous: they stole immigrants' bags as they were checked and offered rip-off exchange rates to the ignorant newcomers. Each family was split up – men sent to one area, women and children to another – while a series of checks weeded out the undesirables and the infirm. The latter were taken to the second floor, where doctors would check for "loathsome and contagious diseases" as well as signs of insanity. Those who failed medical tests were marked with a white cross on their backs and either sent to the hospital or put back on the boat. There was also a legal test, which checked nationality and political affiliations. Steamship carriers had an obligation to return any immigrants not accepted into America to their original port, though according to official records, only two percent of all immigrants were ever rejected, and of those, many jumped into the sea and tried to swim to Manhattan, or committed suicide, instead of going home. On average, eighty percent of immigrants were processed in less than eight hours, after which they headed either to New Jersey and trains to the West, or into New York City, where they settled in one of the rapidly expanding ethnic neighborhoods, such as the Lower East Side.

Ellis Island Museum of Immigration

The island's main building was constructed in 1903 (its predecessor had burned down in 1897), and various additions were built in the ensuing years – hospitals, outhouses, and the like, usually on bits of landfill. During World War II it was used as a detention center for some seven thousand German, Italian, and

△ Registry Room, Ellis Island Museum of Immigration

Japanese people, then finally closed in 1954. The buildings remained derelict until 1984, when $162 million was donated for their restoration; since then, the main, four-turreted central building has been completely renovated as the **Ellis Island Museum of Immigration** (daily 9.30am–5.15pm; free; ☏212/363-3200, ⊛www.nps.gov/elis, ⊛www.ellisisland.com). This is an ambitious museum that eloquently recaptures the spirit of the place with artifacts, photographs, maps, and personal accounts that tell the story of the immigrants who passed through Ellis Island on their way to a new life in America. Some 100 million Americans can trace their roots back through Ellis Island, and, for them especially, the museum is an engaging display. On the first floor, located in the old railroad ticket office, the excellent permanent exhibit "Peopling of America" chronicles four centuries of immigration, offering a statistical portrait of those who arrived at Ellis Island – who they were, where they came from, and why they came. The huge, vaulted **Registry Room** on the second floor, scene of so much immigrant trepidation, elation, and despair, has been left imposingly bare, with just a couple of inspectors' desks and American flags. In the side hall, a series of interview rooms recreate the process that immigrants went through on their way to naturalization; the white-tiled chambers are soberingly bureaucratic. Each room is augmented by recorded voices of those who passed through Ellis Island, recalling their experiences, along with photographs, thoughtful and informative explanatory text, and small artifacts – train timetables, toiletries, and toys from home. Descriptions of arrival and subsequent interviews are presented, as well as examples of questions asked and medical tests given. One of the dormitories, used by those kept overnight for further examination, has been left almost intact. On the top floor, you'll find evocative photographs of the building before it was restored, along with items rescued from the building and rooms devoted to the peak years of immigration.

Among the additional features of the museum are thirty-minute long, hit-or-miss re-enactments of immigrant experiences. Titled "Embracing Freedom," they are based on oral histories from the museum's archives (April–Oct, usually around 7 times daily in the museum's theatre; a small fee; ☎212/561-4500). A short documentary film, *Island of Hope, Island of Tears*, is shown throughout the day; it also lasts thirty minutes, and is free. If you turn up early enough to get a place, you can get a free, 45-minute ranger-guided tour of the museum (they can't be booked in advance).

The museum's **American Family Immigration History Center** (hours same as the museum's; $5 per half-hour to conduct genealogical searches on computer terminals; ⊛www.ellisisland.org) offers an interactive research database that contains information from ship manifests and passenger lists concerning over 22 million immigrants who passed through the entire Port of New York between 1892 and 1924. Outside, the names of over 600,000 immigrants who passed through the building over the years are engraved in copper; while the "Wall of Honor" (⊛www.wallofhonor.com) is always accepting new submissions, it controversially requires families to pay $100 to be included on the list.

Governors Island

"Nowhere in New York is more pastoral," wrote travel writer Jan Morris of **Governors Island**, a 172-acre tract of land across from Brooklyn and with unobstructed views of lower Manhattan and New York Harbor. Until the mid-1990s, the last of the three small islands just south of Manhattan was the largest and most expensively run Coast Guard installation in the world, housing some 1600 service personnel and their families. Active since 1637, it was also the oldest military installation in continuous service in the US. The island is still home to a handful of colonial and nineteenth-century houses, as well as Fort Jay (constructed between 1794 and 1809 and used in the War of 1812) and Castle Williams, which was erected in 1811 to complement the near-identical Castle Clinton on the lower end of Manhattan (see p.59), and was used to house Confederate prisoners during the Civil War. In 1988, Governors Island was the site of a summit between US President Ronald Reagan and Mikhail Gorbachev. However, the island's annual upkeep became too high to justify at the end of the Cold War, so in 1995 it was handed over to the General Services Administration of the Federal Government. The Coast Guard moved to Homeport, Staten Island, and for a few years rumors abounded about the picturesque spot's uncertain future – casinos, parkland, and a City University campus were all discussed as possibilities. However, in 2003 Governors Island was returned to the public to be administered by the City and State of New York, and the National Park Service, and for the moment it is an intriguingly offbeat and bucolic tourist destination, if one of limited access. It's open from June to September, and you can visit, by way of free, two-hour tours only, on Tuesday, Wednesday, or Thursday (10am & 1pm); on Friday and Saturday you can make your own way and join one of the free tours once you're there (ferries leave every hour 10am–3pm). Ferries depart from the Battery Maritime Building at Slip 7 just northeast of the Staten Island Ferry Terminal (see p.287); call ahead or check their website for the schedule (☎212/825-3045, ⓦwww.nps.gov/gois).

The Financial District

With its incredible assemblage of skyscrapers, the **Financial District** in Lower Manhattan has long been synonymous with the New York of popular imagination. What the celebrated skyline doesn't show, though, is the area's layers of dense development – from the prime vantage point of the Brooklyn waterfront or a harbor ferry you would never know that buildings of all vintages, styles, and sizes are packed in along narrow, canyon-like streets. This is where Manhattan first began, and is as good a place as any for visitors to first dive in: the heart of the world's business trade is still home to some of the city's most historic streets and sights as well as some of its most modern corporate headquarters.

Over time, the area has seen more than its fair share of destruction and renewal. Many of the early colonial buildings that once lined these blocks burned down in either the Revolutionary War or the Great Fire of 1835. Big businesses eager to boost their images by building offices on Wall Street have demolished more of the older structures, replacing them with multistory towers. In September 2001, the character of the Financial District was altered radically once again when the attacks on the World Trade Center destroyed the Twin Towers and killed thousands (see box, p.56). Nonetheless, life is rapidly coming back to the area: the site has been cleared of debris, work has begun on the foundations of a new World Trade Center, and a temporary subway station has opened. Complemented by the steady commercial development of South Street Seaport and the construction of new residential buildings, the Financial District is once again in the process of integrating its present and future into its past.

Begin your tour of the Financial District at Wall Street, accessible by the #2, #3, #4, and #5 trains.

Along Wall Street

It was the Dutch who provided **Wall Street** its name when they built a wooden wall at the edge of New Amsterdam in 1635 in an effort to protect themselves from British settlers living to the north. The street has been associated with money for hundreds of years; the eighteenth century saw the creation of homes for the city's most affluent residents, as well as the establishment of the young country's first banks and insurance companies. The purse strings of the capitalist world are controlled behind the Neoclassical facade of the **New York Stock Exchange** at no. 18 (ⓦwww.nyse.com), where 1.3 billion shares are traded and $35 billion changes hands on an average day. The building, with

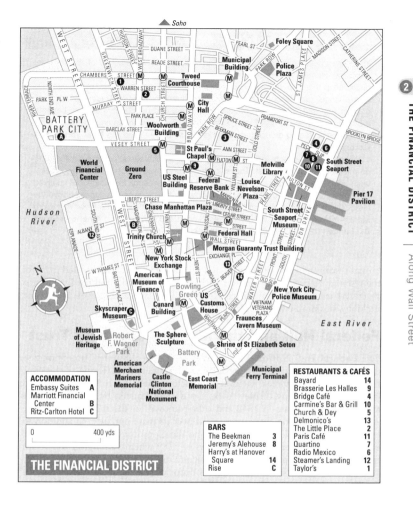

Soho ▲

BATTERY PARK CITY

Hudson River

World Financial Center

Ground Zero

Foley Square

Municipal Building

Police Plaza

Tweed Courthouse

City Hall

Woolworth Building

St Paul's Chapel

Melville Library

South Street Seaport

US Steel Building

Federal Reserve Bank

Louise Nevelson Plaza

Chase Manhattan Plaza

South Street Seaport Museum

Pier 17 Pavilion

Trinity Church

Federal Hall

New York Stock Exchange

Morgan Guaranty Trust Building

American Museum of Finance

Bowling Green

New York City Police Museum

Cunard Building

US Customs House

Skyscraper Museum

Vietnam Veterans Plaza

Fraunces Tavern Museum

East River

Museum of Jewish Heritage

Robert F. Wagner Park

The Sphere Sculpture

Battery Park

Shrine of St Elizabeth Seton

American Merchant Mariners Memorial

Castle Clinton National Monument

East Coast Memorial

Municipal Ferry Terminal

ACCOMMODATION
Embassy Suites   A
Marriott Financial
  Center   B
Ritz-Carlton Hotel C

0   400 yds

BARS
The Beekman   3
Jeremy's Alehouse   8
Harry's at Hanover
  Square   14
Rise   C

RESTAURANTS & CAFÉS
Bayard   14
Brasserie Les Halles   9
Bridge Café   4
Carmine's Bar & Grill   10
Church & Dey   5
Delmonico's   13
The Little Place   2
Paris Café   11
Quartino   7
Radio Mexico   6
Steamer's Landing   12
Taylor's   1

THE FINANCIAL DISTRICT

its six mammoth Corinthian columns and monumental statues representing Integrity surrounded by Agriculture, Mining, Science, Industry, and Invention, dates from 1903, and was designed by famed turn-of-the-century architect James B. Post. Due to security concerns, the public is not allowed to view the frenzied trading floor of the Exchange, although on the rest of Wall Street it's business as usual, with swarms of suited traders and financial movers and shakers coming and going from the Exchange and surrounding buildings like clock-work, Monday through Friday. If you don't care for crowds and want to stroll down Wall Street in relative peace, head to the narrow streets on the weekend, when the whole district is eerily vacant.

Just south of Wall Street, *Delmonico's*, 56 Beaver St, at William Street, is the oldest restaurant in the country. Despite the Great Panic and financial crisis that befell Wall Street in 1837, the Delmonico brothers, Giovanni and Pietro, opened their doors to much acclaim, attracting the city's wealthiest denizens. The build-ing was a bastion of opulence, with its grand portico supported by columns

The early days of stocks and bonds

In order to help America finance the Revolutionary War, Secretary of the Treasury Alexander Hamilton offered $80 million worth of bonds up for sale. Not only did the public snap them up, but merchants also started trading the bonds, along with bills of exchange, promissory notes, and other commercial paper. Trading became so popular that in 1792 a group of 22 stockbrokers and merchants gathered beneath a buttonwood tree on Wall Street, signing the "Buttonwood Agreement" and forming the initial trading group that would go on to be renamed the **New York Stock Exchange** in 1817.

A century later, a more individualistic group of stockbrokers forged a similar bond on the curbs of Broad Street. These "curb brokers," who specialized in risky stocks, were unable to meet the requirements of the New York Stock Exchange, but survived nonetheless, with phone clerks in the windows of buildings several stories above the street using hand signals to relay customers' orders. In 1921, the New York Curb Market moved indoors at 86 Trinity Place and in 1953 became the **American Stock Exchange** (Ⓣ212/306-1000, Ⓦwww.amex.com).

brought from the ruins of Pompeii and a 100-page menu that featured many of the restaurant's culinary inventions, including baked Alaska and the Delmonico steak. *Delmonico's* is now an official New York City landmark, as well as a decent, if clubby, steakhouse (see p.331 for review).

Federal Hall and the Morgan Guaranty Trust

The **Federal Hall National Memorial**, 26 Wall St (Mon–Fri 9am–5pm; free; Ⓣ212/825-6888, Ⓦwww.nps.gov/feha), at the street's head, is one of the city's finest examples of Greek Revival architecture. Built in 1699 as the second city hall of the colony of New York, it was reconstructed by Town and Davis as the Customs House in 1842 and is best known for the monumental statue of George Washington that stands guard over its main entrance. In addition to information on the US Bill of Rights and the Constitution, there's also a small exhibit inside that relates the heady days of 1789 when Washington was sworn in as America's first president from a balcony on this site.

Some sixty years before Washington's historic oath-taking, Federal Hall was the site of an ominous blow to British rule. It was here that in 1735 printer John Peter Zenger was tried and acquitted of libel charges, thereby setting an

The trial of John Peter Zenger

German immigrant **John Peter Zenger** (1697–1746) rapidly established a reputation as a printer and journalist for the *New York Weekly Journal*, which took an anti-British stance and published inflammatory writings in an age when British law maintained that truth was no defense in cases of libel. The *Journal*'s views made him unpopular with the royal authorities in New York, and in 1734 Zenger was arrested for articles considered libelous against the Crown, and spent eight months in prison. Philadelphia attorney **Andrew Hamilton** took Zenger's case pro bono, ensuring that his libel trial became a fight for freedom of the press. Urging the jury to find in Zenger's favor, the fiery Hamilton declaimed that "The laws of our country have given us a right: the liberty of both exposing and opposing arbitrary power by speaking and writing the truth." It took only minutes before the jury reached a verdict of not guilty. After he was acquitted, Zenger was appointed public printer of New York and New Jersey.

important precedent for freedom of press in America (see box, opposite). The documents and models inside are worth a look, as is the hall itself, with its elegant rotunda, and Cretan maidens worked into the decorative railings.

Just across Wall Street at no. 23 is the **Morgan Guaranty Trust Building**, which bears scars from an explosion in 1920, when a horse-drawn cart blew up out front, killing 33 and wounding over a hundred. The bombing has never been explained. One theory holds that it was a premeditated attack on Morgan's financial empire; another claims it was an accident involving the transportation of explosives; yet another alleges the blast was an Italian anarchist taking revenge for the executions of Sacco and Vanzetti. Curiously, or perhaps deliberately, the marks on the building's wall have never been repaired.

Trinity Church

At Wall Street's western end at Broadway sits **Trinity Church** (free guided tours daily at 2pm; ☎212/602-0800, ⊛www.trinitywallstreet.org), a stoic onlooker of the street's dealings. King William III of England granted the church a charter and some land in 1697, and while there's been a church here ever since, this knobby neo-Gothic structure – the third model – only went up in 1846. It was the city's tallest building for fifty years – a reminder of just how relatively recently high-rise Manhattan has sprung up. Trinity has the air of an English country church (hardly surprising, given its architect, Richard Upjohn, was English), especially in the sheltered graveyard, the resting place of many early Manhattanites. A search around the old tombstones uncovers such notables as the first secretary of the Treasury, Alexander Hamilton, steamboat king Robert Fulton, and Declaration of Independence signatory Francis Lewis, to name a few. The church's interior, while pleasant, is not nearly as interesting as its exterior or the graveyard. There is, however, a small museum that details the church's history through multiple fires and landmark events from the Revolutionary War to the Great Depression. Trinity parish, along with St Paul's Chapel, farther north on Broadway, also played an integral role in providing refuge following the September 11 attacks; there are memorials inside and out dedicated to both victims and volunteers.

The Federal Reserve Plaza and around

Four blocks north of Wall Street lies Maiden Lane, which curves across lower Manhattan. Maiden Lane meets Nassau Street at Philip Johnson's and John Burgee's fortress-like **Federal Reserve Plaza**, with its cavernous arched hall. The Federal Reserve Plaza proved to be one of Johnson's last projects with Burgee: he split with the architect soon after, leaving Burgee broke and in the architectural wilderness.

There's good reason for the **Federal Reserve Bank**'s iron-barred exterior: stashed 80ft below the somber neo-Gothic interior are most of the "free" world's gold reserves – 9000 tons of them, occasionally shifted from vault to vault as wars break out or international debts are settled. It is possible to tour the stacks of gleaming gold bricks; contact the Public Information Department, Federal Reserve Bank, 33 Liberty St, NY 10045 (☎212/720-6130, ⊛www .ny.frb.org), several weeks ahead, as tickets have to be mailed. The free tour (hourly Mon–Fri 9.30am–2.30pm) includes visits to the gold vault, as well as

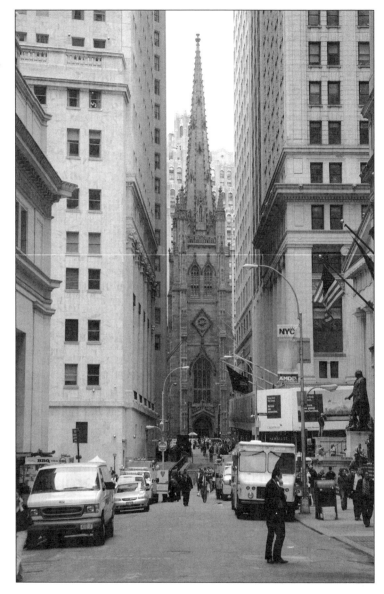

△ Trinity Church, from Wall Street

coin and interactive exhibits. Upstairs, in the bank, dirty money and counterfeit currency are weeded out of circulation by automated checkers that shuffle dollar bills like endless packs of cards.

When you've adjusted to the sight of high finance's gold, you can see more of its glitter at **1 Chase Manhattan Plaza**, immediately to the south between

Pine and Liberty streets. This, the bank's prestigious New York headquarters, was designed by the distinguished firm of Skidmore, Owings & Merrill. It boasts a boxy tower that was the first of its kind in lower Manhattan when built in 1960, and which brought to downtown the concept of the plaza entrance. One block west, at Cedar Street and Broadway, is the **Marine Midland Bank Building**, 140 Broadway, a smaller tower by the same design team, decorated with a cube sculpture by Isamu Noguchi (1967). A more striking display of sculpture lies behind Chase Manhattan Plaza on **Louise Nevelson Plaza**, which divides Maiden Lane and Liberty Street. Here, several of Nevelson's works perch like a mass of shrapnel on an island; a mural of Seurat's *A Sunday Afternoon on the Grande Jatte* sits to one side of the plaza.

Ground Zero and around

The former site of the World Trade Center, **Ground Zero** remains a gaping hole on Manhattan's lower West Side, even as construction workers labor away beneath street level at the foundations of a new World Trade Center. Seven buildings in total were destroyed as a result of the 2001 terrorist attacks, while eleven other structures surrounding the complex, including the Federal Building and the New York Police Command Center, suffered serious damage. Many businesses remained closed in the months after the attacks, but the vast majority have by now reopened and today they are, if anything, invigorated by the brisk Ground Zero visitor traffic.

Many continue to make the pilgrimage to Ground Zero, though there's precious little to see. The viewing platform that stood here immediately after the events of September 11 has been taken down, but you can still get a look at the site by circling the fenced-in perimeter. There is an elevated walkway at the south end that gives you the best view of the area, where construction is ongoing underground. At the time of writing, building has yet to start on the new World Trade Center's Freedom Tower, but ground had just been broken on a new, more permanent subway station, which is scheduled to be completed in 2009.

Dominating lower Manhattan's landscape from nearly any angle, the 110-story **Twin Towers** always loomed over their surroundings; harsher critics charged that, spirited down to a tenth of their size, the towers wouldn't get a second glance. The first tower went up in 1972 and the second one year later, only to be quickly surpassed as the world's tallest skyscrapers by the Sears Tower in Chicago (itself exceeded by Kuala Lumpur's Petronas Towers). The towers were highly celebrated examples of tube buildings – constructions that used exterior columns and beams to form steel tubes able to withstand the mighty winds encountered by buildings of such heights. At 1368 and 1362 feet – over one quarter-mile tall – the towers afforded mind-blowing views; on a clear day, visitors to the observation deck could see 55 miles into the distance. While the Twin Towers became integral parts of the New York skyline, they also evolved into emblems of American power in the eyes of Islamic extremists. On February 26, 1993, a bomb exploded in one of the World Trade Center underground parking lots, killing six people. Radical Muslim cleric Sheikh Omar Abdel-Rahman, along with nine co-defendants, was convicted of the bombing in 1995. It's hard to imagine how inconsequential this attack would seem in light of future events.

September 11 and its aftermath

At 8.46am on September 11, 2001, a hijacked airliner slammed into the north tower of the **World Trade Center**; seventeen minutes later another hijacked plane struck the south tower. As thousands looked on in horror – in addition to hundreds of millions more viewing on TV – the south tower collapsed at 9.50am, its twin at 10.30am. All seven buildings of the World Trade Center complex eventually collapsed, and the center was reduced to a mountain of steel, concrete, and glass rubble. As black clouds billowed above, the whole area was covered in a blanket of concrete dust many inches thick; debris reached several hundred feet into the air. The devastation was staggering. While most of the 50,000 civilians working in the towers had been evacuated before the towers fell, many never made it out of the building; hundreds of firemen, policemen, and rescue workers who arrived on the scene when the planes struck were crushed when the buildings collapsed. In all, **2996 people perished** at the WTC and the simultaneous attack on the Pentagon in Washington DC, in what was, in terms of casualties, the largest foreign attack on American soil in history. Radical Muslim Osama bin Laden's terrorist network, al-Qaeda, claimed responsibility for the attacks.

In the days after the attack, downtown was basically shut down, and the seven-square-block area immediately around the WTC was the focus of an intense rescue effort. New Yorkers lined up to give blood and volunteered to help the rescue workers; vigils were held throughout the city, most notably in Union Square, which was peppered with candles and makeshift shrines. Then-Mayor **Rudy Giuliani** cut a highly composed and reassuring figure as New Yorkers struggled to come to terms with the assault on their city. Life in New York, and the rest of the United States, was irrevocably changed.

Moving forward

In 2003, Polish-born architect **Daniel Libeskind** was named the winner of a competition held to determine the design for the new World Trade Center. Libeskind's visionary plans include the use of windmills, meant as symbols of energy independence, atop the planned **Tower of Freedom** spire, which will soar 1776ft high, making the new World Trade Center the second-tallest structure on earth after the CN Tower in Toronto, though it will not qualify as a skyscraper as the tower itself will not be continuously habitable.

In addition to the tower, there will be two large public spaces: **Park of Heroes** and **Wedge of Light**, which will make use of engineering and astronomy in order that each year on September 11, precisely between the hours of 8.46am, when the first plane hit, and 10.30am, when the second tower collapsed, the sun will shine as "a wedge of light" between the buildings in honor of the victims. Beneath these structures, Libeskind plans to leave space for an official memorial, whose design was determined by another international competition. Finalists Michael Arad of New York City and Peter Walker of Berkeley, California, were chosen for their submission, Reflecting Absence, in January 2004 by a jury that included famed Vietnam Memorial designer, Maya Lin. The World Trade Center Site Memorial will be located in a field of trees and include two enormous voids with recessed pools symbolizing the "footprints" of the twin towers. Libeskind also plans to leave room for a September 11 museum.

Unfortunately, since the inception of Libeskind's design, the new construction has been plagued with controversy. Many people wonder if the Wedge of Light, ideally a shadowless space, will be possible in this skyscraper-dense part of town. One of the more recent debates has been over the content of the proposed museum; federal officials want a broad-ranging exhibit on the fight for freedom against Cold War opponents like Cuba and China, while an organization of surviving families want the focus to remain strictly on the September 11 attack.

St Paul's Chapel

Both the oldest church and the oldest building in continuous use in Manhattan, **St Paul's Chapel**, at Fulton Street and Broadway, dates from 1766, making it almost prehistoric by New York standards. Though the building is American in feel, its English architect used London's St Martin-in-the-Fields as his model for this unfussy eighteenth-century space of soap-bar blues and pinks. George Washington worshipped here and his pew has been preserved. For eight months after the September 11 attacks, St Paul's Chapel served as a sanctuary for the rescue workers at Ground Zero, providing food, a place to nap, and spiritual support. The chapel's excellent exhibit, "Unwavering Spirit," effectively chronicles the church's role in the September 11 recovery efforts, and has had over a million visitors to date.

South along Broadway

At 1 Liberty Plaza, on Liberty Street between Broadway and Church Street, you'll find the **US Steel Building**, a black mass that has justly been called a "gloomy, cadaverous hulk." To make way for it, the famed Singer Building, one of the most delicate features of the Manhattan skyline, was demolished in 1968. When the World Trade Center towers collapsed in 2001, many of the US Steel Building's windows popped out, and it was feared at first that the building itself would tumble; it didn't, but its north wall is still covered as repairs near completion.

The old **Cunard Building**, south along Broadway at no. 25, is a most impressive leftover of the confident days before the Wall Street Crash of 1929. Constructed in 1921, its marble walls and high dome once housed the famous steamship line's trans-Atlantic booking office for such seafaring vessels as the *Queen Mary* and the *Queen Elizabeth* – hence the elaborate, whimsical murals of ships and nautical mythology splashed around the ceiling of the Great Hall. As ocean liners gave way to jets, Cunard could no longer afford such an extravagant shop window. Today, the building houses a post office – one that's been fitted with little feeling for the exuberant space it occupies.

In front of the Cunard Building on the street partition is a sculpture of a **Charging Bull** – not originally envisioned as a symbol of a "bull market" for Wall Street stocks, though that's how it is perceived by New Yorkers today. As the story goes, on December 15, 1989, Arturo Di Modica installed his sculpture in the middle of Broad Street. The city removed the sculpture the next day, but was forced to put it back when public support of the statue was surprisingly vocal.

Across the street, located in the former headquarters of John D. Rockefeller's Standard Oil Company, is the **Museum of American Finance**, 28 Broadway (Tues–Sat 10am–4pm; $2; ☎212/908-4110, ⓦwww.financialhistory.org), though they're set to decamp to 48 Wall St in 2007. This is the largest public archive of financial documents and artifacts in the world, featuring such objects as the bond signed by Washington bearing the first dollar sign ever used on a Federal document, and a stretch of ticker tape from the opening moments of 1929's Great Crash. Also on view are early photographs of Wall Street and furnishings from *Delmonico's* restaurant, many a robber baron's favorite eatery (see p.51). Fortunately, this isn't just a self-congratulatory temple to big business; it also features genuinely educational, rotating exhibits related to global finance.

Bowling Green

Broadway ends at the city's oldest public park, **Bowling Green**. The green was the location of one of Manhattan's more inspired business deals, when Peter Minuit, first director general of the Dutch colony of New Amsterdam, in 1626 bought the whole island from the Native Americans for a bucket of trade goods worth sixty guilders (about $25). The other side of the story (and the part you never hear) was that these particular Native Americans didn't actually own the island – they were from New Jersey; no doubt both parties went home smiling. Later, the park became the site of the city's meat market, but in 1733 it was transformed into an oval of turf used for lawn bowling by colonial Brits, on a lease of "one peppercorn per year." The encircling iron fence is an original from 1771, though the crowns that once topped the stakes were removed during the Revolutionary War, as was a statue of George III. The statue was melted into musket balls – little bits of the monarch that were then fired at his troops. The area was one of the last to be evacuated by the British in 1783, and five years later was the site of celebration when New York ratified the Constitution in 1788. The elegant townhouses that once rimmed the green were replaced, starting in 1850, by such nonresidential structures as the Produce Exchange and the US Customs House. The park itself was neglected for a number of years, but was fully restored by the city in the mid-1970s, and today is a well-maintained patch of green in the midst of downtown's concrete jungle.

The US Customs House and the Museum of the American Indian

The green sees plenty of office folk picnicking in the shadow of Cass Gilbert's **US Customs House**, a monument to the Port of New York and home of the **Smithsonian National Museum of the American Indian**, 1 Bowling Green (daily 10am–5pm, Thurs 10am–8pm; free; ☏212/514-3700, ⓦwww .si.edu/nmai). This excellent collection of artifacts from almost every Native American tribe was largely assembled by one man, George Gustav Heye (1874–1957), who traveled through the Americas picking up such works for over fifty years. Only a small portion of the collection is actually on display here – the majority of it lives in a sister museum on the Mall in Washington DC. The permanent collection in Manhattan includes thousands of pieces selected by curators and different Native American groups, and there are also several temporary shows per year. Items on display include intricate basketry and woodcarvings, feathered bonnets, and objects of ceremonial significance. A rather extraordinary facet of the museum is its repatriation policy, adopted in 1991, which mandates that it give back to Indian tribes, upon request, any human remains, funerary objects, and ceremonial and religious items it may have illegally acquired.

Built in 1907, the Customs House was intended to pay homage to the booming maritime market. The four statues at the front of the building (sculpted by Daniel Chester French, who also created the Lincoln Memorial in Washington DC) represent the African, Asian, European, and North American continents, while the twelve statues near the top personify the world's great commercial centers of the past and present: Denmark, England, France, Genoa, Germany, Greece, Holland, Phoenicia, Portugal, Rome, Spain, and Venice. Each of the building's Corinthian columns features the head of Mercury, the god of commerce. As if French foresaw the House's current use, his statues comment on the mistreatment of Native Americans. The striking work on the left side of the front main staircase depicts a Native American in full headdress timidly peering over the shoulder of "America," who sits grandly on a throne and holds an oversized sheaf of corn on her lap – a symbol of Native American prosperity and contribution to world culture. Equally telling is the sculpture on the opposite side of the stairs, in which "America," her throne decorated this time with Mayan glyphs, rests her foot on the head of Quetzalcoatl, the plumed serpent god worshiped by the Aztecs. Inside the House, on the rotunda, are blue, gray, and brown murals of bustling ships, painted by Reginald Marsh.

Battery Park

Due west of the Customs House, lower Manhattan lets out its breath in **Battery Park**, a breezy, spruced-up space with tall trees, green grass, lots of flowers, and views overlooking the panorama of the Statue of Liberty, Ellis Island, and America's largest harbor. Various monuments and statues, honoring everyone from Jewish immigrants to Celtic settlers to the city's first wireless telegraph operators, adorn the park.

Before a landfill closed the gap, **Castle Clinton** (daily 8.30am–5.30pm), the 1811 fort on the west side of the park, was on an island, one of several forts positioned to defend New York Harbor with its battery of cannons. Not a single shot was ever fired from this fort, and in 1823 it was ceded to the city, which leased it to a group that recreated it as the Castle Garden resort. For a time, it found new life as a prestigious concert venue – in 1850, the enterprising P.T. Barnum sponsored a hugely hyped concert by soprano Jenny Lind, the "Swedish Nightingale," with tickets at $225 a pop – before doing service (pre–Ellis Island) as the drop-off point for arriving immigrants; from 1855 to 1890 eight million

△ Castle Clinton, Battery Park

immigrants passed through the walls. The squat castle is now the place to buy tickets for and board ferries to the Statue of Liberty and Ellis Island (see p.43). South of Castle Clinton stands the **East Coast Memorial**, a series of granite slabs inscribed with the names of all the American seamen who were killed in World War II. To the castle's north, perched ten feet out in the harbor, is the **American Merchant Mariners Memorial**, an eerie depiction of a marine futilely reaching for the hand of a man sinking underneath the waves. Fittingly, both these memorials look out across New York Harbor, and offer tremendous views of the Statue of Liberty and Ellis Island. At the bottom of Broadway, the park entrance holds the city's first official memorial to the victims of September 11; its focal point is the cracked fifteen-foot steel-and-bronze sculpture *The Sphere* – designed by Fritz Koenig to represent world peace. The sculpture once stood in the WTC Plaza and survived the collapse of the towers – the only artwork on the premises not to be destroyed in the attack.

Incorporated into the ground floor of the *Ritz-Carlton Hotel*, 39 Battery Place facing Battery Park, is **The Skyscraper Museum** (Wed–Sun noon–6pm; suggested donation $5; ☎212/968-1961, ⊛www.skyscraper.org). Another fine Skidmore, Owings & Merrill construction, the 5900-square-foot space houses an educational institution devoted entirely to the study of high-rise building, past, present, and future. In an attempt to lend a feel of infinitely receding distance, the floor and ceiling are mirrored. There are exhibits dedicated to skyscrapers like the Empire State Building, the Chrysler Building, and even a few out-of-town examples like the Sears Tower, history panels for the Viewing Wall at Ground Zero, and a virtual walking tour of Lower Manhattan.

Battery Park City, the Museum of Jewish Heritage, and the World Financial Center

The hole dug for the foundations of the former World Trade Center's towers threw up a million cubic yards of earth and rock, which was then dumped into the Hudson River to the west to form the 23-acre base of **Battery Park City**. This self-sufficient island of office blocks, apartments, chain boutiques, and landscaped esplanade – which runs from just northwest of Battery Park up to Chambers Street in Tribeca – feels a far cry from the rest of Manhattan, indeed.

Battery Park City's southern end is anchored by **Robert F. Wagner Jr Park**; zen-like in its peacefulness, the park is a refuge from the ferry crowds, and winner of a National Honor Award for Urban Design in 1998. The spot is still something of a local secret, where many summer afternoons can be spent reading and soaking up the sun on the well-manicured grounds. In the park, a hexagonal, pale granite building will grab your eye. Designed in 1997 by Kevin Roche, the **Museum of Jewish Heritage**, 36 Battery Place, was created as a memorial to the Holocaust; its six sides represent both the six million dead and the Star of David (Sun–Tues & Thurs 10am–5.45pm, Wed 10am–8pm, Fri 10am–5pm; closed Jewish holidays; $7, students $5, children free; ☎646/437-4200, ⊛www.mjhnyc.org). The moving and informative collection, which covers three floors of exhibits, features practical accoutrements of everyday Eastern European Jewish life, prison garb worn by Holocaust survivors in Nazi concentration camps, photographs, and personal belongings. Some of the more notable items include Himmler's personal annotated copy of *Mein Kampf* and a notebook filled by the inhabitants of the "barrack for prominent people" in the Terezín Ghetto. Multimedia montages and archival films catalogue the Jewish experience in the twentieth century: Europe's pre–World War II ghettos, the establishment of Israel, even the successes of entertainers and artists like Samuel Goldwyn and Allen Ginsberg. There's also a healthy schedule of events, including films and debates.

Outside the museum, locals run, rollerblade, or just lazily stroll along the **esplanade**, a path that skirts the edge of the Hudson River for over a mile, ending at the edge of Tribeca. The route is very relaxing and scenic.

The centerpiece of the park is the **World Financial Center** (☏212/945-2600, ⊚www.worldfinancialcenter.com), a rather grand and imposing fourteen-acre business, shopping, and dining complex that looks down into the pit of Ground Zero from just across West Street. The buildings – four chunky, interconnected granite and glass towers with geometrically shaped tops – look like piles of building blocks. Their interiors are more refined, as befits the world headquarters of financial giants Merrill Lynch and American Express: six acres of marble were used for their lobby floors and walls, and jacquard fabric lines the elevators. Two footbridges, the Vesey Street Bridge from building 3 and the South Bridge from building 1, cross over West Street, connecting the center to Ground Zero.

At the middle of the Financial Center is the **Winter Garden**, a huge, glass-ceilinged public plaza that brings light and life into a mall full of shops and restaurants, as well as playing host to concerts, art shows, and the like. It was destroyed almost completely by debris during the September 11 attack, but the plaza reopened a year later after a vigorous restoration effort. Decorated by sixteen palm trees – the originals were transplanted from the Mojave Desert but after September 11 had to be replaced by these forty-foot Washingtonia palms from Florida – the plaza is a veritable oasis. Bask here for a bit, have some lunch or a cocktail at one of the outdoor cafés, and take in a view of the swanky private yachts docked in North Cove.

State Street

State Street curves along Battery Park's east side. A rounded, dark, red-brick Georgian facade identifies the **Shrine of St Elizabeth Seton**, 7 State St (Mon–Fri 6.30am–5pm, Sat & Sun 10am–3pm; ☏212/269-6865), a chapel honoring the first native-born American to be canonized. Before moving to Maryland to found a religious community, St Elizabeth lived here briefly (1800–03) in a small house adjacent to the church that now bears her name. The shrine – small, hushed, and illustrated by pious and tearful pictures of the saint's life – is one of a few old houses in the area that has survived the modern onslaught.

At 17 State St, you'll find **New York Unearthed** (Tues–Fri noon–5pm by advance appointment only; free; ☏212/748-8753, ⊚www.southstseaport .org), the tiny, hands-on annex of the South Street Seaport Museum (see p.63), devoted to the city's urban archeology. Built on the site of Herman Melville's 1819 birthplace, the building's upper floor consists of artifacts excavated from different periods of New York's history. There's a "Pitt and Liberty" plate commemorating William Pitt's opposition to the Stamp Act, Britain's first attempt to tax the colonies; a selection of personal items from Brooklyn's Weeksville, the first free African-American community in New York State after the 1827 abolition of slavery (see p.255); and even 1950s-era luncheonette ware. In the basement, relics from the 1835 fire that ravaged Lower Manhattan are also on display.

Water and Pearl streets

For a perspective of Manhattan's eighteenth-century heart, check out the **Fraunces Tavern Museum**, 54 Pearl St at Broad (Tues–Fri noon–5pm, Sat 10am–5pm; $3, students and seniors $2; ☎212/425-1778, ⊛www.frauncestavernmuseum.org), which escaped the 1835 fire. The ochre-and-red-brick Fraunces Tavern claims to be a colonial inn, although in truth it is more of an expert fake. Having survived extensive modifications, several fires, and a brief stint as a hotel in the nineteenth century, the three-story Georgian house was almost totally reconstructed by the Sons of the Revolution in the early part of the twentieth century to mimic how it appeared on December 4, 1783 – complete with period interiors and furnishings. It was then, after the British had been conclusively beaten, that a weeping George Washington took leave of his assembled officers, intent on returning to rural life in Virginia: "I am not only retiring from all public employments," he wrote, "but am retiring within myself." With hindsight, it was a hasty statement – six years later he was to return as the new nation's president. The Tavern's second floor traces the site's history with a series of illustrated panels.

Head east from Pearl Street to **Water Street**, then turn east down Old Slip, where you'll find the small but ornate building that once housed the **First Precinct Police Station**, now home to a museum dedicated to the force. Staffed by cops from the force's community-affairs department, the **New York City Police Museum**, 100 Old Slip, between Water and South streets (Tues–Sat 10am–5pm, Sun 11am–5pm; suggested donation $5, students and seniors free; ☎212/480-3100, ⊛www.nycpolicemuseum.org), features a collection of New York Police Department memorabilia and is the largest and oldest museum of its kind in the country. Very simply, it showcases the history of New York's Finest by displaying the tools of their trade: night sticks, guns, uniforms, photos, and the like – over 10,000 items in all. There's a copper badge from 1845 of the kind worn by the sergeants of the day, earning them the nickname of "coppers," and a pristine-looking Tommy gun – in its original gangster-issue violin case – that was used to rub out Al Capone's gang leader, Frankie Yale.

A little to the south, off Water Street, stands the **Vietnam Veterans Plaza**, an unattractive assembly of glass blocks etched with troops' letters home. The mementos are sad and often haunting, but the place is a peaceful spot for contemplation – and enjoying a nice view of the East River. If you continue along Water Street you'll reach an attenuated agglomeration of skyscrapers developed in the early 1960s. At that time, the powers-that-were thought that Manhattan's economy was stagnating because of lack of room for growth, so they widened throughways like Water Street by razing many of the Victorian brownstones and warehouses that lined the waterfront. By doing so, they missed a vital chance to allow the old to give context to the new; ironically, a decent chunk of the office buildings they built so ambitiously have since been converted to condos.

South Street Seaport

The **South Street Seaport**, located on the East Side of Manhattan's southern tip between the Battery and Fulton Street, dates back to the 1600s and was the center of New York City's port district from 1815 to 1860, favored by sea captains for providing shelter from the westerly winds and the ice that floated down the Hudson River during the winter.

The Seaport was once New York's primary sailing port: it began when Robert Fulton started a ferry service from here to Brooklyn in 1814, leaving his name for the street and then its market. In fact, New York owes most of what it has become to its access to the sea. The harbor lapped up the trade brought by the opening of the Erie Canal (1825) and by the end of the nineteenth century was sending cargo ships on regular runs to California, Japan, and Liverpool. When the FDR Drive was constructed in the 1950s, the Seaport's decline was rapid. Beginning in 1966, a private initiative rescued the remaining warehouses and saved the historical seaport just in time. Today, the Seaport is a mixed bag: a fair slice of commercial gentrification was necessary to woo developers and tourists, but the presence of a centuries-old working fish market kept things real – at least until it was relocated to Hunt's Point in the Bronx in 2006.

Regular guided tours of the Seaport run from the **Visitors' Center**, an immaculate brick-terraced house located at 12–14 Fulton St.

The Seaport Museum and Paris Café

Housed in a series of painstakingly restored 1830s warehouses, the **South Street Seaport Museum**, 12 Fulton St (daily: April–Oct 10am–6pm; Nov–March 10am–5pm; $5, includes all tours, films, galleries, and **New York Unearthed** (see p.61); ☎212/748-8600, ⊛www.southstseaport.org), offers a collection of refitted ships and chubby tugboats (the largest collection of sailing vessels – by tonnage – in the US), plus a handful of maritime art and trades exhibits, a museum store, and info about the now-gone Fulton Fish Market. The museum also offers daytime, sunset, and nighttime cruises around New York Harbor on the *Pioneer*, an 1895 schooner that accommodates up to forty people (May–Sept; $25, students and seniors $20, children under 12 $15; reservations on ☎212/363-5481). The 1893 fishing schooner *Lettie G. Howard* and the tug *W.O. Decker* will coast you around the harbor for an additional consideration. This "quiet" tour is an exceptional (and educational) alternative to the oft-crowded and noisy Circle Line cruises.

Next door is **Bowne & Co., Stationers**, 211 Water St, near Beekman Street (10am–5pm, closed Wed; ☎212/748-8651), a gas-lit nineteenth-century shop that produces examples of authentic letterpress printing. You can order a set of business cards made by hand with antique handpresses: one hundred will cost you less than $100, single postcards sell for $1.25, notecards are $2.75 each. At 213 Water St on the second floor, the **Melville Library** (open by appointment only; ☎212/748-8648) serves as a reference facility for the public researching any aspect of shipping, the Port of New York, or the South Street Seaport District. It was founded in 1967 and named after the author of *Moby Dick* in an attempt to keep the neighborhood associated with its maritime history in the public mind.

You couldn't ask for a better spot than the **Paris Café**, at 119 South St, located in *Meyer's Hotel* at the end of Peck Slip, one of the last and most important harbor slips. The café played host to a panoply of luminaries in the late nineteenth and early twentieth centuries. Thomas Edison used the café as a second office while designing the first electric power station in the world on Pearl Street; the opening of the Brooklyn Bridge was celebrated on the roof with Annie Oakley and Buffalo Bill Cody as guests; Teddy Roosevelt broke bread here; and journalist John Reed and other members of the Communist Labor Party of America met secretly here in the early 1920s. These days, even without presidents or communists, the elegant square bar, tempting seafood specials, and outdoor seating still pull in a lively crowd. For a stellar **view of the Brooklyn Bridge**, walk out to the narrow, bench-lined waterfront and have your photo taken in front of one the most beautiful backdrops in New York City.

Pier 17 and the rest of the Seaport

As far as tourism is concerned, **Pier 17** is the focal point of the district, created from the old fish-market pier that was demolished and then restored in 1982. A three-story glass-and-steel-pavilion houses all kinds of restaurants and shops; a bit more interesting is the outdoor promenade. It's always crowded in the summer, when you can listen to free music, tour historic moored ships like the *Peking* (1911), the *Ambrose Lightship* (1908), or the *Wavetree* (1855), or book cruises with the New York Waterway (May–Nov; 2hr cruises $24, 50min cruises $11; ☎1-800/533-3779, ⓦwww.nywaterway.com). The views of the Brooklyn and Manhattan bridges from the promenade are fantastic (and free) at any time of year.

Just across South Street, there's an assemblage of up-market chain shops like Ann Taylor, Abercrombie & Fitch, and the Body Shop that line Fulton and Front streets. Keep your eyes peeled for some unusual buildings preserved here, like at **203 Front St**; this giant J. Crew store was an 1880s hotel that catered to unmarried laborers on the dock. Not far away, cleaned-up **Schermerhorn Row** is a unique ensemble of Georgian Federal–style early warehouses, dating to about 1811.

City Hall Park and the Brooklyn Bridge

Since New York's earliest days as an English-run city, **City Hall Park** has been the seat of its municipal government. Though many of the original civic buildings are no longer standing, you can still find some fine architecture here: within the park's borders is stately **City Hall,** with **Tweed Courthouse** just to the north; the towers of **Park Row** and the **Woolworth Building** stand nearby; the **Municipal Building** watches over Police Plaza and the city's courthouses; and the **Brooklyn Bridge**, a magnificent feat of engineering, soars over the East River. NYC Heritage Tourism (☎212/606-4064), which maintains an info kiosk on the west side of City Hall Park, leads a free walking tour of the area every Tuesday at noon, rain or shine. Coming to the park by subway, take the #2 or #3 trains to Park Place; the #4, #5, or #6 trains to Brooklyn Bridge–City Hall; or the #R or #W trains to City Hall. If you arrive on the #6 train, which terminates here, try to stay on board as the train loops around to the uptown track – you'll be rewarded with a ghostly view of the original 1904 City Hall station, designed by architect Rafael Guastavino. The station is closed, so the conductors usually try to clear the train, but if you ask, sometimes they'll let you remain on board. Guastavino's signature tiled arches are still beautiful.

City Hall Park

First landscaped in 1730, **City Hall Park** is bounded by Chambers Street to the north and the intersection of Broadway and Park Row to the south. The triangular wedge of green is often dotted with contemporary sculpture, but renovations, including the incorporation of old-fashioned gaslights, have sought to showcase the park's history. Keep an eye out for panels in the paving that show the borders of old buildings and streets, as well as vintage images etched in stone. In the grassy areas, other stones mark the old foundations of bygone structures, such as the Bridewell, a prison that stood west of City Hall during the colonial period.

Facing City Hall is a statue of the shackled figure of Nathan Hale, who was captured in 1776 by the British and hanged for spying, but not before he'd spat out his famous last words: "I only regret that I have but one life to lose for my

country." On the same spot two months earlier, George Washington had ordered the Declaration of Independence be read in the city for the first time. Initially, New York abstained from voting on the issue of independence, but the Second Continental Congress in Philadelphia nonetheless adopted Thomas Jefferson's eloquent statement of the new nation's rights. It no doubt fired the hearts and minds of the patriots here assembled to hear the declaration read aloud – and perhaps convinced the remaining naysayers to join the American cause:

> We hold these truths to be self-evident, that all men are created equal, that they are endowed by their Creator with certain unalienable rights, that among these are Life, Liberty and the Pursuit of Happiness; that to secure these rights Governments are instituted among Men, deriving their just powers from the consent of the governed; that whenever any Form of Government becomes destructive of these ends, it is the Right of the People to alter or abolish it, and to institute new Government . . . .

City Hall

In the middle of the park sits **City Hall**, which was completed in 1812. Its front and sides are gleaming white marble, but the back of the building, which faces north, is dull red sandstone – allegedly because the architects couldn't imagine anyone peering around behind the structure, which was built when this area was at the farthest north fringe of the city. The building's first moment of fame came in 1865 when Abraham Lincoln's body lay in state here for 120,000 sorrowful New Yorkers to file past. In 1927, the city feted aviator Charles Lindbergh, lately returned from Paris, and the building became the traditional finishing point for tickertape parades down Broadway, over time honoring everyone from astronauts to returned hostages to championship-winning teams. An elegant meeting of arrogance and authority, the building, with its sweeping interior spiral staircase, has unfortunately been closed to the public since the July 2003 shooting of City Councilman James E. Davis here by a political rival. The only way you can see the attractive interior is to take one of the free guided tours offered by the Art Commission, well worth your time (Mon, Wed & Thurs 10am, including visits to Tweed Courthouse Tues 10am & Fri 2pm; ☏212/788-2170, ⓦwww.nyc.gov/artcommission). The Art Commission visits require reservations, but if you haven't planned ahead, you can join a tour that begins at the NYC Heritage Tourism kiosk at the southwestern tip of the park every Wednesday at noon.

Park Row and the Woolworth Building

The southern tip of City Hall Park is flanked on either side by impressive early twentieth-century skyscrapers. **Park Row**, the eastern edge of the park, was once known as "Newspaper Row," and the intersection with Spruce and Nassau streets was Printing House Square. From the 1830s to the 1920s, the city's most influential publishers, news services, trade publications, and foreign-language presses all had their offices on this street or surrounding blocks. The *New York Times* operated from no. 41, a Romanesque structure that grew from five stories to sixteen to accommodate the booming paper until it relocated uptown in 1904. The wildly ornamented brick building at no. 38 dates from 1886, when it was a pioneer in fireproofing, thanks to its ironclad lower floors and durable terracotta trim.

The **Park Row Building**, at no. 15, was completed in 1899; at 391 feet, it was the tallest in the world. Behind the elaborate limestone-and-brick facade were the offices of the Associated Press as well as the headquarters of the IRT subway (investor and gambler August Belmont financed both this tower and the transit system). The Park Row Building towered over its surroundings until 1908, when the Singer Building, at 165 Broadway (now demolished), surpassed it.

By 1913, the tallest building was on the opposite side of City Hall Park: the **Woolworth Building**, at 233 Broadway, held the title until the Chrysler Building topped it in 1929. Cass Gilbert's "Cathedral of Commerce" oozes money and prestige. The soaring, graceful lines are covered in white terracotta tiles and fringed with Gothic-style gargoyles and decorations that are more whimsical than portentous. Frank Woolworth made his fortune from his "five and dime" stores – everything cost either 5¢ or 10¢, strictly no credit. True to his philosophy, he paid cash for the construction of his skyscraper, and reliefs at each corner of the lobby show him doing just that: counting out the money in nickels and dimes. Unfortunately, the lobby is closed to sightseers, but if you feel like risking the wrath of the security guards, do walk in the front doors to bask in the honey-gold glow of the mosaics that cover the vaulted ceilings (and the gaze of Teddy Roosevelt, complete with monocle, staring down from the left). Look quickly – you'll probably only have a few seconds before you get shooed back outside.

Tweed Courthouse and Chambers Street

If City Hall is the acceptable face of New York's municipal bureaucracy, the genteel Victorian-style **Tweed Courthouse**, just to the north with its entrance at 52 Chambers St, is a reminder of the city government's infamous corruption in the nineteenth century. The man behind the gray-marble county courthouse, William Marcy "Boss" Tweed, worked his way up from nowhere to become chairman of the Democratic Central Committee at Tammany Hall (see p.463) in 1856. Through a series of adroit and illegal moves, Tweed manipulated the city's revenues into his pockets and the pockets of his supporters. He consolidated his position by registering thousands of immigrants as Democrats, offering them a low-level welfare system in return, and then paying off a legion of critics. For a while Tweed's grip strangled all dissent (even over the courthouse's budget, which rolled up from $3 million to $12 million during its construction between 1861 and 1881), until political cartoonist Thomas Nast and the editor of the *New York Times* (who'd refused a $500,000 bribe to keep quiet) turned public opinion against him in the late 1860s. Fittingly, Tweed was finally tried in an unfinished courtroom in his own building in 1873, and died in 1878 in Ludlow Street Jail – a prison he'd had built while he was Commissioner of Public Works.

Tweed's monument to greed, which now houses the Department of Education, looks more like a mansion than a municipal building: its long windows and sparse ornamentation are, ironically, far less ostentatious than those of many of its peers. Its interior, however, is flashier, with a grand octagonal rotunda soaring upward in a series of red-and-white arches. Extensive renovations removed eighteen layers of paint and unearthed architectural details long hidden; in the process, the building was simultaneously returned to its former glory and stripped of its unsavory reputation. To see the inside, join a guided tour; they run twice weekly (combined with a City Hall visit; see p.67).

This short block of Chambers Street is also home to a couple of other impressive structures. Across the street from the Tweed Courthouse, the 1912 **Emigrant Industrial Savings Bank** building houses city offices above the lavish central banking hall, which has been used for mayoral inaugurations; it's sporadically open to the public. Next door at 31 Chambers St, the **Surrogate's Court** is a bit more accessible. Its lobby is trimmed in elaborate Beaux-Arts mosaics with zodiacal and ancient Egyptian motifs (they could use a good scrubbing, though); marble statuary depicts the consolidation of New York and the sale of the island of Manhattan. Go through security or peek into the main hall to see a spiral marble staircase that appears to pour onto the floor.

The Municipal Building and around

At the east end of Chambers Street, across Centre Street, stands the 25-story **Municipal Building**, looking like an oversized chest of drawers. Built between 1908 and 1913, it was the first skyscraper constructed by the well-known architectural firm McKim, Mead and White, although it was actually designed by one of the firm's younger partners, William Mitchell Kendall. At its top, an extravagant "wedding cake" tower of columns and pinnacles, including the frivolous eighteen-foot gilt sculpture *Civic Fame*, attempts to

△ Municipal Building

dress up the no-nonsense home of public records. (It's also the destination for civil wedding ceremonies – you can often spot couples in full big-day finery standing in the security line at the south entrance.) The shields decorating the molding above the colonnade represent the various phases of New York as colony, city, and state: the triple-X insignia is the Amsterdam city seal, and the combination of windmill, beavers, and flour barrels represents New Amsterdam and its first trading products, images used on the city seal today. Walk through the building's arch (at the end of Chambers Street) – toward the bright red Bernard Rosenthal sculpture – to reach **Police Plaza** and the **NYC Police Headquarters**, one of New York's more polished modern civic buildings.

Down the diagonal pedestrian stretch of Duane Street to the left, you pass the neo-Georgian Catholic Church of St Andrew, dwarfed by the surrounding structures, and the side of the grandiose **United States Courthouse**, now dedicated to Thurgood Marshall and used as a court of appeals. Its columned facade looks onto **Foley Square**, named for the sheriff and saloonkeeper Thomas "Big Tom" Foley, one of the few admirable figures in the Tammany Hall era. The focal point of the wide concrete plaza is Lorenzo Pace's 300-ton black granite sculpture, *The Triumph of the Human Spirit*, a tribute to the many thousands of enslaved Africans who died on American soil – particularly those whose bodies were discovered in the African burial ground just off the west side of the square (see box, opposite). On the northeast edge of the square (60 Centre St) sits the **New York County Courthouse**, one of the

The Notorious Five Points

East of Foley Square is the area once known as **Five Points**, named for the inter-section of Mulberry, Worth, Park, Baxter, and Little Water streets, the last of which no longer exists. A former swamp, it was filled in as part of a public-works project around 1812. Initially poor but respectable, the district rapidly slipped in status under the pressures of the city's population growth, as a relentless influx of immigrants, sailors, and criminals sought refuge here, and toxic industries were shunted to this unlovely side of town. By the mid-1800s, Five Points' muddy streets – called Bone Alley, Ragpickers' Row, and other similarly inviting names – were lined with flimsy tenements, and diseases like cholera skipped easily from room to overcrowded room.

The neighborhood was further marred by vicious pitched battles among the district's numerous Irish gangs, including the Roach Guards, the Plug Uglies, and the Dead Rabbits (depicted with flair in Martin Scorsese's *The Gangs of New York*). After the Civil War, when the area's Irish majority gave way to the new waves of Ital-ian and Chinese immigrants, the gangs consolidated to form the Five Pointers. The group acted as a strong arm for Tammany Hall, effectively training the top names of organized crime, including Al Capone.

Upper-class sightseers like Charles Dickens, both fascinated and repelled by Five Points, invented the concept of "slumming" in their tours of the neighborhood. They made lurid note of the crime, filth, and other markers of obvious moral depravity, but most New Yorkers were not gravely concerned until 1890, when police reporter and photographer Jacob A. Riis published *How the Other Half Lives*, a report on the city's slums. In particular, his gripping images, which retained his subjects' dignity while graphically showing the squalor all around them, helped convince readers that these people were not poor simply due to moral laxity. The book was remarkably success-ful in its mission to evoke sympathy for the plight of this troubled community, and it's in large part thanks to Riis that Five Points has been relegated to colorful history, replaced by a park and a towering courthouse.

The African burial ground

In 1991, construction of a federal office building at 290 Broadway uncovered the remains of 419 skeletons in what was once a vast African burial ground. Archeologists estimate that as many as 20,000 free and enslaved blacks were buried in this five-block area (between Broadway and Lafayette, and from Chambers to Duane streets) during the 1700s. The site's discovery inspired heated discussions over how best to preserve this find; the debate has yielded a few small but tangible results, including an exhibition on the city's slavery legacy at the New-York Historical Society in 2005 and a massive sculpture based on tribal headdresses of Mali commanding attention on Foley Square. A somber patch of grass next to 290 Broadway has been fenced off; the 419 bodies were reinterred here in 2003 and commemorated with a plaque from Nigerian president Olusegun Obasanjo in 2004. The lobby of the 290 Broadway building also contains a small exhibit about the excavations and the history of Africans in New York.

state's supreme courts. A massive hexagonal building, it merits a quick visit to see its rotunda, decorated with storybook Works Progress Association murals illustrating the history of justice. The 1950s courtroom drama *Twelve Angry Men* was filmed here.

At 100 Centre St, the 1940 Art Deco **Criminal Courts Building**, reminiscent of a Babylonian temple, also contains the Manhattan House of Detention, still nicknamed "The Tombs" after the 1833 Egyptian-funereal-style prison that previously stood across the street and was finally condemned in 1938. Past the small plaza where this first prison stood hulks the fortress-like **New York County Family Court** (60 Lafayette St), a rather unfortunate mid-1970s exercise in cold modernity. All courts – and, handily, the buildings' restrooms – are open to the public (Mon–Fri 9am–5pm), though you will have to pass through metal detectors and occasionally check bags; the Criminal Courts are your best bet for viewing the justice system in action and can expose a fascinating, if sometimes bleak, side of the city.

The Family Court marks the beginning of the end of civic dignity, which fades as you head north. Ramshackle electronics stores and offices offering "Immigrant fingerprinting and photo ID" mark the edge of Chinatown. If you turn back down Centre Street past the Municipal Building, you can catch the footpath that runs over the Brooklyn Bridge.

The Brooklyn Bridge

One of several spans across the East River, today the **Brooklyn Bridge** is dwarfed by lower Manhattan's skyscrapers, but in its day, the bridge was a technological quantum leap, its elegant gateways towering over the brick structures around it. For twenty years after its opening in 1883, it was the world's largest and longest suspension bridge, the first to use steel cables, and – for many more years – the longest single-span structure. To New Yorkers, it was an object of awe, the concrete symbol of the Great American Dream. Italian immigrant painter Joseph Stella called it "a shrine containing all the efforts of the new civilization of America." Indeed, the bridge's meeting of art and function, of romantic Gothic and daring practicality, became a sort of spiritual model for the next generation's skyscrapers. On a practical level, it expanded the scope of New York City, paving the way for the incorporation of the outer boroughs and the creation of a true metropolis.

The bridge didn't go up without difficulties. Early in the project, in 1869, architect and engineer John Augustus Roebling crushed his foot taking measurements for the piers and died of tetanus less than three weeks later. His son Washington took over, only to be crippled by the bends after working in an insecure underwater caisson; he subsequently directed the work from his sickbed overlooking the site. Some twenty workers died during the construction, and a week after the opening day, twelve people were crushed to death in a panicked rush on the bridge's footpath. Despite this tragic toll (as well as innumerable suicides over the years), New Yorkers still look to the bridge with affection, celebrating its milestone anniversaries with parades and respecting it as a civic symbol on a par with the Empire State Building.

The **view** from below (especially on the Brooklyn side) as well as the top is undeniably spectacular. You can walk across its wooden planks from Centre Street, but resist the urge to look back till you're at the midpoint, when the Financial District's giants stand shoulder to shoulder behind the spidery latticework of the cables; the East River slips by below as cars hum to and from Brooklyn; and the Statue of Liberty is visible far out in the harbor. It's a glimpse of the twenty-first-century metropolis, and on no account to be missed, though you may want to wait until a day when you have time to tour Brooklyn as well.

Tribeca and Soho

T he adjoining neighborhoods of **Tribeca** and **Soho** encompass the area from Ground Zero north to Houston Street (pronounced HOW-ston rather than HEW-ston) and east from the Hudson River to Broadway. Acting as a sort of segue between the businesslike formality of the Financial District and the relaxed artiness of the West Village, the district is home to wealthy New Yorkers with a taste for retro-industrial cool and the stores that cater to them. Nineteenth-century warehouses have been converted into vast lofts overlooking cobblestone streets, and the area's cast-iron buildings (and their enormous ground-floor windows) make it a perfect spot for purveyors of fine art, antiques, and luxury goods. Both Tribeca and Soho have changed significantly in the past few decades, first as old factories and storerooms gave way to upstart galleries and artists' studios, then as bars, restaurants, and chic shops filled the ground floors.

The art scenes that flourished here in the 1970s and 1980s have, for the most part, moved on to Chelsea and the outer boroughs, but there are still plenty of reasons to visit the area. Tribeca feels more residential, its sidewalks populated by stylish moms and their hip tots, as well as the occasional celebrity. Soho, by contrast, is a window-shopper's delight, where you can shell out for an Anya Hindmarch or Louis Vuitton handbag, snap up bargains at chain shops like H&M, or buy some handmade earrings directly from a designer on the street.

Tribeca

Tribeca (try-BECK-a), the *Tri*angle *be*low *Ca*nal Street, is a former wholesale-food district that has become an enclave of urban style; its old industrial buildings house the spacious loft apartments of the area's gentry. Back in the early 1900s, sightseers came to this part of the city to gawk at the scrum of commerce at the round-the-clock bulk food markets. It's fitting, then, that now most who trek to Tribeca do so for its restaurants, the best of which can be found along Hudson and Greenwich streets (see "Restaurants," p.331). Less a triangle than a crumpled rectangle, the neighborhood is bounded by Canal and Murray streets to the north and south, and Broadway and the Hudson River to the east and west. It is accessible via the #1 train to Canal Street (for the north edge), Franklin Street (center), and Chambers Street (south side; the #2 and #3 also stop here).

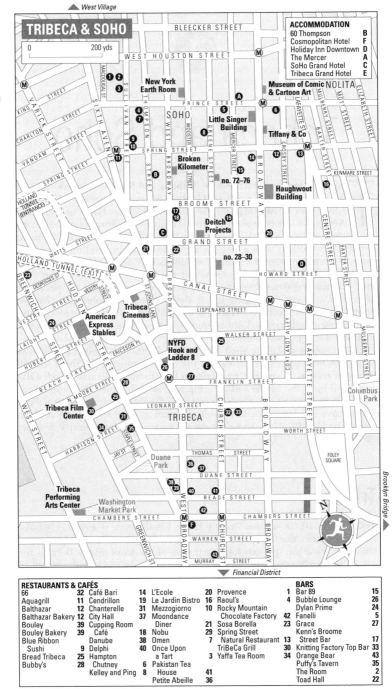

TRIBECA & SOHO

0   200 yds

ACCOMMODATION

60 Thompson	B
Cosmopolitan Hotel	F
Holiday Inn Downtown	D
The Mercer	A
SoHo Grand Hotel	C
Tribeca Grand Hotel	E

West Village

BLEECKER STREET

WEST HOUSTON STREET

New York Earth Room

Museum of Comic & Cartoon Art

NOLITA

PRINCE STREET

SOHO

Little Singer Building

Tiffany & Co

SPRING STREET

Broken Kilometer

no. 72–76

Haughwout Building

KENMARE STREET

BROOME STREET

HOLLAND TUNNEL (ENTRANCE)

Deitch Projects

GRAND STREET

no. 28–30

HOWARD STREET

HOLLAND TUNNEL (EXIT)

CANAL STREET

LISPENARD STREET

American Express Stables

Tribeca Cinemas

WALKER STREET

NYFD Hook and Ladder 8

WHITE STREET

Columbus Park

FRANKLIN STREET

Tribeca Film Center

LEONARD STREET

TRIBECA

WORTH STREET

HARRISON STREET

Duane Park

THOMAS STREET

FOLEY SQUARE

Tribeca Performing Arts Center

Washington Market Park

DUANE STREET

READE STREET

CHAMBERS STREET

WARREN STREET

MURRAY STREET

Brooklyn Bridge

N

Financial District

RESTAURANTS & CAFÉS

66	32	Café Bari	14
Aquagrill	11	Cendrillon	19
Balthazar	12	Chanterelle	31
Balthazar Bakery	12	City Hall	37
Bouley	39	Cupping Room	
Bouley Bakery	39	Café	18
Blue Ribbon		Danube	38
Sushi	9	Delphi	40
Bread Tribeca	25	Hampton	
Bubby's	28	Chutney	6
		Kelley and Ping	8

L'Ecole	20	Provence	1
Le Jardin Bistro	16	Raoul's	4
Mezzogiorno	10	Rocky Mountain	
Moondance		Chocolate Factory	42
Diner	21	Sosa Borella	23
Nobu	29	Spring Street	
Omen	7	Natural Restaurant	13
Once Upon	3	TriBeCa Grill	30
a Tart		Yaffa Tea Room	34
Pakistan Tea	41		
House			
Petite Abeille	36		

BARS

Bar 89	15
Bubble Lounge	26
Dylan Prime	24
Fanelli	5
Grace	27
Kenn's Broome	
Street Bar	17
Knitting Factory Top Bar	33
Orange Bear	43
Puffy's Tavern	35
The Room	2
Toad Hall	22

Some history

The name "Tribeca" is a semiotic construct, a mid-1970s invention of entrepreneurial real-estate brokers who thought the name better suited to the neighborhood's increasing trendiness than its former moniker, **Washington Market**. The namesake market was a massive hall near the river, south of Chambers Street. By the latter half of the nineteenth century, most of the surrounding blocks were involved in the business of feeding New York City. Dozens of depots processed the steady stream of produce, spices, and other foodstuffs that arrived by boat on the Hudson. In the late 1960s, the market building was torn down as part of the scheme for the World Trade Center – though by that time many of the wholesalers had already moved out of the area's cramped streets to the modern Hunts Point complex in the Bronx.

Meanwhile, the blocks around Broadway were the headquarters of the country's largest **textile industry**. Fabric mogul Augustus Juilliard gave both his money and his name to the elite music academy now adjacent to the Metropolitan Opera at Lincoln Center (see p.210). Like the food wholesalers, the cloth dealers also slowly dispersed in the 1960s, when many of their workshops on Worth Street were razed. A few smaller fabric stores are the only trace of the industry today.

The area was a ghost town for more than a decade, until artists such as Richard Serra began using the abandoned warehouses as studios in which to work on large-scale sculptures and canvases. When nearby Soho rapidly turned chic during the art-market boom of the late 1980s, buyers scrambled for more affordable warehouses in Tribeca. Since then, living space in the neighborhood has reached Soho's in status and price, and a zoning loophole allowing for the construction of penthouses has been fully exploited. Recently, the film industry has replaced studio art as the area's main creative medium, and an influx of high-profile residents has provided further impetus for growth and lent the area a certain cachet. One big name in the neighborhood is Robert De Niro, who helped found both the **TriBeCa Film Center**, a state-of-the-art building catering to producers, directors, and editors, and the Tribeca Film Festival. Started in 2002 to aid in the recovery of Lower Manhattan after the September 11 attacks, the event has grown increasingly star-studded and attractive to distributors each April.

Duane Park to Chambers Street

To get a feel for Tribeca's historical roots, start at **Duane Park**, a sliver of green between Duane, Hudson, and Greenwich streets. The second-oldest park in New York City (after Bowling Green), it was also once the site of the city's egg, butter, and cheese markets – the original depots, alternating with new residential buildings, form a picturesque perimeter around the little triangle. Up narrow Staple Street a covered walkway arcs between two buildings, while just off the northwest corner of the park hulks the Art-Deco facade of the Western Union Building. The ornate tops of the Woolworth and Municipal buildings guard the skyline.

Walk a few blocks north on Hudson Street to see a row of Federal-style frame houses, preserved from before the era of the wholesale food industry. Heading back south on Hudson, you'll pass the triangular intersection with West Broadway and Chambers, where a tiny park – more of a large median – is dedicated to James Bogardus, an ironmonger who put up the city's first cast-iron building in 1849. City Hall Park lics about three blocks east on Chambers, but if you turn west, you'll reach **Washington Market Park**, a compact green space that pays tribute, in name at least, to the neighborhood's old function; it's mainly a playground for Tribeca's stroller set. Next door, the Borough of Manhattan Community College houses the **Tribeca Performing Arts Center** (see p.387 for details), the largest arts complex in Lower Manhattan.

Immediately to the west, the **TriBeCa Bridge** is a pedestrian walkway over the busy West Side Highway. On the far side, Stuyvesant High School is perhaps the city's most prestigious public high school, where Irish memoirist Frank McCourt taught for decades. If you continue west to the river, you'll find yourself on the **West Side Greenway**, a jogging and cycling promenade that stretches all the way from the southern tip of Manhattan up to the George Washington Bridge. The areas surrounding the promenade in Tribeca are under construction as part of a larger **Hudson River Park**, slated for completion in 2007 – expect recreation options such as a boathouse and a skate park, as well as an educational center for ecology at Pier 32. From here, you can follow the path south along the Hudson toward Battery Park City, or turn back to Tribeca.

Varick Street and around

Just north of Leonard Street, **Varick Street** splits off from **West Broadway**, one of Tribeca's main thoroughfares, lined with boutiques and restaurants, and angles northwest, becoming Seventh Avenue once it crosses Houston Street. The New York City Fire Department's **Hook and Ladder Company #8**, 14 N Moore St, at Varick, operates from an 1865 brick-and-stone firehouse dotted with white stars. Movie buffs may recognize the building from the *Ghostbusters* films of the 1980s; more recently, it played a role in the rescue efforts of September 11. As it is a working firehouse, you can't do more than admire it from the outside.

Just to the east, at the junction of Church and White streets, one of the area's flashiest social scenes is the lobby lounge of the *Tribeca Grand Hotel* (see listings, p.301). It's topped with a sunny atrium, and the basement contains a plush screening room, in keeping with the neighborhood's cinematic slant. You'll have a better chance of getting into **TriBeCa Cinemas**, 54 Varick St just south of Canal (☎212/941-2000, ⊛www.tribecacinemas.com), an art theater managed by De Niro and partners that also hosts numerous special screenings.

If you cross the pedestrian bridge to the west, over the tangle of traffic headed into the Holland Tunnel, you'll be at the intersection of Laight Street and Hudson, on Tribeca's barely renovated fringes. At Laight and Collister stand the elegant but ruined **American Express Stables**. Built in 1867, they are a relic from the company's first incarnation as a delivery service; so too is the high-relief seal with a dog's head. (You can see another, not quite identical, head on the south face of the building – squeeze down narrow Collister to Hubert Street.) Heading back east to Varick Street then north across Canal Street brings you right into central Soho.

Soho

Like Tribeca to the south, **Soho** (short for *So*uth of *Ho*uston; another of those semiotic constructs) has also undergone a series of transformations in the past few decades. In the 1980s, when cruising the neighborhood's cast-iron warehouse galleries was weekend entertainment for wealthy investors, Soho was the center of New York's art scene. The latest victims of the city's ever-climbing rents, the most forward-looking galleries have relocated to cheaper spaces in West Chelsea and the outer boroughs, and a mostly nonresident crowd uses the area between Houston and Canal streets and Sixth Avenue and Lafayette Street as an enormous outdoor shopping mall. By day a place to buy khakis or trendy trousers, at night the neighborhood becomes a playground for gangs of well-groomed bistro- and bar-goers. The overall effect is one of slickness (except, perhaps, in the southern few blocks of the neighborhood, close to Canal Street, where the stores are farther between).

Despite the commercialism, Soho's artistic legacy hasn't been completely eradicated. If anything, it has been incorporated into the neighborhood's new character. You can still visit a couple of permanent installations tucked away on upper floors, or just cruise the visionary Prada boutique, designed by Dutch architect Rem Koolhaas. The store, at Prince Street and Broadway, acts as a sort of gatekeeper to the area's myriad shopfronts, which showcase everything from avant-garde home décor to conceptual fashion. In a nod to the early Seventies, when the neighborhood's artists-in-residence hung out flags to show which buildings were occupied, many boutiques mark their facades with colorful banners. The #R or #W train to Prince drops you at Prada's front door; the #D, #F, or #V to Broadway–Lafayette deposits you a block north at Houston. For access to the west side of the neighborhood, take the #C or #E to Spring Street.

Some history

In 1644, the area was home to the first settlement of freed slaves in Manhattan. They farmed the land until the end of the eighteenth century, when city planners leveled the then-hilly territory and used the earth to fill in Collect Pond near Five Points. At the same time, Broadway was extended north of Canal Street, and immense development followed. By 1825 this was the most

Soho's cast-iron architecture

In vogue from around 1860 to the turn of the twentieth century, the **cast-iron architecture** that is visible all over Soho initiated the age of prefabricated buildings. With mix-and-match components molded from iron, which was cheaper than brick or stone, a building of four stories could go up in as many months. The heavy iron crossbeams could carry the weight of the floors, allowing greater space for windows.

The remarkably decorative facades could be molded on the cheap, so that almost any style or whim could be cast in iron and pinned to the front of an otherwise dreary building: instant facelifts for Soho's existing structures, and the birth of a whole new generation of beauties. Glorifying Soho's sweatshops, architects indulged themselves in Baroque balustrades and forests of Renaissance columns. But as quickly as the trend took off, it fell out of favor. Stricter building codes were passed in 1899, when it was discovered that iron beams, initially thought to be fireproof, could easily buckle at high temperatures. At the same time, steel proved an even cheaper building material.

With nearly 150 structures still standing, Soho contains one of the largest collections of cast-iron buildings in the world, and the **SoHo Cast-Iron Historic District**, from Houston Street south to Spring Street and from West Broadway to Crosby Street on the east, helps preserve the finest examples. Many more functional, less elaborate structures dot Tribeca as well.

4

TRIBECA AND SOHO | Soho

77

densely populated neighborhood in Manhattan, its sidestreets fringed with elegant Federalist-style townhouses. Broadway was thick with burlesque theaters, crooked casinos, opium dens, high-toned bordellos with exclusive admission policies, the headquarters of the New York Free Love League, and even a short-lived incarnation of huckster P.T. Barnum's American Museum. "Hell's Hundred Acres" was the fond nickname for this district of unabashed entertainment.

After the Civil War, the area turned more commercial, with homes demolished to make way for warehouses and factories, basic functional structures that were prettied up with cast-iron facades, an innovation that was popular until the early twentieth century (see box, p.77). As in Tribeca, textiles were a major industry, but the district was also a hodgepodge of small manufacturers, import-export businesses, and the like. New Yorkers marched farther uptown for their pleasures, and by the middle of the twentieth century the neighborhood was a wasteland; lacking a cohesive identity, it was considered a slum and an eyesore.

In the 1940s, rising rents began to drive artists out of Greenwich Village and into Soho's large, cheap, and light-filled factory floors. However, the buildings were zoned exclusively for light industry, shipping, and warehouses, so these new tenants were technically illegal. They lived in perpetual fear of eviction and without basic services such as garbage collection – in exchange for the freedom to do whatever they pleased. The residents didn't attract much attention until the 1960s, when Robert Moses laid plans for a cross-island expressway that cut right through the district.

In response, city conservationists, including urban advocate Jane Jacobs, teamed with local artists to publicize Soho's attractive cast-iron buildings. They managed to save the quarter (and their accommodations) by having it declared a historic district. When revised building codes specifically opened industrial spaces to "artists in residence," three thousand people moved in during the first year. Thus began contemporary New York's full-scale intertwining of industry and art, paving the way for major uptown dealers such as Leo Castelli to move downtown and the 1980s as the golden age of the Soho art scene. But big money inspired higher rents, effectively pushing out all but the most established or consciously "commercial" galleries and making room for today's retail explosion.

Broadway

Any exploration of Soho's streets entails crisscrossing and doubling back, but an easy enough starting point is the intersection of Houston Street and **Broadway**. Broadway reigns supreme as downtown's busiest drag. On weekends, the sidewalks are thick with shoppers, many dawdling at sidewalk vendors' displays of handmade jewelry, wind-up toys, sunglasses, and paintings. Numerous storefronts, most of them chain shops which look as though they're trying to fit in with the cool kids, make it easy to get swept up in the commercial frenzy. For more visual stimulation, pop upstairs to the **Museum of Comic and Cartoon Art**, on the fourth floor at 594 Broadway (Fri–Mon noon–5pm; $3, under 12 free; ☏212/254-3511, ⊛www.moccany.org), where you may catch a themed exhibit on anything from World War II propaganda to contemporary *anime*.

Broadway is also the place to start a tour of Soho's distinctive **cast-iron architecture**. One of the later examples of the form is the **Little Singer Building**, 561 Broadway, between Prince and Spring streets. The twelve-story terracotta-tiled office and warehouse of the sewing-machine company was

△ Haughwout Building

erected in 1904 by architect Ernest Flagg, who went on to build the record-breaking Singer Tower in the Financial District in 1908, thus rendering this earlier creation "little" in comparison. Here, Flagg used wide plate–glass windows set in delicate iron frames – a technique that pointed the way to the glass curtain wall of the 1950s. Across the street at 550 Broadway is the original location of legendary jewelers **Tiffany & Co.**; the 1854 structure's cast-iron facade was added in 1901. A block and a half south, on the northeast corner of Broome and Broadway, stands the magnificent 1857 **Haughwout Building**, the oldest cast-iron structure in the city, as well as the first building of any kind to boast a passenger elevator – the lift, designed by Elisha Otis, was steam-powered. The facade of the former housewares emporium, which provided Abraham Lincoln's White House with its china, is mesmerizing; ninety-two colonnaded arches are framed behind taller columns. The whole building was painted off-white to mimic marble, but it looks more like an elaborate sculpture in buttercream frosting.

❹ Greene Street and the Cast-Iron Historic District

If you continue down Broadway to Grand Street and turn right (west), you'll be in a prime position to appreciate a couple of architectural gems on **Greene Street**. First dip south to **no. 28–30**, the building known as the "Queen of Greene Street." Architect Isaac Duckworth's five-story French Second Empire extravagance dates from 1873. You may not be able to glimpse all the details, including the mansard roof; as of press time, the facade was in the middle of exhaustive renovations.

Head back north to Grand, where, if you're into installation art, you can detour west to **Deitch Projects**, 76 Grand St (Tues–Sat noon–6pm; ☎212/343-7300, ⓦwww .deitch.com), a singularly edgy gallery in now-staid Soho. Its exhibitions, which range from bead-covered landscapes to the newest graffiti, often call for a complete rebuilding of the interior space, and the opening parties are the stuff of legend in the art world. The gallery also maintains a larger space at 18 Wooster St.

Continuing north on Greene, you'll see more of Duckworth's artistry at **no. 72–76**. Thanks to its mass of columns and peaked cornice, this creation, completed just prior to no. 28–30, has naturally been given the title "King of Greene Street." (Alas, its existence came at the expense of one of the neighborhood's finest bordellos.) Farther on along Greene Street, past Spring, you officially enter the **Cast-Iron Historic District**, where you'll see similarly vivacious facades, as well as curlicue bishop's-crook cast-iron lampposts. None are quite as splendid as Duckworth's, but all are beautifully preserved and make excellent display cases for the dazzling retail offerings inside.

Head west on Prince Street, then north to **The New York Earth Room**, 141 Wooster St (Wed–Sun noon–3pm & 3.30–6pm; free; ⓦwww.earthroom .org), a permanent sculpture installation by land-artist Walter de Maria. Since 1980, this second-floor loft has been some of the most squandered real estate in NYC, as it is covered in almost two feet of dirt, all of which weighs some 280,000 pounds. Commissioned and maintained by the Dia Art Foundation, the dirt is periodically aerated and cleaned, to keep mushrooms and bugs from flourishing.

West Broadway and around

The north–south avenue of **West Broadway**, lined on either side with stately buildings, is the edge of the cast-iron district, though not the end of Soho. The blocks west of West Broadway are smaller and more residential. It's still partially an Italian district; residents shop at small bakeries and attend St Anthony of Padua Church on Sullivan Street (which hosted the 2005 funeral of local resident and mafioso Vincent Gigante, better known as "the Oddfather" because he feigned mental illness for years to avoid prison).

The most famous address on West Broadway is **no. 420**, for a couple of decades the home of the most influential galleries in the city. In 1971, art dealers Leo Castelli, André Emmerich, and John Weber, along with Castelli's ex-wife Ileana Sonnabend, moved here from their offices uptown. The five-story paper warehouse soon became one of the great focal points of contemporary art, introducing deep-pocketed investors to the likes of Sol LeWitt, James Rosenquist, and Gilbert & George, who performed at the space's opening party. Even as Castelli brought dignity and credibility to American contemporary artists, he segued seamlessly into the razzle-dazzle of the 1980s art market: for a time, the building was easily identifiable by a giant blinking neon penis, a sculpture by Bruce Nauman, that hung from the facade. Perhaps the most over-the-top exhibition occurred in 1991 in Sonnabend's gallery, when Jeff Koons debuted his *Made in Heaven* collection, a series of graphic photos and sculptures featuring his porn-star wife, La Cicciolina. The art-market bubble burst a year later, and Castelli died in 1999, at the age of 91; Sonnabend now operates from West Chelsea.

At 393 West Broadway, about a block south, you can find **Broken Kilometer**, another installation by Walter de Maria (Wed–Sun noon–3pm & 3.30–6pm; free; ⓦwww.brokenkilometer.org). This collection of five hundred carefully arranged brass rods is a slightly disorienting study in scale and perspective, as well as a testament to the sturdiness of cast-iron buildings – the collected rods weigh more than eighteen tons.

The southern blocks of West Broadway offer two opportunities to take a rest: either at cozy *Kenn's Broome Street Bar*, set in an 1825 Federalist house on the corner of Broome Street, or the ultra-chic (and ultra-expensive) *SoHo Grand Hotel* (see p.301), which occupies the corner of Canal Street and West Broadway. If you don't want to fork out the dough for a room, at least take a look around the impressive lobby or have a cocktail at the bar. Canal Street links the **Holland Tunnel** with the Manhattan Bridge and marks Soho's southern edge, though in look and feel the street is more like Chinatown than any other area.

Chinatown, Little Italy, and NoLita

With some 200,000 residents (more than half of them of Chinese descent and the rest of other Asian heritage), seven Chinese newspapers, a dozen Buddhist temples, around 500 restaurants, and hundreds of garment factories, **Chinatown** is Manhattan's most densely populated ethnic neighborhood. For generations bounded by Canal Street to the north, over the last twenty years it has pushed across its traditional border into the smaller enclave of **Little Italy**, and today it has begun to sprawl east across Division Street and East Broadway into the periphery of the Lower East Side. On the northern fringes of Little Italy, the hip quarter known as **NoLita** is known for a number of chic restaurants, bars, and boutiques. Together, these three bustling neighborhoods can make for a diverting sidetrip away from Manhattan's more ordered districts.

Chinatown and Little Italy are best reached by taking the #6, #J, #M, #N, #Q, #R, #W, or #Z trains to Canal Street. The Spring Street stop on the #6 is the most direct to NoLita.

Chinatown

On the surface, Chinatown is prosperous – a "model slum," some have called it – with the highest employment and least juvenile delinquency of any city district. Walk through its crowded streets at any time of day and you will find every shop doing a brisk trade. Restaurants are packed full; storefronts display heaps of shiny squid, clawing crabs, and fresh lobsters; and street markets offer overflowing piles of exotic green vegetables, garlic, and ginger root.

Beneath the neighborhood's prosperous facade, however, is a darker legacy. In recent years, some of the most regrettable institutions associated with the area – namely non-union sweatshops – have closed, or at least moved (rising rents in Manhattan have forced these factories out to satellite Chinatowns in Queens and Brooklyn), but other sharp practices continue to flourish. Organized crime is prevalent, illegal immigrants are commonly exploited, and living conditions can be abysmal for poorer Chinese. Many landmark shops have closed, worrying longtime residents and business owners. Gone, too, are attractions like the

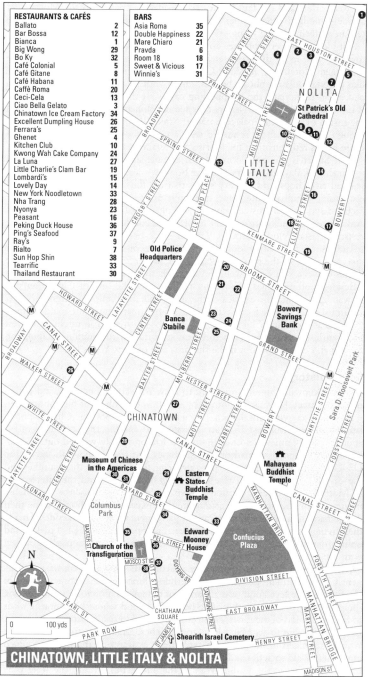

RESTAURANTS & CAFÉS

Ballato	2
Bar Bossa	12
Bianca	1
Big Wong	29
Bo Ky	32
Café Colonial	5
Café Gitane	8
Café Habana	11
Caffè Roma	20
Ceci-Cela	13
Ciao Bella Gelato	3
Chinatown Ice Cream Factory	34
Excellent Dumpling House	26
Ferrara's	25
Ghenet	4
Kitchen Club	10
Kwong Wah Cake Company	24
La Luna	27
Little Charlie's Clam Bar	19
Lombardi's	15
Lovely Day	14
New York Noodletown	33
Nha Trang	28
Nyonya	23
Peasant	16
Peking Duck House	36
Ping's Seafood	37
Ray's	9
Rialto	7
Sun Hop Shin	38
Tearrific	33
Thailand Restaurant	30

BARS

Asia Roma	35
Double Happiness	22
Mare Chiaro	21
Pravda	6
Room 18	18
Sweet & Vicious	17
Winnie's	31

NOLITA

St Patrick's Old Cathedral

LITTLE ITALY

Old Police Headquarters

Banca Stabile

Bowery Savings Bank

CHINATOWN

Museum of Chinese in the Americas

Eastern States Buddhist Temple

Mahayana Buddhist Temple

Columbus Park

Edward Mooney House

Confucius Plaza

Church of the Transfiguration

Shearith Israel Cemetery

N

0   100 yds

CHINATOWN, LITTLE ITALY & NOLITA

pai gow parlors and the famous tic-tac-toe-playing chicken in the Mott Street arcade – modern entertainment revolves around sipping tapioca-filled "bubble tea" in glittering Hong Kong–style cafés.

Outsiders, however, won't see anything sinister, nor will they miss the Chinatown of yore in all the commercial hubbub. The neighborhood is a melange of vintage storefronts, modern Chinese graffiti, and tourist-oriented kitsch, like pagoda roofs on phone booths. Lined with tacky shops and frequently a pedestrian traffic jam, the unappealing east–west thoroughfare of Canal Street is unfortunately often all visitors ever see of Chinatown – perhaps along with the inside of a *dim sum* palace on Mott Street. Explore the narrow sidestreets, though, and you will be rewarded with a taste of a Chinatown that functions more for its residents than for tourists and retains many of its older traditions.

Mott Street is the main north–south avenue, although the streets around it – Canal, Pell, Bayard, Doyers, and the Bowery – also host a glut of restaurants, tea and rice shops, and grocery stores that are fun to browse. While Cantonese cuisine dominates the scene, many restaurants also specialize in the spicier Sichuan and Hunan cuisines, along with Fujian, Suzhou, and Chaozhou dishes. Anywhere you walk into is likely to be good, but do note that many Chinese restaurants start closing around 9.30pm – it's best to go early if you want friendly service. If you're looking for specific recommendations (especially for *dim sum*), some of the best are detailed in Chapter 25, "Restaurants." Nowhere in this city can you eat so well, and so much, for so little.

Besides scoffing down Asian culinary delicacies, the lure of Chinatown lies in wandering amid the exotica of the shops and absorbing the neighborhood's vigorous street life. You can pick up additional maps, brochures, and coupon booklets at the visitors' kiosk at Canal and Baxter streets. You might also invest in a bottle or two of water before you start out: in the summer, population density and congestion can make this area one of New York's hottest.

Some history

The first known Chinese immigrant to New York arrived in 1858, and settled on Mott Street. He was not joined by significant numbers of his countrymen – and they were virtually all men – until the 1870s. By 1880, the Chinese population had risen from just 75 to an estimated 700, and the 1890 census recorded about 12,000 Chinese. Most of these men had previously worked out West on the transcontinental railroad or in gold mines, and few intended to stay in the US. Their idea was simply to make a nest egg, then return to their families and the easy life in China; as a result, the neighborhood around the intersection of Mott and Pell streets became known as the "bachelor society." Inevitably, money took rather longer to accumulate than expected, and though some men did go back, Chinatown soon became a permanent settlement. Residents made their livings as cooks, cigar vendors, sailors, and operators of fan-tan parlors and opium dens (upper-class bohemian New Yorkers were particularly obsessed with the latter cultural contribution).

The authorities did not particularly welcome the development of a permanent Chinatown. The growing neighborhood, built on the swampy ground of the filled-in Collect Pond, was a warren of tenements, flophouses, and saloons; the notorious Five Points slum (see box, p.70) stood where Columbus Park is today. By the end of the nineteenth century, the quarter was notoriously violent, in large part due to its Mafia-like "tongs." These organized-crime operations, which originated in the California gold fields as secret brotherhoods, doubled as municipal-aid societies and thrived on prostitution, gambling, and the opium trade. Beginning in the waning years of the nineteenth century, the Tong Wars

As is true for many of the neighborhoods in New York City, the area that is now known as Chinatown has undergone several transformations over time. Different immigrant groups have come and gone; the pan-Asian mini-metropolis is only the most recent development here. As you tour Chinatown's streets, you'll catch the occasional glimpse of the neighborhood as it was prior to the Chinese influx around 1870.

The first trace of another culture is the **cemetery of Congregation Shearith Israel**, one block south of Chatham Square on St James Place. The oldest Jewish congregation in North America, Shearith Israel was established in New York in 1654 by a small group of Sephardim from Brazil, descendants of Jews who had fled the Spanish Inquisition. This small graveyard was in use from 1683 to 1833, but all that remains today is a collection of seventeenth- and eighteenth-century headstones, which unfortunately lie out of public view. The cemetery is opened every year around Memorial Day, when a special ceremony pays tribute to those Jews interred here who died in the Revolutionary War.

Just around the corner on James Street, the **St James Church** marks the presence of the Irish in the mid-nineteenth century. A big Greek-Revival brownstone, the church was the gathering place of the first American division of the Irish-Catholic brotherhood, the Ancient Order of Hibernians. True to the cultural mixing that is characteristic of Manhattan's slums, St James Church was founded with the help of a Cuban priest, Félix Varela, who was also instrumental in the early Catholic period of the Church of the Transfiguration on Mott Street. If you walk around the corner from St James Church to Oliver Street, you'll see the former church rectory in a row of tenement-style homes, as well as the much-worse-for-wear **Mariners Temple**, the oldest Baptist church in Manhattan.

Perhaps the most overlooked anachronism is the **Edward Mooney House**, a tiny Georgian-style brick building at the corner of Bowery and Pell streets that looks very out of step with its plastic-facade neighbors. Built in 1785, it's the oldest surviving rowhouse in New York City, erected by a merchant who saw this neighborhood's future as a center for commerce.

raged well into the 1930s in the form of intermittent assassinations.

The US government attempted to curtail such crime by passing a series of immigration laws. The Chinese Exclusion Act of 1882 completely forbade entry to Chinese workers for ten years, and in the early twentieth century, additional immigration quotas, particularly the 1924 National Origins Provision (NOP), further restricted the flow of Asians to America. In 1965, the Immigration Act did away with the NOP, and some 20,000 new Chinese immigrants, many of them women, began to arrive in Chinatown. Local businessmen took advantage of the declining midtown garment business and made use of the new, unskilled female workforce to open garment factories of their own. At the same time, many restaurants opened to cater to the workers in the district. When the Wall Street crowd became interested in the area in the early 1970s, investment flowed into the quarter; that capital soon attracted Asian money from overseas. In little time, Chinatown overflowed its traditional boundaries, taking over blocks abandoned by Italians and Jews, and had an internal economy stronger than any other immigrant neighborhood in New York.

The early 1990s saw another major shift, as large numbers of illegal immigrants from the Fujian province of China arrived, upsetting the neighborhood's power structure. Unlike the established Cantonese, who had dominated Chinatown's politics for a century or so, the Fujianese were largely uneducated laborers who spoke Mandarin. Cultural and linguistic differences made it difficult for them to find work in Chinatown, and a large number turned to more desperate means. By 1994, Fujianese-on-Fujianese violence comprised the majority of Chinatown's crime, prompting local leaders to break the neighborhood's traditional bond of silence and call in city officials for help. A network of social agencies and political groups designed to improve the immigrants' plight was also established. Aided by these services, and by the fact that many well-off Cantonese have moved to the outer boroughs, the Fujianese are now the majority here. While Chinatown remains the central Chinese neighborhood in New York City, Chinese communities also flourish in Flushing, Queens, and Sunset Park, Brooklyn.

Columbus Park and the Museum of Chinese in the Americas

The southern limits of Chinatown begin just a few blocks north of City Hall Park at the intersection of Worth and Baxter streets. From here, **Columbus Park** stretches north, a green sward away from Chinatown's hectic consumerism. It's favored by the neighborhood's elderly, who congregate for morning *t'ai chi* and marathon games of *xiangqi* (Chinese chess). The park was laid out by Calvert Vaux, of Central Park fame, but little of his original plan remains today – ball fields take up one end, while craggy rock-gardens are the backdrop on the north side. Facing Bayard Street, an open-air concert pavilion is a relic of the late nineteenth century.

Across Bayard Street, on the northeast corner with Mulberry, stands a brick building, once a public school and now a community center. Through the red double doors and up two flights is the tiny but fascinating **Museum of Chinese in the Americas**, 70 Mulberry St (Tues–Sat noon–6pm; $3, students and seniors $1; ☎212/619-4785, ⊛www.moca-nyc.org), which documents the experiences of immigrants, from the earliest days of hand laundries and garment work through Chinatown residents' experiences during and after September 11. Rotating exhibits focus on contemporary art and culture. Take time to explore a bit with the virtual Chinatown CD-ROM tour, or join a real-life group walk around the neighborhood (make reservations through the museum's education department).

East to Chatham Square

Head east from the park along narrow Mosco Street (past the venerable *Fried Dumpling*, renowned for its five-for-a-dollar pork-filled snacks), and you'll be in the oldest section of Chinatown, where the streets are lined with barely renovated tenements. At the corner of Mott Street, the green-domed **Church of the Transfiguration** is an elegant Georgian building with Gothic details. It opened in 1801 as a Lutheran parish, then was sold to Irish Catholics fifty years later; today, Mass is said daily in Cantonese, English, and Mandarin. On the same block, **32 Mott St** operated as a general store from 1891 to 2004, and was the longest-running store in Chinatown. It has reopened as a generic gift shop, but you can still see some of the original wood trim on the windows and inside.

The next block over (head north on Mott, then east one block on Pell) is crooked **Doyers Street**. Once known as the "Bloody Angle" for its role as a battleground during the Tong Wars, there's little more malicious than barber shops operating here now. In the late nineteenth century, the building directly opposite the post office (6 Doyers St) was the neighborhood's largest Chinese opera house. In 1905, the Hip Sing Tong confronted the On Leong Tong here in a shootout in front of several hundred people. When the police arrived, however, there was scant evidence of the battle, as the gangs had dragged the bodies away through an adjacent tunnel. The underground passage, which had been dug to provide cold storage in the pre-refrigerator era, can be entered through the door to **no. 5–7**, though now it's just a warren of employment agencies; the far end opens onto the Bowery. Also keep an eye out for *Nom Wah Tea Parlor*, 13 Doyers St, which was established in 1920 and has changed little since.

Doyers Street dead-ends at the Bowery and **Chatham Square**, really a tiny triangle, where Fujianese civic organizations have erected a statue of Lin Ze Xu, a provincial official who helped start the Opium Wars in 1839 by confiscating almost 2.6 million pounds of the drug from the British. The Fujianese, often stereotyped as Chinatown's drug lords, have cast their hero as a "pioneer in the war against drugs," according to the inscription. Also in Chatham Square is a small arch that pays tribute to Chinese-Americans killed in World War II. Just to the north looms **Confucius Plaza**, a 1970s housing complex that's still considered some of the best living quarters in Chinatown.

Farther east from Chatham Square, you're in "new" Chinatown – the district expanded by the Fujianese in the past few decades. **East Broadway**, often called Little Fuzhou, is the main commercial avenue. Directly under the Manhattan Bridge, a mob of aggressive touts sells impossibly cheap bus tickets to destinations up and down the Eastern seaboard. The "Chinatown buses," now popular with bargain-lovers of every ethnicity, began as shuttles for Chinese restaurant workers, a by-product of Fujianese employment agencies that supply labor to Chinatowns as far as Chicago, Atlanta, and Maine. Competition among the bus lines became so aggressive that for a time a one-way ticket to Boston was just $5; as an arm of Fujianese racketeering operations, the "bus wars" also provoked several stabbings and shootings. Indictments in 2004 halted the violence, and the bus companies now have at least a veneer of legitimacy.

North along Mott Street

To continue your tour of Chinatown's historical center, return from Chatham Square to **Mott Street** via Pell Street. You'll pass **12 Pell St**, now a salon but once the Chinatown Music Hall and later the *Pelham*, the saloon where Irving Berlin first worked as a singing waiter in 1906. **No. 16** is the headquarters of the United in Victory Association, aka the Hip Sing Tong, where some seventy people were killed when the rival On Leong group raided the place in 1924.

At first glance, Mott Street, the "dragon's spine" of Chinatown, is a strip of tacky gift shops and countless modern tea shops. In this context, even the pagoda roof at **no. 41** looks a bit fake – in fact, it's the last remaining wood roof in the neighborhood; the style was deemed a fire hazard in the early 1900s and summarily banned. Look past the kitsch, though, and you'll also find retailers, like herbal-medicine vendors and furniture dealers, catering to the neighborhood's residents. The **Eastern States Buddhist Temple**, 64 Mott St (daily 9am–6pm), is the oldest temple on the East Coast. Established in 1962 as a social club for unassimilated elderly Chinese men, the room's linoleum floors and dropped ceiling make it more functional than fancy. The temple claims to have a collection of one hundred gold Buddhas, but most are kept out of sight in a back room. Close to Canal Street is *Fay Da Bakery*, 83 Mott St (7am–9pm), a wildly popular source for both Chinese- and Western-style pastries – look for little egg-custard tarts, roasted-pork buns, and steamed sweet-rice rolls.

North of Canal, Mott Street is home to a wild variety of produce stands, seafood shops, and butchers. This is where visitors will feel most strongly the

Chinese culture of today: snow peas, bean curd, assorted fungi, numerous varieties of bok choi, and dried sea cucumbers spill out onto the sidewalks, while racks of ribs, whole chickens, and lacquered Peking ducks glisten in store

△ Fish market, Chinatown

windows. Perhaps even more fascinating than the assortment of foodstuffs are the herbalists, in whose shops you will find myriad drawers and jars, all filled with roots and powders that are centuries-old remedies for nearly every human ailment.

Canal and Grand streets

Say "Canal Street" to most New Yorkers, and they'll think not of a real canal (which this busy thoroughfare was until 1820), but of counterfeit handbags, which you'll see on sale in nearly every shop you pass. A casual stroll here is impossible; the sidewalks are lined with food vendors and hawkers talking up their knock-off bargains – foot traffic often grinds to a halt. This area is an essential strip of Chinatown, but it feels recognizably Chinese only in patches, as the occasional fish market punctuates the legions of souvenir T-shirt stands. West on Canal from Mott Street becomes progressively more unremarkable and commercial, though you may want to make a special trip to the six-floor **Pearl Paint**, 308 Canal St, which claims to be the largest art-supply store in the world.

Toward the east end of Canal, the Chinese influence is more obvious, particularly at the gilded **Mahayana Buddhist Temple**, 133 Canal St (daily 8am–6pm; ☎212/925-8787), which is much more lavish than its counterpart on Mott Street. Drop a dollar in the donation box to grab a fortune, then proceed to the main hall. Candlelight and blue neon glow around the giant gold Buddha on the main altar. Along the walls are 32 plaques that tell the story of Buddha. Despite the assault of red and gold, it's a surprisingly peaceful place.

Canal Street channels its eastbound traffic onto the **Manhattan Bridge**, which crosses the East River to Brooklyn. The grand Beaux-Arts arch over the center lanes looks a bit out of place compared to the neon signs and abandoned Chinese cinemas gathered around the piers below, but it's in good company with the regal **Bowery Savings Bank**, just north of Canal on Bowery, at the corner of Grand Street (the city's main east–west avenue in the 1800s). Designed by Stanford White in 1894, the building is a shrine to the virtue of saving money. Unfortunately, the bank has ceased to trade from this location, and the interior is not open to visitors.

Chinese New Year

During the **Chinese New Year Festival** (see p.440), a two-week period that begins on the first new moon of the first lunar month of the year (generally late January or early February), Chinatown comes alive with even more color than usual. Doors and windows are decorated with red scrolls calling for wealth, happiness, and longevity, and restaurants prepare elaborate banquets loaded with symbolic meaning and special dishes. The highlight is the lion dancers, when more than twenty dance troupes fill the streets with their giant red, green, and gold dragons made of wood frames draped in cloth and *papier-mâché*. The dancers, accompanied by gongs and drummers, parade through the streets, bowing in front of each business to bless it with prosperity for the coming year, and the gutters run with ceremonial dyes and confetti. The firecrackers that traditionally accompanied the parade are now permitted only in a highly controlled, twenty-minute show; locals make do with decorative fireworks strands, some of which even light up and make snapping noises. Fifteen days later, the **Lantern Festival** marks the first full moon in the new year with a display of more than four hundred Chinese lanterns, usually along East Broadway.

From here you could head east one block to Chrystie Street, which forms the nominal border between Chinatown and the Lower East Side, or you could go west down Grand Street, through a few more blocks of Chinatown hubbub and into the area known as Little Italy, once the center of the city's considerable Italian community.

Little Italy

Bounded roughly by Canal Street to the south, Houston Street to the north, Mulberry Street to the east, and Broadway to the west, **Little Italy** is light-years away from the solid ethnic enclave of old, but it's still fun for a stroll, a schmaltzy kick, and a decent cappuccino on the hoof. The area was settled in the latter half of the nineteenth century by a huge influx of Italian immigrants, who supplanted the district's earlier Irish inhabitants and, like their Chinese and Jewish counterparts, clannishly cut themselves off to recreate the Old Country. The neighborhood is smaller and more commercial than it once was, with Chinatown encroaching on three sides – Mulberry Street is the only Italian territory south of Broome Street.

If you walk north on Mulberry from Chinatown to get here, the transition from the throngs south of Canal to Little Italy's somewhat forced Big Tomato hoopla can be a little difficult to stomach. The red, green, and white tinsel decorations along Mulberry Street and the suited hosts who aggressively lure out-of-town visitors to their restaurants are undeniable signs that the neighborhood is little more than a tourist trap. Few Italians still live here, though a number still visit for a dose of nostalgia, some Frank Sinatra, and a plate of fully *Americano* spaghetti with red sauce. For a more vibrant, if workaday, Italian-American experience, you'll want to head to Belmont in the Bronx (see p.281) or even rapidly gentrifying Carroll Gardens in Brooklyn (see p.248).

This is not to advise missing out on Little Italy altogether. Some original bakeries and *salumerias* (Italian specialty food stores) do survive, and there, amid the imported cheeses, sausages, and salamis hanging from the ceiling, you can buy sandwiches made with slabs of mozzarella or eat slices of fresh focaccia. In addition, you'll still find plenty of places to indulge with a cappuccino and a pastry, not least of which is *Ferrara's*, 195 Grand St, the oldest and most popular café. Another establishment of note is the belt-defying *Lombardi's*, 32 Spring St, which is not only the city's oldest pizzeria, but is also one of its finest. (For more on Little Italy's comestibles, see p.316 and p.336.)

Along Mulberry Street

Little Italy's main strip, **Mulberry Street** is an almost solid row of restaurants and cafés – and is therefore filled with tourists. The street is particularly lively, if a bit like a theme park, at night, when the lights come on and the sidewalks fill with restaurant hosts who shout menu specials at passersby. None of the eating places around here really stand out, but the northwest corner of Mulberry and Hester streets, the former site of *Umberto's Clam House* (now relocated two blocks north), was quite notorious in its time: in 1972 it was the scene of a vicious gangland murder when "Crazy Joey" Gallo was shot dead while celebrating his birthday with his wife and daughter. Gallo, a big talker and ruthless businessman, was keen to protect his interests in Brooklyn; he was alleged to have offended a rival family and so paid the price. For a more tangible Mafia vibe, you can't beat the 1908 *Mulberry Street Bar*, at no. 176 1/2, where the back room, all fogged mirrors and tile floors, has been the setting for numerous Mob movies and episodes of *The Sopranos*.

Take a peek through the window of the former **Banca Stabile**, 189 Grand St at Mulberry. It opened in 1885, and offered services to immigrants, including translation, letter writing, wire transfers, and travel booking. Though the bank has been shut for decades, the gilt windows and elaborate interior are still preserved by the building's owner. On the opposite corner, **Alleva Dairy**, established in 1897, claims to be the oldest cheese-maker in the US – perhaps true if the definition of cheese is limited to mozzarella and ricotta.

If you're here in mid-September, the ten-day **Festa di San Gennaro** (see p.445) is a wild and tacky celebration of the patron saint of Naples. Italians from all over the city converge on Mulberry Street, and the area is filled with street stalls and numerous Italian fast-food and snack vendors. The festivities center on the 1892 **Church of the Most Precious Blood**, 109 Mulberry St (main entrance on Baxter St), providing visitors a chance to see the inside of this small church, which is normally closed.

Old Police Headquarters and St Patrick's Old Cathedral

Jog west of Mulberry on Broome Street to see the grandeur of the **Old Police Headquarters**, a palatial 1909 Neoclassical construction at the corner of Centre Street. Meant to cow would-be criminals into obedience with its high-rise copper dome and lavish ornamentation, it was more or less a complete failure: the blocks immediately surrounding the edifice were some of the most corrupt in the city in the early twentieth century. Police headquarters moved to a bland modern building near City Hall in 1973, and the overbearing palace was converted in the late 1980s into up-market condominiums.

St Patrick's Old Cathedral, on Mulberry Street north of Prince Street, is the spiritual heart of Little Italy and the oldest Catholic cathedral in the city. When it was consecrated in 1815, it served the Irish immigrant community and hosted the Roman Catholic archdiocese in New York. Catholic leadership has moved uptown to a newer St Patrick's Cathedral on Fifth Avenue at 50th Street, relegating "old St Pat's" to the status of a parish church. It now serves English-, Spanish-, and Chinese-speaking worshippers. Designed by Joseph-François Mangin, the architect behind City Hall, the building is grand Gothic Revival, with an 85-foot vault, a gleaming gilt altar, and a massive pipe organ that was installed in 1868, when the church was restored following a terrible fire.

Equally notable is the **cemetery** behind the church, which is ringed with a brick wall that the Ancient Order of Hibernians used as a defense in 1835, when anti-Irish rioters threatened to burn down the church. The graveyard was the original resting place of Pierre Toussaint, a Haitian man born a slave who moved to New York with his wife in the 1770s, where they dedicated their lives to charity and helped fund St Patrick's. In 1990, Toussaint was reinterred at St Patrick's uptown, while an application for his sainthood was assessed at the Vatican; he has yet to be canonized. The cemetery is almost always locked, but try to peek through one of the doors – you may recognize the view from a scene in Martin Scorsese's *Mean Streets* (one of the few parts of the movie actually shot here, even though the film was allegedly set in Little Italy).

NoLita

The blocks surrounding Old St Patrick's, particularly north to Houston and east to the Bowery, have been rechristened **NoLita**, or North Little Italy. Stylish shop-owners are the newest variety of immigrant here, as numerous tiny boutiques have taken over former Italian haunts. Most are above Spring Street, but the trendiness has spread south, too. Although this district is not cheap by any means, it is a bit more personal and less status-mad than much of neighboring Soho. The shops showcase handmade shoes, custom swimwear, and items with vintage flair, often sold by the designers themselves, or at least by obsessive buyers who have strong affection for the goodies they've collected from elsewhere.

If you're not interested in shopping, this area is also a good place to put up your feet after a long walking tour. Choose from any of the numerous cafés – the tea shop inside the McNally Robinson bookstore, 50 Prince St (Mon–Sat 10am–10pm, Sun 10am–8pm), is an ideal spot for beautiful-people-watching. From NoLita, you can walk west past Lafayette to the cast-iron grandeur of Soho, north across Houston to the East Village, or east to the Lower East Side.

The Lower East Side

Historically the epitome of the American ethnic melting-pot, the **Lower East Side** – bordered to the north by Houston Street, the south by East Broadway, the east by the East River, and the west by the Bowery – is one of Manhattan's most enthralling downtown neighborhoods. A fair proportion of its inhabitants are working-class Dominicans and Chinese, but among them you're also likely to find small Jewish communities, students, moneyed artsy types, and hipster refugees from the more gentrified areas of Soho and the East Village. With the possible exception of the still somewhat seedy southeastern reaches around East Broadway and Grand Street, the Lower East Side has been considerably maintained in recent years, bringing in all sorts of visitors. Many come for the shopping; most of the city's best vintage-clothing and furniture stores are here, which has in turn attracted a number of emerging designers as well. The plethora of drinking, dancing, and food options also draw large crowds every night of the week.

To begin your tour of the Lower East Side, take the #F train to Lower East Side–Second Avenue, Delancey Street, or East Broadway.

Some history

Some of the first people to live in this area were freed slaves, who farmed small plots of land in the seventeenth century, most of which were confiscated and sold after the American Revolution. The first tenement buildings in the city, which housed Irish immigrants, were constructed on the Lower East Side in 1833, and the development of *Kleindeutschland* (Little Germany) along the Bowery followed closely behind in 1840. The neighborhood attracted international humanitarian attention toward the end of the nineteenth century, when it became an insular slum for over half a million Jewish immigrants and the most densely populated spot in the world. Mainly from Eastern Europe, these refugees came to America in search of a better life, but instead found themselves scratching out a living in a free-for-all of sweatshops and pushcarts.

The area's lank brick tenements (a term which comes from the Latin verb *tenere*, to hold, and literally denotes a human holding-tank) were a bleak destiny for those who crossed the Atlantic. More people crowded into the district every day. Low standards of hygiene and abysmal housing made disease rife and life expectancy low: in 1875, the infant mortality rate was forty percent, mainly due to cholera. It was conditions like these that spurred reformers like Jacob Riis and Stephen Crane to record the plight of the city's immigrants in writing and photographs, thereby spawning not only a whole school of journalism but also some notable changes in urban planning. Not for nothing – and not without some degree of success – did the Lower East Side become known as a

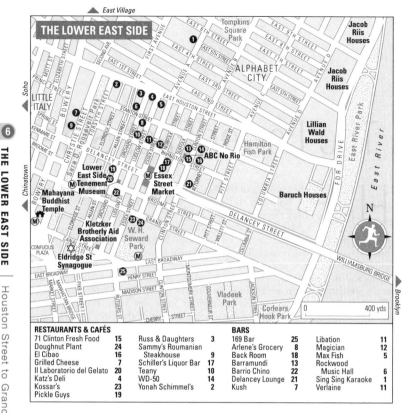

THE LOWER EAST SIDE

RESTAURANTS & CAFÉS				BARS			
71 Clinton Fresh Food	15	Russ & Daughters	3	169 Bar	25	Libation	11
Doughnut Plant	24	Sammy's Roumanian		Arlene's Grocery	8	Magician	12
El Cibao	16	Steakhouse	9	Back Room	18	Max Fish	5
Grilled Cheese	7	Schiller's Liquor Bar	17	Barramundi	13	Rockwood	
Il Laboratorio del Gelato	20	Teany	10	Barrio Chino	22	Music Hall	6
Katz's Deli	4	WD-50	14	Delancey Lounge	21	Sing Sing Karaoke	1
Kossar's	23	Yonah Schimmel's	2	Kush	7	Verlaine	11
Pickle Guys	19						

neighborhood where political battles were fought, from the 1904 and 1908 rent strikes against the appalling housing conditions to the protests in the late 1980s against the district's increased yuppification.

The Chinese and Dominicans also moved to the area in the 1980s, but it wasn't until the 1990s that the Lower East Side saw high-end development. Retro clubs, chic bars, gourmet restaurants, and unique boutiques sprouted up all over, with the neighborhood hitting its zenith of hipness around 2000. Things have mellowed a bit since then, with the more bleeding-edge cool-seekers having decamped for less well-trammelled parts of Brooklyn.

Houston Street to Grand Street

The most readily explorable – and most rewarding – part of the Lower East Side is the area between Houston and Grand streets. In the 1830s and 1840s, this stretch was known as *Kleindeutschland*, and it was home to relatively well-off German and Jewish merchants. While these early immigrants moved onward and upward, a more desperate group of Jews, fleeing poverty and pogroms in

Eastern Europe, flooded in behind them. South of **Houston**, between Orchard and Essex streets, Jewish immigrants indelibly stamped their character with their own shops, delis, restaurants, synagogues, and, later, community centers. Even now, with Chinatown overflowing into the neighborhood, the area still exhibits remnants of its Jewish past.

Ludlow and Orchard streets

When a few artsy types discovered **Ludlow Street** in the early 1990s, it sparked a hipster migration south from the East Village. A half-dozen or so bars dot the block just south of Houston. The street is also home to a number of second-hand stores offering kitschy items – especially gorgeous retro furniture – and slightly worn treasures. Around the intersection of Allen and Stanton streets are several more bar/performance spaces like the no-cover *Arlene's Grocery*, 95 Stanton St (ⓦwww.arlene-grocery.com). For a pre-show tipple, see "Drinking," p.366, for one of the funky watering holes in this area.

Continue west on Houston and you'll arrive at **Orchard Street**, center of the so-called Bargain District. This area is at its best on Sundays, when it's filled with stalls and storefronts hawking discounted designer clothes and accessories. The rooms above the stores used to house sweatshops, so named because whatever the weather, a stove had to be kept warm for pressing the clothes that were made there. The garment industry moved uptown ages ago, though, and today the rooms are often home to pricey apartments.

Vestiges of the Jewish Lower East Side are still apparent around Ludlow and Orchard streets. You'll find *Katz's Deli*, 205 Houston, at the corner of Ludlow – it's famous for its assembly-line counter service and good for a late-night pastrami binge. *Russ & Daughters*, 179 Houston, at the corner with Orchard, specializes in smoked fish and caviar, and *Yonah Schimmel*, farther west at no. 137, has been making some of New York's best knishes since 1910. Rather incongruously, the new arthouse movie theater, the Landmark Sunshine, no. 143, is housed in a restored temple.

Lower East Side Tenement Museum

Even if you don't have the time to tour the Lower East Side extensively, make sure you visit the **Lower East Side Tenement Museum**, 97 Orchard St (Tues–Fri 11am–6pm, Sat & Sun 10.45am–6pm; $10, students and seniors $9; ⓣ212/431-0233, ⓦwww.tenement.org). This local museum does a brilliant job bringing to life the neighborhood's past and present through photographs and community-based displays that concentrate on the area's multiple ethnic heritages. This will probably be your only chance to see the claustrophobic interior of an 1863 tenement (purchased by the museum in 1992, the first tenement ever to be designated as a landmark), with its deceptively elegant entry hall and two toilets for every four families. Various apartments within the tenement have been renovated with period furnishings to reflect the lives of its tenants, from the mid-nineteenth century when there was no plumbing, electricity, or heat, to the mid-twentieth century when many families ran cottage industries out of their apartments. The whole affair is an earnest and sympathetic attempt to document the immigrant experience. The tenement is accessible only by guided tours, which run on the hour and half-hour. For tickets, go to the museum's visitor center, 108 Orchard St. Tours include "Getting By: Weathering the Great Depressions of 1873 and 1929" (Tues–Fri every 40min 1–4pm; $10, students and seniors $8) and the kid-friendly "Confino Family Apartment" (Sat & Sun hourly noon–3pm; $9, students and seniors $7). The museum also offers an hour-long walking tour of the area's ethnic neighborhoods (Sat & Sun 1 & 2.30pm; $10, students and seniors $8); come early or book in advance.

Delancey and Essex streets

Orchard Street bisects **Delancey Street**, once the horizontal axis of the old Jewish Lower East Side, now a tacky boulevard leading to the **Williamsburg Bridge** and Brooklyn. The construction of the bridge in 1903 greatly altered the social demographic of both the Lower East Side and Williamsburg. When it opened, an influx of Jewish settlers crossed the "Jews' Bridge" to Williamsburg, inducing its longtime Irish and German residents to migrate to Queens. In a historical twist, in recent years it's the hipsters who've made the migration to the Lower East Side, and from there to Williamsburg, following in the footsteps of the Jewish immigrants.

Two blocks east of Orchard at Delancey and Essex sprawls the **Essex Street Market** (Mon–Sat 8am–6pm), erected under the aegis of Mayor LaGuardia in the 1930s, when pushcarts were made illegal (ostensibly because they clogged the streets, but mainly because they competed with established businesses). Here you'll find all sorts of fresh produce and fish, along with random clothing bargains and the occasional trinket or piece of tat. If you go a bit farther south of Delancey on Essex you'll find *The Pickle Guys*, 35 Essex St, where people line up outside the store to buy fresh home-made pickles, olives, and other yummy picnic staples from huge barrels of garlicky brine. Nearby are a number of shops that specialize in Judaica; while not flourishing, the Jewish Lower East Side has yet to completely disappear.

East of Essex Street, the historical Jewish Lower East Side gives way to a contemporary, sometimes incongruous mix of Puerto Ricans and Dominicans hanging out at homey Spanish diners and hipster foodies trolling the high-end eateries that line **Clinton Street**. North on Clinton from Delancey, a welded gate composed of old gears and scrap metal identifies **ABC No Rio**, 156 Rivington St (☎212/254-3697, ⓦwww.abcnorio.org), a long-downtrodden but recently renovated and still vibrant community arts center that has hosted gallery shows, raucous concerts, a 'zine library, art installations, and the like. Recent and ongoing events include Hardcore/Punk Matinees, held every Saturday at 3.30pm, and, from February to June, a reading series featuring new works by local neighborhood poets and writers.

The Bowery

The western edge of the Lower East Side is marked by **the Bowery**, which runs north from Chatham Square in Chinatown to Cooper Square in the East Village. This wide thoroughfare has gone through many changes over the years: it took its name from *bouwerie*, the Dutch word for farm, when it was the city's main agricultural supplier. Toward the end of the nineteenth century, it was flanked by music halls, opera houses, vaudeville theaters, hotels, and middle-market restaurants, drawing people from all parts of Manhattan – including opera lover Walt Whitman. The city's only thoroughfare never to have housed a church, it is still somewhat of a skid row, though less glamorous than it was a hundred years ago. The Bowery is known increasingly for its restaurant-supply stores, where you can pick up all manner of kitchen goods for a song.

The Bowery's notoriety immortalized it in literature, with many writers making use of its less than stellar reputation. Theodore Dreiser closed his 1900 tragedy *Sister Carrie* with a suicide in a Bowery flophouse, while fifty years later

More than a century after his death, poet Walt Whitman remains one of New York City's – and America's – most important literary figures. Born in 1819 on Long Island, as a teenager Whitman made his way first to Brooklyn and then Manhattan, where he worked as a journalist, and nightly attended the opera at the houses along the Bowery.

Whitman was born into an era of execrable, highly mannered American verse; he and Emily Dickinson (though they did not know one another) collectively turned such verse on its ear, creating the tradition of American poetry as we know it. Whitman's long, free-verse lines in *Leaves of Grass* – the foundation for virtually all 20th-century poetry written in English – have no real literary precedent. The poems spring from the city itself, capturing the fleeting attractions of passersby in an urban environment and the cacophony of industrial activity that characterizes Manhattan to this day.

In other ways, life in Whitman's New York City seems far different from life here today. It's hard to imagine anyone bathing daily in the East River, as Whitman once did; the later poet Federico García Lorca aptly described New York rivers as "drunk with oil." But Whitman's all-encompassing embrace of humanity, and especially New Yorkers, at times renders the intervening years unimportant, as in his *Crossing Brooklyn Ferry*:

I am with you, you men and women of a generation, or ever so many
  generations hence,
Just as you feel when you look on the river and sky, so I felt,
Just as any of you is one of a living crowd, I was one of a crowd,
Just as you are refreshed by the gladness of the river and the bright flow,
  I was then refreshed,
Just as you stand and lean on the rail, yet hurry with the swift current,
  I stood yet was hurried,
Just as you look on the numberless masts of ships and the thick-stemmed
  pipes of steamboats, I looked.
And you that shall cross from shore to shore years hence are more to me,
  and more in my meditations, than you might suppose.

William S. Burroughs alluded to the area in a story that complained of bums waiting to "waylay one in the Bowery."

Canal Street and East Broadway

Though the southern half of **East Broadway** is now almost exclusively Chinese, the street used to be the hub of the Jewish Lower East Side. To get a feel for the old quarter, start on Canal Street at Eldridge Street, two blocks west of Orchard, and wind your way east. Built in 1887, the **Eldridge Street Synagogue**, 12 Eldridge St, was the first synagogue constructed by Eastern European Orthodox Jews, as a testament to their faith in the New World. In its day it was one of the neighborhood jewels: a brick and terracotta hybrid of Moorish and Gothic influences, it was known for its rich woodwork and stained-glass windows, including the west-wing rose window – a spectacular Star of David roundel. The synagogue is still a functioning house of worship, but the only way for the general public to see the interior is through one of their organized

△ Eldridge Street Synagogue

tours (hourly Tues–Thurs & Sun 11am–4pm; $5, students and seniors $3; ☎212/219-0888). Concerts are also held regularly in this majestic structure; call for current listings.

East on Canal Street at nos. 54–58, above the row of food and electrical stores, is the stately facade of **Sender Jarmulowsky's Bank**, dwarfing the buildings around it. Founded in 1873 by a peddler who made his fortune reselling ship tickets, the bank catered to the financial needs of the area's non-English-speaking immigrants. Around the turn of the twentieth century, as the bank's assets increased, rumors began circulating about its insolvency. As the threat of war in Europe grew, the bank was plagued by runs and riots when panicked patrons tried to withdraw their money to send to relatives back in Europe. In 1914, the bank collapsed; on its closure, thousands lost what little savings they had accumulated.

At the corner of Canal and Ludlow streets and prominently marked with a Star of David and the year 1892, the **Kletzker Brotherly Aid Association** building stands at no. 5. The building is a relic of a time when Jewish towns set up their own lodges (in this case, the town was Kletzk, in modern-day Belarus) to provide community health care and Jewish burials, assistance for widows, and other similar services. The tradition has been schizophrenically preserved by an Italian funeral parlor at the front of the building and a Chinese funeral home at the side.

Continue east, past the junction of Canal Street and East Broadway, to the latter's intersection with Grand Street. Here, adjacent to the bodegas and the eyesore that is Public School 134, proudly stands a cultural anachronism: an operating *mikveh*, or ritual bathhouse, where Orthodox Jewish women must bathe prior to marriage and monthly thereafter.

East Broadway, Essex, and Grand streets frame the pie-slice-shaped complex that comprises **W.H. Seward Park** and its neighboring apartment blocks. Constructed in 1899 by the city in an attempt to provide a bit of green space in the overburdened precincts of the Lower East Side, the park boasted the first public playground in New York and is still surrounded by benevolent institutions set up for the benefit of ambitious immigrants.

Grand Street heads east through housing projects to the messy East River Park – not one of the city's most attractive open spaces, though parts of it have been spruced up. It's better to skip that area and double back up Grand, toward Essex Street, where you'll find more activity.

THE LOWER EAST SIDE | Canal Street and East Broadway

6

The East Village

L ike the Lower East Side to the south, the **East Village**, which extends east from Broadway to Avenue D and north from Houston Street to 14th Street, was once a solidly working-class refuge for immigrants. In the early part of the twentieth century, rents began to rise in the city's traditional Bohemia in Greenwich Village, sending New York's nonconformist intelligentsia scurrying here. By the 1990s, the rents here had begun their own upward climb, and the East Village is now no longer the hotbed of dissidence and creativity that it once was. The last fifteen years have seen it become downright mainstream – you're likely to walk by a pretty standard cross-section of boutiques, thrift stores, and record shops patronized by more tourists, students, and uptowners than authentic bohemians. The area's high standard of living and panoply of restaurants and bars, never mind its proximity to NYU, ensure that rents here are almost – although not quite – as insane as those in the neighboring West Village. Nevertheless, despite the vaudevillian circuses of

The East Village's cultural heritage

Over the years, the East Village has been home to its share of **famous artists, politicos**, and **literati**. In the mid-seventeenth century, Peter Stuyvesant, director-general of New Amsterdam, developed the land between what are now 6th and 16th streets, and from Third Avenue to the East River, for his country estate. Stuyvesant built a small chapel on his estate in 1660, the approach to which can be visited (while employing a generous serving of imagination) by walking east on Stuyvesant Street toward St Mark's Church-in-the-Bowery, which has occupied the lot since 1799.

Fast-forward to the twentieth century: W.H. Auden lived at 77 St Mark's Place; the Communist journal *Novy Mir* operated from the same building, numbering among its contributors Leon Trotsky, who lived for a brief time in New York. In the 1950s, the East Village became one of the main New York haunts of the Beat poets – Kerouac, Burroughs, Ginsberg – who, when not riding trains across the country, would get together at Ginsberg's house on East 7th Street for declamatory readings. Later, Andy Warhol debuted the Velvet Underground at the *Fillmore East*, which played host to just about every band you've ever heard of – and forgotten about – before becoming *The Saint* (also now defunct), a gay disco famous for its three-day parties.

By the 1980s, the East Village was best known for its **radical visual artists**, including Keith Haring, Jeff Koons, and Jean-Michel Basquiat. Toward the end of the decade, the neighborhood was the center of a different kind of attention: the city evicted the homeless from Tompkins Square Park, and the neighborhood's many dead-broke squatter artists were forced out, a story memorialized in the hit Broadway musical *Rent*. With suitable irony, the show has made millions of dollars since its debut in 1996, and was successfully adapted for the big screen in 2005.

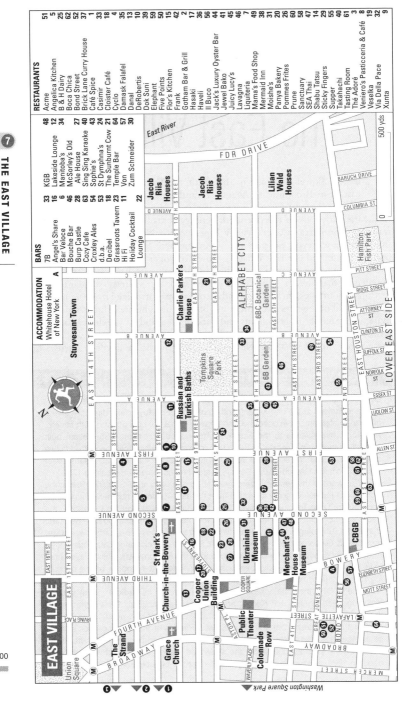

EAST VILLAGE

ACCOMMODATION

| Whitehouse Hotel of New York | A |

BARS

7B	48
Angel's Share	12
Bar Veloce	34
Bouche Bar	6
Burp Castle	46
Cozy Cafe	27
Croxley Ales	28
d.b.a.	63
Decibel	43
Grassroots Tavern	54
Hi Fi	53
Holiday Cocktail Lounge	18
KGB	33
Lakeside Lounge	16
Manitoba's	6
McSorley's Old Ale House	46
Sing Sing Karaoke	40
Sophie's	54
St Dymphna's	53
The Sunburnt Cow	57
Temple Bar	64
Von	11
Zum Schneider	22

RESTAURANTS

Acme	51
Angelica Kitchen	5
B & H Dairy	25
Boca Chica	62
Bond Street	52
Brick Lane Curry House	37
Café Spice	1
Casimir	33
Cloister Café	18
Cyclo	4
Damask Falafel	35
Danal	13
DeRobertis	10
Dok Suni	39
Elephant	59
Five Points	50
Flor's Kitchen	15
Frank	42
Gotham Bar & Grill	2
Hasaki	17
Haveli	36
Il Buco	56
Jack's Luxury Oyster Bar	44
Jewel Bako	41
Juicy Lucy's	45
Lavagna	46
Liquiteria	7
Mama's Food Shop	49
Mermaid Inn	38
Moishe's	31
Panya Bakery	20
Pommes Frites	26
Prune	60
Sanctuary	58
SEA Thai	47
Shabu Tatsu	14
Sticky Fingers	29
Supper	55
Takahachi	40
Tasting Room	61
The Adoré	3
Veniero's Pasticceria & Café	8
Veselka	19
Via Della Pace	32
Xunta	9

500 yds

St Mark's Place and Cooper Square, and several corporate attempts to turn the neighborhood into a *Starbucks* (note the two across from each other at Astor Place), thoughtful resistance to the status quo can still be found from time to time, though even that is changing quickly.

The East Village can best be reached by taking the #6 train to Astor Place, or the #N or #R trains to the 8th Street station.

Astor Place and around

At Third Avenue and East 8th Street, on the western fringes of the East Village, lies **Astor Place**, named for real-estate tycoon John Jacob Astor and, for a very brief few years before the Civil War and high society moved west to Washington Square, the center of one of the city's most desirable neighborhoods. In the 1830s, Lafayette Street, which is a block east of Broadway and runs south from Astor Place, was home to the city's wealthiest residents, not least of whom was John Jacob Astor. Infamous for his greed (supposedly he was still dispatching servants to collect rents even when he was so old and sick he couldn't leave his bed), Astor was also notorious for having won his enormous fortune by deceiving just about everybody he came into contact with, including the president. The old-fashioned kiosk of the Astor Place subway station, a replica, is bang in the middle of the junction. The platforms downstairs discreetly remember Astor with mosaics depicting beavers, representing his first big killings in the fur trade. The brick building with arched windows overlooking Astor Place is where John Jacob conducted business; it now houses a *Starbucks* and pricey loft apartments.

It's hard to believe that the Astor Place district was once home to the wealthy and influential. Today **Lafayette Street** and **Broadway** cut grimy trails along the edge of the East Village and down into Soho. All that's left to hint that this might once have been more than a down-at-heel gathering of industrial buildings is **Colonnade Row**, a strip of four 1833 Greek-Revival houses with twelve Corinthian columns, on Lafayette just south of Astor

△ Astor Place

CBGB (This Ain't No Party)

The New York punk-rock scene began at **CBGB**, 315 Bowery. Despite its initial intentions (CBGB stands for "country bluegrass blues"), this legendary club forged a reputation for itself in the 1970s as a leading venue for the sounds of the underground. **Television** was one of the first bands to play here, back in 1973, when admission was a dollar and the crowd had no spare cash for drinks. Also closely associated with the club are bands like the **Ramones**, **Blondie**, **Patti Smith**, and the **Talking Heads**, all of whom frequented the joint. Few, if any, upgrades were undertaken over the years, and the place became dingy, plastered with posters and littered with decrepit tables and chairs, an aesthetic which actually appealed to its following. But in 2005, the Bowery Residents Committee, the club's landlord, refused to renew *CBGB*'s lease after disputes over back rent. The agreement demands that the club close its doors on October 31, 2006. Though, at press time, it looks like little can be done to keep *CBGB* at the Bowery, owner Hilly Kristal maintains that the fight is still on. Regardless of the outcome, half a block away, you can see another musical landmark: on November 30, 2003, the city renamed the corner of East 2nd Street and the Bowery "Joey Ramone Place," in honor of the late punk legend.

Place. Originally over twice as long, the row was constructed as residences for the likes of Cornelius Vanderbilt; it now holds restaurants and the Astor Place Theater (longtime home to The Blue Man Group; see p.385). The stocky brownstone-and-brick building across Lafayette was once the Astor Library. Built with a bequest from John Jacob Astor between 1853 and 1881, it was the first public library in New York. It became the **Public Theater** in 1967, under the direction of Joseph Papp, founder of Shakespeare in the Park. Since then, the Public has become something of a legend, seeing many of its hit shows, including *Hair*, *A Chorus Line*, and, more recently, *Top Dog/Underdog*, transfer to Broadway. On the first floor, a hip performance space/restaurant/bar, *Joe's Pub*, often hosts concerts, readings, and celebrity-studded private parties. This stretch is also home to a number of expensive furniture shops and a fashion designer or two.

A quick detour east onto 4th Street takes you to the **Merchant's House Museum**, 29 E 4th St (Mon & Thurs–Sun noon–5pm, with guided tours available Sat & Sun; $8, students and seniors $5; ☎212/777-1089, ⊛www.merchantshouse.com). Constructed in 1832, this fine Federalist building is the only nineteenth-century family home in New York whose interior and grounds have both been preserved for the sake of a museum. It cost a bank-breaking $18,000 to build back in 1832, a small fortune at the time – its neighbors are reputedly selling for around $12 million today. The magnificent interior contains the estate's property, including furniture fashioned by nineteenth-century New York's best cabinetmakers, and personal possessions of the house's original inhabitants, the Tredwell family. Weekend tours are led by enthusiastic volunteers, but you can amble through the five floors of sumptuous surroundings alone – just don't miss the perfectly manicured gardens behind the house. From here, the legendary underground music club **CBGB** is just a few blocks south on the Bowery (see box, above).

If you head north on Broadway from Astor Place, you'll find the lacy marble of **Grace Church** at its intersection with East 10th Street. Designed in 1846 by James Renwick (of St Patrick's Cathedral fame), it was built in a delicate neo-Gothic style. Dark and aisled, with a flattened, web-vaulted ceiling, it's one of the city's most beautiful escapes. Two blocks north on Broadway at East

12th Street lies **The Strand** at no. 828. Opened in 1927, the wonderful, yet claustrophobic store sells new, used, rare, and out-of-print books – their famous claim to have "eighteen miles" of titles is fairly easy to believe. Another couple blocks in the same direction will bring you to the blaring traffic cacophony at the southern edge of Union Square (see p.121).

Cooper Square and St Mark's Place

East of Astor Place is **Cooper Square**, a busy crossroads formed by the intersection of the Bowery, Third Avenue, and Lafayette Street, where countless teenagers and out-of-town hipsters mill around, wolfing pizza, drinking cheap beer, or skateboarding. This whole area is dominated by the seven-story brownstone mass of **Cooper Union for the Advancement of Science and Art**, 41 Cooper Square, erected in 1859 as a college for the poor by the wealthy industrialist Peter Cooper, and the first New York structure to be hung on iron girders. Historically, Cooper Union is known as the place where, in 1860, Abraham Lincoln wowed an audience of New Yorkers with his so-called "right makes might" speech, in which he boldly criticized the pro-slavery policies of the Southern states – before going to *McSorley's* on East 7th Street (see p.368) to quench his thirst. Today, Cooper Union remains a prestigious art and architecture school, whose nineteenth-century glory is evoked with a statue of the benevolent Cooper just in front.

   St Mark's Place extends east from Cooper Square. Between Second and Third avenues its independent book and discount record stores compete for space with hippie-chic clothiers and newly installed chain restaurants, signalling the end of the gritty atmosphere that had dominated this thoroughfare for years. To the north and south of St Mark's Place, East 7th and 9th streets boast used-clothing stores as well as several original boutiques, while 6th Street between First and Second avenues, also known as "Indian Row," offers all things curry; however, the street is something of a misnomer, as most of the drag's eating establishments are Bengali.

Second Avenue to Avenue A

If you head south on Second Avenue from St Mark's Place, you'll find the **Ukrainian Museum**, 222 E 6th St (Wed–Sun 11.30am–5pm; $8, students and seniors $6; ☎212/228-0110, ⊛www.ukrainianmuseum.org), which is dedicated to chronicling the history of this area's main immigrant community. The varied collection contains ethnic items such as Ukrainian costumes and examples of the country's famous painted eggs; lectures are held here on a regular basis.

   A few blocks north at East 10th Street is **St Mark's Church-in-the-Bowery**, the oldest church in continuous use in the city. In 1660, "Peg Leg Pete" Stuyvesant built a small chapel here, but the box-like Episcopalian house of worship that currently occupies this space was built in 1799 and sports a Neoclassical portico that was added fifty years later. It was home to Beat poetry readings in the 1950s, and the St Mark's Poetry Project (⊛www .poetryproject.com) was founded here in the 1960s to ignite artistic and social change. It remains an important literary rendezvous, with regular readings, dance performances, and music recitals. Worship services begin at 11am on Sundays, with a pleasant coffee hour afterward.

   If you head east on 10th Street, you'll pass a number of stores belonging to local designers and antique dealers, as well as the old red-brick **Tenth Street Russian and Turkish Baths** (see p.436 for details), its steam and massage services active since 1892. Make sure to wander through these streets, where new shops and old treasures meld without effort. Venture farther east and you'll catch up with Avenue A, the western edge of Alphabet City, which borders the once sketchy Tompkins Square Park and buzzes with thrift stores and trendy bars.

Tompkins Square Park

Fringed by avenues A and B and East 7th and 10th streets, **Tompkins Square Park**, once part of the estate of President James Monroe, has long been a focus for the Lower East Side/East Village community as well as one of New York's great centers for political protest. It was here in 1874 that the police massacred a crowd of workers campaigning against unemployment. In the 1960s, myriad protests took place in the park. The late Yippie leader Abbie Hoffman lived nearby, and residents like him, along with the many incidents in the square, are what have given the East Village its maverick reputation. The first annual **Wigstock**, a celebration of high kitsch and cross-dressing, was held here in 1985. In 2003, Wigstock was folded into the first Howl Annual Festival of East Village Arts, a week-long event in August named for Allen Ginsberg's famous poem and founded to channel the neighborhood's creative spirits.

In recent years, Tompkins Square Park has evolved from its former identity as a place of protests, squatters, and riots (see box, below) to a desirable outdoor space that appeals to both families and drag queens. The cleaned-up park features handball courts and a dog run. There's even a farmers' market on Sundays, as well as free concerts, a regular summer pastime for locals.

One of the few things to see in the area is a small relief showing a woman and child gazing forlornly out to sea, which you can find just inside the brick enclosure on the north side of the park. In 1904, the local community, then mostly made up of German immigrants, was devastated by the burning and sinking of a cruise ship, the *General Slocum*, in Long Island Sound. The relief is designed in commemoration of the 1021 lives lost, mostly women and children. Near the center of the park is the **Hare Krishna elm tree**. Planted in 1965, it was the site of the Hare Krishna movement's first ceremony outside of India.

At 151 Ave B, on the east side of the park, is the famous saxophonist and composer **Charlie Parker's house**, a simple whitewashed structure with a

---

The Tompkins Square riots

Until the early 1990s, Tompkins Square Park was more or less a shantytown (known locally as "Tent City"). Hundreds of homeless people slept on benches or under makeshift shelters between the paths. In the winter, only the really hardy or truly desperate lived here, but when the weather got warmer the numbers swelled, as activists, anarchists, and all manner of statement-makers descended upon the former army barracks, hoping to rekindle the spirit of 1988. That was the year of the **Tompkins Square Riots**, when massive demonstrations in August led the police, badges covered and nightsticks drawn, to attempt to clear the park of people. In the ensuing battle, many demonstrators and a large number of bystanders were hurt. The investigation that followed heavily criticized the police for the violence. In the summer of 1995 another riot erupted as police tried to evict a group of squatters from an empty apartment building nearby. This time, protesters were armed with video cameras, but, though heated, the riot never reached the proportions of 1988. Despite resistance, the park was eventually overhauled, its winding pathways and playground restored; the changes are enforced by an 11pm lock-up and police surveillance.

Gothic doorway. Bird lived here from 1950 until his death of a pneumonia-related hemorrhage in 1954.

Alphabet City

East of Tompkins Square Park and north of Houston Street is **Alphabet City**, one of the most dramatically revitalized areas of Manhattan. Deriving its name from the grid of avenues lettered A–D, where the island bulges out beyond the city's grid structure below 14th Street, Alphabet City is also known to its Puerto Rican residents as **Loisaida**. Like Tompkins Square Park, this used to be a notoriously unsafe corner of town run by drug pushers and gangsters; cars lined up for fixes in the street, shoes hung from lampposts to mark places where someone had been shot, and burned-out buildings served as safe houses for the brisk heroin trade. Most of this was brought to a halt in 1983 with "Operation Pressure Point," a massive police campaign to make the neighborhood livable again. This aim has certainly been achieved: the crime rate is way down, many of the old buildings have been renovated and (unfortunately) supplemented by ugly new ones, and the streets are primarily the haunt of moneyed twenty-somethings and edgier tourist youth. Only Avenue D might still give you some pause, in terms of safety; avenues A, B, and C have some of the coolest bars, cafés, and stores in the city, though the profusion of sushi bars and French *boîtes* are easy indicators of the neighborhood's increasingly up-market image. See Chapters 25, "Restaurants," and 26, "Drinking," for listings of the best in the area.

Comestibles and consumerism aside, it's worth it to wander around this part of town just to see some of the murals and **public art**, including the former Iglesia

Community gardens

In the 1970s, huge parts of the East Village burned to the ground after cuts in the city's fire-fighting budget closed many of the local firehouses. Since then, East Village residents have reclaimed these neglected and empty lots, turning the rubble-filled messes into some of the prettiest and most verdant spaces in lower Manhattan. Not able to leave well enough alone, the city decided that these spaces could be used for something much more valuable than grass – more real estate. Despite a 1999 agreement which ensured the safety of around 100 of the neighborhood's over 600 gardens, the battle reached a fever pitch in February 2000, when El Jardin de la Esperanza (Hope Garden) on East 7th Street between avenues B and C was bulldozed to make way for market-priced housing. Around thirty local residents were arrested while protesting the action; the city began to bulldoze the garden while the last resister was being removed – a mere forty minutes before an injunction was issued to prevent the city from destroying any community gardens.

The fight seems to have been well worth it. There is no nicer way to spend a summer evening or a Sunday afternoon than by grabbing some picnic ingredients and relaxing among the lush trees and carefully planted foliage of these spaces. Of particular note is the East 6th Street and Avenue B affair, overgrown with wildflowers, vegetables, trees, and roses, and home to a spectacular four-story sculpture maintained by a local fanatic. The garden also provides a space for yoga classes in the morning and performance art in the evening during the summer, as well as a forum for bake sales, sing-alongs, and other community events. Other gardens include the very serene 6BC Botanical Garden on East 6th Street between B and C; Miracle Garden on East 3rd Street between A and B; El Sol Brillante on East 12th Street between A and B; and the Creative Little Garden on East 6th Street between A and B.

San Isidro y San Leandro at 345 E 4th St, which is decorated with mosaics and mirrors, and the numerous community gardens (see box, p.105). In addition, you'll find a growing number of micro-galleries and storefront artists' studios. As on the Lower East Side, Hispanic residents have recycled their predecessors' institutions: have a look at 638 E 6th St (between avenues C and B), where a former synagogue has been converted into a colorful community center and Catholic church.

The West Village

W hen the *Village Voice*, the venerable listings/comment/investigative magazine, began chronicling Greenwich Village nightlife in 1955, "the Village" had a dissident, artistic, vibrant voice. And though it's still one of the more progressive neighborhoods in the city, Greenwich Village (now commonly called the **West Village**) has attained a moneyed status over the last four decades and is definitely the place for those who have Arrived. (Perhaps not coincidentally, the *Voice* moved its offices to Cooper Square in the East Village in 1991.) Celebrities seem to snap up properties right and left, and the historic enclave is booming with development. These famous residents – the likes of Nicole Kidman and Gwyneth Paltrow, for example – have come for the same reasons that the intelligentsia did a century ago: quaint sidestreets, charming brownstones, and brick townhouses unrivaled elsewhere in Manhattan. It's quiet and residential, but with a busy streetlife that keeps humming later into the night than in many other parts of the city. Restaurants, cafés, bars, and boutiques clutter most every corner, and Washington Square is a hub of superbly aimless activity throughout the year.

Bounded by 14th Street to the north, Houston Street to the south, the Hudson River to the west, and Broadway to the east, the West Village is easily reached by the #1 train to Christopher Street or the #A, #C, #E, #F, or #V to West 4th Street.

Some history

Greenwich Village was originally designed as a rural retreat away from the frenetic nucleus of early New York City. During the yellow fever epidemic of 1822 it became highly sought after as a refuge from infected downtown streets, and there was even talk of moving the entire city center here when the fever was at its height. Thankfully, the Village was spared that dubious honor, and was instead left in peace to grow into a wealthy residential neighborhood. Before long it had sprouted elegant Federal and Greek Revival terraces and lured some of the city's highest society names.

At the close of the nineteenth century, German, Irish, and Italian immigrants swarmed to jobs in breweries, warehouses, and coal yards along the Hudson River, causing the once-genteel veneer of New York City's refined "American Ward" to disappear. As the immigrants moved in, rents plummeted and the neighborhood took on a much more working-class atmosphere. Left behind when the rich migrated farther and farther uptown, the area's large houses proved a fertile hunting ground for struggling artists and intellectuals on the lookout for cheap rents and a community of free-thinkers. By the end of World War I, Greenwich Village had become New York's Left Bank. Decrepit rowhouses were converted into bohemian-style apartments, and in 1926 the

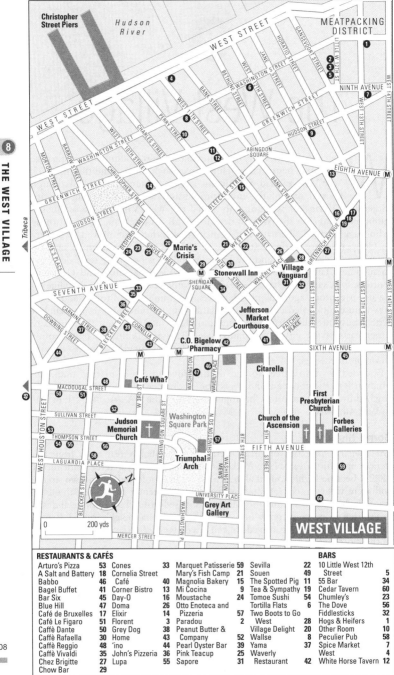

Christopher
Street Piers

Hudson
River

MEATPACKING
DISTRICT

WEST STREET

NINTH AVENUE

EIGHTH AVENUE

SEVENTH AVENUE

SIXTH AVENUE

FIFTH AVENUE

Marie's
Crisis

Stonewall Inn

Village
Vanguard

Jefferson
Market
Courthouse

C.O. Bigelow
Pharmacy

Café Wha?

Citarella

First
Presbyterian
Church

Forbes
Galleries

Church of the
Ascension

Judson
Memorial
Church

Washington
Square Park

Triumphal
Arch

Grey Art
Gallery

0   200 yds

WEST VILLAGE

RESTAURANTS & CAFÉS

Arturo's Pizza	53	Cones	33	Marquet Patisserie	59
A Salt and Battery	18	Cornelia Street		Mary's Fish Camp	21
Babbo	46	Café	40	Magnolia Bakery	15
Bagel Buffet	41	Corner Bistro	13	Mi Cocina	9
Bar Six	45	Day-O	16	Moustache	24
Blue Hill	47	Doma	26	Otto Enoteca and	
Café de Bruxelles	17	Elixir	14	Pizzeria	57
Café Le Figaro	51	Florent	3	Paradou	2
Caffè Dante	50	Grey Dog	16	Peanut Butter &	
Caffè Rafaella	30	Home	43	Company	52
Caffè Reggio	48	'ino	44	Pink Teacup	25
Caffè Vivaldi	35	John's Pizzeria	36	Sapore	55
Chez Brigitte	27	Lupa	55		
Chow Bar	29				

Sevilla	22
Souen	49
The Spotted Pig	11
Tea & Sympathy	19
Tomoe Sushi	54
Tortilla Flats	6
Two Boots to Go	
West	28
Village Delight	20
Wallse	8
Yama	37
Waverly	
Restaurant	42

BARS

10 Little West 12th	
Street	5
55 Bar	34
Cedar Tavern	60
Chumley's	23
The Dove	56
Fiddlesticks	32
Hogs & Heifers	1
Other Room	10
Peculiar Pub	58
Spice Market	7
West	4
White Horse Tavern	12

construction of a luxury apartment block at the northern edge of Washington Square marked a turn toward gentrification.

Among the vast array of early twentieth-century Village characters, Mabel Dodge was perhaps the most influential. Wealthy and radical, she threw parties for the literary and political cognoscenti – parties to which everyone who was anyone was invited. Just about all of the well-known figures who lived in New York during the first two decades of the twentieth century spent some time at Dodge's house at 23 Fifth Avenue, just north of Washington Square. Emma Goldman discussed anarchism with Gertrude Stein and Margaret Sanger; Conrad Aiken and T.S. Eliot dropped in from time to time; and John Reed – who went on to write *Ten Days That Shook the World*, his firsthand account of the Russian Revolution – was a frequent guest. Another wealthy patron of the arts was long-time Village resident Gertrude Vanderbilt, who opened the Whitney Museum of American Art here in the 1930s. Dedicated to modern American art, it eventually moved to much grander digs on the Upper East Side in the 1960s (see p.197).

The Beat movement flourished here after World War II, as did unorthodox "happenings," and bacchanalian parties promoted as "pagan romps." Meanwhile, the neighborhood's cafés, literary and folk clubs, and off-Broadway theaters came to define Village life, laying the path for rebellious, countercultural groups and activities in the 1960s. The mystique and allure of a free-thinking activist Greenwich Village was further enhanced over the years by radicals such as the Weather Underground, history-changing events like the Stonewall Riots (see box, p.114), and the area's invigorating intellectual life, among countless other factors. In recent decades, the Village has grown up, leaving its impassioned youth behind to become the relatively tame, historic, and overdeveloped corner of Manhattan that it is today.

Washington Square and around

The best way to see the Village is to walk, and by far the best place to start is its natural center, **Washington Square**. Memorialized in Henry James's 1880 novel of the same name, it is not an elegant-looking place, but along the square's north-ern edge a line of brick rowhouses – the "solid, honorable dwellings" that James described – remind visitors of the area's more illustrious past. More imposing is Stanford White's famous **Triumphal Arch**, built in 1892 at the southern termi-nus of Fifth Avenue to commemorate the centenary of George Washington's presidential inauguration. In 1913, Dada artist Marcel Duchamp, accompanied by an agitator going by the name "Woe," climbed to the top of the arch via the internal staircase to declare the "Free Republic of Greenwich Village." It is said that while atop the arch they lit a bonfire and toasted their freedom with cham-pagne. Quite another sort of monument stands in the northwest corner of the square. Washington Square Park was used as a site for public executions for many years while New York was a British colony and even after the Revolutionary War; the Hangman's Elm continues to grow in the park today.

Washington Square remains the symbolic heart of the Village and its radicalism – so much so that when Robert Moses, the paver of great chunks of New York City (see p.492), wanted to plow a four-lane roadway through the square's center in 1952, the ensuing protests not only stopped the road but also caused all traffic to be banned from the park, then used as a turnaround point by buses. The square has stayed the same ever since, notwithstanding some battles in the 1960s when the

△ Washington Square Park

authorities decided to purge the park of folksingers and nearly had a riot on their hands. For years the square was something of an open-air drug bazaar, but more recently a heavy undercover police presence has put an end to most of that activity. Not that you should be worried about your safety here; these days, crime is quite rare in this part of town.

During the spring and summer months, the square becomes a combination running track, performance venue, giant chess tournament, and social club, boiling over with life as skateboards flip, dogs run, and guitar notes crash through the urgent cries of performers calling for the crowd's attention.

NYU and south of the square

New York University (NYU) owns many of the buildings around the square, although even nonstudents will be interested in the university's innovative **Grey Art Gallery**, 100 Washington Square E (Tues, Thurs & Fri 11am–6pm, Wed 11am–8pm, Sat 11am–5pm; suggested donation $3; ☎212/998-6780, ⓦwww.nyu.edu/greyart/). The space hosts top-notch traveling exhibitions, which rotate every three months and feature a wide range of media, including sculpture, painting, photography, and provocative video shows. Since the gallery is so small, they do not have room to display their excellent permanent collection, and it is only shown when pieces are included in special exhibits – a shame, considering that the gallery is famous for its New York University Art Collection, which includes several strong American paintings from the 1940s onwards and prints by Picasso, Miró, and Matisse, as well as the Abbey Weed Grey Collection of Contemporary Asian and Middle Eastern Art.

There's little that's evocative of Henry James's day on the south side of the square: only the fussy Judson Memorial Church stands out amid a messy blend of modern architecture. Over the years, though, many notable authors have called Washington Square South home. In the NYU Student Center at Washington Square South and LaGuardia Place lies the site of Madame Katherine Blanchard's House of Genius, a former boarding house where Willa Cather, Theodore Dreiser, and O. Henry lived. Playwright Eugene O'Neill, one of the Village's most acclaimed residents, lived (and in 1939, completed *The Iceman Cometh*) at **38 Washington Square South**, which is now Vanderbilt Hall, an NYU Law School office. O'Neill consumed vast quantities of ale at *The Golden Swan Bar*, which once stood on the corner of Sixth Avenue and West 4th Street and is now a garden. *The Golden Swan* (variously called *The Hell Hole*, *Bucket of Blood*, and other such inviting names) was best known in O'Neill's day for the dubious morals of its clientele – a gang of Irish hoodlums known as the Hudson Dusters – and for the pig in the basement that ate the customers' trash. O'Neill was great pals with this crowd and drew many of his characters from the bar's personalities.

South along MacDougal Street

From the southwest corner of the park, follow MacDougal Street south to no. 133, home of the **Provincetown Players**, who, on the advice of John Reed, moved here from Massachusetts in 1915 and opened this theater in 1918. Continue to 115 MacDougal, which is the site of the famous **Café Wha?**, where "soul food for the ear, mind and body" was offered in the 1960s. Jimi Hendrix and Bill Cosby began their careers here, and Allen Ginsberg and Abbie Hoffman were regular customers. Turn right for an out-and-back detour down pretty Minetta Lane. This area was among the city's first African-American neighborhoods in the early nineteenth century; around the turn of the twentieth century the area saw an influx of Irish and Jewish communities. Charming now, in 1896 *The Red Badge of Courage* author Stephen Crane wrote that this neighborhood was a dangerous slum. Back on MacDougal, continue south until you reach Bleecker Street, with its touristy concentration of shops, bars, restaurants, and people. Here you'll find the European-style sidewalk cafés that have characterized Village cultural life for decades. **Café Le Figaro**, 184 Bleecker St, was made famous by the Beat writers in the 1950s and is generally crowded throughout the day. It's worth the price of a cappuccino to people-watch for an hour or so.

North of Washington Square

This is college country, so throngs of students are a permanent part of the scenery in the area. Running between University Place and Fifth Avenue just north of the square, **Washington Mews** stands out from the legions of coffee shops and quick-fix bodegas. The pin-neat prettiness of the small cobblestone street and old pastel buildings seems out of place amid the grand brownstones that abut the square. This alley was used to stable horses until it was redesigned in the 1930s to stable humans, and most recently NYU professors (not to suggest there's a connection). Also somewhat incongruous in this genteel area is West 8th Street to the west of University Place, a strip of brash shoe stores, tattoo parlors, and cut-price clothing stores. Walk west on West 10th and 11th streets and you'll find some of the best-preserved early nineteenth-century townhouses in the Village, with the exception of the rebuilt facade of **18 W 11th St** (see box, p.112). Between 1933 and 1942, **Eleanor Roosevelt** resided at 20 E 11th St, between University Place and Fifth Avenue, but since this period coincided with her husband's presidency, it's probable that she spent more time talking domestic and foreign policies than playing bridge with her West Village neighbors.

The Triangle Shirtwaist Fire

One of New York's most infamous tragedies occurred on March 25, 1911, at the corner of Washington Place and Greene Street, when a fire started on the eighth floor of the **Triangle Shirtwaist garment factory**, one of the city's most notorious sweatshops. A terrible combination of flammable fabrics, locked doors, collapsing fire escapes, and the inability of fire-truck ladders to reach higher than the sixth floor, resulted in the deaths of 146 workers – almost entirely women, primarily immigrants, and some only 13 years old – in less than fifteen minutes. Although the ensuing outrage spurred the state to institute tougher fire codes and child-labor regulations, as well as laws forcing employers to take account of their employees' safety, there are still sweatshops in New York in which safety conditions are probably little better than they were almost a century ago.

If you head north up Fifth Avenue, off which the neighborhood's low-slung residential streets lead to some eminently desirable apartment buildings, you'll pass a couple of imposing churches. On the corner of West 11th Street stands the **Church of the Ascension**, a small structure built in 1841 by Richard Upjohn (the Trinity Church architect), where a gracefully toned La Farge altar painting and some fine stained-glass are on view Mondays through Saturdays from noon to 1pm. Decidedly more sober, Joseph Wells's bulky, chocolate-brown Gothic-Revival **First Presbyterian Church**, just across 11th Street, features a crenellated tower modeled on the one at Magdalen College in Oxford, England. To look inside at its carved black-walnut pews and Tiffany Rose Window, you need to enter through the discreetly added Church House (ring the bell for attention if the door's locked).

One block farther north you will come to one of the city's best small museums, **Forbes Galleries**, 62 Fifth Ave, at 12th St (Tues, Wed, Fri & Sat 10am–4pm; free; ☎212/206-5548), which contains a treasure-trove of tiny delights, from a 10,000-strong host of tin soldiers from various eras and armies to an impressive collection of over 500 model boats. Also on view are early Monopoly boards, and plenty of historical documents, including the papers of past presidents.

Sixth Avenue and west

Although **Sixth Avenue** is for the most part lined with mediocre stores and restaurants, there are some exceptions, like **C.O. Bigelow Pharmacy**, no. 414, just north of West 8th Street, possibly the city's oldest drugstore, and upscale grocer **Citarella**.

At West 10th Street stands the unmistakable clocktower of the nineteenth-century **Jefferson Market Courthouse**. Erected in 1876, this imposing High Victorian–style edifice, complete with gargoyles, first served as an indoor market but went on to be a firehouse, a jail, and, since 1967, a public library. If you walk around to Greenwich Avenue for a better look, you will see an adjacent garden, which was, until 1971, the site of the Women's House of Detention, a prison known for its abysmal conditions that numbered Angela Davis among its inmates. Across the street from the courthouse and opening onto West 10th Street, **Patchin Place** is a tiny mews constructed in 1848. The rowhouses were home to the reclusive author Djuna Barnes for more than forty years. Supposedly, Barnes's long time neighbor e.e. cummings used to call her "just to see if she was still alive." Patchin Place has also been home to Marlon Brando, Ezra Pound, and Eugene O'Neill.

Off Sixth Avenue's west side are some of the Village's prettiest residential streets, where you can easily spend a couple hours strolling and soaking up the neighborhood's charms, which include many respected and intimate spots to enjoy jazz, such as the *Village Vanguard*, at 178 Seventh Ave (see p.380). To start exploring, cross west over Father Demo Square, at Sixth Avenue and Bleecker Street (until the 1970s there was an Italian open marketplace on this stretch, and it's still lined by a few Italian stores), walk north up Bleecker and turn west down Leroy Street. The houses here, dating from the 1850s, are among the city's most graceful. No. 6 (recognizable by the two gas lamps of honor at the bottom of the steps) is the ex-residence of **Jimmy Walker**, mayor of New York in the 1920s. Walker was for a time the most popular of mayors, a big-spending wisecracker who gave up working as a songwriter for politics and lived an extravagant lifestyle that rarely kept him out of the gossip columns. Nothing if not shrewd, he reflected people's most glamorous, big-living aspirations during an era of unprecedented prosperity. He was, however, no match for the hard times to come, and once the Depression took hold in the 1930s he lost his touch and – with it – his office.

If folk music is your thing, **Bob Dylan** lived for a time at 161 W 4th St, and the cover of his 1963 *Freewheelin'* album was shot a few paces away on Jones Street.

Grove and Bedford streets

Just west of where Bleecker Street meets Seventh Avenue, **Grove Street** runs east into **Bedford Street**. Here you will find Grove Court, one of the neighborhood's most secluded little mews. Along with nearby Barrow and Commerce streets, Bedford Street is one of the quietest and most desirable Village addresses. Edna St Vincent Millay, the young poet and playwright who did a lot of work with the Provincetown Players, lived at no. 75 1/2. At only 9ft wide, it is one of the narrowest houses in the city. The clapboard structure next door, built in 1799, is the oldest house in the Village.

Farther down Bedford from Grove, the former speakeasy *Chumley's*, no. 86 (p.369), is recognizable only by the metal grille on its door – a low profile useful in Prohibition years that makes it hard to find today. Enter through the Bedford door or through the patio garden at 58 Barrow St. If you follow Bedford back onto Grove Street toward Seventh Avenue, keep an eye out for *Marie's Crisis Café*, 59 Grove St. Now a gay bar, it was once home to Thomas Paine, one of the most important and radical thinkers of the American Revolutionary era, and from whose *Crisis Papers* the café takes its name. Though English by birth, Paine was significantly involved in the Revolution on the American side. Following his active support of the French Revolution, Paine was scapegoated by the American government, and by the time he died in 1809, he had been stripped of citizenship by the country he helped found.

Heading back east, Grove Street meets Seventh Avenue at one of the Village's busiest junctions, Sheridan Square – not in fact a square at all unless you count Christopher Park's slim strip of green, but simply a wide and hazardous meeting of several busy streets.

Christopher Street and around

Christopher Street, the main artery of the West Village, runs west from Jefferson Market Courthouse and past Sheridan Square – the traditional center

Stonewall Riots

On June 27, 1969, police raided the **Stonewall gay bar**, and started arresting its occupants – for the local gay community simply the latest occurrence in a long history of harassment. Spontaneously, word got around to other bars in the area, and before long the *Stonewall* was surrounded by hundreds of angry protestors, resulting in a siege that lasted the better part of the night and ended with several arrests and a number of injured policemen. Though hardly a victory for their rights, it was the first time that gay men had stood up en masse to police persecution and, as such, formally inaugurated the gay-rights movement. The event is honored by the Annual Lesbian, Gay, Bisexual and Transgender March (often just referred to as the **Gay Pride March**). Typically the last Sunday in June, this parade is one of the city's most exciting and colorful (see p.443).

of the city's gay community. The square itself was named for Civil War cavalry commander General Sheridan, and holds a pompous-looking statue in his memory. Historically, Sheridan Square is better known, however, as the scene of one of the worst and bloodiest of New York's Draft Riots (see Contexts, p.463), when a marauding mob assembled here in 1863 and attacked members of the black community, several of whom were lynched. Violence also erupted here in 1969, when the **gay community** wasn't as readily accepted as it is now (see box, below).

Nowadays, however, the gay community is fairly synonymous with Greenwich Village life. From Sheridan Square west to the Hudson River is a tight-knit enclave – focusing on Christopher Street – of bars, restaurants, and bookstores used specifically, but not exclusively, by gay men; for complete listings of gay bars and clubs, see pp.399 and 401

The next major thoroughfare west of Seventh Avenue is Hudson Street. From Christopher Street north to Abingdon Square (where it bends to become Eighth Avenue and heads for Chelsea), Hudson is a good place for meandering, with a bevy of unique stores, coffee bars, and restaurants catering to its upwardly mobile and moneyed residential community. The excellent *White Horse Tavern*, no. 567 at West 11th Street, is where legend claims Dylan Thomas had his last drink; see p.370 for details.

Meatpacking District

Located just north of Abingdon Square, below 14th Street and west of Ninth Avenue, the **Meatpacking District** has seen the majority of its working slaughterhouses sell out to French bistros, after-hours clubs, wine bars, galleries, and boutique department stores, despite the lingering stench. Even the city's hottest and most exclusive private club, the **SoHo House**, 29–39 Ninth Ave, lies in a nondescript building at the heart of this postindustrial part of town. Walk a block or two farther to the west for a southerly stroll along the newly landscaped promenade that runs along the Hudson River. As soon as you cross the West Side Highway to the pedestrian-, rollerblade-, and bike-friendly stretch leading south to Soho and north to Chelsea, you will be greeted by the scent of salt air and stunning river views.

Chelsea

A squat grid of renovated tenements, rowhouses, and warehouses, **Chelsea** lies west of Broadway between 14th and 30th streets, though most consider the area between 14th and 23rd streets to be the heart of the neighborhood. For years, these dreary, overlooked buildings and bare streets gave Chelsea an atmosphere of neglect and did not encourage visitors to linger. Over the past few decades, however, Chelsea has become quite commercial, influenced greatly by the arrival of a large gay community in the late 1980s and early 1990s. Today, its districts are filled with affluent townhouses whose inhabitants relish the luxury of extra living space. Stores and restaurants pepper the scene, along with excellent cutting-edge art **galleries** and increasingly up-market real estate. Despite the encroachment of these moneyed forces, some of the long-entrenched Hispanic community has managed to stay put, providing an interesting cultural counterpoint.

To begin your visit to Chelsea, take the #1 train to 23rd Street and Seventh Avenue, or take the #C or #E to 23rd and Eighth.

Some history

The neighborhood, developed on former farmland, began to take shape in 1830 thanks to **Clement Clarke Moore**, famous as the author of the surprise poetic hit *A Visit from St Nick* (popularly known as *'Twas the Night Before Christmas*), whose estate comprised most of what is now Chelsea. That year, Moore, anticipating Manhattan's movement uptown, laid out his land for sale in broad lots. However, stuck as it was between the ritziness of Fifth Avenue, the hipness of Greenwich Village, and the poverty of Hell's Kitchen, the area never quite made it onto the shortlist of desirable places to live. Manhattan's chic residential focus leapfrogged over Chelsea to the East 40s and 50s, and the arrival of the slaughterhouses, an elevated railroad, and working-class poor sealed Chelsea's reputation as a rough-and-tumble no-go area for decades.

In the mid-nineteenth century, Chelsea enjoyed a short respite from gloom when its proximity to glitzy Gramercy Park and Murray Hill made it a center for Manhattan's theater scene. In 1869, 23rd Street between Sixth to Eighth avenues became known as the **theater district**, and even included an opera house. However, in 1871 a riot between Irish Catholics and Protestants, in which fifty people were killed, soured the mood, and in subsequent years an increasing number of jobs in freight handling and the warehouses west of Tenth Avenue returned Chelsea to a mainly working-class neighborhood. Despite all this, theater continued to flourish here well into the 1900s, and many local performers lived in the **Chelsea Hotel**. Bohemians also flocked here for a time,

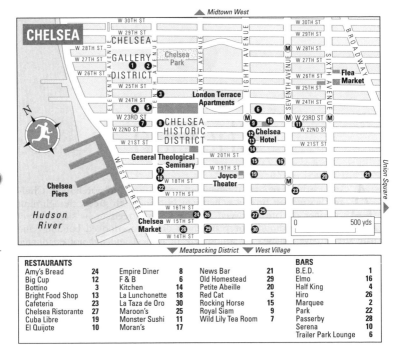

▼ Meatpacking District ▼ West Village

RESTAURANTS						BARS	
Amy's Bread	24	Empire Diner	8	News Bar	21	B.E.D.	1
Big Cup	12	F & B	6	Old Homestead	29	Elmo	16
Bottino	3	Kitchen	14	Petite Abeille	20	Half King	4
Bright Food Shop	13	La Lunchonette	18	Red Cat	5	Hiro	26
Cafeteria	23	La Taza de Oro	30	Rocking Horse	15	Marquee	2
Chelsea Ristorante	27	Maroon's	25	Royal Siam	9	Park	22
Cuba Libre	19	Monster Sushi	11	Wild Lily Tea Room	7	Passerby	28
El Quijote	10	Moran's	17			Serena	10
						Trailer Park Lounge	6

lured by the novelty of down-and-out charm, only to make for the Village at the turn of the twentieth century.

The last few decades have seen a totally new Chelsea emerge. New York's drifting art scene has been extremely influential in the neighborhood's transformation. In the early 1990s, a number of respected **galleries** began making use of the large spaces available in the low-rise warehouses of Chelsea's western reaches, securing the area's cultural edge. This influx has been counterbalanced by the steadily expanding presence of retail superstores, especially along **Sixth Avenue**, and the building of the **Chelsea Piers** mega-sized sports complex. For years now, the neighborhood has been crowded with shoppers, restaurant-goers, and the like, and it shows no signs of quieting down.

Eighth, Ninth, and Tenth avenues

Chelsea's main drag is **Eighth Avenue**, where the more laid-back vibe of the West Village, just to the south, segues at 14th Street into a stretch of vibrant retail energy. Along here, dozens of trendy bars, restaurants, health-food stores, gyms, bookstores, and clothes shops cater to Chelsea's large, out, and proud gay population. At West 19th Street you will also find one of the more important dance theaters in New York, the **Joyce**. The in-residence Feld Ballet and a host of other touring companies keep this Art Deco–style theater (complete with pink and purple neon signs) in business (see p.390).

As you head west to **Ninth Avenue**, the red-brick **Chelsea Market** fills an entire block between 15th and 16th streets. This high-class food temple is housed in the old National Biscuit Company (aka "Nabisco") factory, where legend has it the Oreo cookie was created. Many of the factory's features remain, including

△ Rowhouses, Chelsea

pieces of rail track used to transport provisions. The handpicked retailers inside the market supply most of Manhattan's upscale restaurant trade, and their wares include fresh fruit, fish, bread, wine, brownies, and flowers (for more details, see "Shopping," p.423).

Farther north, on West 20th, 21st, and 22nd streets between Ninth and Tenth avenues, is the **Chelsea Historic District**, which boasts a picturesque variety of predominantly Italianate and Greek Revival rowhouses. Dating from the 1830s to the 1890s, they demonstrate the faith some early developers had in Chelsea as an up-and-coming New York neighborhood. The **oldest house** in the area, at 404 W 20th St, stands out with its 1829 wood siding, predating as it does the all-brick constructions of James Wells, Chelsea's first real-estate developer. The ornate iron fencing heading west along this block is original and quite impressive. However, the nineteenth century runs headlong into the modern era at the corner of West 22nd Street and Tenth Avenue in the aluminum-sided, sci-fi-looking *Empire Diner*, built in the 1930s (see p.343 for review).

The block bounded by 20th and 21st streets between Ninth and Tenth avenues contains one of Chelsea's secrets, the 1817 **General Theological Seminary** on Chelsea Square. Clement Clarke Moore donated this island of land to the institute, and today the harmonious assembly of ivy-clad Gothic structures surrounding a green feels like part of a college campus. Though the buildings still house a working Episcopal seminary – the oldest in the United States – it's possible to explore the park on weekdays and Saturdays at lunchtime, as long as you sign in and keep quiet (the entrance is via the modern building on Ninth Avenue between West 20th and 21st streets). And if you're at all interested in theological history, you should check out the seminary's collection of Latin Bibles – it's one of the largest in the world.

London Terrace Apartments

Just north of the historic district at 405 and 465 W 23rd St is one of New York's premier residences for those who believe in understated opulence. The

London Terrace Apartments, two rows of apartment buildings a full city block long, sit between Ninth and Tenth avenues and surround a private interior garden. The building had the misfortune of being completed in 1930 at the height of the Great Depression, and despite a swimming pool and other posh amenities, many of the 1670 apartments stood empty for several years. The first management, wanting to evoke thoughts of Britain, made the doormen wear London-style police uniforms, thereby giving the building its name. The apartments were later nicknamed "The Fashion Projects" because of their designer, photographer, and model residents (including Isaac Mizrahi, Annie Leibovitz, and Debbie Harry), and for their proximity to Chelsea's real housing projects to the south and east.

West of Tenth Avenue

Tenth Avenue serves as a dividing line between Chelsea's more historic and quainter side to the east and its industrial past to the west. For years there was not much to see or do along this stretch – that is, until the galleries started swarming in. Along 22nd Street between Tenth and Eleventh avenues, as well as farther north on the streets just above West 24th, lie the **galleries** and **warehouse spaces** that house one of New York's most vibrant art scenes. (See "Commercial galleries," p.404, for more details on Chelsea's 150-odd galleries.) The buildings used by Chelsea's galleries are especially imposing above West 23rd Street, and in some cases even stretch for a whole block. This warehouse district can often seem eerily quiet and strictly industrial, but on opening nights or arts weekends, eccentric street parties erupt and it's quite a lively place. With the exception of a few established names in the art world that pay a premium for ground-floor real estate, most of the area's exhibition spaces are off street level. It's best to pick up a *Gallery Guide* to navigate the floors, whose hallways seem to stretch for miles. Even the ovular entryway to Comme des Garçons – the store is just west of Tenth Avenue at no. 520 – masquerades as art in this part of town.

At West 23rd Street and the West Side Highway, you'll find **Chelsea Piers** (ⓦwww .chelseapiers.com), a glitzy, family-friendly, and somewhat incongruous entertainment development stretching from piers 59 to 62. First opened in 1910, this was where passengers would disembark from the great transatlantic liners (it was en route to the Chelsea Piers that the *Titanic* sank in 1912). By the 1960s, however, the piers had fallen into decay through disuse, and as late as the mid-1980s an official report condemned them as "shabby, pathetic reminders of a glorious past." Since then, money and effort has been poured into the revival of this once illustrious area. Reopened in 1995, the new Chelsea Piers, whose commercial aura begs comparison with South Street Seaport (see p.62), is primarily a huge sports complex, with ice rinks and open-air roller rinks, as well as a skate park, bowling alley, and a landscaped golf driving range (for more details, see "Sports and outdoor activities," p.436). If you're not into overpriced athletic activities, there's a nice waterfront walkway of over a mile and a pleasant water's-edge park at the end of Pier 62. While somewhat contrived, these spaces put you as close to the Hudson River as you can (or would want to) get.

For a different sort of diversion, head one block north to Pier 63 to the unusual and very cool venue, *Frying Pan* (ⓣ212/989-6363). This lightship operated between 1929 and 1964 on the North Carolina coast, before it was submerged, abandoned, and finally brought to New York in the 1980s. These days, it acts as a performance space, hosting dance parties (including the excellent, outdoor "Turntables on the Hudson"), theater, and live bands.

The Chelsea Hotel

Double back east along 23rd Street, past Eighth Avenue, to find one of the neighborhood's major claims to fame – the **Chelsea Hotel**, no. 222 (see p.303 for accommodation details). Even though little evidence remains now of Chelsea's theater heyday in the 1870s and 1880s, in 1966 the hotel that put up all the actors, writers, and bohemian hangers-on was the first building in New York to be declared a landmark for both architectural and historical interest. Originally built as a luxury co-operative apartment building, with New York's first penthouses and duplexes, in 1882, the building never attracted many affluent tenants, who at the time scorned co-operative living. Despite its official status as a hotel, more than half the "guests" here are permanent residents, paying for their rooms at a reduced monthly rate.

Since its conversion to a hotel in 1905, the building has been the undisputed residence of the city's harder-up literati. Mark Twain and Tennessee Williams lived here and both Brendan Behan and Dylan Thomas staggered in and out during their New York visits. Actresses Sarah Bernhardt and Lillie Langtry were guests at the *Chelsea* around the turn of the nineteenth century. Thomas Wolfe assembled *You Can't Go Home Again* from thousands of pages of manuscript he had stacked in his room, and in 1951 Jack Kerouac, armed with a specially adapted typewriter (and a lot of Benzedrine), typed the first draft of *On the Road* nonstop onto a 120-foot roll of paper. William Burroughs (in a presumably more relaxed state) completed *Naked Lunch* here, and Arthur C. Clarke wrote *2001: A Space Odyssey* while in residence. Arthur Miller (who was sick of having to put on a tie just to pick up his mail at the stylish *Plaza*) and Paul Bowles have also been guests.

In the 1960s, the *Chelsea* entered a wilder phase. Andy Warhol and his doomed protégées Edie Sedgwick and Candy Darling holed up here and made the film *Chelsea Girls*. The late photographer Robert Mapplethorpe and Patti Smith also lived here in the late 1960s and early 1970s. The hotel's soundproof walls made the rooms attractive to musicians: Nico, Hendrix, Zappa, Pink Floyd, and various members of the Grateful Dead passed through; Bob Dylan wrote songs in and about the hotel; in probably the hotel's most infamous moment, Sid Vicious stabbed Nancy Spungen to death in 1978 in their suite, a few months before he fatally overdosed on heroin. (The owner of the *Chelsea*, in fact, had to divide Sid's and Nancy's old room into several smaller ones because visitors kept leaving wreaths and candles outside the door.) On a more cheerful note, the hotel inspired Joni Mitchell to write her song *Chelsea Morning* – a song that twanged the heartstrings of the young Bill and Hillary Clinton, who named their daughter after it. More recently, Ethan Hawke's 2001 film *Chelsea Walls* was a star-heavy homage to the hotel's durable bohemian legend.

With a pedigree like this it's easy to forget the hotel itself, which has a down-at-the-heel Edwardian grandeur all of its own and, incidentally, is also an affordable, though not always desirable, place to stay. The lobby, with its famously phallic wall-mounted sculpture *Chelsea Dog* and more respectable work by Larry Rivers, is worth a gander.

East Chelsea

Sandwiched between infinitely more interesting blocks, the eastern edge of Chelsea has become a buzzing strip of commerce, concentrated mostly along **Sixth Avenue** between West 17th and 23rd streets. In the last few years, a crush of discount emporiums like Best Buy, and mediocre national chain restaurants have mostly driven out the mom-and-pop businesses, and the trend only seems to be accelerating. On weekends especially, Sixth Avenue teems with bargain hunters lugging oversized bags from places like Bed, Bath and Beyond, the Container Store, and the Sports Authority. Before all the commercialism, a little **literary history** took place near here on West 23rd Street: Stephen Crane spent part of his impoverished twenties at no. 165, while Edith Wharton's birthplace is further east, at no. 14.

North above 23rd Street, away from Chelsea's heart, the city's largest **antiques market** (and surrounding junk sales) takes place on weekends in a few open-air parking lots centered around Sixth Avenue and 26th Street (see "Shopping," p.422).

The area around West 28th Street is Manhattan's **Flower Market** – not really a market as such, more the warehouses and storefronts where potted plants and cut flowers are stored before brightening offices and atriums across the city. There are no signs to mark the strip, and you come across it by chance: the greenery bursting out of drab blocks provides a welcome touch of life in a decidedly industrial neighborhood.

The street's historical background couldn't be more at odds with its present incarnation: from the mid-1880s until the 1950s, the short block between Sixth Avenue and Broadway was the original **Tin Pan Alley**, where music publishers would peddle songs by the likes of Irving Berlin and George Gershwin to artists and producers from vaudeville and Broadway. The name came from the piano-playing racket coming out of the publishing houses here at any time of the day, a sound that one journalist compared to banging on tin pans. After the sale of sheet music declined in the 1920s, the industry began focusing its energies on recording for radio, but it was the popular advent of mainstream motion pictures in the 1930s that truly helped bring Tin Pan Alley songs to the wider public. Sadly, competition from rock'n'roll and folk in the 1950s and 1960s proved too much, and business on the tiny strip dried up at around that time. However, some of the stylistic conventions of some of the best-known songs produced here – such as Fats Waller's *Ain't Misbehavin'* and *Do Nothin' Till You Hear from Me* by Duke Ellington – continue to inspire.

Union Square, Gramercy Park, and the Flatiron District

Downtown and midtown sensibilities collide in the knot of close-knit neighborhoods west of Fifth Avenue, as social protests rub up against some of the city's best restaurants and stores. **Union Square**, between 14th and 17th streets, is a bustling open space that breaks up Broadway's pell-mell dash north. Northeast of there is sedate **Gramercy Park**, with its private clubs and members-only park. Straddling Broadway northwest of Union Square and running up to 23rd Street, the **Flatiron District** was once the center of Manhattan's fine shopping and still retains a certain elegance. It is here, as you head north in the blocks between Third, Park, and Fifth avenues, that midtown Manhattan's skyscrapers begin to rise from downtown's generally low-lying buildings. Before heading on to jaw-droppers like the Empire State Building (see p.129), though, it's certainly worth it to take at least a quick jaunt around these neighborhoods, which offer not only some decent architecture, but also your last glimpse of trees south of Central Park.

Union Square and around

Located at the confluence of Broadway, Fourth, and Park avenues between 14th and 18th streets, **Union Square** is an inviting public space. Take a moment to stroll the park's paths, feed it squirrels, and gaze at its array of statuary. Among the figures are George Washington as equestrian; Gandhi; a Lafayette by Bartholdi (more famous for the Statue of Liberty); and, at the center of the green, a massive flagstaff base whose bas-reliefs symbolize the forces of Good and Evil in the American Revolution. Founded as a park in 1813, the square is still surrounded by a crush of commerce and serves as a welcome respite from crazed taxi-drivers and rushed pedestrians on 14th Street. Mostly, however, Union Square is beloved for its **Farmers' Market**

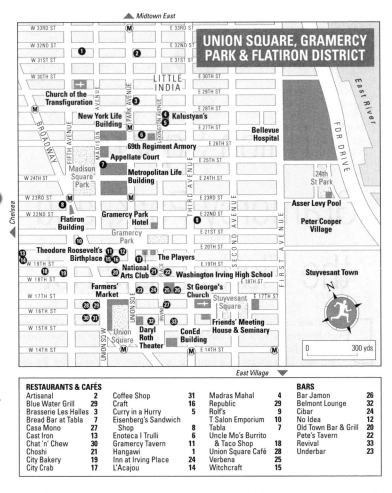

UNION SQUARE, GRAMERCY PARK & FLATIRON DISTRICT

RESTAURANTS & CAFÉS					BARS	
Artisanal	2	Coffee Shop	31	Madras Mahal	4	Bar Jamon	26
Blue Water Grill	29	Craft	16	Republic	29	Belmont Lounge	32
Brasserie Les Halles	3	Curry in a Hurry	5	Rolf's	9	Cibar	24
Bread Bar at Tabla	7	Eisenberg's Sandwich		T Salon Emporium	10	No Idea	12
Casa Mono	27	Shop	8	Tabla	7	Old Town Bar & Grill	20
Cast Iron	13	Enoteca I Trulli	6	Uncle Mo's Burrito		Pete's Tavern	22
Chat 'n' Chew	30	Gramercy Tavern	11	& Taco Shop	18	Revival	33
Choshi	21	Hangawi	1	Union Square Café	28	Underbar	23
City Bakery	19	Inn at Irving Place	24	Verbena	25		
City Crab	17	L'Acajou	14	Witchcraft	15		

– the largest in Manhattan (see box, opposite) – which sells all sorts of seasonal goods and non-edible products, like hand-spun wools and flowers.

Like the generally more rambunctious Washington Square in the West Village, Union Square is also often the site of civil demonstrations. After September 11, hundreds of vigils were held here, and the entire square became a makeshift memorial to the victims until it was finally ordered dismantled by then-Mayor Rudolph Giuliani. Since 2003, the park's southern end has also served as the informal center of Manhattan protest against the war in Iraq, with raggedly dressed protesters brandishing megaphones at passers-by day and night. They're occasionally joined by advocates for miscellaneous causes, everything from animal rights to legalized marijuana.

The square is flanked by a range of excellent restaurants, as well as by buildings in a mismatched hodgepodge of architectural styles, not least of which is the old **American Savings Bank** at 20 Union Square East – now the Daryl Roth Theatre – of which only the grandiose columned exterior survives. The pedimented Union Square Theater just north of here is the former **Tammany**

On Mondays, Wednesdays, Fridays, and Saturdays from 7am until 6pm, the square hosts the city's best and most popular **Farmers' Market** on its northern edge. Farmers and other food producers from upstate New York, Long Island, New Jersey, and even as far away as Pennsylvania Dutch country, sell fresh fruit and vegetables, baked goods, cheeses, eggs, meats, fish, and plants. The quality of the produce is generally very high (an advisory committee sets up and enforces stringent rules on the growers and keeps out wholesalers and brokers). Putting together a picnic at the market is one of the finest things you can do here on a spring or summer day. Prior to the winter holidays, there's also an extensive crafts market toward the square's southern end, where you'll find a good array of handmade treasures.

Hall (see p.463), once headquarters of the Democratic Party and a fine example of Colonial-Revival architecture. The narrow building almost directly across the way at 33 Union Square West was Andy Warhol's original Factory. The **Consolidated Edison** (or ConEd) building, off the southeast corner, is home to the company responsible for providing the city with both energy and steaming manholes.

The area immediately to the west of Union Square is chock-a-block with fine but pricey eateries – including the venerated *Union Square Café* at 21 E 16th St (see p.345 for review) – which are well situated (for those with deep pockets) for breaks from shopping at the many chic clothiers on Fifth Avenue.

Irving Place

East of Union Square, walk the six graceful blocks of **Irving Place** north toward Gramercy Park. Irving Place was named for Washington Irving, the early nineteenth-century writer best known for his creepy tale of the Headless Horseman, *The Legend of Sleepy Hollow*, and also for supposedly being the first American to earn a living from his writing. Although he only lived for a short time at no. 56 (he did make frequent visits to his nephew's house on East 21st Street), this strip nevertheless bears his name. A bust of Irving stands in front of the early nineteenth-century Washington Irving High School at no. 40. Another celebrated author, Pulitzer Prize–winning short-story writer O. Henry, lived at what was once no. 55 for many years. Landmark **Pete's Tavern**, at 18th St and Irving Place, is one of New York's oldest bars, in business since 1864. The tavern promotes itself as the place where O. Henry dreamed up and wrote *The Gift of the Magi* and, although this is disputed, the legend serves the place and its atmosphere well.

Gramercy Park and around

Irving Place comes to an end at the ordered open space of **Gramercy Park**. This former "little crooked swamp" (which is what the Dutch called it before the name was Anglicized) between East 21st and 22nd streets is one of the city's prettiest squares. It is beautifully manicured and, most noticeably, completely empty for much of the day – principally because it is the city's last private park and the only people who can gain access are those rich or fortunate enough to live here. Famous past key-holders have included Mark Twain and Julia Roberts, as well as a host of Kennedys and Roosevelts. Despite the park's exclusivity, it's well worth a walk around the edge for a glimpse of the trim, historic area that was once the city's main theater district.

△ Union Square Farmers' Market

Inside the park gates stands a statue of the actor Edwin Booth (brother of Lincoln's assassin, John Wilkes Booth) in the guise of Hamlet, one of his most famous roles. (Ironically, Edwin rescued Lincoln's son, Robert, from a train accident years before John's fatal action.) In 1887, aided by architect (and Gramercy Park resident) Stanford White, Booth turned his home at 16 Gramercy Park South into the private club **The Players**. Booth also established a Theater Library in the club to chronicle the history of the American stage. The porch railings on this rather forbidding building are decorated with distinctive figures representing Comedy and Tragedy. In the nineteenth century, actors and theater types were not accepted in general society, so Booth created the club for play and socializing – neglecting, however, to admit women, who were not allowed in until 1989. Later members included the Barrymores, Frank Sinatra, and (oddly) Sir Winston Churchill, while more recent inductees are Morgan Freeman and Liv Ullmann. These days it seems to be the club that is trying to keep regular society out – rather than vice versa.

Next door to The Players at no. 15 is the equally patrician **National Arts Club**, fittingly located in the rather grand Tilden Mansion. Built in 1840, the mansion was Victorianized in the 1870s by Central Park co-designer Calvert Vaux at the request of owner Governor Samuel Tilden, and is studded with terracotta busts of Shakespeare, Milton, and Franklin, among others; the National Arts Club moved here in 1906. Art collectors Henry Frick, J.P. Morgan, and Teddy Roosevelt were prominent members of this institution, which was founded to support American artists at home. Unfortunately, the priceless members' dining room, with its vaulted glass dome and stained-glass window panels, is off-limits to the public. The club does, however, host a year-round program of lunch-hour theater called *Food for Thought*, featuring one-act plays by writers as diverse as Anton Chekhov and Tony Kushner and supplemented by a light lunch. The program often feels more like an exclusive salon featuring marquee-name actors, making advance booking highly recommended (shows twice per week on Mon, Wed, Thurs, or Fri; lunch 12.30pm, show 1pm; $45; ☏212/362-2560, ⊛www .foodforthoughtproductions.com).

Have a walk around the square to get a look at the many early nineteenth-century townhouses. The **Visual Arts Foundation**, 17 Gramercy Park S, occupies the former home of Joseph Pulitzer, while at no. 38 on the northeast corner of the square is the mock-Tudor building in which John Steinbeck, then a struggling reporter for the now defunct *New York World*, lived from 1925 to 1926 (it took getting fired from that job to plunge him into fiction). At 2 Lexington Ave and Gramercy Park North is the imposing 1920s bulk of the **Gramercy Park Hotel** (see "Accommodation," p.302), whose elite early residents included Mary McCarthy, a very young John F. Kennedy, and Humphrey Bogart. Once a fairly stodgy, old-fashioned affair, it's recently been renovated by entrepreneur Ian Schrager and turned into a minimalist interior-design masterpiece; hotel guests also get access to Gramercy Park. Lastly, lining Gramercy Park West is a splendid row of brick Greek Revival townhouses from the 1840s with ornate wrought-iron work; James Harper, of the publishing house Harper & Row, lived at no. 4.

East of Gramercy Park

The area between Gramercy Park and the East River is somewhat of a no-man's-land, with a clutch of nondescript apartment buildings and businesses. It is, however, a good place for a stroll, even if only to hop off the beaten path and to check out the neighborhood's few historical points of interest. The land that makes up **Stuyvesant Square**, between East 14th and 18th streets, was a gift to the city from Peter Stuyvesant, the last director-general of New Amsterdam (see Contexts, p.460). As with Gramercy Park, the park in the middle of the square was modeled on the layout of London's Bloomsbury. Though framed by the buildings of Beth Israel Medical Center and bisected by bustling Second Avenue, it still retains something of its secluded quality, especially on the western side. Here there's a smattering of elegant terraces and the **Friends' Meeting Houses and Seminary** (1860), whose austere Greek-Revival facade contrasts with the Romanesque brownstone of St George's Episcopal Church next door. Built on land donated by the Stuyvesants in 1836, the church is best known as the place where J.P. Morgan worshipped. Today it houses a playground as well as an antique furniture and thrift store.

Dominating the blocks just east of First Avenue are **Peter Cooper Village** and **Stuyvesant Town**, possibly the city's most successful examples of densely packed urban housing. Tall, angled apartment buildings are surrounded by peaceful, tree-lined walkways. This is private, not public, housing, though, and the developments' owners, Metropolitan Life, were accused of discriminating against non-whites when the projects first opened around 1947 (after some 500 residences were demolished to make room) for returning soldiers from World War II. The complexes make for a striking contrast with the similarly high-rise public housing complexes a little farther downtown. At the northeast corner of Peter Cooper Village, at East 23rd Street and Avenue A, stands the **Asser Levy Recreation Center**, named for the country's first Jewish citizen and kosher butcher, who arrived in America in 1654. The Asser Levy building was originally constructed in 1908 as a bathhouse – modeled on the Roman public baths – for the huddled, unwashed masses (at the time, East Side tenements supposedly had but one bath for every 79 families). Abandoned in the 1970s, the bathhouse was reopened as a city gym in 1990 (see p.436 for admission info).

The Flatiron District

The small district north and northwest of Union Square, between Fifth and Park avenues up to 23rd Street, is generally known as the **Flatiron District**, taking its name from the distinctive early skyscraper on the southwest corner of Madison Square Park. This area is a nice enough place to stroll around in, though there's little to see besides the proliferation of upscale eateries and antique stores. This stretch of Broadway was once the heart of the so-called "**Ladies' Mile**," which during the mid-nineteenth century was lined with fancy stores and boutiques. The area started losing its luster around the turn of the twentieth century, and by World War I, Ladies' Mile had all but disintegrated due to the department stores' uptown migration. However, a few sculpted facades and curvy lintels remain as mementos of that gilded age, including Lord & Taylor's Victorian wedding-cake of a building at 901 Broadway (the store is now at 38th and 5th).

Standing apart from its rather commercial surroundings at 28 E 20th St is **Theodore Roosevelt's birthplace** (Tues–Sat 9am–5pm; $3; ☎212/260-1616), or at least a reconstruction of it. In 1923, the house was rebuilt as it would have been when Roosevelt was born there in 1858. This rather somber mansion contains many original furnishings, some of Teddy's hunting trophies, and a small gallery documenting the president's life, viewable on an obligatory guided tour.

The lofty, elegant, and decidedly anorexic **Flatiron Building** (originally the Fuller Construction Company, later renamed in honor of its distinctive shape) is set on a narrow, triangular plot of land at the manic intersection of Broadway, Fifth Avenue, and 23rd Street. It is one of the city's most famous buildings, evoking images of Edwardian New York. Though it's hard to believe today, the Flatiron was the city's first true skyscraper (a fact hotly debated by architectural-history buffs), hung on a steel frame in 1902 with its full twenty stories dwarfing all the other buildings around. Its uncommonly thin, tapered structure creates unusual wind currents at ground level, and years ago policemen were posted to prevent men gathering to watch the wind raise the skirts of women passing on 23rd Street. The cry they gave to warn off voyeurs – "23 Skidoo!" – has passed into the language.

Madison Square Park and around

Just northeast of the Flatiron Building, between Park and Fifth avenues, lies **Madison Square Park**. Though enveloped by a maelstrom of cars, cabs, buses, and dodging pedestrians, because of the stateliness of the surrounding buildings and its peaceful green spaces, it possesses a grandiosity and neat seclusion that Union Square has long since lost. Some believe the park to be the birthplace of baseball, as this is supposedly where the country's first ball club, the New York Knickerbockers, was founded in 1845.

On the park's east side, at no. 1 Madison Avenue, stands the tiered, stately **Metropolitan Life Company**, which became the city's tallest building in 1909, and whose tower is visible from blocks away. Just north of the Metropolitan Life building, at 27 Madison Ave, is the Corinthian-columned marble facade of the **Appellate Division** of the **New York State Supreme Court**, resolutely righteous with its statues of Justice, Wisdom, and Peace. The grand structure next to that, the **New York Life Building** proper, was the work of Cass Gilbert, creator of the Woolworth Building downtown (see p.67). It went up in 1928 on the site of the original **Madison Square Garden**, renowned scene of drunken and debauched revels of high and Broadway society.

There is one reminder of the time when this was New York's theaterland: the **Church of the Transfiguration**, just off Fifth Avenue at 1 E 29th St (chapel open daily 8am–6pm). Built in 1849, this dinky, rusticated church, made of brown brick, topped with copper roofs, and set back from the street, has long been a traditional place of worship for showbiz people and other social outcasts. The church was also headquarters to the oldest boys' choir in the city, formed in 1881. Its first rector, Rev George Hendric Houghton, served for 49 years, during which time he maintained a breadline for the unemployed and sheltered escaped slaves during the 1863 draft riots. It was not until 1870, though, that members of the theater profession started coming here to pray. That year, the place was tagged with the name "The Little Church Around the Corner" after a devout priest from a larger, stuffier church had refused to officiate at the funeral of an actor named George Holland, sending the bereaved here instead. Since then, the church has been a haven for actors, and there is even an Episcopal Actors' Guild. The chapel itself is an intimate little building in a gloriously leafy garden, providing comfort and solace away from the skyscrapers on Fifth Avenue. Its interior is furnished in warm wood and lit with soft candlelight. The figures of famous actors (most notably Edwin Booth as Hamlet) are memorialized in the stained glass.

North of Madison Square Park

From here, Lexington Avenue, which begins its long journey north at Gramercy Park, heads uptown, past the lumbering **69th Regiment Armory** at 26th

Stanford White, a partner in the illustrious architectural team of McKim, Mead and White, which designed many of the city's great Beaux-Arts buildings, including the General Post Office, the old Penn Station, and Columbia University, was something of a rake by all accounts. His dalliance with millionaire Harry Thaw's future wife, Evelyn Nesbit, a Broadway showgirl (who was unattached at the time), had been well publicized – even to the extent that the naked statue of the goddess Diana on the top of the Madison Square Garden building was said to have been modeled on her. Thaw was so infuriated by this display that one night in 1906 he burst into the roof garden of White's tower apartment in Madison Square Garden, found the architect surrounded, as usual, by doting women and admirers, and shot him through the head. Thaw was carted away to spend most of his life in mental institutions, and his wife's show-business career took a tumble: she resorted to drugs and prostitution, dying in 1966 in Los Angeles. Madison Square Garden has moved twice since then, first to a site on Eighth Avenue and 50th Street in 1925, and finally in 1968 to its present location in a hideous drum-shaped eyesore on the corner of 32nd Street and Seventh Avenue (see p.155).

Street. The site of the famous Armory Show of 1913, which brought modern art to New York, it is now a venue for antiques shows and art fairs.

One of Manhattan's most condensed ethnic enclaves, **Little India**, runs along Lexington Avenue between East 27th and 30th streets – blink, and you might miss it altogether. Most of New York's Indian population lives in Queens, but there's still a sizable grouping of restaurants and fast-food places – slightly outnumbered by those down on East 6th Street – and a pocket of sweet and spice shops here. *Kalustyan's*, 123 Lexington Ave between East 28th and 29th streets, is a heavenly scented store that has been selling Indian food products, spices, and hard-to-find ingredients since 1944; it also has a selection of foods from around the globe.

Midtown East

argely corporate and commercial, the area known as **Midtown East** rolls north from the 30s through the 50s, and east from Fifth Avenue, the sight- and store-studded spine of Manhattan. Some of the city's chicest boutiques, richest Art Deco facades, and most sophisticated Modernist skyscrapers are in this district, primarily scattered along **Fifth**, **Park**, and **Madison avenues**. Famous for their neck-straining vistas and terrible traffic jams, the streets in this part of town are crammed with yellow cabs and office workers during the day, but once professional nine-to-fivers go home in the evening, much of the activity comes to a screeching halt.

Anchored by **Grand Central Terminal**, Cornelius Vanderbilt's Beaux-Arts transportation hub, Midtown East is a trove of architectural and cultural treasures. Some of its most notable attractions include the **Empire State Building**, the soaring symbol of New York City; the **Seagram Building**; the Art Deco, automobile-inspired **Chrysler Building**; the rambling, geometric bulk of the **United Nations** complex; and the renovated **Museum of Modern Art** (see Chapter 12).

Fifth Avenue

For the last two centuries, an address on **Fifth Avenue** has signified prosperity, respectability, and high social standing. Whether around Washington Square or far uptown around the Harlem River, the boulevard has traditionally been the home to Manhattan's finest mansions, hotels, churches, and stores. Thanks to its show of wealth and opulence, Fifth Avenue has always drawn crowds, and the stretch between 34th and 59th streets is no exception, home to grand institutions like **Rockefeller Center** and the **New York Public Library**. The winter holiday season, when department stores mount elaborate window displays, is particularly crazy. And as if the usual crush of pedestrians wasn't enough, Fifth Avenue is also home to most of the city's many parades and processions (see Chapter 33, "Parades and festivals," for more details).

The Empire State Building

The city's tallest skyscraper, the **Empire State Building**, 350 Fifth Ave, between 33rd and 34th streets, has easily been the most potent and evocative symbol of New York since its completion in 1931. The building occupies what has always been a prime piece of real estate; nearby, between 38th and 39th

MIDTOWN EAST | Fifth Avenue

RESTAURANTS & CAFÉS

Buttercup Bake Shop	13	Hatsuhana	18	Oyster Bar	20
Chez Laurence	21	Jaiya Thai	24	Smith & Wollensky	17
Comfort Diner	19	La Grenouille	10	Solera	9
El Rio Grande	22	L'Annam	25	Tea Box	5
Four Seasons	12	Le Colonial	3	Viand	1
Fresco by Scotto on the Go	11	Luna Piena	8	Vong	6
		Mad Tea Cup	2	Zarela	15

BARS

Campbell Apartment	20
Divine Bar	14
FUBAR	16
Lever House	7
MBC Music Box	23
P.J. Clarke's	4

streets, are the headquarters of Lord & Taylor, and Macy's is just a short stroll away on Herald Square. Before the construction of the Empire State Building, this was the site of the first *Waldorf-Astoria Hotel*, built by William Waldorf Astor to convince his aunt, Caroline Schermerhorn, to move uptown. The hotel opened in 1893 and immediately became a gathering place for the city's rich – "Meet me at the Waldorf" was the catchphrase *du jour*. Though the reputation of the *Waldorf* – at least that of its prices – endures, the establishment didn't remain at its initial premises for very long, moving in 1929 to its current Art Deco home on Park Avenue (see p.142).

Wall Street visionary John Jacob Raskob and his partner Alfred E. Smith, a former governor, began compiling funds in October 1929, just three weeks before the stock market crash. Despite the ensuing Depression, the building proceeded full steam ahead and came in well under budget after just fourteen months. Since the opening, the building has seen its share of celebrity: King Kong clung to it while grabbing at passing aircraft; in 1945, an actual B-25 bomber negotiating its way through heavy fog crashed into the building's 79th story, killing fourteen people; and in 1979, two Englishmen parachuted from its summit to the ground, only to be carted off by the NYPD for disturbing the peace. The darkest moment in the building's history came in February 1997, when a man opened fire on the observation deck, killing one tourist and injuring seven others; as a result there is tighter security upon entrance, with metal detectors, package scanners, and the like. This vigilance has only increased since the attacks on the World Trade Center in 2001.

From toe to TV mast, the building is 102 stories and 1454 feet tall, but its height is deceptive, rising in stately tiers with steady panache. Standing on Fifth Avenue below, it's easy to walk right by without even realizing that it's there; only the crowds outside serve as a reminder of what stretches above. Inside, the basement, finished with delicate Art Deco touches, is an underground shopping mall, featuring newsstands, beauty parlors, cafés, and even a post office. On the second floor is the **New York Skyride**, a pricey, eight-minute simulated flight over the city's landmarks (daily 10am–10pm; $18, kids and seniors $13; ☏212/299-4922 or 1-888/SKY-RIDE, ⊛www.skyride.com). Few people come for either the shopping or the Skyride; neither is as interesting as a trip to the top of the building.

Getting to the top

A first set of elevators takes you to the **86th floor**. The views from the outdoor walkways here are as stunning as you'd expect; on a clear day visibility can be up to eighty miles, but, given the city's air pollution, on most it's more likely to be between ten and twenty. For an additional $14, a second set of elevators will take you to the **102nd floor observatory**, the base of the radio and TV antennas. The space is small, you can't go outside, and the extra sixteen stories don't really add much to the view, but you'll be able to say you've been to the top. This area was initially designed as a mooring post for airships, but the plan was abandoned and the "blimp port" closed after some local VIPs were almost swept away by the wind in one attempted mooring, and a second try, this time made by a Navy blimp, resulted in the flooding of 34th Street – when the wind got hold of the blimp, they had to drop the water used as ballast. (Daily 8am–midnight, last trip 11.15pm; $16, seniors $14, children ages 5–11 $10, children under 5 and military personnel free; combined tickets for New York Skyride and the Observatory $28; audio tour $6; bring photo ID; ☏212/736-3100, ⊛www.esbnyc.com.)

The New York Public Library and around

Several unexceptional blocks north of the Empire State Building on Fifth Avenue is one of midtown Manhattan's most striking buildings: the **New York Public Library** (Tues & Wed 11am–7.30pm, Thurs–Sat 10am–6pm; ☎212/930-0830, ⊛www.nypl.org), which stretches between 40th and 42nd streets. Beaux Arts in style and faced with white marble, it is the headquarters

△ Reading Room, New York Public Library

of the largest public-library system in the world. Its steps, framed by two majestic reclining lions, the symbols of the NYPL, are a meeting point and general hangout for groups of people throughout the year. To explore the library, either walk around yourself or take one of the **free tours** (Tues–Sat 11am and 2pm), which last an hour and give a good all-round picture of the building, including the **Map Room**, which reopened to the public in December 2005 after a $5m renovation project. Tours start at the information desk in Astor Hall (the main lobby). The highlight of the library is the large, coffered 636-seat **Reading Room** on the third floor. Authors Norman Mailer and E.L. Doctorow worked here, as did Leon Trotsky during his brief sojourn in New York just prior to the 1917 Russian Revolution. It was also here that Chester Carlson came up with the idea for the Xerox copier and Norbert Pearlroth searched for strange facts for his "Ripley's Believe It or Not" cartoon strip in the famed research library – the largest with a circulating stock in the world. Its 88 miles of books are stored beneath the reading room on eight levels of stacks, which run the half-acre length of Bryant Park (behind the library; see below).

Bryant Park

The restoration of **Bryant Park**, just behind the library to the west between 40th and 42nd streets, is one of the city's resounding success stories. An eyesore until 1992, it is now a beautiful, grassy block filled with trees, flowerbeds, and inviting chairs (the fact that they aren't chained to the ground is proof enough of revitalization). Like Greeley Square to the south, Bryant Park is named for a newspaper editor – William Cullen Bryant of the *New York Post*, who was also a poet and backer of Central Park. In place since 1847, Bryant Park was the site of the first American World's Fair in 1853, with a Crystal Palace, modeled on the famed London Crystal Palace, on its grounds – an edifice that burned in 1858. In the warmer months, it's easy to imagine yourself in Paris's Jardin du Luxembourg, while the corporate lunch crowd is just grateful for a pleasant place to eat.

You can grab a slice of pizza or an ice-cream cone at one of the park's small, reasonably priced eateries. There's also a rather aggressive singles' scene at the outdoor *Bryant Park Café* (which becomes the indoor *Bryant Park Grill* during colder months). Summertime brings life to the park – there are free dance and yoga classes, as well as various performances throughout the week and free outdoor movies on Monday evenings. Games, lectures, and rallies also take place in the park, and you can even rent a portion of it for your own event (☎212/768-4242, ⊛www.bryantpark.org).

Just across from the park is the swanky **Bryant Park Hotel**, 40 W 40th St. Designed by Raymond Hood for the American Radiator Company and constructed in 1924, the building is noteworthy for its Gothic tower, polished black-granite facade, and gold terracotta detail. Georgia O'Keeffe's painting *Radiator Building – Night, New York* captured its somber beauty. To the north of the park, the **W.R. Grace Building** swoops down at 41 W 42nd St; breaking the rules by stepping out of line with its neighbors, its curved lower walls are set back from the street.

North to Rockefeller Center

The **Chemical Bank**, on the southwest corner of 43rd Street, is an eye-catcher. An early glass'n'gloss box, it teasingly displays its vault (no longer in use) to passers-by. Around the next corner, West 44th Street contains several old-guard New York institutions. The Georgian-style **Harvard Club**, no. 35

The Round Table

All across the globe, the period between World War I and World War II saw an incredible outpouring of creative energy. In America, one of the groups involved in this burst of productivity was the so-called **Round Table**, which originated at the **Algonquin Hotel**. Several writers, many of whom had worked together for the Army newspaper *Stars and Stripes*, met in June 1919 at the hotel to roast *New York Times* drama critic Alexander Woollcott. They had so much fun that they decided to return the following afternoon; it wasn't long before their meeting became a ritual. At the heart of the group were Parker, Robert Benchley, Robert Sherwood, Irving Berlin, Harold Ross (founder of *New Yorker* magazine), George Bernard Shaw, and George S. Kaufman, among others. The members of the Round Table had a profound respect for each other's work, and they often cited each other in their writings. They were outspoken and unafraid to comment on the state of the postwar world. Several of the friends joined forces and worked together on notable projects: Ross hired Parker as a book reviewer and Benchley as a drama critic. By 1925, the Round Table wielded a good deal of power as a social critic; when its members spoke, the country listened. Then the Great Depression arrived, and a decade after the Round Table first met, it faded from the scene. Times have changed considerably since the Round Table's heyday, but over the years the *Algonquin* has continued to attract a stream of famous guests, many with some kind of writerly bent.

(☎212/840-6600, 🌐www.hcny.com), easily identified in the evening by the paparazzi hanging around outside, has an interior so lavish that lesser mortals aren't even allowed to enter (you must be a Harvard alumnus/a). Built in 1894, the Harvard Club was the first of several elite associations in the neighborhood, including the Yale Club and the Century Club, among others. Over the years, the building has gone through a series of expansions to match its growing membership.

The **New York Yacht Club**, 37 W 44th St (☎212/382-1000, 🌐www.nyyc.org), chartered in 1844, is just down the block. In its current location since 1901, this playfully eccentric exterior of bay windows is molded as ships' sterns; waves and dolphins complete the effect of tipsy Beaux-Arts fun. For years this has been the home of the America's Cup, a yachting trophy first won by the schooner *America* in 1851.

"Dammit, it was the twenties and we had to be smarty," said Dorothy Parker of the sharp-tongued wits known as the Round Table (see box, above), whose members lunched and drank regularly at the **Algonquin Hotel**, 59 W 44th St (☎212/840-6800). The bar, the *Oak Room*, is still one of the most civilized in town and hosts an acclaimed cabaret series.

Just down the street from the *Algonquin* is the **Royalton**, 44 W 44th St (☎212/869-4400), one of hotelier Ian Schrager's many unique boutique hotels; it was for media types in the 1990s what the *Algonquin* had been for Parker's set at the beginning of the twentieth century. Designed by Philippe Starck (his first collaboration with Schrager), the lush, velvety style and nautical atmosphere brought the word "trendy" to new heights.

West 47th Street, or **Diamond Row** (described on p.161), is a diverting (though pricey) side-trip from Fifth Avenue, but before heading down there, duck into the **Fred F. French Building** at 551 Fifth Ave. The colorful mosaics on the exterior are a mere prelude to the combination of Art Deco and Near Eastern imagery on the vaulted ceiling and bronze doors of the lobby. Also striking (and indicative of another era) is the facade of what was once **Charles**

Scribner's Sons bookstore, 597 Fifth Ave. The black-and-gold storefront looks like something from an Edwardian engraving, and has been granted historic landmark status. All the more anachronistic, then, that the building now houses a Benetton store; the lone remnant of its literary history is a basement café-cum-salon that hosts frequent readings.

Rockefeller Center

Taking up the entire block between Fifth and Sixth avenues and 49th and 50th streets, **Rockefeller Center** (℡212/332-6868, ✉www.rockefellercenter.com) is one of the finest examples of urban planning in New York. Built between 1932 and 1940 by John D. Rockefeller, Jr, son of the oil magnate, its offices, cafés, theater, underground concourse, and rooftop gardens work together with an intelligence and grace rarely seen. As a city-center shopping mall, it is a combination that leaves you thinking that Cyril Connolly's snide description – "that sinister Stonehenge of Economic Man" – was way off the mark. Just adjacent on the Sixth Avenue side stands the similarly Art Deco–style **Radio City Music Hall**, arguably the most famous theater in the United States (see p.161).

You're lured into the Center from Fifth Avenue down the gentle slope of the **Channel Gardens** (whimsically named because they divide La Maison Française and the British Empire Building) to the focus of the Center – the **GE Building**, formerly the RCA Building and nicknamed "30 Rock" by entertainment insiders aware of the television studios in its towers. Rising 850ft, its monumental lines echo the scale of Manhattan, though they are softened by symmetrical setbacks to prevent an overpowering expanse of wall. At the foot of the building, the **Lower Plaza** holds a sunken restaurant in the summer months – a great place for afternoon cocktails – linked visually to the downward flow of the building by **Paul Manship**'s sparkling sculpture *Prometheus*. In winter this sunken area becomes an **ice rink**; skaters show off their skills to passing shoppers. Many events take place throughout the year at the plaza, with the winter holidays being one of the busiest seasons. Since 1931 a huge lighted tree, now a New York tradition, has been on display here at Christmas time. The lighting of the tree, with accompanying musical entertainment, on a night in early December, draws throngs of locals and tourists alike.

Inside, the GE Building is no less impressive. **José Maria Sert**'s lobby murals, *American Progress* and *Time*, are faded but still in tune with the 1930s ambience – presumably more so than the original paintings by Diego Rivera, which were removed by John D.'s son Nelson Rockefeller when the artist refused to scrap a panel glorifying Lenin. A leaflet available from the lobby desk details a self-guided tour of the Center (also available online).

Among the GE Building's many offices is **NBC Studios**, on 49th Street between Fifth and Sixth avenues, which produces, among other things, the long-running sketch-comedy hit *Saturday Night Live* and the popular morning program the *Today Show* (1hr behind-the-scenes tours Mon–Fri 8.30am–7.30pm, Sat & Sun 9.30am–4.30pm; reservations at the NBC Experience Tour Desk; $18.50, children $15.50; free ticket for a show recording from the mezzanine lobby or out on the street; ℡212/664-7174). Keep in mind that the most popular tickets evaporate before 9am. During the summer the *Today Show* hosts concerts every Friday morning. Adjacent is the old **Associated Press Building**, recognizable by the unusual frieze by Japanese-American artist Isamu Noguchi.

North to Central Park

Return to Fifth Avenue and you'll see another sumptuous Art Deco component of Rockefeller Center, the **International Building**. The lobby looks
out across **Lee Lawrie**'s bronze *Atlas* to **St Patrick's Cathedral**. Designed
by James Renwick and completed in 1888, St Patrick's sits on the corner of
50th Street amid the glitz like a misplaced bit of moral imperative. The exterior seems the result of a painstaking academic tour of the Gothic cathedrals
of Europe: perfect in detail, it's also lifeless in spirit. However, the peaceful
Lady Chapel at the back of the cathedral, with its graceful, simple altar,
captures the mysticism that its big sister lacks. Despite its spiritual shortcom-
ings, St Patrick's is an essential part of the midtown landscape, a foil for Rockefeller Center and one of the most important Catholic churches in America.
In all, the compound's Gothic details are striking and the cathedral's twin
towers certainly a work of art – and made all the more so by the backing of
the sunglass-black Olympic Tower.

Across the avenue from Rockefeller Center are the striped awnings of **Saks
Fifth Avenue**, no. 611, one of the last of New York's premier department stores
to relocate to midtown from Herald Square. With its columns on the ground
floor and yellow-brick-road pathways through fashion collections, Saks is every
bit as glamorous today as it was when it opened in 1924.

Museum of Television and Radio

If your body needs the kind of rejuvenation only an hour in front of a television can offer, visit the **Museum of Television and Radio (MTR)**, 25
W 52nd St between Fifth and Sixth avenues (Tues–Sun noon–6pm, Thurs
noon–8pm; $10, seniors and students $8; ☎212/621-6800, ⊛www.mtr.org).
In a building designed by Philip Johnson, the MTR preserves an archive of
100,000 mostly American TV shows, radio broadcasts, and commercials. The
museum's excellent computerized reference system allows you to research
news, public affairs, documentaries, sporting events, comedies, advertisements,
and other aural and visual selections. To appease wary pop-culture critics, the
museum also conducts educational seminars and screenings in its four theaters.
The MTR becomes unbearably crowded on weekends and holidays, so plan
to visit at other times.

The '21' Club

Right next door to the MTR is the **'21' Club**, 21 W 52nd St (☎212/582-
7200), which has been providing food (and drink) since the early days of
Prohibition. Founded by Jack Kriendler and Charlie Berns, the club quickly
became one of the most exclusive establishments in town, a place where the
young socialites of the Roaring Twenties could spend wild nights dancing the
Charleston and enjoying wines and spirits of the finest quality. Although *'21'*
was raided more than once, federal agents were never able to pin anything
on Jack and Charlie. At the first sign of a raid, they would activate an ingenious system of pulleys and levers, which would sweep bottles from the bar
shelves and hurl the smashed remains down a chute into the New York sewer
system. This bar and restaurant, which is easily recognizable by the colorful
iron jockey statues in front, remains a New York institution, where the
Old Boys meet, surrounded by dark-wood paneling and served by the
consummately professional waitstaff. There's a dress code, so wear a jacket
and tie.

The Museum of Arts & Design and the Museum of American Folk Art

On the next block north, look for the **Museum of Arts & Design**, 40 W 53rd St (daily 10am–6pm, Thurs 10am–8pm; $9, students $7; ☎212/956-3535, ⓦwww .madmuseum.org), whose eclectic collection spans three floors and features everything from blown-glass *objets d'art* to contemporary jewelry. Changing exhibits cover a wide array of mediums (from paper to porcelain to metal to glass) and styles, and are often accompanied by lectures and workshops, which have included such diverse themes as origami and "the kilns of Denmark." The museum is scheduled to move to the 2 Columbus Circle building on the Upper West Side in 2008 (see box, p.207); check the website for details.

Just across the street is the excellent **Museum of American Folk Art**, 45 W 53rd St (Wed & Thurs, Sat & Sun 10.30am–5.30pm, Fri 10.30am–7.30pm; $9, students/seniors $7; ☎212/265-1040, ⓦwww.folkartmuseum.org), which exhibits multicultural folk art from all over America, with a permanent collection that includes over 3500 works from the seventeenth to twentieth centuries. The affiliated Folk Art Institute runs courses, lectures, and workshops.

53rd Street to Grand Army Plaza

After a stint at the art museums, take a break in the authentic tearoom at the New York branch of Japan's largest department store chain, **Takashimaya**, no. 693, at the northeast corner with 54th Street. Northward from here, Fifth Avenue's ground floors shift from mundane offices to an elegant stretch of exclusive shops and art galleries. Taking ostentatious wealth to the extreme is **Trump Tower**, no. 725 at 56th Street. Many visitors, although perhaps not those who frequent the glamorous designer boutiques here, find its outrageously overdone atrium just short of repellent. Perfumed air, polished marble paneling, and a five-story waterfall are calculated to knock you senseless with expensive "good taste." The building itself is clever: a neat little outdoor garden is squeezed high in a corner, and each of the 230 apartments above the atrium provides views in three directions. Donald Trump, the property developer all New York traditionalists love to hate, lives here, along with other hyper-rich worthies, including Yankees captain Derek Jeter and fan-favorite Hideki Matsui.

The stores on these blocks are more like sights than shops, with **Cartier**, **Gucci**, and **Tiffany & Co** among the many gilt-edged names. If you're keen to do more than merely window-shop, Tiffany's at no. 727 is worth a perusal, its soothing green marble and weathered wood interior best described by Truman Capote's fictional Holly Golightly: "It calms me down right away . . . nothing very bad could happen to you there." Farther north at no. 754 is the famed rich people's department store **Bergdorf Goodman**, offering a wedding-cake interior of glossy pastels, chandeliers, and pink curtains. Just next door are the glittering (and virtually priceless) window displays of **Harry Winston Jewelers**, beloved by countless celebrities (see "Shopping," Chapter 31, for more on this area's stores).

At 59th Street, Fifth Avenue reaches **Grand Army Plaza** and the fringes of Central Park, where a golden statue of William Tecumseh Sherman stands guard amid all the highbrow shopping. The copper-edged 1907 **Plaza Hotel** looms impressively on the plaza's western border. The *Plaza* is currently being converted to high-end condominiums; it's still possible to get inside, but only if you're going to the first-floor sales office to inquire about purchasing a unit. Unfortunately, the celebrated lobby and snazzy *Oak Room* bar are closed, too, unless by special appointment. In its heyday, the hotel's reputation was built not just on looks, but on lore: it boasts its own historian, keeper of such tidbits as when legendary tenor Enrico Caruso, enraged with the loud ticking of the hotel's clocks, stopped them all by throwing a shoe at one (they were calibrated to function together). The management apologized with a magnum of champagne.

Madison Avenue

Madison Avenue parallels Fifth with some of the grandeur but less of the excitement. In the East 30s, the avenue runs through the heart of the mundane and residential **Murray Hill** neighborhood, an area distinguished mostly by the presence of the historical **Morgan Library**. Heading north to the East 40s and the Upper East Side, you encounter the Madison Avenue of legend, the center of the international advertising industry in the 1960s and 1970s. Today, this section of town is a major upscale shopping boulevard.

Murray Hill and the Morgan Library

Madison Avenue is the main artery of **Murray Hill**, a tenuously tagged residential area of statuesque, canopy-fronted buildings bounded by East 34th and 40th streets. The district offers little, apart from its WASPish anonymity, to mark it out from the rest of midtown Manhattan. Built on one of the few remaining actual hills in the lower part of Manhattan island, the neighborhood is residential by design – no commercial building was allowed until the 1920s, when greedy real-estate interests successfully challenged the rule in court. It lacks any real center and sense of community, and, unless you work, live, or are staying in Murray Hill, there's little reason to go there at all. Indeed, you're more likely to pass through without even realizing it.

When Madison Avenue was on a par with Fifth as the place to live, Murray Hill was dominated by the Morgan family, including the crusty old financier J.P. and his offspring, who at one time owned a clutch of property here. Morgan Junior lived in the brownstone on the corner of 37th Street and Madison (now headquarters of the American Lutheran Church), his father in a house that was later pulled down to make way for an extension to his library next door. The **Morgan Library**, 29 E 36th St (☎212/685-0610, ⊛www.morganlibrary.org), housed in a mock-Roman villa, still stands here. Morgan would often come to his library to luxuriate among the art treasures he had acquired on his trips to Europe: manuscripts, paintings, prints, and furniture. During a crisis of confidence in the city's banking system in 1907, he entertained New York's richest and most influential men here night after night until they agreed to put up the money to save what could have been the entire country from bankruptcy. Morgan himself gave $30 million as an act of good faith. The library recently underwent a three-year, $106 million renovation, reopening in April 2006. The changes, designed by Pritzker Prize–winner Renzo Piano, have doubled the exhibition space and added several new features to the building, including an entrance on Madison Avenue, a four-story piazza-style gathering space, a performance hall, and a naturally lit reading room. The library's collection is priceless, including nearly 10,000 drawings and prints by such greats as Da Vinci, Degas, and Dürer; manuscripts by Dickens, Austen, and Thoreau; and a copy of the 1455 Gutenberg Bible (the museum owns three out of the eleven that survive).

North of Murray Hill

Leaving behind the relative quiet of Murray Hill, Madison Avenue becomes progressively more commercial the farther north one goes. Several good stores – notably several specializing in men's haberdashery, shoes, and cigars – still cater to the needs of the more aristocratic consumer. Brooks Brothers, traditional clothiers of the Ivy League and inventors of the button-down collar, occupies a corner of East 44th Street. Between 50th and 51st streets the **Villard Houses**, a replica of an Italian palazzo (one that didn't quite make it to Fifth Avenue) by McKim, Mead and White, merit more than a passing glance. The houses have been surgically incorporated into the *Helmsley Palace Hotel*, and the interiors polished up to their original splendor.

Madison's most interesting sites come in a four-block strip above 53rd Street. The tiny, vest-pocket-sized **Paley Park** is on the north side of East 53rd between Madison and Fifth avenues. Its soothing mini-waterfall and transparent water tunnel are juxtaposed with a haunting five-panel section of the former Berlin Wall. Around the corner, the **Continental Illinois Center** looks like a cross between a space rocket and a grain silo, but the **Sony Building** (formerly the AT&T Building), at no. 550 between 55th and 56th streets, has grabbed more headlines. A Johnson–Burgee collaboration, it follows the postmodernist theory of borrowing from historical styles (the idea being to quote from great public buildings and simultaneously return to the fantasy of the early part of the twentieth century): a Modernist skyscraper is sandwiched between a Chippendale top and a Renaissance base. Perhaps Johnson should have followed the advice of his teacher, Mies van der Rohe: "It's better to build a good building than an original one." The first floor is well worth ducking into to soak up the sheer grandeur. It houses a music store and a spate of interactive exhibits on record production and video-game production (ceremoniously named the Sony Wonder Technology Lab). The requisite coffee bar and deli abut a rather somber public seating area.

The **IBM Building**, no. 580–590, between 56th and 57th streets, has a far more user-friendly plaza than the Sony Building. In the calm, glass-enclosed atrium, tinkling music, tropical foliage, yet another coffee bar, and comfortable seating make for a livelier experience. Occupying the first three floors is the **Dahesh Museum of Art** (Tues–Sun 11am–6pm; $10, seniors $8, students $6; ☎212/759-0606, ⊛www.daheshmuseum.org). The small museum features nineteenth- and early twentieth-century European artwork collected by Dr. Dahesh, a Lebanese writer and philosopher passionate about European academic art. The museum is entirely dedicated to showing the works of that period's academically trained artists – the only of its sort in America – and has a permanent collection containing more than three thousand works, including Edwin Long's painting *Love's Labour Lost* and Jean-Jacques Pradier's bronze sculpture *Standing Sappho*.

Across East 57th Street at no. 41–45 is the eye-catching **Fuller Building**. Black-and-white Art Deco, it has a fine entrance and tiled floor. Cut east on 57th Street to no. 57 to find the **Four Seasons Hotel**, notable for sweeping marble and limestone design by I.M. Pei.

Park Avenue

In 1929, author Collinson Owen wrote that **Park Avenue** is "where wealth is so swollen that it almost bursts." Things have changed little since. The focal point of the avenue is the hulking **Grand Central Terminal**, at 42nd Street. South of Grand Central, Park Avenue narrows in both width and interest, but to the north of the building it becomes an impressively broad boulevard. Built to accommodate elevated rail tracks, the area quickly became a battleground, as corporate headquarters and refined residences jostled for prominence. Whatever your feelings about conspicuous wealth, from the 40s north, Park Avenue is one of the city's most awesome sights. Its sweeping expanse, genteel facades, and sculpture-studded medians capture both the gracious and grand sides of New York in one fell swoop.

Grand Central Terminal

Park Avenue hits 42nd Street at Pershing Square, where it lifts off the ground to make room for the massive **Grand Central Terminal** (Ⓦwww .grandcentralterminal.com). More than just a train station, the terminal is a full-blown destination unto itself. When it was constructed in 1913 at the order of railroad magnate Cornelius Vanderbilt, the terminal was a masterly piece of urban planning. After the electrification of the railways made it possible to reroute trains underground, the rail lines behind the existing station were sold off to developers and the profits went toward the building of a new terminal – built around a basic iron frame but clothed with a Beaux-Arts skin. While Grand Central soon took on an almost mythical significance, today its traffic consists mainly of commuters speeding out to Connecticut, Westchester County, and upstate New York, and any claim to being a gateway to an undiscovered continent is purely symbolic.

The most spectacular aspect of the building is its **size**, though it is now dwarfed by the Met Life building at 200 Park Ave. The station's main concourse is one of the world's finest and most imposing open spaces, 470ft long and 150ft high. The **barrel-vaulted ceiling** is speckled like a Baroque church with a painted representation of the winter night sky, its 2500 stars shown back to front – "as God would have seen them," the French painter Paul Helleu reputedly remarked. Stand in the middle and you realize that Grand Central represents a time when stations were seen as miniature cities. Walking around the marble corridors is an elegant experience. You can explore Grand Central on your own or take the excellent **free tour** run by the Municipal Arts Society (see p.35).

In addition to its architectural and historical offerings, there are fifty shops here, including the tantalizing Grand Central Market, which sells every gourmet food imaginable, and over 22 restaurants, many of which are on the terminal's lower concourse. Chief among the restaurants is the *Grand Central Oyster Bar* (☏212/490-6650), which is located in the vaulted bowels of the station and is one of the city's most celebrated seafood eateries; it serves a dozen varieties of oyster and is packed at lunchtime. Just outside of the restaurant is something that explains why the *Oyster Bar*'s babble is not solely the result of the people eating there: two people can stand on opposite sides of any of the vaulted spaces and hold a conversation just by whispering, an acoustic fluke that makes this the loudest eatery in town.

Search out the **New York Racquet & Tennis Club** on the third floor; once a CBS studio it now offers court-time for a membership fee of several thousand dollars a year. For a civilized cocktail, stop into the *Campbell Apartment* (see p.371). The grand one-time home of the terminal's architect, it is found near the terminal's west-side taxi stand. There's also a full calendar of monthly events that in the past has included such diverse goings-on as gospel concerts in the main terminal, lectures by the World Health Organization, and squash tournaments in Vanderbilt Hall.

Around Grand Central

Across East 42nd Street to the south, the former **Bowery Savings Bank**, now *Cipriani's 42nd Street*, echoes Grand Central's grandeur. Like its sister branch downtown, its extravagant design lauds the virtues of sound investment and savings. The Roman-style basilica has a floor paved with mosaics; the columns are each fashioned from a different kind of marble; and, if you look at the elevator doors (through a door on the right), you'll see bronze bas-reliefs of bank employees hard at various tasks. This kind of lavish expenditure is typical of the buildings on this stretch of 42nd Street, which is full of lobbies worth popping inside for a glimpse. Start with the **Philip Morris Building**, at 120 Park Ave right across from Grand Central, which contains a small offshoot of the Whitney Museum of American Art. Situated in the atrium of the Philip Morris Building, the **Whitney at Philip Morris**, a 900-square-foot Whitney Museum satellite, has two sections: a small Picture Gallery (Mon–Fri 11am–6pm, Thurs 11am–7.30pm; free; ☎917/663-2453), with commissioned site-specific works by mid-career or emerging artists on just about any modern theme that you can think of, and a grand 5200-square-foot Sculpture Court (Mon–Sat 7.30am–9.30pm, Sun 11am–7pm; free). About six times per year, contemporary performances (anything from string quartets to dance recitals) are held here. **The Grand Hyatt Hotel**, next to Grand Central Terminal on the south side of 42nd Street, is another notable instance of excess, and perhaps the best (or worst) example in the city of all that is truly vulgar about contemporary American interior design. The thundering waterfalls, lurking palms, and gliding escalators represent plush-carpeted bad taste at its most meretricious.

Just north of Grand Central, impressive more for its size than grandeur, stands the Bauhaus bulk of the **Met Life Building**, 200 Park Ave, which was built in 1963 as the Pan Am Building. Bauhaus guru Walter Gropius had a hand in designing the structure, and the critical consensus is that he could have done better. As the headquarters of the now-defunct international airline, the building, in profile, was meant to suggest an airplane wing. The blue-gray mass certainly adds drama to the cityscape, although it robs Park Avenue of its southern views, sealing off 44th Street and sapping much of the vigor of the surrounding buildings. Another black mark against the building is its rooftop helipad, which was closed in the 1970s after a helicopter undercarriage collapsed and a rotor sheered off, killing four disembarking passengers and injuring several people on the ground.

The Helmsley Building, the Waldorf–Astoria, and north

Standing astride the avenue at 46th Street at no. 230 is the high altar of the New York Central Building (built in 1928 and years later rechristened the **Helmsley Building**). A delicate construction with a lewdly excessive Rococo lobby, it rises up directly in the middle of the avenue; twin tunnels allow traffic to pass beneath it. In its mid-twentieth century heyday it formed a punctuation mark to the avenue, but its thunder was stolen in 1963 by the completion of the Met Life Building, which looms above and behind it.

Wherever you placed the solid mass of the **Waldorf–Astoria Hotel**, no. 301 (see p.305), a resplendent statement of Art Deco elegance between 49th and 50th streets, it would more than hold its own. Duck inside to stroll through a block of vintage grandeur, sweeping marble, and hushed plushness where such well-knowns as Herbert Hoover, Cole Porter, and Princess Grace of Monaco have bunked.

Crouching just across 50th Street, **St Bartholomew's Church** is a low-slung Byzantine hybrid that adds an immeasurable amount of character to the area, giving the lumbering skyscrapers a much-needed sense of scale. Due to the fact that it's on some of the city's most valuable real estate, the church fought against developers for years, and ultimately became a test case for New York City's landmark preservation law. Today, its congregation thrives and its members sponsor many community-outreach programs. It even features an excellent outdoor restaurant, *Café St Bart's*. Directly behind St Bartholomew's, the spiky-topped **General Electric Building** seems like a wild extension of the church, its slender shaft rising to a meshed crown of abstract sparks and lightning strokes that symbolizes the radio waves used by its original owner, RCA. A New York-designated landmark, the building is another Art Deco delight, with nickel-silver ornamentation, carved red marble, and a lobby with a vaulted ceiling (entrance at 570 Lexington Ave).

Among all this architectural ostentation it's difficult at first to see the original-ity of the **Seagram Building**, 375 Park Ave between 52nd and 53rd streets. Designed by Mies van der Rohe and Philip Johnson, and built in 1958, this was the seminal curtain-wall skyscraper: the floors supported internally rather than by the building's walls, allowing a skin of smoky glass and whiskey-bronze metal (the colors of a late-night watering hole, the domain of Seagram's distilled prod-ucts). Sadly, the facade has weathered to a dull black. In keeping with the era's vision, every interior detail, down to the fixtures and lettering on the mailboxes, was specially designed to fit with the building's overall aesthetic. Deceptively simple and cleverly detailed, the Seagram was the supreme example of Modern-ist reason, and its opening was met with a wave of approval. The **plaza**, an open forecourt designed to set the building apart from its neighbors and display it to advantage, was such a success as a public space that the city revised the zoning laws to encourage other high-rise builders to supply similar plazas.

Across Park Avenue between 53rd and 54th streets is **Lever House**, no. 390, the building that set the Modernist ball rolling on Park Avenue when it was constructed in 1952. Back then, the two right-angled slabs that form a steel and glass bookend seemed revolutionary when compared with the surround-ing buildings. Its vintage appeal helps to make the restaurant of the same name one of the hottest places in town to eat, tipple, and be seen. The restaurant-bar interior was conceived by internationally acclaimed designer Marc Newson and features all sorts of Modernist elements from the 1950s.

Lexington Avenue

One block east of Park Avenue, **Lexington Avenue** marks a sort of border between East Side elegance and the everyday avenues closer to the East River.

Starting inauspiciously at the tranquil Gramercy Park, Lexington Avenue trawls quietly north for many indistinguishable blocks through Murray Hill and the East 30s. Closer to 42nd Street and the Chrysler Building, it quickly becomes more active, especially through the mid-40s, where commuters swarm around Grand Central Terminal, and around a well-placed **post office** on the corner of 50th Street. From there, Lexington lurches northward past 53rd Street and the towering aluminum and glass **Citicorp Center**, to the bulk of **Bloomingdale's** department store at 59th Street, which marks the end of the avenue's midtown stretch of highlights.

The Chrysler Building and around

The Chrysler Building, 405 Lexington Ave, dates from 1930, a time when architects married prestige with grace and style. For a fleeting moment, this was the world's tallest building (it was surpassed by the Empire State Building in 1931), and, since the rediscovery of Art Deco, it has become one of Manhattan's best loved. The golden age of motoring is evoked by the building's car-motif friezes, hood-ornament gargoyles, radiator-grill spire, and the fact that the entire structure is almost completely fashioned from stainless steel. Its designer, William Van Alen, indulged in a feud with an erstwhile partner, H. Craig Severance, who was designing a building at 40 Wall St at the same time. Each was determined to have the higher skyscraper: Van Alen secretly built the stainless-steel spire inside the Chrysler's crown; when 40 Wall St was finally topped out a few feet higher than the Chrysler, Van Alen popped the 185-foot spire out through the top of the building, and won the day. In the end, though, Van Alen was hardly rewarded for his achievement as Walter Chrysler accused him of taking bribes from contractors and refused to pay him. He never recovered from the slur and practiced architecture for the rest of his life in obscurity.

The Chrysler Corporation moved out some time ago, and for a while the building was allowed to decline by a company that didn't wholly appreciate its spirit. The current owner has pledged to keep it lovingly intact, and it was renovated in 2000 by Philip Johnson. The lobby, once a car showroom, is all you can see for the moment (there's no observation deck), but that's enough in itself. The opulent walls are covered in African marble and the ceiling shows a realistic, if rather faded, study of airplanes, machines, and brawny builders who worked on the tower.

On the south side of 42nd Street flanking Lexington Avenue are two more noteworthy buildings. The **Chanin Building**, 122 E 42nd St, on the right, is another Art Deco monument, cut with terracotta carvings of leaves, tendrils, and sea creatures. Also interesting is the design of the weighty **Socony–Mobil Building** across the street at no. 150. Built in 1956, it was the largest metal-clad office building in the world at the time. Made from chromium–nickel stainless steel, it was designed this way to enable the wind to keep it clean.

Citicorp Center and around

Just as the Chrysler Building dominates the lower stretches of Lexington Avenue, the chisel-topped **Citicorp Center**, 153 E 53rd St, between 53rd and 54th streets, towers above northern midtown. Opened in 1978, the building, now one of New York's most conspicuous landmarks, looks as if it is sheathed in shiny graph paper. Its slanted roof was designed to house solar panels and provide power, but the idea was ahead of the technology and Citicorp had to content itself with adopting the distinctive top as a corporate logo. The atrium of stores known as **The Market** is pleasant enough, with some food options.

Hiding under the Center's skirts is **St Peter's Lutheran Church**, known as "the Jazz Church" for being the venue of many a jazz musician's funeral and even having a long-running jazz vespers service. The tiny church was built to replace the one demolished to make way for Citicorp, and part of the deal was that the church had to stand out from the Center – which explains the granite material. Explore the thoroughly modern interior, including sculptor **Louise Nevelson**'s **Erol Beaker Chapel**, the venue for Wednesday lunchtime jazz concerts (and evening concerts as well). More Nevelson sculpture can be seen on the median running down Park Avenue.

In direct contrast to the simple, contemporary St Peter's is the reform **Central Synagogue**, 652 Lexington Ave, at East 55th Street. Striking because of its Moorish appearance, this landmark structure was built in 1870–72 by German immigrant Henry Fernbach. The oldest continually used Jewish house of worship in the city, it was heavily damaged in a blaze in 1998, and although repairs were unable to fully restore all the site's features, services still continue as they always have.

Third, Second, and First avenues

The construction of the Citicorp Center provided a spur for the development of **Third Avenue** in the late 1970s. The most interesting section of this avenue is between East 44th and 50th streets – look out for the sheer marble monument of the **Wang Building** (between East 48th and 49th streets), whose cross-patterns reveal the structure within. The area from Third to the East River between East 43rd and 53rd streets is known as **Turtle Bay** (though most New Yorkers would be hard-pressed to tell you just where this area is). Named for the former inhabitants of an adjacent river cove (where the United Nations now sits), it features a scattering of brownstones alongside chirpier shops and restaurants that disappear as you head north.

All the office space that came in the wake of Citicorp hasn't totally removed interest from Third Avenue. There are a few good bars here, notably *P.J. Clarke's*, no. 915 at East 55th Street, a spit-and-sawdust alehouse and New York institution (see p.371), but most life, especially at night, seems to have shifted east to **Second Avenue** – less corporate and more residential, it has any number of bars to crawl between.

Not surprisingly, most of this neighborhood's architectural attractions lie on or around 42nd Street. The stone facade of the somber yet elegant former **Daily News Building**, 220 E 42nd St, fronts a surprising Art Deco interior. The interior was bastardized somewhat in the 1950s: white marble replaced the original golden marble, an annex was added to the building, and stainless-steel elevator doors replaced the original bronze ones. The most impressive remnant of the original 1929 decor is a large globe encased in a lighted circular frame (with updated geography), made famous by Superman movies when the Daily News Building appropriately housed the *Daily Planet*. Various bronze meteorological devices, displayed on the walls, were once connected to a weather station on the roof. The marble floor is inlaid with intersecting bronze lines that give the distances between New York and other major cities. The tabloid after which the building is named has moved to 450 W 33rd St, and the building is not open on weekends.

New York Architecture

New York is a true architectural display case – all of the significant and influential movements of the last two centuries are represented in the city's magnificent structural landmarks. For an up-close look, take a stroll around the concrete jungle – it will leave you with a crick in the neck, but also with a palpable sense of New York's remarkably dynamic and enduring urban landscape.

▲ Woolworth Building

The nineteenth and early-twentieth century

It was the advent of cast-iron constructions in the mid-nineteenth century that really thrust New York to the forefront of architectural sophistication – the technique allowed developers to mimic classical designs by adding cast-iron decorations to pre-cast steel frames (see box, p.77). Several buildings in Soho retain their cast-iron embellishments – the 1859 **Haughwout Building** is one notable model.

The late nineteenth century saw the influence of the industrial age on New York. Structures like the **Brooklyn Bridge** (1876) embody the strength and potential of that era, while still retaining ties to the old styles – witness its huge, soaring Gothic arches. The **Flatiron Building** on Madison Square (1902) is widely regarded as the city's first real skyscraper; though the **Park Row Building** by City Hall Park is in fact older and taller, it was considered a greater feat to make the triangular, iron-frame Flatiron stand up. The **Woolworth Building** (1913), nicknamed the "cathedral of commerce" for its decorative Gothic spires and gargoyles, continued the sky-touching trend, rising several stories higher than the Flatiron, while other contemporary buildings, like the **US Custom House** (1907), the **New York Public Library** (1911), and the vast, block-filling **General Post Office** (1913), stuck firmly to traditional Neoclassical forms. The **Grand Central Terminal** (1919), a glorious shrine to modern transport, is a crowning example from this era.

Five architectural days out in New York

Financial District Where it all began. Come here to see some of the city's oldest buildings, St Paul's and Trinity churches, as well as some of its newest.

Greenwich Village and around Still home to the city's best domestic architecture, with quiet mews, handsome rowhouses, and elegant apartment blocks. This is a good part of town for exploring: start with Washington Square Park in the heart of the Village, and finish up at Gramercy Park, the city's most refined residential square, having taken in Tompkins Square Park and Union Square on the way.

Midtown Manhattan A smorgasbord of architectural styles, including some of the city's greatest skyscrapers (the Empire State and GE buildings), Neoclassical beauties (the New York Public Library and Grand Central Terminal), and Modernist masterpieces (the Seagram Building and Lever House).

Brooklyn Heights This peaceful, low-rise district has a wide selection of domestic styles, from early Federal rowhouses to large neo-Romanesque and neo-Gothic villas.

Harlem Some of the most beautiful residential architecture in the city, exemplified by blocks of brownstones and other styles south of 125th Street, and developments farther north like Strivers' Row and Hamilton Heights.

The glory years

Architects began to experiment in the 1920s, and the artistic liveliness of the Jazz Age permeates many buildings from this period. Ironically, two of the most impressive structures in the city – the **Chrysler Building** (1930) and the **Empire State Building** (1931) – went up just after the 1929 Wall Street Crash. They were complete stylistic visions, right down to the elevator fittings and the shops in the basement. The **Rockefeller Center** complex, which was worked on throughout the 1930s, is perhaps the apogee of this self-contained urban planning. Looming over the center, the **GE Tower** marks the zenith of Art Deco style in New York.

▲ Chrysler Building

The 1950s and 1960s saw the Modernist style further refined with the arrival of European architectural movements like Bauhaus and Le Corbusier, whose mantra of form following function influenced the glass curtain-wall buildings of Mies van der Rohe: the **United Nations Complex** (1950), **Lever House** (1952), and the **Seagram Building** (1958), all in Midtown East. The Seagram remains the best example of a sheer glass tower anywhere in the city. This style culminated in the giant **Rockefeller Center Extension** (1973) and, most famously, the now-destroyed twin towers of the **World Trade Center**.

The modern day

Post-modernism enabled late twentieth-century architects to return to a level of playfulness in their designs – check out the Chippendale pediment on the 1983 **Sony Building** on Madison Avenue. These kinds of conceits are toned down a bit on the **Citicorp Center** (1978) in midtown, though the atrium, with its ground floor given over to public space (a now-popular way to get around zoning regulations), has since been copied in numerous new buildings.

City buildings continue to be at the heart of architectural innovations. The twin towers of the **Time Warner Center** at Columbus Circle stand out mainly for their (gargantuan) size, while the **Condé Nast Building** on Times Square has been a major trendsetter in

▲ The Seagram Building

the move to "green" architecture – the state-of-the-art insulation requires less heating and cooling than other buildings of its size. Plans for the **Ground Zero** site (where the World Trade Center towers once stood) continue to be hotly debated. See the box on p.56 for more on the proposed design for this space. In the meantime, investment bank **Goldman Sachs** has begun work on new headquarters across the road from Ground Zero: it was to have been in New Jersey but Goldmans' bankers refused to relocate – proof, if any was needed, that New York's skyline will continue to change for some time.

Skyscrapers

New York is one of the best places in the world to see **skyscrapers** – Manhattan's puckered, almost medieval skyline is one of the iconic images of the city. With over 40 buildings higher than 200 meters, there are more skyscrapers here than in any other urban center. Somehow, the skyscraper is New York.

The city's skyscrapers peak at two points on the island: downtown, in the Financial District, where the tall structures loom over narrow streets to form slender, lightless canyons, and midtown, with its larger, more bombastic buildings. This is no accident: Manhattan's bedrock lies closest to the surface in these two areas, meaning that early engineers found it easiest to build high-rises there. Skyscraper styles have changed over the years, as the city's zoning laws have placed restrictions on the types of buildings permitted. At first skyscrapers were sheer vertical monsters, maximizing the floor space possible at any given site with no regard to how neighboring buildings were affected. City authorities later invented the concept of "air rights," limiting how high a building could be before it had to be set back from its base. This forced skyscrapers to be designed in a series of steps – a law most elegantly adhered to by the **Empire State Building**, which has no less than ten steps in all – which you'll see repeated all over the city. For more on the city's skyscrapers check out the Skyscraper Museum (see p.60), housed in a contemporary Financial District skyscraper.

Just north and around the corner from the Daily News, at 320 E 43rd St, between First and Second avenues, is one of the city's most peaceful (if surreal) spaces – the **Ford Foundation Building**. Built in 1967, the building featured the first of the atriums that are now commonplace across Manhattan. Structurally, the atrium is a giant greenhouse, gracefully supported by soaring granite columns and edged with two walls of offices visible through the windows. This subtropical garden, which changes naturally with the seasons, was one of the first attempts to create a "natural" environment inside a building, and it's astonishingly quiet. Forty-second Street is no more than a murmur outside, and all you can hear is the burble of water, the echo of voices, and the clipped crack of feet on the brick walkways. The indoor/outdoor experience here is one of New York City's great architectural coups.

First Avenue has a certain rangy looseness that's a relief after the concrete claustrophobia of midtown. **Beekman Place** (49th to 51st streets between First Avenue and the East River) is quieter still, a beguiling enclave of garbled styles. Similar, though not quite as intimate, is **Sutton Place**, which stretches from 53rd to 59th streets between First Avenue and the river. Originally built for the lordly Morgans and Vanderbilts in 1875, Sutton Place increases in elegance as you move north and, for today's *crème de la crème*, **Riverview Terrace** (off 58th Street at the river) is a (very) private enclave of five brownstones. The UN Secretary-General has an official residence on Sutton Place, and the locals are choosy about who they let in: disgraced ex-president Richard Nixon was refused on the grounds he would be a security risk. Two small public parks here afford fine views of the river and Queens' industrial waterfront, which still awaits its own development boom.

At the east end of 42nd Street, steps lead up to the 1925 **Tudor City**, which rises behind a tiny tree-filled park. With coats of arms, leaded glass, and neat neighborhood shops, this area is the very picture of self-contained residential respectability. It's an official historic district, to boot. Head down the steps here and you'll be plum opposite the **United Nations**.

The United Nations

Some see the **United Nations complex** – built after World War II, when John D. Rockefeller, Jr donated $8.5 million to buy the eighteen-acre East River site – as one of the major sights of New York. Others, usually those who've been there, are not so complimentary. Despite the symbolism of the UN, few buildings are quite so dull to walk around. What's more, as if to rationalize the years of UN impotence in international war and hunger zones, the (obligatory) guided tours emphasize that the UN's main purpose is to promote dialogue and awareness rather than enforcement. The organization itself moves at a snail's pace – bogged down by regulations and a lack of funds – which is the general feel of the tour as well.

△ UN Headquarters

For the determined, the complex consists of three main buildings – the thin, glass-curtained slab of the **Secretariat**; the sweeping curve of the **General Assembly Building**, whose chambers can accommodate more than 191 national delegations; and the low-rise **Conference Wing**, which connects the other two structures. Construction on the complex began in 1949 and finished in 1963, the product of a suitably international team of architects that included Le Corbusier – though he pulled out before the construction was completed. Guided tours (daily every 20–30min, Mon–Fri 9.30am–4.45pm, Sat & Sun 10am–4.30pm; tours last 45min–1hr; $11.50, seniors $8.50, students $7.50; bring ID; ☎212/963-8687, ⓦwww.un.org) take in the UN conference chambers and its constituent parts. Even more revealing than the stately chambers are its thoughtful exhibition spaces and artful country gifts on view, including a painting by Picasso. The structure of the tours can vary depending on official room usage.

Other council chambers visited on the tour are the **Security Council**, the **Economic and Social Council**, and the **Trusteeship Council** – all of which are similarly retro (note the clunky machinery of the journalists' areas) and sport some intriguing Marxist murals. Once you've been whisked around all these sites and have seen examples of the many artifacts that have been donated to the UN by its various member states (among them rugs, sculptures, and a garishly colored mosaic based on a Norman Rockwell painting courtesy of Nancy Reagan), the tour is more or less over and will leave you in the basement of the General Assembly Building. Here, a couple of shops sell items from around the world. A **post office** will make you a UN postage stamp to prove that you've been here – though bear in mind it's only valid on mail posted from the UN. A **restaurant** serves a daily lunch buffet with dishes from different UN member countries, but the food, like the tour, is fairly taste-free. Where the UN has real class is in its beautiful **gardens**, with their modern sculpture and views of the East River. Carpets of daffodils and flowering cherry trees in spring and an extensive rose garden in summer make them worth a visit. The many sculptures outside the complex include *Reclining Figure* (1982) by **Henry Moore**.

The Museum of
Modern Art

New York City's **Museum of Modern Art** – **MoMA** to its friends – offers the finest and most complete collection of late nineteenth- and twentieth-century art anywhere, with a permanent collection of more than 100,000 paintings, sculptures, drawings, prints, photographs, architectural models, and design objects, as well as a world-class film archive. Despite its high admission price, it's an essential stop for anyone even remotely interested in the world of modern art.

Founded in 1929 by three wealthy women, including Abby Aldrich Rockefeller (wife of John D., Jr), as the very first museum dedicated entirely to modern art, MoMA moved to its present home ten years later. Philip Johnson designed expansions in the 1950s and 1960s, and in the mid-1980s a steel-pipe and glass renovation by Cesar Pelli doubled its gallery space. In 2002, the museum closed for two years at this site while it underwent massive renovations; it reopened in November 2004, just in time for its seventy-fifth anniversary.

The renovation has clearly been successful. The design, by Japanese architect Yoshio Taniguchi, has doubled the exhibition space available, creating new and vibrant public spaces while expanding the galleries into larger and more accessible venues for the museum's extraordinary permanent collection. The building is quite clever: it's easy to navigate, but it also constantly and deliberately gives glimpses of other levels, like the sculpture garden, the lobby, and the second-floor landing, where Monet's large *Waterlilies* study is displayed. Yet those familiar with the old museum may wonder whether anything has really changed. The collection is still divided broadly into the same categories, and

---

MoMA practicalities

The Museum of Modern Art (℡212/708-9400, ⊛www.moma.org) is located at 11 W 53rd St, just off Fifth Avenue. Take the #E or #V train to 5th Ave–53rd St, or the #B, #D, or #F train to 47–50th Sts/Rockefeller Center. Its hours are Monday and Wednesday through Sunday 10.30am to 5.30pm, Friday until 8pm; it is closed Tuesdays throughout the year, as well as Thanksgiving Day and Christmas Day. Admission is $20, seniors $16, students $12, children 16 and under are free. Thanks to a corporate promotion, the museum is free for everyone on Fridays from 4 to 8pm. Tickets can be booked in advance through Ticketmaster (℡212/220-0505).

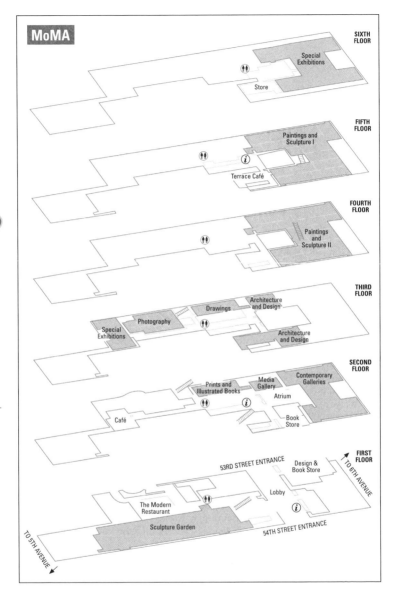

the principal exhibits – at least in the core Painting and Sculpture galleries – are displayed in much the same chronological order as before, albeit with some thematic detours. The main differences come in the museum's ability to display its more peripheral materials – its drawings, photography, etc; to show more contemporary art; and to mount temporary exhibitions without cutting into the permanent exhibition space.

Painting and Sculpture I

The core of the collection is, as before the building's renovation, the Painting and Sculpture galleries. Most visitors head directly for the fifth floor – to **Painting and Sculpture I**. The starting point here is the **Post-Impressionists** of the late nineteenth century, with works by **Cezanne**, **Seurat**, **Van Gogh**, and **Gauguin** mixed in with vivid early paintings by **Derain**, **Braque**, and **James Ensor** that already hint at a more Modernist perspective. This is developed in the next room by **Picasso**, most notably with his seminal *Demoiselles d'Avignon*, as well as by some of his later, more Cubist pieces. More works by Picasso, Braque, and **Leger** follow in the subsequent room, and, beyond them, the big swirling colors of **Boccioni** and the Italian Futurists. If you go straight from here you'll find yourself in an explosion of color, with paintings by **Chagall**,

THE MUSEUM OF MODERN ART | Painting and Sculpture I

△ Marron Atrium, Museum of Modern Art

Kandinsky, and **Kirchner**, and an entire room devoted to **Matisse**. Featured are his *Red Studio*, *Piano Lesson*, and other paintings, as well as his lumpy series of sculpted heads of *Jeanette*. After Matisse is a so-called **"Crossroads" gallery**, which houses some of the most recognizable works of the modern age – Picasso's *Three Women at the Spring*, the same artist's *Three Musicians*, and Leger's *Three Women*, all painted the same year (1921), as well as some haunting works by **de Chirico**. This room leads to galleries devoted to **Duchamp**, **Malevich**, and the paintings of the Dutch *De Stijl* movement. You can trace the development of the movement's leading light, **Mondrian**, from his tentative early work to the pure color abstract of *Broadway Boogie Woogie*, painted in New York in 1943. Oddly enough, Matisse's muscular back studies occupy a room with **Bonnard**'s soft studies, while beyond are paintings by **Diego Rivera** and a room devoted to the Surrealists. Many of the works here will be familiar from popular reproductions: **Miró**'s *Dutch Interiors*, **Magritte**'s *The Menaced Assassin*, and **Dalí**'s *Persistence of Memory*. Finally, there are a few paintings by American artists: **Wyeth**'s *Christina's World*, a couple of pieces by **Hopper**, and one of **Charles Scheeler**'s American industrial landscapes.

Painting and Sculpture II

Painting and Sculpture II, the next floor down, displays work from the 1940s to 1960s and inevitably has a more American feel, starting with works by **Pollock**, **Rothko**, and **de Kooning**. Farther on, **Dubuffet**'s challenging paintings sit with **Giacometti**'s stick-like figures and paintings by **Bacon** – *Study of a Baboon* – and **Picasso** – *The Charnel Room* – the latter inspired by the horrors of World War II. Beyond here the **Abstract Expressionists** hold sway, with vast canvases by **Barnett Newman**, Rothko, and Pollock – all at the height of their influence in the 1950s, when these paintings were done. Later rooms contain lots of work familiar from the modern canon – **Jasper Johns**' *Flag*, **Robert Rauschenberg**'s mixed-media paintings, **Warhol**'s soup cans and *Marilyn Monroe*, **Lichtenstein**'s cartoons, and **Oldenburg**'s soft sculptures.

Photography, Architecture and Design, Drawings

The other sections of the museum's collection are just as impressive and shouldn't be missed. On the third floor, the **Photography** galleries are also chronological in their layout, and begin with a European slant – photos of Paris by **Atget**, **Brassaï**, and **Cartier-Bresson** – before moving on to **Robert Franck**'s and **Robert Capa**'s stunning pictures of the modern-day US. Their realism is mirrored by the hyper-naturalism of the later, more contemporary works in the collection.

MoMA refreshments

If you need to take a break during your tour of the museum, the second-floor café, *Café 2*, does very good, slickly presented Italian-style food. *Terrace 5*, on the fifth floor, is a more formal option, and provides nice views of the sculpture garden. A very swanky full-service restaurant, *The Modern*, sits on the ground floor, if you really want to push the boat out.

Architecture and Design, on the same floor, shows designs from the twentieth century. There are illustrations of modern buildings and town planning by key innovators like **Frank Lloyd Wright**; examples of interior design, with chairs by **Gerrit Rietveld**, **Arne Jacobsen**, and **Charles Rennie Mackintosh**; lots of glass and ceramics; and a series of neat large-scale objects like a 1946 Ferrari, a British motorcycle, and signage from the New York subway.

The **Drawing** galleries, also on the third floor, show works on paper by a glittering array of twentieth-century artists, including **Lucien Freud**, **Jackson Pollock**, **Robert Rauschenberg**, and his old roommate **Willem de Kooning**, as well as studies by **Warhol**, **Jasper Johns**, and **Roy Lichtenstein**. Finally, the second-floor galleries give MoMA the chance to show its **Contemporary Art** in all media, and basically consist of works from the 1970s onward, including pieces by **Bruce Nauman**, **Jeff Koons**, and other stellar names from the world of contemporary art.

Midtown West

B etween West 30th and 59th streets and west of Sixth Avenue, much of midtown Manhattan is enthralling, noisy, and garish, packed with attractions meant to entertain the legions of tourists staying in the area's many hotels. The heart of **Midtown West** is **Times Square**, where jostling crowds and flashing neon signs (some many stories high) assault the senses at all times of the day. It's here that the east side's more sedate approach to capitalism finally overflows its bounds and New York City reaches its commercial zenith. South of Times Square is the bustling, business-oriented **Garment District**, home to Madison Square Garden and Macy's department store, while just north of the once "naughty, bawdy 42nd Street" is the **Theater District**, which offers the most impressive concentration of live theater in the world.

For glimpses of vintage seediness, head west beyond Eighth Avenue to **Hell's Kitchen** – though keep in mind that the buzzing forces of gentrification are hard at work in this part of town, and shiny open-air eateries are far more common than peep-show pavilions these days. There aren't many tourist attractions per se in this direction, though if you hike all the way over to the Hudson River, you'll come upon the massive **Intrepid Sea, Air & Space Museum**, which is housed in a retired aircraft carrier. Back over in the center of the island, **Sixth Avenue**, its architecture melding cultural and corporate New York, is good for a stroll, while **57th Street** has some of the city's most distinctive shops and steadfast clusters of galleries, many of which display some of the world's greatest works of art.

The Garment District

Squeezing in between Sixth and Eighth avenues from West 30th to 42nd streets, the **Garment District**, home to the twin modern monsters of Penn Station and Madison Square Garden, offers little of interest to the casual tourist. The majority of people in this area are here for one of three reasons: to catch a train or bus at Penn Station, to watch wrestling or basketball at the Garden, or to work. It's really only Macy's department store between Herald and Greeley squares that draws a significant number of visitors.

It is in this tiny district that three-quarters of all the women's and children's clothes made in America are put together, though you'd never believe it from walking around. Outlets are almost entirely wholesale, and don't bother to woo customers; the only visible evidence of the industry is the racks of clothes shunted around on the street and occasional bins of off-cuts that give the area the look of an open-air rummage sale.

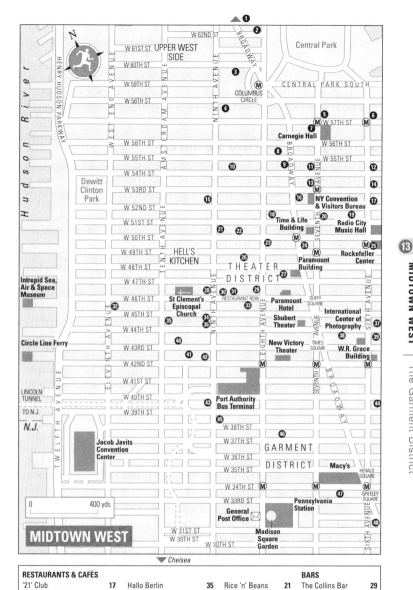

MIDTOWN WEST

RESTAURANTS & CAFÉS				BARS	
'21' Club	17	Hallo Berlin	35	Rice 'n' Beans	21	The Collins Bar	29
Algonquin Hotel	39	Hell's Kitchen	28	Rosa Mexicana	2	Hudson Bar	4
Aquavit	12	HK	43	Ruby Foo's	24	Jimmy's Corner	38
Ariana Afghan Kebab	15	Hourglass Tavern	30	Shun Lee	1	Landmark Tavern	32
Becco	31	Joe Allen	33	Soup Kitchen		MObar	3
Brasserie Central	16	Judson Grill	19	International	9	Rudy's	36
Bryant Park Grill	44	La Maison du Chocolat	25	Stage Deli	13	Russian Vodka Room	18
Carnegie Deli	11	Le Bernardin	20	Sugiyama	8	Stitch	46
Chez Napoleon	22	Le Madeleine	40	Thalia	23	Stout	47
China Grill	14	Little Pie Company	41	Trattoria dell'Arte	7		
Churrascaria Plataforma	26	Petrossian	5	Uncle Vanya Café	10		
Cupcake Café	45	Pongsri Thai Restaurant	27	West Bank Café	42		
db Bistro Moderne	37	Poseidon Bakery	34	Won Jo	48		
Great American Health Bar	6						

One of the benefits of walking through this part of town is taking advantage of the designers' **sample sales**, where floor samples and models' castoffs are sold to the public at cheap prices, though if you can't afford a $750 Donna Karan dress, you probably still can't afford it at $450 (see p.420 for more on sample sales). Any squeamish anti-fur zealots should steer clear of the area around West 30th Street, where you are likely to see the heads and tails of whole minks and foxes peeking from industrial-sized barrels in cooled storefronts, waiting their turn to become winter coats.

Greeley and Herald squares

Sixth Avenue collides with Broadway at West 34th Street at an unremarkable triangle given the somewhat overblown title **Greeley Square**, in honor of Horace Greeley, founder of the *New York Tribune* newspaper. One could make the case that Greeley deserves better: known for his rallying call to the youth of the nineteenth century ("Go West, young man!"), he also supported the rights of women and trade unions, denounced slavery and capital punishment, and commissioned a weekly column from Karl Marx.

The somewhat more interesting **Herald Square** faces Greeley Square in a continuation of the battle between the *New York Herald* newspaper and its arch rival, Horace Greeley's *Tribune*. During the 1890s this was the Tenderloin area, with dance halls, brothels, and rough bars like *Satan's Circus* and the *Burnt Rag* thriving beside the elevated railway that ran up Sixth Avenue. When the *Herald* arrived in 1895 it gave the square a new name and a bit of dignity, though it's perhaps best recognized from George M. Cohan's 1904 song *Give My Regards to Broadway* in which he sang, "Remember me to Herald Square." These days its congested sidewalks and pedestrian commercial appeal won't inspire anyone to sing about it, unless you are moved by the ornate Bennett Clock (named for *Herald* publisher James Gordon Bennett, Jr) or the massive Macy's department store a block south.

Macy's

Macy's, 151 W 34th St (☏212/695-4400, ⊛www.macys.com), bills itself as "the world's largest store," which is not overly hyperbolic, considering the building takes up about a billion square feet, roughly an entire city block. Founded in 1858, for several decades Macy's was one of the anchor stores of the "Ladies' Mile" shopping district at 14th Street and Sixth Avenue. The store moved to its current location in 1902, where, until the mid-1970s, it contented itself with its phenomenal size. In the 1980s, in response to the day's high-rolling lifestyle, Macy's went fashionably up-market as designers – such as Tommy Hilfiger – began building their own shops within Macy's. Brand boutiques were able to showcase sweaters next to silverware and spaces were created to make it easier to mix and match items. By the late 1980s, however, vendors had gained too much control within the establishment, and when the economy went into a tailspin in 1990, the store's fortune declined dramatically, burdened as it was by overexpansion and debt. New Yorkers were stunned when word went around that it was near closure, but Macy's scrambled out of bankruptcy in the nick of time, complete with a debt-restructuring plan that allowed it to continue financing its famed annual Thanksgiving Day Parade. One of the best-attended Manhattan processions, it is known for its giant cartoon-character balloons and the arrival of Santa (see Chapter 33, "Parades and festivals"). Although some would argue that Macy's is not the grandest department store in the world (it's no Harrods), you'll appreciate it all the more if you visit the tacky and characterless Manhattan Mall next door.

Madison Square Garden and Penn Station

The most prominent landmark in the Garment District, the **Pennsylvania Station and Madison Square Garden complex** takes up the whole block between Seventh and Eighth avenues and 32nd and 33rd streets. It's a combined box-and-drum structure: at the same time its train-station belly swallows up millions of commuters, its above-ground facilities house Knicks basketball and Rangers hockey games, as well as pro wrestling and boxing matches (for ticket details, see p.434).

There's nothing memorable about the train station; its grimy subterranean levels are an example of just about everything that's wrong with the subway. The original 1910 Penn Station, which brought an air of dignity to the neighborhood and set the stage for the ornate General Post Office and other elaborate *belle époque* structures, was demolished in 1963 to make way for this monstrous structure. One of McKim, Mead and White's greatest designs, the station's original edifice reworked the ideas of the Roman Baths of Caracalla to awesome effect: the floors of the grand arcade were pink marble, the walls pink granite. Glass floor tiles in the main waiting room allowed light from the glass roof to flow through to the trains and platforms below. Architectural historian Vincent Scully lamented the differences in the two structures in the 1960s, saying, "Through it one entered the city like a god... One scuttles in now like a rat." Some of Penn Station's lost luster may be restored when an expanded station in the General Post Office building opens in 2008, if all goes according to plan.

Glimpses of the original structure are visible in photos hanging in the Amtrak waiting area of today's Penn Station, as well as in the four-faced clock on display in the Long Island Railroad (LIRR) ticket area on 34th Street and Seventh Avenue. Andrew Leicester's 1994 *Ghost Series* lines the walls, including terracotta wall murals saluting the Corinthian and Ionic columns of the old Penn Station. Also look for a rendering of Adolph A. Weinman's sculpture *Day & Night*, an ornate statue surrounding a clock that welcomed passengers at the

Old Penn Station and the Landmarks Preservation Law

When the old **Penn Station** was demolished in 1963 in order to expand the Madison Square Garden sports complex, the notion of conservation was only a gleam in the eye of its middle-class supporters; ten years later a broad-based power group but then few and far between. Despite the vocal opposition of a few, "modernization" was the theme of the day – so much so that almost nothing of the original building was saved. A number of the carefully crafted statues and decorations actually became landfill for New Jersey's Meadowlands complex just across the Hudson River.

At around the same time, the Singer Building, an early, graceful skyscraper in the Financial District, was demolished to make way for the hulking US Steel Building. In the end, it was public disgust with the wanton destruction of these two buildings that brought about the passing of the **Landmarks Preservation Law**. This act ensures that buildings granted landmark status – a designation based on aesthetic value or historical importance – cannot be destroyed or even altered. The law goes beyond protecting buildings, and also applies to districts, such as Fort Greene and Soho, as well as "scenic" landmarks, including Verdi Square at Broadway and West 73rd Street.

old station's entrance. Be sure to look above your head in the LIRR ticket area for Maya Lin's *Eclipsed Time*, a sculpture of glass, aluminum, and fiber optics that alludes to the immeasurability of time with random number patterns.

The General Post Office

Immediately behind Penn Station at 421 Eighth Ave, the **General Post Office** (aka the James A. Farley Post Office) is a 1913 McKim, Mead and White structure that survived the push for modernization, and stands as a relic from an era when municipal pride was all about making statements. The old joke is that the building had to be as big as it is in order to fit in the noteworthy inscription above the columns ("Neither snow nor rain nor heat nor gloom of night stays these couriers from the swift completion of their appointed rounds"), a claim about as believable as the old one that Manhattan's postal district handles more mail than Britain, France, and Belgium combined. There's still a working post-office branch here, although the main sorting stations have moved into more modern spaces farther west. That said, the building is no architectural dinosaur: a new Penn Station for Amtrak is currently being built inside; the original exterior will be preserved. Set to open in 2011 and replace the existing Penn Station, the redevelopment will be named Moynihan Station, after the late US Senator Daniel Patrick Moynihan, who, in his later years, lamented the city's ability to make good on its many planned public-works projects.

Port Authority Terminal

One of midtown's more revived landmarks, the **Port Authority Terminal Building** crouches on Eighth Avenue between West 40th and 42nd streets (for practical details see p.23). Not long ago, the Port Authority had a reputation as a haven for down-and-outs, but it is spruced up and remarkably safe now. Greyhound buses leave from here, as do several other regional services. Randomly, the station holds an exceptional bowling alley, should you have the urge to play a few games immediately upon arrival. Just west of here on 42nd Street are some incongruous luxury apartment buildings, a sign of the neighborhood's changing face, as well as several off-Broadway theaters, stranded far from the neon of Times Square.

Times Square and around

Forty-second Street meets Broadway at the southern outskirts of **Times Square**, the center of the Theater District (see box, p.158), where the constantly pulsating neon conjures up the notion of a beating heart for Manhattan. The area is certainly always alive with activity. Traditionally a melting pot of debauchery, depravity, and fun, for years the quarter was a place where out-of-towners provided easy pickings for petty criminals, drug dealers, and prostitutes (always, seemingly, a companion to theater districts). Most of Times Square's legendary pornography and crime are long gone, replaced by sanitized superstores, highrise office buildings, and boutique hotels that have killed off the square's historically greasy appeal. This doesn't mean, though, that the area is without charm. If you have never seen Times Square, plan your first visit for after dark. Without passing through the square, take a taxi to 57th and Broadway and start walking south. The spectacle will open out before your eyes, slowly at first, and then with a rush of energy and animation.

Like nearby Greeley and Herald squares, Times Square took its name from a newspaper – the *New York Times* built its offices here in 1904. While the *Herald* and *Tribune* fought each other in ever more vicious circulation battles (and eventually both went out of business), the *Times* stood on more restrained ground under the banner "All the news that's fit to print," a policy that has enabled both its survival and its current status as most powerful newspaper in the country. The newspaper's old headquarters, **Times Tower**, is at the southernmost end of the square on a small block between 42nd and 43rd streets.

△ Times Square

The Theater District

Though many of the **theaters** hosting big-budget musicals and dramas considered to be "Broadway shows" are not technically on that avenue, they are, for the most part, located within a couple blocks of it in the West 40s. Sadly, the majority of New York's great theaters have been destroyed (like the vaudeville palaces that preceded them) to make way for office buildings. Thus, for example, the original Paramount Theater was replaced by the majestic 1927 clock-and-globe-topped **Paramount Building** at 1501 Broadway, between 43rd and 44th streets.

However, some of the old grandeur still survives. The **New Amsterdam**, 214 W 42nd St, and the family-oriented **New Victory**, 209 W 42nd St, both between Seventh and Eighth avenues, were refurbished by Disney some years ago, two of the truly welcome results of the massive changes here. The **Lyceum**, 149 W 45th St, retains its original facade, while the **Shubert Theater**, 225 W 44th St, which hosted *A Chorus Line* during its twenty-odd-year run, still occupies its own small space. One of the older theaters is the 1907 **Belasco**, 111 W 44th St, which was also the first of Broadway's theaters to incorporate machinery into its stagings. At 432 W 44th St is a former Presbyterian church that in 1947 became **The Actors Studio**, where Lee Strasberg, America's leading proponent of Stanislavski's method-acting technique, taught his students.

The famous **neon**, so much a signature of Times Square, was initially confined to the theaters and spawned the term "the Great White Way." In 1922, the lights moved G.K. Chesterton to remark, "What a glorious garden of wonder this would be, to anyone who was lucky enough to be unable to read." Today the illumination is not limited to theaters. Myriad ads, forming one of the world's most garish nocturnal displays, promote hundreds of products and services. Businesses that rent offices here are actually required to allow signage on their walls – the city's attempt to retain the square's traditional feel, paradoxically enough, with the most advanced technology possible.

Originally an elegant building modeled on Giotto's Campanile in Florence, the famous zipper sign displaying the news of the world was added in 1928. In 1965, the building was "skinned" and covered with the lifeless marble slabs visible today. The paper's offices have long since moved around the corner to a handsome building with globe lamps on 43rd Street, and most of the printing is done in New Jersey.

Not actually a square at all, Times Square is formed by the intersection between arrow-straight Seventh Avenue and left-leaning Broadway; the latter more or less follows true north through much of the island, which tilts to the northeast. So narrow is the angle between these two thoroughfares that Broadway, which meets Seventh Avenue at 43rd Street, does not begin to strike off on its own again until 48th Street, just above the traffic island of **Duffy Square**. Not much to look at itself, Duffy Square offers an excellent view of Times Square's lights, megahotels, theme stores, and restaurants. The canvas-and-frame stand of the **TKTS booth**, modest in comparison, sells half-price, same-day tickets for Broadway shows (whose exorbitant prices these days make a visit to TKTS a necessity; see p.384 for details). A lifelike statue of Broadway's doyen **George M. Cohan** looks on – though if you've ever seen the film *Yankee Doodle Dandy* it's impossible to think of him in any other form than a swaggering Jimmy Cagney. At eye level, you can find enough gifts in the souvenir shops for your five hundred closest friends.

It's in Times Square and on its immediate sidestreets that, every **New Year's Eve**, hundreds of thousands of deliriously happy people, many of them running on little more than alcohol, camp out to witness a giant sparkling ball drop from the top of Times Tower at midnight. The crowds continue to mass here every year, even with the remarkably tight post–September 11 security.

North of Times Square, the **West 50s** between Sixth and Eighth avenues are populated by businesses that scream to tourists at every opportunity. Edged by Central Park to the north and the Theater District to the south, and with Fifth Avenue and Rockefeller Center within easy striking distance, the area has been invaded by overpriced restaurants and cheapo souvenir stores: should you wish to stock up on "I Love New York" underwear, this is the place. One sight around here worth looking out for, though, is the **Equitable Center**, 787 Seventh Ave, at 51st Street. The building itself is dapper if not a little self-important, and Roy Lichtenstein's 68ft *Mural with Blue Brush Stroke* assaults your eyes as you enter. Closer to Columbus Circle is the **Gainsborough Studios** building, 222 Central Park South, between Broadway and Seventh Avenue. Built in 1905, it became an official city landmark in 1988 and is notable for the Moravian tiles that dominate the top two floors, as well as the double-story windows that peer onto Central Park. Note the bust of the building's namesake, English artist Thomas Gainsborough, which hovers above the entrance on the facade. Walking up Eighth Avenue, **Hearst World Headquarters**, between 56th and 57th streets, had its 597ft tower completed in June 2006. The tower, designed by Lord Norman Foster, is supposed to be one of the most environmentally friendly high-rise buildings ever constructed, employing technologies to reduce pollution and energy consumption, while fully utilizing renewable energy resources. Down West 57th Street toward Sixth Avenue, **no. 130** was designated a landmark in 2000. Constructed in 1907, the bay windows bring in light that has invited artists like William Dean Howells, Jose Ferrer, Woody Allen, and Tony Bennett to live here. But it's the **Ed Sullivan Theater**, 1697 Broadway, between 54th and 53rd streets, that attracts the most people in this neighborhood, as lines wrap around 53rd Street for stand-by tickets to see the *Late Show with David Letterman*.

Hell's Kitchen

Sprawling across the blocks west of Times Square to the Hudson River between 30th and 59th streets lies **Clinton** (named for nineteenth-century Governor Dewitt Clinton), more famously known as **Hell's Kitchen**, an area centered on the restaurants, bars, and ethnic delis of **Ninth Avenue**.

Head to Hell's Kitchen from Eighth Avenue (which now houses the porn businesses long since expelled from the square) by walking west on 46th Street along so-called **Restaurant Row** – the area's preferred haunt for pre- and post-theater dining, even though most of the strip's eateries are mediocre at best. Here you can begin to detect a more laid-back feel, which only increases on many of the sidestreets around Ninth and Tenth avenues, where cramped apartment buildings frequently hide small garden oases. Check out the decidedly unstuffy **St Clement's Episcopal Church**, 423 W 46th St: it doubles as a community theater and its foyer features a picture of Elvis Presley and Jesus with the caption, "There seems to be a little confusion as to which one of them actually rose from the dead."

Among New York's most violent and lurid neighborhoods at one time, Hell's Kitchen was rumored to be named for a tenement at 54th Street and Tenth

Avenue. More commonly, the name has been attributed to a veteran policeman who went by the sobriquet "Dutch Fred the Cop." In response to his young partner's comment – while watching a riot – that the place was hell, Fred reportedly replied, "Hell's a mild climate. This is Hell's kitchen." The area originally contained slaughterhouses and factories that made soap and glue, with sections named "Misery Lane" and "Poverty Row." Irish immigrants were the first inhabitants; they were soon joined by Greeks, Puerto Ricans, and African-Americans. Amid the overcrowding, tensions rapidly developed between (and within) ethnic groups – the rough-and-tumble neighborhood was popularized in the musical *West Side Story* (1957). A violent Irish gang, the Westies, claimed the streets in the 1970s and early 1980s, but the area has since been cleaned up and is far less dangerous than it ever has been (although you should still keep your wits about you). Over the past few decades the neighborhood has been moving up in the same way the East Village did in the late 1990s; it's attracted a new population of musicians, Broadway types, and a growing number of professionals, and the renovation and construction of apartment buildings continues to move at a fast pace.

The Intrepid Sea, Air & Space Museum and around

If you continue west to the river, you will reach the **Intrepid Sea, Air & Space Museum**, 46th St and Twelfth Ave at Pier 86 (April–Sept: Mon–Fri 10am–5pm, Sat & Sun 10am–6pm; Oct–March: Tues–Sun 10am–5pm; $16.50, college students and seniors $12.50, ages 6–17 $11.50, ages 2–5 $4.50, under 2 years free; ☎212/245-0072, ☜www.intrepidmuseum.org). This huge (900-foot-long) old aircraft carrier has a distinguished history: it picked up capsules from the Mercury and Gemini space missions and made several trips to Vietnam. It holds an array of modern and vintage air- and sea-craft, including the A-12 Blackbird, the world's fastest spy plane, and the USS *Growler*, the only guided-missile submarine open to the public. The museum also has interactive exhibits, an on-board restaurant, and the recently retired Concorde, formerly operated by British Airways. If you're visiting at the end of May, **Fleet Week** (the week leading up to Memorial Day) is a big deal here, and deservedly so, with ships visiting from all corners of the globe, as well as military demonstrations and competitions.

Otherwise, there's not too much to see this far west. Ragged Eleventh Avenue is home to the automobile warehouses that once made up Times Square's Automobile Row, and past that is the sleazy West Side Highway. These streets are unremarkable, highlighted only by two well-preserved, old-time restaurants on Eleventh, the *Landmark Tavern* (no. 626, at West 46th Street) and the *Market Diner* (no. 572, at West 43rd Street).

Sixth Avenue

Sixth Avenue is officially named **Avenue of the Americas**, though no New Yorker ever calls it this; guidebooks and maps labor the convention, but the only manifestations of the tag are lamppost flags of Central and South American countries that serve as useful landmarks. The street is distinguished mostly by its width, a result of the elevated railway that once ran along here (now the Sixth

Avenue line runs underground). In its day, the Sixth Avenue "El" marked the border between respectability to the east and dodgier areas to the west, and in a way it's still a divider, separating the glamorous strips of Fifth, Madison, and Park avenues from the brasher western districts. The buildings on either side of the boulevard look like two large sets of dominoes set on end.

The avenue goes into sort of a nondescript slump north of Macy's, then gets more interesting when it passes Bryant Park between 40th and 42nd streets, and again when it reaches the **International Center of Photography**, no. 1133 at 43rd Street (Tues–Thurs, Sat & Sun 10am–6pm, Fri 10am–8pm; $10, students and seniors $7; ☎212/857-0000, ⊛www.icp.org). Founded in 1974 by Cornell Capa (brother of war photographer Robert Capa), this exceptional museum and school sponsors twenty exhibits a year dedicated to "concerned photography," avant-garde works, and retrospectives of modern masters. The permanent archived collection contains most of the greats, and the shows often contain more experimental works from photographers based around the world. The Center also conducts classes and educational trips.

Some of the best things about New York City are the gems you discover when you least expect them. One good example is **Little Brazil Street**, on West 46th Street between Fifth and Sixth avenues, which holds many of the city's (few) Brazilian restaurants and where, during lunchtime on weekdays, you'll hear more Portuguese than English. Even better is **Diamond Row** (marked by the diamond-shaped lamps mounted on pylons at the Fifth- and Sixth-avenue ends of West 47th Street), a strip of wholesale and retail shops chock-full of gems and jewelry first established in the 1920s. These shops are largely managed by Hasidic Jews, who impart much of the street's workaday vibe, making the Row feel less like something just off ritzy Fifth Avenue and more like the Garment District, by way of the Middle East. Come here to get jewelry fixed at reasonable prices.

Back on the avenue, this part of Sixth is a showcase for corporate wealth. There's little of the ground-floor glitter of Fifth or the razzmatazz of Broadway, but the **Rockefeller Center Extension** defines the stretch from 47th to 51st streets. Following the **Time & Life Building** at 50th Street, three near-identical buildings went up in the 1970s. Though they don't have the romance of their predecessor, they at least possess some of its monumentality. Backing onto Rockefeller Center proper, the repeated statement of each building comes over with some power, giving Sixth Avenue much of its visual excitement.

Radio City Music Hall and north

On the corner of Sixth Avenue and 50th Street is **Radio City Music Hall**, a sweeping and dramatic Art Deco jewel box that represents the last word in 1930s luxury. The staircase is positively regal, the chandeliers are the world's largest, and the auditorium looks like an extravagant scalloped shell: "Art Deco's true shrine," as critic Paul Goldberger rightly called it. Believe it or not, Radio City was nearly demolished in 1970; the resulting outcry caused it to be designated a national landmark. To explore, take a tour from the lobby (daily 11am–6pm; hour-long "Stage Door" behind-the-scenes walking tours include a meeting with a Rockette; $17, children under 12 years $10; general info ☎212/307-7171, tour info ☎247-4777, ⊛www.radiocity.com).

A block farther north, enjoy the company of Venus, in the form of three 25ft copper statues, anchoring the fountains in front of the **Crédit Lyonnais Building** at no. 1301. Look out as well for the **AXA Financial Center**, no. 1290, which hosts Thomas Hart Benton's *America Today* murals. This creation

(1931), which dynamically and magnificently portrays ordinary life in the days before the Depression, was celebrated for its representation of Americans from a variety of classes, shown both at work and at leisure. It spurred an interest in murals as public art, and lent momentum to the Federal Arts Project (which provided both employment for artists suffering through the decade, and a morale boost for the rest of the public) in the 1930s.

Keep an eye open for the **CBS Building** on the corner at 51 W 52nd St. Dark and inscrutable, this has been compared to the monolith from the film *2001: A Space Odyssey*; from here Sixth Avenue proceeds grandly and placidly north for several blocks before reaching the green expanse of Central Park.

57th Street

The area just around 57th Street between Fifth and Sixth avenues competes with Soho and Chelsea as a center for **up-market art sales**. Galleries here are noticeably snootier than their downtown relations, and often require appointments for viewings. Two that usually don't include the **Kennedy Galleries**, 730 Fifth Ave (☎212/541-9600), who deal in nineteenth- and twentieth-century American painting, and show a wide variety of styles, and the venerable **Tibor de Nagy Gallery**, 724 Fifth Ave, 12th floor (Tues–Sat 10am–5.30pm; closed mid-August through Labor Day; ☎212/262-5050), which was established in 1950 but still shows exciting works. Also noteworthy is the **Art Students League**, 215 W 57th, built in 1892 by Henry J. Hardenbergh (who later built the *Plaza Hotel*) to mimic Francis I's hunting lodge at Fontainebleau. Today this art school provides inexpensive art classes to the public. For more on galleries in this area, see Chapter 30, "Commercial galleries."

At 154 W 57th St is stately **Carnegie Hall**, one of the world's greatest concert venues, revered by musicians and audiences alike. The Renaissance-inspired structure was built in the 1890s by steel magnate and self-styled "improver of mankind" Andrew Carnegie, and the still-superb acoustics ensure full houses most of the year. Tchaikovsky conducted the program on opening night and Mahler, Rachmaninov, Toscanini, Frank Sinatra, and Judy Garland have all performed here (not to mention Duke Ellington, Billie Holiday, the Beatles, Spinal Tap, and Missy Elliott). If you don't want, or can't afford, to attend a performance, sneak in through the stage door on 56th Street for a quick look – no one minds as long as there's not a rehearsal in progress. Alternatively, catch one of the tours, available September through June only (Mon, Tues, Thurs & Fri 11.30am, 2pm & 3pm; $9, students and seniors $6, children under 12 $3; general info ☎212/903-9600, tours ☎903-9765, tickets ☎247-7800, ⒲www.carnegiehall.org). It's just a couple blocks north of here at the southwestern corner of Central Park that Eighth Avenue and Broadway empty into the swirling maelstrom of traffic and construction that is Columbus Circle, gateway to the Upper West Side and Central Park.

Central Park

"All radiant in the magic atmosphere of art and taste," raved *Harper's* magazine on the occasion of the opening of **Central Park** in 1876. A slight overstatement, perhaps, although today few people could imagine New York City without the park. Devotedly used by locals and visited by travelers, it serves purposes as varied as the individuals who take advantage of it: it's an environmental haven, a theater for all things cultural, a beach, a playground, and a running track. Over the years, the park has occasionally fallen on hard times, experiencing everything from official neglect to some truly horrible crime waves. Recently, though, it has benefited from a series of major renovations, and is now cleaner, safer, and more user-friendly than ever.

Some history

Known today for its bucolic beauty amid the crazed hustle and bustle of midtown Manhattan, Central Park came quite close to never existing at all. Poet and newspaper editor **William Cullen Bryant** is credited with first publicizing the idea for an open public space in Manhattan in 1844; he then spent seven years

---

Park practicalities

General park information can be obtained by calling ☎212/310-6600, or by going to ⊛www.centralparknyc.org. Special events information is available at ☎1-888/NYPARKS.

The **Central Park Conservancy**, founded in 1980, is a nonprofit organization dedicated to preserving and managing the park. It runs three **Visitor Centers**, which have free maps and other helpful literature, as well as feature special events. All are open year-round Tuesday through Sunday 10am to 5pm: The **Dairy** (65th St at mid-park; ☎212/794-6564); **Belvedere Castle** (79th St at mid-park; ☎212/772-0210); and the **Charles A. Dana Discovery Center** (110th St off Fifth Ave; ☎212/860-1370).

Restrooms are available at Hecksher Playground, the Boat Pond (Conservatory Water), Mineral Springs House (northwest end of Sheep's Meadow), Loeb Boathouse, the Delacorte Theater, the North Meadow Recreation Center, the Conservatory Garden, and the Charles A. Dana Discovery Center.

Manhattan Urban Park Rangers (activities info line ☎212/628-2345, ⊛www.nyc.gov/parks) are in the park to help; they lead walking tours, give directions, and provide first aid in emergencies.

In case of emergency, use the **emergency call boxes** located throughout the park and along the park drives (they provide a direct connection to the Central Park Precinct), or dial ☎911 at any payphone.

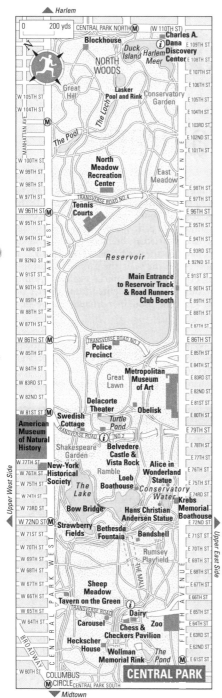

trying to persuade City Hall to carry out the plan. At the same time, property developers leaned heavily on the authorities from the other direction, hoping not to lose any valuable land. Eventually the city agreed with Bryant and his supporters, paying $5 million for 840 acres north of the (then) city limits at 38th Street, a desolate swampy area occupied at the time by scattered shantytowns. The most notable of these was **Seneca Village**, in the area that's now between 81st and 88th streets; this was home to a cluster of African-American property owners who'd snapped up space here several years before in order to get the vote. The residents of these settlements were evicted, and planning began to pick up speed.

In 1857, after a fierce design contest, **Frederick Law Olmsted** and **Calvert Vaux** were chosen to create the rural paradise they called "Greensward," an illusion of the countryside smack in the heart of Manhattan. The idea was that Greensward would bring nature to the increasingly congested city, in an area where developers were already eyeing space for mansions. The sparseness of the existing terrain didn't just attract builders; it also provided Olmsted and Vaux with the perfect opportunity to plan the park according to the precepts of classical English landscape gardening. They designed 36 elegant bridges, each unique, and planned a revolutionary system of four sunken transverse roads to segregate different kinds of traffic; it was this ingenious system which assured their victory, since no other plans solved the cross-park traffic problem so smoothly.

Navigating the park

Central Park is so enormous that it's impossible to miss entirely and nearly as impossible to cover in one visit. The intricate **footpaths** that meander through the park are some of its greatest successes. If you've lost your way among them, though, there are several tricks to finding it again. Every feature has a name in order that rendezvous can be precise. Even the bodies of water are differentiated (a loch, a pool, a lake, and even a meer) so that there can never be confusion. But if you do need **to figure out exactly where you are**, find the nearest **lamppost**. The first two digits on the post indicate the number of the nearest cross street, while the last two show whether you're nearer the east side (odd numbers) or west side (even). It's smart to stop by one of the Visitor Centers to pick up a free park map (see box, p.163); there are now also two dozen free-standing unmanned kiosks throughout the park, all of which provide information on nearby sights as well as a full map.

Car access to the park's drives is severely restricted (closed Mon–Thurs 10am–3pm, 7–10pm, & Fri 7am–Mon 6am). Even if you're visiting during a car-free period, you should still keep a watchful eye: crossing the road amid the hordes of goggled and headphoned rollerbladers, cyclists, and joggers can be trying – just be patient.

Since there are no bus routes in the park and car access is spotty, most people visit on foot or rollerblade. Other options include **renting a bicycle** from the Loeb Boathouse (see p.168), Metro Bicycles, West Side Bikes, or Midtown Bicycles. Bikes from the Boathouse are $9 for the first hour ($10 for 10-speed bikes and $14 for two-seater tandems), and from Metro $7 an hour (or $35 for the day); both require a credit card or refundable cash deposit ($250).

All of the above options are better deals than the famed **romantic buggy rides** ($34 for a 20min trot and $10 for every additional 15min after that; ☎212/736-0680, ⦿www.centralparkcarriages.com). There has long been vocal opposition to these rides, fueled by claims that the incompetence and greed of the buggy drivers can lead to great cruelty to the horses. A law enacted in 1994 mandates that the horses must get fifteen-minute rest breaks every two hours and cannot work more than nine hours a day; they're also not supposed to work at all when the temperature goes above 90°F. Buggy drivers can get their licenses suspended or revoked for disobedience.

As for **safety** in the park, you should be fine during the day everywhere except around the Blockhouse on the northwestern tip, which is best visited only on a tour. Otherwise, just stay alert to your surroundings and try to avoid being alone in an isolated area; after dark, it's safer than it used to be, but it's still not advisable to walk around, especially not by yourself. If you want to look at the buildings of Central Park West lit up, as they were in Woody Allen's iconic film *Manhattan*, the best option is to fork out for a buggy ride. The one exception to the after-dark rule is in the case of a public evening event such as a concert or a summertime Shakespeare in the Park performance; these events are very safe – just make sure you leave when the crowds do.

The **Reservoir** divides Central Park in two. The larger **southern park** holds most of the attractions (and people), but the **northern park** (above 86th St) is well worth a visit for its wilder natural setting and dramatically quieter ambience. Organized walking tours are available from a number of sources, including the Urban Park Rangers and the Visitor Centers (see box, p.163), but almost any stroll, formal or informal, will invariably lead to something interesting.

It took sixteen years and $14 million ($260 million in today's money) to construct the entire park, though the sapling trees planted here didn't reach their full height for five decades. Central Park opened to the public in 1876. So great was the acclaim for Olmsted and Vaux that they were soon in demand as park architects all over the United States. Locally, they went on to design Riverside and Morningside parks in Manhattan, as well as Prospect Park in Brooklyn. Working alone, Olmsted laid out the campuses of Berkeley and Stanford universities in California, and had a major hand in the most televised of American sights, Capitol Hill in Washington DC.

At its opening, the powers that be emphasized that Central Park was a "people's park," available to all – though most of the impoverished masses for whom it was allegedly built had neither the time nor the carfare to come up to 59th Street from their downtown slums and enjoy it. But as New York continued to expand and workers' leisure time increased, people started flooding in, and the park began to live up to its mission, although occasionally in ways that might have scandalized its original builders.

Robert Moses, a relentless urban planner and the power behind some of the city's largest building projects in the mid-twentieth century, tried hard to put his imprint (concrete) on Central Park while he served as parks commissioner from 1935 to 1960. Thankfully, public opinion kept damage from his developments to a minimum; he only managed to pave over a small portion of the park, mostly in the form of unnecessary parking lots (since reconverted to green space). When he tried to tear down a park playground in 1956 to build a parking lot for *Tavern on the Green*, Moses was thwarted by outraged citizens – mothers and their young children stood in the way of the bulldozers, and the city sheepishly backed down.

The park hit rock bottom in 1973, by which point it had degenerated into a vandalized, crime-infested eyesore on which the bankrupt city had no money to spare (see p.467). It was only the threat that the park would be turned over to the National Park Service that mobilized both politicians and local citizens to find funds to refit it. That ongoing effort is now overseen by a feisty nonprofit group called the Central Park Conservancy, which works in conjunction with the city government to maintain the park, increase its policing, and restore areas like Bethesda Terrace (see p.168). Indeed, citing possible environmental damage, the Conservancy for years blocked what turned out to be one of the park's most recent successes, the 2005 staging of *The Gates, Central Park, New York*, an installation by art stuntman **Christo** and his wife/collaborator Jeanne Claude. The artists finally prevailed, however, and for sixteen days in February, 7500 saffron gates, all 161 feet tall with colored fabric panels suspended from the top, were placed at ten- to fifteen-foot intervals throughout the park. The project drew international attention, and visitors from all over came to walk the park's paths.

Despite the advent of motorized traffic, the idea of nature-as-disorder intended by Olmsted and Vaux largely survives. Cars and buses cut through the park in the sheltered, sunken transverses originally intended for horse-drawn carriages, and remain mostly unseen from the park itself. The skyline, of course, has drastically changed, but the buildings that menacingly thrust their way into view are kept at bay by a fortress of trees, adding to the feeling that you're on a green island in the center of a magnificent city.

The southern park

Most visitors enter the park at Grand Army Plaza (Fifth Ave and 59th St; see p.137). From here, **The Pond** lies to the left, and a little farther north is the **Wollman Memorial Rink** (63rd St at mid-park; Nov–March ice skating Mon & Tues 10am–2.30pm, Wed & Thurs 10am–10pm, $9.50; Fri & Sat 10am–11pm, Sun 10am–9pm, $12; ☎212/439-6900, ⓦwww .wollmanskatingrink.com). Hang out above the rink to watch the skaters and contemplate the views of Central Park South and 59th Street's skyline. You can also rent skates here: rollerblades, the most versatile and popular mode of park transportation, and ice skates are both available here (skate rental $5, locker rental $5 plus $5 refundable deposit).

East of the skating rink, at 64th Street and Fifth Avenue, lies the small **Central Park Zoo** (Nov–March daily 10am–4.30pm; April–Oct Mon–Fri 10am–5pm, Sat, Sun & holidays 10am–5.30pm; $6, children ages 3–12 $1, children under 3 free; ☎212/439-6500, ⓦwww.centralparkzoo.com). This welcoming wildlife center's collection is based on three climatic zones – the Tropic Zone, the Temperate Territory, and the Polar Circle. The zoo has over a hundred species on view in mostly natural-looking homes. The animals are as close to the viewer as possible: the penguins, for example, swim around at eye level in Plexiglas pools. Other top attractions include the polar bears, the monkeys, a nocturnal exhibit, and the sea lions, who cavort in a pool right by the zoo entrance. This complex also boasts the **Tisch Children's Zoo**: there's a petting area, interactive displays, and a musical clock just outside the entrance that draws rapt children at the top of each hour. The zoo is a charming stop-off for an hour or two, but if you're a dedicated animal-lover, or have older children, you're better off heading to the Bronx Zoo (see p.282).

Close by stands the **Dairy** (65th St at mid-park), a cutesy yellow neo-Gothic chalet that was built in 1870 as a café. Despite local lore, there were never any cows here, though it did sell milk for children – the name's an early touch of savvy marketing rather than a nod to the building's function. It's now one of the park's Visitor Centers (see p.163), where you can pick up free maps and leaflets or buy books on the park. Weekend walking tours often leave from here – check ⓦwww .centralparknyc.org for times and routes. You can also pick up playing pieces here for the **Chess and Checkers Pavilion** near the zoo.

Just west of the Dairy, you will see the octagonal brick building that houses the **Carousel** (64th St at mid-park; April–Nov daily 10am–6pm; Dec–March Sat & Sun 10am–4.30pm, weather permitting; $1.25; ☎212/879-0244). Built in 1903 and moved to the park from Coney Island in 1951, this is one of the park's little gems. There are fewer than 150 such carousels left in the country (one of the others is still at Coney Island – see p.257). A ride on it is a magical experience: its hand-carved, colorfully painted jumping horses are accompanied by the music of a military-band organ.

Heading north from the Dairy, you'll pass through the avenue of trees known as **The Mall.** The trees, whose branches tangle together to form a "roof" (hence its nickname, "The Cathedral"), are elms, a rarity in America. No one knows for sure why these, and the rest of the park's 1800-odd trees, were not wiped out by the Dutch elm disease epidemic of the 1930s and 1940s that killed the majority of elms across the country. The statues that line the avenue are all literary and artistic greats: Shakespeare arrived first, and others from across the world soon followed, often privately funded by the appropriate immigrant groups – hence Italy's Mazzini and Germany's Beethoven; it's better to gloss over the long-forgotten Fitzgreene Halleck, an American poet who secured his spot thanks to connections to the Astor family. If the weather's good, expect to see street performers of varying caliber cavorting here. At the base of the Mall is the only acknowledgment to either park architect: a small memorial garden in Frederick Law Olmsted's name. Poor Calvert Vaux isn't commemorated anywhere.

To the west lies the **Sheep Meadow** (between 66th and 69th streets), fifteen acres of commons where sheep grazed until 1934, when they were banished to Brooklyn's Prospect Park. In the summer, the meadow is crowded with picnickers, sunbathers, and Frisbee players. Two grass bowling and croquet lawns are maintained on a hill near the Sheep Meadow's northwest corner; to the southeast are a number of very popular volleyball courts (call ☎212/360-8133 for information on lawn bowling; call ☎212/408-0226 for volleyball and other ball-field permit information). On warm weekends, an area between the Sheep Meadow and the north end of the mall is usually filled with rollerbladers dancing to funk, disco, and hip-hop music – one of the best free shows in town. Just west of the Sheep Meadow is the once exclusive, still expensive, but now tacky, landmark restaurant, **Tavern on the Green** (see p.354). The original 1870 building housed a fold for the animals who grazed the nearby meadow. Take a look at the exterior of the eatery, a colorful and intricate design done in the Victorian Gothic style. The street lamps outside the entrance were built in the early 1900s and originally lined the Champs Elysées in Paris. Also check out the amusingly huge fake topiary trees in front of the Crystal Room (you'll know it when you see it).

East of *Tavern on the Green*, at the northernmost point of the Mall, lie the **Bandshell** and **Rumsey Playfield**, the sites of the free SummerStage performance series (see box, p.171). There's also the **Bethesda Terrace and Fountain** (72nd St at mid-park), one of the few formal elements planned by Olmsted and Vaux. The crowning centerpiece of the fountain is the nineteenth-century *Angel of the Waters* sculpture, the only statue included in the original park design. Its earnest puritanical angels, who represent Purity, Health, Peace, and Temperance, continue to watch disappointedly over their wicked city. They were recently made famous again by Tony Kushner's Pulitzer Prize–winning play *Angels in America*, of which the last scene is set here. The subterranean arcade is the subject of a series of major renovations aimed at restoring the intricate Minton tiling that once covered the ceiling. The fountain overlooks **The Lake**, where you can go for a Venetian-style gondola ride or rent a rowboat from the Loeb Boathouse on the eastern bank (March–Nov daily 10am–6pm, weather permitting; rowboats $10 for the first hour, $2.50 each 15min thereafter, $30 refundable deposit; gondola rides available 5–10pm, $30 per 30min per group, requires reservations; ☎212/517-2233, ⊛www.thecentralparkboathouse.com).

The narrowest point on the lake is crossed by the elegant cast-iron and wood **Bow Bridge**. Take this bridge if you want to amble to **The Ramble** on the lake's northern banks, a 37-acre area of unruly woodland, filled with narrow winding paths, rocky outcroppings, streams, and an array of native plant life. Once a favorite spot for drug dealers and anonymous sex, it is now a great place to watch for one of the park's 54 species of birds or take a quiet daytime stroll. Clean-up notwithstanding, steer clear of this area at night.

To the west of Bethesda Terrace, along the 72nd Street Drive, is the **Cherry Hill Fountain**. Originally a turnaround point for carriages, it was designed to have excellent views of the Lake, the Mall, and the Ramble. One of the pretty areas paved by Moses in the 1930s for use as a parking lot, it was restored to its natural state in the early 1980s.

West of here, across the Park Drive, is **Strawberry Fields** (72nd St and Central Park W), a peaceful area dedicated to John Lennon, who was murdered in 1980 in front of his home at the Dakota Building, across the street on Central Park West. (See box on p.212 for more on the death of John Lennon.) Strawberry Fields is always crowded with those here to remember Lennon, at no time more so than December 8, the anniversary of his murder. Near the West 72nd Street entrance to the park is a round Italian mosaic with the word "Imagine"

△ Boating on the Lake, Central Park

at its center, donated by Lennon's widow, Yoko Ono. This is also a favorite spot for picknickers and resting seniors.

Back to the east of Bethesda Terrace is the **Boat Pond** (72nd St and Fifth Ave), officially named the Conservatory Water (though New Yorkers never call it that). This small man-made pond was intended to be the reflecting pool of a large greenhouse to be built on Fifth Avenue – hence the name – but as plans for the park changed, that project was abandoned. Today, the Water is known for its model-boat races, held every Saturday in the summer; you can participate by renting a craft from the cart in front of the **Krebs Memorial Boathouse**, just east of the Water ($10 per hour; more information ☎917/796-1382). The fanciful *Alice in Wonderland* statue at the northern end of the pond was donated by publisher George Delacorte and is a favorite climbing spot for kids. During the summer the New York Public Library sponsors Wednesday-morning (11am) storytelling sessions for children at the *Hans Christian Andersen* statue on the west side of the pond (☎212/340-0906 for more information). A storyteller from the Central Park Conservancy also appears here at 11am on Saturdays throughout the summer.

Central Park has ample **picnicking opportunities**, the most obvious of which is the hectic, perpetually crowded expanse of the Sheep Meadow. For (a very) little more peace and quiet, you might try one of these other fine locations: the western shore of the Lake, near Hernshead; the lawn in front of Turtle Pond, which has a nice view of Belvedere Castle; the Conservatory Garden; the lawn immediately north of the Ramble; Strawberry Fields; the Arthur Ross Pinetum; and the areas around the Delacorte Theater.

Continue north to reach the backyard of the **Metropolitan Museum of Art** to the east at 81st Street (see p.173). Behind the museum to the west stands the **Obelisk**, the oldest structure in the park, which dates from 1450 BC. It was a gift to the city from Egypt in 1881, and, like its twin on the Thames River in London, is nicknamed "Cleopatra's Needle." Immediately west of the needle is the **Great Lawn** (81st St at mid-park). It was the site of the park's original reservoir from 1842 until 1931, when the water was drained to create a playing field. Years later, the lawn became a popular site for free concerts and rallies (Simon and Garfunkel, Elton John, Garth Brooks, Sting, and the Pope, who celebrated mass here in 1995, have all attracted crowds numbering over half a million), but it was badly overused and had serious drainage problems. Reopened in 1998 after a massive two-year, $18.2-million reconstruction, the lawn's engineering and sandy soil now mean that even if there's a heavy downpour at lunchtime, the grass will be dry by evening. Rebuilt, reseeded and renewed, it will hopefully stay that way by only hosting the more sedate free New York Philharmonic and Metropolitan Opera concerts (see box, opposite). The lawn features eight softball fields and, at its northern end, new basketball and volleyball courts and an eighth-mile running track.

The refurbished **Turtle Pond** is at the southern end of the Lawn, with a new wooden dock and nature blind designed for better views of the aquatic wildlife (yes, there actually is wildlife here, including ducks, fish, and frogs). Note the massive statue of fourteenth-century Polish king **Wladyslaw Jagiello** (pronounced Ha-GAY-wuh) on the southeast corner of the pond. It appeared at the New York World's Fair in 1939, and upon the outbreak of World War II remained in New York; once peace was declared in 1945, the Polish government officially donated it to the park as a Holocaust memorial, and today it's the occasional site of Polish folk-dancing displays.

Southwest of the Lawn is the **Delacorte Theater**, the venue of the annual free Shakespeare in the Park festivals (see box, opposite). In another of the park's Shakespearean touches, the theater features Milton Hebald's sculptures of Romeo and Juliet and *The Tempest*'s Prospero, while the tranquil **Shakespeare Garden** next door claims to hold every species of plant or flower mentioned in the Bard's plays. East of the garden is **Belvedere Castle**, a mock medieval citadel first erected on top of Vista Rock in 1869 as a lookout on the highest point in the park. It's still a splendid viewpoint, and houses the New York Meteorological Observatory's weather center, which is responsible for providing the official daily Central Park temperature readings; there's also a handy Visitor Center here (see p.163). For more plays of the puppet kind, check out the **Swedish Cottage Marionette Theater** (79th St at mid-park) at the base of Vista Rock, which holds shows for kids like *The True Story of Rumpelstiltskin* or *Gulliver's Travels* (July–May Tues–Fri 10.30am, Sat 1pm; $6, kids $5; ☎212/988-9093 for reservation).

The northern park

There are fewer attractions, but more open spaces, above the Great Lawn. Much of the northern park is taken up by the **Reservoir** (86th–97th streets at mid-park, main entrance at 90th St and Fifth Ave), a 107-acre, billion-gallon reservoir originally designed in 1862 and no longer active. The reservoir was long hemmed in by an eyesore of a chainlink fence, but renovations have replaced it with iron railings, which mean the views across the water are finally as impressive as they ought to be. It's also a favorite place for active

Seasonal events and activities

SummerStage and **Shakespeare in the Park** are two of the most popular cultural summer programs in Manhattan. Both activities are free and help to take the sting out of New York's infamous hazy, hot, and humid summers. In 1986, **SummerStage** presented its inaugural Central Park concert with Sun Ra performing to an audience of fifty people. When he returned with Sonic Youth six years later, the audience numbered ten thousand. The musical acts are of consistently good quality, and cover pretty much every genre. Located at the Rumsey Playfield near 72nd Street and Fifth Avenue, concerts here are crowded and sticky, but unbeatable – especially given that they're free. Dance performances, spoken word, DJ sets, and (paid admission) benefit shows also share the stage; if you don't manage to snag a spot inside the auditorium, the music usually pours out across the surrounding lawns, so you can lounge there too. More information: ☎212/360-2756 or ⊛www.summerstage.org.

Shakespeare in the Park takes place at the open-air Delacorte Theater, located near the West 81st Street entrance to the park. Pairs of free tickets are distributed daily at 1pm for that evening's performance – you'll have to get in line well beforehand. You can also pick them up at the Public Theater (425 Lafayette St at Astor Place in the East Village) from 1pm on the day of the performance, though again, expect a line to be forming by 7am most days. Two plays are performed each summer (mid-June through early Sept Tues–Sun at 8pm) and though Shakespeare is the festival's focus, the entire cycle of his plays has been performed over the course of more than twenty years, so other works are now produced here as well. More information: ☎212/539-8750 or ⊛www.publictheater.org.

New York Philharmonic in the Park (☎212/875-5709, ⊛www.newyork philharmonic.org) and **Metropolitan Opera in the Park** (☎212/362-6000, ⊛www .metopera.org) hold several evenings of classical music in the summer, often with a booming fireworks display to usher the crowds home.

Horseback-riding lessons are available at Claremont Riding Academy (175 W 89th St at Amsterdam Ave; Mon–Fri 6.30am–10pm, Sat & Sun 6.30am–5pm; ☎212/724-5100, ⊛www.potomachorse.com/clarmont.htm), as are rentals for riders experienced in the English saddle. Private classes run $65 per 30 minutes, group lessons $55 per hour; if you want to ride in the park, you'll need to be at least an intermediate rider, and you can only hire during daylight hours – it's $55 per hour.

The Harlem Meer Festival (110th St between Fifth and Lenox avenues; ☎212/860-1370) offers fairly intimate and enjoyable free performances of jazz and salsa music outside the Charles A. Dana Discovery Center on Sundays from Memorial Day through Labor Day from 4 to 6pm. The new **Parks Library collection** (in the Arsenal, 830 Fifth Ave at 64th St, Room 240; Mon–Fri 9am–5pm; ☎212/360-8240) contains materials on the history of New York and the Parks system, wildlife, and ecological concerns. The photo archive (☎212/360-8110) documents park events and improvements from the 1930s onward, but you must make an appointment (and state your interest and intent) to use the collection.

uptown residents: the raised 1.58-mile track is a great place to get breathtaking 360-degree views of the skyline – just don't block any jogger's path or there will be hell to pay. North of the reservoir are a tennis-court complex and the soccer fields of the **North Meadow Recreation Center** (97th St at mid-park; ☎212/348-4867; for tennis permits and info, call ☎212/316-0800). The landscape north of here, in the aptly named North Woods, feels more like upstate New York than Manhattan: the 90-acre area contains man-made but natural-looking stone arches plus the **Loch**, which is now more of a stream, and the **Ravine**, which conceals five small waterfalls.

If you see nothing else in the park above 86th Street, don't miss the **Conservatory Garden** (daily 8am–dusk; E 103rd–106th streets along Fifth Ave with entrance at 105th). The iron-gated entrance at 105th Street and Fifth Avenue is known as the Vanderbilt Gate; it was the main entry to the Vanderbilt Mansion, previously situated at Fifth Avenue and 58th Street, and is now a favorite spot for weekend wedding-party photographs. The pleasing, six-acre garden is filled with flowering trees and shrubs, planted flowerbeds, fanciful fountains, and shaded benches, and is frequented by families, lovers, painters, and sketch artists. The green space itself is actually three gardens, each landscaped in a distinct style. You'll first walk through the Italian garden, a reserved oasis with neat lawns and trimmed hedges. To the south is the English area, enhanced by the Burnett Fountain, which depicts the two children from F.H. Burnett's classic book *The Secret Garden*. The French garden, the northernmost of the three, hosts sculptor Walter Schott's *Three Dancing Maidens*, known as the Untermyer Fountain for the wealthy Yonkers man who donated it in his will. Visit the French garden for the flowers – 20,000 tulips in spring and 2000 chrysanthemums in fall. North of this green space is the stand-alone **Robert Bendleim Playground** for disabled children, at 108th Street near Fifth Avenue, where physically challenged youngsters can play in "accessible" sandboxes and swings, or work out their upper bodies on balance beams.

At the top of the park is the **Charles A. Dana Discovery Center**, an environmental education center and Visitor Center, with free literature, changing visual exhibits, bird walks every Saturday at 11am in July and August, and multicultural performances (see box, p.163). Crowds of locals fish in the adjacent **Harlem Meer**, an eleven-acre pond created in 1864 and recently restored to undo the determined cement work of Robert Moses. It's stocked with more than 50,000 fish. The Discovery Center provides free bamboo fishing poles and bait, though they have a catch-and-release policy.

In the extreme northeast corner of the park, at 110th Street and Fifth Avenue, is a 1997 monument to **Duke Ellington**, the esteemed musician and composer of such classics as *Mood Indigo*. On top of the three columns that summon the nine muses, the Duke stands before his grand piano, symbolically looking toward Harlem for the next generation of musical vanguards. In the park's northwestern corner stands the **Blockhouse**, one of the few landmarks to still be awaiting renovation: one of several such houses built as a lookout over pancake-flat Harlem during the War of 1812, it's the only one which remains. Now a ruin, it's a picturesque but iffy place to visit even during the daytime – stick to seeing it from one of the park's scheduled tours.

The Metropolitan Museum of Art

The **Metropolitan Museum of Art**, or the **Met**, as it's usually called, is the foremost art museum in America. It started in 1870 in a brownstone downtown before decamping to its present site in Central Park, an area that park designers Frederick Law Olmsted and Calvert Vaux had initially tagged for a ball field. The Gothic-Revival building, unveiled in 1880, stood out from the prevailing notion of the day that a museum should be housed in an awe-inspiring structure – it was important for Vaux and co-architect Jacob Wrey Mould that the building not diminish the features of Central Park. Much of the museum's familiar multi-columned, wide-stepped facade on Fifth Avenue was added by McKim, Mead and White in 1906, and over time various additions to the building have completely surrounded the original structure.

The museum's collection includes over two million works of art from the Americas, Europe, Africa, and the Far East, as well as the classical and ancient worlds. Broadly, its holdings can be broken down into **seven major collections**, and we've followed that breakdown in giving an account of its highlights in this chapter: European Art – Painting and Sculpture; Asian Art; American Painting and Decorative Arts; Medieval Art; Egyptian Antiquities; Ancient Greek and Roman Art; and the Art of Africa, the Pacific, and the Americas. Additionally, we have provided overviews of the Met's often overlooked but impressive modern-art holdings as well as the Lehman Collection, which is housed in a separate wing at the rear of the museum.

There's also plenty to see in some of the **less famous collections**, which range from Islamic Art to the Arms and Armor Galleries, the largest and most important in the western hemisphere. There's also a Musical Instrument Collection, which contains the world's oldest piano, and a Costume Institute, home to many of the museum's glitzier displays. Add to this the half-dozen or so simultaneous temporary exhibitions (recent blockbusters have included solo shows on artists as varied as El Greco and fashion designer Gianni Versace), and the entire experience can turn into a cultural overdose – see the box on p.176 for some tips on how best to enjoy it all without becoming too overwhelmed.

There is one **main entrance** to the museum; it leads to the **Great Hall**, a deftly lit Neoclassical cavern where you can consult floor plans, check tour times, and pick up info on the Met's excellent lecture listings. Straight across from the entrance is the Grand Staircase, which leads to, for many visitors, the museum's single greatest attraction – the European Painting galleries. Make sure

The Met (☎212/535-7710, ⓦwww.metmuseum.org) is on Fifth Avenue at 82nd Street, set into Central Park. Take subway #4, #5, or #6 to 86th St–Lexington Ave. The museum is open Tuesday through Thursday and Sunday 9.30am to 5.30pm, Friday and Saturday 9.30am to 9pm. There is no set admission price, but the suggested donation is $20, $10 for senior citizens and students (includes admission to the Cloisters on the same day; see p.234). Recorded "acoustiguide" tours of the major collections are $6. The museum staff also offer free guided tours daily, including "Highlights of the Met," and periodic tours of specific galleries. Call for up-to-date schedules and a list of rotating gallery closures.

you pick up the detailed room-by-room gallery maps for the European Painting and Nineteenth-Century Painting collections, available at the **main information desk** in the Great Hall.

Note that the Met is currently undergoing some major renovations – mostly on the southern edge of the interior courtyard, facing Fifth Avenue – that will change the layout of the museum during the life of this guide edition. A space that once served as a restaurant is being converted to a sculpture gallery in which to display much of the museum's Roman holdings. It's set to open in late 2007. The museum has also placed most of its Islamic art in storage so that those galleries can be refurbished and reopened by mid-2008; objects on display will be shown in specially commissioned spaces in the building's Great Hall.

European Art

The Met's **European Art** galleries, located on the second floor at the top of the main staircase, are divided in two parts: the European Painting section – which traces several centuries' worth of work – and the more narrowly focused Nineteenth-Century European Paintings and Sculpture section.

The **European Painting galleries** begin with a room full of eighteenth-century French portraits by the likes of Elizabeth Vigée-Lebrun and Marie-Denise Villers; there's also a sad canvas by Jacques-Louis David, which depicts the scientist Lavoisier and his wife. Her preoccupied attitude is hardly surprising, since Lavoisier zigzagged safely through the Revolution only to land under the guillotine in 1794. You have two options from here. If you head right, you'll take in the Italian Renaissance; then several rooms of seventeenth-century Dutch masters; some English paintings; and finally, a clutch of Baroque works from Spain, France, and Italy. Head left, and you'll see a number of rooms stacked with Gothic works, then a raft of Northern Renaissance religious images, and lastly some Italian Mannerist and Baroque paintings. No matter which direction you decide to go, be sure to pause in the preliminary section to see works by **Tiepolo**, many of which are ceiling scenes in which the figures look like ants.

If you want to start with the **nineteenth century** (as many people do, in order to get to the Met's trove of Impressionist works), follow the left-hand corridor at the top of the main staircase; it's immediately outside the Drawings, Prints, and Photographs exhibit. This passage leads to another hall, which is littered with stunning Rodin sculptures in white marble and bronze. Twenty

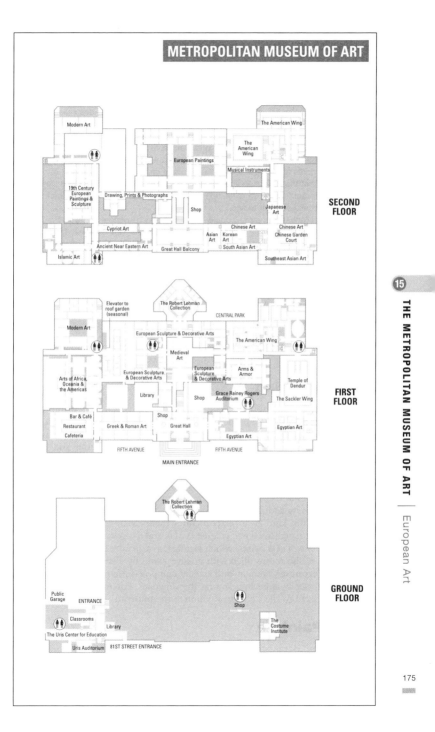

METROPOLITAN MUSEUM OF ART

SECOND FLOOR

Modern Art

The American Wing

The American Wing

European Paintings

Musical Instruments

19th Century European Paintings & Sculpture

Drawing, Prints & Photographs

Shop

Japanese Art

Cypriot Art

Chinese Art

Chinese Art

Asian Art

Korean Art

Chinese Garden Court

Ancient Near Eastern Art

South Asian Art

Islamic Art

Great Hall Balcony

Southeast Asian Art

FIRST FLOOR

Elevator to roof garden (seasonal)

The Robert Lehman Collection

CENTRAL PARK

Modern Art

European Sculpture & Decorative Arts

The American Wing

Medieval Art

Arts of Africa, Oceania & the Americas

European Sculpture & Decorative Arts

European Sculpture & Decorative Arts

Arms & Armor

Temple of Dendur

Library

Shop

Grace Rainey Rogers Auditorium

The Sackler Wing

Bar & Café

Shop

Restaurant

Greek & Roman Art

Great Hall

Egyptian Art

Cafeteria

Egyptian Art

FIFTH AVENUE

FIFTH AVENUE

MAIN ENTRANCE

GROUND FLOOR

The Robert Lehman Collection

Public Garage

ENTRANCE

Shop

Classrooms

Library

The Costume Institute

The Uris Center for Education

Uris Auditorium

81ST STREET ENTRANCE

Making the most of the Met

The Met has developed in a piecemeal way, as benefactors have willed their private holdings to the institution over the course of several decades, often specifying where or how the artwork should be displayed. This has made the museum dauntingly huge. While there's definitely a little something for everyone, the downside of the impressive collection is the amount of choice among the must-see sights. Here are a few tips on making the most of a visit to the Met, no matter how little (or how much) time you have:

• The first thing to do is pick up a map of the museum at the information booth in the main hall; if there's a piece or exhibit you don't want to miss, ask one of the knowledgeable docents at the desk to draw a route to it on your map.

• Be aware that the collection is regularly reorganized and galleries can be closed. Call ahead to confirm which exhibition spaces are under construction if there are particular pieces you want to see.

• As one of Manhattan's most popular attractions (more visitors come to the Met annually than to New York Yankees baseball games), the Met is usually throbbing with people, though it's large enough that the numbers rarely feel overwhelming. If you're determined to avoid the crush, come early in the day, or on Friday and Saturday evenings when – as an added bonus – a string quartet plays in the main hall.

• Don't feel you have to cram everything into a single visit: the suggested admission price is exactly that – a suggestion. Whether you pay 12¢ or $12, the cashier won't flinch, so if you can, spread out your exploration over several days.

rooms branch off from here, leading to an array of Impressionist and Post-Impressionist paintings and nineteenth-century European sculpture.

Italian Painting

A turn to your right from the main gallery brings you to the beginning of the **Italian Painting** gallery. The Italian Renaissance is the Met's Achilles heel – although the collection is fairly large, it includes few showstoppers and no canvases at all by either Michelangelo or da Vinci. Lamentations aside, highlights include **Mantegna**'s dark *Adoration of the Shepherds* and **Carlo Crivelli**'s distended, expressive *Madonna and Child*. It's worth seeking out the chunk of fresco by **Ghirlandaio** entitled *St Christopher and the Infant Christ*: it's in outstanding condition and retains many of the painted-on details – known as "*a secco*" – which were added once the plaster was dry and have eroded by now in other works of this kind. As for later pictures, there's Mannerist master **Bronzino**'s dapper but haughty *Portrait of a Young Man* and a showy **Raphael**, *Madonna and Child Enthroned with Saints*, which features his signature pin-up pretty Virgin Mary. There are also rooms filled with massive works by **Titian** and **Tintoretto**, though it's **Veronese**'s raunchy and artfully composed *Mars and Venus United by Love* that's especially appealing among the Venetians. For more Italian Renaissance works, head to the Lehman Pavilion at the museum's rear.

Dutch Painting

This collection, dominated by the major works of Rembrandt, Vermeer, and Hals, is the high point of the main European galleries – and the finest single group of paintings in the museum.

The Met's enviable stash of works by **Vermeer** – they own five of the existing forty canvases – should not be missed. He was the genius of the domestic interior, drawing quiet drama and deep emotion from everyday events. *Young Woman with a Water Jug* showcases his skill in composition and tonal gradation, not to mention his uncannily naturalistic sense of lighting. *A Maid Asleep* is deeper in its composition, or at least appears to be, the rich fabric separating the foreground from the rooms beyond. Vermeer often used this trick, and you'll see it again in *Allegory of the Faith*, where the drawn curtain presents the tableau and separates the viewer from the woman within. Most haunting of all is the great *Portrait of a Young Woman*: she's an odd-looking creature with huge doleful eyes and twinkly earrings, her enigmatic expression marking her as Vermeer's own Mona Lisa. Fans of Vermeer's work can see more of it a few blocks away in the Frick collection.

While Vermeer's paintings focused on stillness and light, the portraits of **Hals** and **Rembrandt** burst with life. At first, these galleries simply seem full of men in jaunty hats and ruffles, but the personalities of the sitters emerge on closer inspection, from the heavy-lidded world-weariness of Rembrandt's *Portrait of a Man* to Hals' almost-jovial *Portrait of a Bearded Man with Ruff*. Another standout is Rembrandt's beautiful painting of his common-law wife, Hendrike Stoffjels, finished three years before her early death. His tight-lipped *Self-Portrait* dates from 1660, when he went bankrupt, and prefigures the self-examination he brought to later works.

In addition to these three famous artists, the Dutch rooms also display a good selection of works by some of their lesser-known but equally intriguing contemporaries. Most memorable is **Pieter de Hooch**'s masterpiece *Two Men and a Woman in a Courtyard of a House*, with its perfect arrangement of line, form, and color. **Adriaen Brouwer** reveled in the seamier side of Dutch life. His raucous canvases, painted when he wasn't drunk or in prison, include *The Smokers*, a portrait of the artist and his drinking pals.

English Painting

Often overlooked in favor of the Flemish and Dutch works nearby, the Met's elegant collection of English pictures, though small, is of high quality. **Sir Thomas Lawrence**'s study of actress *Elizabeth Farren*, which he painted at the precocious age of 21, is impressive, as much for how well it conveys her spirited personality as for its technical mastery. A patrician counterpoint to the mischievous Farren is **Thomas Gainsborough**'s *Mrs Grace Dalrymple*, who's all long neck, big nose, and sloping shoulders. Several strapping works by **Sir Joshua Reynolds** and some shadowy, more sentimental portraits by **George Romney** complete the room.

Spanish Painting

The **Spanish** works at the Met are also of quite high quality. You'll pass through a smattering of Spanish paintings, including pictures by **Goya** and **Velázquez**, near the end of the Dutch and English masters as you loop back to the entrance of the painting galleries. The pick of Velázquez's work is the piercing and somber *Portrait of Juan de Pareja*, while Goya's widely reproduced portrait of a toddler in a red jumpsuit, *Don Manuel Osorio Manrique de Zuniga*, seems more sinister on second glance, what with the caged birds on the floor being menaced by three wide-eyed cats. Tacked onto the end of the Italian section is a room of freaky, dazzling canvases by **El Greco**, each of which underscores the jarring modernism of his approach – a few Picassos wouldn't look out of place scattered in here. Amid the swathes of El Greco's signature distorted bodies, note his *View of Toledo* – all brooding intensity as the skies seem about to swallow up the ghost-like town – one of the best of his works displayed anywhere in the world.

Early Flemish and Netherlandish Painting

A left turn from the preliminary rooms takes you to the galleries of Early Flemish and Netherlandish Painting from the fifteenth and sixteenth centuries, precursors of both the Northern and Italian Renaissances. Inevitably, the first paintings are by **Jan Van Eyck**, who is usually credited with beginning the

△ *Ugolino and His Sons*, Jean-Baptiste Carpeaux

tradition of North European realism. The freestanding panels of *The Crucifixion* and *The Last Judgment* were painted early in his career and are full of scurrying, startled figures, tightly composed with expressive and even horrific detail.

There are more Gothic allusions in **Rogier van der Weyden**'s *Christ Appearing to His Mother*, the apocryphal visit surrounded by tiny statuary depicting Christ's earlier, and Mary's later, life; its warmth of design and feeling contrast well with Van Eyck's hard draftsman's clarity. Another great Northern Gothic painter, **Gerard David**, used local settings for his religious scenes; the background of his exquisite *Virgin and Child with Four Angels* is medieval Bruges and *The Rest on the Flight to Egypt* features a forest glade, again with the turrets of Bruges visible down below. Head across to **Pieter Bruegel the Elder**'s *Harvesters* to see how these innovations were assimilated. Made charming by its snapshot ordinariness (check the sprawling figure napping under a tree), this is one of the Met's most reproduced pictures and part of the series of six paintings that included his (Christmas-card familiar) *Hunters in the Snow*. The rest of the galleries are packed with standard Flemish portraits, all high cheeks, strong jaws, and earnest expressions, though the penetrating, raised-eyebrow stare of **Hans Holbein the Younger**'s *Portrait of Herman Wedigh* is particularly eye-catching.

Impressionist Painting

15

Most visitors head directly to the Nineteenth-Century European Paintings and Sculpture gallery. To the far left, you'll find a smattering of Barbizon painters like **Millet** and **Corot**, as well as precursors of the **Impressionists** such as **Delacroix** and **Ingres**. The latter is well represented with *Mme Jacques-Louis Leblanc*, a matron with a glancing smile on her lips. Straight ahead are several works by **Manet**, the Impressionist movement's most influential predecessor, whose early style of contrasting light and shadow with modulated shades of black can be firmly linked to the traditions of Hals, Velázquez, and Goya. *The Spanish Dancer*, an accomplished example of this tradition, was well received on Manet's debut at the Paris Salon in 1861. Within a few years, he was shocking the same establishment with the striking *Young Lady in 1866*, thanks to his realistic portrayal of a girl in her peignoir.

The woman who modeled for both these canvases crops up again in the museum's collection of **Courbet**'s erotica: she's the centerpiece of the languid *Woman with a Parrot*, hair tousled as she lies back for the bird to land on her hand, a picture which gave Manet the idea for his later picture. Don't miss Courbet's equally voluptuous *The Woman in the Waves*. **Degas** fans will find studies here in just about every medium, from pastels to sculpture. Many examine one of his favorite themes: dancers. One lovely example is *Dancers Practicing at the Bar*. Also here is a casting of his *Little Dancer*: she's now a little forlorn, her real tutu, hair ribbon, and slippers having discolored over time.

Monet was one of the Impressionist movement's most prolific painters, returning again and again to a single subject in order to produce a series of images capturing different nuances of light and atmosphere. The Met's two-room hoard runs like Monet's Greatest Hits: the museum has a canvas from almost every major sequence by the artist, including *Waterlilies*, *Bridge at Giverny*, *Rouen Cathedral (The Portal in Sun)*, *The Houses of Parliament (Effect of Fog)*, and *Haystacks (Effect of Snow and Sun)*.

Cézanne's technique was very different. He labored long to achieve a painstaking analysis of form and color, an effect clear in the *Landscape of Marseilles*. Of his few portraits, the jarring, almost Cubist angles and spaces of the rather plain *Mme Cézanne in a Red Dress* seem years ahead of their time: she looks clearly pained, as if she'd rather be anywhere than under her husband's gaze. Take a look, too, at *The Card Players*, whose dynamic triangular structure thrusts out, yet retains the quiet concentration of the moment. Though there's also work here by every Impressionist name from **Berthe Morisot** to **Pisarro**, it's **Renoir** who's perhaps the best represented. Sadly, most of his works are from after 1878, when he began to move away from the techniques he'd learned while working with Monet and toward the chocolate-boxy soft focus that plagued his later work. Of these, *Mme Charpentier and Her Children* is a likeable enough piece, one whose affectionate tone manages to sidestep the sentimentality of Renoir's later work.

Post-Impressionist Painting

The rooms devoted to the **Post-Impressionists**, logically enough, follow those of Monet and Cézanne. One of the highlights of the collection is **Gauguin**'s masterly *La Orana Maria*. This Annunciation-derived scene, a Renaissance staple, has been transferred to a different culture in an attempt to unfold the symbolism, and perhaps voice the artist's feeling for the native South Sea islanders. *Two Tahitian Women* hangs adjacent – an example of skillful, studied simplicity.

Toulouse-Lautrec delighted in painting the world Gauguin went to Tahiti to escape: his pastels are displayed in dimly lit galleries much like the demimonde in which he moved. Look for *The Sofa*, which features two ugly, bored prostitutes – sparked by his dislike of posed modeling, it's one of a series of sketches he made in Paris brothels: the women awaiting clients were ideal subjects. Hookers aside, Lautrec loved the grotesques who populated the *fin de siècle* underworld, perhaps because he himself was such an outsider – he suffered from a genetic defect which weakened his bones, and left him only 4ft 11in tall as an adult.

All of this scratches little more than the surface of the galleries – for example, there are also more than a half-dozen canvases by **Van Gogh**. Many of them are fine works, especially his famed *Irises*, and the twisty, thrashing trees of *Cypresses*. Otherwise, make sure to stop by one of the two Pointillist pictures by the master of the technique, **Georges-Pierre Seurat**, who only finished a handful of works before his early death at age 32. This painstaking school of painting took the Impressionists' obsession with color to its natural extreme; its followers believed that mixing bright paints in a palette dimmed their brilliance and instead preferred to apply pure colors in pixel-sized dots, allowing the eye to blend them. The sparkling nighttime scene *Circus Sideshow* was the first attempt to replicate artificial light using these Technicolor dots; there's also a small canvas that was the final study for Seurat's masterpiece *Sunday Afternoon on the Island of La Grande Jatte*.

Asian Art

Also on the second floor are the **Asian Art** galleries, an impressive, schizophrenic collection that includes works in various mediums from most major civilizations (Japan, India, China) as well as an indoor replica of a Chinese garden. As you approach from the Great Hall balcony, there's an exhibit of fifth- to eighth-century Kuran pottery lining the back wall; look for the showy, technically impressive glazed and decorated ceremonial pieces among the everyday jugs and bowls. First up is **Chinese Sculpture**, a collection of stone works arranged around two serene, twenty-foot-high Buddhas. The focal point, however, is the enormous (and exquisite) fourteenth-century mural, *The Pure Land of Bhaishajyaguru*. This piece was carefully reconstructed after being severely damaged in an earthquake and is a study in calm reflection.

Take the right fork from this gallery to arrive at **South Asian Art**. The ancient pair of golden earrings from India are far more rare and precious than you might assume: custom dictated that personal jewelry be melted down after death and recast to avoid passing on that person's karma, so it's rare to find intact pieces like this. There's a vast, if rather monotonous, range of **statues** of Hindu and Buddhist deities here, alongside numerous pieces of friezes, many of which still possess exceptional detail despite years of exposure. *The Great Departure and the Temptation of the Buddha*, carved in the third century, is particularly lively: Siddhartha sets out on his spiritual journey, chased by a harem of dancing girls and grasping cherubs.

Past a set of stairs that leads to a small third-floor gallery (for temporary exhibits) lies **Chinese Art**. This is another overwhelming collection that's been crammed into its space; it may seem easier to skip over rather than tackle head on. Whatever you do, make sure you don't miss *Stele with Paired Bodhisattvas and Thousand Buddha Motif*, dating from the early eighth century AD. It's noteworthy and eye-catching for its use of dramatic black marble and for the painstaking effort in the carving of all those tiny Buddhas.

The highlight in this area is the **Chinese Garden Court**, a serene, minimalist retreat enclosed by the galleries, and the adjacent **Ming Room**, a typical salon decorated in period style with wooden lattice doors. Assembled by experts from the People's Republic, the naturally lit garden is representative of one found in Chinese homes: a pagoda, small waterfall, and stocked goldfish pond landscaped with limestone rocks, trees, and shrubs conjure up a sense of peace.

The Sackler Wing

After meditating in the garden, turn right toward the **Sackler Wing**, part of a cluster of rooms dedicated to **Japanese Art**. This collection has been organized very differently from much of the rest of the Met's holdings. It contains objects from the prehistoric to the present divided not chronologically but thematically, including "Gods and Ancestors," "Spirits and Teachers," "Characters in a Story," and "The Moral and Immoral." Complementing these displays

The Cantor Roof Garden

From May through October, you can ascend to the **Cantor Roof Garden**, located on top of the Lila Acheson Wallace Wing (see Modern Art, p.186). The leafy garden is an outdoor gallery, and each summer it's used to showcase contemporary sculpture (Roy Lichtenstein and Andy Goldsworthy have been recent subjects); it's also nominally a bar, though the mediocre drinks and pricey snacks aren't the reason to come here. The views are what draw most visitors – from this height, you can grasp how vast the park truly is; you're also within close view of Cleopatra's Needle. By far the best time to come for a cocktail is October, when the weather's cooler and the foliage has begun to turn.

To reach the garden, head for the southwest elevators on the first floor, just outside the Modern Art gallery – you'll find them if you head left of the main marble stairs in the entrance hall.

are rotating exhibits of textiles, paintings, and prints. Some of the oldest pieces in the collection are the *dogu*, female figurines dating from between 10,500 BC and 400 BC. Contrast these early works with those that appeared after the advent of Buddhism in the sixth century AD; it shifted the focus of Japanese art to exaggerated depictions of physical perfection, much as Mannerism did in Europe one thousand years later. The resulting distorted and distended figures can be seen in the **Buddhist** painting and sculpture collection.

All these trinkets are but a prelude to the undeniable showstopper here: several galleries of seventeenth- and eighteenth-century hand-painted **Kano screens**. The gorgeous, delicate screens range from the elegantly mundane (books on a shelf) to elaborate scenes of historical allusion and divine fervor. Also make sure to see the recreated *shoin* (study) room, which projects serenity and scholarly virtue. Since all the exhibited paintings, calligraphy, and scrolls of Asian art are rotated every six months or so, the scenes change, but their beauty remains constant.

The American Wing

Close to being a museum in its own right, the **American Wing** is a thorough introduction to the development of fine art in America. Enter from the **Charles Engelhard Court**, a shrub-filled sculpture garden enclosed at the far end by the Palladian *Facade of the Branch Bank of the United States*, salvaged in 1915 from Wall Street when the building was set to be demolished. Step through this facade and you'll be standing in Federal-period rooms, the first of 25 furnished historical rooms. On three floors (ground, first, and second), these rooms lie adjacent to the American Painting galleries and throb with Georgian grandeur. On the first-floor balcony, don't miss the iridescent Favrile glass of **Louis Comfort Tiffany**: an elegant Art Nouveau accompaniment to the decor.

American Painting

The **American Painting** collection begins on the second floor with a maze of rooms of eighteenth-century portraits. There are several works by **Benjamin West**, who worked in London and taught or influenced many of the American painters of his day – *The Triumph of Love* is typical of his Neoclassical, allegorical works. More heroics come with **John Trumbull**, one of West's pupils, in *Sortie Made by the Garrison of Gibraltar*, and the full-blown Romanticism of *Washington Crossing the Delaware* by **Emanuel Leutzes**. This enormous canvas shows Washington escaping across the river in the winter of 1776. Although historically and geographically inaccurate – the American flag, shown flowing dramatically in the background, hadn't yet been created – the picture is nonetheless a national icon.

Early in the nineteenth century, American painters embraced landscape painting and nature. **William Sidney Mount** depicted scenes of his native Long Island, often with a sly political angle, as he did in *Cider Makers* and *The Bet*. The painters of the **Hudson Valley School** glorified the landscape in their vast lyrical canvases. **Thomas Cole**, the school's doyen, is represented by *The Oxbow*, while his pupil **Frederic Church** has the immense *Heart of the Andes*, which combines the grand sweep of the mountains with minutely depicted flora. **Albert Bierstadt** and **S.R. Gifford** concentrated on the American West

– their respective works *The Rocky Mountains*, *Lander's Peak*, and *Kauterskill Falls* have a near-visionary idealism, bound to a belief that the westward development of the country was a manifestation of divine will.

Winslow Homer has most of a gallery to himself – a fitting tribute for the painter who so greatly influenced the late nineteenth-century American artistic scene. Homer began his career illustrating the Civil War – there's a good selection of those works, which show the tedium and sadness of that era. His talent in recording detail carried over into his late, quasi-Impressionistic seascapes, of which *Northeaster* is one of the finest.

The mezzanine below takes American art into the **late nineteenth and early twentieth centuries**. Some of the initial portraiture here tends to the sugary, but **J.W. Alexander**'s *Repose* deftly hits the mark – a simple, striking use of line and light with a sumptuous feel and more than a hint of eroticism. By way of contrast, there's **Thomas Eakin**'s subdued, almost ghostly *Max Schmitt in a Single Scull*; **Childe Hassam**'s *Avenue of the Allies: Great Britain 1918*, patriotic art filled with light and color; and **William Merritt Chase**'s *For the Little One*, an Impressionist study of his wife sewing. The collection is crowned with a selection of works by the best-known American artist of the era: James Abbott McNeill Whistler. The standout is *Arrangement in Flesh Color and Black: Portrait of Theodore Duret*, a realist portrait of one of the Impressionists' most supportive patrons – it's a tribute to Whistler's mastery of his technique that despite labouring on the painting for a long time, it retains the spontaneity of a sketch.

John Singer Sargent's reputation rests on his virtuoso portraits, like that of *Mr and Mrs I.N. Phelps Stokes*, in which the couple is purposefully elongated as if to emphasize their aristocratic characters. *The Portrait of Madam X* (Mme Pierre Gautreau, a celebrated Parisian beauty) was one of the most famous pictures of its day. Exhibited at the 1884 Paris salon, it was considered so improper that Sargent had to leave Paris for London. "I suppose it's the best thing I've done," he said wearily, on selling it to the Met a few years later.

Medieval Art

Although you could move straight to the **Medieval Art** from the American Wing, you'd miss out on the museum's carefully planned approach. Instead, enter these galleries via the corridor from the western end (or rear) of the Great Hall on the left of the main staircase. There you'll see displays of the sumptuous Byzantine metalwork and jewelry that financier **J.P. Morgan** donated to the museum in its early days. At the end of the corridor is the main sculpture hall, piled high with religious statuary and carvings like the tremendous *St Nicholas Saving Three Boys in the Brine Tub*; it's divided by a 52-foot-high *reja* – a decorative open-work, iron altar screen – from Valladolid Cathedral. If you're here in December, you'll see a highlight of New York's Christmas season: a beautifully decorated, twenty-foot-high Christmas tree lit up in the center of the sculpture hall. The **medieval treasury** to the right of the hall has an all-encompassing display of objects religious, liturgical, and secular. Beyond this are the **Jack and Belle Linski Galleries**: Flemish, Florentine, and Venetian painting, porcelain, and bronzes.

Scattered throughout the medieval galleries are **later period rooms**: paneled Tudor bedrooms and Robert Adam fineries from England, florid Rococo boudoirs and salons from France, and an entire Renaissance patio from Velez Blanco in Spain. It's all fascinating, but a bit much, leaving you with the feeling that Morgan and his robber-baron friends would probably have shipped Versailles over from France if they could have. If you want to see more of the Met's medieval holdings, head up to the Cloisters at the northern tip of Manhattan.

The Egyptian collection

The Met hogs a collection of more than 35,000 objects from Ancient Egypt, most of which are displayed to their full potential. Brightly efficient corridors steer you through the treasures of the museum's own digs during the 1920s and 1930s, as well as other art and artifacts from 3000 BC to the Byzantine period of Egyptian culture.

Prepare to be awed as you enter from the Great Hall on the first floor: the large **statuary**, **tombs**, and **sarcophagi** in the first few rooms are immediately striking. As you move into the interior galleries, the smaller, quieter sculptural pieces are also quite eye-catching. A beautifully crafted example is the *Carving of Senbi* in gallery nine; what was probably **Senbi's tomb** is displayed nearby along with other funerary objects like canopic jars. One of the museum's most precious pieces is the remarkably well-preserved cedar statue, *Ritual Figure*, with its jaunty mitre-style hat, the crown of Lower Egypt, and slender, but intact, staff. It was one of the earliest pieces to be uncovered by pioneering Egyptologists in the early twentieth century; one of a pair, its identical twin is in a museum in Cairo. Look, too, for the chipped dark-brown bust, *Face of Senwosret III*: with his realistically hollow cheeks and bug eyes, he stands out amid the idealized portraits of other rulers. In the room next door is the dazzling collection of **Princess Sit-Hathor-yunet jewelry**, a pinnacle in Egyptian decorative art from around 1830 BC.

The Temple of Dendur

At the end of the collection sits the **Temple of Dendur**, housed in a vast airy gallery lined with photographs and placards about the temple's history and its original site on the banks of the Nile. Built by the Emperor Augustus in 15 BC for the Goddess Isis of Philae, the temple was moved here as a gift from the Egyptian government during the construction of the Aswan High Dam in 1965 – otherwise it would have drowned. Though you can't walk all the way inside, you can go in just far enough to get a glimpse of the interior rooms, their walls chock-full of hieroglyphs. The temple itself is on a raised platform and surrounded by a narrow moat, which in the front widens to become a rather pretty reflecting pool, no doubt designed to make visitors think of the Nile – it doesn't, but is a nice touch anyway. The entire gallery is glassed-in on one side, and looks out onto Central Park; the most magical time for the temple is when it's illuminated at night and the gallery seems to glow, lending it an air of mystery that's missing during the day.

Greek and Roman Art

This is one of the largest collections of ancient art in the world, which is set to decamp to new, as-of-yet-unveiled quarters at the museum's southeastern corner sometime in 2007, following the completion of a three-phase renovation project; all pieces should remain on display after the new spaces open, if perhaps in different arrangements. In the meantime, the collection is exhibited in eight galleries on the ground floor, recreated according to original McKim, Mead and White designs. Enter from the southern end of the museum's Great Hall, and you'll soon find yourself in the **Belfer Court**, a sort of preamble to the exhibit. The court displays prehistoric and early Greek art – characterized by simpler, more geometric shapes and patterns, as in the fanciful **Minoan vase** in the shape of a bull's head from around 1400 BC and a charming sculpture of a seated man playing the harp from around 3000 BC. The central hall, which displays sixth- to fourth-century BC marble sculpture, including several large sphinxes, is flanked by three rooms on either side, each fully renovated, with exhibits arranged by theme, medium, and chronology. You'll find everything from large **funerary monuments** to tiny terracotta figures to intricately carved gold jewelry in the same room, with artfully arranged display cases that you can circle to get views from all angles. Standing in the center of the first gallery to the left of the central hall is a marble sculpture of a nude boy – known as the **New York Kouros** – one of the earliest examples of a *kouros*, or funerary statue, to have survived intact. Dating from 580 BC and originally from Attica, it marked the grave of the son of a wealthy family, created according to tradition as a memorial to ensure he would be remembered.

Art of Africa, the Pacific, and the Americas

Michael C. Rockefeller, son of Governor Nelson Rockefeller, disappeared during a trip to West New Guinea in 1961. In 1969, his father donated the entire collection of his **Museum of Primitive Art** – over 3300 works, plus library and photographic material – to the Met. This wing, on the first floor past the Greek and Roman galleries, stands as a memorial to Michael. It includes many Asmat objects, such as carved *mbis* (memorial poles), figures, and a canoe from Irian Jaya, alongside the Met's comprehensive collection of art from **Africa, the Pacific, and the Americas**.

It's a superb set of galleries, the muted, understated décor throwing the exhibits into sharp and often dramatic focus. The **African exhibit** offers an overview of the major geographic regions and their cultures, though West Africa is better represented than the rest of the continent. Particularly awe-inspiring is the display of art from the Court of Benin (in present-day Nigeria) – tiny carved ivory figures, created with astonishing detail.

The **Pacific collection** covers the islands of Melanesia, Micronesia, Polynesia, and Australia, and contains a wide array of objects, including wild, somewhat frightening, wooden masks with all-too-realistic eyes. Sadly, **Mexico, Central, and South America** get somewhat short shrift, though there is a nice collection of pre-Columbian jade, Mayan and Aztec pottery, and Mexican ceramic sculpture. But the best part by far is the entire room filled with South American gold jewelry and ornaments – particularly the exquisite hammered-gold nose ornaments and earrings from Peru and the richly carved, jeweled ornaments from Colombia.

Modern Art

Many people bypass the Met's **Modern Art** collection – housed over two floors in the Lila Acheson Wallace Wing (named in honor of the founder of *Reader's Digest*), directly to the rear of the Rockefeller Wing – in favor of its headline-grabbing Old Masters. That's a shame, since this is a fine hoard that includes several stunning individual works. There's a wide variety of pieces by most of the major names, ranging from mid-century experimental and abstract canvases to contemporary sculpture.

1905 to 1940

The first floor begins with the collection's most recent acquisitions and proceeds with a chronological installation of **American and European art from 1905 to 1940**: look for **Derain**'s Fauvist riot of color, *Fishing Boats, Collioure* and one of **Le Douanier Rousseau**'s creepy naive canvases, *The Repast of a Lion*. There's also visceral, bloody work by **Soutine** like *The Ray*, and **Modigliani**'s firm-breasted *Reclining Nude*, plus a room devoted to **Picasso** and his artistic rival **Matisse**. Works by the former range from the provocative, Blue-Period *The Blind Man's Meal*, through his Cubist Period to more familiar skewed-perspective portraits; there's also the famous 1906 portrait of Gertrude Stein that the writer bequeathed to the museum on her death and was the first Picasso picture to enter its collection. As for Matisse, there are early, more traditional works like *Promenade Along the Olive Trees* as well as later, more graphic canvases, which owe their simplicity to the arthritis that increasingly crippled the artist's hands.

American art from the period is displayed separately, including **Georgia O'Keeffe**'s moody *From the Faraway, Nearby* (which resembles nothing so much as a progressive rock album cover), and **Edward Hopper**'s *Tables for Ladies*. In addition, there is a small design collection, featuring rotating pieces of furniture, ceramics, and almost anything else from the museum's holdings.

1945 to the present

The top floor contains **European and American art from 1945 to the present**, from installations to abstracts. **Rachel Whiteread** is represented with her usual *Untitled* work – this time, two snow-white baths-cum-coffins – as is **Lucian Freud**, with a fleshy *Naked Man*, and **Chuck Close**, whose *Lucas* has the characteristic intense stare of the artist's giant portraits. Other highlights include **Ellsworth Kelly**'s playful *Spectrum V*, a thirteen-panel color-block installation that looks like a child's xylophone, **Andy Warhol**'s camouflage-patterned *Last Self-Portrait* from 1986 and **R.B. Kitaj**'s *John Ford on His Deathbed*, a dreamlike painting of the director of western movies. There's an entire room filled with the gigantic, jagged canvases of grumpy Abstract Expressionist **Clyfford Still** who once "repossessed" a picture by knifing it from its frame when he fell out with the owner. Another Abstract Expressionist, **Mark Rothko**, is represented with one of his signature canvases filled with bright, sketchy boxes of color – *White, Red on Yellow*; don't miss Jasper Johns' *White Flag* either – a monochrome collage of the Stars and Stripes, built up piecemeal using scraps of newsprint, fabric, and beeswax.

The Lehman Pavilion

Another of the Met's many gems, the two-floor **Lehman Pavilion** was tacked on to the rear of the Met in 1975 to house the holdings of Robert Lehman, a relentless collector and scion of the Lehman Brothers banking family. Lehman bequeathed his entire collection – an impressive and eclectic mix – to the museum with the stipulation that it be displayed separately from the rest of the Met's holdings. He also wished the galleries to retain the appearance of a private home rather than a public institution, and approved the plans for this extension – an octagonal building centered on a brilliantly lit atrium – just before his death. Some of the galleries actually resemble rooms in his former mansion, though the layout of artworks is different. The overall impression is of a charmingly cluttered grand old house.

Italian Renaissance art

Lehman's artistic interests fill important gaps in the Met's collection, notably the **Italian Renaissance**. This period was his passion, and his personal hoard includes some standout works like the tiny, easily missed *Annunciation* by **Botticelli**; it's stashed in a glass cabinet in the first room. More impressive are the Venetian works, including a glassy *Madonna and Child* by **Bellini** in which Mary looks like a 1920s screen goddess, and cartoonish wooden icons by **Carlo Crivelli** featuring a grumpy St Peter. There are Byzantine-inflected works from Siena by **Giovanni di Paolo**, notably the *Expulsion from Paradise*, in which an angel gently ushers Adam and Eve from Eden, while white-bearded God, surrounded by feathered blue angels, points to their place of banishment; don't miss the same painter's large and glitzy *Coronation of the Virgin*.

Other Old Master paintings

As for **non-Italian art**, Lehman evidently liked **Ingres**, whose languid, sculptural portrait of the *Princesse de Broglie* in her bright-blue dress sparkles on the wall; similarly impressive is **Goya**'s *Countess of Altamira and Her Daughter*, the soft pink of her outfit contrasting sharply with her plain features. One picture stands out from them all, though: **Rembrandt**'s unflinching *Portrait of Gerard de Lairesse*. Although de Lairesse was supposedly disliked for his luxurious tastes and unpleasant character, his most apparent flaw was his grotesquely disfigured face – his bug eyes and snout-like nose are evidence of the ravages of congenital syphilis.

The final galleries at the rear of the building house **Northern European works**, including a tiny portrait of *Erasmus of Rotterdam* by **Hans Holbein the Younger** – barely six inches high, it still throbs with his usual psychological acuity. Look, too, for **Petrus Christus**'s highly symbolic *A Goldsmith in His Shop*. Banished to the walls of the atrium are the lesser works in Lehman's collection, mostly uninteresting **Impressionist** works from **Derain** and **Cézanne**, two late **Renoirs**, and several canvases by **Edouard Vuillard**; one work worth looking for in the atrium display, however, is **Balthus**'s creamy and disturbing *Nude with a Mirror*.

The Upper East Side

The defining characteristic of Manhattan's **Upper East Side**, a two-square-mile grid that runs from 59th to 96th streets and includes **Fifth**, **Madison**, and **Park avenues**, is wealth. While other neighborhoods have been affected by influxes of immigrant groups and changing artistic trends, this area has remained an enclave of the well-off since they migrated here from downtown in the late nineteenth century. Largely residential, the buildings are all well-preserved and the streets clean and relatively safe; dotted between the luxurious apartments are some of the city's finest museums and upscale shops. Recent squeezes in the housing market have produced waves of high-rise construction and brownstone restoration on the avenues and streets east of **Lexington Avenue**, by far the more affordable part of the neighborhood. Still farther east, in the middle of the East River, sits **Roosevelt Island**, an area distinctly different from the rest of the city, and one that many Manhattanites frequently forget is there.

Fifth Avenue

Fifth Avenue has been the haughty patrician face of Manhattan since Central Park opened in 1876. Wealthy families like the Carnegies, Astors, Vanderbilts, and Whitneys were lured north from lower Fifth Avenue and Gramercy Park by the green space, and they built their fashionable residences alongside the park. Their migration made Upper Fifth Avenue not only an acceptable place to live but also a stylish one; to this day Fifth Avenue addresses remain so prestigious that buildings that front the thoroughfare but lack entrances onto it go by their would-be Fifth Avenue addresses rather than their more accurate sidestreet numbers. The park-side buildings on Fifth Avenue went up when Neoclassicism was the rage, so the surviving originals are cluttered with columns and classical statues. A great deal of what you see, though, is third- or fourth-generation construction; enormous single-family mansions sprouted up here throughout the late nineteenth century, lasting only ten or fifteen years before they were demolished and replaced with apartment buildings.

Upper Fifth Avenue is nicknamed "**Museum Mile**" – it is home to New York's greatest concentration of art museums and other exhibitions, several of which are housed in the area's few remaining mansions. Henry Clay Frick's House at East 70th Street, marginally less ostentatious than its neighbors, is now the intimate and tranquil home of the **Frick Collection**, one of the city's

El Barrio & Harlem

UPPER EAST SIDE

RESTAURANTS & CAFÉS

Aureole	32
Barking Dog Luncheonette	1
Café Boulud	22
Café Sabarsky in the Neue Galerie	9
Caffe Buon Gusto	23
Carino	5
Daniel	29
Dawat	36
Donguri	12
E.A.T.	15
Ecco-La	2
Elaine's	4
Etats-Unis	16
Googie's Diner	19
Heidelberg	10
King's Carriage House	14
Lenox Room	27
Le Refuge	13
Mariella Pizza	34
Maya	30
Mocca Hungarian	17
Payard Patisserie & Bistro	28
Persepolis	25
Pig Heaven	18
Rectangles	26
Rohrs, M.	11
Saigon Grill	7
Serendipity 3	35
Sushi of Gari	20
Taco Taco	3
Tal Bagels	8
Viand	31
Wildgreen Café	6

BARS

American Trash	24
Brother Jimmy's	21
Subway Inn	33

ACCOMMODATION

Mark	A
Wales	B
Wanderers Inn Hostel East	C

Museo del Barrio

Museum of the City of New York

Mount Sinai Hospital

Jewish Museum

YORKVILLE

Cooper-Hewitt Museum

Church of Heavenly Rest

National Academy of Design

Ruppert Park

Guggenheim Museum

Gracie Mansion

Church of the Holy Trinity

Neue Galerie

Henderson Place

Carl Schurz Park

Metropolitan Museum of Art

Cherokee Apartments

John Jay Park

The Cottages

Whitney Museum

Central Park

St James Church

Asia Society

Sotheby's

Frick Collection

Seventh Regiment Armory

Park East Synagogue

Roosevelt House

Cosmopolitan Club

Temple Emanu-El

Museum of American Illustration

Mount Vernon Hotel Museum and Garden

Roosevelt Island Tram

Colony Club

Metropolitan Club

Bloomingdale's

QUEENSBOROUGH BRIDGE

Plaza Hotel

GRAND ARMY PLAZA

Harmonie Club

MIDTOWN EAST

East River

FDR DRIVE

Queens & Roosevelt Island

0   500 yds

16

189

must-see spots, while the controversial, modern structure of the **Guggenheim** is farther north at 89th Street.

Grand Army Plaza to the Frick

Grand Army Plaza marks the shift between Fifth Avenue's fancy shopping – in the blocks to the south – and its fancy living – in the grand mansions to the north. This oval, formed where Fifth Avenue hits Central Park South (as 59th Street is known while it runs along the park's southern edge), is one of the city's most dramatic public spaces, although the buzz of traffic often means pedestrians give it barely a second glance. There's a showy fountain plus a dazzling gold statue of Civil War General William Tecumseh Sherman on horseback. When Sherman was replated in the late 1990s, locals complained that the gold was too bright; New York's pollution has quickly taken care of that problem. To the south stands the extended copper-lined chateau of the **Plaza Hotel** – now being converted to condominiums – with the dark, swooping facade of the **Solow Building** behind it. Across the plaza to the east, you'll see the imposing **General Motors Building**, home to one of the last surviving branches of the fabled toy store F.A.O. Schwarz; the chain declared bankruptcy in 2003, though a white-knight investor snapped up two locations (here and Las Vegas) and relaunched them in 2004. Continuing north, Fifth Avenue and its sidestreets are dotted with **private clubs** that served, and still cater to, the city's wealthy (see box, below).

America's largest reform synagogue, the **Temple Emanu-El**, stands on the corner of 65th Street and Fifth Avenue (Mon–Fri 9.30am–4.45pm; free;

Members only

When industrialists like **J.P. Morgan** and **William and Cornelius Vanderbilt** arrived on the New York social scene in the 1890s, established society still looked askance at bankers and financiers – the city's new money. Downtown social clubs were kept closed to Morgan and anyone else considered less than up to snuff. Not one to be slighted, Morgan commissioned Stanford White to design a club for him – one that would be bigger, better, and grander than all the rest. Such was the birth of the **Metropolitan Club**, 1 E 60th St at Fifth Ave, an exuberant construction with a marvelously outrageous gateway: just the thing to greet its affluent members (both then and now).

Another group of New Yorkers unwelcome in the downtown clubs, prosperous Jews, founded the elegant **Harmonie Club** in the 1850s, building its home at 4 E 60th St (across the road from the Metropolitan) around the same time. The perceived effrontery of so many **parvenus** led to a mushrooming of private societies, including the **Kinckerbocker Club**, a handsome Federal-style structure on the corner of Fifth Avenue and 62nd Street, which was founded in 1913 in response to the "relaxed standards" of the **Union Club**, 101 E 69th St at Park Ave, which had finally admitted several friends of Morgan and the Vanderbilts.

All the clubs, both restrictive and lax, refused to open their doors to women. In 1903, with the opening of the **Colony Club**, 564 Park Ave at 62nd Street, the ladies fought back, founding the first social club for members of their sex. The **Cosmopolitan Club**, 122 E 66th St at Park Ave, also opened as a women's institution. An elaborate Colonial building with extensive gymnasium and spa facilities, it was originally a place for the rich to send their governesses, though the matriarchs eventually claimed the building for their own use. It's a strange, apartment-like structure, with a private garden in the back, and ironwork terraces reminiscent of New Orleans.

☎212/744-1400). The brooding Romanesque-Byzantine cavern – a dark, moody, and contemplative place – manages to feel bigger inside than it looks from outside. There's also a smallish on-site museum on the second floor, accessible via the 65th Street entrance (Sun–Thurs 10am–4.30pm; free); its three rooms hold both temporary exhibits on religious themes like the Kabbalah as well as an artifact-heavy history of the temple itself.

The streets off Fifth Avenue are a trim mix of apartment houses and elegant townhouses. One of the most beautiful private homes in the area is the triple-fronted **Ernesto and Edith Fabbri House**, 11 E 62nd St at Fifth Avenue. It was built around 1900 for a Vanderbilt daughter in a Beaux-Arts style, with curving iron balconies and ornate stonework – note the high security railings that enclose its first floor. The **Sarah Delano Roosevelt Memorial House**, 47 E 65th St at Madison Ave, was commissioned by Mrs Roosevelt as a town-house for her son Franklin in 1908. This street has a decidedly presidential air: after leaving the White House, Richard Nixon lived for a few years at no. 142.

The Frick Collection

A spectacular feat of acquisitive good taste, the **Frick Collection**, 1 E 70th St at Fifth Ave, is one of New York's finest sights (Tues–Sat 10am–6pm, Sun 11–5pm; $15; ☎212/288-0700, ⊛www.frick.org). Housed in his former mansion, the collection consists of the art treasures amassed by **Henry Clay Frick**, one of New York's most ruthless robber barons. Uncompromising and anti-union, Frick broke strikes at his coal and steel plants with state troopers and was hated enough to provoke a number of attempts on his life. The legacy of his ill-gotten gains – he spent millions on the best of Europe's art – is a superb assembly of works, and as good a glimpse as you'll find of the sumptuous life enjoyed by New York's early industrialists.

Opened in the mid-1930s, for the most part the museum has been kept as it looked when the Fricks lived there at the beginning of the twentieth century. What sets it apart from most galleries – and the reason many rate the Frick so highly – is that it strives hard to be as unlike a museum as possible. There is no wall text describing the pictures, though you can dial up info on each piece using the handheld guides available in the lobby (included with the price of admission). There are few ropes, fresh flowers on every table, and chairs provided for weary visitors, even in the most sumptuously decorated rooms. Make sure you pay a visit to the enclosed central courtyard, where marble floors, fountains, and greenery, all simply arranged, exude serenity.

A gallery on the ground level shows temporary exhibits from the permanent collection, as well as pieces on loan from other institutions (other temporary groupings may be shown in the Oval Room or the Garden Court). It's a more modern space; the pale walls and carpets are designed not to compete with whatever is on display. Accessible only by a steep spiral staircase just to the left outside the entry hall, it's easy to miss unless you're looking for it.

The collection

The collection itself was acquired under the direction of Joseph Duveen, a notorious – and not entirely trustworthy – adviser to the city's richest resi-dents in the late 1800s. He seems to have picked out the cream of Europe's post–World War I private art collections for Frick, including a magnificent array of Old Master works. In some ways, the collection here rivals the much larger holdings of the Met, especially in the quality of Italian Renaissance pieces, an area in which the Met is comparatively weak.

Keep an open mind as you start your visit in the **Boucher Room**. With its flowery walls, overdone furniture, and Boucher's Rococo representations of the arts and sciences in gilded frames, it is not to modern tastes. More reserved English pictures pack the nearby **Dining Room**: look for Reynolds' bug-eyed but determined *General Burgoyne* as well as lighter portraits by Romney and Gainsborough, whose *St James's Park* is a study in social mores – there isn't a woman walking under the trees who isn't assessing the competition. The other irresistible painting here is Hogarth's *Miss Mary Edwards*: this portrait of a feisty heiress hums with personality. Outside in **the hall** there's more of Boucher's work, including the cutesy *Four Seasons* canvases, starring his signature doll-eyed women, while in the **Fragonard Room** is the painter's *Progress of Love* series, painted for Louis XV's mistress Madame du Barry but discarded by her soon afterwards.

The **Living Hall** houses one of the most impressive Renaissance pictures anywhere in America: Bellini's sublime *St Francis in the Desert*. Stunningly well preserved, the picture suggests Francis's vision of Christ. This canvas unfairly overshadows the rest of the pieces in the room, although also notable are a couple of knockout portraits by Hans Holbein the Younger, including the masterpiece *Sir Thomas More*, whose world-weariness is graphically evidenced by his eye bags and five-o'clock shadow, as well as El Greco's restrained *St Jerome*. In the **South Hall** hangs Vermeer's saucy and suggestive *Officer and Laughing Girl*, as well as a haughty, highly detailed portrait of *Lodovico Capponi* by Bronzino. Move into the **Library** to see more British pictures, such as Reynolds' *Lady Taylor*, who's dwarfed by her huge blue ribbon and feather hat, and one of Constable's *Salisbury Cathedral* series; there's also a portrait of Frick himself here, as a white-bearded old man. Across in the **North Hall**, look for a beguiling portrait by Ingres, *Comtesse d'Haussonville*; with her heart-shaped face and ample arms, she's a period beauty.

The **West Gallery** is another important space: the long, elegant room is decorated with dark-green walls and carpet, a concave glass ceiling, and ornately carved wood trim. There's a clutch of snazzy Dutch pictures here, including a set of piercing self-portraits by Rembrandt and a couple of uncharacteristically informal portraits of Frans Snyders and his wife by Van Dyck, Frick's favorite artist. This gallery is also the location of the last picture Frick himself bought before his death in 1919: Vermeer's seemingly unfinished *Mistress and Maid*, a snapshot of an intimate moment.

At the far end of the West Gallery is the tiny **Enamel Room**, named for the exquisite set of mostly sixteenth-century Limoges enamels on display. There's also a collection of small altarpieces by Piero della Francesca; it's another sign of Frick's good taste that he snapped up work by this artist, who is now one of the acknowledged Italian masters but was little regarded in the nineteenth century. Though most are done by his workshop rather than della Francesca's own hand, the picture of *St John the Evangelist* is suffused with his characteristic stillness. The **Oval Room** at the other end of the West Gallery is jarringly modern, filled with a quartet of pretty portraits by Whistler, while the **East Gallery** displays a mishmash of styles and periods: look for Van Dyck's *Paolo Adorno* (size alone makes it unmissable) and *Lord Derby and His Family*, whose little girl fizzes with mischief.

Neue Galerie

On the corner of 86th Street stands the former Vanderbilt mansion, which in 2001 was transformed into the **Neue Galerie**, 1048 Fifth Ave (Mon, Thurs, Sat

& Sun 11am–6pm, Fri 11am–9pm; $15; ☏212/628-6200, ⊛www.neuegalerie
.org). The museum is dedicated to the arts, furniture, and crafts of Germany
and Austria from the nineteenth and twentieth centuries, a distinct group of
works. The most impressive part of the collection is on the second floor, where
a host of turn-of-the-century Viennese works focus on the likes of **Egon
Schiele** and **Oskar Kokoschka**, examining their impact on architecture and
design in Austria. Temporary exhibitions are housed upstairs, but when there's
no traveling show in town, expect twentieth-century works from all the major
art movements in Germany, from Bauhaus to the Brücke group, with greats
like Paul Klee and Vasily Kandinsky along the way. At the Neue's *Café Sabarsky*
(see p.323), you can pause for exquisite Viennese pastries before heading back
to Museum Mile.

The Guggenheim Museum

Multistory parking garage or upturned beehive? Whatever you may think of the
collection, it's the **Guggenheim Museum** building, 1071 Fifth Ave at 89th St,
that steals the show (Mon–Wed, Sat & Sun 10am–5.45pm, Fri 10am–8pm; $18,
last ticket sold 5.15pm, Fri 7.40pm; ☏212/423-3500, ⊛www.guggenheim.org).
The structure, designed by **Frank Lloyd Wright** specifically for the museum,
caused a storm of controversy when it was unveiled in 1959, bearing, as it did,
little relation to the statuesque apartment buildings of this most genteel part
of Fifth Avenue. Reactions ranged from disgusted disbelief to critical acclaim
– "one of the greatest rooms erected in the twentieth century," wrote Philip
Johnson, himself no slouch in the architectural genius stakes. Ornery Wright
missed much of the criticism, though, since he died six months before construction was completed. Time has been kinder than his contemporaries – nearly half
a century later, the museum is now a beloved New York landmark.

The institution's namesake, **Solomon R. Guggenheim** (1861–1949), was
one of America's richest men, thanks
to his silver and copper mines. As
with other nineteenth-century
American capitalists, the only problem for Guggenheim was how to
spend his vast wealth; he chose
to collect Old Masters – a hobby
he continued half-heartedly until
the 1920s, when various sorties to
Europe brought him into contact
with the most avant-garde and
influential of European art circles.
Although abstract art was considered little more than a fad at the
time, Guggenheim, always a man
with an eye for a sound investment,
began collecting modern paintings
with fervor. He bought wholesale
the canvases of **Kandinsky**, then
added works by **Chagall**, **Klee**, and
Léger, among others, and exhibited
them to a bemused American public
in his suite of rooms in the *Plaza
Hotel*. The Guggenheim Foundation

△ Guggenheim Museum

was created in 1937; after exhibiting the collection in various rented spaces, it commissioned Wright to design a permanent home. The Foundation now includes museums in Berlin, Bilbao, Las Vegas, and Venice (which is named for Solomon's niece Peggy, another art-collecting magpie).

The building

Collection of art aside, it's the structure that dominates – it's not hard to theorize that the egomaniacal Wright engineered it that way. Most visitors find it difficult to not be impressed (or sidetracked) by the tiers of cream concrete overhead. The circular galleries rise upward at a not-so-gentle slope, so you may prefer to start at the top of the museum and work your way down; most of the temporary exhibits are designed to be seen that way. A word to the wise: restroom facilities are hard to find and lines are long; it's probably best to hit a nearby café before arriving at the museum.

Proposed changes to the Guggenheim have historically caused an uproar, as proved by the debate in the early 1990s over the museum's extension. The building was closed for two years, during which the original Wright structure underwent a $60-million facelift. The whole building was then opened to the public for the first time: offices, storage rooms, and bits of chicken wire were all removed to expose the uplifting interior spaces so that the public could experience the spiral of the central rotunda from top to bottom. At the same time, a clever extension added the sort of tall, straight-walled, flat-floored galleries that the Guggenheim needed to adapt to its distinct shape. Much like the original structure, though the extension's merits were debated at the time, they are now acknowledged to have created a much better, and more visitor-friendly, museum.

More recently, the museum was caught in a fresh storm of controversy after the media-savvy director, **Thomas Krens**, tried to duplicate the museum with outposts in Vegas and Rio. Some of the Upper East Side's arty set called for his scalp after the first new location, in Vegas, failed spectacularly – a partnership with the Hermitage in St Petersburg, Russia, the massive space couldn't attract enough visitors and is now derelict; only a tiny salon remains open to show a capsule collection of pictures. The Rio museum is set to debut in 2007, and patrons are anxiously waiting to see what happens there.

The collection

The museum's permanent holdings have been bolstered since Guggenheim's day via acquisitions and donations – the collection has broadened in scope to span the late 1800s through most of the twentieth century. A significant gift came in 1976 when collector Justin K. Thannhauser handed over works by **Cézanne**, **Degas**, **Gauguin**, **Manet**, **Toulouse-Lautrec**, **Van Gogh**, and **Picasso**, among others, greatly enhancing the museum's Impressionist and Post-Impressionist holdings. It's almost overwhelming to walk into the Thannhauser Collection and immediately see Cézanne's *Still Life: Plate of Peaches*, *Bend in the Road Through the Forest*, and *Bibémus*; that said, things only improve from there. Next in line are a Degas, *Dancers in Green and Yellow*; two works by Van Gogh, *Landscape with Snow* and *Mountains at Saint Remy*; Monet, with *The Palazzo Ducale Seen from San Giorgio*; and several pieces by Picasso. The collection of Picasso highlights the period between 1900 to 1931, with notable works such as *Le Moulin de la Galette* (1900), the bizarre *Accordionist* (1911), and the recognizable *Woman with Yellow Hair* (1931).

Though you'll be able to see the entire museum in an afternoon, two galleries offer a representative sample of the Guggenheim's **permanent collection** if you're really running short on time (though bear in mind that they are often the two busiest galleries in the museum). The first, on the second floor of the tower, gives a quick but comprehensive look at the **Cubists**. The other, in the restored small rotunda, offers a collection of **Impressionist, Post-Impressionist**, and early modern masterpieces, like Picasso's scratchy *Woman Ironing* and a figurative work from Le Douanier Rousseau, *The Football Players*.

Ironically, given Guggenheim's eminent position in the twentieth-century art world, it's not his permanent collection that usually makes the news: it's the magnificent **temporary exhibitions** in the main rotunda. Most temporary shows are linked, albeit tenuously, to pieces in the permanent collection – during his tenure as museum director, Krens has overseen shows on the likes of the motorbike and Giorgio Armani as well as the modern-art surveys the museum was once best known for. Although some may find Krens' headline-chasing grating, he knows how to put on a good show, both literally and figuratively, and the temporary exhibitions rarely disappoint.

The National Academy of Design

A group of artists, including Samuel Morse, founded the little-known **National Academy of Design**, 1083 Fifth Ave at 89th St, in 1825 (Wed & Thurs noon–5pm, Fri–Sun 11am–6pm; $10; ☎212/369-4880, ⊛www.nationalacademy.org). It was intended to ape London's prestigious Royal Academy, and is housed in the Huntington Mansion, a bow-fronted, Beaux-Arts townhouse owned by Archer Huntington, whose father made a fortune in San Francisco overseeing early American railways; Archer's wife, Anna, was a sculptor of some note in her own right and one of her pieces graces the main floor of the rotunda here.

The member list of the National Academy has included big names like **Richard Diebenkorn**, **Chuck Close**, **Robert Rauschenberg**, and **Jasper Johns**. Each artist – famous, notorious, or neither – is required to donate a picture to the place when they join, but the rotating exhibit spaces on the second and fourth floors are filled with fine, if largely unremarkable, pieces, mostly portraits, by maestros few other than art-world insiders would recognize. The Academy is also home to a School of Fine Arts, whose students occasionally exhibit their work here.

The Cooper-Hewitt National Design Museum

The **Cooper-Hewitt National Design Museum**, 2 E 91st St at Fifth Ave, is part of the Smithsonian network, and offers impressive shows, so it's a shame that it's rarely on visitors' itineraries (Tues–Thurs 10am–5pm, Fri 10am–9pm, Sat 10am–6pm, Sun noon–6pm; $12; ☎212/849-8400, ⊛www.ndm.si.edu). The displays are housed in a mansion commissioned by millionaire industrialist Andrew Carnegie; when he decided to build at what was, in 1898, the unfashionable end of Fifth Avenue, he asked for "the most modest, plainest and most roomy house in New York." What he got (after four years and $1.5 million) was a bit more than that: a beautiful, spacious mansion with dark wood-paneled walls, carved ceilings, and parquet floors – too decorative to be plain, too large to be modest. The frilly green copper portico above the main entrance is especially enchanting. Inside, two floors of temporary exhibits focus on the history, nature, and evolution of design and decorative arts – commercial, utilitarian, and high art.

Very little of the large permanent collection is on view to the public, except when pieces are involved in the museum's temporary exhibitions, which run continuously. The temporary shows are worth checking out: recent standouts included a thematic show exploring the design and impact of hotels. Skillful curatorial work and insightful commentaries make a trip to this museum highly entertaining, and the building itself is worth a look, too. Themes vary, so before you go check what's on, to make sure it's to your taste.

The adjacent **Design Resource Center** is open by appointment, and can provide access to the museum's library, archives, and four curatorial departments, which hold 40,000 objects in Applied Arts and Industrial Design, 160,000 Drawings and Prints, and 40,000 examples of Wallcoverings and Textiles, some dating from the first century AD.

The Jewish Museum

Given how Jewish culture has flourished in New York, it is fitting that the **Jewish Museum**, 1109 Fifth Ave at 92nd St, is the largest museum of Judaica outside Israel (Mon–Wed & Sun 11am–5.45pm, Thurs 11am–8pm, Fri 11am–3pm; $10, Thurs 5–8pm pay what you wish; ☎212/423-3200, ⓦwww.jewishmuseum.org). The museum's centerpiece is a permanent presentation of Jewish culture, including Judaism's basic tenets and values, as it has developed over four thousand years. The exhibition seeks to answer the question, "What constitutes the essence of Jewish identity?"; a collection of Hanukkah lamps, on view throughout the year, is a highlight. More vibrant, however, are the changing displays of works by major international artists and the theme exhibitions, both of which sometimes incorporate pieces from the permanent collection. The Jewish Museum also sponsors a varied media program, including a film festival.

The Museum of the City of New York

The sweet, if rather dainty, **Museum of the City of New York**, 1220 Fifth Ave at 103rd St, is housed in another repurposed mansion, this time a smaller and later neo-Georgian example (Tues–Sun 10am–5pm; $7; ☎212/534-1672, ⓦwww.mcny.org). The permanent collection provides a history of the city from Dutch times to the present, displaying prints, photographs, costumes, and furniture across four floors. There's also a film narrated by Stanley Tucci – a quick and painless must-see that puts the museum (and city) into perspective. It runs on a loop and glosses over New York's 400-year history in 25 minutes, so put your seatbelt on. The most engaging of the permanent exhibits is "New York Toy Stories," that consists of all manner of motion toys, board games, sports equipment, and doll houses (look for the one with original artwork by **Duchamp** and **Lachaise**) dating from the late 1800s to today. Only one room in the gallery is currently open; the rest are closed indefinitely for renovations.

Madison Avenue

Immediately east of Fifth Avenue is **Madison Avenue**, the swankiest shopping street in the city. This strip was entirely residential until the 1920s, though you'd never know it now, lined as it is with the offerings of high-end jewelers and designers. It's also where you'll find the establishment-baiting **Whitney Museum of American Art**, as well as the tiny **Margo Feiden Galleries**,

699 Madison Ave at 63rd St, which display the work of the great New York caricaturist Al Hirschfeld, famous for his line drawings of Broadway stars. The other notable exception to the glitz is the stately and elaborate neo-Gothic facade of **St James' Church**, 865 Madison Ave at 71st St (T212/288-4100), with its graceful, gilded Byzantine-inspired altar; it's best known as the place where the funeral service for Jacqueline Kennedy Onassis was held.

The Whitney Museum of American Art

In a gray, arsenal-like building designed in 1966 by Marcel Breuer, the **Whitney Museum of American Art**, 945 Madison Ave at 75th St, has – from the outside at least – a suspiciously institutional air (Wed, Thurs, Sat, & Sun 11am–6pm, Fri 1–9pm; $12; T1-800/WHITNEY or 212/570-3676, www .whitney.org). Once inside the exhibition space, though, first impressions prove wildly off-base: not only does the Whitney incorporate some of the best-designed exhibition space in the city, but the intelligent, challenging shows, designed from its eminent collection of twentieth-century American art, are outstanding.

    Gertrude Vanderbilt Whitney, a sculptor and champion of American art, established the Whitney Studio in 1914 to exhibit the work of living American artists who could not find support in established art circles – she was the first to exhibit Edward Hopper in 1920. By 1929 she had collected more than 500 works by various artists, all of which she offered, with a generous endowment, to the Met. When her offer was refused, she set up her own museum in Greenwich Village in 1930, with her collection as its core exhibit. The small museum soon outgrew its Village home, and, after several interim moves, relocated to its current spot in 1966. The Brutalist building was initially a controversial addition to the neat townhouses of the Upper East Side, but it's a sign of how beloved the structure has become that plans to wreck its integrity with a Neoclassical addition were shouted down in the late 1990s. Forced to find more space, the Whitney kicked its administrative offices off-site and transformed the fifth floor into additional gallery space.

    Like many of the other institutions in this neighborhood, the Whitney is best known for its superb **temporary exhibitions**, to which it devotes most of its time and rooms (and even stairwells). Many of these exhibitions are retrospectives of established artists or debuts of their lesser-known counterparts: Jasper Johns, Cy Twombly, and Cindy Sherman were all given their first retrospectives here, and hipster photographer Ryan McGinley also had a solo show. But the most thought-provoking exhibitions push the boundaries of art as a concept – strong showings of late have been in the realms of video installations (incorporating names such as Bill Viola and Nam June Paik) and computer and digital technology.

    Without a doubt, though, the Whitney is most famous for its **Biennial**, which was first held in 1932 and continues to occur between March and June in even-numbered years. Designed to give a provocative overview of what's happening in contemporary American art, it's often panned by critics, sometimes for good reason. Nonetheless, the Biennial is always packed with visitors: catch it if you can.

The collection

The museum owns more than 12,000 paintings, sculptures, photographs, and films by almost 2000 artists as diverse as Calder, Nevelson, O'Keeffe, de Kooning, Rauschenberg, and LeWitt. For an overview of its holdings, see the

Highlights of the Permanent Collection, a somewhat arbitrary pick of the Whitney's best: the fifth floor takes you from Hopper to the mid-century, while the second floor brings you from Jackson Pollock to today. The works form a superb introduction to twentieth-century American art, best evaluated with the help of the free gallery talks designed to explain the paintings and sculptures, and their place within various movements.

Included in the Highlights is **Gaston Lachaise**'s *Standing Woman*, which greets visitors at the entrance to the fifth floor. The bronze statue is modeled after Isabel Dutaud Nagle, Lachaise's muse. Just over *Standing Woman*'s left shoulder, **George Bellows**' painting, *Dempsey and Firpo*, captures what many sports photographers today try for: the moment of the fallen champion. Though here Jack Dempsey is catapulted from the ring, he actually pulled it together and won the 1923 duel at the Polo Grounds. **Robert Henri**'s 1916 painting *Gertrude Vanderbilt Whitney*, also grouped with the Highlights, is an ode to the woman who defied the rules that defined her generation. While her neighbors collected stuffy, traditional art, Whitney was interested in a more sensuous experience. She appears in pants, a *faux pas* at the time. Consequently, the painting was never shown in her Fifth Avenue mansion.

In deference to its origins, the rest of the permanent collection is particularly strong on **Edward Hopper** (2000 of his works were bequeathed to the museum in 1970), and several of his best paintings are here. *Early Sunday Morning* is typical of many of his works: it focuses on light and shadow, a bleak urban landscape, uneasily tense in its lighting and rejection of topical detail. The street could be anywhere (in fact it's Seventh Avenue); for Hopper, it becomes universal. Additional major bequests include a significant number of works by **Milton Avery**, **Charles Demuth**, and **Reginald Marsh**. You may also find one of **Joseph Cornell**'s intricate shadowboxes, or one of Surrealist **Yves Tanguy**'s alien landscapes.

As if to balance the figurative works that formed the nucleus of the original collection, more recent purchases have included an emphasis on abstract art. **Marsden Hartley**'s *Painting Number 5* is a strident work painted in memory of a German officer friend killed in the early days of World War I. **Georgia O'Keeffe**'s *Abstraction* is gentler, though with its own darkness: it was suggested by the noises of cattle being driven to slaughter. Her flower paintings verge on abstraction while hinting at deeper, more erotic forms.

The **Abstract Expressionists** are a strong presence, with great works by masters **Pollock** and **de Kooning**. **Mark Rothko** and the **Color Field** painters are also well represented – though you need a sharp eye to discern any color in **Ad Reinhardt**'s *Black Painting*. In a different direction, **Warhol, Johns**, and **Oldenburg** each subvert the meaning of their images. Warhol's silk-screened *Coke Bottles* fade into motif; Johns' celebrated *Three Flags* erases the emblem of patriotism and replaces it with ambiguity; and Oldenburg's lighthearted *Soft Sculptures*, with its toilets and motors, falls into line with his declaration, "I'm into art that doesn't sit on its ass in a museum."

The Whitney maintains a satellite museum in the Philip Morris building at 42nd Street and Park Avenue (see p.141).

Park Avenue

Park Avenue, one block east from Madison, is stolidly comfortable and often elegant. On the Upper East Side, it's known for the dozens of swish apartment blocks that line its sides – look for uniformed doormen dotting the sidewalk, sleek black town-cars idling, their drivers still inside, and Chanel-suited women. Aside from glimpses of Manhattan's elite, it's worth wandering down Park for the sweeping view south, where it coasts down to the hulking Grand Central Terminal and Met Life Buildings (see p.140). Its twin arteries sandwich a lush green median – in the low 90s, look for the large black shapes of Louise Nevelson sculptures on the traffic islands. Just above 96th Street, at the point where the subway line emerges from underground, the neighborhood rather joltingly transitions from blocks of quiet, moneyed apartment buildings to **El Barrio**, or **Spanish Harlem**.

The Seventh Regiment Armory

The block on Park Avenue between 66th and 67th streets is dominated by the **Seventh Regiment Armory** (☏212/452-3067). Built in the 1870s, the exterior features pseudo-medieval crenellations, and the interior a grand double staircase and spidery wrought-iron chandeliers. It's noteworthy as the only surviving building from the era before New York's railroad tracks were roofed over; without that innovation, Park Avenue would have remained a clattering, noisy mess. Also on the inside, there are two surviving rooms – the Veterans' Room and the Library – from the building's heyday, Neoclassical masterpieces executed by the firm that included Louis Comfort Tiffany and Stanford White. They're only accessible by special arrangement, so the best way to get a peek is to try to attend one of the frequent art and antique shows staged here, which also showcase the enormous drill hall inside. January's Winter Antiques Show is especially large. Call ahead to find out about upcoming exhibits.

The Asia Society

A prominent educational resource founded by John D. Rockefeller III, the **Asia Society**, 725 Park Ave at 70th St (Tues–Sun 11am–6pm; $10; ☏212/517-ASIA, ⓦwww.asiasociety.org), offers a small but nevertheless enthralling exhibition space dedicated to both traditional and contemporary art from all over Asia. In addition to the usually worthwhile temporary exhibits, ranging from Japanese lacquerware to ancient Buddhist sculpture, a variety of intriguing performances, political roundtables, lectures, films, and free events are frequently held here. Call ahead or visit their website for special-events listings.

Lexington Avenue and east

Lexington Avenue is Madison Avenue's upstart sibling; it was only gentrified in the 1960s, as the western stretches of the neighborhood increased in value, and money-savvy property developers rushed in to snap up real estate farther east. Only forty years later, the signs of its hip economic heyday are already long gone, and this is now one of the cheaper residential areas in the city. The proliferation of small apartments (as well as a generous number of hip restaurants and sports bars) means that the East 60s and 70s are home to a number of young, unattached, and upwardly mobile professionals – for some years now it has been one of the more popular areas with just-out-of-college types looking to make their start in the business world.

Dozens of **foreign consulates** to the United Nations are scattered on Upper East Side blocks in this area: many countries – including poor ones, spending more than they can afford – have purchased handsome homes. The Russians occupy an entire apartment building on East 67th St between Lexington and Third avenues. Here and there you will notice a small kiosk occupied by a police officer, likely as not placed near a consulate of a country whose politics may tend to provoke street protests or unwelcome callers.

The southern stretches

At the southern end of Lexington Avenue's Upper East Side stretch is department store legend **Bloomingdale's**, which takes up the block between 59th and 60th streets; note its Art Deco facade (see p.413).

A few blocks east of here is the **Mount Vernon Hotel Museum and Garden**, 421 E 61st St at York Ave (Tues–Sun 11am–4pm, except June & July Tues 11am–9pm; $8; ☎212/838-6878, ⊛www.mvhm.org). Formerly the Abigail Adams Smith Museum, this wasn't the actual home of the daughter of President John Adams; rather, this building was just the stables, since restored with Federal-period propriety by the Colonial Dames of America (a ragtag association of patriotic history buffs). The furnishings, knickknacks, and the serene little park out back are more engaging than the house itself, but there's an odd sort of pull if you're lucky enough to be guided around by one of the chatty and urbane Colonial Dame docents.

The house is hemmed in by decidedly non-historic buildings and overlooked by the **Queensborough Bridge**, which may stir memories as the 59th Street Bridge of Simon and Garfunkel's *Feelin' Groovy* or from the title credits of TV's *Taxi*. This glut of clanging steel links Manhattan to Long Island City in Queens, but is utterly unlike the suspension bridges that elsewhere lace Manhattan to the boroughs. "My God, it's a blacksmith's shop!" was architect Henry Hornbostel's comment when he first saw the finished bridge in 1909.

If you'd rather spend time dawdling over cartoons than dodging cars, head to the **Museum of American Illustration**, 128 E 63rd St at Lexington

Ave (Tues 10am–8pm, Wed–Fri 10am–5pm, Sat noon–4pm; free; ☎212/838-2560, ⊛www.societyillustrators.org). Rotating selections from the museum's permanent collection of more than 2000 illustrations include everything from wartime propaganda to political and other cartoons and drawings, to contemporary ads. Exhibitions are based on a theme or illustrator; designed primarily for aficionados, they are nonetheless accessible, well presented, and topical.

On East 67th Street, east of Lexington and beyond the rear of the Seventh Regiment Armory, look for a remarkable ensemble of fanciful **Victorian buildings** that resemble a movie set, including the blue-trimmed local Police Precinct, the Fire Station with its red garage doors, and the whimsical ochre Park East Synagogue, with Moorish arches, stained glass, and campanile.

There's not much north of here until you hit the New York auction gallery of London-based **Sotheby's**, 1334 York Ave at 72nd St (☎212/606-7000, ⊛www.sothebys.com), the oldest fine-arts auctioneer in the world. It's weathered a price-fixing scandal in recent years, though the cost was high: the company had to sell this stunning, purpose-built New York headquarters and then lease it back to pay off the fines incurred. If you want to look inside, there's normally a viewing of some kind going on most days, though admission to most of the auctions is by invitation only.

Yorkville and around

It's only in **Yorkville** that the Upper East Side displays minute traces of New York's European immigrant history: this was originally a German–Hungarian neighborhood that spilled out from East 77th to 96th streets between Lexington and the East River. Much of Manhattan's German community arrived after the failed revolution of 1848–49, to be quickly assimilated into the area around Tompkins Square in lower Manhattan. Three near-simultaneous events around 1900 drove the center of German life uptown to Yorkville: the influx of Italian and Slavic immigrants to the Lower East Side; the opening of the island-long Elevated Railway, which ran along Second Avenue; and the tragic sinking of an excursion steamer carrying Tompkins Square residents, killing 1021 and decimating that neighborhood's German community. Other immigrant groups followed not long after, and some splendid little townhouses were built for these newcomers, such as **The Cottages** on Third Avenue between East 77th and 78th streets, whose stylish English Regency facades and courtyard gardens remain intact.

You do have to search hard to detect a German flavor to the area; the prospect of cheap rent with an Upper East Side address has lured many fresh-out-of-college folks, who now blend amicably with the few elderly German-speaking residents who still reside here. Amid all the video stores and fast-food joints, there are a few hints of the old neighborhood, notably the traditional German delicatessens: look for **Schaller and Weber**, 1654 Second Ave at 86th St (☎212/879-3047).

Beginning at East 76th Street and East End Drive is **John Jay Park**, a lovely patch of green built around a beautiful pool and gym – though you need a Parks Department pass ($35 per year) to make use of either (more info ☎212/397-3177). Fronting the park between 77th and 78th streets are the **Cherokee Apartments**, originally the Shively Sanitarium Apartments, an understatedly elegant row with a splendid courtyard. Up the block at 81st Street is **John Finley Walk**, where a concrete promenade named for **Carl Schurz**, a nineteenth-century German immigrant who rose to fame as Secretary of the Interior under President Rutherford B. Hayes and as editor of *Harper's Weekly* and the *New York Evening Post*, runs north into the park. Winding pathways lead through this small, model park – a breathing space for elderly German-speakers and East Siders alike. FDR Drive cuts beneath the green, and there are views of Queens and of the confluence of dangerous currents where the Harlem River, Long Island Sound, and the Harbor meet – not for nothing known as Hell Gate. It's a few blocks west to the **Church of the Holy Trinity**, 316 E 88th St at Second Ave (℡212/289-4100), a picturesque and discreet Victorian building with an enchanting little garden.

Gracie Mansion and Henderson Place

One of the reasons Schurz Park is so exceptionally well manicured and maintained is the high-profile security that surrounds **Gracie Mansion** (East End Ave at 88th St; telephone reservations required for tours, Wed 10am, 11am, 1pm, 2pm; $7; ℡212/570-4751). Built in 1799 on the site of a Revolutionary fort, it is one of the best-preserved colonial buildings in the city. Roughly contemporary with the Morris–Jumel Mansion and the Mount Vernon Hotel Museum, Gracie Mansion has been the official residence of the mayor of New York City since 1942, when Fiorello LaGuardia set up house; the name's a misnomer, since it's more a cramped cottage than a grand residence. The mansion itself isn't particularly compelling, and the tours are perfunctory – frankly, it's most interesting for the stories associated with past mayors than any architectural features.

Small wonder, then, that billionaire mayor Michael Bloomberg opted not to live there full-time – dropping Gracie Mansion from the headlines. It's a far cry from the Rudy Giuliani era when, thanks to an acrimonious split, he and his wife continued to live in the same home even when his new companion was visiting. Eventually – in a tabloid-frothing move – the wife successfully filed a lawsuit to bar his mistress from the house.

Across from the park and just below Gracie Mansion at East 86th Street and East End Avenue is **Henderson Place**, a set of old servants' quarters now transformed into a "historic district" of luxury cottages. Built in 1882 by John Henderson, a fur importer and real-estate developer, the small and sprightly Queen Anne–style dwellings were intended to provide close and convenient housing for servants working in the palatial old East End Avenue mansions, most of which have now been torn down. Ironically, these servants' quarters now represent some of the most sought-after real estate in the city, offering the space, quiet, and privacy that most of the city lacks.

Roosevelt Island

An aerial tramway near the Queensborough Bridge connects Manhattan with **Roosevelt Island**, in the middle of the East River. Though the island was hooked up to the subway system in the 1990s, the tram has long been the more popular way to arrive (trams run every 15min Mon–Thurs & Sun 6am–2am, Fri & Sat 6am–3.30am; every 7 and 1/2 min during rush hours; $2 one way; ℡212/832-4540, ⊛www.rioc.com); from there, take the 25¢ bus to the northern part of the island.

Roosevelt Island's a thorough oddity, perhaps because the place has passed through so many hands and names over the years. Only two miles long and no more than 800ft wide, **Blackwell Island** was first owned, inhabited, and farmed by the family of the same name from 1676 to 1828. At that time, the city of New York snapped up the land and assigned it use as a **quarantine site** for criminals, lunatics, and smallpox victims; by 1921, it was officially known as **Welfare Island**. There are still several reminders of those days: the Octagon Tower at the north end, now off-limits, was once an insane asylum and briefly housed Emma Goldman and even Mae West after a particularly bawdy performance in 1927. On the opposite tip of the island, look for the stabilized ruins of what was once the island's **Smallpox Hospital**, now a ghostly Gothic shell, as well as the Strecker Laboratory, the city's premier laboratory for bacteriological research when it opened in 1892. The ruins can be easily spotted from the Manhattan side of the East River but are all but impossible to see from the island itself, as the area surrounding the hospital is boarded up with rows of corrugated fencing. These derelict buildings are an example of what the whole island looked like by the 1960s: deserted, forgotten, and unloved. Forward-thinking city mayor John Lindsay enlisted architects John Burgee and Philip Johnson to demolish most of the old buildings and create a master plan for new residential living areas in the late 1960s. Duly rechristened Roosevelt Island in 1973, the island received its first new inhabitants two years later. The narrow streets, bold signage, and modular buildings are considered a triumph of **urban planning**, though some may find it reminiscent of the village in the TV series *The Prisoner*.

Paranoid impressions aside, it is nonetheless somewhat cultish. Locals are fiercely protective of their hidden enclave: to snag one of the cheap apartments here, you'll have to join the years-long official waiting list. The island has a small-town feel, notably along the narrow, brick-paved Main Street, though if that's too much and you want to look back at the city, head for the Meditation Steps and the River Walk, a walking and rollerblading path on the west side of the island. The other fine vantage point is the northern tip, which affords excellent views of the upper reaches of the East River and the surging waters of Hell Gate, and Lighthouse Park is a romantic retreat of grassy knolls and weeping willows. This tip is also home to the Roosevelt Island **Lighthouse**, which dates back to 1872 and was built from gray gneiss, a high-grade metamorphic rock indigenous to the island. It's well preserved, but there's no public access to the light at the top.

The Upper West Side and Morningside Heights

W hile the Upper East Side has always been a patrician stronghold, the Upper West Side, only minutes away on the other side of the park, has grown into its position as a somewhat younger, somewhat hipper, but nonetheless affluent counterpart. Later to develop, it has seen its share of struggling actors, writers, and opera singers come and go over the years. In the 1990s, the Upper West Side was the neighborhood of choice for upwardly mobile dot-commers, and though that frenzy has calmed down, young professionals and their stroller-bound children still make up a sizable part of the population.

This isn't to say it lacks glamour; the lower stretches of **Central Park West** and **Riverside Drive** are quite fashionable, while the network of performing spaces at **Lincoln Center** makes the neighborhood New York's de facto palace of culture. As you move north, though, the neighborhood diversifies and loses some of its luster, culminating in **Morningside Heights**, home to **Columbia University** at the edge of Harlem, as well as the monolithic **Cathedral of St John the Divine**.

The Upper West Side

North of 59th Street, the somewhat tawdry Midtown West becomes decidedly less commercial and garish, and then morphs into the largely residential **Upper West Side**. The neighborhood parallels Central Park, running west from the park to the Hudson River, and north from Columbus Circle at 59th Street to 110th Street and the beginning of Morningside Heights. Its main artery is **Broadway**: generally speaking, the farther east or west you stray from here, the more expensive the real estate becomes – the twin pinnacles of prosperity are the historic apartment houses of **Central Park West** and **Riverside Drive**. In

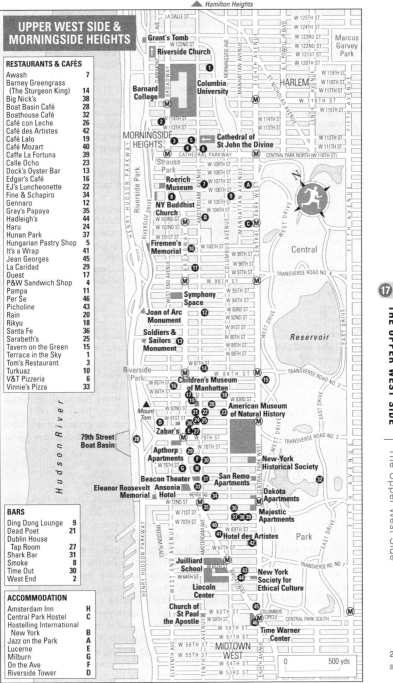

Hamilton Heights

UPPER WEST SIDE & MORNINGSIDE HEIGHTS

RESTAURANTS & CAFÉS

Awash	7
Barney Greengrass (The Sturgeon King)	14
Big Nick's	38
Boat Basin Café	28
Boathouse Café	32
Café con Leche	26
Café des Artistes	42
Café Lalo	19
Café Mozart	40
Caffe La Fortuna	39
Calle Ocho	23
Dock's Oyster Bar	13
Edgar's Café	16
EJ's Luncheonette	22
Fine & Schapiro	34
Gennaro	12
Gray's Papaya	35
Hadleigh's	44
Haru	24
Hunan Park	37
Hungarian Pastry Shop	5
It's a Wrap	41
Jean Georges	45
La Caridad	29
Ouest	17
P&W Sandwich Shop	4
Pampa	11
Per Se	46
Picholine	43
Rain	20
Rikyu	18
Santa Fe	36
Sarabeth's	25
Tavern on the Green	15
Terrace in the Sky	1
Tom's Restaurant	3
Turkuaz	10
V&T Pizzeria	6
Vinnie's Pizza	33

BARS

Ding Dong Lounge	9
Dead Poet	21
Dublin House Tap Room	27
Shark Bar	31
Smoke	8
Time Out	30
West End	2

ACCOMMODATION

Amsterdam Inn	H
Central Park Hostel	C
Hostelling International New York	B
Jazz on the Park	A
Lucerne	E
Milburn	G
On the Ave	F
Riverside Tower	D

Grant's Tomb
Riverside Church
Columbia University
Barnard College
HARLEM
Marcus Garvey Park
MORNINGSIDE HEIGHTS
Cathedral of St John the Divine
Strauss Park
Roerich Museum
NY Buddhist Church
Firemen's Memorial
Symphony Space
Joan of Arc Monument
Soldiers & Sailors Monument
Children's Museum of Manhattan
American Museum of Natural History
Mount Tom
Zabar's
79th Street Boat Basin
Apthorp Apartments
New-York Historical Society
Beacon Theater
San Remo Apartments
Eleanor Roosevelt Memorial
Ansonia Hotel
Dakota Apartments
Majestic Apartments
Hotel des Artistes
Juilliard School
New York Society for Ethical Culture
Lincoln Center
Church of St Paul the Apostle
Time Warner Center
MIDTOWN WEST
Hudson River
Riverside Park
Central Park
Reservoir

0   500 yds

THE UPPER WEST SIDE | The Upper West Side

17

205

Like practically every other neighborhood in the city, the Upper West Side was once fecund farmland. That began to change in 1879, when the opening of the Ninth Avenue elevated train made the open space west of Central Park more accessible to city residents, who mainly still lived downtown. But it was more difficult than developers had envisioned to attract New York's wealthy to the district, as it was dominated by the train, which spewed smoke and made an unholy amount of noise. Cheap tenements began to pop up, and the New York Central Railroad line, which transported livestock to the 60th Street stockyards, went in about a year later, adding the smell of farm animals to what was already a sensory overload. Between 59th and 65th streets, the neighborhood became home to more warehouses than anything else, and the district had the early makings of a soulless slum.

One diamond in the rough, though, was the Dakota Building on 72nd Street, built in 1884. Slowly, other townhouses and high-class living quarters rose around it, displacing some of the hulking warehouses. Ten years later, as Manhattan began to grow north in earnest, the confluence of Eighth Avenue, Broadway, and 59th Street became a hot bed of excitement. Concerts were held at the Majestic Playhouse on Broadway and 60th Street, area theaters showcased popular vaudeville acts, and quality watering holes were quite numerous. By the 1920s, theaters for all types of entertainment (some more risqué than others) lined the Ninth Avenue train circuit. Soon retail stores, unable to resist the smell of prosperity, began to appear, and by 1929, shopping had taken over as the neighborhood's main attraction. The area has hardly looked back since.

between is a checkerboard of modern high-rise buildings and old brownstones; you'll also find gourmet markets, upscale boutiques, and restaurants catering to cliques of young professionals.

Above 90th Street, particularly along **Amsterdam** and **Columbus avenues**, there are enclaves of public housing, some shabby SRO ("single room occupancy") hotels, and a certain amount of downbeat street hustle, all of which increase in volume into the 100s, where you'll find some less-well-off Latino neighborhoods. However, even these areas have begun the gentrification process, as middle-class families have moved into areas farther north that they previously would have shunned.

Columbus Circle and around

Columbus Circle, located at the intersection of Broadway, Central Park West, and 59th Street, is a roundabout, a rarity in Manhattan. It's also a pedestrian's worst navigation nightmare; be careful crossing the street. Amid the hum of traffic it's easy to overlook Columbus himself, who stands uncomfortably atop a lone column in the center island. Recently, the city's attention has turned to this long-ignored intersection for two reasons. Firstly, the glitzy **Time Warner Center**, a massive, multi-million-dollar home for companies like CNN and Warner Books, finally opened here in February 2004, after a highly publicized and problematic construction that included worker deaths and an on-site fire. The business part of the complex squats on top of a multistory mall where, aside from over three dozen shops, you'll find five of the city's priciest restaurants, including *Per Se*, run by Thomas Keller (see p.354). If your budget doesn't allow for $100 per head on dinner, kill some time at the interactive exhibit grafted onto the CNN offices: head to the third floor of the mall for **Inside CNN** (daily 9.30am–5pm; 50min tours depart every 20min;

$15; ☏1-866/4CNN-NYC, ⊛www.cnn.com/insidecnn/). The exhibit is a fun, if gimmicky, way to see behind the scenes of cable news – you can try a teleprompter and blue screen, as well as burn your own interactive news DVD to take home (though it costs an extra $21.99).

Columbus Circle's other point of interest is also architectural, though its attraction is somewhat contentious. The oddball, vaguely Venetian white building at **2 Columbus Circle** looms over the roundabout's southern side, and is considered by some New York residents to be one of the city's grand follies (see box, below).

Opposite Columbus Circle, on the park side, stands the **Maine Monument**, a large stone column with the prow of a ship jutting out from its base; it's crowned by a dazzlingly bright gilded statue of Columbia Triumphant. Erected in 1913, the monument is dedicated to the 260 seamen who died when the battleship *Maine* inexplicably exploded in Havana Harbor in 1898, propelling forward the Spanish-American War. Across the street, at the junction of Broadway and Central Park West, are the glittering **Trump International Hotel** and condos. During construction the 1 Central Park address was touted as "The World's Most Prestigious" – just one of the more recent examples of Trump's braggadocio. A large silver globe sits in the plaza in front of the hotel; it's a glitzy and completely unnecessary replica of the Unisphere, which is on display at the 1964 World's Fair site in Queens.

For aesthetic relief, go west a few blocks and contemplate the **Church of St Paul the Apostle**, 405 W 59th St at Ninth Ave (☏212/265-3495), a beautiful Old Gothic structure housing Byzantine basilica features, including a high altar by Stanford White. A few steps north is the **New York Society for Ethical Culture**, 2 W 64th St at Central Park W (☏212/874-5210, ⊛www.nysec.org), "a haven for those who want to share the high adventure of integrating ethical

Columbus Circle: masterpiece or Modernist mistake?

The controversial building at **2 Columbus Circle** was originally commissioned in 1964 by Huntington Hartford, an art-loving supermarket heir who wanted a place to house his personal art collection. In displaying his somewhat traditional acquisitions in a grandiose setting, Hartford hoped to staunch his contemporaries' gushing flow of support for abstract art, which he considered a waste of time and space. The museum lasted only five years – though the building's facade, made from a screen of concrete studded with filigree portholes and a huge penthouse loggia, may be stunning, the interior is dark, claustrophobic, and ill suited as an exhibition space. Empty since 1997, the building is now also in need of serious repair. Years of neglect have left the facade in a terrible state, and the edifice's structural integrity is questionable.

The **Museum of Arts & Design** (see p.137), set to decamp here in 2008 from cramped quarters on 53rd Street, is currently battling both the building's condition and its design. The museum's administration has plans to gut the whole thing: the redesign will significantly alter the marble exterior, including the lollipop columns, portholes, and loggia, and give the interior galleries views of Central Park. However, at the time of writing, the museum's ambitious aims were opposed by a coalition of anti-development activists and avant-garde aesthetes (including the normally traditional novelist Tom Wolfe), and were mired in multiple lawsuits. At the heart of the debate is the question of whether or not the museum's practical needs should take precedence over the building's architectural and historical importance to the city. Opponents of the proposed changes believe that Hartford's original design should be respected, regardless of the building's (lack of) aesthetic value.

ideals into daily life." Founded in 1876 (though the building itself wasn't built until 1902), this distinguished organization also helped to found the National Association for the Advancement of Colored People and the American Civil Liberties Union. It holds regular Sunday meetings, and organizes occasional recitals and lectures on social responsibility, politics, and other related topics. It also runs an elementary school where J. Robert Oppenheimer, who directed the construction of the first atomic bomb, was once a student.

Lincoln Center

Broadway continues north from Columbus Circle to the **Lincoln Center for the Performing Arts**, an imposing group of six marble-and-glass buildings arranged around a large plaza between 63rd and 66th streets. It's not, as most assume, named for President Abraham Lincoln; rather, it honors the name of the surrounding area in Manhattan's early times, likely named Lincoln for a tenant farmer who tilled the land here. Robert Moses came up with the idea of creating a cultural center here in the 1950s as a way of "encouraging" the area's gentrification, one of his rare exercises in urban renewal that has been extremely successful. A number of architects worked on the plans, and the complex was finally built in the mid-1960s on a site that formerly held some of the city's poorest slums. In a case of life imitating art imitating life, once the slums were emptied and their residents moved to ghettos farther uptown, the deserted area became a movie set: before construction began in 1960, the run-down buildings served as the open-air location for *West Side Story*, which was based on the stage musical set here.

Home to the world-class **Metropolitan Opera**, the **New York City Ballet**, and the **New York Philharmonic**, as well as a host of other smaller companies, Lincoln Center is worth seeing even if you're not catching a performance; the best way is on an **organized tour** – otherwise you'll only be allowed to peek into the ornate lobbies of the buildings. Hour-long tours leave from the booth on the concourse level, and take in the main part of the Center (daily beginning at 10.30am, last tour at 4.30pm; $12.50, students $9; ☎212/875-5350). Be warned that tours can get booked up and times vary, since the tour schedule is made a week in advance; it's best to phone ahead to be sure of a place. Backstage tours of the Met are also available; see p.209 for more information.

If your budget's tight, you may want to stop by here for the **free entertainment** that is often offered: there's the Autumn Crafts Fair in early September, folk and jazz bands at lunchtime, and dazzling fountain and light displays every evening in the summer. In addition, Lincoln Center hosts a variety of affordable summertime events, including Midsummer Night Swing, a dance series that allows you to swing, salsa, hustle, and ballroom dance on an outdoor bandstand at the Lincoln Center Plaza Fountain. Contact **Lincoln Center Information** (☎212/875-5000, ⊛www.lincolncenter.org) for specifics.

The New York State Theater and Avery Fisher Hall

Philip Johnson's spare and elegant **New York State Theater**, on the south side of the plaza, is home to both the New York City Ballet (including its famed annual December performances of the *Nutcracker)* and the New York City Opera. Its foyer is ringed with balconies embellished with delicate bronze grilles and boasts an imposing, four-story ceiling finished in gold leaf. The ballet season runs from late November through February and early April through June; the opera season starts in July and runs through mid-November. Call ☎212/870-5570 for ticket information.

Johnson also had a hand in the **Avery Fisher Hall**, opposite the theater on the north side of the plaza, where the New York Philharmonic plays; he was called in to refashion the interior after its acoustics were found to be below par. The seating space here, though, does not possess the magnificence of his glittery horseshoe-shaped State Theater, and the most exciting visual aspect of Avery Fisher is its foyer, dominated by a huge, hanging metal-and-wire sculpture by Richard Lippold, whose distinctive style you may recognize from an atrium or two downtown. The Philharmonic performs here from September through May, while Mostly Mozart, the country's first and most popular indoor summer chamber-music series, take place in July and August. Call ☎212/875-5030 for performance information.

The Metropolitan Opera House

In contrast to the surrounding Modernist starkness, the plaza's focal point, the **Metropolitan Opera House** (aka "the Met"), is gushingly ornate. Its enormous crystal chandeliers and red-carpeted staircases, designed for grand entrances in evening wear, ooze opulence, while the multilingual titling and translation system is definitely state-of-the-art. Behind two of the high arched windows hang **murals by Marc Chagall**. The artist wanted stained glass, but at the time it was felt that glass wouldn't last long in an area still less than reverential toward the arts, so paintings were hung behind square-paned glass to give a similar effect. These days, they're covered for part of the day to protect them from the sun; the rest of the time they're best viewed from the plaza outside. The mural on the left, *Le Triomphe de la Musique*, is cast with a variety of well-known performers; landmarks snipped from the New York skyline; and a portrait of Sir Rudolph Bing, who ran the Met for more than three decades, outfitted as a gypsy. The other mural, *Les Sources de la Musique*, is reminiscent of Chagall's renowned scenery for the Met production of *The Magic Flute*: the god of music strums a lyre while a Tree of Life, Verdi, and Wagner all float down the Hudson River. You can learn more about the Opera House on one of the **backstage tours** of the building (Sept–June Mon–Fri 3.30pm, Sun 10.30am; reservations required; $12, students $5; ☎212/769-7020). For performance information, see p.387.

The rest of Lincoln Center

Two piazzas flank the Met. To the south there is **Damrosch Park**, a large space facing the Guggenheim Bandshell, where chairs are set up in the summer so you can catch free lunchtime concerts and various performances. To the north you will find a lovely, smaller plaza facing the **Vivian Beaumont Theater**, designed by Eero Saarinen in 1965 and home to the smaller **Mitzi E. Newhouse Theater**. This square is mostly taken up by a rectangular reflecting pool, around which office workers munch their lunches. A lazy Henry Moore figure reclines mid-pond, while a spidery sculpture by Alexander Calder perches on the edge of the pool. The **New York Public Library for the Performing Arts** (Tues, Wed, Fri & Sat noon–6pm, Thurs noon–8pm; free; ☎212/870-1630, ⓦwww .nypl.org/research/lpa/lpa.html) is located behind the Vivian Beaumont and holds over eight million items (everything from performing-arts ephemera to scores and manuscripts), plus a museum that exhibits costumes, set designs, and music scores. At the corner of Broadway and 65th Street is **Alice Tully Hall**, a recital hall that houses the Chamber Music Society of Lincoln Center, and the **Walter E. Reade Theater**, which features foreign films and retrospectives and, together with the Avery Fisher and Alice Tully halls, hosts the annual New

York Film Festival in September (see p.393). The celebrated **Juilliard School of Music** is in an adjacent building (the best way to check it out is via one of the regular concerts by its students; see p.387 for details).

The smallish **Dante Park**, an island on Broadway across from the main Lincoln Center Plaza, features a statue of its namesake; the American branch of the Dante Alighieri Society put it up in 1921 to commemorate the 600th anniversary of the writer's death. But the park's *pièce de résistance* is a piece of art dating from 1999: *TimeSculpture*, a bronze and stone masterwork featuring a series of large clocks, was designed by Philip Johnson and dedicated to the patrons of Lincoln Center. The subject matter is a nod to the company who donated the funds for it – Movado, the Swiss makers of swanky watches.

North on Broadway

Immediately north at 72nd Street, tiny, triangular **Verdi Square** (featuring a craggy statue in the likeness of the composer) makes a fine place to take a break from the marvels of Lincoln Center. From the square, you can fully appreciate the ornate balconies, round towers, and cupolas of the **Ansonia Hotel**, 2109 Broadway at W 73rd St. Never actually a hotel (it was planned as upscale apartments), the Ansonia was completed in 1904 and the dramatic Beaux-Arts building is still the *grande dame* of the Upper West Side: it's been home to luminaries like Enrico Caruso, Arturo Toscanini, Lily Pons, Florenz Ziegfeld, Theodore Dreiser, Igor Stravinsky, and even Babe Ruth. North of here along Amsterdam Avenue is a nondescript retail strip, home to a cluster of Irish pubs, a few pet shops, and some unremarkable eateries.

The enormous limestone **Apthorp Apartments**, 2211 Broadway between 78th and 79th streets, occupy an entire block from Broadway to West End Avenue. Built in 1908 by William Waldorf Astor, the ornate iron gates of the former carriage entrance lead into a central courtyard with a large fountain visible from Broadway, though you won't be allowed to stroll in. The building's in a fair enough state now, though its fortunes have hiccoughed over the years – it was used as the location for the crack factory in the 1991 movie *New Jack City*. The Upper West Side past 79th Street has seen a lot of changes in the last decade as the forces of gentrification have surged northward, bringing with them a proliferation of chains like *Starbucks* as well as girly boutiques and swanky eateries. One of the older establishments in the area is gourmet hub **Zabar's**, 2245 Broadway at 80th St, which has been selling baked goods, cheese, caviar, gourmet coffee and tea, and an exhaustive collection of cooking gadgets since 1934. For more on the store, see p.424.

Nearby, the **Children's Museum of Manhattan**, 212 W 83rd St at Broadway (Wed–Sun 10am–5pm; $8; ☎212/721-1234, ⊛www.cmom.org), fills a delightful five-story space. It offers interactive exhibits that stimulate learning, in a fun, relaxed environment for kids (and babies) of all ages; the Dr. Seuss exhibit and the storytelling room, filled with books kids can choose from, are particular winners.

Weaving your way north through Broadway's invariably crowded sidewalks, you will reach **Symphony Space**, 2537 Broadway between W 94th and 95th streets (☎212/864-5400, ⊛www.symphonyspace.org), one of New York's premier performing-arts centers. Symphony Space regularly sponsors short-story readings called Selected Shorts (featuring everyone from David Sedaris to Walter Mosley), as well as classical and world music performances, screenings of revival and foreign films, and an annual free marathon reading of James Joyce's *Ulysses* every Bloomsday (June 16).

Broadway and West End Avenue converge at 107th Street at the small, triangular **Strauss Park**. The statue by Augustus Lukeman of a reclining woman gazing over a water basin was dedicated by Macy's founder Nathan Strauss to his brother and business partner, Isidor, and Isidor's wife, Ida. Isidor and Ida, who lived nearby, went down with the *Titanic* in 1912 – legend has it that Ida refused to leave Isidor for the lifeboats. Farther down the block, in a manicured brownstone, is the overlooked but appealing **Roerich Museum,** 319 W 107th St (Tues–Sun 2–5pm; suggested donation $5; ☎212/864-7752, ⊛www.roerich .org). It contains a small, weird, and virtually unknown collection of original paintings by Nicholas Roerich, a Russian artist who lived in India and was influenced by Indian mysticism.

Central Park West

Central Park West stretches north from Columbus Circle to 110th Street along the western edge of the park. Home to some of the city's most architecturally distinguished apartment buildings, like the **Dakota** and **Majestic**, as well as the enormous **American Museum of Natural History**, Central Park West bustles with taxis and tour buses. In contrast, the sidestreets between Central Park West and Columbus Avenue in the upper 60s and 70s are quiet, tree-lined, and filled with beautifully renovated brownstones, many of which are single-family homes.

Most of the monolithic, mansion-inspired apartment complexes in this area date from the early twentieth century and rim the edge of the park, hogging the best views. The southernmost of these is the Hotel des Artistes, 1 W 67th St at Central Park W. It was built in 1917 especially for artists (hence the name), and once was the Manhattan address for the likes of Nöel Coward, Norman Rockwell, Isadora Duncan, and Alexander Woollcott. Though the building is now expensive co-op apartments, you can still see the original interior on the ground floor, via the similarly pricey and famous *Café des Artistes* (see p.354). If you can't afford to eat here, dress up for a drink at the renowned bar, where you can absorb the ambience and see the luscious nude-nymph murals by Howard Chandler Christy.

Four blocks north, between 71st and 72nd streets, you'll find the fittingly named **Majestic**. This gigantic, pale yellow, Art Deco landmark was thrown up in 1930 and is best known for its twin towers and avant-garde brickwork. The next block north houses one of New York's more illustrious residences: the **Dakota Building**, 1 W 72nd St. The rather hoary story of its name is that when construction finished in 1884, its uptown location was considered as remote as the Dakota territory by Manhattanites. Whatever the origin of its name, this grandiose hulk of German Renaissance masonry is undoubtedly impressive. Its turrets, gables, and other odd details were all included for one reason: to persuade wealthy New Yorkers that life in an apartment could be just as luxurious as in a private house. For the large part, the developers succeeded: over the years, few of the residents here haven't had some sort of public renown, from Lauren Bacall and Judy Garland to Leonard Bernstein and TV personalities Maury Povich and Connie Chung; of course, it's best known as the home of the late John Lennon (see box, p.212).

Continue north to the **San Remo**, 145–146 Central Park West at 74th St. Another apartment complex, this one dates from 1930 and is one of the most significant components of the skyline here: its ornate twin towers, topped by columned, mock-Roman temples, are visible from most points in Central Park. Architecture aside, the residents' board here is known for its snooty

The Dakota Building, 1 W 72nd St, is most famous as the former home of **John Lennon** – and present home of his widow, **Yoko Ono**, who owns a number of the building's apartments. It was outside the Dakota, on the night of December 8, 1980, that the ex-Beatle was murdered – shot by a man who professed to be one of his greatest admirers.

His murderer, **Mark David Chapman**, had hung around outside the building all day, clutching a copy of his hero's latest album, **Double Fantasy**, and accosting Lennon for his autograph, which he received. This was nothing unusual: fans loitered outside the building and hustled for a glimpse of the singer. But when the couple returned from a late-night recording session, Chapman was still there, and he pumped five .38 bullets into Lennon as he walked through the Dakota's 72nd Street entrance. Lennon was picked up by the doorman and rushed to the hospital in a taxi, but he died on the way from blood loss. A distraught Yoko issued a statement immediately: "John loved and prayed for the human race. Please do the same for him." No one really knows the reasons behind Chapman's actions. Suffice it to say his obsession with Lennon had obviously unhinged him. Chapman was given a sentence of twenty years to life in prison; he has since been denied parole on three separate occasions – Ono told the parole board she wouldn't feel safe with Chapman walking the streets. He's expected to remain behind bars for the foreseeable future.

Fans of Lennon may want to light a stick of incense across the road in **Strawberry Fields** (see p.168), a section of Central Park that has been restored and maintained in his memory through an endowment by Ono. Its trees and shrubs were donated by a number of countries as a gesture toward world peace. The gardens are pretty enough, if unspectacular, though it would take a hard-bitten cynic not to be a little bit moved by the **Imagine** mosaic on the pathway.

---

exclusiveness: they rejected Madonna as a buyer of a multi-million-dollar co-op, though her former boyfriend Warren Beatty did live here with Diane Keaton. A block farther north is the **Central Park Historic District**, from 75th to 77th streets on Central Park West, and on 76th Street toward Columbus Avenue, home to a number of small, turn-of-the-nineteenth-century rowhouses, as well as another block of flats, the **Kenilworth Apartments**, 151 Central Park West at 75th St. Dating from 1908, the Kenilworth is notable for its mansard roof and carved limestone exterior.

The New-York Historical Society

The oft-overlooked **New-York Historical Society**, 170 Central Park West (Tues–Sun 10am–6pm, Fri until 8pm; $10; ☎212/873-3400, ⊛www.nyhistory .org), houses a permanent collection of books, prints, and portraits, as well as a research library. One room focuses on the work of **James Audubon**, the Harlem artist and naturalist who specialized in lovingly detailed paintings of birds: astonishingly, the Historical Society holds all 432 original watercolors of Audubon's landmark *Birds of America*. Other galleries hold a broad cross-section of **nineteenth-century American** painting, principally portraiture and Hudson River School landscapes, among them Thomas Cole's famed and pompous *Course of Empire* series. Another highlight is the permanent children's area called **Kid City**, which offers interactive exhibitions, such as a child-size recreation of a block on Broadway in 1901. More a museum of American than New York history, the society also features various temporary exhibitions that mix high and low culture with intelligence and flair. Don't miss the museum

library either: among its massive holdings – more than two million manuscripts and maps, as well as almost 650,000 books – are the original Louisiana Purchase document and the correspondence between Aaron Burr and Alexander Hamilton that led up to their deadly duel (see p.232).

The American Museum of Natural History

The **American Museum of Natural History**, Central Park W at 79th St, is one of the best museums of its kind in the world, an enormous complex of buildings full of fossils, gems, taxidermy, and other natural specimens (daily 10am–5.45pm, Rose Center open until 8.45pm on Fri; $14 with additional cost for IMAX films, certain special exhibits, and Hayden Planetarium; ☎212/769-5100, ⓦwww.amnh.org). This elegant giant fills four blocks with a strange architectural mélange of heavy Neoclassical and rustic Romanesque styles – it was built in several stages, the first of which was overseen by Central Park designer Calvert Vaux. Founded in 1869, it is one of the oldest natural-history museums in the world as well as one of the largest, and once you've paced its four floors of exhibition halls and seen a fair number of the 32 million items on display, you'll feel the latter fact in your feet. There's a fantastic amount to see, so be selective; depending on your interests, anything from a highly discriminating couple of hours to half a day should be ample. If you're not sure exactly where you are on a floor (and it can easily happen), check the pillars near each staircase and between exhibit halls – they contain good locator maps. Also make sure to check what temporary exhibits are running; there's usually something of interest.

The collection

The museum's vast marble front steps on Central Park West are a great place to read or soak up the sun. An appropriately haughty statue of museum co-founder Theodore Roosevelt looks out toward the park from his perch on horseback, flanked by a pair of Native Americans marching gamely alongside. This entrance (which opens onto the second floor) leaves you well positioned for a loop of the more interesting halls on that level: principally the **Hall of Asian People** and **Hall of African People**, both of which are filled with fascinating, often beautiful, art and artifacts, and backed up with informal commentary and indigenous music. The Hall of Asian People begins with artifacts from Russia and Central Asia, moves on to pieces from Tibet – including a gorgeous recreation of an ornate, gilded Tibetan Buddhist shrine – and then on to China and Japan, with displays of some fantastic textiles, rugs, brass, and jade ornaments. The Hall of African People displays ceremonial costumes, musical instruments, and masks from all over the continent. Another highlight of this floor is the lower half of the **Hall of African Mammals**, a double-height room whose exhibits continue on to the third-floor balcony: don't miss the life-size family of elephants in the center of the room (it's fairly difficult to do so). Once you're on the third floor, stop by the mildly creepy **Reptiles and Amphibians Hall**, filled with samples of almost any species in the category. A little less interesting is the **Eastern Woodlands and Plains Indians** exhibit, a rather pedestrian display of artifacts, clothing, and the like.

The fourth floor is almost entirely taken up by the wildly popular **Dinosaur Exhibit**; spreading across five spacious, well-lit, and well-designed halls, the museum houses the largest dinosaur collection in the world, with more than 120 specimens on display. Here, you can touch fossils, watch robotic dinosaurs, and walk on a transparent bridge over a fifty-foot-long Barosaurus spine. The multi-level exhibits are also supplemented by interactive computer programs and claymation videos, which add a nice hands-on appeal to the exhibit.

Downstairs on the first floor is the **Hall of Gems and Minerals**, which includes some strikingly beautiful crystals – not least the Star of India, the largest blue sapphire ever found. The enormous, double-height gallery dedicated to **Ocean Life** includes a 94-foot-long (life-size) Blue Whale disconcertingly suspended from the ceiling. The exhibit of **North American Mammals** hasn't changed in ages – the dark halls, marble floors, and illuminated diorama cases filled with stuffed specimens have seen over fifty years' worth of children on school trips. The greatest draw on this floor, however, is the **Hall of Biodiversity**. It focuses on both the ecological and evolutionary aspects of biodiversity,

△ Diorama, American Museum of Natural History

with multimedia displays on everything from the changes humans have wrought on the environment (with examples of solutions brought about by local activists and community groups in all parts of the world) to videos about endangered species. The centerpiece of the exhibit is an interactive recreation of a Central African Republic rainforest, accompanied by detailed texts about the ecology of the area and the need for conservation. The **NatureMax Theater**, also located on this floor, presents some interesting nature-oriented IMAX films; check to see what's playing (there is an additional charge).

The Rose Center for Earth and Space

Across from the Hall of Biodiversity is the **Rose Center for Earth and Space**, including the **Hall of Planet Earth**, a multimedia exploration of how the earth works, with displays on a wide variety of subjects such as the formation of planets, underwater rock formation, plate tectonics, and carbon dating. Items on display include a 2.7-billion-year-old specimen of a banded iron formation and volcanic ash from Mount Vesuvius. One of the newer displays is an earthquake monitoring system; a three-drum seismograph and color screen work together to show real-time seismic activity from around the globe. The centerpiece of the room is the Dynamic Earth Globe, where visitors are able to watch the earth go through its full rotation via satellite, getting as close as possible to the views astronauts see from outer space.

The Hall of Planet Earth links visitors to the rest of the Rose Center, which is made up of the **Hall of the Universe** and the **Hayden Planetarium**. The center boasts an enormous sphere, 87ft in diameter, which appears to be floating inside a huge cube above the main entrance to the center. The sphere actually houses the planetarium, which includes two theaters, as well as research facilities and classrooms, and is illuminated rather eerily at night. Inside, the state-of-the-art **Space Theater** uses a Zeiss projector to create sky shows with sources like the Hubble telescope and NASA laboratories.

On the planetarium's second floor, the **Big Bang Theater** offers a multi-sensory recreation of the "birth" of the universe. On the outer walkway stand the Scales of the Universe, an installation which gives a physical presentation of the relative sizes of things, from galaxies, stars, and planets, down through cells and atoms, all in comparison to the central sphere. It is simple and effective, yet frustratingly complex to wrap your brain around.

Follow the **Cosmic Pathway**, a sloping spiral walkway that takes you through thirteen billion years of cosmic evolution via an interactive computerized timeline. It leads to the Hall of the Universe, which offers exhibits and interactive displays on the formation and evolution of the universe, the galaxy, stars, and planets, including a mini-theater where visitors can journey inside a black hole through computerized effects. There is even a display here entitled The Search for Life, which examines the planetary systems on which life could exist – in case you hadn't questioned the meaning of existence enough by this point.

Riverside Park and Riverside Drive

At the western edge of 72nd Street begins the four-mile stretch of **Riverside Park** (⍟www.nycgovparks.org). The entrance is marked by Penelope Jencks' pensive *Eleanor Roosevelt Monument* on the corner of 72nd Street and Riverside Drive, dedicated in 1996 by then–First Lady Hillary Rodham Clinton. Riverside Park was conceived in the mid-nineteenth century as a way of attracting the middle class to the remote Upper West Side and covering the unappealing Hudson River Railway tracks that had been built along the Hudson in 1846.

Though not as imposing or as spacious as Central Park, Riverside was designed by the same team of Frederick Law Olmsted and Calvert Vaux. Begun in 1873, the park took 25 years to finish; rock outcroppings and informally arranged trees, shrubs, and flowers surround its tree-lined main boulevards, and the overall effect is much the same today as it was then. The biggest changes to the park came in the 1960s, when Robert Moses widened it and added some of his usual concrete touches, including the rotunda at the 79th Street Boat Basin. The basin is a delightful place for a break, with paths leading down to it located on either side of 79th Street at Riverside Drive (you'll hit Moses' rotunda first – keep going until you see water). Not on many visitors' itineraries, this is a small harbor where a few hundred Manhattanites live on the water in houseboats, while others just moor their motorboats and sailboats there. It's one of the city's most peaceful locations; and while the views across the water to New Jersey aren't exactly awesome, they can be a tonic after the congestion of Manhattan proper.

A less appealing local landmark is the new forest of skyscrapers overlooking the park from what used to be derelict shipping yards. Although officially named the Penn Yards Project, this cluster of luxury condos is colloquially known as **Trump City** for the billionaire developer who seems to delight in offending local aesthetes. Squabbles over the future of the 75-acre site seemed endless, but now much of the construction is finished and the developer has added yet more stock to his real-estate holdings.

The main artery of this neighborhood is **Riverside Drive**: starting at West 72nd Street, it winds north, flanked by palatial townhouses and multistory apartment buildings, mostly thrown up in the early part of the twentieth century. In the 70s, especially, there is a concentration of lovely turn-of-the-nineteenth-century townhouses, many with copper-trimmed mansard roofs and private terraces or roof gardens. Between 80th and 81st streets you will find a row of historic **landmark townhouses**: classic brownstones, they have bowed exteriors, bay windows, and gabled roofs. You'll also find a number of other architectural surprises in this area, as many of the residences in the 80s between Riverside and West End have stained-glass windows as well as stone gargoyle faces leering from their facades.

Riverside Drive is also dotted with notable monuments: at West 89th Street, look for the **Soldiers and Sailors Monument** (1902), a marble memorial to the Civil War dead. Then there's the **Joan of Arc Monument** at West 93rd Street, which sits on top of a 1.6-acre cobblestone-and-grass park named Joan of Arc Island and located in the middle of the Drive. Finally, you'll hit the **Firemen's Memorial** at West 100th Street, a stately frieze designed in 1913 with the statues of *Courage* and *Duty* at its top.

There are more historic apartment buildings on Riverside Drive as you head north between 105th and 106th streets. **330 Riverside Drive**, now the Riverside Study Center (used by the shadowy Catholic sect Opus Dei) is a glorious five-story Beaux-Arts house built in 1900 – note the copper mansard roof, stone balconies, and delicate iron scrollwork. **331 Riverside Drive** is the current headquarters of the New York Buddhist Church, though it was formerly the home of Marion "Rosebud" Davies, a 1930s actress most famous for her role as William Randolph Hearst's mistress. The newspaper magnate bought the place for her since it was conveniently close to the house he shared with his wife Millicent and five sons (137 Riverside Drive at W 86th St); Hearst spent $1 million spiffing up the place to make it worthy of Marion. Their odd domestic arrangement continued for some years until Hearst and Davies finally decamped to the family's west-coast spread, San Simeon; Millicent and the boys remained in New York.

The odd little building next door to 331 Riverside Drive is also part of the New York Buddhist Church; it showcases a larger-than-life bronze statue of Shinran Shonin (1173–1262), the Japanese founder of the Jodo-Shinsu sect of Buddhism. The statue originally stood in Hiroshima and somehow survived the atomic explosion of August 1945. In 1955 it was brought to New York as a symbol of "lasting hope for world peace" and has been in this spot ever since. When it arrived, local lore had it that the statue was still radioactive, so in the 1950s and 1960s children were told to hold their breath as they went by. The River Mansion, as **337 Riverside Drive** is called, was home to Duke Ellington – and the stretch of West 106th Street between here and Central Park has been tagged Duke Ellington Boulevard in his honor.

Morningside Heights

North of the Upper West Side, **Morningside Heights** stretches from 110th Street to 123rd Street, west to the Hudson River, and east to Morningside Park, which is a small and rather unspectacular green space. The neighborhood has a somewhat funky, college-town aura, and has so far resisted the urge to convert its small stores to large impersonal chains or to build luxury high-rise apartments for mobs of stroller-pushing parents. That's partly thanks to its residents, a diverse mix of academics, professionals, and working-class families, who have banded together in the name of community preservation. Though there are few sights per se here, aside from the massive **Cathedral of St John the Divine** and **Columbia University**, it's worth ambling up here to get a sense of a close-knit neighborhood, a feeling that the Upper West Side lost some time ago.

The Cathedral Church of St John the Divine

The Cathedral Church of St John the Divine, 1047 Amsterdam Ave at 112th St (Mon–Sat 7am–6pm, Sun 7am–7pm except July & Aug 7am–6pm; free; ℡212/316-7540, ⊛www.stjohndivine.org), rises out of its surroundings with a solid majesty – hardly surprising, since it is the largest Gothic-style cathedral in the world, a title it holds even though it remains incomplete.

This Episcopal church was conceived, in 1892, as a Romanesque monolith; when the architect in charge changed in 1911, so did the building's style – it has ended up French neo-Gothic. Work progressed well until the outbreak of war in 1939; it wasn't until the mid-1980s that it resumed. The church's problems aren't limited to timely construction, though: it declared bankruptcy in 1994, fraught with funding difficulties and its legitimacy questioned by people who think the money might be better spent directly on the local community. Church members launched a massive international fundraising drive, which helped clear them from bankruptcy, but in 2001 church finances again became precarious following a fire that did significant damage to the cathedral. Water and smoke damage created the need for an all-out restoration, and even now it is unclear when the repairs will be completed. Don't let the building's raw state put you off visiting – the church is one of New York's most impressive sights. Despite being a regular stop for visiting bigwigs and leaders, including the Dalai Lama, its uptown location ensures the cathedral is rarely crowded.

Though the cathedral appears finished at first glance, take a look up into one of its huge, incomplete towers, and you'll see how much there is left to do. In reality, only two-thirds of the church is finished, and given the problems with funding, it's impossible to estimate when it'll be done – the earliest date is 2050. The one activity that continues is small-scale carving, much of it undertaken by locals who are trained by English stonemasons in the church's own sculpture/ stone workshops. When, or if, it is finished, St John the Divine will be the largest cathedral structure in the world, its floor space – 600ft long by 320ft wide at the transepts – big enough to swallow both the cathedrals of Notre Dame and Chartres whole, or more prosaically, two full-size football fields. For some idea of how the completed cathedral will look, stop in at the gift shop, where there's a scale model of the projected design, as well as an interesting array of books and souvenirs.

The **Portal of Paradise** at the cathedral's main entrance was completed in 1997, and is dazzlingly carved from limestone and painted with metallic oxide. Keep an eye out for the 32 biblical figures depicted (both male and female) and such startling images as a mushroom cloud rising apocalyptically over Manhattan. The portal is evidence of just how slow progress here really is: the carving took ten years. Only after entering the church does its staggering size become clear; the space is awe-inspiring, and definitely adds to the building's spiritual power. The interior shows the melding of the two architectural styles, particularly in the choir, where a heavy arcade of Romanesque columns rise to a high, Gothic vaulting; it is hoped the temporary dome will someday be replaced by a tall, delicate Gothic spire.

Construction aside, St John's is very much a **community church**. It houses a soup kitchen and shelter for the homeless; sponsors AIDS awareness and health outreach initiatives, and other social programs; and has a gymnasium, as well as plans for an amphitheater. The open-minded, progressive nature of the church is readily visible throughout the cathedral building: note the intricately carved wood **Altar for Peace**, the **Poets Corner** (with the names of American poets carved into its stone-block floor), and an altar honoring AIDS victims. The amazing stained-glass windows include scenes from both the Bible and American history. All kinds of art, both religious and secular, grace the interior, from teak Siamese prayer chests, to seventeenth-century tapestries, to a rare religious work by the late graffiti artist Keith Haring.

Outdoors, the cathedral's south side features the **Bestiary Gates**, their grills adorned with animal imagery (celebrating the annual blessing of the animals ceremony held here on the Feast of St Francis), a **Children's Sculpture Garden**, showcasing small bronze animal sculptures created by local schoolchildren, and the rather hideous **Peace Fountain**. This in turn circles Greg Wyatt's scary sculpture *Heaven and Hell*, which symbolically tells a tale of good triumphing over evil. Afterwards, take a stroll through the cathedral yard and workshop where, if work has begun again, you can watch Harlem's apprentice masons tapping away at the stone blocks of the future cathedral.

Public **tours** are given Tuesday through Saturday at 11am and Sunday at 1pm ($5) – meet at the Info Center, the blue booth right inside the main door. Access to the top of the cathedral is restricted, due to the 2001 fire; otherwise, the tour is unaffected.

Columbia University and around

The **Columbia University** campus fills seven blocks between Broadway and Morningside Drive from 114th to 121st streets, with its main entrance at Broadway and 116th Street. It is one of the most prestigious academic institutions in the country and a member of the Ivy League. Established in 1754,

Columbia has a long and venerable history – it is the country's fifth-oldest institution of higher learning, it awarded the first MD degree in America, and sponsored ground-breaking atomic research in the 1940s. The Morningside Heights campus, modeled after the Athenian *agora* (or town square), was laid out by McKim, Mead and White after the university moved here from midtown in 1897.

Amid the campus's Italian Renaissance–style structures, the domed and colonnaded **Low Memorial Library**, 116th Street at Broadway, is most noteworthy. Built in 1902, it's on the New York City Register of Historic Places and is a commanding sight. Tours of the campus leave from the Visitor Center here (Mon–Fri 11am and 2pm; free; ☎212/854-4900, ⊛www.columbia.edu). Across Broadway sits **Barnard College**: now part of Columbia University, it was a women's college until Columbia finally went coeducational in the mid-1980s. Many women still choose to study here, and Barnard retains its status as one of America's elite "Seven Sisters" colleges.

Running alongside the campus, Broadway is characterized by a lively bustle, with numerous inexpensive restaurants, bars, and cafés, and a few bookstores. The **West End**, 2911 Broadway at 113th St, was the hangout of Jack Kerouac, Allen Ginsberg, and the Beats in the 1950s; it still serves a student crowd, although it's undergone a few makeovers in the meantime.

Riverside Church and Grant's Tomb

Several blocks north and east of the university, **Riverside Church**, 490 Riverside Drive at 120th St (daily 9am–4.30pm, Sun service 10.45am; ☎212/870-6600), has a graceful French Gothic Revival tower, loosely modeled on the cathedral at Chartres. Like St John the Divine, it has become a community center for the surrounding parish. Take the elevator to the tower's twentieth floor and ascend the steps around the **carillon** (the largest in the world, with 74 bells) for some great views of Manhattan's skyline, New Jersey, and beyond – plus the rest of the city well into the Bronx and Queens. Make sure to root around inside the body of the church, too: its open interior stands in stark contrast to the mystery of St John the Divine; the one exception is the apse, which is sticky with ornamentation.

Up the block from the church is **Grant's Tomb**, at Riverside Drive and 122nd Street (daily 9am–5pm; free; ☎212/666-1640, ⊛www.nps.gov/gegr/). This Greek-style memorial is the nation's largest mausoleum, home to the bodies of conquering Civil War hero (and blundering eighteenth US president) Ulysses S. Grant and his wife, in two black-marble Napoleonic sarcophagi.

Harlem and above

The most famous African-American community in America (and, arguably, the birthplace of modern black culture), **Harlem** languished as a low-rent, high-crime neighborhood for much of the mid-twentieth century, justly earning a reputation as a place of racial tension and urban decay. Over the past few decades, though, things have begun to look up, and it is far less dangerous than it once was – indeed, pockets of it are among the more up-and-coming areas in Manhattan. Many local observers worry, however, that the influx of investment may come at too high a price in the long run.

While visitors to Harlem's main thoroughfares – **125th Street**, **Adam Clayton Powell, Jr Boulevard**, and **Lenox Avenue** – should have no problem, sightseers in Spanish Harlem (**El Barrio**) will find an undeniably rougher edge. Daytime visits there shouldn't be troublesome as long as you keep your wits about you, but strolling about at night is not recommended. Farther uptown is **Hamilton Heights**, a largely residential spot pepped up by an old Federal-style historic mansion and the campus of the City College of New York. Continuing north from there, you'll hit the Dominican stronghold of **Washington Heights**, a patchy place with few visitor attractions and another area where it pays to take care at night. The northernmost tip of the island, known as **Inwood**, is home to the **Cloisters Museum**, a mock medieval monastery that holds the Metropolitan Museum's superlative collection of medieval art and is the most visited site in the city north of Central Park.

Harlem

Practically speaking, **Harlem**'s sights are too spread apart to amble between: they stretch out over seventy blocks. You'll do best to make several trips if you want to see them all. It can be helpful to take a **guided tour** (see "Tours," p.33) to get acquainted with the area and to get you thinking about what you want to come back and see on your own. If you intend to see Harlem without a tour guide, it will serve you well to familiarize yourself with the areas you plan to visit before you go, and to stick to well-trodden streets and act relaxed once you get there.

Some history

Although the Dutch founded the settlement of **Nieuw Haarlem** in 1658, naming it for a town in Holland, the area remained primarily farmland up until

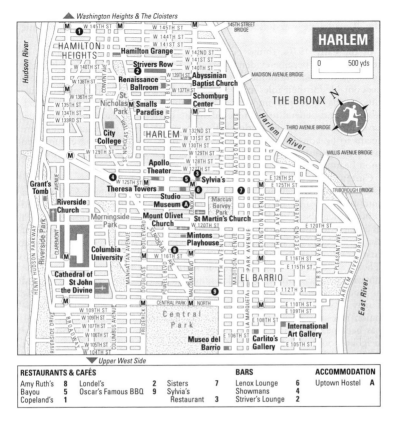

RESTAURANTS & CAFÉS				BARS		ACCOMMODATION	
Amy Ruth's	8	Londel's	2	Sisters	7	Lenox Lounge	6	Uptown Hostel	A
Bayou	5	Oscar's Famous BBQ	9	Sylvia's		Showmans	4		
Copeland's	1			Restaurant	3	Striver's Lounge	2		

the mid-nineteenth century, when the New York and Harlem Railroad linked the area with Lower Manhattan. The new rail line and the steadily developing suburb's new, fashionable brownstones attracted better-off immigrant families, mainly German Jews from the Lower East Side. When work began on the IRT-Lenox line (now the #1, #2, and #3 subway) later in the century, property speculators were quick to build good-quality homes farther north. They were too ambitious, though, for when the line opened in 1904 most of the buildings were still empty, any potential residents uneasy at moving so far from downtown. Black real-estate agents saw their chance: over the next fifteen years they snapped up the empty houses for next to nothing, then rented them to the city's growing community of displaced blacks, which was comprised of former midtown residents who had been driven out by the construction of Pennsylvania Station in 1906–10, and workers who had come from the Deep South for industrial jobs during World War I.

Once this real-estate boom began, the Jewish, German, and Italian populations of Harlem relocated farther north, and the area became predominantly black by the 1920s. The first signs of Harlem's explosion of black culture quickly appeared, and the musical and literary movement known as the **Harlem Renaissance** (see box, p.222) made the streets north of Central Park a necessary destination for anyone interested in the artistic cutting-edge. The Depression and post-war years were not kind to the area, however, and the Renaissance was followed by several decades of worsening economic conditions.

In the early 1970s, things began to turn around, and the beginnings of redevelopment became evident. Years of disgraceful living conditions brought residents to a boiling point, and slumlords and absentee landlords were held accountable for their roles in the area's ruin. A plethora of urban and community grants were put into effect for commercial and retail development, housing, and general urban renewal. Some thirty-odd years later, that initial investment is paying off: Harlem's historic areas are well maintained and there seems to be construction everywhere you turn. Savvy locals have purchased many of the district's nineteenth-century brownstones, which are some of the most beautiful in the city.

Currently, the federally established Upper Manhattan Empowerment Zone, encompassing Harlem and part of the South Bronx, is pumping $550 million into various area projects – many of them retail-driven. The program has helped usher in neighborhood branches of chains like Pathmark and *Starbucks*, as well as a Magic Johnson multiplex cinema. In March 2006, Harlem Lanes opened at the corner of 126th Street and Adam Clayton Powell, Jr Boulevard, marking the first time in more than thirty years that Harlem has had its own bowling alley. There's a certain chic cachet to retail in Harlem these days: fashion chain H&M unveiled a huge shop here, and downtown designer Nicole Miller has opened an outpost nearby. As for community-led changes, an organization involving ninety local churches and spearheaded by the Abyssinian Development Corporation (the development arm of the Abyssinian Baptist Church – see p.229), has become the owner of a number of business sites. Further boosting the neighborhood's visibility was Bill Clinton's decision in 2001 to maintain his first post-presidential office at 55 W 125th St. The questions facing the community now are not about how to drive interest or investment here, but rather how to

The Harlem Renaissance

The **Harlem Renaissance**, during which the talents of such icons as Billie Holiday, Paul Robeson, and James Weldon Johnson took root and flowered, served as inspiration for generations of African-American musicians, writers, and performers. In the 1920s, Manhattan's white residents began to notice Harlem's cultural offerings: after downtown went to bed, the sophisticated set drove north, where **jazz musicians** like Duke Ellington, Count Basie, and Cab Calloway played in packed nightspots like the Cotton Club, Savoy Ballroom, Apollo Theater, and Smalls Paradise, and the liquor flowed freely, despite Prohibition. But the Harlem Renaissance wasn't just about music. It was also characterized by the rich body of **literature** produced by Johnson, Langston Hughes, Jean Toomer, and Zora Neale Hurston, among many others.

Still, all these cultural forces were not enough to sustain a neighborhood where most residents lived below the poverty line. Even before the Great Depression it was hard to scrape out a living here, but the economic downturn of the 1930s drove middle-class blacks out of Harlem. It may be because evening revelers never stayed longer than the last drink that neither they, nor many histories of the period, recall the rampant poverty that went hand-in-hand with Harlem's raunchy, anything-goes nightlife.

One of the lasting legacies of this period, however, has been the neighborhood's sense of racial consciousness. First evidenced during the 1920s and 1930s in the writings and speeches of men like Marcus Garvey, W.E.B. DuBois, and Charles S. Johnson, the same spirit is still alive today in such larger-than-life Harlem firebrands as Al Sharpton and the Reverend Calvin Butts.

manage and control the area's evolution, as well as how to reconcile it with the poverty and unemployment still very much in evidence.

Along 125th Street

To begin exploring Harlem, take the #2 or #3 train to 125th Street; you'll exit the station at 125th Street and Lenox Avenue. The stretch of **125th Street** between Broadway and Fifth Avenue is Harlem's main commercial drag. It's here that recent investment in the area is most obvious – note the presence of fashion retailer H&M. This was Malcolm X's beat in the 1950s and 1960s – he strolled and preached on 125th Street, and photos of him and his followers have passed into legend. If you need a landmark, look for the **Adam Clayton Powell, Jr State Office Building** looming on the corner of Adam Clayton Powell, Jr Boulevard. Commissioned in 1972, it replaced a constellation of businesses that included Elder Louis Michaux's bookstore, one of Malcolm X's main rallying points. When construction began, the protests of squatters were so vehement that the city made several concessions: the bookstore was relocated one avenue eastward, and the building was named in honor of Adam Clayton Powell, Jr, Harlem's first black congressman (see box, p.228).

Apollo Theater and around

Walk a little west from the Powell Building and you reach the legendary **Apollo Theater**, 253 W 125th St at Frederick Douglass Blvd (☎212/531-5300, ⓦ www.apollotheater.com). Although it's not much to look at from the outside, from the 1930s to the 1970s this venue was the center of black entertainment in New York City and the northeast US. Almost all the great figures of jazz and blues played here, along with singers, comedians, and dancers; past winners of its famous Amateur Night have included Ella Fitzgerald, Billie Holiday, Luther Vandross, The Jackson Five, Sarah Vaughan, Marvin Gaye, and James Brown. Since its heyday, the Apollo has served as a warehouse, a movie theater, and a radio station; in its latest incarnation it is the venue for a weekly TV show, *Showtime at the Apollo*. Renovations have been ongoing since 2002: the interior has been overhauled, as have the old sign and marquee. Officially a landmark building, the Apollo offers daily 60-minute tours, but only to groups of twenty or more (call to arrange at ☎212/531-5337).

Across the way, the tall, narrow **Theresa Towers** office building, 2090 Adam Clayton Powell, Jr Blvd at 125th St, was until the 1960s the *Theresa Hotel*. Designed by George and Edward Blum in 1913, it still stands out from the rest of the street, thanks to its gleaming white terracotta patterns topped with sunbursts. Not desegregated until 1940, the hotel became known as the "Waldorf of Harlem." Fidel Castro was a guest here in 1960 while on a visit to the United Nations, when he shunned midtown luxury in a popular political gesture (though there's also a story, most likely apocryphal, that he turned up first at the actual *Waldorf* with a retinue that included his own supply of chickens for dinner – and when spurned by that swanky hotel decamped here). Look, too, for **Blumstein's**, 230 W 125th St at Eighth Ave, which, though no longer in business, still features its dilapidated neon sign. Founded by a German-Jewish immigrant in 1898, this was once the largest department store in the area. Like many white-owned local businesses, for many years Blumstein's refused to hire black workers except as menial laborers. In 1934 it became the focal point of a community-wide boycott led by Adam Clayton Powell, Jr – pointedly called "Don't Buy Where You Can't Work." The campaign was effective: the department store not only began hiring blacks, but it also became the first shop in the area to use black mannequins and feature a black Santa at Christmas.

Studio Museum in Harlem

Founded in 1968, the **Studio Museum in Harlem**, 144 W 125th St at Lenox Ave (Wed–Fri & Sun noon–6pm, Sat 10am–6pm; suggested donation $7; ☎212/864-4500, ⊛www.studiomuseum.org), has over 60,000 square feet of exhibition space dedicated to showcasing contemporary African-American painting, photography, and sculpture. The permanent collection is displayed on a rotating basis and includes works by Harlem Renaissance–era photographer James Van Der Zee, as well as paintings and sculptures by post-war artists. A neighborhood-oriented perspective, skillful curatorial work, and supplementary lectures, author readings, and music performances combine to create an atmosphere more like a community center than a museum.

Lenox Avenue and around

North of Central Park, Sixth Avenue becomes **Lenox Avenue**, one of Harlem's main north–south arteries. It was officially rechristened **Malcolm X Boulevard** in the late 1980s, but is still known to most by its old name.

Mount Morris Park Historic District

The area around Lenox Avenue between West 118th and 124th streets is known as the **Mount Morris Park Historic District**. It was one of the first districts north of Central Park to attract residential development after the elevated railroads were constructed. Initially inhabited by WASPy commuters, the area then became home to the city's second-largest neighborhood of Eastern European Jewish immigrants (after the Lower East Side), and finally shifted to a primarily black neighborhood in the 1920s. This series of complex demographic shifts has created a profusion of diverse religious structures, and has helped place the neighborhood on the National Register of Historic Places. The district has an active community-improvement association, which runs a historic-home tour (call for details ☎212/369-4241, ⊛www.harlemmtmorris.org).

One of the district's most interesting buildings is **Mount Olivet Church**, 201 Lenox Ave at 120th St, a Greco-Roman–style temple that was once a synagogue. Compare its design with the somber, bulky, Gothic **St Martin's**, at the southeast corner of Lenox Avenue and 122nd Street; both these institutions have been fortunate in avoiding the decay that has afflicted much of the area. Elsewhere, the Mount Morris district includes some lovely rowhouses that were constructed during the speculation boom of the 1890s: most outstanding of all are **133–143 W 122nd St** at Lenox Ave. Arguably the finest row of Queen Anne–style homes in the city, they were designed by leading architect Francis H. Kimball in 1885–87. The orange-brick houses have gables, dormers, and some lovely stained-glass. Double back west and pause in front of **Hale House**, 152 W 122nd St (☎212/663-0700, ⊛www.halehouse.org). It was established in 1969 by "Mother" Clara Hale, whose program for substance-addicted (and now HIV-infected) infants and mothers was one of the first in the country; a plaque in front of the house is decorated with bronze renderings of children's faces and encircles a statue of Hale herself.

From Hale House, head east to **Marcus Garvey Park**, formerly Mount Morris Park; it takes its new name from the black leader of the 1920s. The park is situated between East 120th and 124th streets, between Mount Morris Park West and Madison Avenue. As urban green-spaces go, it's a little odd, centered on a low, rocky hill rather than rolling lawns, although it's become a bit nicer, thanks to a series of recent renovations: unnecessary asphalt was replaced with grass, a children's wading pool and spray shower were installed for summertime play, and there's a new sitting area for adults. It's dotted with other public facilities as well, including an amphitheater, which is occasionally used for performances by local arts groups. The park's most notable feature, though, is the elegant octagonal fire tower built in 1857 on a peak in the middle of the space. It is a unique example of the early-warning devices once found throughout the city. Sadly, the tower's observation deck has been removed, so you can no longer enjoy the views, but even so, it's still an impressive structure.

Although there are some noteworthy houses along **Mount Morris Park West**, the park's western border, you may find them hard to appreciate, overshadowed as they are by one of Harlem's great architectural tragedies. Smack dab in the middle of the block is a group of rowhouses so neglected that the facades of several have literally been torn away. Notoriously known as **The Ruins**, this ensemble was callously created by New York State when, under the right of eminent domain, it began stripping down several of the houses to create a drug-rehab center in 1968. Community opposition was fierce: this proposal and later plans were shelved. Today Mount Morris Park West is experiencing gentrification, albeit slowly (restoration efforts began in 1998); the quality of these buildings has attracted developers, who've bought up several and rehabbed them for sale – there's even a day spa here now.

Schomburg Center for Research in Black Culture

If you're more interested in learning about Harlem's past than pondering its uncertain future, it's worth taking a walk up to the **Schomburg Center for Research in Black Culture**, 515 Lenox Ave at 135th St (Tues & Wed noon–8pm, Thurs & Fri noon–6pm, Sat 10am–6pm; free; ☎212/491-2200, ⓦwww.nypl.org/research/sc), a member of the New York Public Library system. Originally a lending branch, the Division of Negro Literature, History and Prints was created in 1925 after the community began rallying for a library of its own. The collection grew dramatically, thanks to Arthur Schomburg, a black Puerto Rican nicknamed "The Sherlock Holmes of Black History" for his obsessive efforts to document black culture. Schomburg had acquired over 10,000 manuscripts, photos, and artifacts, and he sold them all to the NYPL for $10,000; he then worked as curator for the collection, sometimes using his own funds for upkeep, from 1932 until his death six years later. Since that time, the amassing of over five million items has made the center the world's top research facility for the study of black history and culture. Aside from its letters archive and book collections, the center is also the site of the ashes of renowned poet Langston Hughes, best known for penning *The Negro Speaks of Rivers.* That poem inspired Houston Conwill's terrazzo and brass "cosmogram" in the atrium beyond the main entrance; it's a mosaic built over a tributary of the Harlem River. Seven of Hughes' lines radiate out from a circle, and the last line, "My soul has grown deep like the rivers," located in a fish at the center, marks where he is interred.

The Schomburg Center also features community-heritage displays, book readings, and art and music events in its halls, gallery, and two auditoriums – call for information on special events.

Harlem was once home to any number of nightspots. Some were small: housed in private brownstones, they catered solely to black audiences, and have long since been converted for other uses. Others were much larger, and attracted hordes of white patrons from downtown as well as middle-class blacks. Several of these, especially the once-famous **jazz venues**, have survived decades of disuse. Although their current boarded-up state is sobering, many of these beautiful buildings are slated for restoration and refurbishment.

The Abyssinian Development Corporation, the development arm of the Abyssinian Baptist Church, acquired the **Renaissance Ballroom**, Adam Clayton Powell, Jr Blvd at 138th St, as a likely future home for the Classical Theater of Harlem, though plans are moving ahead very slowly. This tile-trimmed, square-and-diamond-shaped dance club hosted Duke Ellington and Chick Webb in the 1920s. Nicknamed the "Rennie," it was a haven for middle-class blacks – look for the original light-up "Chop Suey" sign (once considered an exotic dish) that's now rusting away on the exterior.   The same corporation, in partnership with the city, has transformed another former club, **Smalls Paradise**, Adam Clayton Powell, Jr Blvd at 135th St, into a public school. This finial-topped brick building was built in 1925 and hosted a mixed black and white crowd from the beginning. It was once known as "The Hottest Spot in Harlem" and has claimed to be the birthplace of New York City's nickname. It's said that when jazzmen met on the road in the 1930s, they would call to each other, "See you at the Big Apple," after the name and appropriate illustration still decorating the outside of **Smalls**, and the term entered the vernacular after local journalists started using it.

The ground floor of the **Cecil Hotel**, 206–210 W 118th St at St Nicholas Ave, still displays the light-up sign advertising **Mintons Playhouse**, supposedly the birthplace of bebop. In the 1940s, after finishing their sets at Harlem's clubs, Thelonious Monk, Dizzy Gillespie, Charlie Parker, John Coltrane, and other greats would gather at Mintons for late-night jam sessions that gave rise to the improvised jazz style.   As for the **Cotton Club**, it was originally at 142nd Street and Lenox Ave, and was a segregated establishment – though most of the performers here were black, as was the staff, only whites were allowed to attend as guests. That building was demolished in 1958, but the club reopened in Harlem in 1978 at 666 W 125th St, where it continues to put on a good jazz show at night as well as a Sunday gospel brunch. For more on Harlem's nightlife today, see "The performing arts & film," p.383, and "Nightlife," p.376.

Along 116th Street

It's along **116th Street** that the spirit of the late Malcolm X, founder of a movement that emphasized austerity and African-American self-reliance, is perhaps the most palpable. Look for the green onion-dome of the **Masjid Malcolm Shabazz mosque**, 102 W 116th St at Lenox Ave; it's named for him. Between Lenox and Fifth avenues on 116th Street, you'll pass the bazaar-like **Malcolm Shabazz Harlem Market** (daily 10am–8pm; ☎212/987-8131), its entrance marked by colorful fake minarets. The market's offerings include cloth, T-shirts, jewelry, clothing, and more, all with a distinctly Afro-centric flavor – it's worth stopping by, mostly since what's on sale here differs so much from the usual flea-market staples. Ironically, the vendors, who used to run from police and clash with other local merchants, now pay taxes, accept credit cards, and take accounting courses at the mosque. The market has changed venues a few times; moved from its original street location by city authorities, it was then shifted down the block to make way for several massive construction projects being supervised by the mosque (which plays a huge role in the community, acquiring property and spurring development projects, much like the Abyssinian Development Corporation). One such project is the **Malcolm Shabazz Gardens**, a series of income-capped houses modeled on the derelict brownstones they replaced, lining 117th Street.

The stretch of 116th Street between Lenox and Manhattan avenues has recently become a hub for recent West African immigrants and is unofficially known as **Little Senegal** – listen for snatches of French on the street. It's estimated that at least 25,000 Senegalese have settled in New York in the last few years. They've opened up shops, beauty parlors, and restaurants here to create a thriving neighborhood.

There are also some much older African-influenced buildings nearby, including the fanciful blue-and-white Moorish-style **Corinthian Baptist Church**, 1912 Seventh Ave (Powell Blvd) at 116th St (☎212/864-9526). Originally built as the Regent Theater in 1912, this was one of America's earliest movie palaces before being transformed into a church in 1929. This change of use isn't all that unusual in this area: many of black Harlem's churches have found homes in buildings initially designated for other uses or structures planned by different congregations. If you want to see one of the few churches built by a black architect, head up to 134th Street between Frederick Douglass and Powell boulevards: that's the site of **St Philip's Church**, an elegant brick-and-granite building constructed by Vertner Tandy in 1910–11.

El Barrio

At Park Avenue, Harlem becomes **Spanish Harlem**, which stretches all the way from here to the East River and dips down as far as 96th Street, where it collides head-on with the affluence of the Upper East Side. The area's name is misleading, though, as it has little in common with Harlem proper other than its uptown location. This neighborhood is one of the centers of Manhattan's large Puerto Rican community, and is better known by locals as **El Barrio** – a term that can sometimes imply a slum, but to its residents simply means "the neighborhood."

What's immediately evident as you walk around here is the quality of the buildings or, rather, the lack thereof. There are no swathes of old brownstones waiting to be remodeled and restored. Instead, there are blocks of low-rise, low-income housing that give the area an intimidating atmosphere. El Barrio was originally a working-class Italian area and, indeed, a small number of Italian families still live around 114–116th streets along First Avenue. However, most Italians started moving to the suburbs after World War II, and this stretch has been predominantly Puerto Rican since the early 1950s. That's when the American government offered Puerto Ricans incentives to immigrate to the US under a policy known as "Operation Bootstrap," the idea being to pull Puerto Rico up "by the straps of its boots" by countering its overpopulation problem. Thousands took the US up on its offer, and many Puerto Ricans relocated here. Most ended up working menial jobs and living in poverty – fifty years on, El Barrio is still one of the rougher parts of Manhattan, and has yet to see any significant gentrification, although changes are coming. The area's ethnic focus is shifting, as more Mexicans arrive, and its cultural and creative strengths are being explored by second-generation immigrants, often known as NuYoricans (the word's a blend of New York and Boricua, the original name for the island of Puerto Rico).

The hub of the neighborhood has long been **La Marqueta**, on Park Avenue between 111th and 116th streets, though it's in a sorry state. Originally a five-block street market of Spanish products, it's now largely vacant, as the locals have turned to shopping in supermarkets like everyone else. The remaining occupied storefronts sell everything from tropical fruits and vegetables, jewelry, religious figurines, and clothing to dried herbs and snake oils. Mayor Bloomberg has assigned a task force to look at ways to improve and upgrade La Marqueta and, with it, the entire area.

If you're looking for insight into New York's Latin culture, you're better off heading to the **Museo del Barrio** or even **La Casa de la Herencia Cultural Puertorriqueña**, a Puerto Rican heritage library (☎212/722-2600). To check out the contemporary-art scene here, stop by two notable galleries, the **International Art Gallery**, 309 108th St at Third Ave, and **Carlito's Gallery**, 1701 Lexington Ave at 107th St (☎212/348-7044), both of which are alternative spaces for local artists of Latin, African-American, and Asian origin.

Museo del Barrio

Literally translated as "the neighborhood museum," the **Museo del Barrio**, 1230 Fifth Ave at 104th St, was founded in 1969 by a group of local Puerto Rican parents, educators, and artists who wanted to teach their children about their heritage (Wed–Sun 11am–5pm; $6; ☎212/831-7272, ⊛www.elmuseo .org). In keeping with its "homegrown" vibe, the museum was started in a school classroom and still feels more like a community center than a stuffy cultural institution. In 2004, the museum undertook a major renovation project designed to broaden its focus beyond strictly Puerto Rican subjects, including the expansion of its one permanent exhibit on **the Taino**, a highly developed people from the Caribbean (1200–1500 AD).

Though there are temporary exhibits as well as a theater on site – the **Teatro Hecksher**, which hosts Latin-influenced plays and movies (call for schedules; tickets $10–20) – the best time to visit is for one of the summertime concerts. The museum stays open late one night per week (usually Thursday), while a band plays out front.

Adam Clayton Powell, Jr Boulevard

Above 110th Street, Seventh Avenue becomes **Adam Clayton Powell, Jr Boulevard**, a broad sweep that pushes north between low-built houses – perhaps the only strip in Manhattan on which the sky can break through. Since its conception, Powell Boulevard has vied with 125th Street as Harlem's main commercial concourse, but while big-name retailers are returning to the other thoroughfare, this boulevard remains forlorn. Years of decline show in its graffiti-splattered walls and storefronts and empty lots; there isn't much to see until you reach 138th Street.

Reverend Adam Clayton Powell, Jr

In the 1930s, the **Reverend Adam Clayton Powell, Jr** was instrumental in forcing Harlem's stores, most of which were white-owned and retained a white workforce, to begin employing the blacks whose patronage ensured the stores' survival. Later, he became the first black on the city council, then New York's first black congressional representative, during which time he sponsored the country's first minimum-wage law. His distinguished career came to an embittered end in 1967, when amid strong rumors of the misuse of public funds, he was excluded from Congress by majority vote. This failed to diminish his standing in Harlem, where voters twice re-elected him before his death in 1972. The scandal is almost forgotten now, and there's a fitting memorial on the boulevard that today bears his name.

Harlem's incredible **gospel music** has long enticed visitors, and for good reason: both it and the entire revival-style Baptist experience can be amazing and invigorating. Gospel tours are big business, and churches seem to be jockeying among themselves to see who can attract the most tourists. Many of the arranged tours (see p.35) are pricey, but they usually offer transportation uptown and brunch after the service. If you don't feel like shelling out the cash, or if you're looking for a more flavorful experience, you can also easily go it alone. The choir at the **Abyssinian Baptist Church** is arguably the best in the city, but long lines of tourists make the experience, well, touristy. Another fairly popular option is the **Metropolitan Baptist Church**, 151 W 128th St at Adam Clayton Powell, Jr Blvd (☏212/663-8990, ⓦwww .metropolitan-bc.org). **Mount Nebo Baptist Church**, 1883 Adam Clayton Powell, Jr Blvd at W 114th St (☏212/866-7880), is much less of a circus; worship here is taken seriously and services are not designed as tourist attractions, but the congregation is very welcoming to nonmembers. Wherever you go, dress accordingly: jackets for men and skirts or dresses for women.

Abyssinian Baptist Church

At 132 W 138th St, at Adam Clayton Powell, Jr Blvd, stands the **Abyssinian Baptist Church** (☏212/862-7474, ⓦwww.abyssinian.org), first incorporated in 1808 in what is now Tribeca. Its founders included a group of African-Americans living in New York, as well as some Ethiopian merchants, who were tired of segregated seating at Baptist churches in New York (the church's name comes from the traditional name for Ethiopia). The Abyssinian started becoming the religious and political powerhouse that it is today in 1908, when the **Reverend Adam Clayton Powell, Jr** was appointed pastor (see box, opposite). Construction on the current Gothic and Tudor building was completed in 1923. It's worth a trip here just to see and hear the gut-busting **choir** – see the box, above, for details.

△ Strivers' Row

Strivers' Row

Just west of Powell Boulevard along 138th and 139th streets stands **Strivers' Row**, some of the finest blocks of rowhouses in Manhattan. Sets of houses were commissioned during the 1890s housing boom from three architects: James Brown Lord; Bruce Price and Clarence Luce; and last but definitely not least, the firm of McKim, Mead and White (their building is on the north side of 139th Street). The results are uniquely harmonious, a dignified Renaissance-derived strip that's an amalgam of simplicity and elegance. Note the unusual rear service alleys of the houses, reached via iron-gated cross streets. At the turn of the nineteenth century, this came to be the desirable place for ambitious professionals within Harlem's burgeoning black community (starting with rail porters) to reside – hence its nickname.

Hamilton Heights

The farther uptown you venture, the less like New York your surroundings seem. Much of Harlem's western edge, between 135th and 145th streets, is taken up by the area known as **Hamilton Heights**; like Morningside Heights to the south, there's a blend of campus buildings (in this case, belonging to the City College of New York) and residences here, lightened by a sprinkle of slender parks on a bluff above Harlem. However, one stretch, the **Hamilton Heights Historic District**, bounded by Amsterdam and St Nicholas avenues from 140th to 145th streets, pulls Hamilton Heights well up from the ranks of middle class; this is still a firmly bourgeois residential area – and one of the most attractive uptown. In the early decades of the nineteenth century, Manhattanites bought up the land here and used it as their country estates. By the twentieth century, most of the neighborhood was completed; there are rowhouses in a variety of architectural styles, including Beaux Arts and Romanesque Revival. Other than the Historic District, there's little up here in the way of specific sights.

Visitors wandering up from Harlem or exiting the 135th Street and St Nicholas Avenue #B or #C subway station will therefore be surprised by **Convent Avenue**. From here to 140th street, its secluded, blossom-lined streets have a garden-suburb prettiness that's spangled with Gothic, French, and Italian Renaissance influences in happily eclectic 1890s houses. The feathery span of the Shepard Archway at 140th Street announces **City College**, a rustic-feeling campus of Collegiate-Gothic halls built of gray Manhattan schist dug up during the IRT subway line excavations and mantled with white terracotta fripperies. Founded in 1905, City College didn't charge tuition, and thus became the seat of higher learning for many of New York's poor, including polio-vaccine pioneer Jonas Salk and soldier-turned-statesman Colin Powell. Even though free education here came to an end in the 1970s, three-quarters of the students still come from minority backgrounds.

Hamilton Grange

Convent Avenue also contains Hamilton Heights' single historical lure – the 1798 house of founding father Alexander Hamilton, **Hamilton Grange National Memorial**, 287 Convent Ave at 142nd St (Fri–Sun 9am–5pm; free; ☎212/283-5154, ⊛www.nps.gov/hagr/). The Grange has bounced around the island a couple times: it stood at its original site on 143rd Street until 1889, and is now scheduled to move again from its current location in October 2007. The National Parks Service, which runs the home, has been trying to relocate it for years, and finally received the funds needed to renovate and then transplant the house out of its cramped quarters here, in the shadow of the fiercely Romanesque St Luke's Church, to which it was originally donated. The money

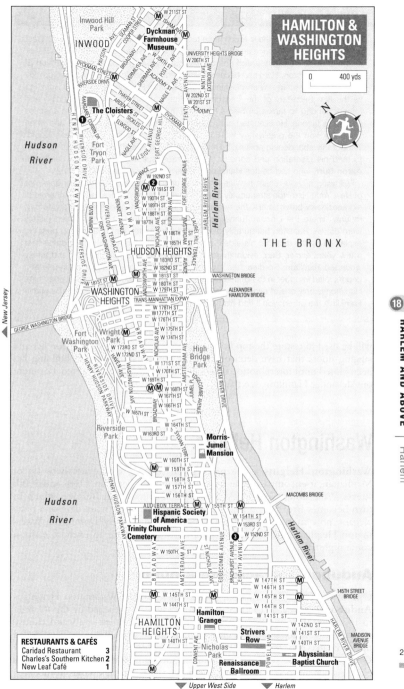

HAMILTON &
WASHINGTON
HEIGHTS

0   400 yds

N

THE BRONX

New Jersey

Hudson
River

Inwood Hill
Park

INWOOD

Dyckman
Farmhouse
Museum

UNIVERSITY HEIGHTS BRIDGE
W 206TH ST

W 202ND ST
W 201ST ST

The Cloisters

Fort
Tryon
Park

HUDSON HEIGHTS

WASHINGTON
HEIGHTS

WASHINGTON BRIDGE

ALEXANDER
HAMILTON BRIDGE

TRANS-MANHATTAN EXPWY

Fort
Washington
Park

GEORGE WASHINGTON BRIDGE

Wright
Park

High
Bridge
Park

Riverside
Park

Morris–
Jumel
Mansion

Hudson
River

MACOMBS BRIDGE

AUDUBON TERRACE
Hispanic Society
of America
Trinity Church
Cemetery

Harlem River

145TH STREET
BRIDGE

HAMILTON
HEIGHTS

Hamilton
Grange

Strivers
Row

MADISON
AVENUE
BRIDGE

Nicholas
Park

Renaissance
Ballroom

Abyssinian
Baptist Church

RESTAURANTS & CAFÉS
Caridad Restaurant   3
Charles's Southern Kitchen 2
New Leaf Café   1

Upper West Side   Harlem

Alexander Hamilton

Alexander Hamilton's life is much more fascinating than his house. Born in the West Indies, he came to America as a young man. He was an early supporter of the Revolution, and his intelligence and enthusiasm quickly brought him to the attention of George Washington. Hamilton became the general's aide-de-camp, and rose quickly through military ranks. When Washington was elected President, he named Hamilton as the first Secretary of the Treasury. Hamilton, quick in both understanding and temper, tended to tackle problems headlong, a propensity that made him enemies as well as friends. He alienated both John Adams and Thomas Jefferson, and when Jefferson won the presidency in 1801, Hamilton was left out in the political cold. Temporarily abandoning politics, he moved away from the city to his grange (or farm) to tend his plantation and conduct a memorably sustained and vicious feud with **Aaron Burr**, who had beaten Hamilton's father-in-law in a Senate election.

Following a short tenure as Vice President under Jefferson, Burr ran for governor of New York; Hamilton strenuously opposed his candidacy and, after an exchange of extraordinarily bitter letters, the two men fought a duel in Weehawken, New Jersey, roughly where the Lincoln Tunnel now emerges, on July 11, 1804. When pistols were drawn, Hamilton honourably discharged his into the air, a happening possibly explained by the fact that his eldest son had been killed in a duel on the same field a few years earlier. Burr, evidently made of lesser stuff, aimed carefully and fatally wounded Hamilton. So died "the most restless, impatient, artful, indefatigable and unprincipled intriguer in the United States," as President John Adams described him. Hamilton is only one of two non-presidents to find his way onto US money (Benjamin Franklin's the other): you'll find his portrait on the $10 bill.

will be used to restore the top floor for visitors, and repair unstable porches and sagging floors that have deteriorated over the years; the current building has been closed until future notice, in an effort to get restorations started. For more on Alexander Hamilton, see the box above.

Washington Heights

Washington Heights is the name given to most of the northern tip of Manhattan; it encompasses the majority of ground between 145th and 200th streets. Walk along Convent Avenue until it joins Sylvan Terrace, which in turn becomes Broadway a few blocks north. This is the main drag of a once elegant, now mostly raggedy neighborhood. The largely Dominican Washington Heights is vibrant and lively by day, but a place to exercise caution come nightfall.

Audubon Terrace and around

One of the few sights worth at least a quick look in Washington Heights is **Audubon Terrace**, at 155th St and Broadway (easily reached by the #1 train to 157th and Broadway). This Acropolis of folly is what's left of a weird, clumsy, nineteenth-century attempt to glorify 155th Street, when museums were dolled up as Beaux-Arts temples. Officially the **Washington Heights Museum Group**, the terrace was originally built in the vain anticipation of New York's elite aristocratic society migrating north. Now the complex stands in mocking contrast to its still-decrepit surroundings; as you might expect, it's little known and little visited.

There is only one museum left here, the **Hispanic Society of America** (Tues–Sat 10am–4.30pm, Sun 1–4pm, Library closed Aug; free; ☎212/926-2234, ⓦwww.hispanicsociety.org), but it makes the trip worthwhile. The Hispanic Society owns one of the largest collections of Hispanic art outside Spain, including over 3000 paintings by masters such as Goya, El Greco, and Velázquez, as well as more than 6000 decorative works of art. The collection ranges from an intricately carved ivory box dating from 965 AD, to fifteenth-century textiles, to Joaquin Sorolla y Bastida's joyful mural series *Provinces of Spain* (commissioned specifically for the society in 1911). Displays of the permanent collection rarely change, so you can be fairly certain you'll see the highlights. The 200,000-book library, which includes over 16,000 works printed before the eighteenth century, is a major reference site for scholars studying Spanish and Portuguese art, history, and literature.

One avenue east, at 155th Street and Amsterdam, lies the **Trinity Church Cemetery** (☎212/368-1600, ⓦwww.trinitywallstreet.org), its large, placid grounds dotted with some fanciful mausolea; robber baron John Jacob Astor is buried up here, as are naturalist James Audubon and Chelsea developer Clement Clark Moore.

The Morris–Jumel Mansion and around

Within easy walking distance of Audubon Terrace and the cemetery is the **Morris–Jumel Mansion**, 65 Jumel Terrace at 160th St and Edgecombe Ave (Wed–Sun 10am–4pm; $4; ☎212/923-8008, ⓦwww.morrisjumel.org). Another uptown surprise, the mansion somehow survived the urban renewal (or better, destruction) that occurred all around it, and is now one of the city's more successful house museums, its proud Georgian outlines faced with a later Federal portico. Inside, the rooms reveal some pieces of engaging history, including the stories of the two men who gave the place their names. Built as a rural retreat in 1765 by Colonel Roger Morris, the house served briefly Washington's as headquarters before falling into the hands of the British. Wealthy wine merchant Stephen Jumel bought the derelict mansion in 1810 and refurbished it for his wife Eliza, formerly a prostitute and his mistress. New York society didn't take to such a past, but when Jumel died in 1832, Eliza married ex–Vice President Aaron Burr – she for his connections, he for her money. Burr was 78 when they married, twenty years older than Eliza: the marriage lasted for six months before old Burr left, having gone through her inheritance, only to die on the day of their divorce. Eliza battled on to the age of 91, and on the top floor of the house you'll find her obituary, a magnificently fictionalized account of a "scandalous" life.

Just opposite the entrance to the mansion's grounds is the quaint block of **Sylvan Terrace**, a tiny cobblestone mews lined with yellow and green wooden houses built in the 1880s – and seeming impossibly out of place just barely off the wide-open intersection of Amsterdam and St Nicholas avenues. North of here at 165th and Broadway is the **Audubon Ballroom**, scene of Malcolm X's assassination in 1965 and now, after some controversy, a part of the Columbia-Presbyterian Hospital complex.

George Washington Bridge

From most western parts of Washington Heights you can get a glimpse of the **George Washington Bridge**, which links Manhattan to New Jersey.

It's arguable that the feeder road to the bridge has created two distinct areas: below is bleakly run-down, one of the biggest areas of illegal drug activity in the city; above, the streets relax in smaller, more diverse, ethnic old-time neighborhoods of Jews, Greeks, Central Europeans, and especially Irish, immigrants, though a major Hispanic community has been growing since the 1970s. A skillful, dazzling sketch high above the Hudson, the bridge skims almost a mile across the channel in massive metalwork and graceful lines, a natural successor to the Brooklyn Bridge. "Here, finally, steel architecture seems to laugh," said Le Corbusier of the 1931 construction. And not only figuratively: the suspension cable looks like a gigantic smile, beaming upon midtown Manhattan's ambitious towers and workers in the distance.

The Cloisters Museum and around

The only reason most visitors come this far uptown is to see **The Cloisters Museum** in Fort Tryon Park (Tues–Sun: March–Oct 9.30am–5.15pm; Nov–Feb 9.30am–4.45pm; suggested donation $15, including same-day admission to the Metropolitan Museum; ☏212/923-3700, ⊛www.metmuseum.org). It stands above the Hudson like some misplaced Renaissance palazzo-cum-monastery, and is home to the Metropolitan Museum of Art's collection of medieval tapestries, metalwork, paintings, and sculpture. Impressive artwork aside, you'll find an additional reward in the park itself, cleverly landscaped by Frederick Law Olmsted, Jr (son of the Central Park planner). The promenade overlooking the river and the English-style garden make for a stunningly romantic spot. Inside the museum, the central cloister, with pink marble arcades and a fountain purchased from the French monastery of Saint-Michel-de-Cuxa, might trick you into believing that you're in southwestern France. Portions of five medieval cloisters (basically, covered walkways and their enclosed courtyards) are incorporated into the structure, the folly of collectors **George Grey Barnard** and **John D. Rockefeller, Jr**. Take the #A train to 190th Street–Fort Washington Avenue.

Some history

Barnard started a museum on this spot in 1914 to house his personal collection of medieval works, mostly sculpture and architectural fragments acquired in France. Later, Rockefeller donated funds to the Met, enabling the museum to purchase the site and its collection, as well as the 66 acres of land around it – now Fort Tryon Park. With commendable foresight, Rockefeller himself purchased 700 acres of land across the way in New Jersey to ensure perpetually good views. Barnard and Rockefeller each shipped over the best of medieval Europe for the museum: **Romanesque chapels** and **Gothic halls**, dismantled and transplanted brick by brick, along with tapestries, paintings, and sculptures. Despite the hodgepodge of styles, it is all undeniably well carried off, superb in detail and offering a great atmosphere. The completed museum opened in 1938, and is still the only museum in the US specializing in medieval art (though, technically, it's not a stand-alone institution, but rather a branch of the Metropolitan Museum of Art).

The collection

The best approach if you're coming from the 190th Street subway is directly across the park: the views are tremendous. Once at the museum, start from the entrance hall and work counterclockwise: the collection is laid out in roughly chronological order. First off is the simplicity of the **Romanesque Hall**, featuring French remnants such as an arched, limestone doorway dating to 1150 and a thirteenth-century portal from a monastery in Burgundy. The frescoed Spanish **Fuentidueña Chapel** is dominated by a huge, domed twelfth-century apse from Segovia that immediately induces a reverential hush. The hall and chapel form a corner on one of the prettiest of the five cloisters here, **St Guilhelm**, which is ringed by Corinthian-style columns topped by carved capitals from thirteenth-century southern France. The nearby **Langon Chapel**, attractive enough in itself, is enhanced by a twelfth-century ciborium (a permanent altar canopy) that manages to be formal and graceful in just the right proportions, and an emotive wooden sculpture of the Virgin and Child beneath.

At the center of the museum is the **Cuxa Cloister**, from the twelfth-century Benedictine monastery of Saint-Michel-de-Cuxa near Prades in the French Pyrenees; its Romanesque capitals are brilliantly carved, with monkeys, eagles, and lions whose open mouths reveal half-eaten human legs. Central to the scene is the garden, planted with fragrant, almost overpowering, herbs and flowers and offering (bizarrely) piped-in birdsong.

The museum's smaller **sculpture** collection is equally impressive. In the **Early Gothic Hall** are a number of carved figures, including one memorably tender Virgin and Child, carved in France in the thirteenth and fourteenth centuries, probably for veneration at a private altar. The next room holds a collection of tapestries, including a rare surviving Gothic work showing the Nine Heroes. The brave men, popular figures of the ballads of the Middle Ages, depict three pagans (Hector, Alexander, and Julius Caesar), three Hebrews (David, Joshua, and Judas Maccabees), and three Christians (Arthur, Charlemagne, and Godfrey of Bouillon). Five of the nine are here, clothed in the garb of the day (around 1385) against a rich backdrop.

The **Unicorn Tapestries** (c.1500, Netherlands) in the following room are even more spectacular – brilliantly alive with color, observation, and Christian symbolism. The entire series is on display to the public: the most famous is the seventh and last, where the slain unicorn has miraculously returned to life and is trapped in a circular pen. It isn't just the creature's resurrection that's mysterious – the entire sequence is shrouded in mystery: aside from the fact that they were designed in France and made in Brussels, little else is known for certain, even who the intended original recipients were (the most plausible claim is Anne of Brittany, wife of King Louis XII). As for the tapestries' allegorical meaning, the unicorn is said to represent both a husband captured in marriage and Christ risen again.

Most of the Met's medieval paintings are to be found downtown, but one important exception is **Campin**'s *Altarpiece*. This fifteenth-century triptych depicts the Annunciation scene in a typical bourgeois Flemish home of the day, and is housed in its own antechamber, outfitted with a desk, chair, cupboard, and other household articles from that period (though from different countries of origin). On the left of the altarpiece, the artist's patron and his wife gaze timidly on through an open door; to the right, St Joseph works in his carpenter's shop. St Joseph was mocked in the literature of the day, which might account for his rather ridiculous appearance – making a mousetrap, a symbol of the way the Devil traps souls. Through the windows behind, life goes on in a fifteenth-century market square, perhaps Campin's native Tournai.

The **Late Gothic Hall** next door is filled with expressively detailed, large sculptural **altarpieces** depicting biblical scenes. Especially noteworthy is the rarely depicted *Death (Dormition) of the Virgin* in dark wood, whose right side displays the girdle of the Virgin being dropped to St Thomas by an angel, conveying her assumption into heaven.

On the first floor, a large Gothic chapel boasts a high vaulted ceiling and mid- to late-fourteenth-century Austrian stained-glass windows, along with the monumental **sarcophagus of Ermengol VII**, with its whole phalanx of (now sadly decapitated) family members and clerics carved in stone to send him off. Also on the first floor are two further cloisters to explore (one with a small café), along with an amazing **Treasury**, literally crammed with items, all worth your gaze. As you amble round this part of the collection, try not to miss the *Belles Heures de Jean, Duc de Berry*, perhaps the greatest of all medieval Books of Hours; it was executed by the Limburg Brothers with dazzling miniatures of seasonal life and extensive border-work in gold leaf. Other highlights are the *Reliquary Shrine of Elizabeth of Hungary*, a luminous enamel and gilded silver piece from the Rhine Valley, and the twelfth-century **altar cross** from Bury St Edmunds in England, containing a mass of 92 tiny expressive characters from biblical stories. Finally, hunt out a golf-ball-sized **rosary bead** from sixteenth-century Flanders: with a representation of the Passion inside, it barely seems possible that it could have been carved by hand (it's made of separate tiny pieces of boxwood painstakingly fitted together with the aid of a magnifying glass).

Inwood

Fort Tryon Park joins **Inwood Park** by the Hudson River; it's possible to walk across Dyckman Street and into Inwood Park. The path up the side of the river gives a beautiful view of New Jersey, surprisingly hilly and wooded this far upstream. Keep walking and you'll reach the very tip of Manhattan, an area known as *Spuyten Duyvil* ("the spitting devil" in Dutch), nowadays Columbia University's athletic stadium. Inwood Park itself is wild, rambling, and often confusing – not to mention a little threatening if you get lost. It was once the stomping ground for Indian cave-dwellers, but unfortunately the site of their original settlement is now buried under the Henry Hudson Parkway. Inwood's main tourist attraction is the **Dyckman Farmhouse Museum**, 4881 Broadway at 204th St (Wed–Sat 10am–5pm, Sun noon–4pm; $1; ☎212/304-9422, ⓦwww.dyckman.org). A pleasant enough period home (an eighteenth-century Dutch farmhouse), it's really only worth going to if you're already up here to see the Cloisters.

19

Brooklyn

"The Great Mistake." So ran local newspaper headlines when **Brooklyn** became a borough of New York in 1898. Then the fourth-largest city in the US, it has since labored in the shadow of its taller but smaller brother across the East River. Over the past few years, though, Brooklyn has started to be looked on with new respect, as a certain cachet has developed around its signature gracious brownstone homes, dynamic street culture, and undeniably beautiful tree-lined streets. Not only have many diehard Manhattanites finally moved to Brooklyn, but some of them have even admitted that they rarely need to leave the borough, what with its world-class museums, lovely parks and beaches, fantastic restaurants, and progressive arts scenes.

Visitors who make the trek across the river will appreciate all these things, too. You'll do best to pick just one or two areas to explore at a time – Brooklyn's attractions are fairly spread out, and if you try to pack too much in at once, you won't be able to savor the distinctiveness of each place. The most accessible district in the borough is pretty, elite **Brooklyn Heights**, a clutch of old mansions abutting the East River directly opposite Lower Manhattan. A little north of here, past the **Fulton Ferry** landing, the once-derelict warehouses of the area known as **DUMBO** have been converted to art galleries and expensive condos.

Though many people never get past this point, the other neighborhoods near the borough's civic center – **Fort Greene**, **Cobble Hill**, and **Carroll Gardens** – offer a lively blend of culture, fine dining, and some of the city's best-preserved brownstones. Just to the south, isolated **Red Hook** is a beautiful, almost empty relic of Brooklyn's shipping heyday.

From the Manhattan Bridge, **Flatbush Avenue**, a road that predates colonization, runs almost to the coast, dividing the borough in two. Following Flatbush, you come to Frederick Law Olmsted and Calvert Vaux's **Prospect Park**, which many consider an improvement on the partnership's more famous bit of landscaping, Central Park. Incorporating the Brooklyn Botanic Garden, the Brooklyn Museum, and Prospect Park Zoo, this is an oasis for both adults and children. West of the park, the neighborhood of **Park Slope** is cultured and kid-saturated. **Bedford-Stuyvesant**, off the other side of the park, is the largest African-American community in New York City, with vibrant street life and beautiful architecture.

Then there's coastal Brooklyn: start in polyglot **Bay Ridge** for a scenic walk or bike ride along the water, then visit **Brighton Beach** and its Russian community as well as **Coney Island**, the venerable seaside center of working-class pleasures that offers a mix of amusements for young and old.

Anyone visiting New York for contemporary art should head north to gallery-dotted **Williamsburg**. Inhabited by artists and musicians, this neighborhood has a healthy mix of independent bookstores, boutiques, and restaurants.

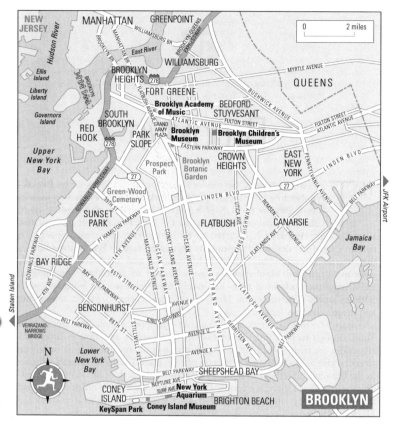

Greenpoint, just north, houses the artsy overflow from Williamsburg but maintains a quieter feel, thanks to the Polish old guard that dominates the area.

Some history

In 1636, **Dutch colonists**, who had already settled New Amsterdam on Manhattan Island under the auspices of the Dutch West India Company, bought farmland from the **Lenape Indians** amid the flat marshes in the southwestern corner of Long Island. The **Village of Breuckelen** received a charter from the company in 1646, and several other villages grew up nearby as other Europeans joined the farmers.

It was in this area that George Washington's Continental Army fought and lost the **Battle of Long Island** (often called the Battle of Brooklyn) in 1776, the first major fight of the American Revolution. Even as Revolutionary leaders espoused freedom, however, Brooklyn was deeply tainted by slavery; by 1790, sixty percent of families in Kings County (as the Brooklyn area was then known) owned slaves, the highest percentage in New York State.

Brooklyn remained little more than a tiny town in the years following the war, separated from neighboring villages by heavy forests and farms. In 1814, though, steamship service linked Long Island with Manhattan, and the town began to take on its present form, starting with the establishment of Brooklyn Heights as a leafy retreat for wealthier Manhattanites. Urban development soon spread through the shoreline towns of Bay Ridge, Red Hook, Williamsburg, and Greenpoint – all of which were absorbed into the growing city during the nineteenth century.

Brooklyn's **incorporation** into the city of New York in 1898, ostensibly so that Manhattan's tax wealth would aid Brooklyn's poor, was a bitterly fought political battle. In the end it was decided by just 277 votes – a tiny percentage of the total 129,000 cast. There was no going back, though: the flood of new residents that had begun with the opening of the **Brooklyn Bridge** in 1883 only increased with the construction of the **Williamsburg Bridge** in 1903, the **Manhattan Bridge** in 1909, and cross-river subway tunnels. By the early years of the twentieth century, Brooklyn had more than one million residents, many of them Jewish and Italian; in 1910, 35 percent of its population was foreign-born (the proportion is similar today).

Even with the population boom, Brooklyn suffered a bit in the twentieth century. Rather than fulfil the main promise of incorporation, New York's central planners encouraged growth elsewhere. The borough saw its strong manufacturing and shipping sectors dwindle, and unemployment climbed steadily, both among white dockworkers and the masses of African-Americans who had come to the borough after World War I. By the 1980s, "white flight," provoked first by racism then by drug-related crime and violence, had left previously nice residential neighborhoods vacant and impoverished.

Fortunately, a city-wide drop in crime beginning in the late 1990s, and some serious gentrification caused by rising rents in Manhattan, have given Brooklyn a chance to rekindle its civic dignity, particularly in its strong contributions to the arts and popular culture. This is, after all, the place that gave the world both "How you doin'?" and "Fuhgeddaboudit," as well as countless talented artists, musicians, writers, and filmmakers. Now with some 2.6 million residents, Brooklyn is still the fourth-largest urban center in America – independent or not – though it probably takes the prize for proudest.

Downtown Brooklyn

This area encompasses the **Brooklyn Bridge**, the **Fulton Ferry District**, **DUMBO**, **Brooklyn Heights**, **Borough Hall**, **Fort Greene**, and **Atlantic Avenue**. It stretches from the East River to the Brooklyn Academy of Music, quickly shifting from warehouses to brownstones to the alternately staid and venerable buildings in the civic center. Downtown Brooklyn is relatively compact, so you can visit most of it on foot in an afternoon; try to be on the DUMBO waterfront or the Brooklyn Heights promenade at sunset. Though the area is a short hop on the subway from Lower Manhattan, a walk across the Brooklyn Bridge is recommended to start your trip in grand style.

Fulton Ferry District

Beneath the glowering shadow of the **Watchtower Building** (for many years the world headquarters of the Jehovah's Witnesses, but sold in 2005) is the **Fulton Ferry District**, where Robert Fulton's steamboat first put in after crossing the East River in 1814. If you're not arriving by ferry (service runs from Pier 11 in Lower Manhattan; ☎212/742-1969, ⓦwww.nywatertaxi.com) or via the Brooklyn Bridge, take the #A or #C to High Street, due east of the pier, or the #2 or #3 to Clark Street, just up the hill in Brooklyn Heights.

Thanks to the ferry, this was Brooklyn's first and most prosperous shipping district. With the opening of the **Brooklyn Bridge** in 1883 (which added the 60,000-ton **anchorage** that now dominates the sky), the ferry fell into disuse, but these days the area is enjoying a bit of a renaissance, as aging

Crossing the Brooklyn Bridge

The **walk** from Manhattan across the **Brooklyn Bridge** is less than a mile and gives some of the best views of the Manhattan skyline and the harbor. The walkway begins at stately City Hall Park next to the Municipal Building (see p.68) and ends in the civic center of Brooklyn. Don't let the scenery distract you from fast-paced bicyclists who will want to pass you – this is also a popular commuter route.

You can follow the pedestrian path straight to its end, at the corner of Adams and Tillary streets, behind the main post office. More convenient for sightseeing, however, is to exit the bridge at the first set of stairs: walk down and bear right to follow the path through the park at Cadman Plaza. If you cross onto Middagh Street, you'll be in the core of Brooklyn Heights; or follow Cadman Plaza West down the hill to Old Fulton Street and the Fulton Ferry District.

If you're not up to walking over the bridge (though it really is the most interesting way), a **taxi** from Lower Manhattan will be about $15.

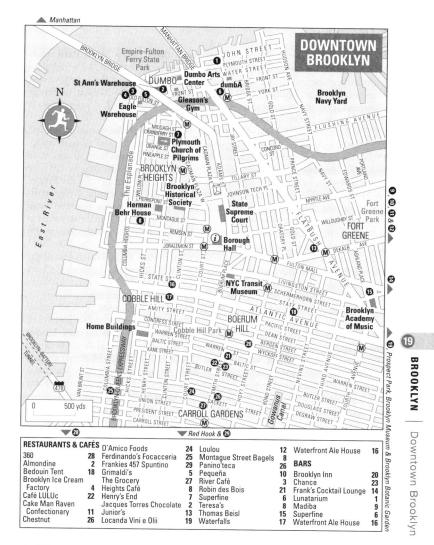

N

BROOKLYN HEIGHTS

FORT GREENE

COBBLE HILL

BOERUM HILL

CARROLL GARDENS

0   500 yds

▼ Red Hook & ㉙

RESTAURANTS & CAFÉS

360	28	D'Amico Foods		Loulou	24
Almondine	2	Ferdinando's Focacceria	25	Montague Street Bagels	8
Bedouin Tent	18	Frankies 457 Spuntino	29	Panino'teca	26
Brooklyn Ice Cream		Grimaldi's	5	Pequeña	10
Factory	4	The Grocery	27	River Café	3
Café LULUc	22	Heights Café	8	Robin des Bois	21
Cake Man Raven		Henry's End	7	Superfine	6
Confectionary	11	Jacques Torres Chocolate	2	Teresa's	8
Chestnut	26	Junior's	13	Thomas Beisl	15
		Locanda Vini e Olii	19	Waterfalls	17

Waterfront Ale House	16	
BARS		
Brooklyn Inn	20	
Chance	23	
Frank's Cocktail Lounge	14	
Lunatarium	1	
Madiba	9	
Superfine	6	
Waterfront Ale House	16	

19 ▶ *Prospect Park, Brooklyn Museum & Brooklyn Botanic Garden*

BROOKLYN | Downtown Brooklyn

buildings are redesigned as lofts. Check out the imposing **Eagle Warehouse**, 28 Old Fulton St; its penthouse, with the huge glass clock-window, is one of Brooklyn's most coveted apartments. The headquarters of *The Brooklyn Eagle*, the newspaper edited for a time by Walt Whitman, previously stood on this spot, and its old press room was integrated into the 1893 warehouse – you can see the separate cornice on the corner of Doughty Street and Elizabeth Place. On the ferry landing, the *Brooklyn Ice Cream Factory* serves up excellent cones, and the adjacent ritzy *River Café*, 1 Water St, lures romantic Manhattanites and Wall Street types alike across the bridge. Locals (and tourists in the know) are more likely to follow their noses to the brick ovens of *Grimaldi's*, 19 Old Fulton St, which turn out some of the best pizza in New York City (see p.357 for review).

DUMBO

Just north of the ferry landing, the **Empire–Fulton Ferry State Park** offers an increasingly rare, river-level view and occasional art exhibits. It's a welcome backyard for residents of the old warehouse district between the Brooklyn and Manhattan bridges known as **DUMBO** (*D*own *U*nder the *M*anhattan *B*ridge *O*verpass). The closest subway is the #F to York Street, which deposits you on the north edge of the neighborhood.

Utterly treeless and perpetually in the shadows of the looming bridge, DUMBO's streets are a patchwork of asphalt, cobblestones, and railroad tracks. Once desolate, the district became quite ritzy in a very short time, thanks to an aggressive development plan on the part of investor David Walentas. In 1981, he purchased some two million square feet of mostly empty property – the major-ity of the neighborhood – for $12 million, then decided to mimic the gentrifi-cation process that had transformed Soho and Tribeca to prime residential real estate. He invented a clever nickname and began to rent loft space to artists at well below market rates; the open studios drew hipsters and wealthy visitors. By 1998, Walentas had converted some artists' studios to residences, and by 2002, river-view condos were routinely selling for more than $1 million. A few of the old galleries and studios remain (see Chapter 30, "Commercial galleries"), now neighbors to a high-end chocolatier (*Jacques Torres*, 66 Water St), ritzy kitchen-appliance showrooms, and a handful of cool restaurants and bars.

The cultural anchor for the area, the **DUMBO Arts Center**, 30 Washington St, hosts five or six yearly shows (Thurs–Mon 10am–6pm; ☎718/694-0831, ⓦwww.dumboartscenter.org). It also puts on the huge **Dumbo Art Under the Bridge Festival**, one weekend in mid-October (see p.445). Also check out the schedule at **St Ann's Warehouse**, 38 Water St (☎718/834-8794, ⓦwww .artsatstanns.org), an intimate space in which you might catch New York rock legends or all manner of experimental music, opera, theater, and even puppetry. For less formal activity, stop by the **dumbA collective**, 57 Jay St (☎718-858-4886), a queer-oriented punk art and party space, to see what shows or parties might be in the works.

To savor what's left of DUMBO's old-fashioned grit, head to **Gleason's Gym** (83 Front St ☎718/797-2872, ⓦwww.gleasonsgym.net), where tomorrow's prizefighters train. Gleason's, first established in Manhattan in 1937, has coached everyone from Jake LaMotta to Muhammad Ali; you can catch a practice bout here for a $3 entrance fee.

Brooklyn Heights

Brooklyn Heights is one of New York City's most beautiful and historical neighborhoods and still the borough's most coveted zip code. The best trains are the #A or #C to High Street or the #2 or #3 to Clark Street. If you're already in the Fulton Ferry District, walk up the hill on Everit or Henry streets. The Brooklyn Historical Society (see p.244) provides a very useful walking-tour map, also available at the Brooklyn Tourism and Visitors Center (see p.239).

Bankers and financiers from Manhattan began building brownstones along the shore here in the early nineteenth century. They traveled across the water daily to their Wall Street offices – the Brooklyn Historical Society calls the Heights "the nation's first commuter suburb." Writers flocked to the Heights after the subway opened in 1908; W.H. Auden, Carson McCullers, Truman Capote, Tennessee Williams, Norman Mailer, and Paul and Jane Bowles (pre-Morocco) all lived in the neighborhood. Although many single-family brownstones were

△ Brooklyn Heights

divided into apartments during the 1960s and 1970s and the streets now feel fairly cosmopolitan, in many ways Brooklyn Heights today is not much different from how it was a hundred years ago.

The north edge, along Henry Street and Columbia Heights, is the oldest part of the neighborhood, where blocks are lined with Federal-style brick buildings. However, it's actually the unassuming wooden structure at **24 Middagh Street** (at the corner of Willow), erected in 1824, that is the area's longest-standing house. Two streets south, on Orange between Hicks and Henry, the simple **Plymouth Church of the Pilgrims** went up in the midnineteenth century and became famous as the preaching base of **Henry Ward Beecher**, abolitionist and campaigner for women's rights (Henry remains less known outside New York than his sister, Harriet Beecher Stowe, author of *Uncle Tom's Cabin*). His fiery orations drew men like Horace Greeley and Abraham Lincoln, and Mark Twain based *Innocents Abroad* on travels with the church's social group. The building was also a stop on the Underground Railroad, where slaves were hidden on their way to freedom. Fitting then, that in 1963, Martin Luther King Jr delivered an early version of his "I have a dream" speech here. These days, you can see the interior only when a service is in progress.

Continuing south, you reach **Pierrepont Street**, one of the Heights' main residential arteries, studded with fine brownstones. At the corner with Clark, the **Herman Behr House**, a chunky Romanesque Revival mansion, has been, successively, a hotel, a brothel, and a Franciscan monastery (the brothers added the horrific canopy); it is currently private apartments. East on Pierrepont, at the corner of Monroe Place, look in if you can on the **First Unitarian Church**, notable for its exquisite neo-Gothic interior, built in 1844. Across the street at no. 128, the **Brooklyn Historical Society** (Wed–Sun noon–5pm; $6, students and seniors $4, under 12 free; ☏718/222-4111, ⊛www.brooklynhistory.org) catalogues the history of Brooklyn in several moving, well-researched multimedia displays.

Walk back west on any street between Clark and Remsen to reach the **Promenade** (more formally known as the Esplanade), a boardwalk with some of the best views in New York. It's hard to take your eyes off the Manhattan skyline, the water, and the Statue of Liberty – if you can, turn around and look at the very large homes set back modestly from the walkway. Had it not been for the efforts of locals in the mid-1940s, this would now be just another stretch of the Brooklyn–Queens Expressway. Protests forced the city to run the highway below the neighborhood, just above the waterfront; the Promenade, which juts over the highway, was finished in 1951.

Near the southern end of the Promenade, **Montague Street** is Brooklyn Heights' main thoroughfare, lined with shops, bars, and restaurants (though for the latter, you can do better elsewhere in the borough).

Borough Hall and Fulton Street

Although the core of downtown Brooklyn saw some hard times during the last few decades, it's well on its way back to being the seat of the borough's government, commerce, and academia. East of Clinton Street, Montague Street is known as **"Bank Row"** – downtown Brooklyn's business headquarters – and leads to the borough's **civic center**, with the end of the residential Heights signaled by the tall Art Deco buildings of Court Street. Directly across the road is the lovely, massive **State Supreme Court** (not actually the highest court in the state – that's the Court of Appeals in Albany). To the south, the Greek-style **Borough Hall** looks tiny in comparison; it was erected in 1849, then topped with its odd cupolated belfry near the end of the century. The north side of the plaza is occupied by the Romanesque central post office, next to which stands a bronze statue of Henry Ward Beecher. The central plaza hosts a farmers' market year-round (Tues & Sat). Just east of Borough Hall, at 250 Joralemon St, stands the **Brooklyn Law School**, founded in 1901. There's little to linger for, but your tired feet should know that this is where to find the Borough Hall subway station (the #2, #3, #4, #5, #M, and #R all stop here).

East of Adams Street, the compact civic grandeur of Joralemon turns into **Fulton Mall**, the portion of Fulton Street that's the borough's principal shopping district, with more than a hundred retail stores. Although there's little more than mainstream goods here, Fulton's energy and crowds make for an invigorating walk. At the end of the street, reward yourself with some cheesecake at the landmark restaurant *Junior's* (see p.357), one block north of Fulton on Flatbush Avenue, or just keep walking toward Fort Greene, which Flatbush neatly divides from Brooklyn Heights and Borough Hall.

New York Transit Museum

Just south of Fulton Mall, Adams Street turns into Boerum Place, and at the corner of Schermerhorn Street an old subway entrance leads to the **New York Transit Museum** (Tues–Fri 10am–4pm, Sat & Sun noon–5pm; $5, children and seniors $3; ⊤718/694-1600, ⊛www.mta.info/mta/museum). Housed in an abandoned station from the 1930s, it offers more than one hundred years of transportation history and memorabilia, including antique turnstiles, restored subway and "el" (elevated) train cars, maps, models, and photographs. In the permanent exhibition, "On the Streets: New York's Trolleys and Buses," you can ride and drive buses and find out about the people behind public transport.

Fort Greene

If you head back east to the corner of Fulton Street and Flatbush Avenue, you'll be at the border between downtown Brooklyn and **Fort Greene**, a historically African-American neighborhood that withstood the brutality of the 1980s better than most places in Brooklyn and is now quite prosperous (thanks in part to director Spike Lee, who gave the place a vote of confidence when he set up his production company here). The area is very easy to reach by subway: the #Q, #R, #B, and #M trains run to the DeKalb Avenue stop at Flatbush, or you can take the #C to Lafayette Avenue, closer to the center of the neighborhood.

Towering above the distinguished brownstones and grand churches is the **Williamsburg Savings Bank** – Brooklyn's tallest building (for now; see box, below) and its most iconic. The tower was sold to Magic Johnson's development corporation in 2005 and redone as luxury condos; the lavish lobby, now dedicated to retail, has been partially preserved. Just north of the bank, down Fulton

---

The new Battle of Brooklyn: Atlantic Yards

In a borough rampant with real-estate development, the **Atlantic Yards** project surpasses all others in scale and controversy. The plan calls for six square blocks east of the intersection of Atlantic and Flatbush avenues to be filled with a 22-acre business-and-residential megalopolis, including a 70-story tower that would dwarf the nearby Williamsburg Savings Bank. At the heart of the proposed undertaking would be an 18,000-seat Frank Gehry–designed stadium for the Nets basketball team (see p.430).

So what's there now? Only a disused MTA rail yard and some condemned buildings – and quite a few occupied homes. Development-minded Mayor Bloomberg supports the project, the people who live within the Atlantic Yards zone are dead set against it, and Brooklyn residents who cherish the current skyline aren't too keen either. The plans have been mired in court since mid-2005, when an environmental-impact report drew virulent criticism and Gehry was sent back to the drawing board to make some new designs. So don't hold your breath: Phase One wouldn't be done until 2009, and that's not counting the time needed for what will be a very long legal battle.

Street or DeKalb Avenue and between Flatbush and Vanderbilt avenues, is the **Fort Greene Historic District**. Home and garden tours can be arranged in summer (☎718/875-1855, ⊛www.fortgreeneny.com); otherwise, just stroll down streets like Oxford and South Portland to see some of the area's nicer homes from the late 1800s.

Fort Greene boasts the reliable yet daring **Brooklyn Academy of Music** – BAM to its fans, who come from all over the city – at 30 Lafayette Ave (☎718/636-4100, ⊛www.bam.org). The oldest performing-arts center in America, established in 1859 and now in its second building, BAM hosts provocative theatrical engagements, as well as avant-garde operas, dance projects, and more. Upstairs, the swanky, glittery *BAMcafé* features local performers, while Rose Cinemas features new (often independent) releases, as well as the BAMcinématek program of classic, rare, art, and foreign films.

If it's lunchtime, get takeout from one of the area's many Caribbean-American cafés for a picnic in **Fort Greene Park**, designed by Olmsted and Vaux in 1867 and situated just north of DeKalb between Fort Greene Place and Cumberland Street. At the park's summit, the 148-foot **Prison Ship Martyrs Monument** (1908) commemorates the estimated 11,500 Americans who died in the floating prison camps maintained by the British during the Revolutionary War. Sixteen squalid ships, rife with smallpox, were moored in old Wallabout Bay (just offshore from what's now the Brooklyn Navy Yard); more people died on board than fell in battle. The bones of the dead, collected as they washed ashore for decades after, are housed in a small crypt at the base of the tower.

At 647 Fulton St, at the corner of Rockwell Place, **UrbanGlass** (daily 10am–6pm; ☎718/625-3685, ⊛www.urbanglass.org) is the East Coast's oldest and largest open glassworking studio. From inside the shop, you can watch an artist heat glass until it's red-hot; for the full experience, come during one of the five or six yearly open houses, visit the gallery, or call ahead for a studio tour.

Heading east into the neighborhood on Lafayette Avenue, at Clermont Avenue you'll see the 1909 **Brooklyn Masonic Temple**, a massive cubic building with a fortress-like air, though decorated with surprising spots of color at the tops of the glazed terracotta columns.

On the farthest eastern fringes of Fort Greene (an area often called Clinton Hill) is another striking building: **Broken Angel**, 4 Downing St, a patchwork house that's a multistoried puzzle of found objects, odd angles, and glinting mirrors. Owner and resident artist Arthur Wood has been working on the place since 1980, and he may give you a free tour if he's around.

Atlantic Avenue

Running from the East River all the way to Queens, **Atlantic Avenue** forms the southern border of Fort Greene and Brooklyn Heights. The stretch west of Flatbush is the center of a thriving Middle Eastern community, where there are some fine and reasonably priced Yemeni, Syrian, and Lebanese restaurants, as well as a good sprinkling of grocers and bakeries. Wander through **Sahadi's**, no. 187, which dates to the 1940s and is known throughout the city for nuts, dried fruit, *halvah* (crushed sesame seeds in a base of honey), cheeses, and more than a dozen varieties of olives, along with delicacies from other parts of the world. Continue east to reach a large concentration of antiques stores featuring Art Deco and Victorian furniture. Otherwise just head south along Court Street into gorgeous South Brooklyn.

South Brooklyn

The neighborhoods of **Cobble Hill**, **Boerum Hill**, and **Carroll Gardens**, whose borders are blurry at best, along with the former industrial zone along the **Gowanus Canal** and the wharves of **Red Hook**, make up the area traditionally known as **South Brooklyn** – confusing, because geographically, much of the borough is actually south of this area. Until 1894, however, this was the southern border of the city of Brooklyn, so the term has stuck. The most popular areas to visit here are Court and Smith streets, which run north–south through Cobble Hill and Carroll Gardens. They're lined with some of Brooklyn's most creative boutiques and, on Smith Street in particular, best places to dine (see Chapter 25, "Restaurants," for reviews). If industrial decay is more your style, don't miss the Gowanus Canal and Red Hook, two areas rich with less-savory urban history.

The #F or #G to Bergen Street deposits you on the border between Cobble Hill and Carroll Gardens; the Carroll Street stop on the same lines leaves you at the southern end of Carroll Gardens, closest to Gowanus and a bus ride (or long walk) to Red Hook. If you're walking here from Brooklyn Heights, simply continue on Court Street; this artery runs from downtown through South Brooklyn and all the way to Red Hook.

Cobble Hill and Boerum Hill

Just south of Atlantic Avenue, the main east–west streets through **Cobble Hill** – Amity, Congress, and Warren – are a mix of solid brownstones and colorful red-brick rowhouses built between the 1840s and the 1880s. The neighborhood name only came about in the 1950s, however, when brownstone enthusiasts renovating the area discovered the name "Cobles Hill" on a map from 1766. The hill, near the corner of Court Street and Atlantic Avenue, was an important fortification during the Battle of Brooklyn, but has since been razed.

South on Clinton Street, which runs parallel to Court Street one block west, sits the lovingly landscaped **Cobble Hill Park**, where couples read newspapers on the sunlit grass on summer mornings. Along the park's southern border is a cobblestone alleyway – **Verandah Place**, a renovated mews built in the 1850s. Writer Thomas Wolfe lived in the basement at no. 40 in the 1930s and described the apartment in his novel *You Can't Go Home Again*: "Here, in winter, the walls . . . sweat continuously with clammy drops of water. Here, in summer, it is he who does the sweating."

Living conditions weren't nearly so dismal in the nearby **Home Buildings** on Warren Place, a tidy row of red-brick cottages lining a pedestrian mews. Built in 1878 as utopian workers' housing, the 44 homes are each only eleven feet wide. The architect, Alfred Tredway White, also designed the adjacent apartment blocks, which are trimmed with wrought iron. To reach the complex, walk south on Clinton or Henry streets to Warren Street and turn right (west).

East of Cobble Hill, **Boerum Hill** is less architecturally impressive than its neighbor, though it has its share of sober Greek Revival and Italianate buildings, developed around the same period. The district was home to Canadian Mohawk steelworkers in the 1930s, then shifted to a largely African-American and Latino population after World War II. In the 1970s, many local buildings were slated for demolition, but preservationists and community organizers united to protect the district. Residents run an aggressive gardening campaign to compete for the title of "Greenest Block in Brooklyn." By contrast, along its southern border, near Union Street, Boerum Hill gives way to the Gowanus Houses, a large, bleak, low-income housing project – a far cry from Alfred White's Home Buildings.

Carroll Gardens and Gowanus

As you walk south along Court Street, Cobble Hill blends into **Carroll Gardens** around DeGraw Street. Built as a middle- and upper-class community between 1869 and 1884, this part of South Brooklyn has been an Italian enclave since dockworkers arrived here in the early 1900s; Al Capone is said to have been married in 1918 at the Saint Mary Star of the Sea Church on Court Street. The area was later named for Charles Carroll, the only Roman Catholic to sign the Declaration of Independence. Though the neighborhood's older Italian residents have moved out to Connecticut and New Jersey, and youthful professionals have moved in from across the water, you'll still find plenty of pizza parlors, Old World pastry shops, and smoky social clubs. A strong sense of community prevails and is reflected in the neighborhood's tidiness (and, some say, its conspicuous lack of integration); look around particularly in the small landmark district bounded by Smith and Hoyt streets, where the deep yards in front of the towering brownstones put the "gardens" in the neighborhood's name.

Carroll Gardens residents are known for their elaborate, often garish **holiday decorations**. Although religious shrines and statues of the Virgin decorate many gardens year-round, Christmas and Easter bring out the festivities in full force, as neighbors try to outdo one another with flashing lights, incandescent monuments, and blaring seasonal music. A much more somber procession is held annually on Good Friday.

The neighborhood is traversed by the **Gowanus Canal**, a name that inspires a bit of a shudder in older Brooklynites. Originally a wetlands area famous for its oysters, it became a fetid stillwater around 1870, thanks to sewers from Park Slope that drained here and oil refineries that sat along its banks. Thomas Wolfe, chronicler of Brooklyn's most miserable moments, wrote that the stench evoked "melted glue, burned rubber, and smoldering rags, the odors of a boneyard horse, long dead, the incense of putrefying offal, the fragrance of deceased, decaying cats, old tomatoes, rotten cabbages, and prehistoric eggs." The stink was so all-pervasive that the whole of South Brooklyn was called Gowanus for several decades.

In 1999, however, city engineers finally repaired the drain pump so water could flow freely through the canal and into Gowanus Bay. No longer known as "Lavender Lake" for the chemical sheen on its surface, the canal now supports a surprising amount of marine life, from small crabs to silvery fish to shrimp. The tongue-in-cheek *Gowanus Yacht Club* (323 Smith St) no longer seems so far-fetched, and needless to say, real-estate agents are claiming they loved the place all along. The **Gowanus Dredgers Canoe Club** (☎718/243-0849, ⊛www .waterfrontmuseum.org/dredgers) runs free tours from March through October, starting at Second Street at the canal; bike trips along the banks are an option for anyone still leery of the water.

Red Hook

South of Carroll Gardens, the maritime ruins of the **Red Hook** waterfront are almost romantic. Very out of the way (take the #B61 bus from Columbia Street or the #B77 bus from Court Street at West 9th) and not exactly hopping with life once you get there, Red Hook is recommended only for serious fans of urban archeology. The views across the river are fantastic, however, and the place is certainly the antidote to Manhattan's crowds, gloss, and modernity. Access to the neighborhood is getting easier: in 2006, the **New York Water Taxi** (☎212/742-1969, ⊛www.nywatertaxi.com) started running here on weekends from Pier 11 in Lower Manhattan.

A small, rounded piece of land (the Dutch called it a *hoek*, or corner) projecting into Upper New York Bay, Red Hook is effectively cut off from the rest of Brooklyn by the Gowanus Expressway. The peninsula is then further divided between the Red Hook Houses, a sprawling project with a predominantly African-American population, and the sparsely inhabited waterfront, where empty piers jut out from shadowy warehouses.

Settled in 1636 and named for the color of the soil, Red Hook eventually became one of the busiest and toughest shipping centers in the US. In the 1950s, the ports inspired Elia Kazan's film *On the Waterfront* and Arthur Miller's play *A View from the Bridge*. By the 1960s, the increasing automation of the docking industry left longshoremen out of work and sent most of the freighters to bigger ports in New Jersey.

Red Hook is now rather marvelously desolate, with the wide, empty streets near the water lined with enormous brick storehouses and abandoned wood-frame homes. Wander down to the bay to see the **Hudson Waterfront Museum** (☎718/624-4719, ⊛www.waterfront-museum.org), housed in a restored barge moored off a small park at the end of Conover Street. From **Valentino Pier** at the end of Van Dyke Street, Governors Island appears almost within wading distance and Lady Liberty hoists her torch just for you. The **Red Hook Recreational Area** (aka the ball fields) is a green space on the water's edge where Latinos gather for ultra-competitive soccer in the shadow of a long string of linked grain silos. On summer weekends, food-stands dole out delicious tacos, *pupusas*, and more. To reach the fields, head back east on Van Dyke Street.

A small arts and restaurant scene, mostly along Van Brunt Street, provides respite after roaming the wharves. *Sunny's* (253 Conover St) is the last of scores of bars that once catered to longshoremen. The **Brooklyn Waterfront Artists Coalition (BWAC)**, 499 Van Brunt St (☎718/596-2507, ⊛www.bwac.org), holds its group shows in May and November in the warehouses at the south end of Van Brunt Street.

Like much of Brooklyn, though, Red Hook is in flux. A giant grocery store opened at the end of Van Brunt in 2006, cruise ships began docking at a new terminal on Pier 12, and plans for an IKEA megamart are slowly working their way through the courts. Although the growth will potentially provide jobs to the underemployed residents of the Red Hook Houses, many of the locals along the water have been fighting the development.

Prospect Park and around

Where Brooklyn really surpasses itself is on Flatbush Avenue in the vicinity of **Grand Army Plaza**, a surprisingly elegant traffic circle around a stately memorial arch. The plaza faces the **Brooklyn Public Library** and the entrance to **Prospect Park**, and immediately east of it, the **Brooklyn Museum** houses, among other things, an excellent ancient Egyptian trove, and the **Brooklyn Botanic Garden** teems with greenery. The plaza also acts as a border to several

19

BROOKLYN | Prospect Park and around

249

very different neighborhoods, including **Crown Heights** and the more serene **Park Slope**. The Grand Army Plaza stop on the #3 train is the most central for the park and the arch, while the museum has its own stop just a few blocks farther down the line.

Grand Army Plaza

Central Park architects Frederick Law Olmsted and Calvert Vaux designed **Grand Army Plaza** in the 1860s and 1870s as an approach to Prospect Park. With one skimpy fountain and swathes of empty space, it was a bit austere and unwelcoming, so additions were made through the 1890s. The largest of them, the triumphal **Soldiers' and Sailors' Memorial Arch**, was unveiled in 1892 by John Duncan in tribute to the Union victory in the Civil War. The 80-foot-tall arch, modeled on Paris's Arc de Triomphe, was still deemed not quite grand enough, so in 1896 bas-reliefs of Abraham Lincoln and General Ulysses S. Grant were installed on the inner walls of the arch. They attracted more criticism than anything else, especially the figure of Lincoln, who appears to be begging and rides a diminutive horse.

The fiery bronze sculptures that top the arch and sit on either side were added in 1898, finally giving the plaza an actual sense of grandeur. At the top, the **Victory Quadriga** depicts the lady Columbia, symbol of the US, escorted by winged victory figures. The groupings on each of the lower pedestals represent the spirit of the Navy (right) and the Army (left). An internal spiral staircase is open only occasionally, as part of the Open House New York program (ⓦwww .ohny.org).

On the east side of the plaza, the immense **Brooklyn Public Library** (ⓦwww.brooklynpubliclibrary.org), started in 1912 with the help of a $1.6-million donation from Andrew Carnegie and finally finished in 1941, is just as

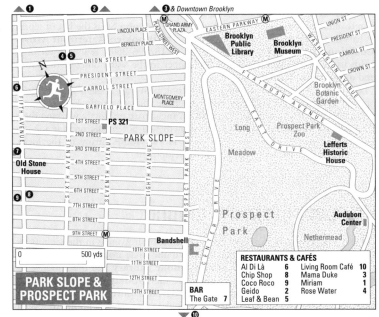

grand, although a bit more serene. Its facade (meant to be the spine of a slightly open book) is covered in declarations on its function as a place of knowledge. Above the entrance fifteen bronze panels depict favorite American literary characters, including Br'er Rabbit, Hester Prynne, and Tom Sawyer. As the flagship branch of the borough's sixty public libraries, the building hosts an array of readings, screenings, and other cultural programs.

Prospect Park

Energized by their success with Central Park, Olmsted and Vaux landscaped **Prospect Park** (☎718/965-8951, ⊛www.prospectpark.org) in the early 1860s. Its 585 acres include a 60-acre lake on the east side, a 90-acre open meadow on the west, and a 3.4-mile park drive primarily reserved for runners, cyclists, and rollerbladers.

Unlike Central Park, Prospect Park has managed to retain its pastoral quality. Despite attractions that have sprung up over the years – an Audubon Center, tennis courts, an ice-skating rink (Nov–March), and a kid-oriented zoo – it remains for the most part remarkably bucolic. The **Long Meadow** cuts through the center of the park, and various quiet corners have been given romantic names like Lullwater and the Vale of Cashmere. The **Lefferts Historic House** (Tues–Sun noon–5pm), an eighteenth-century Dutch farmhouse with programs geared to children, is an architectural focal point, while natural attractions include the lovely **Prospect Park Ravine**, complete with a rushing waterfall. The **Prospect Park Zoo** (April–Oct Mon–Fri 10am–5pm, Sat & Sun 10am–5.30pm; Nov–March 10am–4.30pm; $5, seniors $1.25, under 12 $1; ☎718/399-7339, ⊛www.prospectparkzoo.org) features sea lions, poisonous frogs, baboons, and sundry other fauna, as well as a restored carousel (originally installed in Coney Island in 1912) and a lake with catch-and-release fishing. To get the most out of the park's several nature trails, stop first at the **Audubon Center** (☎718/287-3400) in the Boathouse (at mid-park on the east side), where you can pick up a $3 guide that details the routes and identifies birds and plants.

For less-structured fun, head to the **Drummers' Grove** near the Parkside and Ocean Avenue entrance on the southeast corner of the park; the crowd that gathers on Sunday afternoons is no amateur circle – some very accomplished musicians have been jamming here for decades. Elsewhere in the park, on warm weekends you can find informal soccer and volleyball matches, as well as families hosting picnics and couples reading or romantically entwined.

On weekends and holidays between noon and 6pm, a free faux-trolley **bus** (☎718/287-3400, ⊛www.prospectpark.org) makes the rounds of popular spots in the park. It also goes to Grand Army Plaza, the Brooklyn Museum, and the Botanic Garden. The Boathouse has maps and information on events; the best are during the summer **Celebrate Brooklyn** festival (☎718/855-7882, ⊛www.celebratebrooklyn.org), when the **Bandshell**, just off Prospect Park West at 10th St, hosts consistently excellent international music and dance acts.

The Brooklyn Museum

East of Grand Army Plaza and the Public Library stands the imposing **Brooklyn Museum**, 200 Eastern Parkway (Wed–Fri 10am–5pm, Sat & Sun 11am–6pm, first Sat of every month until 11pm; suggested donation $8, students and seniors $4; ☎718/638-5000, ⊛www.brooklynmuseum.org).

The original McKim, Mead and White vision for the building, designed in the early twentieth century, would have made this the largest museum in the world, but the plans had to be scaled back. Nonetheless, with five floors of galleries it is still a very impressive structure, second only to the Met in terms of exhibit space in NYC. The museum is best known for its distinguished store of Egyptian relics, though it has also been in the spotlight for its controversial contemporary shows, including two that prompted former mayor Rudy Giuliani to threaten funding cuts for alleged anti-Christian content. Whether your interest is ancient or modern, you'll find something to admire here, only without the crowds you'll encounter in Manhattan museums.

The collection

On the first floor, the central element of the architects' grand plan did survive: it is now the main hall, which houses a permanent display of some four hundred pieces of **American Indian traditional art**. Adjacent is the **Arts of Africa** collection, arranged geographically to represent fifty different cultures; particularly splendid is a sixteenth-century ivory gong from Benin.

The second floor is dedicated to the **Asian and Islamic galleries**, with pieces from China, Korea, India, and Japan, as well as Ottoman Turkish and Qajar Persian textiles, manuscripts, and jewelry.

The delicately carved stone "Brooklyn Black Head" of the Ptolemaic period, arguably the museum's crown jewel, is one of 1200 objects in the authoritative **Ancient Egyptian Art** collection, on the third floor. One of the largest outside Egypt, the Egyptian collection is renowned for its jewelry, mummified animals, and sarcophagi. The wall text makes an occasionally labored connection between Egypt and the rest of Africa, but the pieces are nicely complemented by small galleries of Assyrian, Sumerian, and other ancient Middle Eastern art, as well as rotating exhibits that include Classical holdings, such as Jewish mosaics from the Roman Empire. On the same floor, "About Time: 700 Years of European Painting" presents a fine, non-chronological array of **European work** from *The Adoration of the Magi* (c.1480) by Milanese artist Bernardo Butanone to Monet's *Houses of Parliament*.

One floor up, most of the **Decorative Arts collection** is in six evocative **period rooms**; there's an Art Deco Park Avenue apartment and a nineteenth-century Moorish smoking room from John D. Rockefeller's estate, among others. Watch out for the Tiffany lamps and stained-glass pieces. The **Feminist Art** galleries, set to open on this floor in 2007, will have as its centerpiece Judy Chicago's ceramic and textile installation *The Dinner Party*, which was shown here for the first time in the early 1980s.

On the fifth floor, Georgia O'Keeffe's sensual 1948 paean to the borough, *Brooklyn Bridge*, opens the somewhat uneven "American Identities" permanent exhibition, which draws from the museum's extremely varied **Painting and**

First Saturdays at the Brooklyn Museum

Much more than a static display case, the Brooklyn Museum is a vibrant institution that offers myriad performances, films, and educational programs, as well as the not-to-be-missed free **First Saturdays** program. A heady, family-friendly mix of celebration and highbrow culture, the program includes art workshops, discussions, and a huge themed ball (tango, Eighties hits, Mardi Gras, waltzing, and so forth). It draws a diverse crowd on the first Saturday night of each month. These events are all part of the increasingly populist museum's aim to become a meeting place and cultural center for all of Brooklyn, while retaining its status as one of the world's great fine-arts museums.

Sculpture collection. Nineteenth-century American landscapes are one of the museum's strong points, including bucolic paintings by members of the **Hudson River School** (1835–70). In addition, the museum's **Rodin** collection, about fifty pieces of vibrant sculpture, is on long-term display in the rotunda.

The Brooklyn Botanic Garden

Located just behind the museum, the **Brooklyn Botanic Garden** (April–Sept Tues–Fri 8am–6pm, Sat, Sun & holidays 10am–6pm; Oct–March Tues–Fri 8am–4.30pm, Sat, Sun & holidays 10am–4.30pm; $5, students and seniors $3, free Tues, Sat before noon, Nov–Feb weekdays, seniors free Fri; ☎718/623-7200, ⊛www.bbg.org), is one of the most enticing park spaces in the city. Plants from around the world occupy 22 gardens and exhibits, all sumptuous but not overplanted. What you'll see depends largely on the season. March brings color to Daffodil Hill, while April sees the cherry trees bloom in the Japanese Garden, designed in 1914 and the oldest garden of its kind outside of Japan. The Rose Garden starts to flourish in the early summer, the elaborate water-lily ponds are at their best in late summer and early autumn, and the fall colors in the Rock Garden are striking. A winter visit lets you enjoy the warmth of the glittering glass Palm House, the 6000-square-foot Tropical Pavilion, and the Steinhardt Conservatory, filled with orchids and the largest collection of bonsai trees in the West. A gift shop stocks a wide array of exotic plants, bulbs, and seeds.

Park Slope

The western exits of Prospect Park leave you in **Park Slope**, a district of stately nineteenth-century brownstones (a useful walking-tour map is available at the Brooklyn Historical Society – see p.244) inhabited since the 1970s by a notoriously liberal crew of urban pioneers; it's also in an eternal baby boom, and strollers jam the sidewalks. The most central subway station is the Seventh Avenue stop on the #F line, but you can also walk down Fifth or Sixth avenues from the Bergen Street stop on the #2 and #3 trains.

Coming from the park, first cross Prospect Park West, lined with beautiful homes. Some of the finest Romanesque and Queen Anne residences in the US, they helped this area earn the nickname, "The Gold Coast of Brooklyn." As you walk west from the park, the neighborhood grows increasingly commercial and marginally less affluent. Eighth Avenue is still quiet, but **Seventh Avenue** is lined with all the essentials, from florists to wine shops, and a **flea market** is held at P.S. 321 (1st to 2nd streets) every weekend, weather permitting. **Fifth Avenue** is currently the liveliest strip of restaurants and boutiques.

The Slope is a center of lesbian life in the city, and a large number of gay, bisexual, and transgender people live here (see Chapter 29, "Gay and lesbian New York," for hangouts). The Slope hosted Brooklyn's first LGBT Pride Parade in 1997. The **Brooklyn Pride Festival & Parade**, a community-oriented, relatively noncommercial event, takes place every June. Older festival-goers say it resembles New York Pride in its early days.

You can learn about the Slope's history at the **Old Stone House** in J.J. Byrne Park, Fifth Ave at 3rd St (Thurs–Sun noon–5pm; $3; ☎718/768-3195, ⊛www.historichousetrust.org); one of the most dramatic skirmishes of the Battle of Brooklyn took place in and around the building. It was a bit more cheerful in the 1880s, when it served as the clubhouse for a baseball team that would later be known as the Brooklyn Dodgers. Reconstructed in the 1930s using the original stones, it now contains changing exhibits and a diorama of the house as it looked in its early days.

Green-Wood Cemetery

South of Park Slope – down Fifth Avenue and across the Prospect Expressway – is the neighborhood of **Sunset Park**, Brooklyn's Chinatown, as well as the famed **Green-Wood Cemetery** (8am–4pm; ⓦwww.green-wood.com). Take the #R train to 25th Street; the cemetery's main entrance is about a block away at Fifth Avenue.

Founded in 1838 and almost as large as Prospect Park, Green-Wood was very much the place to be buried in the nineteenth century, particularly among city power-brokers, who saw the cemetery as an appropriately grand end to a life lived on Fifth Avenue and in City Hall. A flashy headstone was *de rigueur*; the real statement-makers erected stately marble tombs for the entire family. Interred here are politician and crusading newspaper editor Horace Greeley; famed preacher Henry Ward Beecher; William Marcy "Boss" Tweed, Democratic chief and scoundrel; and the entire Steinway clan of piano fame, at peace in a 119-room mausoleum. Look for a bronze statue of Minerva, set so that she locks eyes with the Statue of Liberty across the harbor; a condo development downhill from the cemetery was forced to alter its plans to keep this view intact.

Central Brooklyn

The neighborhoods within **Central Brooklyn** – most notably **Bedford-Stuyvesant** and **Crown Heights**, to the northeast and east of Prospect Park – are slightly rougher terrain, although they are no longer as defined by interethnic tensions and violence as they were in the mid-1990s. Bed-Stuy, as it's called, is experiencing a real-estate rush on its brownstones, and Crown Heights may not be far behind. You'll feel safe here during daylight hours, and a trip is worth it for the under-appreciated historical appeal.

Bedford-Stuyvesant

Immediately east of Fort Greene, **Bedford-Stuyvesant** is a bit rough around the edges but contains some of the most elegant residential architecture in the city. This expansive neighborhood stretches north–south from Flushing to Atlantic avenues, and east as far as Saratoga; its main arteries include Bedford and Nostrand avenues and Fulton Street. Although Harlem gets more attention as a historically African-American neighborhood, Bed-Stuy is in fact the nation's largest black community after Chicago's South Side. A walk around the area passes beautiful brownstones, stately churches, and a handful of cool boutiques and cafés. The #C train runs through here; the Franklin Avenue and Nostrand Avenue stops put you closest to the center of the neighborhood (Nostrand is also served by the #A).

Originally two separate areas, the neighboring districts of Bedford and Stuyvesant were populated by both blacks and whites. During the Great Migration between 1910 and 1920, large numbers of southern African-Americans moved north and settled in this area. In the 1940s the white population began to leave, taking funding for many important community services with it. Economic decline continued for several decades, reaching an all-time low in the 1980s.

Part of Bed-Stuy was once a thriving, self-contained community of free blacks called **Weeksville**, founded after slavery was abolished in New York in 1827 and named for black landowner James Weeks. For almost a century, this fact was lost to history. Although Weeksville was occasionally referred to in historical documents – including the town's own newspaper, **The Freedman's Torchlight** – and famous residents such as Susan Smith McKinney Steward, the first black woman doctor in the nation, were widely recognized, the town's precise whereabouts were not known until 1968. In that year, a historian flew over central Brooklyn, taking aerial photographs. The images revealed the fragments of a nineteenth-century village: four wood-frame cottages tucked away in an alley on the border between Bedford-Stuyvesant and Crown Heights. An archeological dig followed, in which artifacts like slaves' shackles were unearthed. Local activists petitioned the city to grant old Weeksville landmark status.

One of these petitioners was Joan Maynard, who steered the **Society for the Preservation of Weeksville and Bedford-Stuyvesant History**, 1698–1708 Bergen St (Tues–Fri 10am–4.30pm, Sat & Sun by appointment; $3; ☎718/623-0600, ⑩www .weeksvillesociety.org) until 1999, and was involved in the group until her death in 2006 – less than a year after the society was finally able to open a museum in the only surviving cottages. The modest exhibit space is a fine testament to both Maynard's dedication and the persistence of the black community over centuries. To get to Weeksville, take the #A or #C train to Utica Avenue.

Ironically, this same poverty and neglect has now made the place desirable, as none of its brownstones were ever razed in the name of economic development. The neighborhood has the densest collection of pre-1900 homes in New York, a fact that only dawned on Manhattan investors around 2003. The African-American community here is attempting to reverse Bed-Stuy's decline and take advantage of its architectural heritage. There are numerous arts, culture, and social-service organizations, and many young professionals, both black and white, have been redoing the area's brownstones.

Gothic, Victorian, and other classic brownstones abound, especially inside the **Stuyvesant Heights Historic District**, which includes parts of MacDonough, Macon, Decatur, Bainbridge, and Chauncey streets primarily between Tompkins and Stuyvesant avenues; an annual five-hour house tour is conducted in late October (☎718/574-1979). On the north side of the neighborhood, the **Magnolia Tree Earth Center**, 677 Lafayette Ave (☎718/387-2116), is a community-based environmental education, arts, and activism center anchored by a *Magnolia grandiflora*, one of only two registered living landmarks in the city.

Crown Heights

South of Bedford-Stuyvesant and east of Prospect Park is thrumming **Crown Heights**, bounded by Atlantic Avenue and Empire Boulevard to the north and south, and Ralph and Washington avenues to the east and west. This community is home to the largest **West Indian** community in New York as well as an active, established population of about ten thousand **Hasidic Jews**, most of them belonging to the Russian Lubavitcher sect. To many New Yorkers, the words "Crown Heights" still conjure tense days in 1991, when the accidental death of a black child set off race riots. The neighborhood is generally not too dangerous now, and a wander here is by turns gritty and lively. Eastern Parkway, a large throughway, is the main traffic artery, but the real activity is on smaller streets to the south, particularly around the subway stops at Franklin Avenue (#2, #3, and #4 trains), Nostrand Avenue, and Kingston Avenue (both #3 only). Dedicated noshers will want to visit the string of dirt-cheap, largely vegetarian Caribbean snack joints along Nostrand Avenue. For a glimpse of Hasidic life – and surprisingly spacious New York real estate – stroll past the crumbling mansions on President Street between Kingston and Nostrand, where "Welcome Moshiach" banners blow in the breeze.

The most public face of the Hasidic community is the **Jewish Children's Museum**, on Eastern Parkway at Kingston Ave (Mon–Thurs 10am–4pm, Sun 10am–6pm; $10; ☎718/907-8833, ⍟www.jcmonline.org), a glitzy new building that looks quite bizarre on this older, slightly run-down corner. It presents Jewish traditions with every bell and whistle possible, including an educational mini-golf course. North of Eastern Parkway, the **Brooklyn Children's Museum**, 145 Brooklyn Ave at St Mark's Ave (July–Aug Tues–Fri 1–6pm, Sat & Sun 11am–6pm; Sept–June Wed–Fri 1–6pm, Sat & Sun 11am–6pm; open most school holidays; suggested donation $4; ☎718/735-4400, ⍟www.bchildmus.org), has a broader focus. Founded in 1899, it was the city's first museum of its kind; galleries, which are undergoing major renovations through 2007, hold thought-provoking and fun hands-on exhibits concentrating on science, the arts, the environment, and much more. The free bus from Grand Army Plaza and the Brooklyn Museum runs by both museums on weekends and holidays.

On Labor Day, Crown Heights hosts the annual **West Indian–American Day Parade and Carnival** (aka West Indian Day Parade or Labor Day Parade), an almost overwhelming cultural event, when almost two million revelers dance, eat, and applaud colorful floats and steel-drum outfits. The parade, which organizers claim is the biggest in the nation, runs west along Eastern Parkway from Rochester Avenue in Crown Heights to Grand Army Plaza (see Chapter 33, "Parades and festivals," for more information).

Coastal Brooklyn

It's possible, in theory, to walk, rollerblade, or bike almost the entire southern **coast** of Brooklyn. On occasion, paths disappear, and you must share the service road off the highway with cars, but you'll never be on the highway itself. Even those of less sturdy stock will find this area, which stretches east from **Bay Ridge** through **Coney Island**, **Brighton Beach**, and several smaller neighborhoods all the way to maritime **Sheepshead Bay**, worth visiting for the breathtaking views, carnival amusements, good shopping, and varied cuisine. If you're not on a bike or similarly speedy transport, though, you'll do best to focus on Brighton Beach and adjacent Coney Island, which make an easy afternoon trip by subway.

Bay Ridge

The last few stops of the #R train are in the neighborhood of Bay Ridge, the farthest corner of southwest Brooklyn. The Dutch West India Company bought Bay Ridge from the Nyack Indians in 1652; its ochre soil earned it the name Yellow Hook, but that was changed in 1853 after New York City suffered a bout of yellow fever. It's now notable for its ethnic and economic mix, in which Chinese, Irish, Italians, Scandinavians, and Lebanese coexist in a sort of low-crime paradise; senior citizens, many of them longtime residents, make up a large chunk of the population.

Bay Ridge is a bit too large to traverse on foot; for this reason, it's really recommended as a destination for bicyclists. The **Shore Road Bike Path** offers a glorious ride along the bay, including views of the shimmering **Verrazano Narrows Bridge** (1964), which flashes its minimalist message across the entry to Upper New York Bay. At 4260ft, this slender, beautiful span was, until Britain's Humber Bridge opened in 1981, the world's longest. The tops of the towers are an inch or so out of parallel to allow for the curvature of the earth. The bridge, which connects Brooklyn to Staten Island, is named for the first European explorer of New York Harbor, Giovanni da Verrazano.

To reach the bike path, get off the #R train at Bay Ridge Avenue (locals know it as 69th Street) and ride west toward the water (if you are on foot, the #B1 and #B9 buses can take you this way). At the pier, a path leads south right along the water's edge, but to see some of Bay Ridge's nicest homes, turn left before the water on Shore Road. Wind through Shore, Narrows, and River roads between 75th and 83rd streets, where you'll see some Greek and Gothic Revival houses. Most distinctive is the **Gingerbread House** (8220 Narrows Ave at 83rd St); the 1916 structure, done in a rare style known as Black Forest Art Nouveau, looks like a witch's backwoods lair, all piled-up stones and drooping eaves.

A bit less pastoral but still worth a visit, the **US Army Garrison Fort Hamilton** is a historic military base at 101st Street and Fort Hamilton Parkway. The **Harbor Defense Museum** of Fort Hamilton (Mon–Fri 10am–4pm, Sat 10am–2pm; free; ☏718/630-4349, ⊛www.harbordefensemuseum.com) is in an 1840 stone structure once used to protect the fort from any possible rear attack. Artifacts and weapons – guns, mines, missiles, cannons – tell the official history of the defense of New York Harbor.

Coney Island

Accessible to anyone for the price of a subway ride, the beachfront amusement spot of **Coney Island** has given working-class New Yorkers a holiday ever since a kerosene-lit carousel opened here in 1867. Buster Keaton movies and early twentieth-century photos provide a sense of the fantasyland it was, an "Electric Eden" aglow with millions of lights.

The fantasy dissipated by the 1960s, when landmarks like Steeplechase Park closed after repeated bankruptcies and fires, although today's Coney Island, boosted by arts organizations and neo–freak shows, exudes a certain rickety, retro charm. To see for yourself, take the #D, #F, #N, or #Q train to the last stop at Stillwell Avenue; the station itself, designed a century ago to handle floods of visitors, was made over in 2005 with a light-trimmed marquee that nods to the place's old glamour.

The entertainment has substantially changed since those days: in the high season, between Memorial Day and Labor Day, hip-hop blares over the sound systems, the language of choice on the boardwalk is Spanish or Russian as often as English, and the rides are state-of-the-art circa 1985. You have to be in the right frame of mind; this is not your typical corporate fun-park. On weekdays, rainy days, and in the off-season, the festive atmosphere can totally disappear, making for an experience that's bittersweet, if not downright depressing and even a bit creepy. The beach can be overwhelmingly crowded on hot days, and it's never the cleanest place.

But step out into the sunshine on a summer day and you'll feel the initial burst of excitement that has filled generations of kids about to ride the Cyclone roller coaster, the Parachute Jump, or the Wonder Wheel for the first time. On Friday nights from July 4 to Labor Day, the boardwalk is packed for the impressive **fireworks**, which at times feel too close for comfort. At the annual **Mermaid Parade** on the first Saturday of summer (ⓦwww.coneyislandusa .com/mermaid), you'll get caught up in one of the oddest, glitziest small-town festivals in the country, where participants dress (barely) as mermaids, King Neptunes, and other sea-dwellers.

Upon arrival, head straight for **Nathan's**, on the corner of Surf Avenue when you get off the subway. This is the home of the "famous Coney Island hot dog," advertised in branches elsewhere in the US, and even if you'd otherwise skip this all-American delicacy, only vegetarians have an excuse for missing it here. *Nathan's* holds a well-attended annual **Hot Dog Eating Contest** on July 4;

△ The Cyclone, Coney Island

slender repeat-champion Takeru "Tsunami" Kobayashi set the record of 53 and three-quarters dogs in 2006. One block from *Nathan's* is the famous **boardwalk**, where all the beach-goers promenade (some in outfits that will make you wonder whether the Mermaid Parade is an ongoing event).

The thrill-ride section, on the inland side of the boardwalk, actually consists of several separately managed parks. Nearly all the children's rides are in **Deno's Wonder Wheel Park** (☎718/372-2592, ⚇www.wonderwheel.com), where you might want to buy a pack of ten tickets for $20. The **Wonder Wheel** ($5, plus a free children's ticket to the New York Aquarium) is a must. An official New York City landmark, the 1920 ride is the world's tallest Ferris wheel aside from the London Eye, and the only one on which two-thirds of the cars slide on serpentine tracks, shifting position as the wheel makes its slow circle twice around. Coney Island's most iconic ride is the almost 80-year-old **Cyclone** roller coaster, in Astroland ($5; ☎718/265-2100, ⚇www.astroland.com). The low-tech, creaky wooden coaster is not for the faint of heart – as you wait in the snaking line, you can actually see the cars lose contact with the metal rails at one point. Sit in front for the most terrifying view, in back for an extra-strong sense of vertigo. Repeat rides go for $4 or $3, depending on the operators' whim, so you can work your way up to the seat you want.

Another great summer attraction is **KeySpan Park**, on Surf Avenue between West 17th and 19th streets, the scenic oceanside baseball-stadium that has helped lend a more prosperous air to the neighborhood. The park is home to the **Brooklyn Cyclones** (see p.428), a New York Mets–affiliated minor-league team that draws a dedicated crowd. Seating is intimate, beer flows freely, and tickets are inexpensive, making it a comfortable place to wallow in Americana under the glow of the stadium lights.

Coney Island Museum and New York Aquarium

East of Stillwell Avenue, the nonprofit **Coney Island Museum**, 1208 Surf Ave (Fri & Sat noon–5pm; 99¢; ☎718/372-5159, ⚇www.coneyislandusa.com), is one indoor destination you don't want to miss. You can tour relics of Coney Island past, hear a lecture on the beach's history, or catch a nighttime burlesque performance. The staff here can point you to nifty outdoor art installations and murals that change every season; you may also see the same folks pop up at **Sideshows by the Seashore**, on W 12th St at Surf Ave. Full-cast sideshows ($5) run from 2 to 10pm summer Fridays and 1–11pm summer weekends. Other, less artistically minded shows (such as the Two-Headed Baby, the Headless Woman, and the Giant Killer Rat) abound on the sidestreets, but don't expect much for your money.

Continue east on the boardwalk, halfway to Brighton Beach, to reach the seashell-shaped **New York Aquarium**, Surf Ave and W 8th St (hours vary by season; $11, under 12 and seniors $7; ☎718/265-FISH, ⚇www.nyaquarium .com). Run by the Wildlife Conservation Society, which also administers New York's four excellent zoos, the aquarium features more than eight thousand creatures from all over the world. It's worth a visit, especially for the dolphin shows or during feeding hours.

Brighton Beach

East along the boardwalk from Coney Island, at Brooklyn's southernmost end, **Brighton Beach** was once an affluent seaside resort of its own. Often called Little Odessa, it is now home to the country's largest community of immigrants from Russia and the former Soviet states, who started relocating here in the

1970s. The eldest of them pack the boardwalk benches to soak up the sun and gossip, dressed in shorts in the summer and swaddled in fur coats in the winter. Reach the neighborhood by riding the #B or #Q train to the Brighton Beach stop, or just walk down the boardwalk from Coney Island.

Brighton Beach Avenue runs parallel to the boardwalk; the street is a bustling mixture of Russian souvenir shops and **food outlets**, including elaborately stocked delis; pick up picnic fixings at the large **M & I International**, 249 Brighton Beach Ave (☎718/615-1011), which has all sorts of smoked fish, sausages, cheeses, pickles (many soaked in vodka rather than vinegar), and breads. Sit-down food is also readily available at restaurants on the boardwalk, though you might want to wait until evening, when the **supper clubs** open up. These cavernous places offer a near-parody of a rowdy Russian night out, complete with lots of food, loud music, surreal floor shows, and plenty of vodka. One of the most popular spots is *National*, 273 Brighton Beach Ave (☎718/646-1225, ⊛www.come2national.com).

Sheepshead Bay

One stop closer to Manhattan on the #B or #Q subway lines is **Sheepshead Bay**, which claims to be "New York's only working fishing village" (though City Island in the Bronx might beg to differ – see p.286). It is quieter and more conservative than other beach communities, and **Emmons Avenue** maintains a salty charm.

In the early evening, the adventurous shop the boats at the Emmons Avenue pier for what may be the **freshest fish in the city**. At about 4pm on weekdays, boats unload heaps of bluefish, flounder, and mackerel. Fish fanatics can go out on one of the many boats that take visitors. Try the *Dorothy B VIII* (7am–4pm, schedule varies; $42 and up; ☎718/646-4057, ⊛www.dorothyb .com) or the *Sea Queen III* (Oct–March Fri–Sun 8am–noon & Mon–Thurs 1–5.30pm; $28 and up; ☎347/723-3092, ⊛www.seaqueenfleet.com). Many boats also conduct sunset cruises to various points of interest in New York Harbor. Show up at the pier at about 5pm on weekdays from spring to fall to see who's going out.

Northern Brooklyn

Northeast of downtown and past Fort Greene are the neighborhoods of **Williamsburg**, which is divided among artsy refugees from Manhattan and sections that are strongly Hasidic or Latino, and working-class Polish and Puerto Rican **Greenpoint**. While short on typical tourist attractions, these districts are rich in atmosphere, whether you want to ogle tattooed twenty-somethings or immerse yourself in the sounds of Spanish, Yiddish, or Polish.

Williamsburg

Step off the #L train at the Bedford Avenue stop and you'll be in the heart of hip Williamsburg, where the sidewalks teem with a particular breed of self-consciously down-market bohemian, decked out in vintage clothes and hopping from coffee shop to record store to nifty boutique. The area from North 12th Street to the Williamsburg Bridge is made up mostly of low-rise

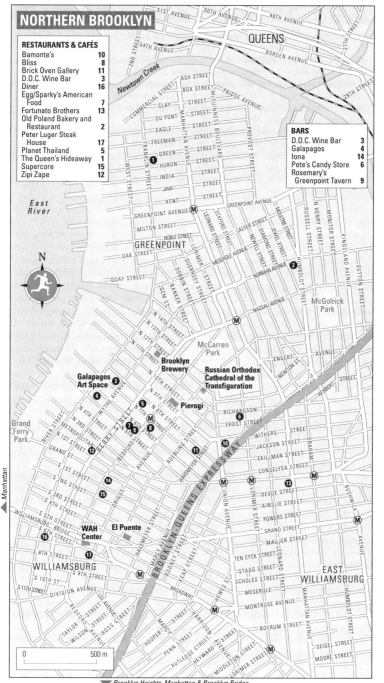

NORTHERN BROOKLYN

RESTAURANTS & CAFÉS

Bamonte's	10
Bliss	8
Brick Oven Gallery	11
D.O.C. Wine Bar	3
Diner	16
Egg/Sparky's American Food	7
Fortunato Brothers	13
Old Poland Bakery and Restaurant	2
Peter Luger Steak House	17
Planet Thailand	5
The Queen's Hideaway	1
Supercore	15
Zipi Zape	12

BARS

D.O.C. Wine Bar	3
Galapagos	4
Iona	14
Pete's Candy Store	6
Rosemary's Greenpoint Tavern	9

Brooklyn Heights, Manhattan & Brooklyn Bridge

converted warehouses – the perfect spaces for studios and galleries, making the area home to the most respected art scene outside of Chelsea.

According to one local curator, Williamsburg (sometimes called Billyburg, but don't try it yourself) boasts more than 100,000 resident artists – which would make it the largest geographical cluster of artists in the world. Of the seventy or so galleries in the neighborhood, ranging in ambience from ultra-professional to makeshift, perhaps the most influential is **Pierogi**, 177 N 9th St (noon–6pm Thurs–Mon; T718/599-2144, W www.pierogi2000.com), two blocks north of the subway. See p.406 for additional gallery recommendations. Amble back down Bedford or Driggs avenues, the two main north–south thoroughfares, to the imposing Kings County Savings Bank, 135 Broadway at Bedford Ave, now home to the **Williamsburg Art and Historical Center** (Sat & Sun noon–6pm or by appointment; T718/486-7372, W www.wahcenter.net). One of several landmark nineteenth-century banks in Williamsburg, the building opened as an arts center in 1996; it hosts beautiful and challenging exhibits.

At night, Williamsburg hosts a thriving club, performance, film, and music scene at venues like *Galapagos Art Space*, 70 N 6th St (T718/782-5188, W www .galapagosartspace.com), and *Pete's Candy Store*, 709 Lorimer St (T718/302-3770, W www.petescandystore.com).

But the cutting-edge feel of Williamsburg is already changing: waterfront high-rises are sprouting up, capitalizing on views like the one from tiny **Grand Ferry Park**, where Grand Street dead-ends and the Williamsburg Bridge soars over the river. Even neighborhood loyalists are already picking up and moving farther down the #L line, seeking cheap rent and space in which to pursue creative interests. By the time you read this, Bedford Avenue may be completely awash in khaki-wearing professionals, and the revolution regrouped to the east, in Bushwick.

South-side Williamsburg, by contrast, seems frozen in time. The roughly triangular area formed by the Williamsburg Bridge and the Brooklyn–Queens Expressway, most easily reached by #J, #M, and #Z trains at Marcy Avenue, is bisected by **Division Avenue**, the traditional border between a long-standing Puerto Rican community and the **Hasidic Jewish** part of Williamsburg. In the latter section, men wear black suits and breeches, and long *payot* (curls) hang from under their big fur hats; women dress in long skirts, with scarves or wigs. The Jewish community has been here since the bridge linked the area to the

Lower East Side in 1903, and many Jews from that neighborhood left for better conditions across the East River. At the end of World War II a further settlement of Yiddish-speaking Hasidic Jews, mainly from Romania, became the majority, and now more than 45,000 Satmar Hasidim live in Williamsburg.

The best place to start exploring Jewish Williamsburg is **Lee Avenue** or Bedford Avenue, which run parallel. Kosher delicatessens line the streets; signs are written in Yiddish and Hebrew. Don't take it personally if you're ignored. Farther south on Lee Avenue, you'll find yourself far from any subway – the #B44 bus will get you back to the Williamsburg Bridge; the #B61 will take you to downtown Brooklyn, or north via Bedford Avenue.

After World War II, Puerto Ricans displaced by development in other parts of Brooklyn began to arrive, settling north and east of the Hasidim, and the two populations coexist today in a state of strained tolerance. **El Puente**, 211 S 4th St (☎718/387-0404), is the center of the Latino community, which now also includes large numbers of Mexicans and Central Americans.

On the waterfront, the vast **Brooklyn Navy Yard** (☎718/907-5900, ⓦwww .brooklynnavyyard.org) forms a barrier between North and South Brooklyn. Established in 1801, the yard was where the *Monitor*, built in nearby Greenpoint (see below), was clad in iron; during World War II, some 71,000 workers made it a crucial construction ground for battleships such as the *Iowa*, *New Jersey*, *Arizona*, and *Missouri*. No vessels have been built here since 1966, and the docks and warehouses are home to a number of creative businesses, including the 280,000-square-foot Steiner Studios, which opened in 2005 and has helped reinvigorate TV and film production in the city.

Greenpoint

Quiet **Greenpoint**, which hugs the northern border of the borough, has the distinction of being the childhood home of Mae West, the birthplace of the oft-ridiculed Brooklynese accent, and home to the largest Polish community in New York City; there's also a substantial Puerto Rican contingent. Reachable by the #G train to Greenpoint Avenue or the #L to Bedford Avenue, the pretty, low-rise area has absorbed some of the artsy feel of Williamsburg to the south, but the younger residents haven't diluted the Polish character of the businesses along its tidy main strip, **Manhattan Avenue**.

Greenpoint and neighboring areas were known in the mid-seventeenth century as Boswijck (later Bushwick), meaning "wooded district." Later, the Industrial Revolution took the "green" out of Greenpoint, as the area became home to the "Black Arts" – printing, pottery, gas, glass, and iron. The abandoned **ironworks**, on West Street between Oak and Calyer streets, was the site of the historic launching of the ironclad ship *Monitor*, which went to sea on January 30, 1862, to fight the Confederate armored *Merrimac*. In 1950, refineries caused a 17-million-gallon underground oil spill, larger than the *Exxon Valdez* disaster in Alaska. It's not immediately visible except as an occasional slick on the surface of Newtown Creek, which separates Greenpoint from Queens.

These things aside, Greenpoint bears a visit, especially if you're in nearby Williamsburg or Long Island City, which is just a short walk over the Pulaski Bridge. It represents a quintessential sort of Brooklyn neighborhood, strong in its local pride and distinctive in its character. If you want to pick up some Polish sausages or *pierogi* dumplings, local restaurants and markets – notably **Steve's Meat Market**, 104 Nassau Ave (☎718/383-1780) – claim to make the best *kielbasa* in America.

From Manhattan Avenue, turn right (west) on Nassau Avenue to reach **McCarren Park**, often considered the line between Greenpoint and Williamsburg. While the physical border might well be the park, the mental one is a little blurry, particularly with "North Williamsburg" (some of which was formerly considered Greenpoint) becoming such a hotspot. At the south end of the park, five green-copper onion domes hover above the trees. This Byzantine Revival structure, consecrated in 1922, is the **Russian Orthodox Cathedral of the Transfiguration**, N 12th St at Driggs Ave, a New York City landmark. Its design echoes the Cathedral of the Dormition in the Kremlin, and its parishioners are largely Russian and Polish.

Queens

O
f New York City's four outer boroughs, **Queens**, named for Catherine
of Braganza, queen consort of Charles II, was for many years probably the least visited – not counting when outsiders passed through
Queens' airports, JFK and LaGuardia. If Brooklyn, with its strong
neighborhood identities and elegant architecture, represents the old, historic
city, then aesthetically challenged, sprawling Queens puts the "new" in New
York.

Some 46 percent of the borough's 2.2 million residents hail from more than 150
foreign countries, bringing an incomparable diversity and dynamism to the city.
You can travel from Greek and Eastern European **Astoria** through Irish **Woodside** to Indian and Latino **Jackson Heights** and finally Asian **Flushing**. You'll
find no shortage of delicious foods in Queens – just follow the #7 train, aka the
"International Express," which traces a five-mile route across the borough. The
elevated train affords drab views of rooftops and graffiti, giving little indication of
the veritable feast to be had below: Turkish breads, Romanian sausages, Indonesian

Navigating Queens

One reason many New Yorkers have no love for Queens is the deeply unsettling
street-number system, which can leave you baffled on the corner of 30th Road and
30th Street. But the so-called "Philadelphia method" of addressing, applied borough-
wide in the 1920s, does have an underlying logic.

Basically, **streets** run north–south, while **avenues, roads, and drives** run east–
west. Avenue numbers get higher as you head south, while First Street is on the
East River, and 180th in Jamaica. (If it helps, this system is precisely the opposite
of Manhattan's.) Moreover, in house numbers, the digits before the hyphen indicate
the cross street: 20-78 33rd Street, for instance, is between 20th and 21st avenues.
This can be handy on the major thoroughfares that have retained their historic names
– 74-15 Roosevelt Avenue, for example, is near 74th Street.

Humorist Ellis Parker Butler captured the essential details in a 1926 mnemonic
verse:

In Queens to find locations best,
Avenues, roads and drives run west
But ways to north or south 'tis plain
Are streets or place or even lane;
While even numbers you will meet
Upon the west or south of street.

If you can't commit this to memory, just make sure to check the MTA neighborhood
map before you leave the subway station. Above ground, you can also often orient
yourself by the Citicorp tower in Long Island City, the borough's tallest building.

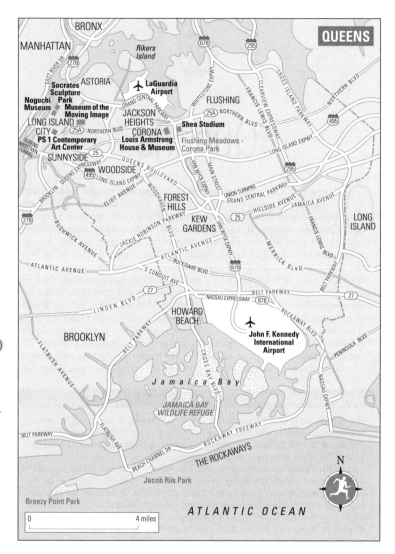

BRONX
MANHATTAN
Rikers Island
678
295
EAST RIVER DR
278
ASTORIA
LaGuardia Airport
Socrates Sculpture Park
WHITESTONE EXPWY
FLUSHING
CROSS ISLAND PARKWAY
NORTHERN BLVD
Noguchi Museum
Museum of the Moving Image
GRAND CENTRAL PARKWAY
JACKSON HEIGHTS
25A NORTHERN BLVD
FRANCIS LEWIS BLVD
495
LONG ISLAND CITY
25A NORTHERN BLVD
CORONA
Shea Stadium
Flushing Meadows-Corona Park
LONG ISLAND EXPWY
QUEENS MIDTOWN TUNNEL
PS 1 Contemporary Art Center
Louis Armstrong House & Museum
VAN WYCK EXPWY
MAIN STREET
295
SUNNYSIDE
25
WOODSIDE
QUEENS BOULEVARD
495 LONG ISLAND EXPWY
ELIOT AVENUE
WOODHAVEN BLVD
UNION TURNPIKE
GRAND CENTRAL PARKWAY
HILLSIDE AVENUE
JAMAICA AVENUE
LONG ISLAND
278
FOREST HILLS
BUSHWICK AVENUE
JACKIE ROBINSON PARKWAY
KEW GARDENS
VAN WYCK EXPWY
25
FRANCIS LEWIS BLVD
ATLANTIC AVENUE
ATLANTIC AVENUE
ROCKAWAY BLVD
678
MERRICK BLVD
S CONDUIT AVE
BELT PARKWAY
BELT PARKWAY
27
LINDEN BLVD
27
NASSAU EXPRESSWAY
878
ROCKAWAY BLVD
HOWARD BEACH
BROOKLYN
BELT PARKWAY
John F. Kennedy International Airport
PENINSULA BLVD
FLATBUSH AVENUE
FLATBUSH AVE
CROSS BAY BLVD
Jamaica Bay
NASSAU EXPWY
JAMAICA BAY WILDLIFE REFUGE
BELT PARKWAY
ROCKAWAY FREEWAY
BEACH CHANNEL DR
THE ROCKAWAYS
N
Jacob Riis Park
Breezy Point Park
0   4 miles
ATLANTIC OCEAN

noodles, Tibetan dumplings, Argentine steaks, Indian curries, and Cantonese *dim sum* all await the adventurous visitor. The borough also boasts a few underrated museums, as well as **Shea Stadium**, home of the New York Mets, and **Flushing Meadows–Corona Park**, which holds the Queens Museum of Art and the annual US Open Tennis Championships. At the southeast end of the borough (accessible via the #A train), in **Jamaica Bay** and the **Rockaways**, lie pristine parks and beaches that feel miles from the city.

For information on the borough and discounts at local merchants, contact Discover Queens (☎718/263-0546, ⓦwww.discoverqueens.info) or the Queens Council on the Arts (☎718/647-3377, ⓦwww.queenscouncilarts.org).

Long Island City and Astoria

The neighborhoods of **Long Island City** and **Astoria**, only a few minutes by subway from midtown Manhattan, comprise the northwest corner of Queens, a region edged by the East River on the west and north, the Brooklyn–Queens Expressway to the east, and Northern Boulevard and Newtown Creek to the south – though the dividing line between the two neighborhoods is less clearly defined. This area has managed to become the hippest part of Queens without sacrificing its long-standing diversity and relatively low housing prices: many artists live and work in the warehouses of Long Island City, and Astoria counts Greeks, Brazilians, Egyptians, Moroccans, Bengalis, Italians, Czechs, Croatians, and Japanese among its residents. The communities are by no means physically gorgeous – in fact, you could consider this a tour of America's most creative vinyl-siding architecture – but they contain enough museums and great cheap restaurants to make it well worth a day-trip.

Long Island City

The less-than-lovely mishmash of warehouses and homes in **Long Island City** pales in comparison to the majestic view of midtown Manhattan that you'll see when the #7, #N, and #W trains pull above ground here. The neighborhood is largely industrial; the biggest residential community, known as **Hunters Point**, is around the Vernon Boulevard stop on the #7. This area is cut off from the rest of LIC proper by **Queens Plaza**, a mass of traffic-packed lanes at the foot of the Queensborough Bridge lined with strip clubs (they decamped here from Times Square when that district was cleaned up in the 1990s) and the Queensbridge Houses, one of the city's oldest and largest projects. North of here, LIC hugs the water, roughly west of 21st Street, all the way up to the Triborough Bridge. Because the neighborhood is spread out, you can't visit all of its sights via one subway stop, and you may even want to take a bus to northerly attractions like Socrates Sculpture Park.

Hunters Point and Gantry Plaza State Park

The neighborhood of **Hunters Point**, on the East River at the border with Brooklyn, demonstrates how far off Manhattanites' radars Queens has been – how else could a place with eye-level views of the UN building and one-stop subway access to Manhattan lie ungentrified for decades? The motley warehouse district has finally become more desirable in recent years, and now sports a clutch of cool cafés along its main drag, Vernon Boulevard (running north of the #7 train stop). By the river, locals relax at **Water Taxi Beach**, where 400 tons of sand acts as a play-spot for families, a cheap-drink destination for hipsters, and the dock for the NY Water Taxi (W www.nywatertaxi.com) **ferry** – service here is erratic, but if the boat is running, it's a scenic alternative to the subway. Farther north, **Gantry Plaza State Park** showcases Long Island City's shipping past – the original gantries look like windows onto Manhattan; the adjacent neon Pepsi-Cola sign is the unofficial symbol of the neighborhood.

PS 1 Contemporary Art Center and around

Just steps from the 45th Road–Court Square stop on the #7 (as well as the #E, #V, and #G trains at 23rd Street–Ely Avenue), or an easy walk from Hunters Point, the renowned **PS 1 Contemporary Art Center**, 22-25 Jackson Ave at 46th Ave (Mon & Thurs–Sun noon–6pm; $5 suggested donation;

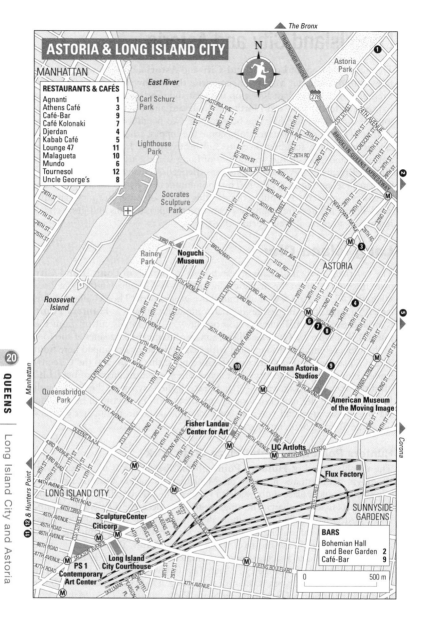

ASTORIA & LONG ISLAND CITY

MANHATTAN

RESTAURANTS & CAFÉS

Agnanti	1
Athens Café	3
Café-Bar	9
Café Kolonaki	7
Djerdan	4
Kabab Café	5
Lounge 47	11
Malagueta	10
Mundo	6
Tournesol	12
Uncle George's	8

The Bronx

East River

Carl Schurz Park

Lighthouse Park

Socrates Sculpture Park

Astoria Park

Rainey Park

Noguchi Museum

ASTORIA

Roosevelt Island

Queensbridge Park

Kaufman Astoria Studios

American Museum of the Moving Image

Fisher Landau Center for Art

LIC Artlofts

Flux Factory

LONG ISLAND CITY

SculptureCenter

Citicorp

SUNNYSIDE GARDENS

Long Island City Courthouse

PS 1 Contemporary Art Center

BARS

Bohemian Hall and Beer Garden	2
Café-Bar	9

0 ————— 500 m

QUEENS | Long Island City and Astoria

20

①⑫ & Hunters Point

Manhattan

Corona

718/784-2084, www.ps1.org), occupies a cavernous nineteenth-century brick schoolhouse. Founded in 1971, PS 1 is now affiliated with the Museum of Modern Art, which has given the former nonprofit organization some much-needed financial stability while leaving it the curatorial freedom that has made it one of the most consistently exciting contemporary-arts spaces in the city. Except for a few site-specific installations, there is no permanent collection, just rotating exhibits. Particularly good are the "Greater New York" survey shows, as well as the presentations by participants in the museum's studio program. On Saturdays in July and August, the popular "Warm Up" party series brings in excellent DJs and other performers to the courtyard; these days are also the only time during the summer that you can see James Turrell's subtle and mesmerizing light installation *Meeting* on the top floor.

Directly across Jackson Avenue from PS 1, the warehouse called **5 Pointz** (⊛www.5ptz.com) is covered with graffiti art – some six hundred people have worked on the facade over the course of a decade. Walk around at street level to see some amazing work, but also keep an eye out while you're on the #7 – the train crosses directly over the building. A few blocks north along Jackson Avenue, past the Neoclassical **Long Island City Courthouse**, the **Sculp-tureCenter**, 44-19 Purves St (Mon & Thurs–Sun 11am–6pm; free; ☎718/361-1750, ⊛www.sculpture-center.org), shows innovative exhibits in a former trolley-repair shop. The center makes interesting use of the space, with pieces on display in a grand open hall as well as down in the warren-like basement, which was cleverly renovated by architect Maya Lin.

North of Queens Plaza

The **Fisher Landau Center for Art**, 38-27 30th Street (Mon & Thurs–Sun noon–5pm; free; ☎718/937-0727, ⊛www.flcart.org), is an easy walk from the numerous subway stops at Queens Plaza or from the 39th Avenue stop on the #N or #W trains. You'll almost certainly have this airy space to yourself as you contemplate works by Jenny Holzer, Jasper Johns, Matthew Barney, and Yinka Shonibare – or whatever other contemporary masters happen to be currently selected from real-estate heiress Emily Fisher Landau's thousand-item personal stash.

Farther afield but definitely worth the detour, the **Noguchi Museum**, 9-01 33rd Ave (Wed–Fri 10am–5pm, Sat & Sun 11am–6pm; $10, students and seniors $5; ☎718/204-7088, ⊛www.noguchi.org), is devoted to the works of Japanese-American abstract sculptor Isamu Noguchi (1904–88). At its center is a garden filled with his stone sculptures, while the surrounding galleries include a special section on his design work. Particularly intriguing are his blueprints of proposed playgrounds that conjure a variety of unconventional yet organic shapes in place of the usual seesaws and slides. To get to the museum, take the #N or #W train to the Broadway (Queens) station; head west to Vernon Boulevard, then south two blocks to 33rd Avenue – about a fifteen-minute walk or a five-minute ride on the #Q104 bus. You can also take the #Q103 bus from Hunters Point.

While you're out this way, stop in at **Socrates Sculpture Park**, one block north of the Noguchi Museum, on Broadway at Vernon Boulevard (daily

△ Courtyard, Noguchi Museum

10am–sunset; ☎718/956-1819, ⓦwww.socratessculpturepark.org). The park was an abandoned landfill until 1986, when sculptor Mark di Suvero transformed it into an outdoor studio, with space for artists to build on a massive scale. The resulting works range from ingenious kinetic installations to bizarre structures that appear to be growing out of the lawn. In the summer, a popular film series highlights Astoria and Long Island City's cultural mix, and kayak rides around the waterfront take off from the park's informal **LIC Community Boathouse** (free, but reserve ahead; ⓦwww.licboathouse.org).

Astoria

Northeast of Long Island City is bustling **Astoria**, bounded to the south (roughly) by 36th Avenue and to the east by the BQE. Astoria is extremely ethnically diverse, though it is best known for being home to the largest concentration of Greeks outside Greece, or so it has claimed for many years (whatever Melbourne, Australia, says to the contrary). The #N and #W trains from Manhattan run north through the middle of the neighborhood, stopping at all of the major avenues, each of which forms its own community: 30th Avenue and Broadway are the liveliest, with European grocers and butchers, Greek-style coffee joints, and glitzy nightclubs; quieter 36th Avenue has a growing Brazilian population alongside Bengali shops; and Ditmars Boulevard is home to some of Astoria's oldest residents – the Italians predate the Greeks – and is near **Astoria Park**, which has beautiful views of Manhattan and a huge public pool. You can also take the #R to Steinway Street, which accesses the east side of the neighborhood; between 28th Avenue and Astoria Boulevard, Steinway is a strip of Egyptian- and Moroccan-run businesses, including a glut of hookah cafés where you can watch Arabic TV, sip tea, and savor sweet apple tobacco (though thanks to the city's smoking ban, you still have to go outside to smoke a cigarette).

Historically, Astoria was a center for the arts. The country's premier piano-making family gave its name to Steinway Street, where it still keeps its workshop, north of 19th Avenue (tours by appointment; ☎718/721-7600,

Between 1920 and 1928, Astoria was the capital of America's **film industry**. Paramount Pictures got its start here, drawing stars such as Rudolph Valentino, Tallulah Bankhead, and the Marx Brothers to its studio on 36th Street. In the 1930s, however, movie titans were lured west to Hollywood by more reliable weather, largely abandoning Astoria Studio. During World War II, the US Army commandeered the place for its Signal Corps Pictorial Center, which provided propaganda films for the troops long after the war ended. The studios were empty for several years in the 1970s, but were named a national historic landmark before reopening in 1977 to stage Sidney Lumet's **The Wiz**.

In recent decades, Hollywood's stranglehold on filmmaking has weakened, and New York in general – and Astoria in particular – is seeing more business. Now called **Kaufman Astoria Studios**, 34-12 36th St, the filmmaking complex occupies fourteen acres. Though it doesn't look like much (and isn't open to visitors), it's extremely busy: in addition to long-running **Sesame Street**, HBO's **Angels in America** was shot here, as was the 2006 remake of **The Pink Panther**. The city is even considering closing off some of the streets in the area to create a more formal "movie lot" that could accommodate bigger productions.

@www.steinway.com). The first commercial moving pictures were produced here, before the industry moved to Hollywood. The **American Museum of the Moving Image**, a tribute to this legacy, is Astoria's single most popular destination, though you're strongly advised to visit one or two of the neighborhood's delicious and affordable restaurants. See Chapter 25, "Restaurants," for reviews.

American Museum of the Moving Image

Part of the Kaufman Astoria complex at 35th Avenue and 36th Street (see box, above) is dedicated to the **American Museum of the Moving Image** (Wed & Thurs 11am–5pm, Fri 11am–8pm, Sat & Sun 11am–6.30pm; $10, students and seniors $10, children $7.50, free Fri 4–8pm; ☎718/784-0077, @www .ammi.org). Take the #R or #V train to Steinway on weekdays (the #E or #R on weekends), walk south on Steinway to 35th Avenue, turn right, and walk three blocks down to the museum at the corner of 36th Street.

The museum's stellar collection contains more than a thousand objects, including posters, film stills, and the complete diner set from *Seinfeld*. Equipment, dating from Astoria's golden age up to recent digital innovations, is on view and set up to be played with. Kids will love the vintage video-game collection and "Tut's Fever Movie Palace," where old adventure serials are screened. On weekends, free tours run at 2pm; your admission ticket also gets you into showings of rare, restored, and classic films.

Sunnyside, Woodside, and Jackson Heights

After Astoria, the #E, #R, and #V trains run north of **Sunnyside** and **Woodside**, historically Irish enclaves now also home to many Asian and Latino immigrants. You're not missing too much if you skip these neighborhoods on your way to the more interesting **Jackson Heights**, though planning enthusiasts may want to see the **Sunnyside Gardens** development, a utopian working-class "garden city" built in 1924 with encouragement from Eleanor Roosevelt and Lewis Mumford; take the #7 train (which runs straight through Sunnyside and Woodside) to the 46th Street stop and walk north on 46th (the opposite direction from the Art Deco "Sunnyside" sign on Queens Boulevard).

Jackson Heights

East of Sunnyside, the #7 train swings away from Queens Boulevard and heads up narrower Roosevelt Avenue. Get off at 74th Street or 82nd Street (or take the #E, #F, #R, or #V to Roosevelt Avenue), and you'll find yourself in central **Jackson Heights**, where English is rarely the tongue of choice. Developed after the construction of the elevated train in 1917, the area was laid out in a united plan of tidy brick homes, apartment blocks with attractive garden court-yards, and orderly shopping streets, lending the area a cohesiveness that's rare in Queens. The area has seen several major population shifts over the decades: in the 1960s, Colombians, Ecuadorians, and Argentines came to the neighbor-hood, seeking to escape the poverty, unemployment, and unstable politics of their various home countries; South Asian emigrants began to arrive at about the same time, and Jackson Heights is equally well known for its community of Indian, Pakistani, Bangladeshi, and Sri Lankan families, the largest in New York City. During Historic Jackson Heights Weekend each June (@www.jhbg.org), you can tour the gardens and historic district (north of 37th Avenue). Roosevelt and 37th avenues, which run parallel between 74th Street and Junction Boul-evard, are the neighborhood's main streets, and this is a great part of Queens for trying out new and exciting **cuisines**. You'll find Argentine steakhouses, street vendors selling treats such as *arepas* (savory corn cakes), and bakeries displaying stacks of bread and pastries operate along both avenues.

Little India at 74th Street is something of a contrast. This is the largest Indian community in New York, and South Asians from all over come here to find colorful saris, elaborate gold jewelry for weddings, groceries, music, and perhaps a pungent betel leaf from a street cart. The restaurants here far surpass the more quotidian fare on better-known East 6th Street in Manhattan: *Jackson Diner*, 37-47 74th St, is one of the best – see p.360 for reviews of this and other notable eateries. The **Eagle Theater**, 73-07 37th Rd (☎718/205-2800), shows Bollywood movies in Hindi with English subtitles.

Corona and Flushing Meadows

East of Jackson Heights is gritty **Corona**, immortalized in Queens-native Paul Simon's song *Me and Julio Down by the Schoolyard*. Once entirely Italian (*corona* is Italian for "crown"), the neighborhood is now mostly first-generation immi-grants from the Dominican Republic, Mexico, Ecuador, and Colombia, and about a fifth of households live below the poverty line. It's not an unpleasant neighborhood, but there's little incentive to wander aimlessly and you'll do best heading straight for the main sights: the Louis Armstrong House, Shea Stadium, or **Flushing Meadows–Corona Park**.

To get to the **Louis Armstrong House**, 34-56 107th St, between 34th and 37th avenues (Tues–Fri 10am–5pm, Sat & Sun noon–5pm; $8, under 12, students and seniors $6; ☎718/478-8274, ⊛www.satchmo.net), take the #7 train to 103rd Street–Corona Plaza, walk north on 104th Street, turn right on 37th Avenue, and then left on 107th Street. The great jazz artist's home has been preserved just as he and his wife, Lucille, left it. Lucille was a wallpaper fan, and bold 1970s prints wrap the house; the downstairs bathroom, covered in mirrors, has something of a Versailles vibe. Armstrong, who lived here from 1943 until his death in 1971, made audio recordings of the day-to-day goings-on in the house, and these play inside, creating a ghostly atmosphere. Guided tours, which show off Armstrong's trumpets and various other artifacts, start every hour on the hour. It's interesting that the Armstrongs, who could have lived anywhere, chose to stay in this working-class neighborhood, a fact that hasn't escaped the museum's enthusiastic staff. If you'd like to learn more about Queens' substantial jazz history, you can also see the house as part of the **Queens Jazz Trail Tour**, which runs from Flushing Town Hall (see p.275) on the first Saturday of every month and visits the neighborhoods where Ella Fitzgerald, Count Basie, and others lived.

Several blocks east of the Armstrong house stands **Shea Stadium**, home to the **New York Mets** baseball team. Like many buildings in the area, the stadium went up as part of the 1964 World's Fair (see box, p.274). The Beatles played here in 1965 (whence the concept of the stadium rock concert). The Mets have a loyal fan base, if for no other reason than that many Queens and Brooklyn residents can't stand the Yankees. For details on the Mets and when they play, see Chapter 31, "Sports and outdoor activities." The stadium has its own stop on the #7 train.

Flushing Meadows–Corona Park

Immediately south of Shea Stadium across the LIRR tracks, **Flushing Meadows–Corona Park** is an enormous swath of green first laid out in the 1930s. Its few key attractions – a couple of interesting museums, as well as some relics of the two World's Fairs held here – make for a good afternoon out, especially if you have children who need space to run around. Take the #7 train to the Shea Stadium stop and walk south past the tennis complex; or, you can bypass much of the park and head directly to the museums by walking south from the 111th Street station until you hit the park's northwest corner.

Flushing Meadows literally rose out of ashes, replacing an old dumping ground known to locals as "Mount Corona" and described by F. Scott Fitzgerald in *The Great Gatsby* as "a fantastic farm where ashes grow like wheat into ridges and hills and grotesque gardens." The park is now the site of the US Tennis Association's **National Tennis Center**, the largest facility in the world, with more than forty indoor and outdoor courts. The main event, the US Open Tennis Championships, take place at the end of each summer. Tickets to the early matches are easy enough to come by; closer to the finals, you may have to buy from scalpers (see p.433).

Walking south on 111th Street from the subway, you reach the **New York Hall of Science**, 111th St at 46th Ave (July & Aug Mon–Fri 9.30am–5pm, Sat & Sun 10am–6pm; Sept–June Tues–Thurs 9.30am–2pm, Fri 9.30am–5pm, Sat & Sun 10am–5pm; $11, students and children $8, free Sept–June Fri 2–5pm & Sun 10–11am; ☎718/699-0005, ⊛www.nyhallsci.org), a concrete and stained-glass structure retained from the 1964 World's Fair. This is an interactive science museum kids will love; it's fun but can be exhausting for adults. Parking is not available during the US Open.

The adjacent **Queens Zoo**, 53-51 111th St (April–Oct Mon–Fri 10am–5pm, Sat & Sun 10am–5.30pm; Nov–March daily 10am–4.30pm; $6, ages 5–12 $2, seniors $2.25; ☎718/271-1500, ⊛www.queenszoo.org), is not nearly as spectacular as those in Central Park and the Bronx, although it has transformed Buckminster Fuller's 1964 geodesic dome into a dizzying aviary, and some beautiful big animals, including bison, Shetland cattle, and elk, roam the grounds.

East of the zoo, the **Unisphere** is a 140-foot-high, stainless-steel globe that weighs 380 tons – probably the main reason why it was never moved after the 1964 fair. Robert Moses intended this park to be the "Versailles of America," but the severe, perfectly symmetrical pathways radiating out from the sphere, the anachronistic and often bizarrely ugly architecture, and the roaring Grand Central Parkway all feel more Eastern Bloc than French – particularly when you look south and see the rusting towers of Philip Johnson's 1964 **New York Pavilion**. The whole thing is softened a bit on sunny days, when the park swarms with kids on bikes and rollerblades. The best way to get around the vast space beyond the museums, which includes two lakes and a botanic garden, is to rent a bicycle yourself, from a kiosk at the park entrance near the tennis center.

The park's finest attraction is the **Queens Museum of Art**, housed right next to the Unisphere in a building from the 1939 fair that served briefly as the first home of the United Nations (Wed–Fri 10am–5pm, Sat & Sun noon–5pm; suggested donation $5; ☎718/592-9700, ⊛www.queensmuseum.org). The one must-see item in the museum is the **Panorama of the City of New York**, a product of the 1964 fair. With a scale of one inch to one hundred feet, the panorama is the world's largest architectural model; its 835,000 buildings – as well as rivers, harbors, bridges, and even tiny planes buzzing into the airports – are scrupulously updated to reflect the city's growth. Guided tours of the panorama run weekends at 2 and 3pm, though you can visit any time the museum is open. Occasionally the lights go out to create a night view, bathing you in the blissful and somewhat creepy darkness of streetlamp-lit New York. The rest of the museum is almost as fascinating: excellent contemporary art;

aerial photos, games, toys, and other paraphernalia from the World's Fairs; plus a collection of glassworks by Louis Comfort Tiffany, who established his design studios in Corona in the 1890s.

For refreshment after seeing the park, visit the *Lemon Ice King of Corona*, 52-08 108th St, which has been dishing out refreshing handmade fruit ices since shortly after the 1939 fair.

Flushing

Beyond the eastern edge of the park, at the end of the #7 line, lies **Flushing**, most notable as New York's second Chinatown (followed by Brooklyn's Sunset Park), with 55 percent of its population claiming Asian ancestry, mainly from China and Korea. Busy shoppers, school kids, and professionals walk **Main Street**, which feels like the downtown of its own small city, complete with large banks and heavy traffic. It doesn't have the tourist-friendly, ramshackle air of Manhattan's Chinatown, but visitors will still find plenty to see and do. Chinese, Taiwanese, Japanese, Korean, Malaysian, and Vietnamese eateries, along with pastry shops and fruit stalls selling a variety of sweets, line Main Street and its sidestreets. See Chapter 25, "Restaurants," for specific recommendations.

The neighborhood, established as **Vlissingen** (named for a town in the Netherlands) in 1645, was an early Quaker community. You'll pass a couple of old Quaker landmarks, as well as a few other historical buildings, by heading north on Main Street from the subway stop. Together they form the "Flushing Freedom Trail," an overrated trek on its own, but a nice break from the otherwise modern storefronts, the glitziest of which is the **Flushing Mall**, on 39th Avenue two blocks west of Main Street (daily 10am–9pm). The food court here is an almost paralyzing array of pan-Asian foods.

On the west side of Main Street between 39th and 38th avenues is **St George's Church**, an elegant 1854 Gothic landmark with a tall central tower. Peek around the side for a long view of the angular body and simple rectory. If you make it up to Northern Boulevard (a few long blocks north), keep an eye out for **Flushing Town Hall**, at 137-35 Northern Blvd (Mon–Fri 9am–5pm, Sat & Sun noon–5pm; ☎718/463-7700, ⓦwww.flushingtownhall.com), now a cultural center with a very sophisticated calendar. Just across the street is a shingle cottage, the **Friends Meeting House**, which dates from 1694, making it the oldest surviving house of worship in the city and the second-oldest Quaker institution in the country. It is open Sundays at 11am for services and noon for tours, on which you can also see the centuries-old cemetery (sans headstones, per Quaker tradition).

Flesh out the Quaker story with a quick visit to the **Kingsland Homestead**, 145-35 37th Ave (Tues, Sat & Sun 2.30–4.30pm; $3; ☎718/939-0647 ext 17, ⓦwww.queenshistoricalsociety.org), a small wooden farmhouse maintained by the Queens Historical Society. You can see the house from Bowne Street (which runs south from Northern Boulevard), where it is set back in **Weeping Beech Park**. The eponymous tree was planted here in 1847 (just east of the Kingsland House), after being shipped from Belgium; every weeping beech in the United States descends from it. South of the park on Bowne Street, the 1661 Quaker-style **Bowne House** was the home of John Bowne, who helped Flushing acquire the tag "birthplace of religious freedom in America" by resisting discrimination at a time when the Dutch persecuted anyone who wasn't Calvinist.

Alternatively, you might head south from the Main Street subway station; the intersection of Main Street and Kissena Avenue is flush with gastronomic options, and boasts the sleek **Queens Public Library** Flushing branch, the busiest in the borough's library. If you continue down Kissena, you'll pass the stately **Free Synagogue of Flushing**, no. 41-60 (☎718/961-0030, ⌨www .freesynagogue.org), on your right. The oldest surviving Reform Jewish synagogue in the US, it looks like a small-town courthouse, but with brick additions and blue stained-glass windows.

The #Q65 bus runs south from the synagogue into an Indian community, passing the impressive **Sri Mahã Vallabha Ganapati Devasthãnam**, 45-59 Bowne St (Mon–Fri 8am–9pm, Sat & Sun 7.30am–9pm; ☎718/460-8484, ⌨www .nyganeshtemple.org). Also known as the **Ganesh Temple**, this building honors the elephant-headed Hindu god. The facade is adorned with ornate elephantine imagery; take your shoes off to enter the sanctuary, which contains embedded wall sculptures and brightly colored altars to various deities. *Dosa Hutt*, next door on Bowne Street, provides tasty south Indian snacks while you're down this way.

Jamaica Bay and the Rockaways

The southern edge of Queens is the place to take a break from urban life. **Jamaica Bay Wildlife Refuge** (☎718/338-3338, ⌨www.nps.gov/gate) is named for the Jameco Indians, whose territory this once was. Near Broad Channel on the largest of these islands (take the #A train to Broad Channel and walk a half-mile north; the #Q53 bus from Rockaway Park or Jackson Heights also stops here), you can hike trails through the diverse habitats of more than 325 varieties of migrating **birds**, including several endangered species. A unit of the 26,607-acre Gateway National Recreation Area, which extends through coastal areas of Queens, Brooklyn, Staten Island, and New Jersey, this is one of the most important urban wildlife areas in the United States. The refuge's teeming avian population can cause problems, though: at nearby JFK Airport, a crew patrols the tarmacs with falcons to help keep smaller birds away so they don't fly into planes taking off and landing.

Partly enclosing the bay, the spit of **Rockaway** stretches for ten miles southwest of Brooklyn – most of it is strollable along a waterfront promenade. You'd expect beach property within the city limits to be ritzy, but the Rockaways, as the neighborhoods here are collectively called, are really quite gritty, with single-room occupancy hotels and adult-care homes mixed in with old rental cottages. If you're curious about this fringe of the city (it's the only place to surf in New York), head to the center, at Beach 116th Street in **Rockaway Park** (a subway stop serviced by the #A or the #S Rockaway Shuttle, depending on the time of day).

By contrast, the lovely beach of **Jacob Riis Park** (☎718/318-4300) on the western end of the spit is quieter and more pristine, because it's part of the Gateway NRA. The subway doesn't go there – instead, take the #Q22 bus from Beach 116th or the #Q35 from Flatbush Avenue in Brooklyn; the latter is by far the faster option from Manhattan. This is widely considered to be New York City's best beach, and it features a brick bathhouse and an outdoor clock that have been New York City landmarks since the 1930s. At the westernmost tip of the peninsula, beyond the reach of public transit but an easy bicycle ride from the end of the train line, the heavily Irish cooperative community of **Breezy Point** feels like a beach town imported from another state – come here to truly escape New York.

The Bronx

"The Bronx? No thonx!" Poet Ogden Nash eventually recanted his two-line witticism, but most New Yorkers still unapologetically harbor similar feelings. The city's northernmost borough, **The Bronx** has long fought a reputation (admittedly deserved) as tough and crime-ridden; indeed, until the late 1990s, no other part of the city so inspired people to roll out their most gruesome horror stories. Although its poorer reaches still suffer from urban deprivation, much of the borough has undergone a civic and economic transformation, even the notorious **South Bronx**, where landlords once burned their own buildings to collect insurance money. Casual tourists don't usually come up this way, but there are a number of worthy attractions: beautiful parks, historic homes, a world-class botanic garden, a fabulous zoo, and, of course, **Yankee Stadium**.

With a unique landscape that ranges from greenery to high-rises, the Bronx is New York's only mainland borough. As might be expected, its hilly geography is more like neighboring Westchester County than Long Island and Manhattan. Economically, the Bronx developed – and declined – in a shorter period than any other part of the city. First settled in the seventeenth century by a Swedish land-owner named **Jonas Bronck**, like the other outer boroughs, it only became part of New York City at the turn of the nineteenth century. This happened in two stages: the area west of the Bronx River was annexed in 1874, and the area east in 1895. After 1900 things moved fast, and for a time real estate in the Bronx was some of the most sought-after in the city. Luxurious Art Deco apartment buildings lined its main thoroughfare, the **Grand Concourse**. This avenue runs the length of the borough; many places of interest lie on it or reasonably close by.

Unlike Brooklyn, the Bronx doesn't lend itself to extensive wandering from neighborhood to neighborhood. Some of the borough's main draws (including the **Bronx Zoo** and the **New York Botanical Garden**) take a long time to explore, while others (like **Wave Hill** and **Orchard Beach**) take a long time to get to. It's easiest to go by bus; the #Bx12, in particular, winds a useful west–east route, connecting many of the Central Bronx sights and linking the north–south subway lines. Pick up a Bronx bus map in any subway station. You may also find the Metro North trains handy, especially when heading to the northeast Bronx and Riverdale.

Find out more about the borough from the **Bronx Tourism Council** (☏718/590-3949, ⊛www.ilovethebronx.com) or the **Bronx Council on the Arts**, 1738 Hone Ave at Morris Park Ave (☏718/931-9500, ⊛www.bronxarts .org), originators of the **Bronx Cultural Card** ($25, students and seniors $15), which provides ten to fifty-percent discounts on a couple dozen of the Bronx's best attractions. The two organizations also run a **free trolley** service: on weekends, it's dedicated to major sights like the zoo and botanic garden; the

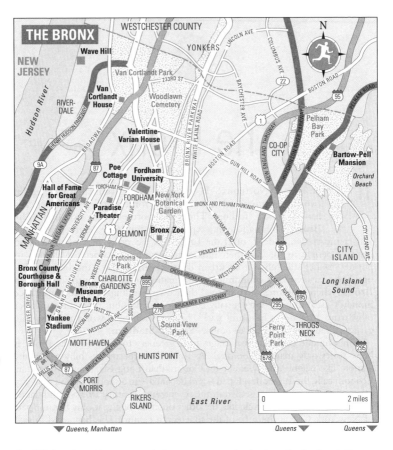

WESTCHESTER COUNTY

N

NEW
JERSEY

Wave Hill

YONKERS

Van Cortlandt Park

233RD ST

22

BOSTON ROAD

95

RIVER-
DALE

Van
Cortlandt
House

Woodlawn
Cemetery

Pelham
Bay
Park

Valentine-
Varian House

CO-OP
CITY

Bartow-Pell
Mansion

Orchard
Beach

9A

87

Poe
Cottage

Fordham
University

GUN HILL ROAD

Hall of Fame
for Great
Americans

FORDHAM RD

FORDHAM

New York
Botanical
Garden

BRONX AND PELHAM PARKWAY

Paradise
Theater

1

BELMONT

Bronx Zoo

CITY
ISLAND

Crotona
Park

TREMONT AVE

95

Bronx County
Courthouse &
Borough Hall

CHARLOTTE
GARDENS

895

CROSS BRONX EXPRESSWAY

WESTCHESTER AVE

Long Island
Sound

Bronx
Museum
of the Arts

161ST ST

BRUCKNER EXPRESSWAY

895

695

278

295

Yankee
Stadium

Sound View
Park

Ferry
Point
Park

THROGS
NECK

295

MOTT HAVEN

HUNTS POINT

678

87

PORT
MORRIS

RIKERS
ISLAND

East River

0   2 miles

Queens, Manhattan   Queens   Queens

first Wednesday of every month, it runs past arts institutions in the South Bronx and Mott Haven; and on the first Friday of the month, it makes a circuit around City Island and Orchard Beach.

The South Bronx

When most people hear the words "the Bronx," they think of the **South Bronx**, the area roughly south of the Cross-Bronx Expressway. Here, **Yankee Stadium**, where Babe Ruth reigned supreme, is a pilgrimage site for baseball fans, while the streets of **Hunts Point** and other burnt-out neighborhoods of "the Boogie Down" (as the Bronx is known in hip-hop parlance) were the birthplace of rap, break-dancing, and graffiti art in the late 1970s. Aside from the stadium and the elegant stretch of the **Grand Concourse** around Borough Hall, there are few formal sights. Anyone interested in street culture should just do a lot of random strolling, preferably by day, or join a tour with **A Hip Hop Look at New York** (⊕212/714-3527, ⊛www.hushtours.com; $75, students $50), led by scene insiders.

Yankee Stadium and Grand Concourse

Off the 161st Street–Yankee Stadium stop on the #B, #D, and #4 trains, **Yankee Stadium** rises snow-white above the South Bronx. Home to the legendary **New York Yankees** baseball team (see box, below), this imposing structure holds an iconic place in American sports history. The stadium opened April 18, 1923, just in time for the Yankees to win their first World Series; it has expanded over the decades, and now almost 60,000 fans can pack the seats overlooking the bright green grass. In early 2006, the city voted to rebuild the place from scratch on a neighboring lot, but construction won't be finished for years.

You can take an hour-long tour of the stadium that includes field access, visits to the dugout and press box, and a look at memorials to Babe Ruth, Joe DiMaggio, and other baseball heroes (schedules vary; $14, under 14 and seniors $7; ☎718/579-4531, ⊛newyork.yankees.mlb.com). Attending a game is highly recommended, if potentially expensive – see p.434 for ticket information. For the full Bronx Bombers experience, ride the **ferry** from midtown to the stadium (game days only; $18; ☎1–800/533-3779, ⊛www.nywaterway.com). If you can't get tickets, the next best place to watch is with the fans at the *Yankee Tavern*, E 161st St at Gerard St, which drips with team paraphernalia collected since the bar opened in 1928.

A trip on the elevated #4 train up to the 161st Street stop affords a good view of the South Bronx, and a short walk in the blocks around the stadium will introduce you to the surprising beauty and strong community feel here. From the stadium, walk east up to the aptly named **Grand Concourse**, which is a rather low-income area, though you wouldn't guess it from the street's architecture. In its southern reaches, the concourse is a magnificent wide boulevard marked by tree-lined medians and opulent Art Deco buildings that now house apartments, social-service organizations, and retirement homes. Also at 161st Street is the massive **Bronx County Courthouse and Borough Hall**, a 1933 construction that combines Neoclassical columns with Art Deco friezes and statuary. North of here stretches **Joyce Kilmer Park**, named for the man who penned the lines "I think that I shall never see / A poem lovely as a tree..." A monument to Louis J. Heintz, who first proposed the Grand Concourse, and the white Lorelei Fountain form a gracious backdrop for residents, who come here to take in the sun on benches and stroll at sunset.

At Grand Concourse and East 165th Street, the **Bronx Museum of the Arts** (Wed noon–9pm, Thurs–Sun noon–6pm; suggested donation $5, students

The Bronx Bombers

The **Yankees**, who inspire love and loathing in New York (and mostly the latter outside the city), moved from north Manhattan to the Bronx in 1923. Leading the way was **George Herman "Babe" Ruth**, who had joined the team in 1920 (from the Boston Red Sox, still the team's arch rivals). The original "Bronx Bomber," Ruth hit the stadium's first home run – soon enough, Yankee Stadium was known as "**The House That Ruth Built.**"

Playing alongside Ruth, **Lou Gehrig** earned the nickname "The Iron Horse" by playing in 2130 consecutive games. **Joe DiMaggio**, **"Yogi" Berra**, **Mickey Mantle**, and **Reggie Jackson** also all wore the famous Yankee pinstripes.

The Yankees won the World Series an amazing nineteen times between 1927 and 1962 and finished the twentieth century with three straight titles, but despite the largest payroll in baseball (nearly twice that of the team with the next highest), the Yankees haven't won the World Series since 2000. For their devoted fans (and devoted enemies), though, they remain the team to beat.

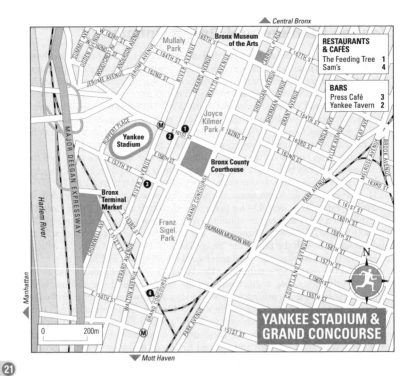

Mullaly Park

Bronx Museum of the Arts

RESTAURANTS & CAFÉS
The Feeding Tree 1
Sam's 4

BARS
Press Café 3
Yankee Tavern 2

Joyce Kilmer Park

Yankee Stadium

Bronx County Courthouse

Bronx Terminal Market

Harlem River

Franz Sigel Park

Manhattan

0   200m

N

YANKEE STADIUM & GRAND CONCOURSE

▼ Mott Haven

and seniors $3, under 12 free, Wed free; ☎718/681-6000, ⓦwww.bronxmuseum .org) occupies a converted synagogue. A renovation in 2006 more than doubled the space for the eclectic exhibits of contemporary art by Asian, Latino, and African-American artists. Its highly respected "Artists in the Marketplace" program, an annual spring show by young New York–based participants, is always compelling.

Hunts Point, Charlotte Gardens, and Mott Haven

Anyone interested in urban development may want to explore the South Bronx on foot – potentially intimidating, but generally not threatening during the day. Thanks to community activists and private development corporations such as the Mid-Bronx Desperadoes, this part of the borough is considerably improved from the dark days of the mid-1970s, when paid arsonists destroyed more than 40,000 buildings. A stroll around formerly notorious **Hunts Point** (Simpson Street on the #2 or #5, or Hunts Point Avenue on the #6), for instance, shows a neighborhood in various phases of renewal, where graffiti is no longer a sign of decay but a point of pride, and the Bronx River flows rather than stagnates.

The most successful example of community regeneration is **Charlotte Gardens**, off the southeast side of Crotona Park (take the #2 or #5 to 174th Street). President Carter despaired here on a visit in 1977, but its tenements have been replaced by almost eerily suburban ranch-style homes. A mall – the ultimate symbol of prosperity in an area where retailers previously refused to invest – opened nearby in 2004. **Mott Haven**, with its historic district around Alexander Road between 137th and 141st streets (near the #6 stop at 3rd

Ave–138 St) and a clutch of studios near the water by the Third Avenue Bridge, is currently the most gentrified area, as artists have moved in and helped renovate the Dutch-style apartment buildings and abandoned factories, and opened a few cafés and antiques shops.

The Central Bronx

The **Central Bronx**, north of the Cross-Bronx Expressway and south of Gun Hill Road, has neither the intense grit of the South Bronx nor the quiet ritz of the borough's extreme north. As in much of the Bronx, its inhabitants are working-class African-Americans, Puerto Ricans, and Dominicans, though its historical center is prestigious **Fordham University**, founded in 1841 and set on lush green lawns. The main east–west artery through this part of the borough is the busy but unremarkable low-end shopping district of **Fordham Road**. One spot of glamour along the way is the recently restored **Paradise Theater**, 2413 Grand Concourse, a 3800-seat movie palace built in 1929 that now hosts salsa concerts and the like; its gorgeous interior is open for tours (Sat 11am & 1pm; $6; ☏718/220-6143, ⊛www.theparadisetheater.com).

The #B or #D trains to Fordham Road drop you a block north of the theater, and at the starting point of a (longish) walk past several top-flight attractions: **Belmont**, better known as the Bronx's Little Italy, and intoxicating **Bronx Park**, home to the city's prized **Bronx Zoo** and **New York Botanical Garden**. Serious sightseers can loop back and visit the **Poe Cottage** and the **Hall of Fame for Great Americans**.

Belmont

If you take East Fordham Road downhill from the subway station (or get on the #Bx12 bus, which will do it for you), you'll arrive at the Fordham University campus; a couple of blocks farther east, **Arthur Avenue** begins on your right. This is the main thoroughfare of **Belmont**, one of New York's largest Italian-American communities. It's bordered to the east by the Bronx Zoo and the west by Third Avenue, with the intersection of Arthur Avenue and 187th Street at its center.

The neighborhood dates to the late nineteenth century, when Italian craftsmen building the Bronx Zoo settled here, and although Haitians, Mexicans, and Albanians also operate businesses on Arthur Avenue, the Italian community still dominates. It feels decidedly more Old World than Little Italy in Manhattan, especially during the Ferragosto di Belmont, on the second Sunday in August, when residents turn out in their festive best to dance, eat, and compete in the annual cheese-carving contest. **Our Lady of Mount Carmel Church**, E 187th St at Belmont Ave (☏718/295-3770), holds daily masses in Italian, and the **Enrico Fermi Cultural Center** (the Belmont branch of the New York Public Library), 610 E 186th St, at Hughes Ave (☏718/933-6410, ⊛www.nypl .org), has a significant Italian and Italian-American culture collection.

There's also no better part of the Bronx if you want to **eat**. But choose restaurants on Arthur Avenue with care: swanky *Mario's*, no. 2342, is popular but pricey. You're better off heading around the corner to *Roberto's*, 603 Crescent Ave, for heaps of pasta served family-style. If you just want a snack, opt for clams or oysters on the half-shell from *Cosenza's* (no. 2354) or *Randazzo's* (no. 2327) seafood stores. Or stop in to the **Arthur Avenue Retail Market**, no. 2331, an indoor collection of vendors, created by Mayor LaGuardia in 1940 as part of his campaign to rid the city of pushcarts. The market is a small maze of salami, mozzarella, and sides of beef; you can get a platter of antipasti here, or a messy eggplant parmesan sandwich, in addition to pantry staples.

Bronx Zoo

If you're walking from Arthur Avenue, follow 187th Street east to reach the main entrance to the **Bronx Zoo**, at Southern Boulevard (April–Oct Mon–Fri 10am–5pm, Sat & Sun 10am–5.30pm; $11, kids and seniors $8; Nov–March daily 10am–4.30pm; $8, kids and seniors $6, free Wed year-round, parking $7, some additional charges; ☎718/367-1010, ⌦www.bronxzoo.org). Coming to the zoo by subway, the closest stop is West Farms Square–East Tremont Avenue on the #2 or #5, three blocks south of the Asia Gate at the southeast corner of the zoo. Another option is the #BxM11 express bus ($5, exact change), which runs from Madison Avenue in midtown Manhattan, dropping visitors near the Bronx River Gate, on the northeast corner.

The zoo is one of the Bronx's main attractions, and often the only reason New Yorkers from other boroughs ever travel north. Opened in 1899, it has significantly expanded from its small cluster of original buildings. It was among the first zoos in America to realize that animals both looked and felt better out in the open – something that has been achieved through a variety of natural-looking habitats. Games and activities provided by zookeepers are an important part of the zoo's mission, and offer a glimpse of the animals at play. Visit in spring to see the new babies (up to a thousand are born each year) or in summer to appreciate the most animals outside.

The forty-acre **Wild Asia** exhibit (May–Oct), where tigers, elephants, and gaur (big cows) roam relatively freely, is accessible either on foot or via the Bengali Express Monorail train ($3). Highlights include a simulated village bazaar complete with camel rides, and JungleWorld (open year-round, unlike the rest of Wild Asia), an indoor Asian rain forest. The **African Plains** nearby are home to lions, zebras, and gazelles.

The innovative **Congo Gorilla Forest** (additional fee, varies by season) houses more than 15,400 African animals and plants, including tiny colobus monkeys, mandrill baboons, and the largest population of western gorillas in the country. Look in also on the **World of Darkness** (a collection of nocturnal species), the **Sea Bird Colony**, and a simulation of a Himalayan mountain area, home to endangered species like the red panda and the snow leopard. Although the entire zoo is, clearly, popular with youngsters, kids will also appreciate the **Children's Zoo** (summers only), where they can climb with lemurs and learn camouflage skills from tortoises. A shuttle covers the sizable distances in the park, but the **Skyfari cable-car** ($3) provides some of the most memorable views; both operate only in summer months.

In winter, many animals are kept in indoor enclosures without viewing areas, but the endangered Siberian tigers love a snowy day, and if you visit the three-acre **Tiger Mountain** habitat then, it may just be you and these enormous cats, separated by inconspicuous barriers. You'll also find all of the indoor exhibits operating – and pleasantly warm and humid – with very few crowds. In the month and a half before Christmas, **holiday lights** transform the zoo into a winter wonderland.

New York Botanical Garden

Adjacent to the zoo, just north of Fordham Road, is a quieter but equally worthwhile attraction: the lush **New York Botanical Garden** (Tues–Sun

& Mon holidays: April–Oct 10am–6pm; Nov–March 10am–5pm; $13, students and seniors $11, under 12 $5, free Sat mornings & Wed, parking $7; ☎718/817-8700, ⓦwww.nybg.org). Prices are for all-access tickets; at certain times of the year or for short visits, you may want to buy less-expensive admission to individual sections of the park. The main entrance, on Kazimiroff Boulevard opposite Fordham University, is a short walk north from the zoo along Southern Boulevard, which changes to Kazimiroff Boulevard; the gates will be on your left. The nearest subway stop is Bedford Park on the #B or #D lines (about a twenty-minute walk).

The glittering glass Enid A. Haupt Conservatory, built when the park opened in 1891, acts as a dramatic entrance,

△ New York Botanical Garden

magnificently showcasing rainforest, aquatic, and desert ecosystems. It also houses a palm court with towering old trees and a fern forest. Cherry, lilac, maple, conifer, crab apple, and rock gardens edge a 50-acre core of native forest. Structures that might actually be found in these ecosystems – a healer's hut and a research station, for instance – lend verisimilitude. Even in winter, much of the scenery is breathtaking, and indoor facilities more than make up for the cold.

Kids can head to the Everett Children's Adventure Garden, twelve acres of plant and science exhibits and some nifty mazes. Programs let kids cook, taste, and draw popular plants such as peppermint, chocolate, and vanilla. The Botanical Garden also offers classes for all ages, tours via tram or on foot, nursery plants for sale, and enough land to wander around happily for hours.

Poe Cottage and the Valentine-Varian House

West of the garden, just off the Kingsbridge Road stop on the #B and #D trains, is the **Edgar Allan Poe Cottage**, Grand Concourse and East Kingsbridge Road (Sat 10am–4pm, Sun 1–5pm; $3; ☎718/881-8900, ⓦwww.bronxhistoricalsociety .org), built in 1812. This white-clapboard anachronism on a twenty-first-century working-class Latino block was Edgar Allan Poe's rural home from 1846 to 1849, just before he died in Baltimore. It originally sat on East Kingsbridge Road near East 192nd Street, but was moved here when threatened with demolition. Never a particularly stable character and dogged by financial problems, Poe also had to contend with the death of his wife, Virginia, shortly after they moved in. In his gloom, he did manage to write the short, touching poem *Annabel Lee* (an homage to his wife) and other famous works during his stay. The cottage displays several rooms as they were in Poe's time, as well as a small gallery of 1840s artwork.

The Bronx Historical Society also runs the **Valentine–Varian House**, 3266 Bainbridge Ave (Sat 10am–4pm, Sun 1–5pm; $2; ☎718/881-8900, ⓦwww .bronxhistoricalsociety.org), an eighteenth-century Georgian stone farmhouse that was occupied by the British during the American Revolution. Only recommended for serious history buffs (it requires an extra jaunt north two stops on the #D to Norwood–205th Street), the museum stands in a small park and contains numerous old photographs that show just how rapidly the Bronx shifted from an agrarian landscape to an urban one.

Hall of Fame for Great Americans

On the campus of the Bronx Community College lies the **Hall of Fame for Great Americans**, one of the Bronx's most overlooked monuments – perhaps because it's not on the way to any of the borough's other sights (take the #4 to Burnside Avenue and walk west on 180th Street, or ride the #Bx12 bus to University Avenue and walk south). The first "hall of fame" of any kind, it's a time capsule of cultural influence in 1900, when the hall was dedicated: painter Gilbert Stuart is in the same league as his portrait subject, George Washington, for instance. The Sanford White–designed outdoor colonnade, studded with bronze busts of the honorees, is set on the highest point in the Bronx, so the views are impressive.

The North Bronx

The **North Bronx**, shorthand for the area above 225th Street in the west and Gun Hill Road in the east, is the northernmost area of the city; anyone who makes it up here usually wants to see the stately **Riverdale** neighborhood, the rolling hills of **Woodlawn Cemetery** or **Van Cortlandt Park**, or the ocean views of **City Island** and **Orchard Beach** – in short, all the suburban and rural splendor you find in few other places in New York City. Getting up this way by public transport is not impossible, but if you have access to a car, this is a good time to use it.

Woodlawn Cemetery

With entrances at Jerome Avenue at Bainbridge (last stop, Woodlawn, on the #4) or at Webster Avenue and East 233rd Street (#2 or #5 to 233rd Street), venerable **Woodlawn Cemetery** (daily 8.30am–5pm; ☎718/920-0500, ⊛www.thewoodlawncemetery.org) is a huge place. Like Green-Wood in Brooklyn, it boasts a number of tombs and mausolea that are memorable mainly for their gaudiness, although a few monuments stand out: Oliver Belmont, financier and horse dealer, rests in a Gothic fantasy modeled on the resting place of Leonardo da Vinci in Amboise, France; F.W. Woolworth built himself an Egyptian palace guarded by sphinxes; and sculptor Patricia Cronin's 2002 marble *Memorial to a Marriage* depicts the artist and her partner, Deborah Kass, locked in a sleepy embrace. Walking tours run on weekends in spring and fall ($5; ☎718/920-1469), or you can pick up a map from the office at the Webster Avenue entrance or one of the security booths to locate the many famous individuals buried here. They include Herman Melville, Irving Berlin, Madame C.J. Walker, Elizabeth Cady Stanton, Fiorello LaGuardia, Robert Moses, Celia Cruz, Miles Davis, and Duke Ellington.

Van Cortlandt Park

Immediately west of the cemetery across Jerome Avenue (you can also take the #1 train to the end of the line at 242nd Street and Broadway) lies vast **Van Cortlandt Park**, a forested and hilly all-purpose recreation space. Apart from the pleasure of hiking and running through its woods, the best thing here is the **Van Cortlandt House Museum** (Tues–Fri 10am–3pm, Sat & Sun

11am–4pm; $5, students and seniors $3, Wed free; ☎718/543-3344, ⓦwww
.vancortlandthouse.org), nestled in the park's southwest corner not far from the
#1 subway station. This is the Bronx's oldest building, an authentically restored
Georgian structure built in 1748, complete with a historically accurate herb
garden. During the American Revolution the house and farmland (now the
city park) was used as operations headquarters by both the British and Continental armies. New York City's archives were buried for safekeeping on the hills
above, and it was in this house that George Washington slept before marching
to victory in Manhattan in 1783.

Riverdale and Wave Hill

The lovely, moneyed heights of **Riverdale** – one of the most desirable neighborhoods in the city – rise above Van Cortlandt Park. It's a bit of a chore to get
here without a car: Metro North to Riverdale provides the best access; otherwise, take the #1 train to 231st Street, then the #Bx7 or #Bx10 bus up the
Henry Hudson Parkway. From there, it's a short walk west to **Palisade Avenue**,
lined with mansions from the late nineteenth and early twentieth centuries.

In the northeastern part of Riverdale, close to the Henry Hudson Parkway (take
the bus to 252nd Street), the spectacular country estate of **Wave Hill**, 249th St
at Independence Ave (mid-April to mid-Oct Tues–Sun 9am–5.30pm, June &
July Wed until 9pm; Oct 15–April 14 Tues–Sun 9am–4.30pm; $4, seniors and
students $2, Dec–Feb and Sat morning & Tues free; ☎718/549-3200, ⓦwww
.wavehill.org) overlooks the Hudson River and the towering Palisades. At various
times home to Teddy Roosevelt (as a child), Toscanini, and Mark Twain, the Wave
Hill house was donated to the city in 1960 and now contains contemporary art
installations, usually with a natural theme. The grounds contain thriving green-
houses, beautifully landscaped flowerbeds, peaceful pools of water lilies, and a tasty
café that uses herbs grown on-site. The busy events calendar includes everything
from guided tours (every Sun) to family art classes to beekeeping workshops.

City Island

On the east side of the Bronx, 230-acre **City Island** juts into Long Island
Sound. The #Bx29 bus – pick it up at the Pelham Bay Park subway stop at the
end of the #6 – runs over a short causeway to and from the mainland, but it
is far easier to drive here if you can. Though shingled City Island looks as if it
were imported from New England, the community was built here as a fishing
and shipbuilding center in the eighteenth century. That maritime spirit persists
in the form of yacht clubs and meticulously preserved Victorian homes. One
of these contains the **City Island Nautical Museum**, 190 Fordham St (Sun
1–5pm; donation; ☎718/885-0008, ⓦwww.cityislandmuseum.org), which touts
all of the island's claims to fame – the yachts that won the America's Cup from
1958 through 1987 were built here, for instance – and often hosts interesting
lectures by local historians.

Most people come for the **restaurants**, many of which traffic in seafood
of the deep-fried variety. They're good for kitsch and a water view – in fact,
the only way to get near the water, as it's mostly blocked by private clubs and
homes. On summer weekends the eateries overflow with off-islanders; you'll
do better on a weekday, when the fish is also fresher. Try the venerable *Lobster
Box*, 34 City Island Ave, for old-school seafood, or romantic *Le Refuge Inn*, 586
City Island Ave, for French country ritz; a few of the fishing piers sell fried
clams and beer. If you'd like to catch your own dinner, rent a boat and pick up

some bait at Jake's Bait and Tackle, 551 City Island Ave (boats $40 Mon–Fri, $50 Sat & Sun, including gear; ☎718/885-2042, ⊛www.jacksbaitandtackle .com), or head out on a day-long fishing trip aboard the *Riptide III* (daily 8am; ☎718/885-0236, ⊛www.riptide3.com) for $47 per person.

Pelham Bay Park and Orchard Beach

From City Island, it's an easy walk to **Orchard Beach**, the easternmost part of expansive **Pelham Bay Park** and one of the few really pleasant additions Robert Moses made to the city. Just make a right after the causeway, then follow the path along the water. Beach and boardwalk pulse constantly with a salsa beat, and **free concerts** are common in summer.

At the northern end of the boardwalk, a sign for the **Kazimiroff Nature Trail** points the way into a wildlife preserve named for Theodore Kazimiroff, co-founder of the Bronx County Historical Society and an amateur naturalist who helped stop these wetlands from being turned into a landfill. The network of trails, which winds through 189 acres of meadow, forest, and marsh, is serene and peaceful – a stark contrast with the rest of Pelham Bay Park, now criss-crossed by highways.

The Greek Revival **Bartow-Pell Mansion Museum** (Wed, Sat & Sun noon–4pm; $5, students and seniors $3, under 6 free, free Wed in winter; ☎718/885-1461, ⊛www.bartowpellmansionmuseum.org) is a national land-mark worth seeing for its beautifully furnished interior, which gives a glimpse of how the other half lived in the 1800s (Mayor LaGuardia wisely comman-deered the place for his summer office in 1936); the lavish gardens overlook Long Island Sound. To get there, go back to the Pelham Bay Park subway #6 station and take Westchester Bee-Line bus #45 (no service Sunday), or the free Bronx Culture Trolley, which runs by here on the first Friday of every month (when the museum is open 5.30–9.30pm). You might also bicycle between the station and the museum along the Bronx Greenway.

The Bronx's phantom theme-park

Pelham Bay Park looks to the west over **Co-op City**, a seemingly endless tract of middle-class housing that is one of the Bronx's bleaker icons. Few residents know that their homes stand on New York's great, lost amusement park: **Freedomland**.

Built in the shape of the United States, the 205-acre park opened in 1960 with entertainments based on American history: the great fire of 1871 raged in Chicago, gunfights blazed in the Old Southwest, and earthquakes rocked San Francisco. Loco-motives and carriages connected the rides, cafés, and even a working cornfield.

Reporters loved Freedomland because it inspired such headlines as "Stagecoach Wreck Injures 10 in the Bronx." But the public was not so enthralled, despite promo-tions on **The Ed Sullivan Show** and the addition of more typical amusements like roller coasters (as well as a rendition of the Last Supper in wax). Park developers blamed competition from the 1964 World's Fair in Flushing, though the expo had barely begun when Freedomland declared bankruptcy late in the year. By 1965, the first phase of Co-op City was being laid out, and Freedomland had vanished without a trace.

Staten Island

L
ike the rest of New York City, Staten Island was first settled by the Dutch in the seventeenth century (the name derives from *Staten-General*, the States General, Holland's governing body). The colonists faced more resistance here than in other parts of the city, as the Lenape inhabitants repelled them in the Pig, Whiskey, and Peach wars, and they did not take full control until 1661. Three years later, the island and the rest of New York City were in British hands, and in 1783, it saw the last shot of the American Revolution. Like the other boroughs, it joined New York City in 1898, but for decades Staten Islanders enjoyed an insular, relatively rural life – the stretch of water between here and Manhattan marks a cultural as much as a physical divide.

The island could be reached only by ferry or a long drive through New Jersey (to which it's physically closer) until 1964, when the opening of the **Verrazano Narrows Bridge** changed everything: land-hungry Brooklynites swarmed over to buy parcels of what quickly became suburbia. Staten Island has swollen into tightly packed residential neighborhoods, formed by endless backwaters of tidy homes. The roughly triangular island is almost 14 miles long and 7.5 miles wide – more than twice the size of Manhattan. Its topography includes marshes, hardwood forests, and beaches, and it remains the city's most verdant borough (Henry David Thoreau, who lived on Staten Island as a private tutor, likened the place to a garden).

Crossing the harbor

The **Staten Island ferry** (T311, www.nyc.gov/dot) sails from a glittering modern terminal at the southern tip of Manhattan, built directly above the end of the #1 train (you must be in the first two cars of the train to disembark here). The #R or #W trains to Whitehall Street and the #4 and #5 to Bowling Green also let you off within easy walking distance. Weekday departures occur every 15–20 minutes during rush hours (7–9.30am and 4–8pm), every half-hour middays, evenings, and late nights. On weekends, boats run every half-hour from Manhattan, but slightly less frequently on the return trip. If you'll be traveling at odd hours, check the schedule online, as the timetable printed on the MTA's Staten Island bus map is seldom updated.

The 25-minute ride is truly New York's best bargain: it's absolutely **free**, with wide-angle views of the city and the Statue of Liberty becoming more spectacular as you retreat. You also pass very close to Governors Island (near Manhattan, east of the boat) and the 1883 Robbins Reef Lighthouse (closer to Staten Island, off to the west). By the time you arrive on Staten Island, the Manhattan skyline stands mirage-like: the city of a thousand and one posters, its skyscrapers almost bristling straight out of the water.

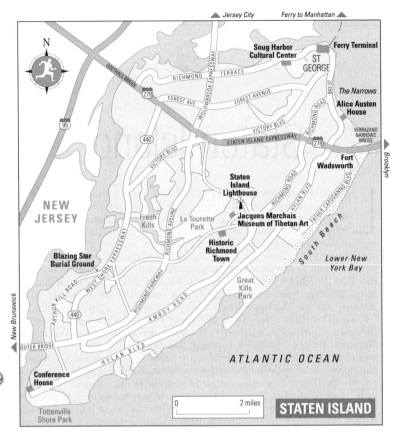

The majority of tourists take the **Staten Island ferry** (see box, p.287) for the views it provides of Manhattan and the Statue of Liberty, then promptly hop the next boat back to the big city. While it's hard to fault anyone for this, Staten Island does offer a respite from the bustle of Manhattan, complete with a handful of interesting museums, expansive green spaces, and some great pizza. Only a few of the sights described here are within walking distance of the **ferry terminal**. For the rest, you'll need to take a bus or the single-line Staten Island Railway (SIR), all of which conveniently leave from the terminal; arm yourself with a transit map (free from the information booth in the Manhattan ferry terminal). The system is integrated with the rest of the city – you get free transfers between buses and the train, as well as the subway system in Manhattan. The SIR is $2, but only if you get on or off at the first stop; at all other stations, it's free.

For more information on Staten Island events and attractions, contact the **Council on the Arts & Humanities for Staten Island** at Snug Harbor, 1000 Richmond Terrace (☎718/447-3329, ⊛www.statenislandarts.org). The council's website includes the handy downloadable *Cultural Tourism Map* and a *St George Walking Tour* map.

St George and around

Passengers disembark the ferry on the northeast corner of the island, in the village of **St George**, which stretches from Westervelt Avenue in the west to Bay Street on the hill above the ferry terminal and is bordered on the south by Victory Boulevard. Reputedly named for George Law, the investor who held the land before it was built up near the end of the nineteenth century, it's no waterfront paradise because its views of lower Manhattan and Brooklyn are severely compromised by high-rises. It is, however, the one city-like section on the otherwise suburban island, with densely packed buildings and a fascinating mixture of inhabitants: everyone from Wall Street bankers to members of Ganas, the only commune in New York City.

Just northeast of the ferry terminal, the **Richmond County Bank Ballpark**, home of the Staten Island Yankees, is about as beautiful as a ballpark can get, with a view from the bleachers straight out to the open harbor (see p.428 for more information). On the south side of the ferry depot are the decaying remnants of the center of lighthouse operations on the East Coast from 1860 to around 1960. A group of maritime-history buffs has been struggling to transform the area into a national lighthouse museum.

St George has a **historic district** that includes portions of St Mark's Place, Carroll Place, Westervelt Avenue, Hamilton Avenue, and stretches of Richmond Terrace. The wonderful residential buildings here include examples of shingle, Queen Anne, Greek Revival, and Italianate styles – many of them designed by local architect Edward Alfred Sargent (1842–1914). The 1906 Beaux-Arts **Borough Hall** (Mon–Fri 9am–5pm; ☎718-816-2000), straight ahead as you walk out of the ferry terminal, has a lobby adorned with WPA murals illustrating the island's history. You may also want to stop in at the grandly named **Staten Island Institute of Arts & Sciences**, 75 Stuyvesant Place (Tues–Sat 9am–5pm, Sun 1–5pm; $2; ☎718-727-1135), really a modest museum with exhibits on the history of the ferry, the island's geology, and the Lenape Indians.

The world's largest landfill

To most New Yorkers, Staten Island is little more than the site of **Fresh Kills Landfill**. Opened in 1948 on 3000 acres in the wetlands on Staten Island's western shore, it was the world's largest trash dump until it closed in 2001. The place was allegedly only a temporary dumping-ground, but over several decades, Staten Island more or less became New York City's garbage can. At the height of the landfill's operation, more than 75,000 tons a week were dumped here, forming the tallest man-made summit on the East Coast; even when the area eventually shrunk to 2200 acres, Fresh Kills still occupied more than ten percent of the island. In 1996, the New York State Senate moved to shut the landfill, but it took another five years for it to finally close. Just a few months later, after the September 11 attacks, the dump was temporarily reopened to serve as the repository of the Twin Towers' remains; it also housed a crime lab in which police sifted through the wreckage.

Since 2003, Fresh Kills has been undergoing a very slow transformation into parkland, a process that should be complete within a couple of decades, when the waste has fully settled. The first phase of construction on the most stable parts of the landfill was approved in 2005 – Owl Hollow Fields will be a 28-acre network of nature trails and playing fields, set to open in late 2007. Additional proposed designs include a network of canals and a wildlife refuge. The city reports progress on the renovation at ⓦ www.nyc.gov/freshkills.

Snug Harbor Cultural Center

In contrast to the more urban area around the ferry terminal, the atmosphere of the **Snug Harbor Cultural Center**, 1000 Richmond Terrace (☎718/448-2500, ⊛www.snug-harbor.org), in nearby New Brighton, is one of bucolic calm. To get there, take the #S40 bus from the terminal, a five-minute ride east along the waterfront (about two miles, if you're up for a long walk). Established in 1833 as a retirement community for "aged, decrepit, and worn-out sailors," the campus of Snug Harbor (of which Thomas Melville, brother of Herman, was the first director) still feels like a haven, even though the last salty dogs moved to North Carolina in 1976.

The complex's remaining 28 buildings, ranging in style from grand Greek Revival halls to cozy cottages, are now home to museums, galleries, and artists' studios. The annual Summer Sculpture Festival is a big event, as are summer performances by the Metropolitan Opera and New York Philharmonic – great music in outdoor surroundings more intimate than anywhere in Manhattan. The oldest building functions as the **visitor center** (Tues–Sun 10am–5pm), and the Staten Island Institute of Arts & Sciences mounts informative **exhibits** in the large downstairs hall and side rooms ($3). Go in at least to admire the beautiful stained-glass over the doors and the elaborate ceiling in the cupola; along the balcony are doors leading to rooms where sailors slept under comforting phrases such as "port after stormy seas." In one of the other Greek Revival halls, the **Noble Maritime Collection** (Thurs–Sun 1–5pm; $5; ☎718/447-6490, ⊛www.noblemaritime.org) displays the work of nautical painter John Noble, as well as his restored houseboat studio and one of the original sailors' dorm rooms.

South of the museum buildings, the **Staten Island Children's Museum** (Tues–Sun noon–5pm, open most school holidays; $5, grandparents free Wed; ☎718/273-2060, ⊛www.statenislandkids.org) offers exhibits such as "Bugs and Other Insects," animal feedings, and arts-and-crafts programs – enough to divert kids, if not utterly enthrall them. The rest of the Snug Harbor grounds are given over to the **Staten Island Botanical Garden** (daily dawn to dusk; free; ☎718/273-8200, ⊛www.sibg.org). This 86-acre sanctuary, built in 1977, includes a section of all-white blooms, flowers catering to butterflies, an antique rose garden, and a children's maze entered through a medieval-look castle ($2 admission). The best attraction, though, is the **New York Chinese Scholar's Garden** (April–Oct Tues–Sun 10am–5pm; Nov–March Wed–Sun 10am–4pm; $5, students, under 12, and seniors $4, free Tues 10am–1pm), a complex of pagoda-roofed halls, including a traditional tea-house, linked by artfully planted courtyards and pools. Perhaps the most beautiful bit of landscaping in New York, it is well worth seeing in any weather. The admission price also includes entrance to the maze.

If you want to get a bite to **eat** while touring the grounds, you can choose from *Café Botanica* (Jan–Oct Tues–Sun 9am–5pm; Nov–Dec Tues–Fri 11am–4pm, Sat & Sun 10am–4pm), near the entrance to the Chinese garden, which does full breakfasts and inventive sandwiches at lunchtime, or *Melville's* (Mon–Fri 11am–2pm), which has basic salads and sandwiches.

The Alice Austen House

Southeast of St George along the coast, the **Alice Austen House**, 2 Hylan Blvd (March–Dec Thurs–Sun noon–5pm; suggested donation $2; ☎718/816-4506, ⊛www.aliceausten.org), is the home of one of the island's most celebrated residents. The Victorian cottage faces the Verrazano Narrows, and the spectacular view from the front lawn takes in the Verrazano Bridge as well as the Brooklyn shore. Reach the house on the #S51 bus from the ferry dock to Hylan Boulevard (walk down the hill), or take the Staten Island Railroad to Clifton Station, then head south on Edgewater Street.

Austen (1866–1952) was a pioneering amateur photographer whose work comprises one of the finest records of American daily life in the early twentieth century. At a time when photography was both difficult and expensive, she developed her talent and passion for the art expertly. Tragically, she never considered going professional, even when the stock-market crash of 1929 lost Austen the family home and left her and her partner, Gertrude Tate, destitute; Austen's work was rediscovered only shortly before her death in 1952. The dignified house exhibits only a small selection of her photos (the Staten Island Historical Society owns the whole collection of more than 3000 negatives), but they're fascinating, and the home's beautiful location is a sight in and of itself.

Along the east coast and inland

At the base of the Verrazano Narrows Bridge, a critical position for the defense of the New York Harbor, the vast complex called **Fort Wadsworth** (Wed–Sun 10am–5pm; free; ☏718/354-4500, ⓦwww.nps.gov/gate) marks the north end of Staten Island's eastern coast. The fort, which housed a missile-defense system during the Cold War and was in use until 1996, is attractively ruined and overgrown and provides fantastic views; take the #S51 bus, or walk fifteen to twenty minutes from the Alice Austen House. South of here (the same bus continues along Father Capodanno Blvd), are several public beaches, not as nice as the Rockaways in Queens, but often less crowded. You first reach **South Beach**, a once thriving resort for New York's wealthy that's known for the two-and-a-half-mile **FDR Boardwalk**, a great place to jog or rollerblade. Farther down the coast, wilder-feeling **Great Kills Park** is, along with Fort Wadsworth, part of the Gateway National Recreation Area. In addition to the beach, which is on a long spit, you'll find nature trails amid scrubby coastal forest. This part of the coast is more easily accessible via the Bay Terrace stop on the SIR.

The Jacques Marchais Museum of Tibetan Art and around

In the middle of Staten Island's residential heartland, the **Jacques Marchais Museum of Tibetan Art**, 338 Lighthouse Ave (Wed–Sun 1–5pm; $5, seniors and students $3, kids $2; ☏718/987-3500, ⓦwww.tibetanmuseum.com), is an unlikely find. Take the #S74 bus and ask to be let off at Lighthouse Avenue (the bus driver may not know of the museum), then hike about ten minutes up the steep hill. A cab from the ferry terminal will run you $12–14.

Jacques Marchais was the alias of Edna Coblentz, a New York art dealer who reckoned she'd get on better with a male name in the 1920s and 1930s. She did, and used her comfortable income to indulge her passion for Tibetan art. Eventually she assembled the largest collection in the Western world, and in 1947 she bought this house on the hillside – perhaps because its location forces the visitor into the humility-inspiring trek uphill often found en route to Buddhist monasteries. Inside, she reproduced a *gompa*, or temple, thus presenting the artwork in its spiritual context and not merely as an assemblage of exotic artifacts. The collection is small enough to be accessible, with magnificent statues of spiritual figures, musical instruments, dance masks, and other objects from Tibet, Nepal, and Mongolia dating as far back as the seventeenth century. In early October, monks in maroon robes perform ritual ceremonies, and food and crafts are sold at the annual Tibetan Festival.

While you're on this small hill, take a look at the 91-foot-tall **Staten Island Lighthouse**; it's a strange thing to see so far inland. Ship captains once lined it up with other lighthouses on the water as a guide into New York Harbor, and it has been in near-constant use since it was erected in 1912. Head a few blocks north to enjoy sprawling **La Tourette Park**, part of the **Staten Island Greenbelt** (☎718/667-2165, ⓦwww.sigreenbelt.org), 2800 acres of wilderness and more manicured spots, like the lovely golf course at La Tourette. Greenbelt highlights include four forested **hiking trails** (one starts at the golf clubhouse); the **Native Plant Center Demonstration Garden**, northwest of La Tourette at 2252 Richmond Ave, where you can picnic and relax among hundreds of indigenous flora species; and the 260-acre **William T. Davis Wildlife Refuge**, northwest of the garden along Travis Avenue, a mixture of forest and wetlands that attracts birds (and bird-watchers). Greenbelt maps and a brochure are available from the Parks Department website (ⓦwww.nycgovparks.org).

Historic Richmond Town

On the main Richmond Road at St Patrick's Place, a short walk west and south from the Tibetan museum (or a ride on the #S74 bus from the ferry terminal) brings you to **Historic Richmond Town**, 441 Clarke Ave (July & Aug Wed–Sat 10am–5pm, Sun 1–5pm; Sept–June Wed–Sun 1–5pm; $5, seniors $4, children $3.50; ☎718/351-1611, ⓦwww.historicrichmondtown. org). Home to the Staten Island Historical Society, it's a "reinvention" of the

△ Historic Richmond Town

village of Richmond, a frontier outpost and center of the island's government from the seventeenth to the late nineteenth century. The 25 original houses (some relocated from spots nearby) are often staffed by costumed volunteers who use traditional techniques to make wooden water buckets, bake bread, and weld tin – it's all carried off to surprisingly picturesque and un-gimmicky effect. Enter through the 1837 building that served as Staten Island's third courthouse, then explore the dirt roads and buildings on your own. Or join the free guided tour that runs weekdays at 2.30pm and on weekends at 2pm and 3.30pm, visiting such gems as the 1695 Dutch-style **Voorlezer's House**, the nation's oldest existing school building; a picture-book general store; and the atmospheric **Guyon–Lake–Tysen House** of 1740. Kids will appreciate the multi-seat outhouse.

Conference House

At the far southern end of the island, in the quiet seaside neighborhood known as **Tottenville**, the **Conference House**, 7455 Hylan Blvd (SIR to Tottenville; tours April–mid-Dec Fri–Sun 1–4pm; $3, seniors and children $2; ☎718/984-0415, ⊛www.theconferencehouse.org), is a stately seventeenth-century stone manor. Its claim to fame is acting as host to failed peace talks, led by Benjamin Franklin and John Adams, during the American Revolution. The house certainly feels like it hasn't seen much action since, other than perhaps the manicuring of its rolling lawns, which offer a lovely view of Perth Amboy, New Jersey. Step inside for a peek at period furnishings, the original kitchen, which has been restored to working order, and the occasional art show or colonial music concert. The surrounding grounds are the lovely nine-acre **Tottenville Shore Park**, which has two public pools (sometimes quite crowded) as well as the shoreline. The famed oyster beds of Tottenville are no more, but you can still see a lot of black ducks and other native birds.

The west coast

For the intrepid only: Staten Island's west coast is home to the **Arthur Kill boat graveyard**, a stretch of shoreline dotted with rotting hulls of tugboats, barges, ferries, and other once-graceful ocean-going craft. Although the place looks completely abandoned, it's still in use, with new boats dumped here all the time. It's the sort of vision that could provoke real tears in nautical fanatics – for others, it's just an eerie vision of industrial decay. To add to the spooky effect, the **Blazing Star Burial Ground**, named for the ferry that used to run from here to New Jersey, is nearby. Some gravestones date from the 1700s, and many of Staten Island's best families are interred here. Take the #S74 bus from St George to just past Huguenot Avenue – look for the cemetery sign.

Listings

Listings

㉓ Accommodation 297

㉔ Cafés and light meals 314

㉕ Restaurants 329

㉖ Drinking 363

㉗ Nightlife 376

㉘ The performing arts and film 383

㉙ Gay and lesbian New York 396

㉚ Commercial galleries 403

㉛ Shopping 408

㉜ Sports and outdoor activities 427

㉝ Parades and festivals 440

㉞ Kids' New York 447

㉟ Directory 454

Accommodation

Accommodation in New York definitely eats up the lion's share of most travelers' budgets. Many **hotels** in the city charge in the neighborhood of $150–200 a night, and most go well beyond that price (these are pre-**tax** rates – see p.300). It is possible to get a safe, clean room for $150 or less, but it's almost always easier to find a place to splurge on than it is to find a bargain.

Anywhere you're going to want to stay is going to require **reservations**; make them as far in advance as possible, especially for visits during the high season (May to September and November to early January) – you're likely to find everything chock-full if you wait until the last minute. Most hotels in New York only hold reservations until 5 or 6pm unless you've warned them that you'll be arriving late.

There are three ways to book a room: directly through the hotel, on a travel website, or through a travel agent. If you're going to do it yourself, try to use the local phone number, as it can be much more expedient than going through the national service at the "800" number. Inquire about discounts; prices are often reduced on weekends (especially downtown choices, as they tend to be devoid of their usual business travelers then), in the low season (February to April and October), and via corporate promotions. Travel websites list all-included flight and hotel package vacations and occasionally offer special deals; Ⓦ www.nycvisit.com has a good selection of specials (which come with a list of restrictions, and require that you pay with an American Express card). Travel agents provide more or less the same services. If you're looking for lodging in a particular area, refer to the Accommodation map, pp.298–99, for help.

There are plenty of **hostels** with dormitory accommodation for the young or budget-minded. Other moderately priced options include **bed and breakfasts**, which basically entail staying in somebody's spare room with all the amenities of a private apartment. These rooms go for approximately $75 and up for a double and can be booked through an agency listed in the appropriate section below.

Wherever you stay, you'll be expected to **pay in advance**, or at least provide a deposit for the first night. If you're booking over the phone or on the Internet, be prepared to give a credit-card number. Most places also ask for a credit-card imprint when you arrive, but they'll also accept cash, and occasionally travelers' checks.

Keep in mind that even though there are thousands of guest rooms in New York City, there are still not enough to go around. Most properties have a steady parade of occupants, and as a result show a lot of wear and tear. Unless you're checking into a luxury hotel – and sometimes even then – don't be surprised to see chipped furniture and scuffs on the wall. That said, there is a difference

ACCOMMODATION	
Alex Hotel	37
Algonquin	41
Ameritania Hotel	17
Beekman Tower	24
Big Apple Hostel	35
Broadway Inn	33
Bryant Park Hotel	50
Carlton	66
Casablanca	42
Chambers Hotel	13
Chelsea Center Hostel	64
Chelsea Hotel	70
Chelsea International Hostel	73
Chelsea Lodge	74
Chelsea Savoy Hotel	71
Comfort Inn Chelsea	69
Comfort Inn Manhattan	55
Dylan	49
Edison	27
Essex House	6
Fitzpatrick Manhattan	12
Flatotel	18
Gansevoort	77
Gershwin	67
Giraffe	68
Gramercy Park	72
Hampton Inn Times Square	19
Herald Square	58
Hilton Times Square	46
Hotel 41	48
Hotel QT	36
Hotel Pennsylvania	56
Hudson	8
Iroquois	40
Jolly Madison Towers	51
Larchmont	78
Le Parker Meridien	10
Library	47
Mandarin Oriental	5

Mansfield	44
Marriot Marquis	34
Mayfair	25
Metro	54
Michelangelo	21
Milburn	1
Milford Plaza	38
Millennium Broadway	39
Morgans	52
Murray Hill Inn	63
Muse	32
Novotel	20
Paramount	30
Park Savoy	7
Pickwick Arms	22
Pierre	3
Portland Square	28
Roger Smith	29
Roger Williams	59
Royalton	43
Salisbury	11
Seventeen	76
Shelburne Murray Hill	53
Sherry Netherland	4
Shoreham	15
Southgate Tower	60
Stanford	57
Thirty-One	62
Thirty Thirty	65
The Time	26
Vanderbilt YMCA	31
W Union Square	75
Waldorf-Astoria	23
Warwick	16
Washington Square Hotel	79
Wellington	14
Westin New York at Times Square	45
Westpark	9
Westside YMCA	2
Wolcott	61

MANHATTAN HOTELS & HOSTELS

between continuous use and unsanitary conditions; if you feel your room is dirty or unsafe, don't hesitate to talk to the management.

Hotels

Most of New York's **hotels** are in midtown Manhattan, in close proximity to many of the main tourist sights, though there are also a growing number of options downtown. The Upper West or Upper East sides should do if your taste runs more to Central Park and the high culture of museums and Lincoln Center. The latest fad in New York's hotel design and marketing is the so-called "boutique" hotel. These establishments are typically fairly intimate (100 or fewer rooms), with less square footage per room but more in the way of guest amenities.

Most hotels do not offer free **breakfast**, though complimentary continental breakfasts are becoming increasingly popular. If you have to pay for breakfast, you'll do better at a nearby diner. Tipping is expected at upmarket hotels: unless you firmly refuse, a bellhop will grab your bags when you check in and expect $5 to carry them to your room. The cleaning staff will really appreciate your tip when you leave (figure $2 minimum per day for cheaper hotels, $5 a day for the nicer establishments). Minibars, stocked with booze and chocolate goodies at astronomical prices, are formulated to appeal to your sense of laziness; these and the hotel shops that sell basic necessities at three times the street price should be avoided.

Taxes are added to your hotel bill, and hotels will nearly always quote you the price of a room before tax. Taxes will add 13.375 percent to your bill (state tax 8.375 percent, city tax 5 percent), and there is also a $3.50 per night "occupancy tax" and a $5.50 "hospitality" tax. All told, this will add about $35 to a $200 room.

The following selection of hotels runs the gamut from the city's cheapest to most luxurious and/or hippest. Unless noted, the prices quoted at the end of each listing represent the price of the hotel's cheapest double room, excluding all taxes, during the high season when rates are at a premium. Hotels are listed alphabetically within each geographical region below. For a visual overview of where to find a listed hotel, see the Accommodation map on pp.298–99, or the downtown neighborhood maps.

Downtown: below 14th Street

60 Thompson 60 Thompson St, between Spring and Broome sts ☎1-877/431-0400, ⓦwww.60thompson.com. Designed by Thomas O'Brien's Aero Studio, rooms at this boutique property ooze sophistication and tempt guests with countless in-room amenities, including DVD players and gourmet minibars. In summer there's a rooftop lounge with views of Soho. $505

Cosmopolitan 95 W Broadway, at Chambers St ☎1-888/895-9400 or 212/566-1900, ⓦwww.cosmohotel.com. A great Tribeca location, smart, well-maintained rooms, and incredibly low prices make the *Cosmopolitan* a steal. $189

Embassy Suites 102 North End Ave, at Vesey St ☎1-800/EMBASSY or 212/945-0100, ⓦwww.embassysuites.com. Near the quiet Battery Park City esplanade, the *Embassy Suites* is a little out of the way, but the roomy bedroom and living areas have tons of amenities, and a cook-to-order breakfast is included (virtually unheard of). Weekend stays are discounted. $449

Holiday Inn Downtown 138 Lafayette St, at Howard St ☎1-800/HOLIDAY or 212/966-8898, ⓦwww.holiday-inn.com. Just north of busy Canal St, this member of the well-known chain is also a stone's throw from Soho and Tribeca. Though the rooms are small for the price, the rates fluctuate according to availability so booking early should get you a better deal. $219

Hotel Gansevoort 18 Ninth Ave, at W 13th St ☎212/206-6700, ⓦwww.hotelgansevoort.com. Preservationists were

Hotel booking services

Central Reservations Service ☎1-800/555-7555 or 407/740-6442, ⓦwww.reservation-services.com

Express Hotel Reservations ☎1-800/407-3351, ⓦwww.express-res.com

Express Reservations (weekdays only) ☎1-800/356-1123 or 303/440-8481, ⓦwww.expressreservations.com

Hotel Reservations Network ☎1-800/964-6835, ⓦwww.hoteldiscount.com

Meegan's Services ☎1-800/441-1115 or 718/995-9292

aghast when cobblestone streets in the Meatpacking District were torn up to make room for this sleek hotel. Rooms are small but spiffy; you're really paying for the 360-degree views, the full spa, and the heated rooftop pool – the only one in the city. $435

Larchmont 27 W 11th St, between Fifth and Sixth aves ☎212/989-9333, ⓦwww.larchmonthotel.com. A budget hotel, in a terrific location on a tree-lined street in Greenwich Village. Rooms are small but nice and clean. Prices go up slightly on weekends. $119

Marriott Financial Center 85 West St, between Carlisle and Albany sts ☎212/385-4900, ⓦwww.marriott.com. This civilized business hotel has superb views of the Hudson River and New York Harbor. The service is excellent. $359

Mercer 147 Mercer St, at Prince St ☎212/966-6060, ⓦwww.mercerhotel.com. Housed in a Romanesque Revival building in Soho, the *Mercer* is one of the top accommodation choices of visiting celebs. Some rooms have massive, 90-square-foot baths, and the *Mercer Kitchen* restaurant is excellent (see p.333). $440–2450

Ritz-Carlton 2 West St, Battery Park City ☎212/344-0800, ⓦwww.ritzcarlton.com. The views of New York Harbor and the Statue of Liberty don't get much better than from the rooms here. The hotel features a bar that serves some of the city's best margaritas, 425-square-foot rooms with soothing muted tones, and "bath butlers" to draw baths and warm towels. $475

SoHo Grand 310 W Broadway, at Grand St ☎212/965-3000, ⓦwww.sohogrand.com. In a great location at the edge of Soho, this hotel draws guests of the model/actor variety. The stylish rooms are a bit small, but there's also a good bar, a restaurant, and a fitness center. $596

Tribeca Grand Hotel 2 Ave of the Americas, between White and Walker sts ☎1-877/519-6600 or 212/519-6600, ⓦwww.tribecagrand.com. The sister property of the *SoHo Grand*, the *Tribeca Grand* is unlabeled and

ACCOMMODATION | Hotels

(23)

▽ Mandarin Oriental New York

301

tucked behind a brick facade. Inside, the striking *Church Lounge*, a great place to have a drink, beckons with a warm glow. Rooms are chicly understated, though bathrooms boast phones and TVs, and the staff is extra attentive. Off-season weekends can be several hundred dollars cheaper. $599

Washington Square 103 Waverly Place, at Washington Square Park ☎212/777-9515, ⒲www.washingtonsquarehotel.com. In the heart of Greenwich Village, this hotel is quite close to the area's many nightlife options. Don't be deceived by the posh-looking lobby – the rooms are surprisingly shabby for the price. Continental breakfast is included. $210

The East Side: E 14th to 36th streets

Carlton 88 Madison Ave ☎1-800/601-8500 or 212/532-4100, ⒲www.carltonhotelny.com. A modernized hotel in a Beaux-Arts building. Two pluses: the location, in the safe residential area of Murray Hill, and the room and valet services. $549

Giraffe 365 Park Ave S, at 26th St ☎1-877/296-0009 or 212/685-7700, ⒲www.hotelgiraffe .com. Similar in tone and amenities to sister hotels *Library* (see p.304) and *Casablanca* (see p.305), *Giraffe*'s rooms borrow their décor from the sleek, colorful 1920s and 1930s. Prices include complimentary breakfast, afternoon wine and cheese, and a 24hr espresso bar. $359

Gramercy Park 2 Lexington Ave, at E 21st St ☎212/475-4320, ⒲www.gramercyparkhotel .com. *Gramercy Park* reopened in 2006 following a series of major renovations by the Ian Schrager Company. With its lovely location, guests also get a key to the adjacent private park. $250

Murray Hill Inn 143 E 30th St, between Lexington and Third aves ☎1-888/996-6376 or 212/683-6900, ⒲www.murrayhillinn.com. It's easy to see why young travelers and backpackers line the *Inn*'s narrow halls. Although the inexpensive rooms are smallish, they all have a telephone, a/c, and cable TV; some also have private bathrooms. $119

Roger Williams 131 Madison Ave, at E 31st St ☎1-888/448-7788 or 212/448-7000, ⒲www.hotelrogerwilliams.com. The first thing you'll notice at the *Roger* is the use of color. Utilizing both mellow and vibrant tones, these Scandinavian/Japanese fusion rooms are well worth the extra bucks. $450

Seventeen 225 E 17th St, between Second and Third aves ☎212/475-2845, ⒲www.hotel17ny .com. *Seventeen*'s rooms feature basic amenities (a/c, cable TV, and phones) and shared baths. It's clean, friendly, and nicely situated on a pleasant tree-lined street just minutes from Union Square and the East Village. Check out the excellent weekly rates. $150

Thirty-One 120 E 31st St, between Lexington and Park aves ☎212/685-3060, ⒲www .hotel31.com. An affordable Murray Hill location run by the folks who own *Seventeen*. The rooms are clean and the street is quiet and pleasant; some rooms share a bath. $155

Thirty Thirty 30 E 30th St, between Park and Madison aves ☎1-800/804-4480 or 212/689-1900, ⒲www.thirtythirty-nyc.com. Small, welcoming hotel, with a few minor but welcome design touches, including framed black-and-white scenes of old New York in all the rooms. $269

W 201 Park Ave S at E 17th St ☎212/253-9119, ⒲www.whotels.com. This stylish chain of luxury hotels – there are five other locations in Manhattan – offers top-to-bottom comfort and prides itself on having all the amenities a business traveler could ever need (and if they're missing something, they'll get it). Many *W* hotels feature trendy bars and restaurants; this one, on the northeast corner of Union Square, features a branch of celebrity chef Todd English's *Olives* restaurant. $539

The West Side: W 14th to 36th streets

Chelsea Hotel 222 W 23rd St, between Seventh and Eighth aves ☎212/243-3700, ⓦwww.hotelchelsea.com. One of New York's most notorious landmarks, this aging neo-Gothic building boasts a fabulously seedy and artistic past (see p.119). Avoid the older rooms by asking for one that's been renovated. They have wood floors, log-burning fireplaces (though you'll have to bring your own screen), and plenty of space. $235

Chelsea Lodge 318 W 20th St, between Eighth and Ninth aves ☎212/243-4499, ⓦwww .chelsealodge.com. The *Lodge* is a gem of a place: upon entrance, you'll be greeted by Early American/Sportsman décor. As a former boarding house, normal rooms, which offer in-room showers and sinks (there's a shared toilet down the hall), are a little small for two, but the few deluxe rooms are great value and have full bathrooms. A three-day cancellation policy applies. $114

Chelsea Savoy Hotel 204 W 23rd St, at Seventh Ave ☎212/929-9353, ⓦwww.chelseasavoynyc .com. A few doors away from the *Chelsea Hotel*, the *Savoy* has none of its neighbor's funky charm. The rooms, though small, are clean and nicely decorated and the staff is helpful. Try to avoid rooms facing the main drags outside; they can be noisy. $250

Comfort Inn Chelsea 18 W 25th St, between Sixth Ave and Broadway ☎212/645-3990, ⓦwww.comfortinn.com. Formerly the *Arlington*, the *Comfort Inn Chelsea* is a solid hotel with very good prices and clean rooms.

Near Madison Square Park, it's equidistant from downtown and midtown. Off-season rates drop significantly. $259

Comfort Inn Manhattan 42 W 35th St, between Fifth and Sixth aves ☎1-800/228-5150 or 212/947-0200, ⓦwww.comfortinnmanhattan .com. The best thing about this hotel is the free, deluxe continental breakfast and complimentary newspapers in the elegant lobby each morning. It's a good value but the management can be unhelpful; it's not always possible to see a room before you decide to bunk here. $234

Herald Square 19 W 31st St, between Fifth Ave and Broadway ☎1-800/727-1888 or 212/279-4017, ⓦwww.heraldsquarehotel.com. The original home of *Life* magazine, *Herald Square* still features Philip Martiny's sculpted cherub *Winged Life* over its Beaux-Arts doorway. The inside is meticulously clean, but somewhat soulless and without much in the way of extras. $159

Hotel Pennsylvania 401 Seventh Ave, at W 32nd St ☎212/736-5000 or 1-800/223-8585, ⓦwww.hotelpenn.com. Boasting the same telephone number since 1917 (the "Pennsylvania six five thousand" of the Glenn Miller song), this hotel across from Madison Square Garden offers a range of amenities in its 1705 rooms, though you can't help thinking things probably looked better back in Glenn's day. $279

The Metro 45 W 35th St, between Fifth and Sixth aves ☎1-800/356-3870 or 212/947-2500, ⓦwww.hotelmetronyc.com. A very stylish hotel, with old Hollywood posters on the walls, a delightful seasonal rooftop terrace, clean rooms, and free continental breakfast. It includes a few more extras (like a fitness room and a restaurant) than would normally be expected for the price. $295

Southgate Tower 371 Seventh Ave, at W 31st St ☎1-866/233-4642 or 212/563-1800, ⓦwww .affinia.com. At the upper end of mid-range hotels, *Southgate Tower* is in a 1929 building

Expense-account hotels

Make sure the bill goes to someone else so you can enjoy these lavish locations without worrying about your wallet:

Bryant Park Hotel 40 W 40th St, between Fifth and Sixth aves; p.306

Mercer 147 Mercer, at Prince St; p.301

Sherry Netherland 781 Fifth Ave, at E 59th St; p.304

SoHo Grand Hotel 310 W Broadway, at Grand St; p.301

opposite Penn Station and Madison Square Garden. Interiors are comfortable and classically decorated. All double rooms have kitchens. $339

Stanford 43 W 32nd St, between Broadway and Fifth Ave ☎1-800/365-1114 or 212/563-1500, ⓦwww.hotelstandford.com. A clean, moderately priced hotel on the block known as Little Korea. The rooms are a tad small, but attractive and very quiet. Free continental breakfast, valet laundry, and an efficient, friendly staff. $229

🏃 **Wolcott** 4 W 31st St, between Fifth Ave and Broadway ☎212/268-2900, ⓦwww.wolcott.com. You get more than your money's worth at the *Wolcott*. The lobby, full of Louis XVI–style mirrors and leonine reliefs, is quite lavish, while the rooms, although staid, are more than adequate. $280

Midtown East: E 36th to 59th streets

Alex Hotel 205 E 45th St, between Second and Third aves ☎212/867-7878 or 1-888/765-2370. By the same owners as the *Flatotel*, this beige-toned spot is a serene, though pricey, midtown oasis. Rooms are Mod with Scandinavian touches, and the award-winning chef from *Aquavit* (see p.349) heads the restaurant-bar *Riingo*. $325

Beekman Tower 3 Mitchell Place, at E 49th St and First Ave ☎1-866/233-4642 or 212/320-8018, ⓦwww.affinia.com. One of the more stylish and expensive hotels in the city's largest all-suite hotel group. Suites come with fully equipped kitchens. $279

Dylan 52 E 41st St, between Park and Madison aves ☎1-866/55-DYLAN or 212/338-0500, ⓦwww.dylanhotel.com. The hardwood floors, inviting lighting, and vaguely lemon-scented air in the lobby are indicative of the whole *Dylan* experience – classy and clever. The rooms show attention to detail and design, and 11ft ceilings make them look quite large. If you're looking to splurge, book the Alchemy Suite, a one-of-a-kind Gothic bedchamber with a vaulted ceiling and stained-glass windows. $329

Fitzpatrick Manhattan 687 Lexington Ave, between E 56th and 57th sts ☎212/355-0100 or 1-800/367-7701, ⓦwww.fitzpatrickhotels.com. This handsome Irish-themed hotel is perfectly situated for visits to midtown stores, Upper East Side museums, and Central Park. A hearty Irish breakfast is served all day. $429

Jolly Madison Towers 22 E 38th St, at Madison Ave ☎212/802-0600, ⓦwww.jollymadison.com. Italian chain hotel with restful, clean, fairly spacious rooms and a nautical-themed bar. $285

Library 299 Madison Ave, at E 41st St ☎1-877/793-READ or 212/983-4500, ⓦwww.libraryhotel.com. The *Library* must have the most bizarre concept in New York hoteldom: each floor is devoted to one of the ten major categories of the Dewey Decimal System, and the artwork and books in each room reflect a different pursuit within that group. Colored in shades of brown and cream, the rooms are average in size but nicely appointed and with big bathrooms. The *Library*'s quirky, sumptuous appeal is worth spending a few extra dollars. $345

Morgans 237 Madison Ave, between E 37th and E 38th sts ☎1-800/334-3408 or 212/686-0300, ⓦwww.morganshotel.com. One of the chicest hotels in town, and although the black-white-gray décor is starting to look self-consciously 1980s, stars still frequent the place. Rooms come with CD/DVD systems. Continental breakfast included. $499

Pickwick Arms 230 E 51st St, between Second and Third aves ☎212/355-0300, ⓦwww.pickwickarms.com. This pleasant budget hotel is one of the best deals in midtown. All 370 rooms have a/c, cable TV, and room service. The open-air roof deck has stunning views, and there are two restaurants (one French, one Mediterranean) downstairs. $229

Roger Smith 501 Lexington Ave, at E 47th St ☎212/755-1400, ⓦwww.rogersmith.com. Popular with bands, this midtown hotel offers both a stylish décor and helpful service. Rooms are individually decorated in contemporary American style with whimsical touches, and bold, colorful artwork is on display in public spaces. In sum, lots of personality. Breakfast is included. $369

Shelburne Murray Hill 303 Lexington Ave, between E 37th and 38th sts ☎212/689-5200, ⓦwww.affinia.com. Luxurious hotel in the most elegant part of Murray Hill. All the rooms have kitchenettes, and there's a new restaurant on the premises specializing in gourmet hamburgers. $419

Sherry Netherland 781 Fifth Ave, at E 59th St ☎212/355-2800, ⓦwww.sherrynetherland.com. If a large sum of money ever comes your way, rent a whole floor here and live in permanently (many of the guests do) – the

stunning views of Central Park are worth
it. The service excellent; room service is by
renowned restaurateur Harry Cipriani. $530

Waldorf-Astoria 301 Park Ave, at E 50th St ☎1-
800/WALDORF or 212/355-3000, ⓦwww
.waldorf.com. One of the city's first grand
hotels (see p.142), the *Waldorf* has been
restored to its 1930s glory and is a wonderful place to stay, if you can afford it. It's no
wonder this is a favorite pick for presidents
and visiting heads of state – the spacious
accommodations feature the latest electronic gadgets, triple sheeting, and marble
baths. At least drop by for a drink at the
legendary mahogany bar, a peek at one of
the opulent banquet halls, or a treatment at
the full-service spa. $459

Midtown West: W 36th to 59th streets

🏃 **Algonquin** 59 W 44th St, between Fifth
and Sixth aves ☎212/840-6800, ⓦwww
.algonquinhotel.com. One of New York's
famed literary hangouts (see p.134). The
quirky décor remains little changed from
the days of Dorothy Parker and her fellow
wits, though the bedrooms (named for
Roundtable regulars like Robert Benchley
and George S. Kaufman) have been refurbished to good effect and the lobby has
had a mini-facelift. Ask about summer and
weekend specials. $599

Ameritania Hotel 54 230 W 54th St, at Broadway
☎1-800/922-0330 or 212/247-5000, ⓦwww
.nychotels.com. With sleek, angular furnishings and a bold color-palette, this is one
of the coolest-looking hotels in the city. All
rooms have cable TV and CD players, and
luxury rooms feature marble baths. There's
also a bar/restaurant off the lobby. $427

Broadway Inn 264 W 46th St, between Broadway and Eighth Ave ☎1-800/826-6300 or
212/997-9200, ⓦwww.broadwayinn.com. A
cozy budget hotel in the heart of the theater
district, just a skip away from Times Square.
All rooms have private bathrooms and cable
TV, and continental breakfast is included in
the price. Guests get a 20 percent discount
at the adjacent restaurant. No elevator. $369

Bryant Park Hotel 40 W 40th St, between Fifth
and Sixth aves ☎1-877/640-9300 or 212/869-
0100, ⓦwww.bryantparkhotel.com. This hotel
shows off its edgy attitude in its stylish rooms,
luxurious 70-seat film-screening room, and
funky *Cellar Bar*, which is always filled with
media types. $575

Casablanca 147 W 43rd St, between Sixth Ave
and Broadway ☎1-888/9-CASABLANCA or
212/869-1212, ⓦwww.casablancahotel.com.
Moorish tiles, palm fronds, and *Rick's Café*
are all here in this theme hotel. While the
décor is 1940s Morocco, the rooms all have
up-to-date amenities. Three-night minimum
stay. $299

🏃 **Chambers Hotel** 15 W 56th St, between
Fifth and Sixth aves ☎1-866/204-5656
or 212/974-5656, ⓦwww.chambershotel.com.
Designed by architect David Rockwell, this
luxe hotel features over 500 original works
of art in its gallery-size hallways (past exhibitions have included pieces by John Waters
and Do-Ho Suh). Earth tones dominate the
modern and comfortable rooms, which are
also packed full of amenities. Inside the
hotel is *Town*, a very good, if pricey, restaurant. $285–$6000

Edison 228 W 47th St, between Broadway and
Eighth Ave ☎212/840-5000, ⓦwww
.edisonhotelnyc.com. The most striking thing
about the 1000-room *Edison* is its beautifully restored Art Deco lobby, built in the
same style as Radio City Music Hall. The
rooms, while not fancy, are clean and relatively new. Prices are quite reasonable for
midtown. $190

Essex House 160 Central Park S, between
Sixth and Seventh aves ☎1-877/854-8051 or
212/247-0300, ⓦwww.jumeirahessexhouse
.com. A beautiful hotel for a special occasion, *Essex House* has been restored to
its original Art Deco splendor. The best
rooms have spectacular Central Park views.
Despite the excellent service and marble
lobby, the atmosphere is quite relaxed.
$599

Flatotel 135 W 52nd St, between Sixth and
Seventh aves ☎1-800/352-8683 or 212/887-
9400, ⓦwww.flatotel.com. A comfortable,
stylish hotel in the heart of midtown featuring motifs inspired by architect Frank Lloyd
Wright and lots of earth tones. Sprawling
three-bedroom suites available in addition to
standard rooms. $469

Hampton Inn Times Square 851 Eighth Ave,
between W 51st and 52nd sts ☎212/581-4100,
ⓦwww.hamptoninn.com. This reliable chain
took over a former *Howard Johnson* space.
No-frills rooms with coffee makers and
movie channels. $389

Hilton Times Square 234 W 42nd St, between
Seventh and Eighth aves ☎1-800/HILTONS
or 212/840-8222, ⓦwww.hilton.com. On a

㉓

famous block, this gorgeous property starts on the building's twentieth floor, giving awesome views in all directions. The rooms (done in chocolate, tan, and cream) are good-sized, with an attractive desk and dresser in light wood. Ask about packages or specials. $339

Hotel 41 at Times Square 206 W 41st St ☎1-877/847-4444 or 212/703-8600, ⓦwww.hotel41.com. With just 47 rooms, this boutique hotel blends classic and contemporary styles to pleasing effect. Rooms come with high-speed Internet access, Aveda bath products, bottled water, and Frette robes. Every guest gets a complimentary *New York Times* and espresso/cappuccino each day of their stay. A terrific value for the area. $359

Hotel QT 125 W 45th St, between Sixth and Seventh aves ☎212/354-2323, ⓦwww.hotelqt.com. A new hotel in the heart of Times Square, boasting ultra-modern rooms with platform beds and, in some cases, bunk beds. All rooms are pet-friendly, and feature many amenities, including flat-screen TVs and sound systems. Great deal for the price. $175

Hudson 356 W 58th St, between Eighth and Ninth aves ☎1-800/444-4786 or 212/554-6000, ⓦwww.hudsonhotel.com. Once you get past the *Hudson's* chartreuse-lit escalators and space-shuttle-esque bar, the rooms are surprisingly tasteful (though miniscule). The library and sky terrace add significant charm. Rates are lower during the week than on weekends. $479

Iroquois 49 W 44th St, between Fifth and Sixth aves ☎1-800/332-7220 or 212/840-3080,

ⓦwww.iroquoisny.com. Once a haven for rock bands, this reinvented boutique hotel has comfortable, tasteful rooms with Italian-marble baths as well as a fitness center and library. The lounge is named for James Dean, one of the hotel's noted visitors. He lived here from 1951 to 1953, and some claim his room (#803) still retains an element of magic. $459

Le Parker Meridien 119 W 56th St, between Sixth and Seventh aves ☎212/245-5000, ⓦwww.parkermeridien.com. This hotel maintains a shiny, clean veneer, with comfortably modern rooms, a huge fitness center, rooftop swimming pool, and 24hr room service. Inquire about discounted weekend rates. $519

Mandarin Oriental New York 80 Columbus Circle, between Columbus and Amsterdam aves ☎212/805-8800, ⓦwww.mandarinoriental.com. The pampering is on par with the astronomical rates at the *Mandarin Oriental*, a favorite with entertainment-industry execs. The spacious, handsome rooms in this plush palace come with Frette linens, twice-daily housekeeping, and hi-def TVs. $747

Mansfield 12 W 44th St, between Fifth and Sixth aves ☎1-877/255-5167 or 212/277-8700, ⓦwww.mansfieldhotel.com. One of the nicest little hotels in the city, the *Mansfield* manages to be both grand and intimate. With a copper-domed salon, clubby library, and nightly jazz, there's a charming, slightly quirky feel. Rates are fair, especially considering the complimentary European breakfast and all-day cappuccino. $459

Marriott Marquis 1535 Broadway, at W 45th St ☎212/398-1900, ⓦwww.nymarriottmarquis .com. It's worth dropping by here even if only to gawk at the split-level atrium and ride the glass elevators to New York's only revolving bar and restaurant. The hotel is well-designed for conference or convention guests, though the rooms themselves are modest for the high price. $429

Mayfair 242 W 49th St, between Broadway and Eighth Ave ☎1-800/556-2932 or 212/586-0300, ⓦwww.mayfairnewyork.com. This boutique-style hotel, across the street from the St Malachay Actors' Chapel, has beautifully decorated rooms, its own restaurant, and a charming, old-fashioned feel. Historic photographs on loan from the Museum of the City of New York are on display everywhere, and add a nice touch to the décor. $159

Michelangelo 152 W 51st St, between Sixth and Seventh aves ☎1-800/237-0990 or 212/765-0505, ⓦwww.michelangelohotel.com. A veritable

▽ Mercer Kitchen, at the Mercer Hotel

palazzo on Broadway, this hotel, part of an Italian chain, features acres of marble. No expense is spared in the luxurious and super-large "standard" rooms. Suites come in Art Deco, Empire, or Country French styles – take your pick. $425

Milford Plaza 270 W 45th St, at Eighth Ave ℡1-800/221-2690 or 212/869-3600, ⓦwww.milfordplaza.com. Rooms are tiny and the atmosphere is impersonal in this *Ramada* hotel, but hordes of theater-goers still flock here for the "Lullabuy [sic] of Broadway" deals, which include theater tickets. Packages vary; best to call or visit their website. $279

Millennium Broadway 145 W 44th St, between Broadway and Sixth Ave ℡1-800/622-5569 or 212/768-4400, ⓦwww.millenniumhotels.com. Black marble and modern Italian wall-to-ceiling artwork dominate the *Millennium Broadway* lobby; the sleek lines continue in the beautiful off-white bedrooms. Rates are high but justifiably so. $429

Muse 130 W 46th St, between Sixth and Seventh aves ℡1-877/NYC-MUSE or 212/485-2400, ⓦwww.themusehotel.com. A small hotel in the center of the Times Square area, *Muse* caters to Europeans. The slightly chilly staff and off-putting lobby (it looks like the reception area at a brokerage house) contrast with the more traditional rooms, which are very airy, plainly decorated, and feature feather beds. $449

Novotel 226 W 52nd St, at Broadway ℡212/315-0100 or 1-800/221-3185, ⓦwww.novotel.com. This chain hotel is large enough to offer a decent range of facilities, including special rooms for the disabled, while small enough to avoid anonymity. The décor is clean, featuring uncluttered wood with blue accents, and the food good (as you would expect from a French-owned establishment). $359

Paramount 235 W 46th St, between Broadway and Eighth Ave ℡212/764-5500, ⓦwww.nycparamount.com. A former budget hotel renovated into a boutique bolt-hole by Ian Schrager (co-founder of *Studio 54*), the *Paramount* offers chic, closet-size rooms. It also boasts a trendy (and sometimes raucous) bar. $369

Park Savoy 158 W 58th St, between Sixth and Seventh aves ℡212/245-5755, ⓦwww.parksavoyhotel.com. Colorful, cozy rooms, all with private baths and just a block from Central Park, make this hotel a good value for the area. $155

Portland Square 132 W 47th St, between Sixth and Seventh aves ℡1-800/388-8988 or 212/382-0600, ⓦwww.portlandsquarehotel.com. A theater hotel since 1904 and the former home of Jimmy Cagney, the *Portland* has a few more comforts than its sister hotel *Herald Square* (see p.303), but it is still a budget operation. $269; small singles available for less.

Royalton 44 W 44th St, between Fifth and Sixth aves ℡212/869-4400, ⓦwww.royaltonhotel.com. Philippe Starck combined minimalist techniques with ocean-liner chic in the *Royalton*'s comfortable rooms; the lobby serves as an elegant stage for those who like to see and be seen. $559

Salisbury 123 W 57th St, between Sixth and Seventh aves ℡212/246-1300, ⓦwww.nycsalisbury.com. Good service, large rooms with kitchenettes, and proximity to Central Park and Carnegie Hall are the attractions here. They offer a discount program in which you get a free night for every 15 you spend here. $319

Shoreham 33 W 55th St, between Fifth and Sixth aves ℡212/247-6700, ⓦwww.shorehamhotel.com. The *Shoreham* is everything it proclaims itself to be: "Urbane. Mindful. Discreet. Comfortable." The lobby, featuring cool white marble, blue wall accents, polished steel columns, and a black-clad, spiky-haired staff, only emphasizes the motto. The rooms are of average size, but as with other boutique hotels, you get amenities galore, including high-speed wireless Internet. $459

The Time 224 W 49th St, between Broadway and Eighth Ave ℡1-877/TIME NYC or 212/246-5252, ⓦwww.thetimeny.com. *Tempus fugit* – and everything here reminds you of this fact, from the waist-level clock in the lobby to the hallways bedecked with Roman numerals. Smallish rooms are tricked out with the latest accoutrements (multi-line phones, ergonomic work station, fax). Not terribly expensive for what you get. $439

Warwick 65 W 54th St, at Sixth Ave ℡1-800/223-4099 or 212/247-2700, ⓦwww.warwickhotelny.com. Stars of the 1950s and 1960s – including Cary Grant, Rock Hudson, the Beatles, Elvis Presley, and JFK – stayed here as a matter of course. Although the hotel has lost its showbiz cachet, the elegant lobby, restaurant, and cocktail lounge still make it a pleasant place to stay. The staff is helpful and friendly. $375

Wellington 871 Seventh Ave, at W 55th St ☎1-800/652-1212 or 212/247-3900, @www.wellingtonhotel.com. Close to Carnegie Hall and Lincoln Center, the *Wellington* is highly reasonable for this stretch of town. Some of the rooms have kitchenettes, and family rooms offer two bathrooms. $299

Westin New York at Times Square 270 W 43rd St, at Eighth Ave ☎1-800/WESTIN-1, @www.westinnewyork.com. The copper-and-blue-glass building seems a little out of place (it was designed by Miami architects), but it's nonetheless a welcome addition to the selection of Times Square hotels. A high-tech high-rise, the rooms have comfortable beds and double-headed showers. $319

Westpark 6 Columbus Circle, between Eighth and Ninth aves ☎1-866/WESTPARK or 212/445-0200, @www.westparkhotel.com. The best rooms here look out over Columbus Circle and the southwestern corner of Central Park. The staff is somewhat reserved but helpful. Overall, it's a great deal. $189

Upper East Side: above E 59th Street

Mark 25 E 77th St, at Madison Ave ☎212/744-4300, @www.themarkhotel.com. This hotel really lives up to its claims of sophistication and elegance. The lobby is decked out in Biedermeier furniture and sleek Italian lighting, and there's a pervasive sense of refinement in the plush guest rooms, restaurant, and invitingly dark bar. $655

Pierre 2 E 61st, between Fifth and Madison aves ☎1-800/743-7734 or 212/940-8101, @www.fourseasons.com. The *Pierre* is consistently named as one of New York's top hotels. It was Salvador Dalí's favorite in the city, though the only surreal aspects today are

△ The Pierre

the prices. If these prohibit a stay, afternoon tea in the glorious frescoed Rotunda is highly recommended. $640

Wales 1295 Madison Ave, between E 92nd and 93rd sts ☎212/876-6000, @www.waleshotel.com. Just steps from "Museum Mile," this Carnegie Hill hotel has hosted guests for over a century. Rooms are attractive with antique details, thoughtful in-room amenities, and some views of Central Park. There's also a rooftop terrace, fitness studio, and café

Boutique hotels

You'll find fewer rooms, more amenities, and an emphasis on design at these intimate properties:
60 Thompson 60 Thompson St, between Spring and Broome sts; p.300
Alex Hotel 205 E 45th St, between Second and Third aves; p.304
Chambers Hotel 15 W 56th St, between Fifth and Sixth aves; p.305
Dylan 52 E 41st St, between Park and Madison aves; p.304
Hotel Gansevoort 18 Ninth Ave, at W 13th St; p.300
Library 299 Madison Ave, at E 41st St; p.304
Mansfield 12 W 44th St, between Fifth and Sixth aves; p.306
Mercer 147 Mercer St, at Prince St; p.301

with live harp music during breakfast and brunch. $399

The Upper West Side: above W 59th Street

Amsterdam Inn 340 Amsterdam Ave, at W 76th St ⊤212/579-7500, ⓦwww.amsterdaminn.com. From the owners of the *Murray Hill Inn* (see p.302), the rooms here are basic but clean (no closets, but TVs and phones) and the staff is friendly and helpful. $139

Lucerne 201 W 79th St, at Amsterdam Ave ⊤1-800/492-8122 or 212/875-1000, ⓦwww .thelucernehotel.com. This beautifully restored 1904 brownstone, with its extravagant Baroque terracotta entrance, charming rooms, and accommodating staff, is just a block from the Museum of Natural History (see p.213) and close to the liveliest stretch of Columbus Avenue. $310

Milburn 242 W 76th St, between Broadway and West End ⊤212/362-1006, ⓦwww.milburnhotel.com. The presence of a library of children's books and a selection of family movies make this welcoming and well-situated hotel great for families. $204

On the Ave 222 W 77th St, between Amsterdam and Broadway ⊤1-800/509-7598 or 212/362-1100, ⓦwww.ontheave-nyc.com. Modern *On the Ave* feels a bit clichéd, with stainless-steel sinks in the minimalist baths and dark-wood platforms for the beds. Although light on amenities, it is still clean, comfortable, and relatively inexpensive. $249

Riverside Tower 80 Riverside Drive, at W 80th St ⊤1-800/724-3136 or 212/877-5200, ⓦwww.riversidetowerhotel.com. The hallways here are plain as can be and the rooms – all with small refrigerators and private baths

– are ultra-basic, but *Riverside Tower*'s location can't be beaten. In the exclusive and safe Riverside Park neighborhood, it's adjacent to one of the city's most beautiful green spaces. $99

Brooklyn

Marriott Brooklyn 333 Adams St, Brooklyn Heights ⊤718/246-7000, ⓦwww.marriott .com. A favorite among those doing business on Wall Street, this modern hotel features wired rooms, a 12,000-square-foot pool, and amazing views of the Brooklyn Bridge. Keep in mind that many of the rooms here are built more for comfort and ease of work for its business-traveler clientele than for luxury. $329

Airport hotels

If your flight gets in at an ungodly hour, or if you have difficulty waking up in a timely manner, it may benefit your sanity to stay at one of the area's **airport hotels**. Usually comfortable and conveniently near the tarmac (though not always quiet), these offerings exist simply to ease the getting-to-the-airport stress associated with inconvenient traffic delays and hearing-impaired taxi drivers ("You wanted Newark? I thought you said JFK…").

JFK

Holiday Inn JFK 144–02 135th Ave, Queens ⊤718/659-0200

Radisson 135–30 140th St, Queens ⊤718/322-2300

Ramada Plaza JFK Building 144, Van Wyck Expressway S, Queens ⊤718/995-9000

Apartment swapping

If you're coming to New York for more than a few nights, and you happen to own a place in your home city/country, the least expensive and most authentic accommodation option by far is **apartment swapping**. You'd be amazed at the number of New Yorkers who would like to get out of the city for a few days or weeks; what's more, your humble Dublin or Seattle flat may seem spacious and exotic to a Manhattanite. Don't be afraid to play up your dwelling's positive features – the mountain view or medieval church that you take for granted may be just what your swap-partner's doctor ordered – and to ask for pictures and references of the potential swap in return. One of the most reputable exchange organizations is **Home Exchange** (⊤310/798-3864 or 1-800/877-8723, ⓦwww.homeexchange.com).

LaGuardia

Crowne Plaza LaGuardia 104–04 Ditmars Blvd,
Queens ☎718/457-6300
Sheraton LaGuardia East 135–20 39th Ave,
Queens ☎718/460-6666
Wyndham Garden 100–15 Ditmars Blvd, Queens
☎718/426-1500

Newark

Courtyard 600 Rt 1–9 South off Rt 78, Newark
☎973/643-8500
Holiday Inn 160 Frontage Rd, Newark
☎973/589-1000
Marriott Airport Behind tower at the airport,
Newark ☎973/623-0006

Hostels

Hostels are just about the only option for backpackers in New York. While hostels can vary greatly in quality, most are fine as long as you don't mind sleeping in a bunk bed and sharing a room with strangers (though if you're traveling in a group of four or six you can often book a room for yourselves). Average rates run $25–60.

Some hostels are part of organizations that require that you be a member in order to stay, so be sure to ask when calling to make a reservation. Although not all hostels require memberships, it's a good rule of thumb that the ones which do are generally cleaner, safer, and more affordable. For hostels that do not participate in the larger budget-travel community, always ask about safety, security, and locker availability before checking in and bunking down.

Hostels in New York are especially busy – and fairly rowdy – in August and September when the legions of summer backpackers descend on the city. The following is a small selection of the best hostels and YMCAs in the city, all of which have rooms for well under $100.

Big Apple Hostel 119 W 45th St, between Sixth and Seventh aves ☎212/302-2605, ⓦwww .bigapplehostel.com. You can't beat this hostel's Times Square location – it's easily the city's best budget pick. There's a secure luggage room, communal refrigerator, and even an outdoor deck with barbeque. All rooms have a/c and shared baths. Dorms $35, private double rooms $95–180, including tax.

Central Park Hostel 19 W 103rd St, at Central Park W ☎212/678-0491, ⓦwww .centralparkhostel.com. Upper West Side hostel in a renovated five-story walk-up has dorm beds for 4, 6, 8, or 10 people, as well as private rooms. All rooms share clean bathrooms, and lockers are available (bring a padlock). Sheets and blankets are included, payment in cash or travelers' checks only; you must have a passport or international student ID. Dorms $29–95, private rooms $109–149, includes tax.

Chelsea Center Hostel 313 W 29th St, at Eighth Ave ☎212/643-0214, ⓦwww.chelseacenterhostel .com. This small, clean, safe, private hostel has beds for $35 (including tax), including sheets, blankets, and breakfast. Reservations are essential in high season. Cash only.

Chelsea International Hostel 251 W 20th St, between Seventh and Eighth aves ☎212/647-0010, ⓦwww.chelseahostel.com. A smart choice located in the heart of Chelsea. Share the clean, rudimentary rooms with 3 or 5 other people, or book a private double room. All guests must leave a $10 key deposit. No curfew; passport required. Dorms $28, private rooms $70, including tax.

Gershwin 7 E 27th St, between Fifth and Madison aves ☎212/545-8000, ⓦwww.gershwinhotel .com. This hostel/hotel is geared toward young travelers, with Pop Art décor, a bar/ cocktail lounge, and dormitories with 2, 6, or 10 beds per room. Reservations highly recommended. Dorms $40, private rooms $109, including tax.

Hostelling International-New York 891 Amsterdam Ave, at W 103rd St ☎212/932-2300, ⓦwww.hinewyork.org. Dorm beds cost $29 (in 10-bed rooms) to $38 (in 4-bed rooms); members pay a few dollars less per night. The massive facilities – 624 beds in all – include a restaurant, library, travel shop, TV room, laundry, and kitchen. Reserve well in advance – this hostel is very popular.

Jazz on the Park 36 W 106th St, at Central Park W ☎212/932-1600, ⓦwww.jazzonthepark.com.

This groovy bunkhouse boasts a TV/games room, a café, and lots of activities, including live jazz on weekends. Rooms sleep between 2 and 14 people, are clean, bright, have a/c. Reserve at least one week in advance. Dorms $32, private double rooms with bath $130.

Uptown Hostel 239 Lenox Ave, at W 122nd St ⓣ212/666-0559, ⓦwww.uptownhostel.com. Clean, comfortable beds in the heart of Harlem. Bunk rooms sleeping 4–6 people, singles, and doubles are available. Inquire about $105 weekly rates at the kindly owner's annexed property, where the rates are otherwise the same. Dorms $20, singles $35, doubles $65.

Vanderbilt YMCA 224 E 47th St, between Second and Third aves ⓣ212/756-9600, ⓦwww.ymcanyc.org. Smaller and quieter than most of the hostels listed here, and neatly placed in midtown Manhattan, only five minutes' walk from Grand Central. Inexpensive restaurant, swimming pool, gym, and laundromat on the premises. All rooms have a/c but also shared baths. Singles $80, doubles $90.

Wanderers Inn Hostel East 179 E 94th St, between Third and Lexington aves

ⓣ212/289-8083, ⓦwww.wanderersinn.com. Located in a brownstone just blocks from Museum Mile, this excellent budget option provides linens, towels, Internet, TV, a fully equipped kitchen, Wed-night pizza parties, and rooms with high ceilings and a/c. All baths are communal, and you need to bring your own padlock. Dorms $25, private double rooms $65.

West Side YMCA 5 W 63rd St, at Central Park W ⓣ212/441-8800, ⓦwww.ymcanyc.org. This "Y" is steps from Central Park and housed in a landmark building that boasts pool tiles gifted from the King of Spain. It has two floors of rooms, an inexpensive restaurant, swimming pool, gym, and laundry. All rooms have a/c. Singles $80, doubles with private bath $115.

Whitehouse Hotel of New York 340 Bowery, at Bond St ⓣ212/477-5623, ⓦwww.whitehouse hotelofny.com. This is the only hostel in the city that offers single and double rooms at dorm rates. Unbeatable prices combined with an ideal downtown location, and amenities such as a/c, ATMs, cable TV, and linens, make this hostel an excellent pick. Singles $28, doubles $54.

Bed and breakfasts

Staying at a **bed and breakfast** can be a good way of visiting New York at an affordable price. But don't go looking for B&Bs on the streets: most rooms – except for a few which we've found off the beaten track (listed below) – are let out via the following official agencies, which all recommend making your reservations as far in advance as possible, especially for the cheapest rooms. Rates run about $80–100 for a double, or $100 and up a night for a studio apartment. Don't expect to socialize with your temporary landlord/lady, either. In the case of a "hosted" room, chances are your space will be self-contained, and you'll hardly see them. Renting an "unhosted" apartment means that the owner won't be there at all.

B&B agencies

Affordable New York City 21 E 10th St ⓣ212/533-4001, ⓦwww.affordablenyc.com. Detailed descriptions are provided by this established network of 120 properties (B&Bs and apartments) around the city. B&B accommodation from $85 (shared bath) and $100 (private bath), unhosted studios $135–160, and one-bedrooms $175–225. Cash or travelers' checks only; three-night minimum. Very customer-oriented and personable staff.

Bed and Breakfast Network of New York 130 Barrow St ⓣ1-800/900-8134 or 212/645-8134, ⓦwww.bedandbreakfastnetny.com. Call at least one month in advance, and ask about weekly and monthly specials. Lists hosted doubles for $150.

City Lights Bed & Breakfast ⓣ212/737-7049, ⓦwww.citylightsbandb.com. There are more than 400 carefully screened B&Bs (and short-term apartment rentals) on this agency's books. Many of the hosts are involved in theater and the arts, which means there's a little more artistic flair to these accommodations than your run-of-the-mill variety. Hosted doubles are $80–130; unhosted apartments cost $135–300 and up per night depending on size. Hosts are paid directly. Two-night minimum stay, with some exceptions.

CitySonnet.com ☎212/614-3034, ⊛www.citysonnet.com. This small, personalized, artist-run B&B/short-term apartment agency offers accommodation all over the city, but specializes in Greenwich Village. Singles start at $80, doubles are $110–165, and unhosted studio flats at $135.

Colby International 21 Park Ave, Eccleston Park, Prescot L34 2QY, UK, ☎0151/292-2910, ⓕ0151/292-2911, ⊛www.colbyinternational .com. Guaranteed accommodation can be arranged from the UK. Book at least a fortnight ahead in high season for these excellent-value apartments (studios to 3-bedrooms $100–350) and B&B singles ($80–90) and doubles ($95–105).

New World Bed & Breakfast Suite 837, 150 5th Ave, NY 10011 ☎212/675-5600, outside city 1-800/443-3800. Hosted singles ($100) and doubles ($120). Larger apartments are available from $150 up; call for a brochure.

Urban Ventures 38 W 32nd St, Suite 1412, NY 10001 ☎212/594-5650, ⓔreservations@gamutnyc.com. Now operated by Gamut Realty, this outfit provides flexibility; you can book up until the last minute for nightly, weekly, or monthly rentals, and there's a minimum stay of only two nights. Budget doubles from $75, "comfort range" rooms from $149.

B&B properties

Inn at Irving Place 56 Irving Place, at E 17th St ☎1-800/685-1447 or 212/533-4600, ⊛www .innatirving.com. Frequented by celebrities, this handsome pair of 1834 brownstones ranks as one of the most exclusive guesthouses in the city. It costs $325–495 a night

Brooklyn B&B properties

The outer boroughs of New York City may be much larger than Manhattan, but you'll be hard-pressed to find a hotel in them. This is especially true for Brooklyn: if you are looking for accommodation there, B&Bs are your best bet. There are quite a few to choose from, many of which are housed in townhouses and provide a welcome change to the corporate high-rise accommodation available in Manhattan.

Akwaaba Mansion 347 MacDonough St, at Stuyvesant Ave, Bedford-Stuyvesant ☎718/455-5958, ⊛www.akwaaba.com. A New York Landmark, this Victorian mansion is one of a kind, featuring Afrocentric details like Daffodil rag dolls, Adrinkra fabrics, and *Ebony* magazines from the 1950s and 1960s. A tearoom, sunny porch, and Southern-style breakfast will make anyone feel right at home. In case you were wondering, the name means "welcome" in Ghana. The beautiful rooms go for $165 per night.

Angelique Bed & Breakfast 405 Union St, between Smith and Hoyt sts, Carroll Gardens ☎718/852-8406, ⊛www.angeliquebedandbreakfast.com. A four-room Victorian brownstone in a historic area. Singles $100, doubles $150 (two-night minimum).

Baisley House 294 Hoyt St, between Union and Sackett sts, Carroll Gardens ☎718/935-1959, ⊛www.brooklynx.org/tourism/baisleyhouse/. Another charming Victorian brownstone, this one dates from 1865. Singles $95, doubles $125–150, all with shared bath. There is a two-night minimum stay.

Bed & Breakfast on the Park 113 Prospect Park W, between 6th and 7th sts, Park Slope ☎718/499-6115, ⊛www.bbnyc.com. A handsome 1892 limestone townhouse with views over Prospect Park. There are five double rooms with private baths ranging $195–300 a night (two-night minimum).

Foy House 819 Carroll St, at Eighth Ave, Park Slope ☎718/636-1492, ⓔmlee1024@nyc.rr.com. Small, beautiful 1894 brownstone (with only three guest rooms) in the heart of Park Slope's Historic District. Rooms range from $125 to $155. Smoking not permitted. Close to subways.

to stay in one of the twelve rooms – each named for a famous architect, designer, or actor. The *Inn* also offers five-course high teas ($30 per person).

Inn on 23rd St 131 W 23rd St, between Sixth and Seventh aves ☎1-877/387-2323 or 212/463-0330, ⌨www.innon23rd.com. This 14-room family-run B&B is adorned with heirlooms and comfortable furniture. Rooms feature pillow-top mattresses and private

baths. A good base for exploring the Chelsea art scene. Rooms start at $219.

New York Bed and Breakfast 134 W 119th St, at Lenox Ave ☎212/666-0559, ⌨www.newyork guesthouse.com. A lovely old brownstone just north of Central Park in Harlem, this B&B features nice double rooms for $65 a night for two people. Double rooms at an annexed property go for $70, including access to a community kitchen.

Cafés and light meals

Eateries geared toward people on the go are omnipresent in New York. Travelers will be hard pressed to find an area that doesn't offer something in the way of a small meal; as you walk the streets you'll come across shops selling breads, pastries, pizzas, sandwiches, bagels, meats, cheeses, juices, ice creams, and vegetarian goodies, to name but a few of the myriad comestible options available. Every neighborhood has several favorite haunts; this chapter details establishments good for breakfast, lunch, and snacks. See Chapter 25, "Restaurants," if you're in the mood for a larger, sit-down affair.

New York's **cafés** and **bakeries** have been greatly influenced by the city's diverse ethnic populations; American, French, and Italian establishments are the most visible throughout the city. Many of the more long-established cafés are in downtown Manhattan, and are perfect for lingering or just resting up between sights. A good number of them are quite European in feel – the grouping at the junction of Bleecker and MacDougal streets in the West Village is determinedly Left Bank, for example.

New York also has a number of **coffeehouses** and **tearooms** that provide fresh coffee and tea, fruit juices, pastries, and light snacks. There are **coffee shops** or **diners** on just about every block that serve cheap, decent breakfast specials. The more upscale midtown hotels are good places to stop for formal tea, too, if you can afford the prices they charge for the English country-house atmosphere they often try to contrive.

Financial District

Bakeries and cafés

Taylor's 156 Chambers St, between Greenwich Ave and W Broadway ☎212/378-3401. The enormous muffins and oatmeal cookies here are guaranteed to lift spirits and satisfy, as is the thick hot chocolate. Everything is baked fresh and reasonably priced.

Sandwiches and snacks

The Little Place 61 Warren St, at W Broadway ☎212/528-3175. Tiny, smartly priced Mexican joint known for its authentic egg dishes, tacos, and fajitas.

Tribeca and Soho

Bakeries and cafés

Balthazar Bakery 80 Spring St, between Crosby St and Broadway ☎212/965-1414. Run by the same management as the *Balthazar* brasserie next door (see p.334), this bakery has wonderful breads (including a dark

Specialty eating

We've highlighted particular types of snacks and lighter meal options and listed them in boxes on the following pages.

Bagels p.317
Breakfast: coffee shops and diners p.322
Bubble tea in Chinatown p.316
Ice cream p.325
Pizza by the slice p.323
Some atmospheric cafés p.320

chocolate loaf) and pastries of all sorts, minus the attitude or the smoke present at the larger restaurant. They also serve great home-made fizzy lemonade.

Bouley Bakery 120 W Broadway, between Duane and Reade sts ☏ 212/964-2525. Wunderkind David Bouley's latest addition to the culinary scene is a tiny bakery/restaurant with truly great breads and baked goods, as well as reasonably priced sandwiches. You really can't go wrong with any of the pastries.

Once Upon a Tart 135 Sullivan St, between Houston and Prince sts ☏ 212/387-8869. A good place to come for a light lunch or to satisfy a sugar craving. The interior is a bit cramped, but intimate and oh-so-quaint.

Yaffa Tea Room 353 Greenwich St, at Harrison St ☏ 212/274-9403. Hidden in an unassuming corner of Tribeca, this restaurant serves Mediterranean-style dinners, good brunch spreads, and a cozy high tea (reservations required). The eclectic décor is composed of flea market bric-a-brac.

Sandwiches and snacks

Café Bari 529 Broadway, at Spring St ☏ 212/431-4350. Among the cornucopia of wholesome offerings at this Soho spot are many variations on the popular wrap (sandwich in a soft tortilla), like goat cheese with grilled chicken. There's a wide selection of soups and salads, and anything made with their mozzarella is sure to please. Juices and yogurt-infused smoothies are good if you're in the mood for something sweet. Head to the upstairs section of the shop for full entrees.

Hampton Chutney 68 Prince St, at Crosby ☏ 212/226-9996. The American sandwich takes a detour through Indian breads and ingredients here. Naan and chickpea-based chapati breads mix nicely with spicy chutneys, cool yogurt, and traditional western sandwich stuffings. Out of the ordinary, and quite good.

Rocky Mountain Chocolate Factory 125 Chambers St, between W Broadway and Church St ☏ 212/349-7553. Chocolate (and other sweets) in every configuration you can think of – even sugar-free. This is a great place to satisfy your cocoa cravings.

Chinatown, Little Italy, and NoLita

Bakeries and cafés

Café Gitane 242 Mott St, between Prince and Houston sts ☏ 212/334-9552. Come here to brush up on your French and settle into a bowl of delicious café crème. For those looking for a bite to eat, excellent Moroccan-influenced food is also on offer. Chock-full of posers, but still one of the best cafés around.

Caffè Roma 385 Broome St, at Mulberry St ☏ 212/226-8413. Old Little Italy *pasticceria*, ideal for a drawn-out latte and traditional Italian pastry. Try the nutty home-made cookies, the exceptionally good cannoli (plain or dipped), or the gelato available at the counter in back.

Ceci-Cela 55 Spring St, between Mulberry and Lafayette sts ☏ 212/274-9179. Tiny French patisserie with tables in the back

Bubble tea in Chinatown

The Chinese, who have always revered tea, have given their traditional drink a contemporary twist: bubbles (actually pearl tapioca). The following teahouses feature bubble teas – milk-added or fruit-flavored teas enhanced with tapioca beads. These beads, which come in white or purple-black, impart only a minor flavor, but they change the texture of the drink significantly. Sucked up through wide straws, the chewy bubbles either pop into the mouth or are easily gulped down with the liquid. Though a bit unsettling at first, it does make drinking tea interesting. Be sure to sample some traditional nutty biscuits with your bubble tea.

Fay Da Bakery 83 Mott St, at Canal St ☎212/791-3884

Green Tea Café 45 Mott St, at Bayard St ☎212/693-2888

Saint's Alp Teahouse 20 Elizabeth St, at Canal ☎212/227-2880

Tearrific 51 Mott St, at Lafayette St ☎212/393-9009

for those who want to linger, as well as a stand-up counter and bench out front designed for those who can't wait to devour their delectable baked goods. The almond croissants and *palmiers* (elephant-ear-shaped, sugar-coated pastries) are divine, as are the cocoa-dusted truffles. The *croque-monsieurs* are a bit more filling.

Ciao Bella Gelato 285 Mott St, at Houston ☎212/431-3591. Heavenly takeout gelato and sorbet, some of the best in the city; the blood-orange sorbet is to die for and the coffee gelato equally delicious.

Ferrara's 195 Grand St, between Mott and Mulberry sts ☎212/226-6150. The best-known and most traditional of Little Italy's coffeehouses, this neighborhood landmark has been around since 1892. Try the cheesecake, cannoli, or, in summer, *granite* (Italian ices). Outdoor seating is available in warmer weather.

Kwong Wah Cake Company 210 Grand St, at Mott St ☎212/431-9575. This bakery on teeming Canal Street serves traditional Chinese items, like crisp almond "moon" cookies, and savory roast-pork buns.

Sandwiches and snacks

Chinatown Ice Cream Factory 65 Bayard St, between Mott and Elizabeth sts ☎212/608-4170. An essential stop after dinner at one of the restaurants nearby (see p.335), even though the wondrously unusual flavors are good any time. Specialty flavors include green tea, ginger, almond cookie, and lychee.

Ray's 27 Prince St, between Mott and Elizabeth sts ☎212/966-1960. While countless pizzerias in the city claim to be the "original *Ray's*," this Little Italy mainstay is perhaps the most distinctive and unchain-like of the bunch (note, though: it's not actually a chain). The thick Sicilian slices ($2.50) are particularly good.

Lower East Side

Bakeries and cafés

Kossar's 367 Grand St, at Essex St ☎212/473-4810. A Jewish bakery. The *bialys* at *Kossar's* just may be the best in the city.

Teany 90 Rivington St, between Orchard and Ludlow ☎212/475-9190. Nice Lower East Side stop-off for a wide selection of teas and classic high-tea sandwiches, as well as vegan scones and baked beans on toast.

Yonah Schimmel's 137 E Houston St, between Forsyth and Eldridge sts ☎212/477-2858.

The knishes, rounds of vegetable- or meat-stuffed dough, are baked fresh on the premises, as are the wonderful bagels. Patronized by a mixture of old men wise-cracking in Yiddish and – on Sundays, especially – young uptowners wading through the *New York Times*.

Sandwiches and snacks

Doughnut Plant 379 Grand St, between Essex and Norfolk sts ☎212/505-3700,

(24)

Bagels

Theories abound as to the **origin of the modern bagel**. Most likely, it is a derivative of the pretzel, with the word "bagel" coming from the German *biegen*, "to bend." Whatever their birthplace, it is certain that bagels have become a **New York institution**. Until the 1950s bagels were still handmade by Eastern-European Jewish immigrants in cellars scattered around New York's Lower East Side. In the last half-century, though, bagels have become common fodder. You'll even find all sorts of bagel spin-offs, including thinly sliced bagel chips.

Modern-day bagels are softer and have a smaller hole than their ancestors – the hole made them easy to carry on a long stick to hawk on street corners. Their curiously chewy texture is a result of being boiled before they are baked. They are most traditionally (and famously) served with cream cheese and lox (smoked salmon). The last decade or so has brought an expansion in the roster of bagel varieties; while many swear by such flavors as blueberry and cheese, purists decry the invention of the new types, which, they say, turn their revered bagel into a low-class muffin alternative.

Though bagels are now an American dietary staple, New Yorkers would say only a few places serve **the real thing**. Here is a list of some of the city's better bagelsmiths. (And if you prefer *bialys*, a drier and flatter bagel without a hole, head straight to *Kossar's*; see p.316.)

Bagel Buffet 406 Sixth Ave, between W 8th and 9th sts ⊕212/477-0448

Bagels on the Square 7 Carmine St, between Bleecker St and Sixth Ave ⊕212/691-3041

David's Bagels 228 First Ave, between 13th and 14th sts ⊕212/533-8766

Ess-A-Bagel 359 First Ave, at E 21st St ⊕212/260-2252

H & H Bagels 2239 Broadway, at W 80th St ⊕212/595-8000

Hot & Crusty 2387 Broadway, between 87th and 88th sts ⊕212/496-0632

Yonah Schimmel's 137 E Houston St, between Forsyth and Eldridge sts ⊕212/477-2858

ⓦ www.doughnutplant.com. Serious (and seriously delicious) donuts; make sure to sample the seasonal flavors and glazes, including pumpkin and passion fruit.

Grilled Cheese 168 Ludlow St, between Houston and Stanton sts ⊕212/982-6600. Great grilled-cheese sandwiches any way you want them – very fresh fillings include everything from pickles and portabello mushrooms to olive pesto and bacon. The salads are good, too. Get your sandwich to go, as the dining space is quite tiny.

Il Laboratorio del Gelato 95 Orchard St, at Broome St ⊕212/343-9922. This shrine to cream and sugar serves up over 75 flavors, including fig, lavender, and malt. The owner

can often be seen mixing his fine creative concoctions in stainless-steel vats.

The Pickle Guys 49 Essex St, between Grand and Hester sts ⊕212/656-9739. Come here to sate your craving for all things briny: pickles, peppers, and olives are only a few of the salty items displayed outside the store in huge barrels.

Russ & Daughters 179 E Houston St, between Allen and Orchard sts ⊕212/475-4880. Technically, this store is known as an "appetizing." The original Manhattan gourmet shop, it was set up around 1900 to sate the appetites of homesick immigrant Jews with smoked fish, pickled vegetables, cheese, and bagels – it still does a great job delivering the goods.

East Village

Bakeries and cafés

Cloister Café 238 E 9th St, between Second and Third aves ⊕212/777-9128. This café is worth

frequenting for its spacious garden dining area and good coffee. Don't come for the food, which hovers somewhere between mediocre and truly terrible. It's a popular late-night spot.

🏃 **DeRobertis 176 First Ave, at 10th St** ☎212/674-7137. A traditional Italian bakery/café that's been around since 1904. The old New York vibe is so good that the establishment has been featured in multiple Woody Allen flicks. Wonderful ricotta cheesecake and espresso.

Moishe's 115 Second Ave, between E 6th and 7th sts ☎212/505-8555. Excellent prune danishes, *hamantashen*, seeded rye, and other kosher treats.

Sticky Fingers 121 First Ave, between E 7th St and St Mark's Place ☎212/529-2554. Friendly, quiet East Village spot with kids' artwork on the wall. Good coffee, pastries, and breads.

Thé Adoré 17 E 13th St, between Fifth Ave and University Place ☎212/243-8742. A charming little tearoom on two floors. Downstairs is a counter with excellent pastries, Japanese scones, and croissants; upstairs is a small café that serves baguette sandwiches and tasty bowls of soup. Daytime hours only; closed Sun; generally closed Sat in Aug, but it varies, so, call ahead.

Veniero's Pasticceria & Café 342 E 11th St, between First and Second aves ☎212/674-7070. An East Village bakery and neighborhood institution since 1894, *Veniero*'s desserts and décor are fabulously over-the-top. The ricotta cheesecake and home-made gelato are great in the summer.

Sandwiches and snacks

B & H Dairy 127 Second Ave, between E 7th St and St Mark's Place ☎212/505-8065. A tiny luncheonette that serves home-made soup, challah, and latkes. You can also create your own juice combinations (carrot-beet, for example, is surprisingly flavorful, if strictly for hard-core juiceaholics). This is a good option for vegetarians.

Damask Falafel 89 Ave A, at E 6th St ☎212/673-5016. *Damask* is one of the better Middle-Eastern eateries in the area. Try the tender chicken shawarma, beef gyro, or generous falafel combo platter; they're all under $10.

Juicy Lucy's 85 Ave A, between E 5th and 6th sts ☎212/777-5829. This very small and congested but congenial juice bar has a wide range of standard juices and yogurt-based smoothies, along with tofu chili dogs and other vegan treats.

🏃 **Liquiteria 170 Second Ave, at E 11th St** ☎212/358-0300. The smoothies here are by far the best in Manhattan (try the "Orangasm" or the "Reggae Rumba"). There are over 30 smoothie combos, and loads of supplement shots. You can also get delicious, healthy lunches like oatmeal with fresh fruit or organic PB&Js.

Panya Bakery 10 Stuyvesant St, between Third Ave and E 9th St ☎212/777-1930. A Japanese take on the sandwich shop with some unique and yummy pastries – try the chocolate sponge cake with green-tea filling. The bakery itself is tiny – look for the logo, a cute, Hello Kitty–style animal.

Pommes Frites 123 Second Ave, between E 7th St and St Marks Place ☎212/674-1234. Arguably the best fries in the city, with gooey, Belgian-style toppings available.

Sanctuary 25 First Ave, between E 1st and 2nd sts ☎212/780-9786. This breezy lunch café is a haven for both foodies and the health-conscious. All their dishes are made with extra-flavorful natural ingredients, and you can take a yoga class upstairs after you eat.

Veselka 144 Second Ave, corner of E 9th St ☎212/228-9682. East Village mainstay that offers fine home-made borscht (hot in winter, cold in summer), latkes, pierogi, and great burgers and fries. Open 24 hours.

Via Della Pace 48 E 7th St, at Second Ave ☎212/253-5803. Dark and cozy East Village café with good Argentine pastas and sandwiches, plus a great selection of coffees and desserts. The tiramisu is excellent.

West Village

Bakeries and cafés

A Salt and Battery 112 Greenwich Ave, between Jane and Horatio sts ☎212/691-2713. Manhattan's only true chippie, run by the Brits from *Tea & Sympathy* (see opposite) next door. It's an authentic enough affair, with decent battered fish, great chips, mushy peas, and mugs of tea, but it may also be the world's most expensive chippie – fish suppers cost a good $20. There's minimal counter seating; most get their fish to go.

Café Le Figaro 184 Bleecker St, at MacDougal St ☏212/677-1100. A Beat hangout during the 1950s, this warm and invitingly worn place still draws a bookish crowd, but is better known now for its respectable cappuccino and pastries. A sure bet, even if it is a shade touristy.

Caffè Dante 79 MacDougal St, between Bleecker and Houston sts ☏212/982-5275. A morning stop-off for many locals since 1915. It's often jammed with NYU students and professors sipping cappuccinos, espressos, and caffè alfredo with ice cream.

Caffè Rafaella 134 Seventh Ave ☏212/929-7247. This great little café serves a blood-orange sorbet that shouldn't be missed. Also notable for a cozy armchair ambience and a variety of excellent cappuccino drinks.

Caffè Reggio 119 MacDougal St, between Bleecker and W 3rd sts ☏212/475-9557. This is one of the first Village coffeehouses, dating back to the 1920s. It's always crowded; in warm weather there are outdoor tables for people- or tourist-watching.

Caffè Vivaldi 32 Jones St, at Bleecker St ☏212/691-7538. An old-fashioned Viennese-style coffeehouse with fireside coziness.

Doma 17 Perry St, at Seventh Ave S ☏212/929-4339. A corner window, good brews, and linger-all-day vibe make this a neighborhood favorite; it's the anti-*Starbucks*.

Grey Dog 33 Carmine St, at Bleecker St ☏212/462-0041. Casual, stay-all-afternoon

▽ Magnolia Bakery cupcakes

café specializing in sandwiches. Try the awesome Philly cheese steak or light quiche with salad, both $7.50.

Magnolia Bakery 401 Bleecker St, at W 11th St ☏212/462-2572. There are lots of baked goods on offer here, but everyone comes for the heavenly and deservedly famous cupcakes (celebrated in both *Sex and the City* and *Saturday Night Live*). At night the lines can stretch around the block.

Marquet Patisserie 15 E 12th St, between Fifth Ave and University Place ☏212/229-9313. Thanks to its convenient location, ample tables, excellent menu, and low-key atmosphere, this is the perfect mid-Village place to warm up or cool down and rest your feet. There's an emphasis on café fare but they serve more substantial meals, too.

Tea & Sympathy 108 Greenwich Ave, between W 12th and 13th sts ☏212/807-8329. Self-consciously British tearoom, serving an afternoon high tea full of traditional staples like jam roly-poly, treacle pud, shepherd's pie, and scones. Perfect for British tourists feeling homesick.

Sandwiches and snacks

Bagel Buffet 406 Sixth Ave, between W 8th and 9th sts ☏212/477-0448. Wide selection of fillings and good-value bagel and salad platters for around $5. Open 24 hours.

Cones 272 Bleecker St, between Seventh Ave and Morton St ☏212/414-1795. Wonderful gelatos by two Argentine brothers. Flavors like tiramisu and rich chocolate attract long lines, especially on warm summer nights.

Elixir 523 Hudson St, at W 10th St ☏212/352-9952. Casual, friendly joint where you can order juices, smoothies, and seasonal "elixirs" with health-promoting ingredients. Notable blends include the "Femme," which blends peppermint, rosemary, nettle, and dandelion; and the "Belly," a mixture of spearmint, fennel, and even catnip.

Peanut Butter & Company 240 Sullivan St, between Bleecker and W 3rd Sts ☏212/677-3995. Peanut butter in ways you never imagined. Try the "Elvis" – a grilled peanut butter and honey sandwich with bananas, or the slightly more adventurous "Spicy Peanut Butter Sandwich," made with pineapple jam and grilled chicken. Sandwiches are $5–6.50.

Two Boots to Go West 75 Greenwich Ave, at Seventh Ave ☏212/633-9096. Great thin-crust

CAFÉS AND LIGHT MEALS

(24)

pizzas with a cornmeal dusting and Cajun flavor. Try a slice of the "Newman" (sopressata, sweet sausage, and ricotta) or the "Mrs (Emma) Peel" (round vegetable Sicilian). Also at 42 Ave A.

Village Delight 323 Bleecker St, between Christopher and Grove sts ☎212/633-9275. Healthy-sized whole turkey or roast beef sandwiches, with falafels and an assortment of Middle-Eastern side dishes.

Waverly Restaurant 385 Sixth Ave, at Waverly Place ☎212/675-3181. The *Waverly* is a comfy neighborhood diner. It's especially good for a late-night burger, a bacon and egg breakfast, or an egg cream.

Chelsea

Bakeries and cafés

Big Cup 228 Eighth Ave, between W 21st and 22nd sts ☎212/206-0059. Popular gay hangout coffee shop with fresh muffins and (big) hot cups of joe. Comfortable couches and chairs make it the perfect place to read the papers and ease into your day.

News Bar 2 W 19th St, between Fifth and Sixth aves ☎212/255-3996. Tiny, minimalist café with a very good selection of pastries and periodicals. It's a good spot to people-watch; many of the patrons are photographers and models.

Wild Lily Tea Room 511 W 22nd St, between Tenth and Eleventh aves ☎212/691-2258. Convenient for a gallery tour of west Chelsea, the shop has over forty different brews, along with a sweet-pea purée soup, poached ginger chicken salad, and tea sandwiches.

Sandwiches and snacks

Amy's Bread 75 Ninth Ave, between W 15th and 16th sts ☎212/462-4338. You can find *Amy*'s breads in fine stores citywide, but it's freshest here in the Chelsea Market. Their grilled-cheese sandwiches, made with chipotle peppers, are some of the best in the city.

F&B 269 W 23rd St, between Seventh and Eighth aves ☎646/486-4441. Terrific European-influenced street food (namely gourmet hot dogs, bratwurst, and knockwurst) at digestible prices. Other items include salmon dogs, and mouthwatering Swedish meatballs. Vegetarians should not fear: there's a surprisingly good selection of meatless offerings, as well.

Kitchen 218 Eighth Ave, between W 21st and 22nd sts ☎212/243-4433. Tasty Mexican cuisine and authentic flavors, with a slew of daily burrito specials. Takeout only.

Petite Abeille 107 W 18th St, at Sixth Ave ☎212/604-9350. French for "little bee," this charming Belgian place is perfect for a lunch or light snack after a morning spent shopping at any of the department stores in the area. The mussels, cold poached salmon, and soups are all good bets.

(24)

Union Square, Gramercy Park, and the Flatiron District

Bakeries and cafés

City Bakery 3 W 18th St, between Fifth and Sixth aves ☎212/366-1045. A good place to come for a filling lunch or to satisfy your sweet tooth (or both). The vast array of pastries is head and shoulders above most in the city. Try the tortilla pie, the idiosyncratic pretzel croissant, or the beer hot-chocolate with home-made marshmallows (it tastes better than it sounds).

Inn at Irving Place 56 Irving Place, at E 17th St ☎212/533-4600. At this small inn set in a handsome pair of brownstones, classic five-course high English teas are served in the afternoon, complete with silver service and a tower of sandwiches ($35 per person).

T Salon Emporium 11 E 20th St, at Broadway ☎212/358-0506. A lovely, inviting spot to relax with a pot of tea or a full load of finger sandwiches and pastries. $31 per person or $41 for two. Daily 10am–8pm.

Sandwiches and snacks

Bread Bar at Tabla 11 Madison Ave, at 25th St ☎212/889-0667. This little sister to pricier *Tabla* (upstairs; see p.345) serves delicious Indian tapas and cocktails perfumed with Southeast Asian spices.

Cast Iron 641 Sixth Ave, between W 19th and 20th sts ☎212/462-2244. *Cast Iron* is an Italian-style joint that serves thick-crust pizzas with savory sauces and an excellent selection of sandwiches on amazing breads. Take a look up at the soaring tiled ceilings while you wait for your food.

Eisenberg's Sandwich Shop 174 Fifth Ave, between 22nd and 23rd sts ☎212/675-5096. A colorful luncheonette, this shop serves great tuna sandwiches, matzoh-ball soup, and old-fashioned fountain sodas at a well-worn counter.

Uncle Mo's Burrito & Taco Shop 14 W 19th St, between Fifth and Sixth aves ☎212/727-9400. Authentic Mexican fare; these tortilla-wrapped goods (available for takeout) are some of the city's best.

Wichcraft 49 E 19th St, between Broadway and Park Ave S ☎212/780-0577. If you can't afford the steep prices at award-winning *Craft* next door (run by the same owner; see p.344), this gourmet sandwichery is a fine wallet-friendly runner-up. Tuck into a moist Sicilian tuna sandwich ($9) or one of their excellent veggie sides ($4).

Midtown East

Bakeries and cafés

Buttercup Bake Shop 973 Second Ave, between 51st and 52nd sts ☎212/350-4144. This *Magnolia Bakery* off-shoot is similarly known for its 1950s-style comfort sweets, especially the moist cupcakes and banana pudding.

Chez Laurence 245 Madison Ave, at 38th St ☎212/683-0284. Well-placed, friendly little patisserie that makes cheap breakfasts, decent, inexpensive lunches, and good coffee at any time of the day. Closed Sun.

Mad Tea Cup Burberry, 3rd Floor, 9 E 57th St, between Fifth and Madison aves ☎212/371-5010. Escape all the plaid at this swanky midtown boutique by ducking upstairs for a fine cup of tea and a savory or sweet gourmet snack. A great hidden place to find some peace and quiet.

Sandwiches and snacks

Fresco by Scotto on the Go 40 E 52nd St, between Madison and Park aves ☎212/935-3434. This welcoming Italian takeout spot serves up fresh pastas, home-made pizzas, and toothsome sandwiches.

Tea Box Takashimaya, 693 Fifth Ave, between 54th and 55th sts ☎212/350-0180. Despite its location at the city's chicest Japanese department store (see p.414), this basement tearoom is very quiet. The small but pricey menu features both Asian and Western snacks; a pot of tea here can be an elixir after a long day shopping and sightseeing.

Viand 673 Madison Ave, at E 61st St ☎212/751-6622. Affordable little coffee shop serving rich brews, awesome turkey sandwiches, and all-around delicious snacks. Service is speedy and the prices sweet.

Breakfast: coffee shops and diners

Grungy American coffee shops have long been a part of the Manhattan legend from television, film, and potboiler fiction. The ones below deliver both a quality breakfast and a classic New York experience.

Downtown Manhattan

Brasserie Centrale 1700 Broadway, at W 53rd St ☎212/757-2233; below
Chez Laurence 245 Madison Ave, at E 38th St ☎212/683-0284; p.321
Marquet Patisserie 15 E 12th St, between Fifth Ave and University Place ☎212/229-9313; p.319
Veselka 144 Second Ave, at E 9th St ☎212/228-9682; p.318
Waverly Restaurant 385 Sixth Ave, at Waverly Place ☎212/675-3181; p.320

Uptown Manhattan

EJ's Luncheonette 447 Amsterdam Ave, between W 81st and 82nd sts ☎212/873-3444; p.324
Googie's Diner 1491 Second Ave, at E 78th St ☎212/717-1122; p.324
Tom's Restaurant 2880 Broadway, at W 112th St ☎212/864-6137; p.325
Viand 673 Madison Ave, at E 61st St ☎212/751-6622; p.321

Midtown West

Bakeries and cafés

Algonquin Hotel lobby, 59 W 44th St, between Fifth and Sixth aves ☎212/840-6800. The archetypal American interpretation of the English drawing room, located in the airy, attractive lobby of the hotel by the same name (see p.305), and reeking of faux nineteenth-century robber-baron splendor. Good for afternoon tea (not high tea, though), or a drink.

Brasserie Centrale 1700 Broadway, at W 53rd St ☎212/757-2233. This is a good place to linger over a coffee or a meal – a rarity in midtown. The menu offers a range of burgers, soups, salads, pastas, and average French-tinged brasserie standards (stick with the simpler items on the menu). Large outdoor seating area. Open 24 hours.

Cupcake Café 522 Ninth Ave, at W 39th St ☎212/465-1530. A delightful, if shabby, little joint, offering great cakes, cupcakes, and pies, as well as decent soups and sandwiches at bargain prices. Anything with fruit is a must, and the birthday cake with buttercream frosting is a city fave.

La Maison du Chocolat 30 Rockefeller Concourse, between 49th and 50th sts ☎212/265-9404. The French vibe here is palpable: the original *Maison* is in Paris. The three hot chocolates on the menu are so thick you'll need a spoon to eat them (but they're not as sweet as you might expect). Their fruit plates, chock-full of market-fresh berries, grapefruit, and pineapple, are must-tastes too.

Poseidon Bakery 629 Ninth Ave, between W 44th and 45th sts ☎212/757-6173. Known best for the phyllo dough hand-rolled on the premises and supplied to many of the city's restaurants, *Poseidon* also sells decadent *baklava*, strudel, cookies, spinach-and-meat pies, and assorted other sweet Greek pastries. Closed Sun and Mon.

Sandwiches and snacks

Little Pie Company 424 W 43rd St, between Ninth and Tenth aves ☎212/736-4780. True to its name, the *Little Pie Company* serves pies to die for. The peach-raspberry, available only in summer, has earned quite a passionate following. Unfortunately, there never seem to be quite enough pastries to go around and they often sell out around mid-afternoon; if you're on your own, pick up a five-inch personal pie and let everyone else fight over the bigger ones.

Soup Kitchen International 259a W 55th St, between Seventh and Eighth aves ☎212/757-7730. The real-life version of *Seinfeld*'s Soup Nazi establishment, with rich blends that range from spicy chilis to cool fruit soups to lobster bisque. All highly priced but worth it. Closed in summer.

Upper East Side

Bakeries and cafés

Café Sabarsky in the Neue Galerie 1048 Fifth Ave, at E 86th St ☎212/288-0665. Sumptuous décor that harkens back to Old Vienna fills the handsome parlor of the former Vanderbilt mansion. The menu reads like that of an upscale Eastern-European *Kaffeehaus*; it includes superb pastries, like Klimt torte and strudels, and small sand-wiches, many made with cured meats.

Payard Patisserie & Bistro 1032 Lexing-ton Ave, between 72nd and 73rd sts ☎212/717-5252. This is real French pastry – buttery, creamy, and over the top. The cookies, cakes, and crème brûlée are made to the exacting standards of the very finest Parisian patisseries, and while it's a bit pricey it's also worth every dime. The café is separate from the main dining room, and is a civilized place to stop for tea, coffee, and something sweet.

Rohrs, M. 303 E 85th St, between Second and Third aves ☎212/396-4456. Coffee connois-seurs say this cozy spot serves some of the city's best brews. The company has been around since 1896, but their current digs are fairly new.

Serendipity 3 225 E 60th St, between Second and Third aves ☎212/838-3531. Adorned with Tiffany lamps, this long-established eatery and ice-cream parlor has been a favorite spot for sweet-sixteen parties and first dates for years. The frozen hot chocolate, a trademarked and copyrighted recipe, is out of this world, and the wealth of ice cream offerings are a real treat, too.

▽ Serendipity 3

Wildgreen Café 1555 Third Ave, at 88th St ☎212/828-7656. A small-town feel adds to the draw of this shop "where natural foods become gourmet." It's justly known for its muffins, salads, wraps, and juices.

Upper East Side

CAFÉS AND LIGHT MEALS

(24)

Pizza by the slice

New Yorkers are passionate about their pizza, but that's where agreement on the topic largely ends. There are many strongly held opinions when it comes to **defining a good slice**, and one man's mozzarella epiphany is often his neighbor's tasteless cardboard triangle. Fortunately, the city is home to restaurants that serve all kinds of delicious variations on the theme, from hunky pieces smothered in red sauce and dripping with cheese to cornmeal-dusted dough with gourmet toppings to authentic Neapolitan pizza with wafer-thin crusts. Here are some places to sample New York's myriad pizza possibilities:

Mariella Pizza 151 E 60th St, between Lexington and Third aves ☎212/319-5999; p.324

Patsy's Pizza 2287 First Ave, between 117th and 118th sts ☎212/534-9783; p.325

Ray's 27 Prince St, between Mott and Elizabeth sts ☎212/966-1960; p.316

Two Boots to Go West 75 Greenwich Ave, at Seventh Ave ☎212/633-9096; p.319

Vinnie's Pizza 285 Amsterdam Ave, between W 73rd and 74th sts ☎212/874-4382; p.325

Sandwiches and snacks

Googie's Diner 1491 Second Ave, at E 78th St ⊤212/717-1122. A long-time fave with Upper East Side yuppies, who flock here on weekends for the terrific brunches.

Mariella Pizza 151 E 60th St, between Lexington and Third aves ⊤212/319-5999. The fine, generously proportioned slices here are more like a full meal than a snack. A great spot to grab a bite while hoofing it around midtown.

Tal Bagels 333 E 86th St, between First and Second aves ⊤212/427-6811. The bagels may be a little too chewy, but the spread selection at this family institution is to die for, especially the smoked fish. Don't let the lines scare you; they move fast.

Upper West Side and Morningside Heights

Bakeries and cafés

Café Lalo 201 W 83rd St, between Amsterdam and Broadway ⊤212/496-6031. Reminiscent of Paris, down to the cramped tables and inconsistent service. Try the "shirred" eggs (made fluffy with a cappuccino machine) with all sorts of herbs and other add-ins, or the wonderful Belgian waffles. Great desserts, too.

Café Mozart 154 W 70th St, between Columbus Ave and Broadway ⊤212/595-9797. This faded old Viennese coffeehouse serves rich tortes and apple strudel, among dozens of other cavity-inducing items.

🏃 **Caffè la Fortuna 69 W 71st St, between Central Park W and Columbus Ave** ⊤212/724-5846. The walls in this dark and comfy café are covered with records and black-and-white photos of opera personalities. In warm weather, you can sip a coffee all day long in the shade of their peaceful garden. The Italian pastries are heavenly.

Edgar's Café 255 W 84th St, between West End Ave and Broadway ⊤212/496-6126. A pleasant coffeehouse with good (though expensive) desserts and light snacks, great hot cider in the winter, and well-brewed coffees and teas all the time. Named for Edgar Allan Poe, who at one time lived a block or so farther east on 84th Street.

Hadleigh's 1900 Broadway, between W 63rd and 64th sts ⊤212/580-0669. Imported edible delicacies and upscale sandwiches. Take your choices outside and eat at one of the shaded tables.

🏃 **Hungarian Pastry Shop 1030 Amsterdam Ave, between W 110th and 111th sts** ⊤212/866-4230. This simple, no-frills coffeehouse is a favorite with Columbia University affiliates. You can sip your espresso and read Proust all day if you like (madeleines, anyone?); the only problem is choosing among the pastries, cookies, and cakes, all made on the premises.

Sandwiches and snacks

Barney Greengrass 541 Amsterdam Ave, between 86th and 87th sts ⊤212/724-4707. The "sturgeon king" is an Upper West Side fixture; the deli (and restaurant) have been around since time began. The smoked-salmon section is a particular treat, and the cheese blintzes are tasty too.

EJ's Luncheonette 447 Amsterdam Ave, between W 81st and 82nd sts ⊤212/873-3444. This retro, family-friendly diner serves huge BLT sandwiches and the best Cobb salads in the city.

Fine & Schapiro 138 W 72nd St, between Broadway and Columbus Ave ⊤212/877-2721. Long-standing Jewish deli that's open for lunch and dinner and serves delicious old-fashioned kosher fare – an experience that's getting harder to find in New York. The chicken soup is also good.

Gray's Papaya 2090 Broadway, at W 72nd St ⊤212/799-0243. Open 24/7, this insanely popular hot-dog joint is an NYC institution, famous for their long-running "Recession Special": 2 dogs and a drink for $3. Call for their several other locations around the city.

It's a Wrap 2012 Broadway, between W 68th and 69th sts ⊤212/362-7922. The wrap sandwiches (stuffed and rolled flour tortillas) with funny names like "Fuhgedaboudit" (prosciutto, salami, and provolone) and "Cover me Brie" are more filling than you'd expect.

P&W Sandwich Shop 1030 Amsterdam Ave, between W 110th and 111th sts ⊤212/222-2245. A luncher run by the people from the *Hungarian Pastry Shop* next door (see opposite), serving a few good Eastern-European specialties.

Tom's Restaurant 2880 Broadway, at 112th St ☎212/864-6137. The greasy-spoon diner made famous by *Seinfeld*. This corner eatery, where Jerry, George, Elaine, and Kramer kvetched about nothing, is no great shakes, food-wise, but the prices almost make up for the quality. Often filled with Columbia University students who come for the great breakfast deals (under $6).

Vinnie's Pizza 285 Amsterdam Ave, between W 73rd and 74th sts ☎212/874-4382. These are the best, cheesiest pizzas on the Upper West Side, and some of the best in the whole city. They're also surprisingly cheap – a plain slice is $2.

Zabar's 2245 Broadway, at W 80th St ☎212/787-2000, ⓦwww.zabars.com. An Upper West Side institution, this beloved family store offers a quintessential taste of New York: bagels, lox, and all manner of schmears, as well as a dizzying selection of gourmet goods at reasonable prices.

Harlem and above

Bakeries and cafés

M & G Diner 383 W 125th St, between Morningside and St Nicholas aves ☎212/864-7326. Ideally located for a filling breakfast (try the pancakes) before a day of touring Harlem, this soul-food diner is also great for a plate of fried chicken before closing time – which sometimes never arrives.

New Leaf Café 1 Margaret Corbin Drive, Fort Tyron Park ☎212/568-5323. An airy, renovated 1930s building with views of Fort Tyron Park, the *New Leaf* offers very reasonably priced and fresh dishes like arugula-stuffed ravioli, mostly to visitors coming from the nearby Cloisters. Closed Mon and Tues.

Patsy's Pizza 2287 First Ave, between 117th and 118th sts ☎212/534-9783. Legend has it that Frank Sinatra craved their thin-crust pies so badly he had them flown out to Hollywood. Around since the 1930s, this is one of the last vestiges of Italian Harlem. Unlike most of the old-fashioned thin-crust pie joints, they offer slices to go.

Saurin Parke Café 301 W 110th St, between Manhattan Ave and Frederick Douglass Blvd ☎212/222-0683. If your ramble through Central Park leaves you at its northwest corner, plop down on a leather chair at this roomy café for an excellent coffee or grilled sandwich.

CAFÉS AND LIGHT MEALS

㉔

Ice cream

There's a whole range of rich and delicious choices that fall under the great "**ice cream**" canopy in New York City. In recent years, ice-cream makers have become more creative, and there's a growing emphasis on fresh ingredients. Gelato, the dense Italian ice cream made with less air than its American counterpart, has entered the everyday lexicon, with sorbets, Italian "ices" (shaved ice with flavored syrups), and frozen yogurt following close behind as lighter options. The current craze is Tasti D-Lite, a low-calorie ice cream alternative available on almost every city block. As a departure from the chain-store ice creams (Ben & Jerry's, Häagen-Dazs) found in freezers everywhere, check out the following establishments:

Chinatown Ice Cream Factory 65 Bayard St, between Mott and Elizabeth sts ☎212/608-4170; p.316

Ciao Bella Gelato 285 Mott St, at Houston ☎212/431-3591; p.316

Gerri's Ice Cream 3974 White Plains Rd, at 225th St, Bronx ☎718/652-8095; p.328

Il Laboratorio del Gelato 95 Orchard St, at Broome St ☎212/343-9922; p.317

Ralph's Famous Italian Ices 501 Port Richmond Ave, at Catherine St, Staten Island ☎718/273-3675; p.328

Brooklyn

Fulton Ferry District and DUMBO

Almondine 85 Water St, at Main St ☏**718/797-5026.** This reasonably priced patisserie produces all kinds of buttery, flaky treats, as well as sandwiches on crusty baguettes. Closed Tues.

Brooklyn Ice Cream Factory 1 Water St, at the Fulton Ferry pier ☏**718/246-3963.** An old fireboat house contains the perfect reward for the walk across the Brooklyn Bridge: super-rich ice cream with toppings created by the pastry chef at the neighboring *River Café*. Closed Mon.

Jacques Torres Chocolate 66 Water St ☏**718/875-9772.** Warm up in winter with the super-thick hot chocolate, enjoy a flaky *pain au chocolat*, or just pig out on truffles.

Brooklyn Heights

Bedouin Tent 405 Atlantic Ave, at Bond St ☏**718/852-5555.** Original and best branch of a small Middle-Eastern chain. Try the *merguez* sandwich or one of the "pitzas," made on fluffy home-made pita bread ($5). The same owners operate *Tutt Café*, 47 Hicks St, at Cranberry St (☏718/722-7777), in the center of Brooklyn Heights.

Montague Street Bagels 108 Montague St, at Hicks St ☏**718/237-2512.** Brisk service and fantastic, doughy bagels. Perfect place to grab a snack before heading down to the Esplanade and parking yourself on a bench. Avoid the coffee, though. Open 24 hours.

Fort Greene

🏃 **Cake Man Raven Confectionery 708A Fulton St, at Hanson Place** ☏**718/694-CAKE.** The Cake Man is best known for his stunning red velvet cake, which he has baked for everyone from Harry Belafonte to Spike Lee. You can also pick up a delicious coconut cream pie and other sweets.

Cobble Hill and Carroll Gardens

D'Amico Foods 309 Court St, between Sackett and Degraw sts ☏**718/875-5403.** All sorts of Italian provisions, but best known for its espresso, served since 1948. Closed Sun.

Panino'teca 275 Smith St, between Sackett and Degraw sts ☏**718/237-2728.** Affordable and tasty pressed Italian sandwiches – as well as white-bread *tramezzini*, salads, and *bruschette*, served at an old wooden bar. Closed Mon.

Robin des Bois 195 Smith St, between Warren and Baltic sts ☏**718/596-1609.** Stop in at this antiques shop/café for a filling *croque-monsieur* or the "Sherwood Special," a charcuterie selection served on a rustic wood board. A pretty garden out back continues the forest theme.

Park Slope

Chip Shop 383 Fifth Ave, at 6th St ☏**718/832-7701.** Upscale chippie beloved by UK expats as well as non-carb-conscious New Yorkers. Kid-friendly atmosphere. Another branch in Brooklyn Heights, 129 Atlantic Ave, between Clinton and Henry sts.

Leaf & Bean 83 Seventh Ave, between Union St and Berkeley Place ☏**718/638-5791.** Exotic coffees and teas plus excellent homemade soups and gourmet truffle candies. Brunch for about $12 on weekends. Outdoor seating when the weather cooperates.

🏃 **Living Room Café 188 Prospect Park W, between 14th and 15th sts** ☏**718/369-0824.** Fun, cozy place where the locals go

▽ Nathan's, Coney Island

for strong coffee and a good selection of teas. It really does feel like home.

Bay Ridge

Hinsch's Confectionery 8515 Fifth Ave, between 85th and 86th sts ☎718/748-2854. A Bay Ridge icon, as famous for its ice cream (try the fresh strawberry syrup topping) and old-fashioned diner food as for its beautiful, unchanged luncheonette setting.

Coney Island

Nathan's 1310 Surf Ave, at Stillwell Ave, Coney Island ☎718/946-2202. Right there when you get off the subway, this is the home of the "famous Coney Island hot dog." Serving since 1916, *Nathan's* holds an annual Hot Dog Eating Contest on July 4.

Williamsburg

Bliss 191 Bedford Ave, between N 6th and N 7th sts ☎718/599-2547. Vegans can get their fix at this crunchy, no-meat, no-dairy spot. They even serve a full vegan breakfast. Others might find the fare a little bland.

Egg/Sparky's American Food 135 N 5th St, between Bedford Ave and Berry St ☎718/302-5151. From 7am, Williamsburg's few early risers enjoy *Egg*'s all-breakfast menu with hearty plates like biscuits and gravy; after noon, *Sparky*'s does high-end hot dogs, milk shakes, and more.

Fortunato Brothers 289 Manhattan Ave, at Devoe St ☎718/387-2281. Old World Italian coffee shop with character to spare.

Supercore 305 Bedford Ave, between S 1st and S 2nd sts ☎718/302-1629. Standard hipster coffee hangout, with an added layer of Japanese cool – you can get some home-style *beni-tori* (chicken soup), as well as a cappuccino and a goat-cheese sandwich.

Queens

Astoria and Long Island City

Athens Café 32-01 30th Ave, Astoria ☎718/626-2164. The place to see and be seen on 30th Ave. On warm days the prime sidewalk tables are packed full of young Greeks all nursing frappes – foamy, Greek-style iced coffees. It's also great for spinach pies and desserts.

🏃 **Café Kolonaki** 3302 Broadway, Astoria ☎718/932-8222. Catering to an elderly Greek crowd on the ground floor and hipper twenty-somethings upstairs, this staple on Astoria's main drag is a great spot for a strong coffee or pastry after dinner at one of the many nearby restaurants. Treat yourself to the tiramisu.

🏃 **Djerdan** 34-04 31st Ave, Astoria ☎718/721-2694. *Burek* – savory meat or cheese pies – are the specialty of this Bosnian house. Try the "special" version, drizzled with garlicky yogurt.

Lounge 47 47-10 Vernon Blvd, Long Island City ☎718/937-2044. LIC's unofficial living room, this funky café and bar offers simple American basics like mac and cheese and juicy hamburgers, as well as more international morsels, like Indian pakoras and a lamb sandwich with yogurt sauce.

Jackson Heights and Corona

Empanadas del Parqe 56-27 Van Doren St, at 108th St, Corona ☎718/592-7288. Traditional Latin-American meat-filled pies are just the tip of the iceberg. Sample the Italian-ish combos, then have a milk caramel for dessert. Nothing costs more than $1.50.

Shaheen's Sweets & Cuisine 72-09 Broadway, Jackson Heights ☎718/639-4791. Pakistani treats, many sticky and syrup-soaked, along with chai.

Flushing

🏃 **Sweet-n-Tart Café** 136-11 38th St, at Main St ☎718/661-3380. Wonderfully cheap and popular Chinese café with a modern vibe, but also authentic dishes like congee, braised noodles, and sautéed duck tongue. For an afternoon refresher, try anything from the *tong shui* ("sweet soup") category – hot, milky almond tea is especially rich and delicious. Open till midnight daily.

(24)

The Bronx

Gerri's Ice Cream 3974 White Plains Rd, at 225th St ☎718/652-8095. For over three decades, Gerri has been serving up ice cream inspired by the local Caribbean community. Go for the unusual treat of a soursop ice-cream cone, or one of the many other island flavors. East of Woodlawn Cemetery, at E 225th St.

The Feeding Tree 892 Gerard Ave, at 161st St ☎718/293-5025. Wash down the spicy jerk chicken at this friendly Jamaican takeout spot with a cool sorrel drink. Plenty of vegetarian options too.

Staten Island

Ralph's Famous Italian Ices 501 **Port Richmond Ave, at Catherine St** ☎718/273-3675. In business since 1928, this beloved place has spawned a few franchises. Its unusual and wide selection of water ices (honeydew, root beer, and blueberry) and sherbets (spumoni, cremalata, and cannoli) have won many a heart and taste bud.

Restaurants

A large part of visiting New York City is experiencing not just the food but the **culture of dining**. As a port city, New York has long received the best foodstuffs from around the globe and, as a major immigration gateway, it continues to attract chefs who know how to cook all the world's cuisines properly, even exceptionally, as well as populations who know the real thing. Then there are the "foodies," locals who make it their business to seek out the best, most unique, and newest dining establishments in the city, and aren't shy about sharing the fruits of their labors. Travelers will soon find that restaurant-hopping is one of the city's most popular pastimes.

This chapter includes eateries that offer everything from fried chicken to foie gras (and sometimes both), though you should keep in mind that New York's culinary scene is extremely dynamic – even the most food-obsessed locals have a hard time keeping up. Restaurants are always opening and closing, and the establishment *du jour* can change in the blink of an eye; gastronomes and those on the prowl for something new turn to publications like *Time Out New York*, *New York* magazine, or the *New York Times*' Wednesday *Dining Out* section for the lowdown on what's good. More serious foodies dig a little deeper and look to sites on the Web, like Ⓦ www.chowhound.com, Ⓦ www.citysearch.com, and Ⓦ www.dailycandy.com, for opinions and leads on sizzling new chefs and gourmet hotspots. For travelers, the most important aspect of plumbing the city's diverse culinary landscape, though, is having a sense of adventure – eating is one of the great joys of being in New York, and it would be a shame to waste time on the familiar.

Cuisines

American cooking is an umbrella term for a vast array of dishes. It includes such standards as steaks, burgers, fried chicken, and macaroni and cheese, but it also refers to menus that highlight local and seasonal ingredients, and recipes that draw on years of tradition as well as new culinary concepts. You'll find many American restaurants offering a rich array of regional specialties: everything from New England clam chowder and Cajun jambalaya to Southern grits and Southwestern barbecue ribs. **Continental** cuisine is generally a hybrid of American, Italian, and French influences, featuring pastas, meats, poultry, and fish or seafood in light sauces and a variety of nightly specials.

You'll encounter an astonishing range of **ethnic cuisines**. **Chinese** food, at its best in Chinatown but available all over the city, is comprised of familiar Cantonese dishes as well as spicier Sichuan and Hunan ones – most restaurants specialize in one of the three. **Japanese** food runs the price gamut from super cheap to extremely expensive; there are a plethora of sushi establishments in

Specialty eating

We've highlighted particular types of restaurants and listed them in boxes in the text. We've also picked out a few favorites in the city, which is very hard to do; most of the places recommended in this chapter are exactly that – recommended – though this might give you an easy guide:

Favorites
Burgers p.331
Haute cuisine p.351
Pizza (by the pie) p.353
Quintessential New York p.343
Sushi p.332

Types
Brunch p.346
Restaurants with views p.348
Vegetarian restaurants p.334

the city. Other Asian cuisines are also in abundance, including **Indian** (best in Jackson Heights, Queens), **Indonesian**, **Korean**, **Thai**, and **Vietnamese**.

Italian cooking is widespread and not terribly expensive, especially if you stick to pizza or pasta. **French** restaurants tend to be pricier, although there are an increasing number of bistros and brasseries turning out less costly but authentic and reliable French dishes.

There is also a whole range of **Eastern European** restaurants – Russian, Ukrainian, Polish, and Hungarian – that serve well-priced, filling fare (emphasis on the filling), including *pierogi* (meat-, potato-, or cheese-stuffed dumplings). Nothing dominates New York's culinary scene more than **Jewish food**, to the extent that many specialties – bagels, pastrami, lox, and cream cheese – are common fare.

Central and South American and **Caribbean** restaurants are a steadily growing presence in New York. The large, satisfying, frequently spicy meals on offer are often good deals.

While the **fusion** fad, combining influences and ingredients from different foreign cuisines (often Asian), has waned, there are still places featuring hybrids like Chinese-Peruvian and Japanese-Brazilian. Numerous **vegetarian** and **wholefood** eateries cater to any taste or health trend.

Financial District and City Hall area

Financial District restaurants cater to Wall Street crowds: most are takeout feeding troughs or overpriced power-lunch spots. Locals tend to deem this part of town a culinary wasteland; we've included some places that prove the exception to that rule. Remember, the neighborhood revolves around trading hours at the stock exchange (8am–4pm), so many restaurants close early and either have reduced hours or are closed on weekends.

American and Continental

Bridge Café 279 Water St, at Dover St ☎212/227-3344. You wouldn't guess from this café-restaurant's up-to-the-minute interior that it is the city's oldest surviving tavern, dating from 1794. The crabcakes are excellent, as is the list of microbrew beers. Entrees $20–30.

Church & Dey Millennium Hilton, 55 Church St, 3rd floor ☎212/312-2000. The immense dining room at this casual American brasserie overlooks the World Trade Center site. The menu includes first-rate regional favorites, as well as dishes like good old-fashioned meatloaf. The sea scallops with basil risotto cakes, and pecan pie are also standouts.

Delmonico's 56 Beaver St, at William St ☎212/509-1144. Many a million-dollar deal has been made at this 1837 landmark steakhouse (check out the pillars from Pompeii). Patrons tend to come more for its historic charms – including classic dishes like Lobster Newburg and Baked Alaska (which was invented here) – than its pricey Porterhouses. Closed Sat.

Paris Café 119 South St ☎212/240-9797. Established in 1873, this old-fashioned bar and restaurant has played host to a panoply of luminaries, from Thomas Edison to Buffalo Bill. These days, the elegant square bar, tempting seafood specials, outdoor seating, and stellar views of the Brooklyn Bridge still pull in a lively crowd, mostly tourists; entrees $15–25.

Steamer's Landing 375 South End Ave, between Albany and Liberty sts ☎212/432-1451. Outdoor terraces and great views of the Hudson make this a fine spot to enjoy dishes like the delicious seafood stew ($24), though it can get crowded during peak dining times.

French

Bayard 1 Hanover Square, at Pearl St ☎212/514-9454. In the 1851 India House,

this maritime-themed French-American restaurant earns rave reviews for its inspired seasonal cuisine (past standouts have included an autumnal venison with poached pears and a spring rack of lamb with a honey-mustard glaze), expert service, and "Gilded Age" atmosphere. Be forewarned: such features warrant high prices.

Brasserie Les Halles 15 John St, between Broadway and Nassau St ☎212/285-8585. One of two *Les Halles* in New York, this French bistro serves "French Beef, American Style." The Rive Gauche fantasy of *Kitchen Confidential* chef Anthony Bourdain, the menu strives for authenticity but often ends up including over-the-top Gallic dishes, like escargots in garlic butter and duck confit shepherd's pie. Entrees $20–30.

Italian

Carmine's Bar and Grill 140 Beekman St, at Front St ☎212/962-8606. In business since 1903, this decently priced place specializes in Northern Italian–style seafood and exudes a comfortable, if run-down, ambience. Try a glass of the house wine and a bowl of linguini in clam sauce.

Quartino 21–23 Peck Slip, at Water St ☎212/349-4433. Slightly off the beaten path, this eatery features wholesome dishes from the Liguria region of Italy, like authentic home-made pappardelle with pesto ($12) and a tuna appetizer with string beans and potatoes ($8). Desserts include a small selection of creamy *gelati* ($5).

Latin American

Radio Mexico 259 Front St, at Dover St ☎212/791-5416. Decent Tex-Mex food in enjoyable surroundings, though the nearby South Street Seaport often draws large crowds. It's the only place in ten blocks to get good margaritas. Entrees are moderately priced – try the fish tacos.

Tribeca

While **Tribeca**'s enclave of very fine restaurants have long attracted Manhattan's "beautiful people," dining in this part of town can leave serious eaters hungry for both a better selection and quality. Most eating establishments are fairly upscale, and you often pay for the view, the overly decorated dining room, or the prospect of dining in famous company rather than the victuals. A bit of exploration will almost certainly turn up a delicious and decently priced meal, but you have to be willing to look for it.

American and Continental

Bread Tribeca 301 Church St, at Walker St ☎212/334-8282. During the day, this spot features a great selection of toothsome sandwiches served on crusty bread. At dinner, the mixed fried seafood ($15) and pasta with fresh clams ($18) get raves, though the patrons who flock here for the evening meal can be overbearing.

Bubby's 120 Hudson St, between Franklin and N Moore sts ☎212/219-0666. A relaxed place serving American comfort food, like matzoh-ball soup ($8) and pulled pork ($13). It's the pies, though, that really pull in the crowds – try a slice of the Key Lime. The weekend brunch menu is very popular.

City Hall 131 Duane St, between Church St and W Broadway ☎212/227-7777. With a nod toward old-time New York City, *City Hall* is all class, serving amazing steaks and always-fresh oysters. Though a little pricey, the open-room ambience, great service, and frequent opportunities to rub shoulders with celebs make the splurge worth it. Look to spend $50 per person.

TriBeCa Grill 375 Greenwich St, at Franklin St ☎212/941-3900. The *Grill* is owned by Robert De Niro; no doubt some people come for a glimpse of the actor, though it's really the food – fine American cooking with Asian and Italian accents – they should be concentrating on. The setting is nice, too: an airy, brick-walled eating area around a central Tiffany bar. Entrees are around $30.

Asian

66 241 Church St, between Worth and Leonard sts ☎212/925-0202. Located in the Textile Building – one of Tribeca's most beautiful historic structures – this Chinese hotspot serves inspired fusion dishes with influences from a variety of provinces. Communal tables make the atmosphere lively and you can peek in on the master chefs as they work – there's a window into the kitchen. Menu highlights include sweet corn and crab soup ($8), squab à l'orange ($14), and lobster sautéed in black-bean sauce ($28).

Nobu 105 Hudson St, at Franklin St ☎212/219-0500. *Nobu*'s lavish woodland décor complements its superlative Japanese cuisine. Try the black cod with miso – one of the city's best dishes – and chilled sake served in hollow bamboo trunks. Prices can be prohibitive, and reservations hard to get; if you can't get in, try your luck at the somewhat less expensive *Next Door Nobu*, located just next door.

Austrian

Danube 30 Hudson St, between Duane and Reade sts ☎212/791-3771. Old Vienna lives on: schnitzel is taken to heavenly heights at this opulent pastry-puff of a restaurant. It's expensive, but a terrific spot for an evening on the town.

French and Belgian

Bouley 120 W Broadway, between Duane and Reade sts ☎212/964-2525. Modern French food made from the freshest ingredients by one of the city's most storied chiefs, Daniel Bouley. Popular with city celebs, the prices are fairly steep; soften costs by opting for one of the prix-fixe options.

Chanterelle 2 Harrison St, at Hudson St ☎212/966-6960. Some say that visitors to New York should live on stale bread, then spend all their money here. The haute French cuisine (options include roast asparagus with black truffles and *crêpinette* of guinea hen) is of the finest order, and the wines are so rare that patrons are advised to reserve a bottle ahead of time so that it can be properly decanted. Very pricey.

Petite Abeille 134 W Broadway, between Duane and Thomas sts ☎212/791-1360. *Tintin* comic

Rough Guide favorites

Sushi
Bond Street East Village, p.338
Donguri Upper East Side, p.351
Hasaki East Village, p.339
Omen Soho, p.334
Sushi of Gari Upper East Side, p.352
Tomoe Sushi West Village, p.341

books cover the walls at this nice little Belgian spot. It's notable for its $16 special of mussels, *pommes frites*, and a beer; on Wednesdays the mussels are all-you-can-eat. The menu also includes a fine selection of Continental drafts.

Greek

Delphi 109 W Broadway, at Reade St ☎212/227-6322. The solid menu, great portions, and unbeatable prices at this accommodating restaurant make it the best place in Manhattan for bargain Greek eating. Try the antipasti and fish ($11–13), kebabs ($14), or sandwiches ($7 and up).

Latin American

Sosa Borella 460 Greenwich St, between Desbrosses and Watts sts ☎212/431-5093. Tucked away on a quiet sidestreet, this moderately priced Argentine-Italian eatery is a longtime favorite of locals. Call to ask about tango nights, but go any time for its savory miniature pizzas or hearty brunch.

South Asian

Pakistan Tea House 176 Church St, at Reade St ☎212/240-9800. Great, cheap Pakistani tandooris, baltis, and curries. The staff will also create made-to-order flatbreads. Main dishes average $12.

Soho

Though best known for its posh boutiques and upscale galleries, a number of the city's top restaurants still make their home here. While in the heart of Soho you should expect to pay top dollar for the more venerable hotspots. A pilgrimage to this area is especially warranted if you're looking for great fresh seafood.

American and Continental

Aquagrill 210 Spring St, at Sixth Ave ☎212/274-0505. The moderately expensive seafood at this cozy Soho spot is so fresh it's practically still flopping. The raw bar and Sunday brunch are excellent, yet not prohibitively priced. Oysters run around $2 a pop, clams $1.

Cupping Room Café 359 W Broadway, between Broome and Grand sts ☎212/925-2898. Snuggle in at this affordable American bistro for comfort food, but avoid visiting on weekends – the brunch line can stretch around the block. Good bets are the blackened cod with chickpeas and eggplant ($20) or Mediterranean rice and lentils with yogurt ($13). Live music on Wednesday and Friday nights.

Mercer Kitchen *Mercer Hotel*, 99 Prince St, at Mercer St ☎2122/966-5454. This hip basement eatery entices hotel guests and scenesters alike with the casual creations of Jean-Georges Vongerichten, who makes ample use of his raw bar and wood-burning oven. Try the roasted lamb sandwich ($15). Pricey, but a guaranteed good time.

Moondance Diner 80 Sixth Ave, between Grand and Canal sts ☎212/226-1191. This authentic old diner car turns out cheap and filling meals, including great burgers, onion rings, omelets, and apple cinnamon pancakes ($7). Open 24 hours on weekends, to midnight all other nights.

Spring Street Natural Restaurant 62 Spring St, at Lafayette St ☎212/966-0290. Though not wholly vegetarian, this restaurant serves up freshly prepared health-food in a large, airy space. Try the "Mayan" eggs ($8), served with tortillas, black beans, and guacamole, for brunch. The heavy crowds hinder the service, which is invariably slow.

Asian

Blue Ribbon Sushi 119 Sullivan St, between Prince and Spring sts ☎212/343-0404. Though the sushi is excellent, the focus here is actually more on the outstanding raw bar, with a wide selection of oysters, littleneck clams, and other tempting bivalves. They don't take reservations and the lines for a table can be long, but never fear: the kitchen is open until 2am.

Cendrillon 45 Mercer St, between Broome and Grand sts ☎212/343-90123. This fine pan-Asian restaurant, run by a passionate Filipino couple, serves consistently

RESTAURANTS | Soho

㉕

333

exceptional food (try the vinegary *adobo*; $10), not to mention creative cocktails with rare fruits and spice infusions ($8–10). The prices are decent, and the desserts swoon-worthy.

Kelley and Ping 127 Greene St, between Prince and Houston sts ☎212/228-1212. Sleek pan-Asian tearoom and restaurant that serves tasty bowls of noodle soup and other dishes at moderate prices. Dark wood cases filled with Thai herbs and cooking ingredients add to the casual setting, which feels a bit like a bustling market.

Omen 113 Thompson St, at Prince St ☎212/925-8923. Traditional Kyoto eatery with lovely decorative touches, including beautiful crockery and menus made from rice paper. Though named for a noodle dish, it serves by far the best sushi in the area (try the bluefin sashimi platter; $25), with a rotating seasonal menu and an extensive sake list. Salmon and fig ($25), cucumber and eel ($8), and tuna tartare ($19) are favorites. If you only go to one Japanese restaurant in New York, make it this one.

French

Balthazar 80 Spring St, between Crosby St and Broadway ☎212/965-1414. After years in operation, this is still one of the hottest restaurants in town. The tastefully ornate Parisian décor keeps your eyes busy until the food arrives; then all you can do is savor the fresh shellfish and exquisite pastries. A meal here is well worth the money. Entrees $17–30.

L'Ecole 462 Broadway, at Grand St ☎212/219-3300. Students of the French Culinary Institute serve up affordable French delights at *L'Ecole* – even the bread basket deserves reverence. The three-course prix-fixe dinner is $30 per person for dinner, $21 for lunch; book in advance. Closed Sun.

Le Jardin Bistro 25 Cleveland Place, between Kenmare and Spring sts ☎212/343-9599. A romantic spot, this unpretentious bistro boasts a trellised garden in the back and reliably good fare, including cassoulet and fresh seafood. Prices are moderate for the neighborhood, with entrees around $18.

Provence 38 MacDougal St, between Prince and Houston sts ☎212/475-7500. This very popular Soho bistro serves excellent seafood, including a delicious coquilles St Jacques. It features a lovely, airy eating area and a garden for the summer, as well as a wait-staff with thick French accents. Main dishes $18–25.

Raoul's 180 Prince St, between Sullivan and Thompson sts ☎212/966-3518. *Raoul's* is a sexy French bistro seemingly lifted from Paris. The food, especially the steak au poivre ($30) and the artichoke vinaigrette ($8), is wonderful – a fact your wallet won't let you forget. The service is great, too. Reservations recommended. Closed Aug.

Italian

Mezzogiorno 195 Spring St, at Sullivan St ☎212/334-2112. This bright Soho restaurant is as much a place to people-watch as it is a place to eat. The good and inventive menu, including excellent pizzas ($13–16), great salads ($10–14), and carpaccio (thinly sliced raw beef served in various ways; $15) make up for the slightly higher prices.

Vegetarian restaurants

Anjelica Kitchen 300 E 12th St, between First and Second aves ☎212/228-2909; p.340

Great American Health Bar 35 W 57th St, between Fifth and Sixth aves ☎212/355-5177; p.351

Madras Mahal 104 Lexington Ave, between E 27th and 28th sts ☎212/684-4010; p.345

Souen 210 Sixth Ave, at Prince St ☎212/807-7421; p.343

Spring Street Natural Restaurant 62 Spring St, at Lafayette St ☎212/966-0290; p.333

Chinatown, Little Italy, and NoLita

If you're after authentic (not to mention affordable) Chinese, Thai, or Vietnamese food, head for the bustling streets of **Chinatown**, where you can sample a little bit of everything. Weekends are especially busy, as New Yorkers come to this neighborhood for *dim sum* brunch, literally "your heart's delight" in Cantonese. Not surprisingly, Chinese food dominates the area, and the streets are lined with dumpling houses, windows festooned with roasted Peking ducks, and regional mom-and-pop eateries.

Mulberry Street is **Little Italy**'s main drag, and though often crowded with weekend tourists from New Jersey and Westchester County, the mostly Southern Italian eateries and carnival-like atmosphere can make for an entertaining dinner or dessert excursion. It's best not to have high culinary hopes for the neighborhood, however: Little Italy's many red-sauce restaurants are fair, but not great.

The **NoLita** strip at the north end of Little Italy is notable for its popular budget restaurants, which are often packed to the gills with aspiring fashionistas and film-industry hipsters.

African

Ghenet 284 Mulberry St, between Houston and Prince sts ☎212/343-1888. This atmospheric and relatively inexpensive Ethiopian restaurant serves a changing menu of unusual spicy dishes that you eat with your hands and sop up with a cold, sponge-like bread. Utensils are available on request, though they seem vaguely frowned upon by the waitstaff.

American and Continental

Rialto 265 Elizabeth St, between Houston and Prince sts ☎212/334-7900. Serious home-style American cooking in unlikely surroundings – an elegant room filled with curved red-leather banquettes and frequented by beautiful, chic people. The food isn't as expensive as the clientele might have you believe, though: a burger will run you around $10, a steak frite $18.

Asian

Big Wong 67 Mott St, between Bayard and Canal sts ☎212/964-0540. This cheap, cafeteria-style Cantonese BBQ joint serves some of Chinatown's tastiest duck and congee (savory rice stew).

Bo Ky 80 Bayard St, between Mott and Mulberry sts ☎212/406-2292. The inexpensive noodle soups are very good at this cramped Chinese-Vietnamese eatery. The house specialty is a big bowl of rice noodles with shrimp, fish, or duck.

Excellent Dumpling House 111 Lafayette St, between Canal and Walker sts ☎212/219-0212. The dumplings at this busy Chinese restaurant are excellent – they come filled with meat or vegetables, and in soup – but they aren't the only things on offer. Everything else is tasty, too; try the fried scallion pancake. Prices are low enough that you could sample a number of dishes.

Kitchen Club 30 Prince St, at Mott St ☎212/274-0025. This oddly integrated Japanese-Dutch eatery features an eclectic, if somewhat expensive, menu. Entrees include miso-marinated steak with huckleberries, and the dessert menu features Linzer torte; the sake list at the adjacent bar is also good. You can often see the restaurant's friendly owner cruising the tables with her French bulldog.

Lovely Day 196 Elizabeth St, between Prince and Spring sts ☎212/925-3310. Frequented by the Soho/Lower East Side hipster set, this budget restaurant is jam-packed and lively at all hours. The Asian-leaning menu lists nicely priced pad thai, satays, and grilled pork chops with roasted apples.

New York Noodletown 28 Bowery, at Bayard St ☎212/349-0923. Noodletown is best during soft-shell crab season (May–Aug), when the crustaceans are crispy, salty, and delicious. The roast meats and soups are good year-round (try the baby pig). Entrees $8–10.

Nha Trang 87 Baxter St, between Bayard and Canal sts ☎212/233-5948. Despite the rushed service, this Chinese-Vietnamese restaurant offers some of the neighborhood's most

RESTAURANTS | ㉕

delicious and affordable meals. The chefs specialize in seafood dishes.

Nyonya 194 Grand St, between Mott and Mulberry sts ☎212/334-3669. The grub at this Malaysian restaurant is superb, and comes at wallet-friendly prices. Try the chicken curry, spicy squid, or clay-pot noodles. If you're in the mood for something sweeter, order some coconut milk – it's served chilled in the shell.

Peking Duck House 28 Mott St, between Chatham Square and Pell St ☎212/227-1810. This chic and shiny-clean eatery dishes up – you guessed it – duck; the crispy fried birds are carved tableside. If you can ignore the shouts of the commanding owner, you're in for an amazing meal. It's slightly more expensive than other neighborhood restaurants, but worth it.

Ping's Seafood 22 Mott St, between Chatham Square and Pell St ☎212/602-9988. While this Hong Kong–style seafood restaurant is good any time, it's most enjoyable on weekends for *dim sum*, when carts of tasty, bite-size delicacies whir by every 30 seconds. This place offers superb bang for your buck.

Sun Hop Shin 21 Mott St, at Mosco St ☎212/267-2729. Not much to look at (really a diner) but this *dim sum* spot has some of the best seafood in Chinatown, including sizzling stir-fried calamari with salt.

Thailand Restaurant 106 Bayard St, at Baxter St ☎212/349-3132. Patrons at this restaurant eat well-priced Thai food at long communal tables. The whole-fish dishes, crispy and spicy, are standouts.

Italian

Ballato 55 E Houston, between Mulberry and Mott sts ☎212/274-8881. Serving by far the best Italian in the area, *Ballato* has a great low-key atmosphere, a spicy penne *arrabbiata*, tasty spaghetti vongole, and veal chops so tender they melt in your mouth.

Bianca 5 Bleecker St, between Bowery and Elizabeth St ☎212/260-4666. This great little Italian spot offers an array of excellent pastas, though most people come here for the delicious Mediterranean white fish and the fried artichokes – house specialties. It's a nice place for those who want an intimate dinner without a lot of the ambient noise found in other area eateries.

La Luna 112 Mulberry St, between Canal and Hester sts ☎212/226-8657. One of Little Italy's

longest-established restaurants, it's also one of the neighborhood's best values. Though the waiters are gruff and the food only middling, it's a popular place in the evening, and the atmosphere is quite fun.

Little Charlie's Clam Bar 19 Kenmare St, at Bowery ☎212/431-6443. The clams are delicious, but a full range of Southern Italian specialties is also available, including a standout lasagna and tasty sautéed shrimp with hot sauce. Great atmosphere and friendly staff.

🏃 **Lombardi's 32 Spring St, between Mott and Mulberry sts** ☎212/941-7994. The oldest pizzeria in Manhattan, *Lombardi*'s serves some of the best pies in town, including an amazing clam pizza; no slices, though. There's open-air dining upstairs.

▽ Lombardi's

Peasant 194 Elizabeth St, between Prince and Spring sts ☎212/965-9511. Patrons here should expect to pay $22–30 for self-consciously rustic and hearty grilled entrees, such as *osso buco* or grilled branzino, served from an open kitchen with a wood-burning oven. Closed Mon.

Latin American

Bar Bossa 232 Elizabeth St, between Prince and Houston sts ☎212/625-2340. The great ambience at this South American eatery complements the extremely yummy food, including tomato-laden *bruschette*, several outstanding fish dishes, and a very rich Guinness chocolate cake.

Café Colonial 276 Elizabeth St, at Houston St ☎212/274-0044. A low-key Brazilian café with good food. On weekends it's a top brunch spot for its omelets; at night go for

25

Ethnic
New York

Historically a gateway to America, New York City can stake a fair claim to being the most ethnically diverse metropolis in the world. A remarkable third of today's Americans can trace their roots to Ellis Island, in New York Harbor, where their ancestors arrived during the nineteenth and early twentieth centuries. Many immigrants stayed in New York and built a life in the city, with the result that just about every ethnic community in the United States is now present here. Ellis Island closed long ago, but as the largest city in America and its commercial hub, New York remains one of the principal magnets that draw people to the US, and the manifestation of the American Dream.

Downtown Manhattan

New York City is in some ways a giant processing machine – it assimilates its newcomers, and then they move on to other parts of the city or country. Nowhere is this more evident than

in downtown Manhattan, where neighborhoods settled by ethnic groups in the nineteenth century have long since become home to others. One exception is **Chinatown**, which has always been one of the city's most buoyant ethnic quarters. Recently bolstered by new immigration from mainland China and Hong Kong, as well as Vietnam, it is spilling over its traditional boundaries into nearby longstanding enclaves like Little Italy and the Jewish Lower East Side. Even though

▲ Ukrainian Museum

Little Italy now has only a handful of Italians – most former residents have relocated to Belmont, in the Bronx – it's still riotously decorated with red, white, and green. Eastern European Jews settled the **Lower East Side** in the nineteenth century, but the city's Jewish

Ethnic eats

For visitors, New York's ethnic diversity means not only interesting sites and cultural history, but also the chance to sample just about every cuisine imaginable. Try these neighborhoods for their top-notch ethnic fare.
Chinatown, for a *dim sum* brunch (see p.82)
The **Lower East Side** and the **Upper West Side**, for Jewish or American deli fare (see pp.93 and 204)
Brighton Beach (often called "Little Odessa"), in Brooklyn, for an authentic Russian supper club experience (see p.259)
Astoria, in Queens, for the best Greek dishes in the city (see p.270)
Jackson Heights, in Queens, for a red-meat fix at an Argentine steakhouse or curry in Little India (see p.272)
Flushing, in Queens, for Korean BBQ or Vietnamese noodle soups (see p.275)

population has dispersed over the last few decades, and the neighborhood has become increasingly Hispanic. Nonetheless, there are still remnants of the area's history: most, like knish shops, are food-related, but there is the odd synagogue or market in between the more common Puerto Rican delis and Chinese restaurants. Just north of the Lower East Side is the **East Village**, where the city's Ukrainian population has traditionally resided. The neighborhood also features a tiny enclave of Indian restaurants, though the city's largest Indian community is in Jackson Heights, Queens.

Uptown Manhattan

Midtown Manhattan is resolutely WASPish and white, as is the Upper East Side until 100th Street, where it becomes gritty **El Barrio**, or **Spanish Harlem**, the city's largest Puerto Rican neighborhood. The **Upper West Side**, on the other side of Central Park, retains vestiges of its roots as the home of a large Jewish population. North of the park, **Harlem** is the most famous African-American community in the United States. Vilified for years as a no-go area for whites, it is now enjoying something of a renaissance as its rows of

▲ Temple Emanu-El

beautiful brownstones are refurbished and big retailers snap up its commercial real estate. Still farther north, at the tip of Manhattan, lie **Washington Heights** and **Inwood**, thriving Hispanic neighborhoods with large Dominican populations.

Brooklyn

◄ Polish kielbasa store in Greenpoint

Today, many of New York's ethnic communities flourish in the outer boroughs. In Brooklyn, **Crown Heights** is home to both the city's largest West Indian population and a significant number of Hasidic Jews – at times it is an uneasy mix, but every year on Labor Day animosities are put on hold for the West Indian-American Day Parade and Carnival, one of the city's most colorful festivals. Trendy **Williamsburg** is similarly divided, as hipster galleries established in the last few years vie for space with the area's long-standing Jewish population and a small but growing Latino community. Just north of Williamsburg, **Greenpoint** is quieter, with an older Polish population. At

Parades and festivals

New York's ethnic communities celebrate their heritage in parades and festivals held throughout the year. Most last a day, but some go for a week – or even a month. Visitors to New York will be hard-pressed to miss these events, as they often take over whole neighborhoods and main transportation arteries. Some of the best are:

Lunar (Chinese) New Year, the first full moon between Jan 21 and Feb 19 (see p.440)
St Patrick's Day Parade, March 17 (see p.441)
Greek Independence Day Parade, late March (see p.441)
National Puerto Rican Day Parade, second Sun in June (see p.443)
West Indian-American Day Parade and Carnival, Labor Day (see p.445)
Feast of San Gennaro, ten days in mid–Sept (see p.445)

▲ National Puerto Rican Day Parade

the southern end of the island, oceanside **Brighton Beach**, sometimes called "Little Odessa," boasts the largest community of Russian immigrants in the United States, and is worth a visit for its restaurants, with their glamorous, over-the-top entertainment.

Queens and the Bronx

Queens, the city's largest borough, is also the most ethnically varied. In **Astoria**, just across the East River from midtown Manhattan, you'll find the largest number of Greeks in the world (outside of Greece, of course). Large communities of South Americans and South Asians live in **Jackson Heights**, and are slowly moving south into **Sunnyside** and **Woodside**, historically Irish neighborhoods. **Flushing** is known as the city's second Chinatown, though Koreans, Malaysians, and Vietnamese also make up a sizeable percentage of the population. In the Bronx, **Belmont** is now home to more Italians than Little Italy, and the main drag, Arthur Avenue, bustles with salumerias and Italian-American eateries.

▼ Greek storefronts in Astoria

the chicken Veracruz or the grilled tilapia. Avoid the steaks; their cuts are not the best. **Café Habana 17 Prince St, at Elizabeth St** ☎212/625-2001. Small and always crowded,

this Cuban–South American eatery features some of the best skirt steak ($11) and fried plantains ($3) this side of Havana. They also have a takeout window next door that serves great *café con leche*.

Lower East Side

The trendy **Lower East Side**, once dominated by immigrant tenements and sweatshops, has turned into something of a culinary destination, with **Clinton Street** as the main thoroughfare. Along this far-eastern drag you'll find some inviting gastronomic *boîtes*, such as *WD-50*, that have garnered dedicated fans for their sophisticated and unusual menus. There are also some terrific little Latin *comedores*, along with some stalwart old-time joints selling Jewish and Eastern European delicacies.

American and Continental

71 Clinton Fresh Food 71 Clinton St, between Rivington and Stanton sts ☎212/614-6960. Popular with foodies and hipsters alike, this cozy spot serves some of the best French-inflected food in the city. The mostly organic menu is strictly seasonal, with entrees averaging $25–30.

Schiller's Liquor Bar 131 Rivington St, at Norfolk St ☎212/260-4555. Fairly high-end restaurant made up to look like a Prohibition-era speakeasy. Menu offerings are eclectic and self-consciously "American," including pan-fried trout and pork chops smothered in sautéed onions.

WD-50 50 Clinton St, between Rivington and Stanton sts ☎212/477-2900. To critics, this experimental haute spot crammed into a retrofitted corner bodega is either the future of gourmet food or the emperor's new clothes. Sample the creations of chef Wylie DuFresne, of *71 Clinton Fresh Food*, who "goes diva" with unconventional entrees like venison tartare with edamame ice cream and pork belly with black soy beans and turnips, then decide for yourself.

Jewish

Katz's Deli 205 E Houston St, at Ludlow St ☎212/254-2246. *Katz*'s overstuffed pastrami or corned beef sandwiches, doused with mustard and complemented by a side pile of pickles, should keep you going for about a week. The egg creams are also delicious. Don't lose your meal ticket or you'll be charged an arm and a leg.

▽ Sammy's Roumanian Steakhouse

Sammy's Roumanian Steakhouse 157 Chrystie St, at Delancey St ☎212/673-0330. This basement Jewish steakhouse offers much more than many customers are prepared for, including schmaltzy songs, delicious-but-heartburn-inducing food (complete with home-made rugelach and egg creams for dessert), and vodka chilled in blocks of ice. Keep track of your tab, if you can, because bills can skyrocket quickly.

Latin American

El Cibao 72 Clinton St, at Rivington St ☎212/228-0873. *El Cibao* is the best of a slew of Dominican restaurants on the Lower East Side. The fare is hearty and inexpensive; the sandwiches, particularly the *pernil* (pork) toasted crisp in a sandwich press, are great.

East Village

Over time, the **East Village**'s mix of radicals, professionals, and immigrants has produced one of the most potent dining scenes in the city. While variety and quality are high, the prices here are a good bit lower than you'll find elsewhere in Manhattan. The range of culinary options makes dining in this neighborhood exciting: you can peruse menus on Indian Row; sample dishes at the handful of Ukrainian eateries; or go out on a limb and try something a little more off-beat, like Afghani, Tibetan, or Persian cuisine. Most New Yorkers come to the East Village for its American and Continental dining scene, which, while not as exotic, is far and away the best of all.

American and Continental

Acme 9 Great Jones St, at Lafayette St ℡212/420-1934. Come here for authentic Southern and Cajun grub; the menu features po-boys, corn bread, and jambalaya. It's especially popular for weekend brunch – the fried catfish filet with two eggs is a local favorite.

Five Points 31 Great Jones St, between Bowery and Lafayette St ℡212/253-5700. Upscale New American cuisine, including some of the best brunch below 14th Street. Try the salt and poached eggs ($14) or the *dulce de leche* French toast ($9).

Gotham Bar & Grill 12 E 12th St, between Fifth Ave and University Place ℡212/620-4020. This restaurant is generally reckoned to be one of the city's best New American restaurants; if you don't want to splurge on a full meal, at least go for a drink at the bar, where you can watch the beautiful patrons drift in. Truffle-crusted halibut is a highlight ($25).

Jack's Luxury Oyster Bar 246 E 5th St, between Second and Third aves ℡212/673-0338. The deconstructed dishes (Oysters Rockefeller becomes oysters with spinach and pancetta) and intimate, 12-seat dining room at this husband- and wife-owned eatery make for an interesting and full-on romantic experience. Pricey but worth it.

Mama's Food Shop 200 E 3rd St, between aves A and B ℡212/777-4425. *Mama*'s dishes out whopping portions of tasty and cheap homestyle cooking. Specialties include meatloaf, macaroni and cheese, and a good selection of roasted vegetables.

Mermaid Inn 96 Second Ave, between E 5th and 6th sts ℡212/674-5870. This restaurant takes its seafood seriously, serving simple and fresh dishes in an elegant yet unpretentious dining room (also has outdoor seating in summer). The raw bar is excellent, and specials change daily depending on the catch.

Prune 54 E 1st St, between First and Second aves ℡212/677-6221. With a menu full of surprises, this Mediterranean restaurant delivers one of the city's most exciting dining experiences, serving dishes like sweetbreads wrapped in bacon, seared sea bass with Berber spices, and buttermilk ice cream with pistachio puff-pastry. It's pricey but not as expensive as you might think.

Tasting Room 72 E 1st St, between First and Second aves ℡212/358-7831. A longtime foodie favorite for its casual fine dining. While the ostensible purpose of the menu here is to complement the enviable wine list (hence the name), the food itself is definitely worth going out of your way for: try the braised pork tongue, the poached trout, or the sautéed blowfish.

Asian

Bond Street 6 Bond St, between Broadway and Lafayette St ℡212/777-2500. Very hip, super-suave Japanese restaurant on multiple stories (there's a happening lounge on the ground floor). The sushi is amazing, the miso-glazed sea bass exquisite, and the steak a treat. Steep prices.

Cyclo 203 First Ave, between 12th and 13th sts ℡212/673-3957. *Cyclo* serves a wide range of well-prepared, reasonably priced Vietnamese dishes in a snazzy setting. The crispy whole red snapper with spicy lime sauce is especially good, as are the desserts.

Dok Suni 119 First Ave, between E 5th and 6th sts ℡212/477-9506. Hip around the edges with great prices to boot, this is a fine bet (and longtime local favorite) for Korean home cooking, including *bibimbop* and *kim chee* rice. The only real drawbacks here are the metal chopsticks, which can retain heat and can be frustratingly slippery.

Elephant 58 E 1st St, between First and Second aves ☎212/505-7739. The menu at this eclectic East Village favorite features a delicious fusion of fairly priced Thai and French delicacies, including innovative fish specials and superb noodle dishes. Look for the blue-and-yellow awning.

Hasaki 210 E 9th St, at Third Ave ☎212/473-3327. Some of the best sushi in the city is served at this popular but mellow downstairs cubby-hole. Sit at the bar and the chefs will try to tempt you with a variety of improvised dishes not found on the menu.

Jewel Bako 239 E 5th St, between Second and Third aves ☎212/979-1012. Come here for exotic Japanese delicacies, including a lot of sushi/sashimi offerings that you can't get elsewhere in New York – like live raw lobster (not for the faint of heart). A memorable dining experience, though very expensive.

SEA Thai 75 Second Ave, between E 4th and 5th sts ☎212/228-5505. This high-energy basement Thai restaurant flaunts fab food at killer prices. Try the SEA Caesar salad ($3), the patpong green curry with shrimp ($8), or the pad thai ($8).

Shabu Tatsu 5216 E 10th St, between First and Second aves ☎212/477-2972. This place offers tasty, moderately priced Korean barbecue. Choose a combination of meat or seafood platters, then cook them yourself right at your table.

Takahachi 85 Ave A, between E 5th and 6th sts ☎212/505-6524. Superior sushi at affordable prices. You'll probably have to wait for a table at dinner – they don't take reservations.

French

Casimir 103 Ave B, between E 6th and 7th sts ☎212/358-9683. This dark, spacious French bistro specializes in straightforward fare at decent prices. Try the filet mignon or the thick-cut pork chop, both excellent – and surprisingly well-priced – cuts of meat.

Danal 90 E 10th St, between Third and Fourth aves ☎212/982-6930. A charming and cozy French café, *Danal* is great for dinner, brunch (try the French toast made with croissants and topped with cinnamon apples), or high tea on weekends (4 to 6pm, by reservation only; $20 per person).

Indian

Brick Lane Curry House 343 E 6th St, between First and Second aves ☎212/979-2900. Hands down the best Indian in the East Village, thanks to its wide selection of traditional favorites, including some fiery *phaal* curries. It's more expensive than other Indian eateries in the neighborhood, but it's still a bargain.

Café Spice 72 University Place, between E 10th and 11th sts ☎212/253-6999. This popular, funky Indian eatery has an expansive and affordable menu of flavorful offerings; try the *dosas*. Be sure to ask for a booth, if you intend to have a conversation over dinner. Otherwise, it's too hard to hear over the din.

Haveli 100 Second Ave, between E 5th and 6th sts ☎212/982-0533. Far superior to most of its neighbors on E 6th Street (with the notable exception of *Brick Lane*), this roomy Indian restaurant serves creative and well-executed classics, although it's not cheap.

Italian

Frank 88 Second Ave, between E 5th and 6th sts ☎212/420-0202. A tiny neighborhood favorite, where basic, traditional American-Italian dishes are served at communal tables. It's packed every night with hungry locals. No credit cards.

Il Buco 47 Bond St, between Lafayette St and Bowery ☎212/533-1932. This antiques-filled Mediterranean eatery delivers authentic dishes from southern Europe with creative, wholesome flair. The wine cellar is alleged to have inspired Edgar Allan Poe's *The Cask of Amontillado*. It's quite expensive, and they don't accept credit cards.

Lavagna 545 E 5th St, between aves A and B ☎212/979-1005. This red-hued hideaway seduces East Villagers with potato-cheese gratin, pasta with sausage, and succulent pork dishes. It's been described by local regulars as perfect from beginning to end, and that includes the check.

Supper 156 E 2nd St, between aves A and B ☎212/477-7600. Great little Italian restaurant with oversized, medieval-looking tables and benches, and some of the best Italian around. Try the "priest strangler" pasta (shaped like little nooses) with marinara and fresh ricotta. No reservations or credit cards.

Latin American

Boca Chica 13 First Ave, at E 1st St ☎212/473-0108. This is authentic South American food,

East Village | **RESTAURANTS**

(25)

piled high and washed down with black beer and tropical drinks. It gets crowded, especially late at night and on weekends, and the music is loud. Bring your dancing shoes and be ready to party.

Flor's Kitchen 149 First Ave, between 9th and 10th sts ℡212/387-8949. Four-table Venezuelan *comedor*. The shredded beef and grilled chicken with saffron rice and beans are delicious and inexpensive. Don't miss the fruit shakes.

Spanish

Xunta 174 First Ave, between E 10th and 11th sts ℡212/614-0620. This gem of a restaurant

buzzes with hordes of young people, all perched on rum barrels, downing pitchers of sangría, and choosing from the dizzying tapas menu. You can eat (and drink) very well for around $20; the dates with bacon ($5) are especially tasty.

Vegetarian

Angelica Kitchen 300 E 12th St, between First and Second aves ℡212/228-2909. Vegetarian macrobiotic restaurant with various daily specials for a decent price. Patronized by a colorful downtown crowd and serving some of the best veggie food in New York.

West Village

Restaurants in the **West Village** must cater to the neighborhood's many and varied residents – everyone from students to celebrities – so the culinary scene is fairly diverse. You'll find loads of takeout spots and places with prix-fixe meals around New York University. Farther west, dining rooms get snazzier, menus more interesting, and prices higher, particularly along Seventh Avenue and into the Meatpacking District, where there's a preponderance of French bistros, and your *cassoulet* is often garnished with a sniffy attitude.

American and Continental

Blue Hill 75 Washington Place, between MacDougal and 6th sts ℡212/539-1776. *Blue Hill* is one of the better restaurants in the West Village. Patrons crowd in for the rustic American fare, including parsnip soup and braised cod. Don't miss the rich chocolate bread pudding.

Corner Bistro 331 W 4th St, at Jane St ℡212/242-9502. A down-home pub with cavernous cubicles, paper plates, and maybe the best burger in town. It's a long-standing haunt for West Village literary and artsy types, with a mix of locals and die-hard fans queuing up nightly for excellent and inexpensive grub and a chance to play the great jazz jukebox; don't be discouraged – the line moves quickly.

Home 20 Cornelia St, between Bleecker and W 4th sts ℡212/243-9579. One of those rare restaurants that manages to pull off cozy with flair. The creative and reasonably priced American food is always fresh and tasty, though it may be a better deal at lunch (around $10 per person) than dinner ($30–40 per person). Try the spice-crusted pork chops ($17).

Mary's Fish Camp 64 Charles St, at W 4th St ℡646/486-2185. Lobster rolls, bouillabaisse, and grilled whole fish adorn the menu at this small, noisy West Village spot. Go early, as they don't accept reservations and the line lasts into the night. Definitely one of the best seafood spots in the whole city – you can almost smell the salty air.

Pearl Oyster Bar 18 Cornelia St, between Bleecker and W 4th sts ℡212/691-8211. You may have to fight for a table here, but the top-notch raw bar and thoughtfully executed seafood dishes are worth it. You won't shell out as much as you expect.

The Pink Teacup 42 Grove St, between Bleecker and Bedford sts ℡212/807-6755. A Southern soul-food institution in the heart of the Village, serving good smothered pork chops, cornbread, and anything fried. They do a good brunch, too. No credit cards.

The Spotted Pig 314 W 11th St, at Greenwich St ℡212/620-0393. New York's first gastro-pub, courtesy of chef Mario Batali, among other culinary giants. The menu is several steps above ordinary bar food – think smoked-haddock chowder and sheep's ricotta gnudi – and the wine list is excellent.

△ The Spotted Pig

Asian

Chow Bar 230 W 4th St, at Seventh Ave
☏ 212/633-2212. This reasonably priced pan-Asian restaurant supplies a creative selection of dishes and killer cocktails.

🥢 **Tomoe Sushi 172 Thompson St, between Bleecker and Houston sts** ☏ 212/777-9346. The nightly lines may look daunting, but there's a good reason to join them: this is some of the best, freshest sushi in Manhattan, and it's affordable, to boot. There are some seasonal dishes (like a soft-shell crab roll) on the menu, but the impossibly fresh fluke and other fish on offer is what draws the crowds – you can be sure the quality is superb.

Yama 38–40 Carmine St, between Bedford and Bleecker sts ☏ 212/989-9330. This intimate yet bustling Japanese restaurant serves great sushi, and everything else is tasty, too – try the "Sushi for Two" special, which could feed an army. In warm weather, see if you can get a table in the small garden out back.

Austrian

Wallse 344 W 11th St, at Washington St
☏ 212/352-2300. The Austrian fare offered here has been updated for the 21st century, and the dining room is adorned with Julian Schnabel canvases. The uniquely crafted menu features light-as-air schnitzel, frothy Riesling sauces, and fantastic strudels, and the wine list includes some notable rare vintages.

French and Belgian

Bar Six 502 Sixth Ave, between 12th and 13th sts ☏ 212/691-1363. Patrons flock to this small bistro for its hopping happy hour and inventive, reasonably priced French-Moroccan fare. There's outdoor seating in nice weather.

Café de Bruxelles 111 Greenwich Ave, at W 13th St ☏ 212/206-1830. Taste the city's most delicious *frites* (served with home-made mayo) and mussels at this affordable Belgian establishment. There's also a nice selection of Belgian beers, including peach- and strawberry-infused brews.

Chez Brigitte 77 Greenwich Ave, between Bank St and Seventh Ave ☏ 212/929-6736. Only a dozen people fit in this tiny restaurant at one time. The stews and roast-meat dinners go for under $10, and the simple menu features a number of other bargains as well, like the $5 Provençal omelet.

Cornelia Street Café 29 Cornelia St, between Bleecker and W 4th sts ☏ 212/989-9319. As much American as French, there is no more comfortable café in NYC. The pastas, salads, and weekend brunch offerings are great, and the prices aren't bad either.

RESTAURANTS

25

Downstairs is a cabaret featuring occasional jazz, poetry, and performance art.

Florent 69 Gansevoort St, between Washington and Greenwich sts ☎212/989-5779. See and be seen at this fashionable eatery in the heart of the Meatpacking District. The menu features great, moderate-to-pricey French bistro fare; the goat-cheese salad is a staple, and the mussels are always a good bet. Open 24 hours, it's a favorite late-night hangout for clubbers and low-level celebrities.

Paradou 8 Little W 12th St, between Greenwich and Washington sts ☎212/463-8345. This underrated Provençal-style French bistro is a far better (and more authentic) option than some of the more exposed options in the area. Great wines by the glass, and good prices.

Italian

Arturo's Pizza 106 W Houston St, at Thompson St ☎212/677-3820. Coal-oven pizzas (no slices) that may be the best in town. While-you-eat entertainment often includes live jazz, and there are a couple of outdoor tables on busy Houston Street.

Babbo 110 Waverly Place, between MacDougal St and Sixth Ave ☎212/777-0303. The super-high-end Italian cuisine at this Washingon Square spot is deservedly touted as some of the best in the city. Try the mint love-letters or goose-liver ravioli, or go for one of the expensive tasting menus. You won't get a reservation less than two months in advance, so just show up and either eat at the bar or try for an open table along the window – they don't take reservations for those. Arrive around 5:30pm if you don't want to wait.

'ino 21 Bedford St, between Downing St and Sixth Ave ☎212/989-5769. Duck in here for a satisfying and nicely priced meal; choose from a list of *bruschette, tramezzine* (a hearty cousin of the tea sandwich), and Italian wines.

John's Pizzeria 278 Bleecker St, between Sixth and Seventh aves ☎212/243-1680. This full-service restaurant serves some of the city's most popular pizzas, thin with a coal-charred crust. Be prepared to wait in line for a table; they don't do slices, and there is no takeout.

Lupa 170 Thompson St, between Bleecker and Houston sts ☎212/982-5089. *Lupa* serves hearty, rustic Italian specialties such as *osso buco, saltimbocca,* and *gnocchi* with fennel sausage. Hint: go before 6.30pm and you'll have no problem getting a table.

Otto Enoteca and Pizzeria 1 Fifth Ave, at Washington Square N ☎212/995-9559. One of the cheaper members of Italian chef Mario Batali's restaurant empire, this popular pizza and antipasti joint has a superb wine list and caters to a beautiful crowd. The acoustics aren't great, but the atmosphere is festive and you can't beat the *lardo* (lard) and *vongole* (clam) pizza.

Sapore 55 Greenwich Ave, at Perry St ☎212/229-0551. This casual corner restaurant is always busy on account of its low prices and dependable Italian dishes, including an always-fresh *caprese* salad and *fusilli* pasta with four-cheese sauce. No credit cards.

Latin American

Day-O 103 Greenwich Ave, at W 12th St ☎212/924-3161. A lively atmosphere and good, affordable food draw a young crowd to this Caribbean/Southern joint. Menu highlights include fried catfish, jerk chicken, and coconut shrimp. Stay away from the tropical drinks if you have a weak head/stomach – they are quite strong.

Mi Cocina 57 Jane St, at Hudson St ☎212/627-8273. Come here for authentic Mexican food in an upscale setting; the spiced meat-stuffed poblano chillis (*chiles en nogada*) are especially good. It's often packed, so be prepared to wait.

Tortilla Flats 767 Washington St, at W 12th St ☎212/243-1053. This Mexican dive has great margaritas, a loud sound system, and plenty of kitsch, including hula-hoop contests. Be careful, it gets really crowded.

Middle Eastern

Moustache 90 Bedford St, between Grove and Barrow sts ☎212/229-2220. A small, cheap spot specializing in "pitzas" (pizzas of pita bread and eclectic toppings); also offers great hummus, chickpea and spinach salad, and bargain lamb chops ($12).

Spanish

Sevilla 62 Charles St, at W 4th St ☎212/929-3189. A longstanding Village favorite, *Sevilla* is dark, fragrant (from garlic), and serves

(25)

good, moderately priced food. Try the garlic soup, the fried calamari, and the large pitchers of strong sangría.

Vegetarian

Souen 210 Sixth Ave, at Prince St ☎212/807-7421. This vegetarian and macrobiotic restaurant uses only organic produce, fish, shrimp, and grains. The food is tasty enough that meat-eaters will like it, too.

Chelsea

Once characterized by retro diners and places to people-watch rather than eat, in recent years **Chelsea** has sprouted some respectable eating establishments that manage to please the palate as well as the wallet. There's a mosaic of cuisines – Thai, Creole, Mexican, Italian, and traditional American, among others – and atmospheres available, with something for just about everyone.

American and Continental

Cafeteria 119 Seventh Ave, at W 17th St ☎212/414-1717. Don't let the name fool you: *Cafeteria* may be open 24 hours and serve great chicken-fried steak, meatloaf, and macaroni and cheese, but it's nothing like a truckstop. The modern, plastic-accented interior is always packed with beautiful diners and a sexy waitstaff. Even the prices are nice to look at.

Empire Diner 210 Tenth Ave, between W 22nd and 23rd sts ☎212/243-2736. With its gleaming chrome-ribbed Art Deco décor, this is one of Manhattan's original diners, still open 24 hours and still serving up plates of simple (if not much better than average) American comfort food. Prices can be a bit high for the quality of the meal.

Moran's 146 Tenth Ave, at W 19th St ☎212/627-3030. You can get good swordfish and lobster (priced per pound) here, but it's the steaks and chops ($22–40) that are most impressive. The plush, stained-wood seating area is tasteful; try and get a table in the cozy back room – it's especially nice in winter, when the fireplace is roaring.

The Old Homestead 56 Ninth Ave, between W 14th and 15th sts ☎212/242-9040. Steak. Period. But really gorgeous steak, served in an almost comically old-fashioned walnut dining room by waiters in black vests. Expensive, but portions are huge.

Red Cat 227 Tenth Ave, between W 23rd and 24th sts ☎212/242-1122. Superb service, a fine American-Mediterranean kitchen, and a warm atmosphere all make for a memorable dining experience at *Red Cat*. Book early, it's getting more popular by the day.

Asian

Bright Food Shop 218 Eighth Ave, at W 21st St ☎212/243-4433. The fusion of Asian and Mexican food at this Chelsea eatery provides diners with a unique culinary experience. It's always crowded, and while prices are low, they're certainly not a steal.

Monster Sushi 158 W 23rd St, between Sixth and Seventh aves ☎212/620-9131, ⓦwww .monstersushi.com. "Monster" portions of sushi are on offer here (hence the name), though it's their creative rolls that are the real draw. Not the cheapest sushi in town, but good. They have several other locations around Manhattan.

Royal Siam 240 Eighth Ave, between W 22nd and 23rd sts ☎212/741-1732. This reasonably priced Thai restaurant has come up with surprisingly flavorful renditions of the old standards.

French

La Lunchonette 130 Tenth Ave, at W 18th St ☎212/675-0342. Even though it's tucked away in a remote corner of Chelsea, this understated little restaurant is always

㉕

343

packed with loyal patrons. The menu features the best of French country cooking, including steak *au poivre*, rabbit stew, and lamb sausage with sautéed apples.

Italian

Bottino 246 Tenth Ave, between W 24th and 25th sts ⓣ 212/206-6766. One of Chelsea's most popular restaurants, *Bottino* attracts the in-crowd looking for authentic Italian food served in a slick, downtown atmosphere. The homemade leek tortellini (winter months only) is truly tantalizing. Be sure to visit the ATM before you go, as it's a bit pricey. **Chelsea Ristorante** 108 Eighth Ave, between W 15th and 16th sts ⓣ 212/924-7786. This brick-walled restaurant is as enjoyable for its relaxed and unpretentious ambience as it is for its Northern Italian food.

Latin American

Cuba Libre 165 Eighth Ave, between 18th and 19th sts ⓣ 212/206-0038. Tapas, mojitos, and hip-swinging music make this airy, affordable eatery a favorite with Chelsea's gay crowd. **La Taza de Oro** 96 Eighth Ave, between W 14th and 15th sts ⓣ 212/243-9946. Come here for

a tasty, filling Puerto Rican meal. Specials change daily, but are always served with a heap of rice and beans. Don't miss the delicious *café con leche*.

Maroon's 244 W 16th St, between Seventh and Eighth aves ⓣ 212/206-8640. Memorable Caribbean and Southern food in a hot and hopping basement space. The cocktails are some of the best in blocks, and the prices are good, too. **Rocking Horse** 182 Eighth Ave, between W 19th and 20th sts ⓣ 212/463-9511. Wash down inventive Mexican cuisine with deliciously potent mojitos and margaritas from the bar. Try to keep track of the tab, if you can; drinks make the bill go up quickly.

Spanish

El Quijote 226 W 23rd St, between Seventh and Eighth aves ⓣ 212/929-1855. *El Quijote* has changed very little over the years (it needed only a minimal makeover when it appeared in the 1996 film *I Shot Andy Warhol*, though the movie was set in 1968). It still serves decent *mariscos* and fried meats, but the bland paella should be avoided.

Union Square, Gramercy Park, and the Flatiron District

The neighborhoods of **Union Square**, **Gramercy Park**, and the **Flatiron District** are heavily trafficked, and are therefore prime spots for restaurants. Some of the city's best dining establishments are in this part of town, the finest of which have come to help define New American cuisine. There are also plenty of places to grab a cheap meal, but the neighborhood notables definitely lean toward upscale.

American and Continental

Blue Water Grill 31 Union Square W, at 16th St ⓣ 212/675-9500. All-around high-quality seafood restaurant. It's hard to go wrong here, whether you choose the grilled fish, caviar, or delicacies from the raw bar. Prices are commensurately high. **Chat 'n' Chew** 10 E 16th St, between Fifth Ave and Union Square W ⓣ 212/243-1616. Come for large portions of standard American comfort food served in a colorful diner setting. Menu classics include macaroni and cheese, fried chicken, and yummy sweet-potato fries. It's a good budget option. **City Crab** 235 Park Ave S, at E 19th St ⓣ 212/529-3800. This large and very popular

eatery prides itself on its large selection of fresh East Coast oysters and clams. Most people come to consume great piles of these bivalves (and pints of ale). Roughly $20–30 per person for a full dinner. **Craft** 43 E 19th St, between Broadway and Park Ave S ⓣ 212/780-0880. Very trendy (read: crowded) but otherwise quite relaxed. The kitchen here serves up some of New York's most inventive food. Among the popular dishes are roast foie gras, daybow scallops, and tasty sides of sautéed wild mushrooms.

Gramercy Tavern 42 E 20th St, between Broadway and Park Ave S ⓣ 212/477-0777. The neo-Colonial décor, exquisite New American cuisine, and perfect service make for a memorable meal at one of the city's best restaurants. The seasonal tasting menus are well worth the steep prices, but if you don't want to splurge, you can also drop in for a drink or more casual meal in the lively front room.

Union Square Café 21 E 16th St, between Fifth Ave and Union Square W ☎ 212/243-4020. Choice California-style dining in a classy but comfortable atmosphere. No one does salmon like the chefs here, and the polenta with gorgonzola is incredible. Meals aren't cheap – prices average $100 and up for two – but the creative menu is a real treat.

Verbena 54 Irving Place, between E 17th and 18th sts ☎ 212/260-5454. This simple and elegant restaurant serves a seasonal menu of creative (and pricey) New American food. Don't miss the crème brûlée with lemon verbena (one of the eatery's signature dishes). Try to get seated in the garden, and definitely reserve in advance.

Asian

Choshi 77 Irving Place, at E 19th St ☎ 212/420-1419. Don't worry about wearing a T-shirt and jeans to this casual Japanese establishment. The fresh sushi is first-rate.

Hangawi 12 E 32nd St, between Fifth and Madison aves ☎ 212/213-0077. An elegant, vegetarian and vegan-safe Korean restaurant. The emperor's rolls (thin pancakes of carrots, zucchini, and mushroom) are a great starter. A little pricey, but quite good.

Republic 37 Union Square W, between 16th and 17th sts ☎ 212/627-7172. The pleasant décor, fast service, low prices, and serviceable noodle dishes at *Republic* make it a popular pan-Asian spot. The tasty dumpling appetizers are the best part.

French and Belgian

Artisanal 2 Park Ave, at E 32nd St ☎ 212/725-8585. Cheese is the name of the game here – there's a cave with 700 varieties. If you don't want the full stinky experience, grab a small table at the bar and try the *gougeres* (Gruyère puffs) with one of the excellent wines on offer. The food is upscale with prices to match.

Brasserie Les Halles 411 Park Ave S, between E 28th and 29th sts ☎ 212/679-4111. *Les Halles* is a noisy, bustling, would-be Left Bank bistro – complete with carcasses dangling in a butcher's shop in the front. The menu

includes rabbit, steak *frites*, and other staples, with entrees $15–25.

L'Acajou 53 W 19th St, between Fifth and Sixth aves ☎ 212/645-1706. This small, homey bistro has attracted an eclectic clientele for years. The bar gets crowded at happy hour and the tables are often full for lunch and dinner. Daily specials, including omelets and dinner tarts, are an excellent value for the neighborhood.

German

Rolf's 281 Third Ave, at E 22nd St ☎ 212/473-8718. An Old-World feeling dominates this dark, chintz-covered East Side institution. The schnitzel and sauerbraten are always good, but somehow they taste better at the generous bar buffet, which commences around 5pm all through the week.

Indian

Curry in a Hurry 119 Lexington Ave, between E 27th and 28th sts ☎ 212/683-0900. A local favorite, *Curry in a Hurry* offers inexpensive and delicious buffet-style Indian food. You can eat well for around $10.

Madras Mahal 104 Lexington Ave, between E 27th and 28th sts ☎ 212/684-4010. This eatery is a kosher vegetarian's dream, but everyone else will like it, too. Entrees are around $11.

Tabla Metropolitan Life Building, 11 Madison Ave, at E 25th St ☎ 212/889-0667. This restaurant's swanky, *nouveau* Indian fare is served in an elegant, glassed-in second-floor dining room. Start off with the duck samosas and move on to the pan-seared skate with baby artichokes and chickpeas. The food is memorable enough to block out the young banker types that tend to crowd the place. *Bread Bar at Tabla*, on the first floor, serves Indian tapas (see p.321).

Italian

Enoteca I Trulli 122 E 27th St, between Lexington and Park aves ☎ 212/481-7372. Just next to a lovely wine bar of the same name, this gourmet Italian restaurant features robust entrees like *orecchiette* with rabbit ragù ($19) and wild boar with fennel ($36). Service can be a bit stiff, but for dishes like these it's worth it.

Brunch

Weekend brunch is a competitive business in New York. The selections below (reviewed in more detail elsewhere) all offer a good weekend menu, sometimes for a price that includes a free cocktail or two – though offers of freebies are to be treated with suspicion by those more interested in the food than getting blitzed. Don't regard this as a definitive list: there are excellent brunch possibilities all over the city.

Downtown Manhattan

Acme 9 Great Jones St, at Lafayette St ☎212/420-1934; p.338

Balthazar 80 Spring St, between Broadway and Crosby St ☎212/965-1414; p.334

Bubby's 120 Hudson St, at N Moore St ☎212/219-0666; p.332

Cupping Room Café 359 W Broadway, between Broome and Grand sts ☎212/925-2898; p.333

Danal 90 E 10th St, between Third and Fourth aves ☎212/982-6930; p.339

Five Points 31 Great Jones St, between Bowery and Lafayette St ☎212/253-5700; p.338

Home 20 Cornelia St, between Bleecker and W 4th sts ☎212/243-9579; p.340

Midtown Manhattan

Brasserie Les Halles 411 Park Ave S, between E 28th and 29th sts ☎212/679-4111; p.345

Cafeteria 119 Seventh Ave, at W 17th St ☎212/414-1717; p.345

Uptown Manhattan

Copeland's 547 W 145th St, between Broadway and Amsterdam Ave ☎212/234-2357; p.356

E.A.T. 1064 Madison Ave, between E 80th and 81st sts ☎212/772-0022; p.351

EJ's Luncheonette 447 Amsterdam Ave, between W 81st and 82nd sts ☎212/873-3444; p.353

Oscar's Famous BBQ 1325 Fifth Ave, at 111th St ☎212/996-1212; p.356

Sarabeth's 423 Amsterdam Ave, between W 80th and 81 sts ☎212/496-6280; p.354

Sylvia's Restaurant 328 Lenox Ave, between W 126th and 127th sts ☎212/996-0660; p.356

Latin American

Coffee Shop 29 Union Square W, at 16th St ☎212/243-7969. Reasonably priced fare (especially the turkey burgers) at this Brazilian establishment, though the staff can be a bit snooty at times. It's a solid lunch spot as well as a good late-night hangout; the kitchen is open until 5:30am Wed–Sat and they serve great *caipirinha* drinks.

Spanish

Casa Mono 52 Irving Place, at E 17th St ☎212/253-2773. This eclectic tapas bar both challenges and enchants the palate with such dishes as lemon-scented miniature squid and cockles with scrambled eggs and Serrano ham ($3–12). The adjacent and sherry-heavy *Bar Jamon* (125 E 17th St; see p.370) is open until 2am daily.

Midtown East

Catering mostly to weekday office crowds, **Midtown East** overflows with restaurants, many of them nondescript and overpriced. You probably won't want to make the eateries in this neighborhood the focal point of too many excursions, but, that said, there are a few timeworn favorites in the area, such as the *Oyster Bar* in Grand Central Terminal and *Smith & Wollensky*.

American and Continental

Comfort Diner 214 E 45th St, between Second and Third aves ☏ 212/867-4555. One of the friendliest spots in town, this retro diner serves up hearty staples like meatloaf, fried chicken, and macaroni and cheese. It's a great place to fill up empty stomachs and rest weary toes, not to mention save a few bucks.

El Rio Grande 160 E 38th St, between Lexington and Third aves ☏ 212/867-0922. Long-established Murray Hill Tex-Mex place with a gimmick: you can eat Mexican, or if you prefer, Texan, by simply crossing the "border" and walking through the kitchen. Personable and fun – and the margaritas are earth-shattering ($7 and up).

Four Seasons 99 E 52nd St, between Lexington and Park aves ☏ 212/754-9494. The face of New York's fine dining for decades, this timeless Philip Johnson-designed restaurant delivers on every front. If you can't swing the grotesque prices of the dishes on the French-influenced American menu, go for a cocktail and peek at the famous pool room. Housed in the Seagram Building, it is much stuffier than other top restaurants in the city.

Oyster Bar Lower level, Grand Central Terminal, at E 42nd St and Park Ave ☏ 212/490-6650. This wonderfully distinctive place is down in the vaulted dungeons of Grand Central. Midtown office workers who pour in for lunch come to choose from a staggering menu – she-crab bisque, steamed Maine lobster, and sweet Kumamoto oysters top the list. Prices are moderate to expensive; you can eat more cheaply at the bar.

Smith & Wollensky 797 Third Ave, at E 49th St ☏ 212/753-1530. A grand, if clubby, steakhouse, where waiters – many of whom have worked here for twenty years or more – serve you the primest cuts of beef imaginable. Quite pricey – you'll pay at least $33 per steak – but it's worth the splurge. Go basic with the sides and wines.

Asian

Hatsuhana 17 E 48th St, between Fifth and Madison aves ☏ 212/355-3345. *Hatsuhana* was one of the first restaurants to introduce sushi to New York many moons ago, and it's still going strong. Despite the spartan décor, this place is not at all cheap, so try to go for the mid-week prix-fixe lunch.

Jaiya Thai 396 Third Ave, between E 28th and 29th sts ☏ 212/889-1330. The food at this affordable restaurant is spicy and delicious. Pad thai goes for $10.

L'Annam 393 Third Ave, at E 28th St ☏ 212/686-5168. Solid Vietnamese in a hip dining room. Good for a quick meal, as the service is quite fast. The $6 lunch specials can't be beat.

Le Colonial 149 E 57th St, between Third and Lexington aves ☏ 212/752-0808. Colonial exploitation never looked as good as it does at this high-end homage to French Indochina, with its bamboo-fan interiors and excellent Vietnamese dishes like *choa tom* (grilled shrimp wrapped around sugar cane), *bo luc lac* (seared filet mignon, watercress, and pickled onions), and *vit quay* (ginger-roast duck with tamarind sauce).

Vong 200 E 54th St, at Third Ave ☏ 212/486-8664. The best Southeast Asian food in midtown, served in a trendy dining room in the bowels of the appropriately named Lipstick Building (it's shaped like a lipstick cylinder). Great early evening prix-fixe meals; don't miss the crab cakes or the rabbit entree.

French

La Grenouille 3 E 52nd St, between Fifth and Madison aves ☏ 212/752-1495. The haute French cuisine here has melted hearts and tantalized palates since 1962. All the classics are done to perfection, and the service is beyond gracious. Its prix-fixe lunch is $45, pre-theater $55, and dinner is $85 per person without wine.

▽ Oyster Bar

Restaurants with views

This is a brief list of (mainly Manhattan) restaurants that draw patrons just for their views or location. The restaurants are covered in more detail in other sections; note that the quality of the views will almost invariably be reflected in the size of your bill.

Boat Basin Café W 79th St, at the Hudson River ☎212/496-5542; p.353

Boathouse Café Central Park Lake, east side, near E 72nd St entrance ☎212/517-2233; p.353

River Café 1 Water St, at Furman St on the East River, Brooklyn ☎718/522-5200; p.357

Tavern on the Green W 67th St, at Central Park W ☎212/873-3200; p.354

Terrace in the Sky 400 W 119th St, between Amsterdam Ave and Morningside Drive ☎212/666-9490; p.354

Italian

Luna Piena 243 E 53rd St, between Second and Third aves ☎212/308-8882. One of the better Italian restaurants in a neighborhood awash in mediocre eateries. The food is filling and the service friendly, and there's an enclosed garden for warm summer evenings.

Mexican

Zarela 953 Second Ave, between E 50th and 51st sts ☎212/644-6740. If you've ever wondered what home-cooked Mexican food really tastes like, this festive restaurant is the place to go. It's noticeably more expensive than most Mexican places, but it's worth every cent.

Spanish

Solera 216 E 53rd St, between Second and Third aves ☎212/644-1166. Tapas and other Spanish specialties are served here in a stylish townhouse setting. As you'd expect from the surroundings and the ambience, it can be expensive, but it's one of the city's better Iberian eateries.

Midtown West

While many of Manhattan's best dining establishments are located downtown, manifold good meals await you in **Midtown West**. The eateries in Little Brazil (West 46th Street) serve up some excellent, if meat-heavy, dishes, while Restaurant Row (West 46th Street between Eighth and Ninth avenues) is a frequent stopover for theater-goers seeking a late-night meal. Cheaper (and often better) alternatives can be found along Ninth Avenue and farther west into Hell's Kitchen. Be advised that many restaurants in the Times Square area (not the ones we have included here) are overpriced and not of the highest quality.

Afghani

Ariana Afghan Kebab 787 Ninth Ave, between W 52nd and 53rd sts ☎212/262-2323. A casual neighborhood restaurant serving inexpensive kebabs (chicken, lamb, and beef) and vegetarian meals.

American and Continental

'21' Club 21 W 52nd St, between Fifth and Sixth aves ☎212/582-7200. This is simply one of New York's most enduring institutions – the city's Old Boys come here to meet and eat. There's a dress code, so wear a jacket and tie. Three-course early dinner prix-fixe menus are $37 per person in the Bar Room, which is a pretty good deal, considering one entree (such as crushed-fennel rack of lamb) goes for $42 all on its own.

Aquavit 13 W 54th St, between Fifth and Sixth aves ☎212/307-7311. Exquisite fish dishes abound at this superb Scandinavian restaurant, though the menu also features more exotic dishes, like reindeer. A meal here is a real treat, and it's priced accordingly. Reserve well ahead.

Bryant Park Grill 25 W 40th St, between Fifth and Sixth aves ☎212/840-6500. Most patrons come to this restaurant for its enviable location in leafy Bryant Park. Enjoy lovely views from inside the spacious dining room or al fresco on the terrace. The food is prosaically standard upscale (Caesar salad, rack of lamb).

db Bistro Moderne City Club Hotel, 55 W 44th St, between Fifth and Sixth aves ☎212/391-2400. Famous chef-owner Daniel Boulud gives average Joes a chance to taste his creations at this bistro, which is decidedly more affordable than his other culinary shrines. A few items do toe the expense line, however, including the sublime $29 foie gras– flecked hamburger.

HK 523 Ninth Ave, at W 40th St ☎212/947-4208. This shiny industrial eatery has lots of light and a smartly priced American and Mediterranean menu. Try the fresh grilled-calamari salad ($6.95).

Joe Allen 326 W 46th St, between Eighth and Ninth aves ☎212/581-6464. The tried-and-true formula of checkered tablecloths and reliable American food at moderate prices works well at this popular pre-theater spot. Make a reservation, unless you plan to arrive after 8pm.

Judson Grill 152 W 52nd St, between Sixth and Seventh aves ☎212/582-5252. This sophisticated and pricey contemporary American restaurant enjoys a loyal fan base. The smoked trout in blini ($13) is a standout, as are any of the foie gras dishes. The braised shortribs ($35) are another delicious pick, and there's always a vegetarian entree or two on the menu made with seasonal green-market produce.

Stage Deli 834 Seventh Ave, between W 53rd and 54th sts ☎212/245-7850. Genuine New York attitude and gigantic, overstuffed sandwiches ($12) are what's on the menu at this open-all-night rival to the better-known *Carnegie Deli*. The food (and the prices) are better here.

Thalia 828 Eighth Ave, at W 50th St ☎212/399-4444. *Thalia* is a solid choice for imaginative, New American cuisine in the Theater District. The 5000-square-foot eating area is full of color and the prices aren't bad either. Try the spiced sweet-potato soup ($7) and the New York Blackout Cake ($8).

West Bank Café 407 W 42nd St, at Ninth Ave ☎212/695-6909. The menu here features some American dishes and some French dishes, all of which are delicious and not as expensive as you might think – entrees range $12–22. It's very popular with theater people, especially after performances.

Asian

China Grill CBS Building, 60 W 53rd St, between Fifth and Sixth aves ☎212/333-7788. An eclectic, pretentious, see-and-be-seen pan-Asian eatery that always seems to be busy. It's a fun destination whether you're seeking lunch, dinner, or drinks.

Pongsri Thai Restaurant 244 W 48th St, between Broadway and Eighth Ave ☎212/582-3392. This restaurant is popular with local businesspeople for its extensive and good-value lunch menu – especially the rice and noodle combos. The dinner menu is massive.

Ruby Foo's 1626 Broadway, at W 49th St ☎212/489-5600. The best dining option in Times Square, *Ruby Foo's* has a wide-ranging Asian menu that includes everything from sushi platters to *dim sum* to Thai noodle dishes, all done surprisingly well. There's another branch at 2182 Broadway, at W 77th St (☎212/724-6700).

Shun Lee 43 W 65th St, at Columbus Ave ☎212/371-8844. The service and table settings here are strictly formal, but you should feel free to dress casually. This venerable local institution – conveniently across the street from Lincoln Center – has top-notch Chinese food. Steer yourself toward the menu's many seafood delicacies.

Sugiyama 251 W 55th St, between Broadway and Eighth Ave ☎212/956-0670. Though you may want to take out a loan before dining at this superb Japanese restaurant, you're guaranteed an exquisite experience, from the enchanting *kaiseki* (chef's choice) dinners to the regal service.

Won Jo 23 W 32nd St, between Broadway and Fifth Ave ☎212/695-5815. Budgeteers will like this "K-town" favorite for its excellent BBQ, wallet-friendly prices, and round-the-clock Korean menu. The service, however, could stand some improvement.

RESTAURANTS | Midtown West

(25)

French

Chez Napoleon 365 W 50th St, between Eighth and Ninth aves ℡212/265-6980. One of several authentic Gallic eateries that sprung up in this area during World War II, when it was a hangout for French soldiers. A friendly, family-run bistro, it continues to serve solid, high-quality food. Not cheap, though – bring plenty of cash.

Hourglass Tavern 373 W 46th St, between Eighth and Ninth aves ℡212/265-2060. This tiny French eatery on Restaurant Row features a three-course prix-fixe menu for $18. The gimmick is the hourglass above each table, the emptying of which means you're supposed to leave and make way for someone else. In reality, the glasses seem to last more than an hour, and to be only rarely enforced. Cash only.

Le Bernardin 155 W 51st St, between Sixth and Seventh aves ℡212/554-1515. The most storied seafood restaurant in the United States, serving incomparable new angles on traditional Brittany fish dishes in elegant surroundings. This is one dinner you'll never forget, though you may cry when the bill arrives.

Le Madeleine 403 W 43rd St, between Ninth and Tenth aves ℡212/246-2993. Charming bistro with stand-up service, slightly above average food (though the desserts are outstanding), and moderate to expensive prices. It's usually crowded pre-theater; get a seat in the outdoor garden if you can.

German

Hallo Berlin 626 10th Ave, between W 44th and W 45th sts ℡212/977-1944. Come to *Berlin* to enjoy all manner of German sausages and unusual ales in a pleasant bench-and-table beer-garden setting. The prices aren't bad.

Italian

Becco 355 W 46th St, between Eighth and Ninth aves ℡212/397-7597. Catering to the pre-theater crowd, *Becco* is most notable for its $22 all-you-can-eat pasta dinner.

Trattoria dell'Arte 900 Seventh Ave, between W 56th and 57th sts ℡212/245-9800. Unusually nice restaurant for this stretch of midtown, with an airy interior, excellent service, and good food. Great, wafer-thin crispy pizzas, decent and imaginative pasta dishes for around $20, and a mouth-watering antipasto bar – all eagerly patronized by an elegant, out-to-be-seen crowd.

Jewish and Russian

Carnegie Deli 854 Seventh Ave, between W 54th and 55th sts ℡212/757-2245. The most generously stuffed sandwiches in the city are served by the rudest of waiters at this famous Jewish deli. Still, it's a must-have experience, if you can stand the inflated prices.

Petrossian 182 W 58th St, at Seventh Ave ℡212/245-2214. Pink granite and etched mirrors set the mood at this decadent Art Deco establishment, where champagne and caviar are the norm. That said, wow! is this place expensive. The most affordable option (sans caviar, sans champagne) is the $39 prix-fixe dinner.

Uncle Vanya Café 315 W 54th St, between Eighth and Ninth aves ℡212/262-0542. Moderately priced Russian delicacies, including more than the obligatory borscht and caviar.

Latin American

Churrascaria Plataforma 316 W 49th St, between Eighth and Ninth aves ℡212/245-0505. Meat (the fare of choice) is served in this huge, open Brazilian dining room by waiters carrying swords stabbed with succulent slabs of grilled pork, chicken, and lots of beef. The $50 prix-fixe (your only option) covers all of these various grilled meats and more. Don't miss the addictive *caipirinhas* (Brazil's national drink).

Hell's Kitchen 679 Ninth Ave, between W 46th and 47th sts ℡212/977-1588. Lively atmosphere aided and abetted by six different kinds of frozen margaritas and sophisticated renderings of Mexican cuisines. Start with the coriander tuna tostadas and move on to the red snapper in *chipotle* and corn broth. For dessert, the carmelized banana *empanadas* are unbeatable.

Rice 'n' Beans 744 Ninth Ave, between W 50th and 51st sts ℡212/265-4444. Narrow, no-frills space serving up affordable and delicious Brazilian fare. In addition to the namesake dish, there are grilled steaks, hearty soups, and some tasty seafood offerings.

Rosa Mexicano 61 Columbus Ave, between W 62nd and 63rd sts ℡212/977-7700. Right across from Lincoln Center, it's the perfect location for a post-opera meal. Try the guacamole, which is mashed at your table, and their signature pomegranate margaritas.

Vegetarian

Great American Health Bar 35 W 57th St, between Fifth and Sixth aves ☎212/355-5177. This Manhattan chain comes highly praised, but the food can be rather bland and uninviting. For committed vegetarians only. Moderately priced.

Upper East Side

Upper East Side restaurants mostly exist to serve a discriminating mixture of Park Avenue matrons and young professionals; many of the city's best Japanese and French restaurants call this area home. Otherwise, the cuisine here is much like that of the rest of Manhattan: a middling mixture of Asian, standard American, and reasonable Italian cafés. More and more family–oriented restaurants are popping up here all the time.

American and Continental

Barking Dog Luncheonette 1678 Third Ave, at E 94th St ☎212/831-1800. This diner-like place offers outstanding, cheap American food (like mashed potatoes and gravy). Kids will feel at home, especially with the puppy motif. Adults will appreciate the excellent Cobb salad.

E.A.T. 1064 Madison Ave, between E 80th and 81st sts ☎212/772-0022. Owned by restaurateur and gourmet grocer Eli Zabar, *E.A.T.* is expensive and crowded but the food is excellent, especially the soups, breads, ficelles, and Parmesan toast. The mozzarella, basil, and tomato sandwiches are fresh and heavenly.

Etats-Unis 242 E 81st St, between Second and Third aves ☎212/517-8826. This pocket-size, New American restaurant is perfect for an intimate evening on the town. There's a nicely curated wine list and menu to match. Pricey but a reasonable splurge.

King's Carriage House 251 E 82nd St, between Second and Third aves ☎212/734-5490. You'll feel as if you've been transported to the country at this romantic, converted carriage-house. With reliable Continental cuisine, it's a fine place for an afternoon pick-me-up cup of tea or an unwind-me-down glass of wine.

Lenox Room 1278 Third Ave, between E 73rd and 74th sts ☎212/772-0404. A fairly swanky seafood spot with an expansive raw bar (over a dozen varieties of oyster), delicious tuna tartare, and other interesting *fruits de mer*.

Viand 673 Madison Ave, between E 61st and 62nd sts ☎212/751-6622. Though pricier than most diners, *Viand*'s chicken *souvlaki* platters, remarkable burgers, and tasty vanilla Cokes are worth the few extra dollars.

Asian

Donguri 309 E 83rd St, between First and Second aves ☎212/737-5656. Sushi lovers won't want to miss this little five-table, family-run spot featuring some of the best bluefin tuna in town, as well as superb Kumamoto oysters, mushroom tempura, and broiled whitefish. There are only two seatings per night (7 and 9pm) and they tend to hustle out the early shift ASAP, so don't plan on lingering.

Pig Heaven 1540 Second Ave, between E 80th and 81st sts ☎212/744-4333. A good-value Chinese restaurant. The accent is on pork (it's decorated with images of pigs, and spare ribs are the featured items on the menu), but everything else is good, too.

Saigon Grill 1700 Second Ave, at E 88th St ⊤212/996-4600. If you can put up with the hectic service and in-and-out attitude, then head here for affordable, well-executed Vietnamese dishes.

Sushi of Gari 402 E 78th St, between First and York aves ⊤212/517-5340. Amiable neighborhood sushi shop with top-quality fish. The tasting menu is full of unusual offerings, including *toro* and pickled radish.

French

Aureole 34 E 61st St, between Madison and Park aves ⊤212/319-1660. *Aureole*'s French-accented American food is unbelievable. It's also quite expensive: the prix-fixe options should bring the cost down to $79 per head, or $89 for the five-course tasting menu. Stop by just for the show-stopping desserts, or the truly affordable late-lunch special (2–2.30pm; $20).

Café Boulud 20 E 76th St, between Madison and Fifth aves ⊤212/772-2600. The muted but elegant interior of chef Daniel Boulud's second Manhattan eatery (there are three) makes this an exceedingly pleasant place to savor the sublime concoctions that emerge from the kitchen. Save room for dessert: the lime-grapefruit soup with lemon-vodka sorbet or coffee profiteroles with chocolate sauce are equally delicious.

Daniel 60 E 65th St, between Madison and Park aves ⊤212/288-0033. Upscale and expensive fare from chef Daniel Boulud – think truffle-crusted lobster and cod confit with fennel and grapefruit. There's even an elaborate, seasonal vegetarian prix-fixe menu ($88). One of the best French restaurants in New York City.

Le Refuge 166 E 82nd St, between Lexington and Third aves ⊤212/861-4505. Quiet, intimate, and deliberately romantic old-style French restaurant in an old city brownstone. The bouillabaisse and other seafood dishes are delectable. Expensive but worth it; save trips here for special occasions. Closed Sun during the summer.

Indian and Middle Eastern

Dawat 210 E 58th St, between Second and Third aves ⊤212/355-7555. One of the most elegant gourmet Indian restaurants in the city. The chicken *tikka masala* ($17) is superbly marinated and spiced. It can be a bit pricey – entrees average about $20.

Persepolis 1423 Second Ave, between E 74th and 75th sts ⊤212/535-1100. One of the few places in New York City for Persian food, this is also one of the best. Smells of rose, cherry, and cardamom fill the dining room. It's affordable, too.

Rectangles 1431 First Ave, between E 74th and 75th sts ⊤212/744-7470. Probably the best Middle Eastern food in the city, this Yemeni-Israeli restaurant features tasty standards like hummus, *baba ghanoush*, and a spicy chicken soup that can instantly cure the common cold. Closed Sat.

Italian

Caffè Buon Gusto 243 E 77th St, between Second and Third aves ⊤212/535-6884. The Upper East Side has no shortage of middling Italian restaurants, but the food at *Buon Gusto* is a notch better than its peers (and a notch lower in price). The vodka sauce is excellent.

Carino 1710 Second Ave, between E 88th and 89th sts ⊤212/860-0566. Family-run Upper East Side Italian joint, with low prices, friendly service, and good food. Two can eat here for under $30.

Ecco-La 1660 Third Ave, at E 93rd St ⊤212/860-5609. Moderate prices make this place one of the Upper East Side's most popular Italian eateries, though the pasta offerings are pretty standard. Reservations are a good idea.

Elaine's 1703 Second Ave, between E 88th and 89th sts ⊤212/534-8103. Remember the opening shots of Woody Allen's film *Manhattan*? That was *Elaine's*, and the wood-panelled Italian restaurant remains something of a favorite with New York celebrities – though it's hard to see why. The food is solid enough but absurdly over-priced. Nevertheless, if you want to star-gaze there's no better place to go.

Eastern European

Heidelberg 1648 Second Ave, between E 85th and 86th sts ⊤212/628-2332. The atmosphere here is *mittel*-European kitsch, with gingerbread trim and waitresses in Alpine goatherd costumes. The food, though, is the real deal, featuring excellent liver-dumpling soup, *Bauernfrühstück* omelets, and pancakes (both sweet and potato). And they serve *Weissbier* the right way, too – in giant, boot-shaped glasses.

Mocca Hungarian 1546 Second Ave, between
E 80th and 81st sts ☎212/734-6470. This
Yorkville restaurant dishes out hearty portions
of Hungarian comfort food – schnitzel, cherry
soup, goulash, and chicken paprikash,
among others. Be sure to come hungry.

Latin American

Maya 1191 First Ave, between E 64th and 65th
sts ☎212/585-1818. Excellent, high-end
Mexican entrees are served in a large, colorful, and noisy dining room. The rock shrimp
ceviche, chicken *mole*, and grilled dorado
filet make this one of the best restaurants
on the Upper East Side – and among the
best Mexican spots in the whole city.
Taco Taco 1726 Second Ave, at E 90th St
☎212/289-8226. High-quality, super-cheap

taco depot with some unconventional fillings (beef tongue and sautéed cabbage) in
addition to the standards. The fish tacos are
especially good.

Upper West Side and Morningside Heights

The **Upper West Side** is yuppie-residential, and the cuisine on offer is tailored
to local tastes. There are lots of generous burger joints, Chinese restaurants,
friendly coffee shops and delectable, if a bit pricey, brunch spots. You'll never be
at a loss for good, comforting dishes, but don't expect many memorable meals.

African

Awash 947 Amsterdam Ave, between 106th and
107th sts ☎212/961-1416. Ethiopian expats
flock to this brightly colored restaurant offering sumptuous vegetarian and meat combo
platters ($10–17). Dig in with your hands,
but lay off the too-sweet honey wine.

American and Continental

Big Nick's 70 W 71st, at Columbus Ave
☎212/799-4444. If you want a hamburger
or pizza on the Upper West Side, this is a
fun place to go. Big Nick has been serving
them up all night long to locals for years
in his crowded, chaotic little wooden-table
restaurant.
Boat Basin Café W 79th St, at the Hudson
River with access through Riverside Park
☎212/496-5542. An outdoor restaurant,
the *Boat Basin* is only open May through
September. The informal tables are covered
in red- and white-checked cloths, and the
food is standard – burgers with fries, hot
dogs, sandwiches, and some more serious
entrees like grilled salmon – but inexpensive
considering the prime location. On weekend

afternoons a violin trio adds to the pleasant
ambience.
Boathouse Café Central Park Lake, at W 72nd St
entrance ☎212/517-2233. A peaceful retreat
after a hard day's trudging around the Fifth
Avenue museums. You get great views of
the famous Central Park skyline and decent
American/Continental cuisine, but at very
steep prices. Closed Oct to March.
Dock's Oyster Bar 2427 Broadway, between W
89th and 90th sts ☎212/724-5588. This popular uptown seafood restaurant has a raw
bar with great mussels, though it can be
noisy and the service slow. Reservations are
recommended on weekends.
EJ's Luncheonette 447 Amsterdam Ave,
between W 81st and 82nd sts ☎212/873-3444.
Diner that does its best to look retro, with
mirrors, booths upholstered in turquoise
vinyl, and walls adorned with 1950s photographs. Unpretentious, affordable American
food that includes waffles in many guises
(over 14 toppings to choose from), a peanut
butter chocolate pie ($4) to die for, and
great salads and French-fried sweet potatoes. Expect long lines for brunch.
Ouest 2315 Broadway, between W 83rd and
84th sts ☎212/580-8700. This New American

㉕

restaurant has earned a loyal following for its exceptional gourmet comfort food, such as bacon-wrapped meatloaf with wild-mushroom gravy; there's also a $26 three-course pre-theater menu (weekdays only). Celebs are frequently spotted enjoying a bite to eat here.

Per Se 1 Central Park W, 10 Columbus Circle, Time Warner Center ☎212/823-9335. Standard dishes are utterly transformed in a series of tasting menus (from five to nine courses, $125–150). Mushroom soup becomes "Cappuccino of Forest Mushrooms" and is served in a *café au lait* cup; "Macaroni and cheese" is the name for a dish that includes poached lobster, orzo, and a thin sliver of parmesan. Reservations accepted only by phone two months prior to the day.

Santa Fe 73 W 71st St, between Columbus Ave and Central Park W ☎212/724-0822. Upscale Southwestern cuisine in lovely surroundings – muted earth tones, large arrangements of fresh flowers, and a cozy fireplace in the bar. The food is first-rate and the prices steep; be prepared to spend about $50 per person.

Sarabeth's 423 Amsterdam Ave, between W 80th and 81st sts ☎212/496-6280. Best for brunch, this country-style restaurant serves delectable baked goods and impressive omelets. Expect to wait in line for a table.

Tavern on the Green Central Park W, between W 66th and 67th sts ☎212/873-3200. This fantastical, tacky tourist trap remains a New York institution. The American and Continental cuisine is dependable if not extraordinary, and during warmer months there's dancing Thursday evenings on the terrace overlooking the park.

Asian

Haru 433 Amsterdam Ave, between W 80th and 81st sts ☎212/579-5655. A solid stand-by in this part of town if you're craving sushi. It's extremely popular, so you should expect to wait for a table.

Hunan Park 235 Columbus Ave, between W 70th and 71st sts ☎212/724-4411. Some of the best Chinese food on the Upper West Side is served here, in a large, crowded room, with typically quick service and moderate prices. Try the spicy noodles in sesame sauce and the dumplings.

Rain 100 W 82nd St, between Amsterdam and Columbus aves ☎212/501-0776. A safe pick for pan-Asian cuisine. The little-bit-of-everything menu is decent, as is the pricing. Quite a lively atmosphere.

Rikyu 483 Columbus Ave, between W 83th and 84th sts ☎212/799-7847. A wide selection of Japanese food, including sushi made to order. Inexpensive lunches and early-bird specials make this place a relative bargain.

French and Belgian

Café des Artistes 1 W 67th St, between Columbus Ave and Central Park W ☎212/877-3500. Charming, fantastical restaurant with richly hued murals and an international menu; its $25 prix-fixe lunch is a good option for those on a budget.

Jean Georges Trump International Hotel, 1 Central Park W, between W 60th and 61st sts ☎212/299-3900. French fare at its finest, crafted by star chef Jean-Georges Vongerichten. The gracious service is a throwback to another, more genteel, era. It's definitely the place for a special occasion; for the more money-conscious, the front-room *Nougatine* has a prix-fixe summer brunch for $20. The wine list includes bottles ranging $22–12,000.

Picholine 35 W 64th St, between Broadway and Central Park W ☎212/724-8585. This French favorite gets rave reviews, especially for its cheese plate. A terrific spot for a special dinner.

Italian

Gennaro 665 Amsterdam Ave, between W 92nd and 93rd sts ☎212/665-5348. A tiny, bustling outpost of truly great Italian food. The excellent menu includes such moderately priced favorites as a warm potato, mushroom, and goat cheese tart and braised lamb shank in red wine. Don't forget to save room for dessert. Open for dinner only.

Terrace in the Sky 400 W 119th St, between Amsterdam Ave and Morningside Drive ☎212/666-9490. Enjoy harp music, marvelous Mediterranean fare, and bird's-eye views of Morningside Heights from this romantic uptown spot.

V&T Pizzeria 1024 Amsterdam Ave, between W 110th and 111th sts ☎212/663-1708. Checked tablecloths and a low-key, down-home feel describes this pizzeria near Columbia University, with predictably college-aged patrons. Good and inexpensive.

25

Jewish and Eastern European

Barney Greengrass (The Sturgeon King) 541 Amsterdam Ave, between W 86th and 87th sts ☎212/724-4707. West Side deli and restaurant that's been around since time began. The smoked-salmon section is a particular treat. Cheese blintzes are tasty, too. Closed Mon.
Fine & Schapiro 138 W 72nd St, between Broadway and Columbus ☎212/877-2721. Longstanding Jewish deli that's open for lunch and dinner, serving delicious old-fashioned kosher fare. Great chicken soup.

Latin American

Café con Leche 424 Amsterdam Ave, at W 80th St ☎212/595 7000. This great neighborhood Dominican restaurant serves roast pork, rice and beans, and some of the hottest chilli sauce you've ever tasted. Cheap and very cheerful. Also at 726 Amsterdam Ave, between 95th and 96th sts.
Calle Ocho 446 Columbus Ave, between W 81st and 82nd sts ☎212/873-5025. Very tasty Latino fare, including *ceviche* (there's a wide

selection priced $12–15) and *chimchuri* steak ($25) with yucca fries, served in an immaculately designed restaurant with a hopping lounge. The mojitos ($8) are as tasty and potent as any in the city.
La Caridad 2199 Broadway, at W 78th St ☎212/874-2780. This no-frills eatery – something of an Upper West Side institution – doles out Cuban-Chinese food to hungry diners (the Cuban is better than the Chinese). Expect to wait in line.
Pampa 768 Amsterdam Ave, between 97th and 98th sts ☎212/865-2929. Some of the most tender *lomo* and *entrana* steaks in the city are served at this pricey Argentine *parilla*. In nice weather, ask for one of the garden tables. No credit cards or reservations.

Middle Eastern

Turkuaz 2637 Broadway, at W 100th St ☎212/665-9541. Sip a glass of *raki* in *Turkuaz*'s cavernous dining room and linger over such Turkish delicacies as grape leaves stuffed with salmon cubes. The *baklava* is unparalleled.

Harlem and above

While visitors to **Harlem** will find plenty of cheap Caribbean and West African eateries, it would be unthinkable not to try the soul food for which the area is justifiably famous. Whether it's ribs or fried chicken and waffles you're craving, you simply can't go wrong. Many of these restaurants are run by passionate chef-owners who pride themselves on their delicious, calorie-rich dishes.

American and Continental

Amy Ruth's 113 W 116th St, between Lenox and Seventh aves ☎212/280-8779. The honey-dipped fried chicken is more than enough reason to travel to this casual family restaurant. It gets especially busy after church on Sundays.

Bayou 308 Lenox Ave, between W 125th and 126th sts ☎212/426-3800. Head to this upscale spot, a favorite of Bill Clinton's, for good New Orleans–style shrimp and okra gumbo ($5 per cup) or crawfish étouffée ($15). *Bayou* gets its dishes right.

Charles' Southern Style Kitchen 2841 Frederick Douglass Blvd ☎212/926-4313. Fried chicken is the specialty at this tiny Harlem spot, but the filling macaroni and cheese is equally good. There's a $10 open buffet on Wed.

Copeland's 549 W 145th St, between Broadway and Amsterdam Ave ☎212/234-2357. Not much thought went into the interior decorating here, but the excellent soul food at good prices more than makes up for it. Try the Louisiana gumbo. Live jazz on Fri and Sat nights.

Londel's 2620 Eighth Ave, between W 139th and 140th sts ☎212/234-0601. A little soul food, a little Cajun, a little Southern-fried food. This is an attractive, down-home place where you can eat upscale items like steak Diane or more common treats such as fried chicken ($14); either way, follow it up with some sweet-potato pie. Jazz and R&B on Fri and Sat evenings at 8pm and 10pm.

Oscar's Famous BBQ 1325 Fifth Ave, at 111th St ☎212/996-1212. This convivial joint still serves some of the best pulled-pork sandwiches ($7) in New York. Good for weekend brunch.

Sylvia's Restaurant 328 Lenox Ave, between W 126th and 127th sts ☎212/996-0660. The most well-known Southern soul-food restaurant in Harlem – so famous that Sylvia herself even has her own packaged-food

line. While some find the barbecue sauce too tangy, the fried chicken is exceptional and the candied yams are justly celebrated.

▽ Sylvia's Restaurant

Also famous for its Sunday gospel brunch, but be prepared for a long wait.

Caribbean

Caridad Restaurant 4311 Broadway, at W 191st St ☎212/781-1880. In the heart of Washington Heights, this place serves mountains of Dominican food at cheap prices. Try the *mariscos*, the specialty of the house, with lots of *pan y ajo* (thick slices of French bread grilled with olive oil and plenty of garlic). Be sure to go with an appetite.

Sisters 47 E 124th St, between Park and Madison aves ☎212/410-3000. Spicy, inexpensive Caribbean classics like jerk chicken, goat curry, callaloo, and oxtail stew in an unassuming diner. Best for lunch or an early dinner, as the favorite dishes start selling out as the evening wears on.

Brooklyn

Over the past several years **Brooklyn** has turned into a seriously food-centric borough, with many ambitious young chefs taking chances on cheap storefront spaces and dreaming of culinary stardom; Park Slope, Carroll Gardens, Cobble

Hill, and Fort Greene all have expanding restaurant rows. Additionally, Atlantic Avenue offers some of the city's best Middle Eastern food, and Brighton Beach features the most authentic Russian food in NYC.

Downtown Brooklyn

Junior's 386 Flatbush Ave, at DeKalb Ave ☎718/852-5257. Open 24hr and with enough lights to make it worthy of Vegas, *Junior's* offers everything from chopped-liver sandwiches to ribs to a full cocktail bar. Most of it is just so-so – the real draw is the cheesecake, for which the place is justly famous. The servings are mammoth.

Fulton Ferry District

Grimaldi's 19 Old Fulton St, between Water and Front sts ☎718/858-4300. People line up down the sidewalk for the delicious, thin, and crispy pizza pies, legendary throughout the city. Lunchtime is a better bet for avoiding crowds. Cash only.

River Café 1 Water St, between Furman and Old Fulton sts ☎718/522-5200. This genteel eating establishment at the base of the Brooklyn Bridge provides spectacular views of Manhattan. Individual dishes like the potato-crusted oysters are excellent, but the three-course $75 prix-fixe (dinner only) is a little steep. Order the "Chocolate Marquise," which comes with a chocolate-laced version of the Brooklyn Bridge.

Superfine 126 Front St, between Jay and Pearl sts ☎718/243-9005. *Superfine*'s ever-changing menu has a fresh, Mediterranean bent, with lots of big salads, and Sunday brunch features New Mexican green chillis, a nod to the chef's Southwestern roots. Closed Sun night and Mon.

Brooklyn Heights

Heights Café 84 Montague St, at Hicks St ☎718/625-5555. Near the Esplanade, this mainstay offers a pleasant environment for a drink and appetizers; for a full dinner, you can do better elsewhere.

Henry's End 44 Henry St, at Cranberry St ☎718/834-1776. Neighborhood bistro with a wide selection of reasonably priced seasonal dishes, appetizers, and desserts. Normally crowded, and don't expect it to be all that cheap. Known for its wild-game festival in fall and winter.

Teresa's 80 Montague St, at Hicks St ☎718/797-3996. A tidy little Eastern

European–influenced diner, serving *pierogi*, blintzes, and, for breakfast, fat slices of French toast.

Atlantic Avenue

Waterfalls 144 Atlantic Ave, at Henry St ☎718/488-8886. Middle Eastern specialties with a Syrian touch, touted by many as the best in the city, and certainly the finest on Atlantic Ave. Consistency is an issue – stick with salads and other *mezes* to be on the safe side.

Waterfront Ale House 155 Atlantic Ave, between Clinton and Henry sts ☎718/522-3794. This inexpensive and fun old-style pub serves good spicy chicken wings, ribs, and killer Key Lime Pie.

Fort Greene

Locanda Vini e Olii 129 Gates Ave, at Cambridge Place ☎718/622-9202. Gorgeous, inventive Italian fare served in a restored pharmacy, all gleaming dark wood and glass. Duck *papardelle*, fluffy *gnocchi*, and even beef tongue in parsley sauce may show up on the menu. Very affordable, and worth the walk to the far reaches of Fort Greene (aka Clinton Hill). Closed Mon.

Loulou 222 Dekalb Ave, between Adelphi and Clermont sts ☎718/246-0633. Reliably delicious French fare, with a dinner menu that can be heavy on seafood (the female half of the husband-and-wife ownership team hails from Brittany), and very good brunch (think lots of Nutella).

Pequeña 86 S Portland Ave, at Lafayette Ave ☎718/643-0000. Super-friendly and cheap, this bohemian neighborhood Mexican joint satisfies urges for both cheesy quesadillas and big green salads. The pork enchiladas with chile verde are excellent.

Thomas Beisl 25 Lafayette Ave, between Ashland Place and St Felix St ☎718/222-5800. Directly across the street from BAM (see p.246), this recreated Viennese café is just elegant enough to set the tone for a pre-show dinner. Rich beef-cheek goulash, sauerkraut-and-trout crêpes, fantastic desserts, and a year-round patio are all highlights. It's open for lunch, too.

Brooklyn

RESTAURANTS

(25)

Cobble Hill and Carroll Gardens

Café LULUc 214 Smith St, at Baltic St ☎718/625-3815. Wide-ranging, crowd-pleasing, French-influenced menu, with pastas as well as croissant sandwiches. The same owners operate *Porchetta*, 241 Smith St, renowned for its cheap and delicious brunches.

Chestnut 271 Smith St, at Degraw St ☎718/243-0049, ⊛www.chestnutonsmith .com. This yellow-hued neighborhood eatery hits the spot with homey, as-organic-as-possible cuisine with influences ranging from Italian to Mexican. Appetizers run $5–9, and main courses top out at $23, with prix-fixe specials on Tues & Wed. Closed Mon.

Ferdinando's Focacceria 151 Union St, between Hicks and Columbia sts ☎718/855-1545. Authentic stick-to-your-ribs Italian, including such gut-busters as *arancini* (deep-fried, cheese-filled rice balls) and a sandwich of chickpea-flour fritters, ricotta, and marinara sauce. Not for the faint of heart (or stomach), but one of the best survivors from Carroll Gardens' pre-gentrification days. Closed Sun.

Frankies 457 Spuntino 457 Court St, at Luquer St ☎718/403-0033. Co-chefs Frank and Frank revive and refine Italian-American favorites on the south side of Carroll Gardens. Don't miss the marinara (better known as "gravy" to Brooklynites), the sausage sandwiches, or the dandelion salad. A big selection of vegetable antipasti, good cheeses, and a couple of pasta options make the place vegetarian-friendly. Enjoy your meal on the breezy garden patio out back.

The Grocery 288 Smith St, between Sackett and Union sts ☎718/596-3335. Loyal fans are obsessed with this place, which helped establish Smith Street's restaurant row. The owners combine seasonal ingredients in simple but satisfying ways (lentils with poached eggs and bacon, for instance). Try the home-made sausages. Six-course tasting menu is $70. Closed Sun.

Red Hook

360 360 Van Brunt St, at Wolcott St ☎718/246-0360. Market-fresh ingredients, a bohemian ambience, and an excellent list of organic wines make this French restaurant worth the adventure of finding it. The prix-fixe menu ($25) changes every day. Closed Mon & Tues.

Park Slope

Al Di Là 248 Fifth Ave, at Carroll St ☎718/783-4565. Venetian country cooking at its finest at this husband-and-wife-run eatery. Standouts include beet ravioli, grilled sardines, *saltimbocca*, and salt-baked striped bass. Early or late, expect at least a 45-minute wait (they don't take reservations).

Coco Roco 392 Fifth Ave, between 6th and 7th sts ☎718/965-3376. Succulent Peruvian-style rotisserie chicken, roast pork, *ceviche*, and really good desserts, all very reasonably priced.

Geido 331 Flatbush Ave, at Seventh Ave ☎718/638-8866. Graffiti-covered walls and wobbly tables belie the wonderfully fresh sushi prepared by a chef with a cult-like following. Try the *okomiyaki*, a seafood pancake not found on other Japanese menus in the city.

Mama Duke 243 Flatbush Ave, at Bergen St ☎718/857-8700. Southern soul food, from collard greens to grits to red velvet cake. The place just so happens to be owned by Sean "Puffy" Combs's mom.

Miriam 79 Fifth Ave, at Prospect Place ☎718/622-2250. A range of refined Middle Eastern flavors are on the menu at this welcoming, inexpensive café, from couscous to artichoke-and-halloumi salad.

Rose Water 787 Union St, at Sixth Ave ☎718/783-3800. Intimate Mediterranean-American bistro, serving excellent seasonal dishes with flavorful accents, like Moroccan *charmoula* sauce (coriander, garlic, and lemon). A little pricey, with entrees around $20, though you'd pay much more back in Manhattan. Excellent brunch too.

Bay Ridge

Agnanti Meze 7802 Fifth Ave, at 78th St ☎718/833-7033. Come to the bigger branch of the Astoria, Queens' favorite (see p.360) for exceptionally fresh Greek food.

Nouvelle 8716 Third Ave, at 87th St ☎718/238-8250. A former executive chef of *Nobu* (see p.332) runs this flashy pan-Asian lounge, favored by locals for its miso-marinated cod and melt-in-your-mouth sashimi.

Coney Island

Gargiulo's 2911 W 15th St, between Surf and Mermaid aves ☎718/266-4891. A gigantic, noisy, family-run Coney Island restaurant famed for its large portions of cheap and hearty Neapolitan food.

Totonno's 1524 Neptune Ave, between 15th and 16th sts ☎718/372-8606. This ancient pizza joint, notable for its use of fresh mozzarella, inspires fierce debates among aficionados – if you're in the area, stop in for a slice.

Brighton Beach

Café Glechik 3159 Coney Island Ave, between Brighton Beach Ave and 10th St ☎718/616-0494. A refreshing break from the ritzier places in this neighborhood, this casual restaurant is decorated with folk art and serves many of its homestyle dishes in clay pots. The lamb kebab and rabbit stew are particularly good.

Primorski 282 Brighton Beach Ave, between 2nd and 3rd sts ☎718/891-3111. Perhaps the best of Brighton Beach's Russian hangouts, with a huge menu of authentic Russian dishes, including blintzes and stuffed cabbage, at absurdly cheap prices. Live music in the evening.

Rasputin 2670 Coney Island Ave, at Ave X ☎718/332-8333. Outstanding multi-course meals (two fish courses, one meat) for a fairly reasonable price, plus way-over-the-top cheeseball Rockette-style entertainment. One of the truly great "only in New York" experiences.

Williamsburg

Bamonte's 32 Withers St, between Lorimer St and Union Ave ☎718/384-8831. Red-sauce restaurants abound in NYC, but this is one of the legends, serving traditional Italian-American dishes like giant cheese ravioli since 1900. Closed Sun & Tues.

Brick Oven Gallery 33 Havemeyer St, between N 7th and 8th sts ☎718/963-0200. The perfect pit-stop before heading to nearby *Pete's Candy Store* (see p.374), this unassuming eatery serves superb wood-fired pizzas, best washed down with not-quite-superb $2 glasses of table wine. A giant back garden is a bonus.

Diner 85 Broadway, at Berry St ☎718/486-3077. A fave with artists and hipsters, this groovy eatery in a Pullman diner-car serves tasty American bistro grub (hangar steaks,

roasted chicken, fantastic fries) at good prices. The kitchen is open till midnight.

D.O.C. Wine Bar 83 N 7th St, at Wythe St ☎718/963-1925. Shaved-artichoke salad, honey-drizzled sheep's-milk cheese, and assorted cured meats are but a few of the light but intensely savory treats available at this rustic, wood-paneled spot; with the addition of friendly service from the Sardinian owners, it's one of the nicest ways to spend an evening in Williamsburg.

Peter Luger Steak House 178 Broadway, at Driggs Ave ☎718/387-7400. Catering to carnivores since 1887, *Peter Luger* may just be the city's finest steakhouse. The service is surly and the décor plain, but the porterhouse steak – the only cut served – is divine. Old-school sides like creamed spinach are just a distraction. Cash only; expect to pay at least $60 a head.

Planet Thailand 133 N 7th St, between Bedford Ave and Berry St ☎718/599-5758. A longtime favorite of Williamsburg's stylish-yet-cash-strapped set, this enormous restaurant serves Thai and Japanese food at attractive prices. The food is dependable, and there's a DJ to ensure the party (and sake) flows into the night.

Zipi Zape 152 Metropolitan Ave, at Berry St ☎718/599-3027. Crowd in at this skinny, popular tapas bar to savor a delightful range of Spanish snacks, such as garlicky razor clams or shrimp. The tab can add up quickly, but happy hour (5–8pm) helps a little. Closed Mon.

Greenpoint

Old Poland Bakery and Restaurant 190 Nassau Ave, at Humboldt St ☎718/349-7775. Cheap and delicious Polish food as served in the old country. Pork shank with mashed potatoes and vegetables is the way to go.

The Queen's Hideaway 222 Franklin St, at Green St ☎718/383-2355. There's Led Zeppelin on the vintage turntable and plenty of cast-iron skillets in the closet-size kitchen of this idiosyncratic restaurant. The menu changes nightly, but you can count on some sort of pork dish, amazing black bean fritters, and barbecue on Tuesdays. Vegetarians will have a bit of a hard time. Closed Mon.

Brooklyn

RESTAURANTS |

(25)

Queens

The most ethnically diverse of all the boroughs, **Queens** offers some of the city's best opportunities to sample a wealth of authentic foreign flavors, from Greek to Colombian. To enjoy them, however, you have to be willing to invest the time it takes to get there – in some cases, restaurants can be a 45-minute subway ride away from Manhattan. Those who do make the trek, however, are sure to be rewarded with culinary delights.

Long Island City and Astoria

Agnanti 19-06 Ditmars Blvd, Astoria ⊤718/545-4554, ⓦwww.agnantimeze .com. Specializing in Greek *meze* – small plates for snacking – this restaurant overlooks Astoria Park. Don't miss the "specialties from Constantinople" section of the menu, with goodies like *bekri-meze*, wine-soaked cubes of tender meat.

Kabab Café 25-12 Steinway St, Astoria ⊤718/728-9858. The culinary highlight of Steinway Street's "Little Egypt," this hole-in-the-wall is the domain of Chef Ali, who lavishes regulars with traditional Middle Eastern goodies (smoky *baba ghanoush*, lighter-than-air falafel) as well as his own creations – don't miss the honey-glazed duck or the marinated sardines. Closed Mon.

Malagueta 25-35 36th Ave, Astoria ⊤718/937-4821. Refined (but reasonably priced) Brazilian cuisine served in a sleek, white corner space with striking artwork on the walls. If you want to spice up the *moqueca de camarão* (shrimp in coconut milk), ask for a side of hot *molho* sauce. BYOB.

Mundo 31-18e Broadway, entrance on 32nd St, Astoria ⊤718/777-2829, ⓦwww.mundoastoria .com. A charming Turkish and Argentine duo team up to offer flaky *empanadas*, yogurt-covered *manti* (tiny dumplings), and a delicious array of other international treats, in a tiny, cool space. Very vegetarian-friendly.

Tournesol 50-12 Vernon Blvd, Long Island City ⊤718/472-4355. Warm French bistro in Hunters Point, steps from the Vernon Blvd #7 stop and an easy walk from PS 1. Staples like steak *frites*, duck confit, and garlicky escargots are reliably good, the wine list is small but well chosen, and brunch is very tasty.

Uncle George's 33-19 Broadway, at 34th St ⊤718/626-0593. This 24hr joint serves excellent and ultra-cheap authentic Greek food, including some of the top Greek BBQ and *spanakopita* in the city.

Sunnyside and Woodside

Hemsin 39-17 Queens Blvd, Sunnyside ⊤718/937-1715. Perfectly prepared Turkish food, from delicate salads to grilled kebabs. Don't forget the bread, exceptionally fluffy and chewy.

Spicy Mina 64-23 Broadway, Woodside ⊤718/205-2340. Absolutely the best Indian and Bangladeshi food in all five boroughs – the samosa *chaat* appetizer, the Bengali-style mustard fish, and the *daal* fry (split peas) are exceptionally good. Be prepared for a wait, as the eponymous Mina cooks entirely from scratch. BYOB.

Sripraphai 64-13 39th Ave, Woodside ⊤718/899-9599. Truly authentic Thai food that puts anything in Manhattan to shame – sweet, sour, (very) spicy, and astoundingly cheap. Try the "drunken" noodles with beef and basil, and staples like papaya salad and lemongrass soup, or flip through the photo menu for inspiration. An outdoor patio is open in the summer.

Jackson Heights and Corona

Green Field Restaurant 108-01 Northern Blvd, between 108th and 109th sts ⊤718/672-5202. A huge Brazilian meatery, where waiters swarm your table offering every sort of grilled meat under the sun, for the low all-you-can-eat price of $26. Don't get distracted by the salad bar.

Jackson Diner 37-47 74th St, between 37th and Roosevelt aves ⊤718/672-1232. Manhattan foodies make regular pilgrimages to this distant but locally famous Indian restaurant, with outstanding versions of classics like tandoori chicken, goat curry, and shrimp *biryani*. If you love spicy food, don't miss the *vindaloo*. Cash only.

La Pequeña Colombia 83-27 Roosevelt Ave, at 84th St ⊤718/478-6528. Literally "Little Colombia," this place doles out heaping portions of seafood casserole, pork, and *arepas* (fat corn cakes). Try the fruit drinks, such as *maracuya* (passion fruit) or *guana-bana* (soursop).

Flushing and Kew Gardens

East Lake 42-33 Main St, at Franklin St ☎718/539-8532. Fantastic and very inexpensive *dim sum*, plus a selection of over fifty teas. Start out with shrimp dumplings and taro cakes and then move on to sautéed frog's legs and sizzling grilled calamari.

Jang Tuh Sutbulgui 136-93 37th Ave, at Union St ☎718/359-1227. Korean barbecue over real charcoal – a rarity these days. Generous and varied *pan chan* dishes to start, and attentive service. Open 24hrs.
Spicy and Tasty 39-07 Prince St ☎718/359-1601. Tea-smoked duck is the signature dish at this Sichuan specialist; prepare yourself for plenty of spicy noodle dishes as well. Open till 3am.

The Bronx

In the **Bronx**, and the whole of the city, Belmont is *the* place to taste old-school Italian-American "red sauce" cuisine, while City Island, whose coastline seems worlds away from a typical New York neighborhood, serves up some of the freshest seafood in the city. The family establishments here have churned out fish dishes for years, with diners flocking from all over the city, especially on warm summer evenings when the waterside dining is at its most scenic.

South Bronx

Sam's 596–598 Grand Concourse, at 150th St ☎718/665-5341. About a ten-minute walk from Yankee Stadium, *Sam*'s makes for a tasty, cheap pre-game meal, whether you want American soul food or Caribbean standards: chicken comes jerked or fried. Closes at 7pm on Tues and Wed.

Belmont

Dominick's 2335 Arthur Ave, at 187th St ☎718/733-2807. All you would expect from a Belmont neighborhood Italian: communal family-style seating, hearty food, and (usually) low prices – sometimes hard to gauge, as there's no printed menu or written check. Just listen closely to your waiter. Cash only.
Roberto's 603 Crescent Ave, between Arthur Ave and Hughes St ☎718/733-9503. Not quite so stuck in a time warp as other Belmont favorites, *Roberto*'s is renowned for its rich pastas, served on giant plates or, sometimes, baked in foil. Chef's specials are always the best option.

City Island

JP's Waterside Restaurant 703 Minnieford Ave, between Bridge and Terrace sts ☎718/885-3364.

Open 365 days a year, this breezy spot features half-decent seafood, but the real reason to go is to enjoy views of City Island from the back terrace.
Le Refuge Inn 586 City Island Ave, at Cross St ☎718/885-2478. A romantic getaway at a historic B&B, this place might be a little frilly for some, but the French-inflected menu, with dishes like bouillabaisse, is a nice change from standard City Island fare. Reasonable prix-fixe lunch, brunch, and dinner deals. Closed Mon.
Lobster Box 34 City Island Ave, at Rochelle St ☎718/885-1952. Don't mess around with appetizers or sides at this City Island old-timer at the south end of the island – lobster fried, broiled, or steamed is the way to go ($29–41); prices are a little lower at lunch.

Riverdale

The Riverdale Garden 4576 Manhattan College Parkway, at 242nd St ☎718/884-5232. If you do make the hike to Riverdale, splash out at this garden restaurant with a seasonal menu, which features many interesting game dishes. A few blocks from the last stop on the #1 train.

RESTAURANTS

㉕

Staten Island

Staten Island is so far out of the way that you won't be heading there just for the food. But if you're here sightseeing, you can end your day with a romantic dinner in a garden, or with a quality helping of schnitzel.

Aesop's Tables 1233 Bay St, at Maryland Ave ☏718/720-2005. The leafy back garden is a main attraction at this whimsical Mediterranean restaurant that locals call one of Staten Island's best. Entrees are rarely above $20. Right across from the Alice Austen House. Closed Sun & Mon.

Denino's Tavern 524 Port Richmond Ave ☏718/442-9401. A Staten Island favorite since 1937, serving pizza with a slightly thicker, chewier crust than most brick-oven joints in the city.

Killmeyer's Old Bavaria Inn 4254 Arthur Kill Rd, at Sharrott's Rd ☏718/984-1202. A full-tilt German beer-garden near the south end of the island, complete with schnitzel, *sauerbraten*, and giant steins of beer, and live oompah music outside on the weekends. Entrees are large enough to feed two.

The Parsonage 74 Arthur Kill Rd ☏718/351-7879. This upscale Continental restaurant tucked in Historic Richmond Town is a prom-night favorite and a bit spendy – but you could do worse for a post-sightseeing splurge. Appetizers are generally better than the mains.

Drinking

The **bar scene** in New York City is quite eclectic, with a broader range of places to drink than in most American cities, and prices to suit most pockets. Bars generally open their doors at noon and close them in the early hours of the morning – 4am at the latest, when they have to close by law. Bar kitchens tend to stop operating around midnight or a little before.

In a basic bar you'll pay around $4–5 for a pint of beer "on tap" (also referred to as "on draft"), while if you want something cheaper, you can head to a local dive and go for a can of beer. At the other end of the spectrum are the city's plush hotel and rooftop bars (see box, p.369), where **prices** tend to top out at around $15 per drink. Keep an eye out for "happy hour" bargains and two-for-one drink deals (see box, below). Wherever you go, you'll be expected to tip about a buck per drink.

The most obvious drink choice is typically **beer**. You'll see the usual American standards – Budweiser, Sam Adams, etc – alongside such European staples as Stella Artois and Heineken pretty much everywhere. Bars with bigger selections often feature **microbrews** from across the country; all are usually of high quality, and quite tasty. You should also definitely try some of the **local brews**: the *Brooklyn Brewery* does a fine range of beers in all styles (lager, pilsner, wheat, and so on; see p.373); *McSorley's*, the oldest bar in the city (see p.368), serves just two flavors of its own beer, light and dark; and the *Blue Point Brewery*, on Long Island, does several excellent seasonal ales.

Wine demands a better-filled wallet than beer does. When in a restaurant or bar, expect a 100 percent mark-up (at least!) on the cost of a bottle. Many establishments do sell wine by the glass, though if you're planning on having a few drinks it's better to just go ahead and spring for the bottle.

DRINKING

26

Happy hour

At the turn of the nineteenth century, barkeepers on the Bowery offered a "free lunch" of pickles and boiled eggs to attract workingmen during their midday break. This practice has evolved into **happy hour**, now designed to pull in the after-work crowd. It's generally a two-hour period (often 5–7pm), Monday to Friday only. Discounts are offered, either in two-for-one deals, special prices on specific drinks – "well" drinks, for example, which are the cheapest "house" liquors – or a buck or two off everything. A diminishing number of bars put out thirst-inducing snacks like popcorn or pretzels during happy hour, and a few glitzy midtown joints offer free hors d'oeuvres, though this practice is also on the decline.

There are a couple of points of potential confusion for overseas visitors when it comes to **liquor**. Bear in mind that whether you ask for a drink "on the rocks" or not, you'll most likely get it poured into a glass filled with ice; if you don't want it like this ask for it "straight up." Also, American shots are approximately double the size of British and European shots, meaning you get more bang for your buck.

When **buying your own liquor or wine**, you'll need to find a liquor store – supermarkets only sell beer. You must be over age 21 to buy or consume alcohol in a bar or restaurant (and you'll be asked to provide photo ID if there's any dispute), and it's against the law to drink alcohol on the street (which is why you may see people furtively swigging from brown paper bags). Note that the brown bags don't make the drinking any more legal. Also by law, all NYC bars must serve **nonalcoholic drinks**, though you shouldn't expect to pay less for them; sodas, juices, and sparkling waters often sell for the same price as beer.

The bar scene

New York's watering holes are much more interesting below 14th Street than above. Some of the best establishments are located in the **East Village**, the **West Village**, **NoLita**, **Soho**, and the farther western reaches of the **Lower East Side**. There's a decent mix of **midtown** drinking spots, though bars here tend to be geared to tourists and an after-hours office crowd and, consequently, can be pricey and rather dull (there are a few notable exceptions). The **Upper East Side** is home to quite a few raucous sports and Irish bars, while the **Upper West Side** has a serviceable array of bars, although most tend to cater to Columbia University students and more of a clean-cut yuppie crowd. Farther uptown, the bars of **Harlem**, while not numerous, offer some of the city's most affordable jazz in a relaxed environment.

While most visitors to New York may not have time or occasion to check out the bar scenes in the outer boroughs, those who venture to **Williamsburg**, **Park Slope**, **Brooklyn Heights**, and **Fort Greene** in Brooklyn or to **Astoria** in Queens will find bars that range in feel from neighborly to über-hip.

The listings that follow are grouped, approximately, according to the chapter divisions outlined in the Guide. Bear in mind that many places double as bar and restaurant, and you may therefore find them listed not here but in the previous chapter, "Restaurants." For ease of reference, however, all specifically **gay and lesbian bars** are gathered together in "Gay and lesbian New York," Chapter 29.

The smoking ban

In May 2003, New York City's **smoking ban** went into effect for places of employment, including restaurants and bars. This legislation states that smoking is only permitted at establishments that draw more than ten percent of their revenue from the sale of tobacco – meaning that just a handful of cigar bars fall into that category. Smoking is also allowed in 25 percent of outdoor "consumption" areas in gardens, at sidewalk tables, and the like. Violations incur $2000 penalties, so owners have a strong incentive to follow the rules. For better or for worse, New York City is now a smoke-free town.

The Financial District

The Beekman 15 Beekman St, between Nassau and William sts ☎212/732-7333. This Wall Street landmark's great selection of more than twenty draught beers is complemented by frequent live music.

Harry's at Hanover Square 1 Hanover Square, between Pearl and Stone sts ☎212/425-3412. Open only on weekdays, this clubby bar hits its stride when the floor traders come in after work. Great burgers, too.

🏃 **Jeremy's Alehouse** 228 Front St, at Peck Slip ☎212/964-3537. *Jeremy*'s stands in the shadow of the Brooklyn Bridge and the nearby South Street Seaport, serving well-priced pints of beer (there are 15 or so to choose from) and excellent fish dishes. The fried clam strips ($7) have received rave reviews in the press.

Rise at the Ritz-Carlton Hotel, 2 West St, 14th floor, Battery Park ☎212/344-0800. Try this plush hotel lounge for swanky sunset drinks, tiered trays of gourmet tapas, and unsurpassed views of the Statue of Liberty.

Tribeca and Soho

Bar 89 89 Mercer St, between Spring and Broome sts ☎212/274-0989. Soft blue light spills over the bar, giving this sleek, modern place a trippy, pre-dawn feel. Check out the clear liquid-crystal bathroom doors that go opaque when shut ($10,000 each, reportedly). Drinks are predictably pricey.

Bubble Lounge 228 W Broadway, between Franklin and White sts ☎212/431-3433. Swanky place to pop a cork or two. There's a long list of champagnes and sparklers, but beware the skyrocketing tabs.

Dylan Prime 62 Laight St, at Greenwich St ☎212/334-4783. Dim, romantic, and slightly off the beaten Tribeca path. Try the stellar Martinis.

🏃 **Ear Inn** 326 Spring St, between Washington and Greenwich sts ☎212/226-9060. "Ear" as in "Bar" with half the neon "B" chipped off. This cozy pub, a stone's throw from the Hudson River, has a good mix of beers on tap, serves basic, reasonably priced American food, and claims to be the second oldest bar in the city.

Fanelli 94 Prince St, at Mercer St ☎212/226-9412. Established in 1872, *Fanelli* is one of the city's oldest bars. Relaxed and informal, it's a favorite destination of the not-too-hip after-work crowd.

Grace 114 Franklin St, between Church St and W Broadway ☎212/343-4200. *Grace* teems with old-school class – there's a 40ft mahogany bar. It's a nice place for a cocktail; try a Pimm's Cup.

Knitting Factory Tap Bar 74 Leonard St, between Church St and Broadway ☎212/219-3006. The street-level bar is fun, but the cozy downstairs taproom is where things really hum, with numerous draft microbrews and free live music – usually some out-there form of jazz – that usually gets going after 11pm. (For details on the jazz venue, see "Nightlife," p.378.)

Orange Bear 47 Murray St, between Church St and W Broadway ☎212/566-3705. This funky bar may need a facelift, but it's still a great place to check out local rock bands and singer-songwriters, plus the occasional spoken-word event.

Puffy's Tavern 81 Hudson St, between Harrison and Jay sts ☎212/766-9159. This small dive serves cheap booze without a single ounce of attitude, rare in this area. The cool jukebox specializes in old 45s.

The Room 144 Sullivan St, between Houston and Prince sts ☎212/477-2102. Dark, homey two-room bar with exposed brick walls and comfortable couches. No spirits, but an impressive array of domestic and international beers.

Toad Hall 57 Grand St, between W Broadway and Wooster St ☎212/431-8145. With a pool table, good service, and excellent bar snacks, this stylish alehouse is a little less hip and a little more of a local hangout than some of its neighbors.

Chinatown, Little Italy, and NoLita

Double Happiness 173 Mott St, at Broome St ☏212/941-1282. Low ceilings, dark lighting, and lots of nooks and crannies make this downstairs bar an intimate spot. If the décor doesn't seduce you, one of the house specialties – a green-tea Martini – should loosen you up.

Happy Ending 302 Broome St, between Eldridge and Forsythe sts ☏212/334-9676. This duplex hotspot milks its past incarnation as a massage parlor of ill repute; a drink in one of its shower-stall alcoves feels fairly naughty.

Mare Chiaro 176-1/2 Mulberry St, between Broome and Grand sts ☏212/226-9345. Though it looks like a backroom hangout from *The Sopranos*, it's actually a friendly local dive bar open to all. Also known as the *Mulberry Street Bar*.

Pravda 281 Lafayette St, between Prince and Houston sts ☏212/226-4944. This chic Russian lounge serves stiff vodka drinks and hard-boiled eggs for snacking. Now that its heyday has passed, there are fewer crowds, and hence a more relaxed vibe, but it's still a great place. Try the coconut vodka.

Room 18 18 Spring St, between Elizabeth and Mott sts ☏212/219-2592. Somehow, this inexpensive, romantic Asian tapas bar has slipped under the radar. Best go before it becomes insanely popular.

Sweet & Vicious 5 Spring St, between Bowery and Elizabeth St ☏212/334-7915. A neighborhood favorite, *Sweet & Vicious* is the epitome of rustic chic, with exposed brick, lots of wood, and antique chandeliers. The back garden is just as cozy as the inside bar.

Lower East Side

169 Bar 169 E Broadway, at Rutgers St ☏212/473-8866. This urban hangout features a pool table, kicking DJs, and, occasionally, live performers.

Back Room 102 Norfolk St, between Delancey and Rivington sts ☏212/677-9489. With a hidden, back-alley entrance, this former speakeasy was reputedly once a haunt of gangster Meyer Lansky. The adjacent steakhouse serves a succulent bone-in rib-eye, though most come for the drinks.

Barramundi 67 Clinton St, between Stanton and Rivington sts ☏212/529-6900. Though the interior is just fine, it's *Barramundi*'s magical, fairy-lit garden that's the real selling point. Come early, as the garden closes at 10pm.

Barrio Chino 253 Broome St, at Orchard St ☏212/228-6710. Don't be confused by the Chinese lanterns or drink umbrellas here – the owner's specialty is tequila, and there are a dozen brands to choose from. Shots are served with a traditional sangría chaser, made from a blend of tomato, orange, and lime juices.

Delancey Lounge 168 Delancey St, at Clinton St ☏212/254-9920. Williamsburg hipsters meet Lower East Side chic at this rooftop lounge. Things can get frisky in the basement, which pulsates with loud music.

Kush 191 Chrystie St, between Stanton and Houston sts ☏212/677-7328. Beguiling Moroccan bar with live music,

excellent, salty bar snacks, and even belly dancing. Exempt from the smoking ban, *Kush* offers hookah pipes.

Libation 137 Ludlow St, between Stanton and Rivington sts ☏866/216-1263. A sexy lounge spanning two floors. It's a bit eclectic, with $10 cocktails, an American tapas menu, and DJs spinning '80s, hip-hop, and everything in between.

Magician 118 Rivington St, between Essex and Norfolk sts ☏212/673-7881. Dark and sedate, couples come here as much for the intimate atmosphere as for the drinks, which are all of average price.

Max Fish 178 Ludlow St, between Houston and Stanton sts ☏212/529-3959. Local hipsters come here in droves, lured by the unpretentious but arty vibe and the jukebox which, quite simply, rocks any other party out of town. Cheap beers, too.

Rockwood Music Hall 196 Allen St, between Houston and Stanton sts ☏212/477-4155. Seven nights of live music draw hordes of locals to this tiny space. Though there are no bad seats, it's a good idea to come early – it's often packed.

Verlaine 100 Rivington St, between Ludlow and Essex sts ☏212/614-2494. This Asian-Latin joint features high ceilings, local art, and soft couches. The specialty drinks are quite good, too.

Karaoke

Despite the potential to make participants both hoarse and more than a little embarrassed, **karaoke** is still going strong. If you have the guts (and the stamina) to join in, these places will all give you a memorable night:

Arlene's Grocery 95 Stanton St, between Orchard and Ludlow sts ℡212/358-1633. For something completely different, check out their punk and heavy metal karaoke. Every Monday night a live band backs anyone willing to get up and give it their all, wailing tunes from the Ramones to Guns 'N' Roses.

Asia Roma 40 Mulberry St, between Worth and Bayard sts ℡212/385-1133. Despite the fact that this is one of the few places in the city where you can sing for free (after the $15 cover charge), it's often devoid of crowds (and atmosphere). Good to practice that rendition of *Cry Me a River*, though.

MBC Music Box 25 W 32nd St, between Broadway and Fifth Ave ℡212/967-2244. This Little Korea spot has twelve sound-proofed rooms for private tune-filled parties. Choose from very long song lists.

Planet Rose 219 Ave A, between E 13th and 14th sts ℡212/353-9500. The funky living room décor and casual atmosphere here should ease any stage fright. Most singers don't even get attention.

🎤 **Sing Sing Karaoke** 81 Ave A, between E 5th and 6th sts ℡212/674-0700. A little divey but fun, though the drinks are expensive. Fifteen rooms in which to sing to your heart's content.

Winnie's 104 Bayard St, between Mulberry and Baxter sts ℡212/732-2384. Tiny Chinatown bar where the most dedicated New Yorkers go to belt out a few tunes. It's pretty seedy, but nowhere else in the city will you find such a social hodgepodge united in a common cause: bad singing.

East Village

🎤 **7B** 108 Ave B, at E 7th St ℡212/473-8840. A quintessential East Village hangout, *7B* has often been used as the sleazy set in films and commercials. It features deliberately mental bartenders, cheap pitchers of beer, and one of the best punk and rock'n'roll jukeboxes in the Village.

Angel's Share 8 Stuyvesant St, between E 9th St and Third Ave ℡212/777-5415. This serene, candlelit haven is a great date spot: it's kept deliberately romantic by the entry rules – parties larger than four will not be admitted. The cocktails are reputed to be some of the best in the city.

Bar Veloce 175 Second Ave, between E 11th and 12th sts ℡212/260-3200. Tiny, slick wine bar fit for the Mod Squad, with excellent hors d'oeuvres and a fine wine list; look for the Vespa parked out front.

Bouche Bar 540 E 5th St, between aves A and B ℡212/420-9265. The close seating arrangements, dark lighting, and creative drink menu make *Bouche Bar* a good place to bring a date. Try the Girl Scout or Playmate.

Burp Castle 41 E 7th St, between Second and Third aves ℡212/982-4756. A delightfully weird place: the bartenders wear monks' habits, choral music is piped in, and you are encouraged to speak in tones below a whisper. Oh, and there are over 550 different types of beer.

Cozy Cafe 43 E 1st St, between First and Second aves ℡212/475-0177. Comfortable sofas and soft pillows make this subterranean Middle Eastern hookah bar all the more relaxing. Belly dancers Fri and Sat nights.

Croxley Ales 28 Ave B, between E 2nd and 3rd sts ℡212/253-6140. This top-notch sports bar smells strongly of wings and has a great selection of 30 draft and 75 bottled brews, all reasonably priced. Countless TVs are tuned into all the night's big games.

🎤 **d.b.a.** 41 First Ave, between E 2nd and 3rd sts ℡212/475-5097. A beer-lover's paradise, *d.b.a.* has at least 60 bottled beers, 14 brews on tap, and an authentic hand-pump. Garden seating (with a small smoking section) is available in the summer.

Decibel 240 E 9th St, between Second and Third aves ☎212/979-2733. A rocking atmosphere (with good tunes) pervades this beautifully decorated underground sake bar. The inevitable wait for a wooden table will be worth it, guaranteed.

Grassroots Tavern 20 St Mark's Place, between Second and Third aves ☎212/475-9443. This wonderful, roomy underground den has cheap pitchers, Brooklyn Brewery beers for $3, baskets of popcorn for a buck, an extended happy hour, and at least three of the manager's pets roaming around at all hours of the day or night.

Hi Fi 169 Ave A, between E 10th and 11th sts ☎212/420-8392 Formerly a live-music venue, this spot has been stripped of its stage, but is still great for music, featuring an mp3 jukebox with over 19,000 albums. Great-looking hipster boys and girls pack this place, drinking hard pretty much every night of the week.

Holiday Cocktail Lounge 75 St Mark's Place, between Second and Third aves ☎212/777-9637. Unabashed dive with a mixed bag of customers, from old-world grandfathers to young professionals, and a bona-fide character (more or less) tending bar. Good place for an afternoon beer. Closes at 1am.

KGB 85 E 4th St, at Second Ave ☎212/505-3360. On the second floor, this dark bar is set in what was the HQ of the Ukrainian Communist Party in the 1930s. Better known now for its marquee literary readings.

Lakeside Lounge 162 Ave B, between E 10th and 11th sts ☎212/529-8463. The owners, a local DJ and a record producer, have stocked the *Lakeside* jukebox with old rock, country, and R&B records. Live performers frequently pack into one small corner.

Manitoba's 99 Ave B, between E 6th and 7th sts ☎212/982-2511. Run by Dick Manitoba, lead singer of the punk group The Dictators, the kickin' jukebox and rough-and-tumble vibe at this spot make it a favorite among East Villagers who really just like to drink.

McSorley's Old Ale House 15 E 7th St, between Second and Third aves ☎212/473-9148. Yes, it's touristy and often full of local frat boys, but you'll be drinking in history along with your beer at this cheap, landmark bar: *McSorley's* served its first brew in 1854. Try the turkey sandwich with hot mustard; it's one of the best bar snacks in the city.

Sophie's 507 E 5th St, between aves A and B ☎212/228-5680. Inexpensive draft beer and oh-so-cheap mixed drinks make this bar one of the most popular East Village hangouts. The crowd around the pool table can get very raucous.

St Dymphna's 118 St Marks Place, between First Ave and Ave A ☎212/254-6636. With a tempting, filling menu and some of the city's best Guinness, this snug Irish watering-hole is a favorite among young East Villagers.

The Sunburnt Cow 137 Ave C, between E 8th and 9th sts ☎212/529-0005. *The Sunburnt Cow* is like nothing else in the neighborhood. The popular Aussie bar uses wooden stumps for stools and has lighting designed to resemble sunsets. Cocktails are decidedly strong.

Temple Bar 332 Lafayette St, between Bleecker and Houston sts ☎212/925-4242. One of the most discreet and romantic spots for a drink downtown, this sumptuous, dark lounge evokes the glamour of the early 1940s. They take their Martinis very seriously; the guacamole appetizer is the best dish on the short snack menu.

Von 3 Bleecker St, between Bowery and Lafayette St ☎212/473-3039. Like an old pair of jeans, this wine-and-beer-only bar is comfortable (and welcoming) through and through. The prices are pretty nice, too.

Zum Schneider 107–109 Ave C, at E 7th St ☎212/598-1098. A German beer-hall (and indoor garden) with a mega-list of brews and *wursts* from the Fatherland. It can be a bit packed with frat-boy types; in the early evening, though, the old-world vibe is sublime.

West Village

10 Little W 12th St 10 Little W 12th St, between 9th Ave and Washington St ☎212/645-5370. The Meatpacking District's 'tude hasn't affected this establishment (aka *The Nameless Bar*). There's a large outdoor patio out back, and the spacious indoor bar gives off an al fresco vibe, as well.

55 Bar 55 Christopher St, between Sixth and Seventh aves ☎212/929-9883. A gem of an underground dive bar that's been around since the days of Prohibition, *55* is a much-loved local spot, with a great jukebox, congenial clientele, and live jazz music seven nights a week.

Cedar Tavern 82 University Place, between W 11th and 12th sts ⊤212/741-9754. The original *Cedar Tavern*, situated just a block away, was a legendary Beat and artists' meeting point in the1950s. The new version, a homey bar with decent food, reasonably priced drinks, and occasional poetry readings, retains the bohemian feel. You can eat outside in their covered roof-garden all year round.

Chumley's 86 Bedford St, between Grove and Barrow sts ⊤212/675-4449. It's not easy to find this former speakeasy, owing to its unmarked entrance, but the Prohibition-era ambience and good choice of affordable beers and food make it worth the effort.

The Dove 288 Thompson St, between Bleecker and W 3rd sts ⊤212/254-1435. Filled with the post-college crowd, this subterranean bar is always chill. Jazzy happy hours evolve into upbeat late nights.

Fiddlesticks 54–58 Greenwich Ave, at Perry St ⊤212/463-0516. Don't be put off by the Irish kitsch here. Not only is the owner the real deal, but the Guinness is poured well and there are Gaelic lessons and Quiz Night every week.

Hogs & Heifers 859 Washington St, at W 13th St ⊤212/929-0655. "Hogs" as in the burly motorcycles parked outside; "heifers" as in, well, ladies. Though officially there's no more bar dancing (Julia Roberts was famously photographed doing so), those bold enough to venture into this rough-and-tumble Meatpacking District joint can still drink to excess.

Other Room 143 Perry St, between Washington and Greenwich sts ⊤212/645-9758. The cozy-cool atmosphere, excellent drink menu, and "way-west" location of this wine and beer bar have guaranteed it a special place in locals' hearts.

Hotel bars

When you're feeling fabulous in New York, there's no better place to go for a Martini, Cosmo, or mojito than a **hotel bar**. These posh watering-holes are for the well-bred and well-maintained. Expensive drink in hand, sink back into a comfy banquette and watch the parade of foreign dignitaries, royalty, well-groomed businesspeople, media celebs, chic socialites, and mysterious strangers conducting important affairs. The experience will be worth the price.

Bemelman's Bar *The Carlyle Hotel*, 35 E 76th St, at Madison Ave ⊤212/744-1600

The Blue Bar *The Algonquin Hotel*, 59 W 44th St, between Fifth and Sixth aves ⊤212/840-6800

Cellar Bar *Bryant Park Hotel*, 40 W 40th St, between Fifth and Sixth aves ⊤212/642-2260

Church Lounge *Tribeca Grand Hotel*, 2 Sixth Ave, at White St ⊤212/519-6600

Grand Bar *SoHo Grand Hotel*, 310 W Broadway, between Grand and Canal sts ⊤212/965-3000

King Cole Bar *St Regis Hotel*, 2 E 55th St, between Fifth and Madison aves ⊤212/339-6721

North Square *Washington Square Hotel*, 103 Waverly Place, at MacDougal St ⊤212/254-1200

Pen-Top Bar *Peninsula Hotel*, 700 Fifth Ave, at E 55th St ⊤212/956-2888

Thom's Bar *60 Thompson*, 60 Thompson St, between Broome and Spring sts ⊤212/219-2000

Twist Lounge *Ameritania Hotel*, 230 W 54th St, between Broadway and Eighth Ave ⊤212/247-5000

View Bar *The Marriott Marquis*, 1535 Broadway, at W 45th St ⊤212/929-2243

Wet Bar *W Court Hotel*, 130 E 39th St, at Lexington Ave ⊤212/592-8844

Whiskey Blue *The W*, 541 Lexington Ave, between E 49th and 50th sts ⊤212/407-2947

West Village | DRINKING | 26

Peculier Pub 145 Bleecker St, between LaGuardia Place and Thompson St ☎ 212/353-1327. Local bar popular with NYU students. The establishment's main claim to fame is the number of beers it sells – more than 500 in all, with examples from just about any country you can think of.

Spice Market 403 W 13th St, at Ninth Ave ☎ 212/675-2322. Moderate-to-expensive Southeast Asian food is done with finesse at this Meatpacking District hotspot, but if you're not here to eat, head downstairs to the swanky lounge and sip a ginger margarita ($14), kumquat mojito ($12), or tamarind rum punch ($11).

West West Side Highway, at W 11th St ☎ 212/242-4375. Design-forward cement floors, Moderne furniture, and exceptional bartenders make this monochromatic bar/cocktail lounge a happening place to watch the sun set over the Hudson River.

White Horse Tavern 567 Hudson St, at W 11th St ☎ 212/243-9260. A Greenwich Village institution: Dylan Thomas supped his last here before being carted off to the hospital with alcohol poisoning. The beer and food are cheap and palatable, and outside seating is available in the summer.

Chelsea

B.E.D. 530 W 27th St, between Tenth and Eleventh aves ☎ 212/594-4109. People come to *B.E.D.* to see and be seen among three walls of beds/sofas in an expensive Latin American–themed setting.

Elmo 156 Seventh Ave, between W 19th and 20th sts ☎ 212/337-8000. Chelsea has been a trendy neighborhood for years, and nothing captures that better than this swanky spot, where hot socialites drink cocktails and little is cheap.

Half King 505 W 23rd St, between Tenth and Eleventh aves ☎ 212/462-4300. This popular Irish pub is owned by a small group of writer/artists and features good food and regular literary events. They've been known to book some heavy hitters, like Sebastian Junger (one of the owners) and Michele Wucker.

Hiro in the Maritime Hotel, 363 W 16th St, at Ninth Ave ☎ 212/242-4300. Chic, spacious indoor/outdoor lounge in one of the city's latest (and most successful) architectural conversions.

Marquee 289 Tenth Ave, between 26th and 27th sts ☎ 646/473-0202. Everyone's a celebrity of some sort at *Marquee*, one of the hottest velvet-rope spots in town. Dress for success and make sure your paycheck cleared.

Park 118 Tenth Ave, between W 17th and 18th sts ☎ 212/352-3313. It's easy to get lost in *Park*'s vast warren of rooms filled with fireplaces, geodes, and even a Canadian redwood in the middle of the floor. The garden is a treat, and the black-clad patrons are invariably stunning.

Passerby 436 W 15th St, between Ninth and Tenth aves ☎ 212/206-7321. Tiny, funky space with a lighted floor that looks like it came straight out of *Saturday Night Fever*. Perennially full of rail-thin, long-legged lovelies, weird mirrors, and art-world gossip.

Serena in the *Chelsea Hotel*, 222 W 23rd St, between Seventh and Eighth aves ☎ 212/255-4646. This retro basement bar is a fairly recent addition to the *Chelsea Hotel*, bringing in a younger and infinitely more self-assured brand of local. The drinks can be somewhat pricey, and although the bouncers seem threatening, they're really puppy dogs in disguise.

Trailer Park Lounge 271 W 23rd St, between Seventh and Eighth aves ☎ 212/463-8000. In a neighborhood full of clout and pout, anything goes here. They serve margaritas by the pitcher.

Union Square, Gramercy Park, and the Flatiron District

Bar Jamon 125 E 17th St, at Irving Place ☎ 212/253-2773. A superb place to sip on sherry and nosh on Spanish tapas. Be forewarned though: there are only 14 stools. Closed Mon.

Belmont Lounge 117 E 15th St, between Park Ave S and Irving Place ☎ 212/533-0009. Oversized couches, dark cavernous rooms, and an outdoor garden reel in a continuous stream of twenty-something singles. The strong drinks help liven things up.

Cibar in the *Inn at Irving Place*, 56 Irving Place, between E 17th and 18th sts ☎212/460-5656. The strong, innovative cocktails, elegant décor and pretty, well-tended herb garden make this cozy hotel bar the place of choice for a tryst.

No Idea 30 E 20th St, between Broadway and Park Ave S ☎212/777-0100. This bizarre palace of inebriation has something for everyone, from $5 pints of mixed drinks to a pool room, TV sports, and even a drink-for-free-if-your-name's-on-the-wall night. Check the website, ⓦwww.noideabar.com, to see if your name is coming up.

Old Town Bar & Grill 45 E 18th St, between Broadway and Park Ave S ☎212/529-6732. This atmospheric Flatiron District bar is popular with publishing types, models, and photographers. The burgers are tasty.

Pete's Tavern 129 E 18th St, at Irving Place ☎212/473-7676. Opened in 1864, this former speakeasy now trades unashamedly on its history, which has included such illustrious patrons as O. Henry, who allegedly wrote the short story *The Gift of the Magi* in his regular booth here.

Revival 129 E 15th St, between Irving Place and Third Ave ☎212/253-8061. Walk down the stairs and into this friendly narrow bar

▽ Pete's Tavern

with great outdoor seating in the backyard. Popular with fans waiting for concerts at Irving Plaza (see p.379) around the block.

Underbar in the *W Union Square Hotel*, 201 Park Ave S, between E 17th and 18th sts ☎212/358-1560. A fashionable meatmarket hotel bar for beautiful people. Red-velvet ropes keep out the riff-raff and the ill-dressed.

Midtown East

Campbell Apartment southwest balcony in Grand Central Terminal ☎212/953-0409. Once home to businessman John W. Campbell, who oversaw the construction of Grand Central, this majestic space – built to look like a Florentine palace – was sealed up for years. Now, it's one of New York's most distinctive bars. Go early, bring a chunk of cash, and don't wear sneakers.

Divine Bar 244 E 51st St, between Second and Third aves ☎212/319-9463. Although often packed with corporate types communing with their cellphones, this swanky tapas lounge has a great selection of wines and imported beers, not to mention tasty appetizers and outdoor seating.

FUBAR 305 E 50th St, between First and Second aves ☎212/872-1325. Midtown isn't known

for its dive-bar scene, so it's no wonder that *FUBAR* is the coolest around; it even challenges those in the Village. Great happy hours and $5 margarita pints on Wednesdays.

Lever House 390 Park Ave, at E 53rd St ☎212/888-2700. This NYC power-drinking stalwart is in a 1950s landmark. The interior strikes a balance between retro and futuristic; it's worth a look and a cocktail or two – you never know who you'll rub elbows with here.

P.J. Clarke's 915 Third Ave, at E 55th St ☎212/317-1616. Friendly bartenders serve thirty varieties of wine (12 by the glass) and a moderate selection of beers at *P.J. Clarke's*, one of the city's most famous watering holes. The bar is casual, though there is a pricey restaurant out back.

Midtown West

The Collins Bar 735 Eighth Ave, between W 46th and 47th sts ☎212/541-4206. Sleek, stylish bar has choice sports photos along one side, original artworks along the other, and what might be perhaps the most eclectic jukebox in the city bridging the gap between.

Hudson Bar in the *Hudson Hotel*, 356 W 58th St, between Eighth and Ninth aves ☎212/554-6000. Philippe Starck (designer of the *Paramount* and *Royalton* hotels) mixes Louis XV décor with modern lighting here, with attractive results. Try the Cosmos and lemongrass cocktails.

Jimmy's Corner 140 W 44th St, between Broadway and Sixth Ave ☎212/221-9510. The walls of this long, narrow corridor of a bar, owned by ex-fighter/trainer Jimmy Glenn, are a virtual boxing hall of fame. You'd be hard-pressed to find a more characterful dive anywhere in the city – or a better jazz/R&B jukebox.

Landmark Tavern 626 Eleventh Ave, at W 46th St ☎212/757-8595. Off-the-beaten-path but long-established Irish tavern with great Guinness and a tasty menu with large portions – the Irish soda bread is baked fresh every day.

MObar in the *Mandarin Oriental*, 80 Columbus Circle, at W 60th St ☎212/805-8826. On the 35th floor of the *Mandarin Oriental*, this *boîte* is a cozy alternative to the hotel's main lobby lounge, serving 20 wines by the glass along with cocktails that will surely put a dent in your wallet.

Rudy's 627 Ninth Ave, between W 44th and 45th sts ☎212/974-9169. One of New York's cheapest, friendliest, and liveliest bars, a favorite with local actors and musicians. *Rudy's* offers free hot dogs, a backyard that's great in the summer, and some of the cheapest pitchers of beer in the city.

Russian Vodka Room 265 W 52nd St, between Broadway and Eighth Ave ☎212/307-5835. As you might expect, they serve several different types of vodka here. The patrons are mostly Russian and Eastern European expats.

Stitch 247 W 37th St, between Seventh and Eighth aves ☎212/852-4826. A loud, crowded midtown sports bar within stumbling distance of all MSG events. Large plasma TV above the bar, with others scattered about. Decent pub fare and upstairs lounge.

Stout 133 W 33rd St, between Sixth and Seventh aves ☎212/629-6191. With more than 20 beers on tap,125 by the bottle, and an equally expansive menu, this Euro-styled bar is another great after-work, pre-MSG option.

Upper East Side

American Trash 1471 First Ave, between E 76th and 77th sts ☎212/988-9008. Don't let the name put you off: this self-styled "professional drinking establishment" has a friendly bar staff, a pool table, a sing-along jukebox, an always-in-use photo booth, and a happy hour dedicated to getting you pleasantly intoxicated.

Brother Jimmy's 1485 Second Ave, between E 77th and 78th sts ☎212/288-0999. A raucous beer and sports bar that serves some mighty good barbecue. Be ready to belch with the rest of the crowd, mostly college-team-cap-wearing recent graduates.

Metropolitan Museum of Art 1000 Fifth Ave, at E 82nd St ☎212/535-7710. It's hard to imagine a more romantic spot to sip a glass of wine, whether on the Cantor Roof Garden (open only in warm weather), which has some of the best views in the city, or on the Great Hall Balcony, where you can listen to live chamber music (Fri & Sat 5–8.30pm).

Subway Inn 143 E 60th St, at Lexington Ave ☎212/223-8929. This neighborhood dive bar, across from Bloomingdale's, is great for a late-afternoon beer.

Upper West Side

Dead Poet 450 Amsterdam Ave, between W 81st and 82nd sts ☎212/595-5670. You'll wax poetical and then drop dead if you stay for the duration of this sweet little bar's happy

DRINKING | Midtown West • Upper East Side • Upper West Side

hour: it lasts 4–8pm and offers draft beer at $3 a pint. The backroom has armchairs, books, and a pool table.

Ding Dong Lounge 929 Columbus Ave, between 105th and 106th sts ☎212/663-2600. This punk bar with a DJ and occasional concerts attracts a vibrant mix of graduate students, neighborhood Latinos, and stragglers from the nearby youth hostel. On Sundays, the pint-sized margarita special is one of the best bargains in the city.

Dublin House Tap Room 225 W 79th St, between Broadway and Amsterdam Ave ☎212/874-9528. This lively Upper West Side Irish pub, which pours a very nice Black & Tan, is dominated at night by the young, inebriated, and rowdy.

Shark Bar 307 Amsterdam Ave, between W 74th and 75th sts ☎212/874-8500. Ultra-elegant African-American lounge with great soul food and a beat to go with it.

🏃 **Smoke 2751 Broadway, at W 106th St** ☎212/864-6662, 🖥www.smokejazz.com.

A real neighborhood treat. Jazz sets start at 9pm, 11pm, and 12.30am; check the website for performers. There's also a retro happy hour with $4 cocktails and $2 beers, Mon–Sat 5–8pm. Cover $16–25 Fri & Sat.

Time Out 349 Amsterdam Ave, between W 76th and 77th sts ☎212/362-5400. How strange… a sports bar with a pleasant atmosphere! There's a good selection of cheap beers and pub grub, friendly bonhomie, and 24 screens of sporting entertainment. $10 cover for special events.

West End 2911 Broadway, between W 113th and 114th sts ☎212/662-8830. Once the hangout of Jack Kerouac, Allen Ginsberg, and the Beats in the 1950s (see p.219). While it still serves the Columbia student crowd, the West End has had several makeovers since those days, and stand-up comedy and karaoke have replaced *Howl* as the performances of choice.

Harlem

Lenox Lounge 288 Lenox Ave, at W 125th St ☎212/427-0253, 🖥www.lenoxlounge.com. Entertaining Harlem since the 1930s, this renovated, historic jazz lounge has an over-the-top Art Deco interior (check out the Zebra Room), and features three sets nightly; cover $15, with a one-drink minimum.

Showmans 375 W 125th St, at Morningside Ave ☎212-864-8941. This small, long-established

blues, jazz, and gospel music haunt is often packed with Harlemites and occasionally with tourists. Jazz shows Tues–Thurs at 8.30pm, Fri and Sat at 10.30pm; no cover charge.

Striver's Lounge 2611 Frederick Douglass Blvd, at W 139th St ☎212/491-4422. Just west of Strivers Row, this bar-café comes alive at night with spoken-word acts and open-mic nights. The soul food's also worth the trip.

Brooklyn

Brooklyn Brewery 1 Brewers Row, 79 N 11th St, Williamsburg ☎718/486-7422. More a store than a bar, the *Brooklyn Brewery* is New York's most well-known microbrewery. They host a number of community-based events throughout the year, as well as happy hours every Fri (beers $3) and free Sat tours, with a beer-tasting at the end. See box, p.262, for more information.

🏃 **Brooklyn Inn 148 Hoyt St, at Bergen St, Boerum Hill** ☎718/625-9741. Locals – and their dogs – gather at this convivial favorite with high ceilings and friendly bar-staff. Great place for a daytime buzz or shooting pool in the back room.

▽ Brooklyn Brewery

Chance 223 Smith St, at Butler St, Boerum Hill
☏718/242-1515. Expect sexy lighting and
sleek furnishing at this French-Chinese bar.
The wine selection complements the light
menu. Closes at 11pm.

D.O.C. Wine Bar 83 N 7th St, at Wythe St,
Williamsburg ☏718/963-1925. A popular
wine bar that also offers authentic Italian
food. Patrons include both posh celebs
and neighborhood hipsters. Expect
bottles to cost around $30; the staff is
quite knowledgeable, so ask their opinion
if you're having trouble deciding on a
vintage.

Frank's Cocktail Lounge 660 Fulton St, between
Hudson Ave and Rockwell Place, Fort Greene
☏718/625-9339. A stone's throw from BAM
(see p.246), this mellow bar with a clas-
sic-to-modern R&B jukebox comes alive at
night when DJs spin hip-hop and the party
spreads upstairs.

Galapagos 70 N 6th St, between Wythe and Kent
aves, Williamsburg ☏718/782-5188, ⓦwww
.galapagosartspace.com Gorgeous design –
this converted factory features placid pools
of water and elegant candelabras – as well
as excellent avant-garde movies on Sunday
nights. Live music, literary readings, or some
other oddball event most nights of the
week. Check the website for a schedule.

The Gate 321 Fifth Ave, at 3rd St, Park Slope
☏718/768-4329. An extensive array of beers
and patio seating lure Park Slopers to this
roomy, congenial staple of the Fifth Avenue
bar scene.

Iona 180 Grand St, between Bedford and Driggs
aves, Williamsburg ☏718/384-5008. An Irish
bar for hipsters, *Iona* provides a calm,
tasteful respite from the moody lighting and
incestuous cool of all the other bars around.
A sweet outdoor garden and a great selection of beers only add to this gem's appeal.

Lunatarium 10 Jay St, at John St, downtown
Brooklyn ☏718/813-8404. A 20,000-square-
foot industrial space that's part dance club
and part cocktail party. Things get downright crazy after dark here; the place is open
until 6am most mornings.

Madiba 195 Dekalb Ave, at Carlton Ave,
Fort Greene ☏718/855-9190. Go to the
community shelf, grab the chessboard,
and announce the challenge at this South
African haunt. Potent mojitos and sangría
make for a great afternoon at one of their
tables outside. The staff – mostly expats – is
remarkably kind.

Pete's Candy Store 709 Lorimer St, between
Frost and Richardson sts, Williamsburg
☏718/302-3770, ⓦwww.petescandystore
.com. This terrific little spot to tipple was
once a real candy store. There's free live
music every night, poetry on Mondays,
Scrabble and Bingo nights, and even an
organized "Stitch and Bitch" knitting group.

Rosemary's Greenpoint Tavern 188 Bedford
Ave, between N 6th and 7th sts, Williamsburg
☏718/384-9539. Rosemary runs a tight ship
at the *Greenpoint Tavern* – a major achievement, considering the 32oz styrofoam cups
of Budweiser continually slung over the bar
counter. Come for the big beers; stay for the
friendly, hip neighborhood vibe.

Superfine 126 Front St, between Jay and Pearl
sts, DUMBO ☏718/243-9005. The restaurant, which serves Mediterranean and
American fare, is inconsistent, but the bar
is awesome, with an orange-felt pool table
and "superfine" drink selection.

Waterfront Ale House 155 Atlantic Ave, between
Clinton and Henry sts, Brooklyn Heights
☏718/522-3794. This inexpensive and fun
old-style pub serves good spicy chicken-
wings, ribs, and excellent, locally made Key
Lime Pie.

Queens

Bohemian Hall and Beer Garden 29-19 24th Ave,
between 29th and 30th sts, Astoria ☏718/721-
4226. This old Czech bar is the real deal,
catering to old-timers and serving a good
selection of pilsners, as well as other hard-to-
find brews. In back, there's a very large beer
garden, complete with picnic tables, trees,
burgers, and sausages, and a bandshell for
polka groups. Great fun in good weather, and
well worth the trip from Manhattan.

Café-Bar 32-90 36th St, at 34th Ave, Astoria
☏718/204-5273. With its plush couches and
outdoor seating, the ultra-relaxed *Café-Bar*
is the perfect place to kill time before a
matinee at the nearby American Museum of
the Moving Image (see p.271).

Rapture Lounge 34-27 28th Ave, at 35th St,
Astoria ☏718/626-8044. A Mexican-style
cocktail lounge and tapas bar with welcoming armchairs and sofas. Theme nights

26

(like Martini Madness Mondays) and drinks (try the "Sex-on-the-Sofa" or "Tie-Me-to- the-Bedpost") bring in crowds of young patrons.

The Bronx

Press Café 114 E 157th St, between River and Gerard aves ☎718/401-0545. Strong cocktails, draft beers, and oh-so-tasty pressed sandwiches in the shadows of Yankee Stadium. Prices are in the downtown Manhattan range, but they're open after the game.

Yankee Tavern 161st St, at Gerard Ave ☎718/292-6130. Everyone wears their pinstripes on their sleeves in this dive. Yankees employees blow off steam here after games – they're suits by the taps. Be sure to buy them a round – after a day of The Boss's tirades, they'll need it.

The Bronx

DRINKING

26

375

Nightlife

A s the city that never sleeps, New York is undeniably a **nightlife** hotspot. Bars don't start to fill up until 11pm, if not later, and clubs look like empty rooms until midnight or 1am. Even confirmed early birds should try to stay out late at least a few times during their stay, as the city's legendary energy is most obvious when most other cities have bedded down for the night.

For the past few years, New York's **live music** scene has been undergoing a rock'n'roll revival, fueled by residents and bands from the East Village, the Lower East Side, and Williamsburg in Brooklyn. On any night of the week you take your pick from several good clubs in these neighbourhoods, and be sure to hear something exciting. The city also continues to set the standard in jazz, with a number of venues where you can hear the most popular contemporary performers.

The city's **nightclubs** are currently recovering from a string of closures and police raids that occurred in the winter of 2006, though new joints throughout the city have since opened their doors. West Chelsea remains the nerve center for the city's club scene – the area overflows with wild party-goers once the sun goes down. Depending on what events are being thrown that night, you can count on hearing virtually any kind of music, no matter the club: very few slavishly devote themselves to one style.

Whatever you're planning to do after dark, remember to **carry ID** at all times to prove you're over 21 – you'll likely be asked by every doorman. Note that some venues do not even allow under-21s to enter, let alone drink – call to check if you're concerned.

The sections that follow provide accounts of the pick of the city's venues. Since the music and club scenes are constantly changing, it's a good idea to get up-to-date info once you hit the ground. The listings magazine *Time Out New York* is pretty reliable; you can pick up the current week's issue for a few bucks from virtually any newsstand. Otherwise, grab a freesheet like *The Village Voice* (Ⓦ www.villagevoice.com), *The Onion* (whose cultural listings are excellent), or the monthly club-sheet *Flyer*. These can be found on street corners in self-serve newspaper boxes, as well as in many music stores; all of them contain detailed **listings** for most scenes.

Rock, pop, and eclectic music

New York's **rock scene** currently leans heavily toward garage- and dance-rock, with bands like The Strokes, The Rapture, and the Yeah Yeah Yeahs leading the charge. Foreign acts – especially British bands – invariably play the city as a

> For most of the large venues listed below, tickets are sold through **Ticketmaster** (ⓦwww.ticketmaster.com). For many mid-sized and small venues, tickets are sold through **Ticketweb** (ⓦwww.ticketweb.com).

tryout before they set about "cracking" America; whatever band is hot in the UK's weekly *NME* music magazine will probably be playing NYC soon.

As for **venues**, rising rents have forced many smaller and medium-sized places to close or decamp to Brooklyn and New Jersey. Historic club *CBGB* in the East Village is but one victim of this syndrome, its continued existence endangered by battles with its rent-chasing landlord (see box, p.102). Most of the best performance spaces are still in Manhattan, though; there's a large cluster of exceptionally good venues in the East Village and Lower East Side.

Large venues

Beacon Theatre 2124 Broadway, at W 74th St ⓣ212/496-7070. This beautifully restored theater caters to a more mature rock and pop crowd, hosting everyone from Tori Amos to Radiohead. Tickets $25–100.

Hammerstein Ballroom 311 W 34th St, at 9th Ave ⓣ212/564-4882, ⓦwww .mcstudios.com. This grand 1906 building has seen many incarnations: it's been an opera house, a vaudeville hall, and a Masonic temple, and it now hosts indie and rock bands. Capacity is 3600, but the sound system and acoustics are of high enough quality that most seats are pretty good. Tickets $20 and up.

Madison Square Garden Seventh Ave, at W 32nd St ⓣ212/465-6741, ⓦwww.thegarden.com. New York's principal big stage, the Garden hosts not only hockey and basketball games but also a good portion of the stadium rock and pop acts that visit the city. Seating capacity is 20,000-plus, so the arena's not exactly the most soulful place to see a band – but for big names, it's the handiest option.

Radio City Music Hall 1260 Sixth Ave, at 50th St ⓣ212/247-4777, ⓦwww.radiocity.com. Not the prime venue it once was; it occasionally hosts a terrific concert, but for the most part its schedule is clogged with cutesy tribute shows and schlocky musicals. The acoustics are flawless and the building itself has a great sense of occasion – it seems to inspire the artists who play here to put on a memorable show.

Roseland Ballroom 239 W 52nd St, at Broadway ⓣ212/247-0200, ⓦwww.roselandballroom .com. This historic ballroom opened in 1919 and was once frequented by Adele and Fred Astaire, among others. Although now a ballroom-dancing school, six times per month it turns into a concert venue, putting on big names in rock and pop. Tickets $10–50.

Mid-sized and small venues

Arlene's Grocery 95 Stanton St, at Ludlow St ⓣ212/473-9831, ⓦwww.arlenesgrocery.com. An intimate, erstwhile *bodega* (hence the name) that hosts nightly gigs by local, reliably good indie bands. Regularly patronized by musicians, talent scouts, and open-minded rock fans. Go on Monday nights for punk and heavy metal karaoke, when you can sing along with a live band. Free week-nights; cover $3 Fri & Sat, $5 Sun.

▽ Arlene's Grocery

The Bitter End 147 Bleecker St, at Thompson St ⓣ212/673-7030, ⓦwww .bitterend.com. Young MOR bands in an intimate club setting, mostly folky rockers in

㉗

the Dylan mold. A catalogue of the famous people who've played the club is posted by the door – it's a pretty long list. Cover $5–10, with a two-drink minimum.

Bowery Ballroom 6 Delancey St, at Bowery ☎212/533-2111, ⓦwww .boweryballroom.com. No attitude, great acoustics, and even better views have earned this site praise from both fans and bands. Major labels test their up-and-comers here, so it's a great place to catch the Next Big Thing of any genre. Highly recommended. Tickets $10–20.

Continental 25 Third Ave, between St Mark's Place and E 9th St ☎212/529-6924, ⓦwww .continentalnyc.com. Loud metal and rock, with the odd guest appearance by the likes of Iggy Pop. Shows start on the hour; buy a beer and get $2 shots at all times. Free entrance Sun–Tues, $5 Wed–Sat.

Irving Plaza 17 Irving Place, at 16th St ☎212/777-6800, ⓦwww.irvingplaza .com. Once home to off-Broadway musicals (hence the dangling chandeliers and blood-red interior), *Irving Plaza* now features an impressive array of rock, electronic, and techno acts. The main room has wildly divergent acoustics; stand toward the back on the ground floor for the truest mix of sound. Tickets $10–25.

Knitting Factory 74 Leonard St, between Church St and Broadway ☎212/219-3055, ⓦwww.knittingfactory.com. While this intimate downtown space is known for its avant-garde jazz, you can hear all other kinds of aural experimentation here too, everything from art rock to electronica. Tickets $10–25.

The Living Room 154 Ludlow St, between Stanton and Rivington sts ☎212/533-7235, ⓦwww.livingroomny.com. Comfortable couches (hence the name) and a friendly bar make for a relaxed setting in which to hear local, low-key folk and rock. No cover, suggested $5 donation, one-drink minimum.

Maxwell's 1039 Washington, at 11th St, Hoboken, New Jersey ☎201/798-0406, ⓦwww.maxwellsnj.com. This neighborhood rock club hosts up to a dozen bands a week, including some big indie names. This is one of the best places to check out the tri-state scene. Brave the PATH train (or a cab ride) out to Jersey, and you won't regret it. Tickets $8–20.

Mercury Lounge 217 E Houston St, at Essex St ☎212/260-7400, ⓦwww .mercuryloungenyc.com. Dark Lower East Side mainstay features a mix of local, national, and international rock and pop acts. It's owned by the same crew as the *Bowery Ballroom*, and is similarly used as a trial venue by major labels for up-and-coming artists. Tickets $10–20.

Northsix 66 N 6th St, at Kent, Williamsburg ☎718/599-5103, ⓦwww.northsix.com. A large performance space with "charming" touches like ratty red-velvet curtains and a set of high-school-gym bleachers to chill out on – it has the hipster feel of a downtown club in the early 1980s. Expect all sorts of different acts, from reggae to rock. Patrons are the standard Brooklyn blend of scruffy, arty intellectuals and a few curious Manhattanites. One of Brooklyn's really great venues. Tickets $10–20.

NuBlu 62 Ave C, at 4th St ☎212/979-9925, ⓦwww.nublu.net. This bar – marked only by a small blue light above the door – is owned by the mavens who run the record label of the same name. Jamming jazz and funk bands from their roster regularly play in the front room. No cover.

Pianos 158 Ludlow St, at Rivington St ☎212/505-3733, ⓦwww.pianosnyc.com. There's no cover to get in the door at this converted piano factory (hence the name), but to get into the tiny back room – where the music is – you'll need to fork out extra ($8–15). The sound system's a standout, and the endless roster of mostly rock bands (expect four choices nightly) means the place is usually packed. Drink prices are somewhat high, and the line to get in habitually long.

Sin-e 148–150 Attorney St, at Stanton St ☎212/388-0077, ⓦwww.sin-e.com. Despite its location (a bleak block of the Lower East Side), this venue (pronounced shin-AY; the name's Gaelic for "that's it," a favorite phrase of the Irish owner) nightly packs in patrons to hear three or four performances on its small stage. The usual mix of rock, folk, and jangle-pop. Cover $7–10.

SOB's (Sounds of Brazil) 204 Varick St, at W Houston ☎212/243-4940, ⓦwww .sobs.com. Premier place to hear hip-hop, Brazilian, West Indian, Caribbean, and world-music acts within the confines of Manhattan. Vibrant and danceable, with a high quality of music. Two shows nightly, times vary. Tickets $10–25.

Village Underground 130 W 3rd St, at Sixth Ave ☎212/777-7745, 🌐www .thevillageunderground.com. Tiny basement performance space that is one of the most intimate and innovative clubs around. Big names have been known to crash the party: Guided by Voices and RL Burnside have both appeared, among others. Cover $10–15.

Jazz

Jazz in New York has seen a bit of a resurgence in the last ten years. The last decades of the twentieth century saw the city's clubs go through a rough patch, but new owners are now breathing life into older venues, and the establishment of a clutch of performance spaces in the late 1990s has helped reinvigorate the scene. There are more than forty locations in Manhattan that present jazz regularly. You'll find the best of these clubs in the West Village and Harlem, though midtown venues have steadily been improving in quality; there are also a few fine sites in Chelsea and the East Village.

To find out **who's playing**, check the usual sources, notably *The Village Voice* (🌐www.villagevoice.com) and *Time Out New York* (🌐www.timeoutny.com); other good jazz rags are the monthlies *Hothouse*, a free magazine sometimes available at venues, and *Down Beat* (🌐www.downbeat.com).

Price policies vary from club to club, but most places have a hefty cover ($10–30) and a minimum charge for food and drinks. An evening out at a major club will cost at least $15 per person, $25–30 per person if you'd like to eat. Piano bars – smaller and often more atmospheric – come cheaper; some have neither an admission fee nor a minimum, though expect to pay inflated drink prices.

Jazz venues

Birdland 315 W 44th St, at Ninth Ave ☎212/581-3080, 🌐www.birdlandjazz .com. Not the original place where Charlie Parker played, but nonetheless an established supper club that plays host to some big names. Sets nightly at 9 and 11pm. Music charge of $20–40; at a table, you'll need to spend a minimum of $10 or more on food or drink, while at the bar, the cover includes your first drink.

Café Carlyle in The Carlyle Hotel, 35 E 76th St, at Madison Ave ☎212/744-1600. This intimate, dressy spot was home to legendary crooner Bobby Short, and Woody Allen still plays clarinet here most Mon nights in the fall, winter and spring; it's a chic, Upper East Side scene, and well worth the ticket price. $30–60 cover, no minimum.

Detour 349 E 13th St, at First Ave ☎212/533-6212, 🌐www.jazzatdetour.com. East Village coffee and cocktail bar with Parisian pretensions, featuring avant-garde experimentation nightly. Unquestionably the best place to catch free jazz in the city.

Iridium Jazz Club 1650 Broadway, at W 51st St ☎212/582-2121 🌐www .iridiumjazzclub.com. Contemporary jazz performed seven nights a week in a Surrealist décor described as "Dolly meets Disney." The octogenarian godfather of electric guitar Les Paul plays every Mon. Cover $20–35, $10 food and drink minimum; Sun jazz brunch.

Jazz at Lincoln Center 33 W 60th St, at Columbus Circle ☎212/258-9800, 🌐www.jazzatlin colncenter.org. There are three different spaces at this venue in the Time Warner Center. The two larger auditoria, Rose Hall and Allen Room, are nice, but the smallest one is the pick of them all: the 140-seater Dizzy's Club Coca-Cola. It has panoramic views, a speakeasy-style atmosphere, and inventive programming.

Jazz Standard 116 E 27th St, at Park Ave S ☎212/576-2232, 🌐www.jazzstandard.net. A spacious underground room with great sound and even better performers has earned this club high praise and a loyal clientele. Sets Mon–Thurs at 8 and 10pm, Fri and Sat 8, 10.30pm, and midnight, Sun at 7 and 9pm. Mon $15; Tues–Thurs

& Sun $18; Fri & Sat $25; all with $10 minimum.

Joe's Pub 425 Lafayette St, at Astor Place
☎212/539-8777, ⊚www.joespub.com. Stylishly classic bar in Joe Papp's Public Theater attracts a hipper crowd than many jazz/cabaret spots; there are performances six days a week, ranging from Broadway songbooks to readings from the *New Yorker*'s fiction issues. Mon nights are often given over to a big name from Broadway in solo concert. $10–25.

Kavehaz Jazz Club 37 W 26th St, at Broadway
☎212/343-0612, ⊚www.kavehaz.com. Sweet little Chelsea gallery/club that plays host to decent jazz and decent drinks for no cover charge.

Lenox Lounge 288 Malcolm X Blvd, at 124th St
☎212/427-0253, ⊚www.lenoxlounge.com. This Harlem staple is elegant yet laid-back, and retains the area's legendary aura as it hosts jazz on the weekends and jam sessions on Mon nights. Known more for contemporary riffs than traditional jazz standards. Cover $15, with a one-drink minimum.

Louis 649 E 9th St between aves B and C ☎212/673-1190. With no cover and live performances seven nights a week, *Louis* is a must if you love jazz. Mon and Thurs are lively, and weekends get downright hectic. They serve gourmet bottled beer and a number of excellent vintages, but no cocktails.

Smoke 2751 Broadway, at 106th St ☎212/864-6662, ⊚www.smokejazz.com. This Upper West Side joint is a real neighborhood treat, with plush couches, lavish chandeliers, and a retro, upscale feel. Sets start at 9, 11pm,

▽ Lenox Lounge

and 12.30am; stop by for happy hour and $3 cocktails daily 5–8pm. Cover varies.

Village Vanguard 178 Seventh Ave, at 11th St
☎212/255-4037, ⊚www.villagevanguard.com. A NYC jazz landmark, the *Village Vanguard* celebrated its seventieth anniversary in 2005. There's a regular diet of big names. Mon–Thurs admission is $15, while Sat & Sun entry is $20; $10 drinks minimum on all nights.

Zinc Bar 90 W Houston St, at LaGuardia Place
☎212/477-8337, ⊚www.zincbar.com. Great jazz venue with strong drinks and a loyal bunch of regulars. The blackboard above the entrance announces the evening's featured band. Cover is $5 with a one-drink minimum. Hosts both new talent and established greats, with an emphasis on Latin American rhythms.

Nightclubs

New York's **nightlife** has come a long way since its decadent, devil-may-care disco years. The city's after-dark party places are now corporate businesses, with many megaclubs, like *Crobar*, for example, as part of multi-city chains. While DJs continue to spin, the venues they frequent shift and change, opening and closing according to finances, fashion, and the enforcement of anti-drug laws.

Former city mayor Rudy Giuliani paid special attention to New York's nightlife as part of his efforts to clean up Manhattan: his reviled **cabaret license laws** effectively ensured that bars couldn't hire a DJ to get drinkers dancing without an expensive permit, thereby stifling club music's fringe. The current mayor, Michael Bloomberg, is much less restrictive about fun after dark, although the fact that he has neither repealed nor reworked the laws hasn't made it much easier to run a nightclub in the city.

In terms of what you can expect to find at a club, New York's DJs still rely on a steady diet of deep house **music** that came from Chicago in the 1980s and never left, though there's a growing cadre of inventive hip-hop venues. As in any large city, **illegal drugs** are a part of clubbing here – expect door searches to be thorough, and heavy penalties if you're caught with any kind of banned substance. That said, alcohol fuels New York's nightlife just as much as ecstasy does, so staying legal doesn't mean you'll be left out of the fun. Regarding **dress codes**, New York is a casual kind of town where clubs are concerned – unless noted in our reviews, you can usually turn up in smart-casual dress (no sneakers or baseball caps) and be fine. If you arrive at a club before midnight, expect a longish wait till the dance floor gets going: nothing really starts to happen until after midnight.

Below is a list of the current hot venues, plus a few perennials; of course, since clubs come and go constantly, it's important to check up-to-date info with one of the free magazines/newspapers like *HX* or *The Village Voice*, or pick up a copy of *Time Out New York*. Fliers are always the best way to hear about the latest nightspots: see the list of record stores on p.424 for places to pick them up.

6s & 8s 205 Chrystie St, at Stanton St ☎212/477-6688. There's no cover at this Lower East Side club, a plus that is often negated by long lines and expensive drinks. The club itself is festive and has an active dance-floor, orchestrated by persnickety DJs. The décor is Vegas red, with a downstairs bar reminiscent of a high-stakes card table, and leather booths along the sides of the main floor.

Apt 419 W 13th St, at Ninth Ave ☎212/414-4245, ⓦwww.aptwebsite.com. Tucked behind an unmarked doorway, this well-hidden bar/club is known for its inventive, eclectic DJ roster (including iPod-powered DIY nights). There are two spaces: a lounge-like upstairs room and a sleek, wood-panelled downstairs bar. Cover $5–10.

Avalon 47 W 20th St, at Sixth Ave ☎212/807-7780. This beauty of a space – a converted church designed by Trinity Church–builder Richard Upjohn – is somewhat scandal-plagued; latest occupant *Avalon* was busted during the NYPD's 2006 city-wide club sweep, although it cleaned up and reopened shortly thereafter. The smallish dance-floor makes it much more intimate than many of Manhattan's megaclubs. You can rest for a while on the large balconies overlooking the crowd. Cover $10.

🏃 **Cielo** 18 Little W 12th St, at Ninth Ave ☎212/645-5700, ⓦwww.cieloclub.com. Expect velvet rope-burn at this super-exclusive see-and-be-seen place: there's only room for 250 people. Though run by Nicolas Matar, a former DJ at Ibiza's legendary *Pacha* club, it's the Monday-night reggae and dub party from François K that most people talk about. Usually free (if you can get in).

Club Shelter 20 W 39th St, at Fifth Ave ☎212/719-4479, ⓦwww.clubshelter.com. Big but friendly venue harking back to the heyday of Chicago house, with graffiti-covered walls, a warehouse floor, and absolutely no attitude. Soulful house guru Timmy Regisford spins on Sat. No dress code. Cover $15–20.

🏃 **Crobar** 530 W 28th St, at Eleventh Ave ☎212/629-9000, ⓦwww.crobar.com. The New York outpost of the chain of super-clubs. With room for 3000 people, it's one of the largest private spaces in the city. There are warrens of VIP rooms to discover, as well as a stylish bar decorated with what look like giant glowsticks; the main dance-floor is huge, and has a spectacular sound-system. The one downside is the crowd, which tends to be rather mainstream, due to the building's massive capacity. Cover $25.

Don Hill's 511 Greenwich St, at Spring St ☎212/219-2850, ⓦwww.donhills.com. Drag queens, creative types, and those nostalgic for the 1980s still congregate at this club on the outskirts of Soho. It's a dive, yes, but friendly and great fun. Picks of the week are Röck Cändy punk night (Wed) and the ever-popular MisShapes (Sat), when DJs spin everything from indie, rock, and punk to pop and new wave. Cover $5–20.

Lotus 409 W 14th St, at Tenth Ave ☎212/243-4420, ⓦwww.lotusnewyork.com. This rocking basement bar/club plays deep house and soul from 11pm onwards. Hip-hop classics blare for Gold Digger Tuesdays, but the club's reputation is based on their Fri- and Sat-night parties. ($10 reduction for guest list; ☎212/539-3916). Cover $20, free if you dine at the Asian fusion restaurant upstairs.

NA 246 W 14th St, at Eighth Ave ☎212/675-1567. Despite the number of celebs caught behaving badly at *NA*, an evening here will be one well spent, if you can work your way past the doormen. The main floor of this bi-level space was designed by indie actress Tara Subkoff. The upstairs balcony offers extraordinary people-watching views while you rest up for round two. Cover $5–15.

Roxy 515 W 18th St, at Eleventh Ave ☎212/645-5156, ⓦ www.roxynyc.com. It is technically a gay club most of the time, but there are few venues in the city that are more welcoming or better places to dance. The main floor is usually hard house, while the upstairs lounge has a poppier playlist; Sat is a circuit party-style marathon. In a nod to its origins as a roller-rink, the powers that be here have finally started a rollerskating night every Wed, when you can rent skates and boogie like it's 1979.

Sapphire Lounge 249 Eldridge St, at Houston St ☎212/777-5153, ⓦ www.sapphirenyc.com. DJ bar and lounge, with an arty, sleazy, sexy vibe, created by the dark lights and enhanced by the moody Lower East Side regulars. The programming is inventive, offering music of almost every genre on different nights, from reggae to hip-hop to breakbeat – as a plus, it's open every night of the week, and the cover is usually mini-mal (expect around $5 or so).

Show 135 W 41st, at Sixth Ave ☎212/278-0988, ⓦ www.shownightclub.com. This glammy throwback to 1980s performance clubs is intended to invoke a burlesque hall: there's gold ormolu everywhere, a stage for P.A.s with a red-velvet curtain, and the servers are even decked out like showgirls. The crowd's much hipper during the week than at week-ends – and the music, for what it's worth, is mainstream house. Cover $30.

Speak 28 E 23rd St, between Park and Madison aves ☎212/673-0100. Modeled after Holly-wood in the 1930s, *Speak* has a unique vibe not often seen in this area of town. The bar offers bottled beers and tasty cocktails: try the "Blood Red Martini" or the "Fury's Cocoa." If you need to take a breather, there are playground swings in back.

Spirit 530 W 27th St, at Eleventh Ave ☎212/268-9477. *Spirit* is a new-agey, late-night superclub split into three sections. There's "Mind," an all-night spa where you can get massages and aromatherapy treat-ments; "Soul," a 180-seat organic restau-rant (also open during the day); and "Body,"

a dance floor with a 1200-person capacity that's open for house and trance nights every Sat. Cover $30, $5 off if you call and are put on the guest list the day before.

Spy 17 W 19th St, at Fifth Ave ☎212/352-2001. Formerly *Discotheque*, and more recently *go-go*, this space changes names frequently, but retains the same ownership. After all, a new club – or at least one with a new name – is hot. The party always comes here, ranging from rock to disco to hip-hop. The kitchen is open late to fuel you for the dance floor. Drinks aren't cheap and neither is the $25 weekend cover.

Stereo 512 W 29th St, between Tenth and Elev-enth aves ☎212/244-1965. The DJ is king here, and when big-time spinners like DJ AM show up, no one sits down, especially not with the surround-sound music threatening to shake your clothes off. Expect to hear '80s, hip-hop, and rap, with a few contem-porary beats thrown in the mix. Like most clubs in this area, the door is the worst part of the experience, but once you're in, you're a part of the "cool crowd." Cover $20.

Stonewall 53 Christopher St, at Seventh Ave ☎212/463-0950. The gay civil-rights move-ment began outside this club in the late 1960s and it doesn't look like it's changed much since. The patrons haven't changed much either, though pop music invades Thursday nights during the weekly dance party, keeping things more or less fresh and current. The crowd is mostly tourists and men, but everyone is made to feel welcome.

Sullivan Room 218 Sullivan St, at Bleecker St ☎212/252-2151, ⓦ www.sullivanroom.com. Hidden basement club for serious dancing. Tronic is the very well-known, long-running Mon night techno party, while Fri and Sat, popular with students from nearby NYU, are good for house music. The only downside: two bathrooms for the whole place. Cover $5–15.

The Warehouse 141 E 140th St, at Walton Ave, The Bronx ☎718/992-5974. Even the most dedicated Manhattanites make an effort to come way up here, where the attitude is nonexistent, the décor is school-disco, and the music classic hip-hop and Chicago house. The patrons are mostly black and largely gay, especially at weekends. Take a cab, or the #4 or #5 subway to 138th Street–Grand Concourse. Cover $14–16.

The performing arts and film

"**P**erforming arts" is really an all-encompassing title for New York's legion of cultural offerings. While many travelers tend automatically to think of the glittery Broadway productions housed on and around Times Square, locals will inform you that such a heading also includes more experimental Off-Broadway theater companies, as well as comedy clubs, cabarets, dance troupes, and the opera, to name but a few of the city's options.

Prices for live performances vary wildly: expect to pony up $150 for a night at the opera, while Shakespeare is performed for free in Central Park every summer. The high prices of many shows can be off-putting; see the box on p.384 for some tips on how to see Broadway blockbusters on a budget.

The silver screen is just as important a part of New York's art scene as its live performances are. New York gets the first run of most American **films** as well as many foreign ones, often long before they open in Europe (or the rest of America). There's also a very healthy arthouse and revival scene.

Listings for the arts can be found in a number of places. The most useful sources are the clear and comprehensive listings in *Time Out New York*, the free *New York Press*, and the "Voice Choices" section of the free *Village Voice*. Tonier events are usually touted in *New York* magazine's "Cue" section, "Goings On About Town" in the *New Yorker*, or Friday's "Weekend" or Sunday's "Arts and Leisure" sections of the *New York Times*. You'll find specific Broadway listings in the free *Official Broadway Theater Guide*, available at theater and hotel lobbies or at the New York Convention and Visitors' Bureau (see Basics, p.33).

If you want to plan your itinerary before you leave home, websites such as Ⓦwww.newyork.citysearch.com and Ⓦwww.timeoutny.com have information on arts events in New York. You can also check the useful sites Ⓦwww.nytheatre.com, Ⓦwww.broadway.com, and Ⓦwww.offbroadwayonline.com for up-to-date info on both major Broadway shows and local theater listings. The best sites to purchase tickets from are Ⓦwww.telecharge.com and Ⓦwww.ticketmaster.com.

THE PERFORMING ARTS AND FILM

28

Theater

Theater venues in the city are referred to as being "**Broadway**," "**Off-Broadway**," or "**Off-Off-Broadway**." These groupings don't necessarily mean a theater's address is physically on or off Broadway; instead they represent a descending order of ticket prices, production polish, elegance, and comfort. In theory at least, the further off-Broadway and down the price scale you go, the more innovative productions are.

Although **Broadway** shows have diversified somewhat of late, they remain predominantly grandiose tourist-magnet musicals, packing in the biggest crowds and boasting the biggest-name stars. A recent trend has been megahit musicals adapted from movies, including multiple Tony Award–winners *The Producers* and *Spamalot* – a popular theatrical rendition of *Monty Python and the Holy Grail*. The majority of Broadway theaters are located in the blocks just east or west of Broadway (the avenue) between 41st and 53rd streets, conveniently near the larger Times Square tourist hotels.

Off-Broadway, a bit less glitzy, is the best place to discover new talent and adventurous new American drama and musicals. Off-Broadway theaters are home to lower-budget social and political dramas, satire, ethnic plays, and repertory – in other words, anything that can make money without having to fill a huge hall each night (most of these theaters seat between 100 and 500). Lower operating costs also mean that Off-Broadway often serves as a forum to try out what sometimes ends up as a big Broadway production.

Off-Off-Broadway is the fringe of New York's theater world. Off-Off venues (often with fewer than 100 seats) aren't bound by union regulations to use professional actors, and shows range from shoestring productions of the classics to outrageous and experimental performance art. Prices range from free to cheap, and the quality can vary from execrable to electrifying. Frankly, there's a lot more of the former than the latter, so it's best to use weekly reviews as your guide.

Hot tickets

Tickets for Broadway shows can cost as much as $100 for orchestra seats at the hottest shows, and as little as $25 for day-of-performance rush tickets (often standing room only) for some of the long-runners; check listings magazines for availability. Off-Broadway's best seats are cheaper than those on Broadway, averaging $25–55. Off-Off-Broadway tickets should rarely set you back more than $20.

The best places to go for bargains are the **TKTS booths** (℡212/768-1818, ⊛www .tdf.org), which offer cut-rate, day-of-performance tickets for many Broadway and Off-Broadway shows. Expect to pay half the face value, plus a $2.50 service charge (cash or travelers' checks only). The booth at Duffy Square, located at Broadway between 45th and 47th streets is open Mon–Sat 3–8pm plus 10am–2pm for Wed and Sat matinees, and 11am–7pm for all Sunday performances. The lines are very long – go early.

If you're prepared to pay full price for tickets, you can, of course, go directly to the theater (or the theater website) or call one of the following **ticket sales agencies**. **Telecharge** (℡1-800/432-7250 or 212/239-6200, ⊛www.telecharge.com) and **Ticketmaster** (℡1-800/755-4000 or 212/307-4100, ⊛www.ticketmaster.com) sell Broadway tickets over the phone; note that no show is represented by both these agencies. **Tickets Central** (℡212/279-4200; daily 1–8pm) sells tickets to many Off-Broadway theaters. Expect a $5–7 surcharge per ticket. When buying tickets, always ask where your seats are located, as once you get to the theater and find yourself in the last row of the balcony, it's too late (for most seating plans, check ⊛www.playbill.com).

We've picked out a smattering of reliable Off- and Off-Off venues (the Broadway theaters generally book whatever shows they can, and therefore don't offer a consistent type of production).

Off-Broadway

Astor Place Theater 434 Lafayette St, at Astor Place ☎212/254-4370. Showcase for exciting work since the 1960s, when Sam Shepard's *The Unseen Hand* and *Forensic and the Navigators* had the playwright himself playing drums in the lobby. For the last fifteen years, however, the theater has been the home of the comically absurd but very popular performance artists Blue Man Group (Ⓦwww.blueman.com).

Atlantic Theater Company 336 W 20th St, at Eighth Ave ☎212/645-8015, Ⓦwww .atlantictheater.com. As you'd expect from a theater founded by David Mamet and William H. Macy, this place is known for accessible, intelligent productions of modern dramatic classics, works by everyone from Harold Pinter to Martin McDonagh. The ATC also runs an acting school nearby on 16th Street, and you can sometimes catch student performances here, too.

Barrow Street Theater 27 Barrow St, at Seventh Ave S ☎212/243-6262. Until late 2003, this small theater inside a landmark West Village building was the long-term home of Off-Broadway favorite the Drama Dept. That company has been replaced by a more profit-minded organization, which is generating artistically excellent but more commercially viable productions, like Austin Pendleton's *Orson's Shadow*.

🏃 **Brooklyn Academy of Music 30 Lafayette Ave, Brooklyn** ☎718/636-4100, Ⓦwww .bam.org. Despite its name, Brooklyn Academy of Music (usually referred to as BAM) regularly presents theatrical productions on its three stages, often touring shows from Europe and Asia. Every autumn BAM puts on the Next Wave festival of large-scale performance art (see p.445). Not so much Off-Broadway as Off-Manhattan, but well worth the trip.

City Center 131 W 55th St, at Seventh Ave ☎212/581-1212, Ⓦwww.citycenter.org. This large, midtown venue is best known for its Encores! series. These readings and studio performances usually run for one weekend only, and are designed to revive long-forgotten or overlooked musicals, from Gilbert & Sullivan to modern dance.

John Houseman Theater 450 W 42nd St, at Tenth Ave ☎212/239-6200. Named for the man who created Juilliard's drama department, this theater complex has three spaces: the largest one is known for producing quality musicals and mainstream drama (not to mention having good sightlines), while the smaller spaces (Studio and Studio Too) showcase more experimental pieces.

🏃 **The Joseph Papp Public Theater 425 Lafayette St** ☎212/239-6200, Ⓦwww .publictheater.org. This major Off-Broadway institution delivers thought-provoking and challenging productions from new, mostly American, playwrights. It's also the city's primary presenter of Shakespeare plays. In the summer, the Public produces the free Shakespeare in the Park series at the open-air Delacorte Theater in Central Park (see p.171).

Manhattan Theater Club 131 W 55th St ☎212/581-1212, Ⓦwww.mtc-nyc.org. An important midtown venue for serious new theater featuring major American actors. Many productions eventually transfer to Broadway; see them here first, though prices aren't that much cheaper. Wheelchair-accessible.

Orpheum Theater 126 Second Ave, at St Mark's Place ☎212/477-2477. One of the East Village's biggest theaters, once known for hosting David Mamet and other influential new American shows, but more recently the home of the percussion group Stomp. Wheelchair-accessible.

Playwrights Horizons 416 W 42nd St, at Ninth Ave ☎212/564-1235, Ⓦwww.playwrightshorizons.org. This well-respected drama-centric space is located smack in the center of Times Square, though its mission remains the same as it was when it was founded in a YMCA in 1971 – championing works by undiscovered playwrights. They also get top-line actors.

Vivian Beaumont Theater and the Mitzi E. Newhouse Theater Lincoln Center, Broadway, at W 65th St ☎212/239-6200, Ⓦwww.lct.org. Technically Broadway theaters, these stages are far enough away from Times Square in distance and, usually, quality, to qualify as Off. A great place to see stimulating new work by playwrights like Tom Stoppard and John Guare.

(28)

Westside Theatre 407 W 43rd St, at Tenth Ave T 212/315-2244, W www.westsidetheatre.com. Two small theaters, known for productions of Shaw, Wilde, and Pirandello. The downstairs one has wheelchair access.

Off-Off-Broadway and performance-art spaces

Adobe Theater Company 138 S Oxford St, Brooklyn T 718/398-3690, W www.adobe.org. Hip, smart theater, where original productions are designed to draw in twentysomethings more likely to watch TV than catch a Broadway show. The program is highly varied, ranging from pulp-inspired *noir* thrillers to artsier performances.

Bouwerie Lane Theater 330 Bowery, at Bond St T 212/677-0060, W www.jean-cocteaurep.org. Home of the Jean Cocteau Repertory, which produces works by playwrights like Brecht, Genet, Ibsen, Molière, Sophocles, and Sartre.

Dixon Place 258 Bowery, at Stanton St, 2nd floor T 212/219-0736, W www.dixonplace .org. Very popular small venue dedicated to experimental theater, dance, and literary readings.

The Flea 41 White St, at Church St T 212/226-2407. Cutting-edge drama space run by Jim Simpson, Sigourney Weaver's husband. The program stretches from performance art and drama to acrobatics. Though many of the actors here are not professionals, the quality remains impressively high.

Franklin Furnace Archive 80 Hanson Place #301, at Portland Ave, Brooklyn T 718/398-7255, W www.franklinfurnace.org. An archive dedicated to installation work and performance art, the Franklin Furnace has launched the careers of performers as celebrated and notorious as Karen Finley and Eric Bogosian. Performances take place at various downtown locations – check the website or call for updated schedules.

Here 145 Sixth Ave, at Spring St T 212/647-0202, W www.here.org. A very open-minded, intriguing space supporting both new artists and established performers like Suzanne Vega. Puppetry and performance art are special strengths.

Kraine 85 E 4th St, at Second Ave T 212/777-6088, W www.httheater.org/kraine.html. This 99-seat East Village theater is home to twelve different residential companies and is mostly known for presenting unusual comedies. Another plus for this budget space is the raked seating, which makes for good sightlines. It's in the basement of the same building as artsy *KGB*, a bar known for its author readings (see p.368).

La Mama E.T.C. (Experimental Theater Club) 74A E 4th St, at Second Ave T 212/475-7710, W www.lamama.org. The mother of all Off-Off venues, founded more than 40 years ago. A real gem with four different auditoria, La Mama is known for politically and sexually charged material as well as visiting dance troupes from overseas. For raw amateur performances, check out The Galleria space a few blocks away.

Ludlow Ten 113 Ludlow St, at Delancey St W www.ludlowten.org. Lower East Side performance group, formerly known as Expanded Arts, that's best known for producing the summer-long Shakespeare in the Park(ing Lot) series of free performances at the Municipal Parking Lot at Broome and Ludlow.

New York Theater Workshop 79 E 4th St, at Second Ave T 212/460-5475, W www.nytw .org. An eminent experimental workshop that often chooses cult hit shows and has presented plays by Tony Kushner, Susan Sontag, and Paul Rudnick; best known these days as the place the global musical megahit *Rent* was first shown to the public.

Ontological-Hysteric Theater St Marks Church, 131 E 10th St, at Second Ave T 212/420-1916, W www.ontological.com. Produces some of the city's best radical shows; especially famous for the work of independent theater legend Richard Foreman.

Performing Garage 33 Wooster St, at Grand St T 212/966-3651, W www.thewoostergroup.org. The famous Wooster Group (which includes Willem Dafoe) performs regularly in this Soho space. Tickets are like gold dust (very hard to come by), but the effort to find them is worth it.

P.S. 122 150 First Ave, at 9th St T 212/477-5288, W www.ps122.org. A converted school in the East Village that is perennially popular for its jam-packed schedule of revolutionary performance art, dance, and one-person shows in their two theaters.

St Ann's Warehouse 38 Water St, Brooklyn T 718/254-8779, W www.artsatstanns.org. Housed in a hulking industrial space, St Ann's is in a part of DUMBO relatively far from the subway (see p.242). Brave the walk, though, as the main stage is consistently impressive for both drama and music – there are Broadway tryouts here and musicians like Lou Reed often play *intime* sets. There's also a café and gallery space in the entrance.

Theater for the New City 155 First Ave, at 10th St ☎212/254-1109, ⓦwww.theaterforthenewcity.net. This major performance venue is best known as the site where Sam Shepard's Pulitzer Prize–winning *Buried Child* premiered in 1978. It's still churning out fine drama through its emerging-playwrights program. TNC also performs outdoors for free at a variety of venues throughout the summer and hosts the Lower East Side Festival of the Arts at the end of May.

Tribeca Performing Arts Center 199 Chambers St, at Greenwich St ☎212/220-1460, ⓦwww .tribecapac.org. TriPac, as it's known, is owned by the Community College of Manhattan, a fact reflected in its programming: mostly high-end local theater and dance groups, plus kids' workshops and multicultural events. It's also known for fine jazz performances and being one of the primary venues for the Tribeca Film Festival.

Worth St Theater Company 111 Reade St, at W Broadway ☎212/571-1576. Now housed at the Tribeca Playhouse, this small collective focuses on modern classics in productions that often move quickly up the food chain to more high-profile Off-Broadway venues.

Classical music and opera

New Yorkers take their **classical music and opera** seriously. Long lines form for anything popular, many concerts sell out, and summer evenings can see a quarter of a million people turning up in Central Park for free performances by the New York Philharmonic. Tickets can be somewhat easier to come by for performances by the city's top-notch chamber-music ensembles (most of the patrons are members of the city's geriatric crowd).

Opera venues

Amato Opera Theater 319 Bowery, at 2nd St ☎212/228-8200, ⓦwww.amato.org. This Bowery venue presents an ambitious and varied repertory of classics performed by up-and-coming young singers and conductors. The Opera in Brief series on Sat mornings (Sept–May) is enchanting for kids. Performances at weekends only, Sept–May.

Juilliard School 60 Lincoln Center Plaza, at 65th St ☎212/799-5000, ⓦwww.juilliard.edu. Located right next door to the Met (see below), Juilliard students often perform under the direction of a famous conductor, usually for low ticket prices.

🏃 **Metropolitan Opera House** Lincoln Center, Columbus Ave, at 64th St ☎212/362-6000, ⓦwww.metopera.org. More popularly known as the Met, New York's premiere opera venue is home to the world-renowned Metropolitan Opera Company from Sept to late April. Tickets are expensive (up to $295) and can be well-nigh impossible to snag, though 175 standing-room tickets for each performance go on sale at 10am every Saturday for the following week's show: weekday tickets are $12–16, Sat $15–20.

The limit is one ticket per person, and the line has been known to form at dawn.

The New York State Theater Lincoln Center, 65th St, at Columbus Ave ☎212/870-5570, ⓦwww .nycopera.com. This is where the New York City Opera plays David to the Met's Goliath. Its wide and adventurous program varies wildly in quality depending on the production (check out a *NY Times* review before purchasing) – some quite creative, others boringly mediocre – but seats go for less than half the Met's prices.

Concert halls

92nd Street Y Kaufman Concert Hall 1395 Lexington Ave, at 92nd St ☎212/996-1100, ⓦwww.92y.org. This wood-panelled space is especially welcoming since performers are usually available to chat or mingle with the audience after shows. Great line-up of chamber music and solo events.

The Alice Tully Hall Lincoln Center, Broadway and W 65th St ☎212/721-6500. A smaller Lincoln Center hall for the top chamber orchestras, string quartets, and instrumentalists. The weekend chamber series are deservedly popular, though the crowd is composed almost exclusively of the 65-and-over set. Prices similar to those in Avery Fisher (see below).

Avery Fisher Hall Lincoln Center, Broadway and W 65th St ☎212/875-5030, ⊛www.lincolncenter .org. The permanent home of the New York Philharmonic. Ticket prices for the Philharmonic range $12–50. The open rehearsals (9.45am on concert days) are a great bargain; tickets are just $14. Avery Fisher also hosts the very popular annual Mostly Mozart Festival (☎212/875-5103) in August.

🏃 **Bargemusic** Fulton Ferry Landing, Brooklyn ☎718/624-4061, ⊛www .bargemusic.org. Chamber music in a wonderful river setting on a moving barge below the Brooklyn Bridge. Thurs and Fri 7.30pm, Sun 4pm. Tickets are $35, $20 for full-time students.

Brooklyn Academy of Music 30 Lafayette Ave, Brooklyn ☎718/636-4100, ⊛www.bam.org. The BAM Opera House is the perennial home of Philip Glass operatic premieres and Laurie Anderson performances. It also hosts a number of contemporary imports from European and Chinese companies, often with a large modern-dance component.

Carnegie Hall 154 W 57th St, at Seventh Ave ☎212/247-7800, ⊛www.carnegiehall.org. The greatest names from all schools of music have performed here, from Tchaikovsky

▽ Brooklyn Academy of Music

(who conducted the hall's inaugural concert) to Toscanini to Gershwin to Billie Holiday. The tradition continues, and the stunning acoustics – said to be the best in the world – lure big-name performers (such as Renée Fleming and Katya Labèque) at sky-high prices. Check website for up-to-date admission rates and schedules. To learn more about the building itself, head to the Rose Museum on the 2nd floor here.

Cathedral of St John the Divine 1047 Amsterdam Ave, at 112th St ☎212/662-2133, ⊛www .stjohndivine.org. A magnificent Morningside Heights setting that hosts occasional classical and New Age performances. Also home to the Early Music Foundation (⊛www.earlymusic.org), which performs scores from the eleventh through the eighteenth centuries.

Lehman Center for the Performing Arts 250 Bedford Park Blvd, Bronx ☎718/960-8833, ⊛www.lehmancenter.com. First-class concert hall drawing the world's top performers, as varied as alumni of the Bolshoi Ballet and Ladysmith Black Mambazo.

Merkin Concert Hall 129 W 67th St, at Broadway ☎212/501-3330, ⊛www.merkinconcerthall .org. This intimate and adventurous venue in the Elaine Kaufman Cultural Center is a great place to hear music of any kind. Plays host to the New York Guitar Festival in September.

🏃 **Symphony Space** 2537 Broadway, at 95th St ☎212/864-5400, ⊛www .symphonyspace.org. The Symphony Space has a jazz and classical performance schedule, a world-music center, and a free annual 12-hour music marathon.

Town Hall 123 W 43rd St, at Sixth Ave ☎212/840-2824, ⊛www.the-townhall-nyc.org. This midtown hall has an unusual history: it was designed by Stanford White (the mastermind of the original Madison Square Garden) and commissioned by suffragettes as a protest-friendly space. One of the egalitarian innovations in the design was the omission of any box seats in order to provide better acoustics and sightlines from every seat in the house. As for programming, it's best known for an eclectic policy – from its Sunday Afternoon Opera series to cutting-edge new classical music and world-music shows.

Free summer concerts

Concert prices just keep getting higher, but in summer there are often budget-priced or free alternatives.

Lincoln Center Out-of-Doors (℡212/875-5108, ⊛www.lincolncenter.org) hosts a varied selection of daily free performances of music and dance events on the plaza throughout the summer.

Bryant Park (℡212/768-4242, ⊛www.bryantpark.org) is home to free Broadway and Off-Broadway musical performances every Thursday lunchtime in the summer, as well as short pop concerts staged by the TV show *Good Morning America* early on Friday mornings.

SummerStage Festival (℡212/360-2777, ⊛www.summerstage.org) in Central Park puts on an impressive range of free concerts of all kinds of music throughout the summer; performances take place at the Rumsey Playfield (near the 72nd St and Fifth Ave entrance). A highlight here is the occasional Wednesday-night performance of Verdi by the **New York Grand Opera**.

Central Park is also one of the many open-air venues for the **New York Philharmonic's Concerts in the Park** (℡212/875-5709, ⊛www.nyphilharmonic.org) series of concerts and fireworks displays that turns up all over the city and the outer boroughs in July. Similarly, there's the **Met in the Parks** series (℡212/362-6000, ⊛www.metopera.org) in June and July.

For other free classical music and jazz performances, try the **Washington Square Music Festival** (℡212/252-3621, ⊛www.washingtonsquaremusicfestival.org) on Tuesdays at 8pm throughout July, or the **Celebrate Brooklyn Festival** (℡718/855-7882, ⊛www.brooklynx.org/celebrate) at Prospect Park Bandshell in Brooklyn, on July and August weekends.

Dance

As favorites like Bill T. Jones, Mark Morris, and Savion Glover continue to show, **dance** – especially experimental or avant-garde performance – is still surging in popularity in New York. The city has five major ballet companies, dozens of modern troupes, and untold thousands of soloists; all performances are listed in broadly the same periodicals and websites as music and theater, though you might also want to pick up *Dance Magazine* (⊛www.dancemagazine.com) for extra specifics. The official dance season runs from September through January and April through June.

The following is a list of some of the major dance venues in the city, though a lot of the smaller, more esoteric companies and solo dancers also perform at spaces like Dixon Place and P.S.122, listed on p.386 under Off-Off Broadway. Dance fans should also note that the annual Dance on Camera Festival (℡212/727-0764, ⊛www.dancefilmsassn.org) of dance films takes place over three weekends at the Walter Reade Theater at Lincoln Center in January.

92nd Street Y Harkness Dance Center 1395 Lexington Ave, at 92nd St ℡212/415-5500, ⊛www.92y.org. Hosts performances and discussions, often for free.

Brooklyn Academy of Music 30 Lafayette St, Brooklyn ℡718/636-4100, ⊛www.bam.org. America's oldest performing-arts academy is still one of the busiest and most daring dance producers in New York. In the autumn, BAM's Next Wave festival features the hottest international attractions in avant-garde dance and music, and each spring since 1977 BAM has hosted the annual DanceAfrica Festival, America's largest showcase for African and African-American dance and culture.

City Center 131 W 55th St, at Seventh Ave ℡212/581-1212 or 581-7907, ⊛www.citycenter.org. This large, midtown venue hosts some of the most important troupes in modern dance, including the Paul Taylor Dance Company, the Alvin Ailey American Dance Theater, and the American Ballet Theater.

Cunningham Studio 55 Bethune St, at Washington St ☎212/255-8240, 🔵www.merce.org. The home of the Merce Cunningham Dance Company stages performances once a week by emerging modern choreographers, usually on Fri and Sat nights.

Dance Theater Workshop 219 W 19th St, at Seventh Ave ☎212/924-0077, 🔵www.dtw.org. Founded in 1965 as a choreographers' collective to support emerging artists in alternative dance, DTW is now housed in a multimillion-dollar building. There's a mid-sized main stage, an art gallery, and smaller workshop spaces, all of which boast more than 175 performances from nearly 70 artists and companies each season. The relaxed, friendly vibe and reasonable ticket prices (around $20) haven't changed.

Danspace Project St Mark's-Church-in-the-Bowery, 131 E 10th St, at Second Ave ☎212/674-8194, 🔵www.danspaceproject.org. Experimental contemporary dance, with a season running from September to June in one of the more beautiful performance spaces.

The Joyce Theater 175 Eighth Ave, at 19th St ☎212/242-0800, 🔵www.joyce.org. Situated in Chelsea, the Joyce is one of the best-known downtown dance venues. It hosts short seasons by a wide variety of acclaimed dance troupes such as Pilobolus, the Parsons Dance Company, and Donald Byrd/The Group. The Joyce also gives performances at their Soho space, a former firehouse (155 Mercer St, at Prince St; ☎212/431-9233).

Juilliard Dance Workshop 155 W 65th St, at Broadway ☎212/799-5000, 🔵www.juilliard .edu. The dance division of the Juilliard

School often holds free workshop performances, and each spring six students work with six composers to present a Composers and Choreographers concert.

🏃 **Lincoln Center's Fountain Plaza** 65th St, at Columbus Ave ☎212/875-5766, 🔵www.lincolncenter.org. Open-air venue for the enormously popular *Midsummer Night Swing*, where each night you can learn a different dance style en masse (everything from polka to rockabilly) and watch a performance – all for $12. Tickets go on sale at 5.45pm the night of the show; the season runs June–July.

Metropolitan Opera House Lincoln Center, 65th St, at Columbus Ave ☎212/362-6000, 🔵www.metopera.org. Home of the renowned American Ballet Theater (🔵www.abt.org), which performs at the Opera House from early May into July. Prices for ballet at the Met range from $275 for the best seats at special performances to $12–16 for standing-room tickets, which go on sale the morning of the performance.

New York State Theater Lincoln Center, 65th St, at Columbus Ave ☎212/870-5570, 🔵www .lincolncenter.org. Lincoln Center's other major ballet venue is home to the revered New York City Ballet (🔵www.nycballet.com), which performs for a nine-week season each spring.

Pace Downtown Theater Schimmel Center for the Arts Spruce St, at Park Row ☎212/346-1715, 🔵appserv.pace.edu/execute/home_ culture.cfm. Venue for the Yangtze Repertory Theatre Company, which stages work by Asian choreographers, as well as the Hudson Stage Company and the Tribeca Film Festival.

Cabaret and comedy

New York is one of America's **comedy** capitals, and there are several major clubs that feature professional performers, some of whom you'll recognize from television and film. There are also a good number of alternative comedy venues in downtown Manhattan that eschew the standard "comedy routine" fare for zanier "conceptual" comedy. Most mainstream clubs have shows every night, with two or more on weekends; it's usual to be charged a cover plus a two-drink minimum fee.

    Cabaret has cooled off a bit since the late 1990s, when it was a bit of a local fad, but there are still a couple of top venues where you can see some truly amazing stuff from the likes of Woody Allen, Elaine Stritch, and Eartha Kitt.

The list below represents the best-known comedy and cabaret venues in town, but performances can also be found at a multitude of bars, clubs, and art spaces all over the city. Check *Time Out New York* and *Village Voice* for the fullest and most up-to-date listings.

Comedy clubs

Carolines 1626 Broadway, at 49th St ☎212/757-4100, ⓦwww.carolines.com. Even after moving to Times Square from the South Street Seaport, *Carolines* still books some of the best stand-up acts in town; this is where most of the biggest names perform. Cover $15–30 Sun–Thurs, $25–40 Fri and Sat. Two-drink minimum. Also has a restaurant, *Comedy Nation*, upstairs.

Chicago City Limits Theater 1105 First Ave, at 61st St ☎212/888-5233, ⓦwww.chicagocity limits.com. The oldest improvisation theater in New York. $15 admission with a two-drink minimum.

Comedy Cellar 117 MacDougal St, at Bleecker St ☎212/254-3480, ⓦwww.comedycellar .com. Popular Greenwich Village comedy club now in its third decade. It's a good late-night hangout. $10–15 cover plus two-drink minimum.

Comic Strip Live 1568 Second Ave, at 81st St ☎212/861-9386, ⓦwww.comicstriplive.com. Famed showcase for stand-up comics and young singers going for the big time. Cover $15–20 plus two-drink minimum.

Dangerfield's 1118 First Ave, at 61st St ☎212/593-1650, ⓦwww.dangerfields.com. Vegas-style new-talent showcase founded by Rodney Dangerfield. $15–20 cover with, unusually, no minimum drink charge.

Gotham Comedy Club 208 W 23rd St, between Seventh and Eighth aves ☎212/367-9000, ⓦwww.gothamcomedyclub.com. A swanky comedy venue in the Flatiron District, highly respected by New York media types and those who scout up-and-coming comics. Cover $15–30 plus two-drink minimum.

Stand-Up New York 236 W 78th St, at Broadway ☎212/595-0850, ⓦwww.standupny.com. Upper West Side all-ages-forum for established comics, many of whom have appeared on *Leno* and *Letterman*. Hosts the Toyota Comedy Festival in June. Cover $12–16 plus two-drink minimum – you're required to arrive a half-hour before showtime, so call or check the website for the night's schedule before arriving.

🏃 **Upright Citizens Brigade Theater** 161 W 22nd St, at Seventh Ave ☎212/366-9176,

ⓦwww.ucbtheater.com. Consistently hilarious sketch-based and improv comedy, seven nights a week. You can sometimes catch *Saturday Night Live* cast members in the ensemble. Cover $5–8.

Cabarets

🏃 **Café Carlyle** inside Carlyle Hotel, 35 E 76th St, at Madison Ave ☎212/744-1600, ⓦwww.thecarlyle.com. Though long-term resident musician Bobby Short may have passed away, there's still ample reason to come here – it's where Woody Allen plays clarinet every Monday, and divas like Eartha Kitt and Elaine Stritch drop by for a week's residency. If you don't want to eat (the food's expensive and unexciting), standing at the bar is just as fun – though it's still a pricey night out. Cover $55–90, jacket required.

Don't Tell Mama 343 W 46th St, at Ninth Ave ☎212/757-0788, ⓦwww.donttellmama.com. Lively and convivial Midtown West piano bar and cabaret featuring rising stars and singing waitresses. Cover free–$20, two-drink minimum.

Duplex 61 Christopher St, at Seventh Ave ☎212/841-5438, ⓦwww.theduplex.com. West Village cabaret popular with a boisterous gay and tourist crowd; Joan Rivers was discovered here. Has a rowdy piano bar downstairs and a cabaret room upstairs. Open 4pm–4am. Cover free–$20 plus two-drink minimum.

Fez 2330 Broadway, at 85th St ☎212/579-5100. Trendier-than-usual cabaret space in a restaurant basement that features singer/songwriters, revues, and kitschy cabaret like Kiki & Herb. Try to get a seat in one of the comfy booths lining the back walls, rather than the long tables crammed together closer to the stage. Cover $10–20.

🏃 **Joe's Pub** 425 Lafayette St, between Astor Place and 4th St ☎212/239-6200, ⓦwww .publictheater.org. The hipper, late-night arm of the Joseph Papp Public Theater, this is one of the sharpest and most popular music venues in the city, with a wide range of cabaret acts nightly, from Broadway crooner Donna McKechnie to Norwegian folk icon and Hardanger fiddle virtuoso Annbjrg Lien, and everything else in between.

Film

Despite steadily rising prices (locals grumbled when ticket prices broke $10 in 2004), New York is a movie-lover's dream. There are plenty of state-of-the-art **movie theaters** all over the city; most are multiscreen complexes, and have all the charm of large airports, but they also have the advantages of superb sound, luxurious seating, and perfect sightlines. This is even the case for Times Square's cinemas, which in the past have tended to be small and noisy but now are typified by the towering megaplexes on 42nd Street.

For listings, your best bets are freesheets like the *Village Voice* or the *New York Press*; otherwise, check the local papers on Fridays, when the papers publish new reviews and schedules for the following week. For accurate showtimes, and to book a ticket in advance, call ☎212/777-FILM or check ⓦwww .fandango.com and ⓦwww.moviefone.com. Despite the per-ticket surcharge of around $1.50, it's often worth booking ahead: hot new releases usually sell out on opening weekend, and since there's no reserved seating it pays to get tickets to a must-see show well in advance. We've highlighted our pick of New York's best movie theaters below, divided into those showing first-run mainstream and indie fare and the venues that specialize in revivals and more obscure and experimental flicks, though the list is by no means exhaustive.

First-run movies

AMC Empire 25 234 W 42nd St, at Eighth Ave ☎212/398-3939. One of the few skyscraper multiplexes: 25 screens, all with stadium seating, soaring upward. Though it's usually crowded on weekends, it offers a decent mix of mainstream and arthouse films, and even has its own restaurant.

Angelika Film Center 18 W Houston St, at Mercer St ☎212/995-2000, ⓦwww.angelikafilmcenter. Six-screen arthouse venue, with a rather overhyped reputation – screens are tiny, and the subway tends to rumble past at inopportune moments, rattling the subterranean rooms. Still, it's one of the few surviving venues for smaller films in the city and has a regular line-up of top-notch indies on offer.

BAM Rose Cinemas 30 Lafayette Ave, at Ashland Place, Brooklyn ☎718/777-3456, ⓦwww .bam.org. There are four screens at BAM's film site. The programming is mostly classics and rarities; the year-round BAMcinématek series usually offers the most interesting choices.

Clearview's Ziegfeld 54th St, at Sixth Ave ☎212/765-7600. Sitting on the site of the old *Ziegfeld Follies* (hence the name), this midtown movie palace with its massive screen (one of the biggest in the country) is the place locals come to for an old-fashioned cinema experience. Numerous film premieres also take place here.

Landmark Sunshine Cinema 143 E Houston St, at

First Ave ☎212/330-8182, ⓦwww.landmark theatres.com. When this former Yiddish vaudeville house opened as a cinema in 2001, it quickly seized the Angelika's crown as the best place to see indie films, thanks to larger screens, better seating, and a less threadbare building.

Lincoln Plaza 1886 Broadway, at 62nd St ☎212/757-2280. This six-screen theater is as close as the Upper West Side gets to an arthouse venue. While it plays a lot of mainstream Hollywood stuff, it's also known for favoring foreign and independent films.

Paris Fine Arts 4 W 58th St, at Fifth Ave ☎212/688-3800. An old-fashioned cinema (there's even a balcony) that specializes in foreign films as well as well-reviewed mainstream fare.

Sony Lincoln Square IMAX 1998 Broadway, at 68th St ☎212/336-5000, ⓦwww.imax.com. More and more mainstream films are being converted to IMAX technology and are being re-released on the huge screens here in high resolution just months after their original theatrical debuts. Worth checking out for sci-fi spectaculars, if nothing else.

Revivals

New York used to be one of the best cities in the world to see **old movies**, but the cinema landscape has changed considerably in recent years. Most of the old repertory houses that showed a regular menu of scratchy prints of old chestnuts and recent favorites have gone. In their place have sprung up an impressive selection of museums and revival houses. These new venues show an imaginatively programmed series of films – retrospectives of particular directors and actors, series from different countries, and programs of specific genres. In the case of visitors, what you get to see is a matter of chance: if you're lucky your trip may coincide with a retrospective of your favorite director or movie heartthrob.

Schedules can be found at the websites listed in the previous section (see opposite), and all the following revival houses and museums publish calendars available at their box offices. **The American Museum of the Moving Image 35th Ave, at 36th St, Astoria, Queens** ☏718/784-0077,

ⓦwww.ammi.org. Despite only showing films during the days on weekends, AMMI is still well worth a trip out to Queens (it's not as far as it sounds; call ☏718/784-4777 for directions) either for the pictures – which are often serious director retrospectives and silent films, with a strong emphasis on cinematographers – or for the cinema museum itself (see p.271 for review). Tickets $10.
Anthology Film Archives 32 Second Ave, at 2nd St ☏212/505-5181, ⓦwww.anthologyfilmarchives .org. A bastion of experimental filmmaking. Programs of mind-bending abstraction, East Village grunge flicks, and auteur retrospectives all rub shoulders here. Tickets $8.
Cinema Classics 332 E 11th St, at Second Ave ☏212/677-6309, ⓦwww.cinemaclassics.com. It's a grungy, sit-on-folding-chairs affair, but the film selections are excellent, the café's sofas comfortable, and cakes divine, and the prices are low (tickets $6). There's also an esoteric collection of cult videos for sale.

Film festivals and seasonal screenings

There always seems to be some **film festival** or other running in New York. The granddaddy of them all, the **New York Film Festival**, starts at the end of September and runs for two weeks at the Alice Tully Hall at Lincoln Center. It's well worth catching if you're in town, though tickets for the most popular films can sell out very quickly. If you're determined to see something, watch the reviews in the *New York Times* each morning – when movies are panned, there's usually a cluster of people trying to sell off their tickets outside the theater that night. More info: ⓦwww.filmlinc .com.

See Chapter 33, "Parades and festivals," for info on the larger filmfests; here's a list of some of the smaller, but still worthwhile, festivals and seasonal screenings:
Asian American Film Festival ⓦwww.asiancinevision.org; July

Bryant Park Summer Film Festival (free; outdoor screenings of old Hollywood favorites on Monday nights at sunset) ⓦwww.bryantpark.org; June–August

DocFest (International Documentary Festival) ⓦwww.docfest.org; spring

GenArt Film Festival of American Independents ⓦwww.genart.org; April

Human Rights Watch Film Festival ⓦwww.hrw.org; June

Margaret Mead Festival (anthropological films at the Museum of Natural History) ⓦwww.amnh.org; October

New Fest: Lesbian & Gay Film Festival ⓦwww.newfestival.org; June

New York Jewish Film Festival at Lincoln Center ⓦwww.filmlinc.com; January

New York Video Festival at Lincoln Center ⓦwww.filmlinc.com; July

River Flicks at Chelsea Piers (free screenings of cult crowd-pleasers) ⓦwww .hudsonriverpark.org; July–August

Socrates Sculpture Garden Film Festival (free screenings of classics every Wed starting at sunset in Long Island City, Queens) ⓦwww.socratessculpturepark.org; July–August

Tribeca Film Festival ⓦwww.tribecafilmfestival.org; May

㉘

Film Forum 209 W Houston St, at Sixth Ave ☎212/727-8112, ⓦwww.filmforum .org. The cozy three-screen Film Forum has an eccentric but famously popular program of new independent movies, documentaries, and foreign films, as well as a repertory program specializing in silent comedy, camp classics, and cult directors. Film Forum is one of the best alternative spaces in town. IFC Center 323 Sixth Ave, at 3rd St ☎212/924-7771, ⓦwww.ifccenter.com. Multiple revivals and a good number of very small indie films daily. Features a much larger screen and a better sound system than you'll find at most other arthouses. The Museum of Modern Art 11 W 53rd St, at Fifth Ave ☎212/708-9400, ⓦwww.moma.org. MoMA is famous among local cinephiles for its vast collection of films, its exquisite programming, and its regular audience of cantankerous senior citizens. The movies themselves range all the way from Hollywood screwball comedies to hand-painted Super 8. Tickets $6.

Ocularis 70 N 6th St, at Wythe Ave, Williamsburg, Brooklyn ☎718/388-8713, ⓦwww.billburg .com/ocularis. This small space inside the *Galapagos* bar (see p.374) is transformed into an independent cinema on Sunday nights, screening rarely seen cult classics, foreign gems, and pioneering work by new directors. Ticket prices vary. Two Boots Pioneer Theater 155 E 3rd St, at Ave A ☎212/254-3300, ⓦwww.twoboots.com. Sunday nights are for short films, Tuesdays for rarely seen and underrated gems, and the rest of the week is devoted to themed programming throughout the year. Tickets $9. Walter Reade Theater Lincoln Center, 165 W 65th St at Broadway ☎212/496-3809, ⓦwww.filmlinc .com. Programmed by the Film Society of Lincoln Center, the Walter Reade is simply the best place in town to see great films. This beautiful, modern theater has perfect sightlines, a huge screen, and impeccable acoustics. The emphasis is on foreign films and the great auteurs; it's also home to many of the city's festivals (see box, p.393). Tickets $9.

Literary events and readings

New York has long been viewed as a **literary mecca**. The city's proliferation of competitive bookstores means that you can see someone performing wordy

Poetry slams and readings

Poetry and story slamming is a literary version of freestyle rapping, in which performers take turns presenting stories and poems (often mostly or entirely improvised) on stage. At their best, slams can be thrilling, raw, and very funny (not to mention competitive – many feature a judges' panel). We've pulled out the three best places to sample New York slams, including the eatery where it all began, the *Nuyorican Poets Café*.

Bowery Poetry Club 308 Bowery, at Houston St ☎212/614-0505, ⓦwww .bowerypoetry.com. A combination café/bar/bookstore with a small stage at the back, this community-focused space is owned by Bob Holman, who used to run *Nuyorican* (see below). There are occasional big names on stage, but it's mostly impressively enthusiastic amateurs.

The Moth The Players Club, 16 Gramercy Park S, at Park Ave S ⓦwww.themoth .org. Offbeat literary company that's known for its story slams – open-mic nights where amateurs vie for a five-minute on-stage storytelling spot. There's also a resident company that performs longer monologues; though most events take place at the Moth's home base of *The Players Club*, there are also sporadic offshoots round town – check the website for schedules.

Nuyorican Poets Café 236 E 3rd St, at Ave B ☎212/505-8183, ⓦwww.nuyorican. org. Alphabet City's *Nuyorican* remains one of the most talked-about performance spaces in town. Its poetry slams are what made it famous, but there are also theater and film-script readings, occasionally with well-known downtown stars.

wonders any night of the week. (For recommendations on specific stores, see Chapter 31, "Shopping," and see Chapter 33, "Parades and festivals," for book festivals.)

92nd Street Y Unterberg Poetry Center 1395 Lexington Ave ☎ 212/415-5500, ⒲ www.92ndsty .org. Quite simply, the definitive place to hear all your Booker, Pulitzer, and Nobel prize–winning favorites, as well as many other exciting new talents. Name almost any American literary great – from Tennessee Williams to Langston Hughes – and they're likely to have appeared here; expect the current line-up to be just as blockbusting.

Barnes & Noble The city's numerous B&Ns host a surprisingly diverse range of readings almost every night of the week. See p.411 for store locations and contact details; the Union Square branch generally gets the most high-profile authors and events.

Half King 505 W 23rd St, at Tenth Ave ☎ 212/462-4300, ⒲ www.thehalfking.com. Large, divey bar owned by macho author Sebastian Junger (*The Perfect Storm*): it's not surprising, then, that most Monday nights are devoted to free readings by a big-name contemporary author – Jerry Stahl and Edna O'Brien have both appeared here. The second Monday of each month

is a more intriguing program centered on great magazine writing read by a group of journalists.

KGB 85 E 4th St ☎ 212/505-3360, ⒲ www .kgbbar.com. Grubby but welcoming little bar that hosts free readings 7–9pm every Sunday and Tuesday (though there are often readings other nights as well). To read here is a highly prestigious honor. Expect to see top names like Michael Cunningham slumming it for the sake of intellectual chicness – call or check the website for up-to-date schedules.

Makor 35 W 67th St ☎ 212/601-1000, ⒲ www .makor.org. This Jewish spirituality/arts center has been one of the hottest spots in New York's art world for some years now. Its programming is superb, and the poetry-reading series perhaps the best in the city.

Symphony Space 2537 Broadway, at 95th St ☎ 212/864-5400, ⒲ www.symphonyspace .org. The highly acclaimed Selected Shorts series, in which actors read the short fiction of a variety of authors (everyone from James Joyce to David Sedaris), usually packs the Symphony Space theater.

Literary events and readings | THE PERFORMING ARTS AND FILM

28

Gay and lesbian New York

There are few places in America – indeed in the world – where **gay culture** thrives as it does in New York. Open gays and lesbians are considered mainstream here – so much so that the city is one of the few places that Republican administrations avidly court gay voters. By some estimates, about twenty percent of New Yorkers identify themselves as gay or lesbian; when you add bisexual and transgender individuals, the figure climbs even higher – as they do when you take into account the number of gay visitors who come to New York each day.

The largely liberal orientation of New York politics has been generally beneficial to the gay community since the 1969 riots at the *Stonewall Bar* marked the onset of the gay-rights movement (see box, p.114). Nonetheless, significant issues still remain hotly disputed, **marriage equality** most of all. The New York State Supreme Court ruled gay marriage illegal in 2006; the city has flimsy domestic-partner legislation in place, but many same-sex couples have opted for Vermont civil unions and Canadian marriages, even though they are not yet recognized here. The rights of **transgender** individuals are also contentious – New York City has a 2002 law prohibiting discrimination on the basis of gender identity or expression, but transgender people are commonly prevented from using public bathrooms. Within the New York City gay community itself, today's major battles revolve largely around the nihilistic practice of "barebacking" (having unprotected sex with strangers), as well as gay-identity issues within the African-American community, where homophobia is surprisingly prevalent (though by no means omnipresent).

Socially, gay men and lesbians are fairly visible in the city, and while it's not recommended that gay couples hold hands in public before checking out the territory, there are a few **neighborhoods** where the gay community makes up the majority of the population. **Chelsea** (especially Eighth Avenue between 14th and 23rd streets), the **East Village/Lower East Side**, and Brooklyn's **Park Slope** are the largest of these, and have all but replaced the West Village as gay New York's hub. A strong gay presence still lingers in the vicinity of **Christopher Street** in the West Village, but it's in Chelsea that gay male socializing is most ubiquitous and open. Lesbians will find large communities in laid-back Park Slope and around East Houston Street. Other neighborhoods with strong gay and lesbian presences are Morningside Heights (Columbia University's college town), Queens's Astoria, and Brooklyn's Prospect Heights (mainly residential), DUMBO, and Williamsburg. All of the city's alternative communities come together in major events like **Pride Week** in late June (Pride Month), which includes a rally, Dyke March, Dyke Ball, Brooklyn Pride, Black Pride, innumerable parties, and the infamous (if commercialized and sweltering) **Lesbian & Gay Pride Parade** (see p.443).

Several free weekly **newspapers and magazines** serve New York's gay community: *Gay City News* (ⓦwww.gaycitynews.com), *New York Blade* (ⓦwww.nyblade.com), *Next* (for men; ⓦwww.nextmagazine.net), *HX* (for men; ⓦwww.hx.com), and *GO NYC* (for women; trans-friendly; ⓦwww.gonycmagazine.com). You'll find these at the LGBT Community Services Center (see below), at street-corner boxes, bars, cafés, lesbian and gay bookstores, and occasionally at newsstands, where glossy national mags such as *Out*, *POZ*, *Girlfriends*, *Diva*, *MetroSource*, and others are also available. The listings in *Time Out New York* are helpful as well. If you're looking for a date, some action, or just people to party with while you're here, post a personal (or respond to someone else's) on craigslist (free; ⓦnewyork.craigslist.org), a popular online message-board. Other useful resources are listed throughout this chapter.

Resources

The Audre Lorde Project 85 S Oxford St, Brooklyn ☎718/596-1328, ⓦwww.alp.org. Center for LGBT people of color.

Callen-Lorde Community Health Center 356 W 18th St, between Eighth and Ninth aves ☎212/271-7200, ⓦwww.callen-lorde.org. Mon 12.30–8pm, Tues, Thurs & Fri 9am–4.30pm, Wed 2.30–8pm. LGBT medical center and clinic. A good place to seek privacy-sensitive medical attention, with sliding price plan based on income.

Gay Men's Health Crisis (GMHC) 119 W 24th St, between Sixth and Seventh aves ☎212/367-1000, ⓦwww.gmhc.org. Despite the name, this incredible organization – the oldest and largest not-for-profit AIDS organization in the world – provides testing, information, and referrals to everyone: gay, straight, and transgender.

The Lesbian, Gay, Bisexual & Transgender Community Services Center 208 W 13th St, west of Seventh Ave ☎212/620-7310, ⓦwww.gaycenter.org. The Center's monthly newsletter, *Center Voice*, has a circulation of 60,000, which should give you an idea of how this space has grown since it opened here in 1983. The Center houses well over a hundred groups and organizations, sponsors workshops, parties, 12-step programs, movie nights, guest speakers, youth services, programs for parents and kids, an archive and library, and lots more. Even the bulletin boards are fascinating.

SAGE: Senior Action in a Gay Environment 305 Seventh Ave, at 27th St, 16th floor ☎212/741-2247, ⓦwww.sageusa.org. Support and activities for gay seniors. Also at the Center, 208 W 13th St (see above).

Sylvia Rivera Law Project ☎646/602-5638, ⓦwww.srlp.org. Legal services and organization for transgender and intersexed individuals.

Accommodation

These places to stay are friendly to gays and lesbians and convenient for the scene. The prices at the end of each listing represent the lowest price for a double in high season, excluding taxes.

Chelsea Pines Inn 317 W 14th St, between Eighth and Ninth aves ☎1-888/546-2700, ⓦwww.chelseapinesinn.com. Housed in an old brownstone on the Greenwich Village/ Chelsea border, this hotel offers clean, comfortable, attractively furnished rooms. Guests are mostly gay. Best to book in advance. $159

㉙

Chelsea Savoy Hotel 204 W 23rd St, at Seventh Ave ☎212/929-9353, ⓦwww.chelseasavoynyc .com. The *Savoy* makes up for its modern lack of charm with clean rooms full of amenities. $135

Colonial House Inn 318 W 22nd St, between Eighth and Ninth aves ☎212/243-9669, ⓦwww .colonialhouseinn.com. You won't mind that this B&B is a little worn around the edges – its attractive design and work with the GMHC make for a feel-good experience. The townhouse property boasts gay and straight clientele. $104

Hotel 17 255 E 17th St, between Second and Third aves ☎212/475-2845, ⓦwww.hotel17ny .com. Woody Allen's *Manhattan Murder Mystery* was filmed here, and the 120 rooms have been tastefully redone, though some of them still share baths. In a good neighborhood, too. $150

Incentra Village House 32 Eighth Ave, between 12th and Jane sts ☎212/206-0007. Some of the rooms in this twelve-room town-house come with kitchenettes. Book far in advance. Three-night minimum stay at weekends. $179

Arts and culture

There's always a good amount of gay and gay-friendly performance and visual art on in New York, much of it in mixed venues: check the listings in *The Village Voice*, *Time Out New York*, and the free papers noted in the introduction to this chapter. You'll only be able to scratch the surface of New York's gay scene on a brief visit; if you're here for a longer trip, and are so inclined, check out sports teams and women's self-defense organizations, which provide a terrific opportunity to meet people. Contact the LGBT Community Services Center for more information (see p.397).

Center for Lesbian and Gay Studies CUNY Graduate Center, 365 Fifth Ave, between 34th and 35th sts ☎212/817-1955, ⓦwww.clags .org. Fascinating talks and seminars featur-ing luminaries such as Judith Butler. Particular attention is paid to international, transgender, and disability studies.

dumbA Art Collective 57 Jay St, between Water and Front sts, Brooklyn ☎718/858-4886, ⓦwww.holytitclamps.com/dumba. Queer performance space and arts center that hosts politically radical, sexually charged events, including all-gender play parties (see p.401). Call for events.

Dyke TV ☎718/230-4770, ⓦwww.dyketv .org. Media and arts center with half-hour show (Manhattan: Wed 5.30pm, channel 34; Brooklyn: Sat 4pm, channel 54 or 69; contact for other areas) covering lesbian, bi, and trans activism, news, arts, politics, sports, and other features. Hosts numerous special events (volunteering is an excellent way to meet people) and offers training for lesbians and bisexual women in video and Web production.

Lesbian Herstory Archives Park Slope, Brook-lyn ☎718/768-DYKE, ⓦwww.lesbianher storyarchives.org. Original materials on dyke life, mostly throughout the past century.

Old-school and inspiring. Requires an appointment; call ahead.

Leslie-Lohman Gay Art Foundation 127b Prince St, between Wooster St and W Broadway ☎212/673-7007, ⓦwww.leslielohman.org. The Foundation maintains an archive and perma-nent collection of lesbian and gay art, with galleries open to the public during shows.

MIX (the New York Lesbian and Gay Experi-mental Film/Video Festival) ☎212/742-8880, ⓦwww.mixnyc.org. This celebrated annual festival, which takes place in November, offers politically radical and technically avant-garde films.

Museum of Sex 233 Fifth Ave, at 27th St ☎212/689-6337, ⓦwww.mosex.org. Provoca-tive explorations of sex throughout history; plenty of LGBT material, plus talks and workshops. Admission $14.50; ages 18 and up only.

National Archive of Lesbian & Gay History at the LGBT Community Services Center (see p.397) ☎212/620-7310, ⓦwww.gaycenter .org/resources/archive. Terrific archive of gay life in America. Requires an appointment; call ahead.

New Festival (aka New York Lesbian and Gay Film Festival) ☎212/571-2170, ⓦwww.new festival.org. This not-to-be-missed annual

29

festival kicks off Pride Month (also known as June). Volunteer as an usher to get in free.

New York City Gay Men's Chorus ☎212/242-1777, ⓦwww.nycgmc.org. Wildly popular 185-member gay men's choral group that has sung with Cyndi Lauper and other famous names. Call or check website for concert schedule and membership information.

WOW Café 59 E 4th St, between Second Ave and Bowery ☎212/777-4280, ⓦwww.wowcafe.org. Feminist performance space that hosts a number of cutting-edge queer plays.

Cafés and restaurants

Big Cup 228 Eighth Ave, between 21st and 22nd sts ☎212/206-0059. Extremely popular gay coffee shop in the heart of Chelsea, famous for its abundance of body builders and some requisite attitude.

Bluestockings 172 Allen St, between Stanton and Rivington sts ☎212/777-6028. Fair-trade café and lefty bookstore that functions as an informal center of the lesbian and bi community. Hosts Dyke Knitting Circle, as well as readings, performances, meetings, and screenings.

Deborah 43 Carmine St, between Bleecker St and Bedford Ave ☎212/242-2606. Trendy, excellent American restaurant, popular with gay men, owned and operated by the namesake lesbian chef. Moderately priced.

The Factory Café 104 Christopher St, between Bleecker and Hudson sts ☎212/807-6900. On the Christopher Street strip, popular with grown-up gay men.

Tea Lounge 837 Union St, between Sixth and Seventh aves, Brooklyn ☎718/789-2762. Spacious Park Slope café, and the de facto headquarters of a community of gays and lesbians, tea aficionados (it offers about 90 varieties), knitters, and small children. One of two Slope locations.

Bars

Gay men's bars cover the spectrum from relaxed pubs to hard-hitting clubs full of glamour and attitude. Most of the more-established places are in Greenwich Village and Chelsea, and along Avenue A in the East Village. The areas around Murray Hill and Gramercy Park (the east 20s and 30s) are up-and-coming. Park Slope in Brooklyn and the East Village are the centers of the **lesbian** universe, while dyke bars and club nights are cropping up at a crazy rate in Chelsea and along Hudson Street in the West Village. Things tend to get raunchier as you head farther west to the bars and cruisers of the wild West Side Highway, though this area is slowly being tamed as the famed Meatpacking District transforms from transgendered streetwalker turf to upwardly mobile baby-stroller playland. In Brooklyn, Williamsburg has become a major hotspot for young, hip, mixed LGBT club nights. Check local weeklies for current listings.

Mainly for men

Barracuda 275 W 22nd St, between Seventh and Eighth aves ☎212/645-8613. A favorite spot in New York's gay scene, and as laid-back as you'll find in Chelsea. Two-for-one happy hour 4–9pm during the week, crazy drag shows and pick-up lines, and a hideaway lounge out back.

The Boiler Room 86 E 4th St, between First and Second aves ☎212/254-7536. Used to be one of the hottest bars in the city, but now it's really just a local NYU bar with a pool table. Still a good hangout, mostly gay but with some lesbian presence.

Brandy's Piano Bar 235 E 84th St, between Second and Third aves ☎212/744-4949. Handsome uptown cabaret/piano bar with a crazy, mixed, and generally mature clientele. Definitely worth a visit.

Dick's 192 Second Ave, at 12th St ☎212/475-2071. Local bar with a pool table, an

29

interesting jukebox, and a good age mix. Hardly much of a "scene," and a good spot for those seeking to avoid one.

The Dugout 185 Christopher St, at Weehawken St ☎212/242-9113. Right by the river, this friendly West Village hangout with TV, pool table, and video games is probably the closest thing you'll find to a gay sports bar.

The Eagle 554 W 28th St, between Tenth and Eleventh aves ☎646/473-1866. Really the place for leather-bar fans, with a super-cool industrial décor and bi-level, multi-room layout, plus a smoker's airshaft that's inevitably the most packed part of the bar. Dress code some nights.

Excelsior 390 Fifth Ave, between 6th and 7th sts, Park Slope, Brooklyn ☎718/832-1599. The amusingly versatile jukebox, friendly rather than overtly cruisy clientele, and two outside spaces make this Brooklyn's best bar for guys.

g 223 W 19th St, between Seventh and Eighth aves ☎212/929-1085. Nearly as stylish as its "guppie" clientele, this large and deservedly very popular lounge also features a DJ nightly.

Hell 59 Gansevoort St, between Greenwich and Washington sts ☎212/727-1666. A friendly, upscale lounge in the hip Meatpacking District. Swish décor, with over-the-top chandeliers and thick velvet curtains, and a mixed crowd of the super-trendy and college kids, as well as a bit of the bridge-and-tunnel crowd on weekends.

Marie's Crisis 59 Grove St, between Seventh Ave S and Bleecker St ☎212/243-9323. Well-known cabaret/piano bar popular with tourists and locals alike. Features old-time singing sessions nightly. Often packed, always fun.

Phoenix 447 E 13th St, between First Ave and Ave A ☎212/477-9979. This relaxed East Village favorite is much loved by the so-not-scene-they're-scene boys and guys who want reasonably priced drinks and a fun crowd.

Rawhide 212 Eighth Ave, at 21st St ☎212/242-9332. Hell-bent for leather, Chelsea's Rough Rider Room is one of the most popular stand-bys in the city – it's been here literally forever and still draws good but aging crowds seven nights a week. Opens at 10am for those who like beer for breakfast. Closes fairly late, too.

Slide Bar 356 Bowery, at 4th St ☎212/420-8885, ⓦwww.theslidebar.com. An original underground nineteenth-century gay bar with the feel of a roaring-twenties speakeasy. Unique atmosphere, great shows, and high-speed, assembly-line-like cruising. The crowd is mostly college-age on weekends.

Stonewall 53 Christopher St, between Waverly Place and Seventh Ave S ☎212/463-0950. Yes, that *Stonewall*, site of the seminal 1969 riot, mostly refurbished and flying the pride flag like they own it – which, one could say, they do.

Mainly for women

An Beal Bocht 445 W 238th St, between Greystone and Waldo aves, Bronx ☎718-884-7127. With a crowd made up of equal parts students, lesbians, and Irish expats, this Riverdale favorite serves up Guinness, oatmeal, and frequent live music until all hours. Definitely worth the trip north.

Chueca 69-04 Woodside Ave, at 69th St, Queens ☎718-424-1171. Despite its inconvenient

△ Stonewall Bar

outer-borough location, this happening Latina dyke bar with a good Colombian restaurant attached has the hottest (and hottest-headed) clientele in town.

Cubbyhole 282 W 12th St, between Greenwich Ave and W 4th St ☎212-243-9041. This welcoming, kitschy, small but famous West Village dyk e bar is something of a required stopover, as it's been here forever.

Ginger's 363 Fifth Ave, between 5th and 6th sts, Park Slope, Brooklyn ☎718/788-0924. The best dyke bar in New York is this dark, laid-back Park Slope joint with a pool table, outdoor space, and plenty of convivial company.

Rubyfruit Bar & Grill 531 Hudson St, at 10th St ☎212/929-3343. Cozy, friendly place for grown-up dykes, with a calming interior that includes a real working fireplace and skylights.

Clubs

Gay and lesbian **club nights** in New York (often held weekly at nondenominational nightspots) can be some of the most outrageous in the world. Check *Time Out New York*, *HX* (Ⓦ www.hx.com), and *GO NYC* (Ⓦ www.gonycmagazine.com) for the latest in homosexual hip. The clubs and nights listed below seem likely to be around for a while; all have their coveted cabaret license, so go forth and dance.

2i's 248 W 14th St, between Seventh and Eighth aves ☎212/807-1775, Ⓦ www.2isnightclub.com. Thursday is dyke night at this chic, low-key African-American joint. Dancers, open mic, and other diversions (call for schedule) get the girls going.

Don Hill's 511 Greenwich St, at Spring St ☎212/334-1390, Ⓦ www.donhills.com. An open-to-all-up-for-anything place, where you will find Britpop drag queens, mod rock dominatrixes, and mohawked Johnny Rotten wannabes. Pole dancers and porn complete the vibe. Thurs 1980s theme night attracts the largest crowds.

Heaven 479 Sixth Ave, at 16th St ☎212/539-3982, Ⓦ www.juliesnewyork.com. Women-owned and -operated club with Wed Noche Latina dyke night and multiracial Kaleidoscope Fri.

Henrietta Hudson 438 Hudson St, between Morton and Barrow sts ☎212/924-3347, Ⓦ www.henriettahudsons.com. Laid-back in the afternoon but brimming by night, especially on weekends, this is the top dyke club in Manhattan. Weekly theme nights include

Latin and baby dyke. Lounging, pool, and dancing areas are all separated.

La Nueva Escuelita 301 W 39th St, at Eighth Ave ☎212/631-0588. This is one of the city's very best gay clubs, and is also popular with the Jersey crowd. It's all about kitsch, dress-up, salsa, cruising, and drag. Expect to wait in line for a while. Eighteen and over; VIP seats available.

The Monster 80 Grove St, at Sheridan Square ☎212/924-3558. Large, campy bar with drag cabaret, piano, and downstairs dance floor. Very popular, especially with tourists, yet has a strong "neighborhood" feel. Every night brings something different, from professional go-go boys and amateur strippers to Latin grooves and a Sunday-afternoon tea dance (5.30pm).

Roxy 515 W 18th St, between Tenth and Eleventh aves ☎212/645-5157. Still the hottest dance spot after two decades, so packed with men on Saturday nights that it's sometimes difficult to breathe. Also possibly the cruisiest men's room on the planet, and with a truly massive dance floor.

Sex

A number of delightful and perfectly legal sex ("play") parties and establishments have sprung up throughout the city. Some are invitation–only; some welcome LGBT men and women to play in the same space; many are BDSM-oriented. Alcohol is not served at any.

29

dumbA Art Collective 57 Jay St, between Water and Front sts, Brooklyn ⊤718/390-6606, ⓦwww .holytitclamps.com/dumba. Hosts all-gender play parties and other envelope-pushing events. Call for events.

New York Renegades ⓦwww.nyrenegades .com. Hard-core gay men's BDSM organization that hosts play parties, bar nights, and retreats.

SPAM 210 Fifth Ave, at Union St, Brooklyn ⊤718/789-4053. Monthly Park Slope play party for the entire LGBT community.

Underwear only. Fourth Sat each month, 10pm–5am (doors close at 2am).

Submit 253 E Houston St, between aves A and B ⊤718/789-4053, ⓦwww.submitparty.com. This trendy, hot-and-heavy S&M girl party welcomes novices, voyeurs, serious players, and anyone who can't afford such good play equipment. Demos and theme nights abound. Women and trans only, 18 and over. First Thurs each month, 9pm–2am (doors close at 1am).

Religion

There are numerous **gay religious organizations** in New York; many of these have regular meetings and services at the LGBT Community Services Center (see p.397).

Congregation Beth Simchat Torah 57 Bethune St, at Washington St ⊤212/929-9498, ⓦwww .cbst.org. LGBT synagogue with Fri 8.30pm and Sat 10am Shabbat services, plus larger services (Fri 7pm) at the Church of the Holy Apostles in Chelsea, 296 Ninth Ave, at 28th St (⊤212/924-0167).

Dignity New York ⊤646/418-7039 or 212/627-6488, ⓦwww.dignityny.org. Large gay

Catholic organization that holds numerous events, including services on Sun at 7.30pm at St John's Episcopal Church, 218 W 11th St, at Waverly Place.

Metropolitan Community Church 446 W 36th St, between Ninth and Tenth aves ⊤212/242-7440, ⓦwww.mccny.org. Services each Sun at 10am and 7pm and Wed at 7pm.

Shops

Bluestockings 172 Allen St, between Stanton and Rivington sts ⊤212/777-6028. Radical Lower East Side bookstore with a sizable collection of LGBT books.

Housing Works Used Book Café 126 Crosby St, between Houston and Prince sts ⊤212/334-3324. An old library, this store holds more than 45,000 used books and records and a café. It also hosts performances and readings. All profits go to Housing Works, which provides housing, health care, etc for homeless New Yorkers with HIV and AIDS.

The Oscar Wilde Memorial Bookshop 15 Christopher St, between Sixth and Seventh aves ⊤212/255-8097. An unbeatable selection

of gay and lesbian-themed books and a major community spot.

Out of the Closet Thrift Shop 220 E 81st St, between Second and Third aves ⊤212/472-3573. This excellent fundraising thrift store for AIDS groups sells everything from books to designer apparel.

Toys in Babeland 94 Rivington St, between Orchard and Ludlow sts ⊤212/375-1701; also 43 Mercer St, between Grand and Broome sts ⊤212/966-2120, ⓦwww.babeland.com. Superlative, sophisticated feminist (and queer) sex-toy store, perhaps the best in the nation. Sex workshops fill up quickly.

Commercial galleries

A rt, especially contemporary art, is big in New York. Although the city is frankly no longer the center of the world art scene – the twentieth century, with artists like Willem DeKooning, Jackson Pollock, Mark Rothko, Andy Warhol, Ellsworth Kelly, and Agnes Martin all living in the city, was really the city's creative heyday – there's still plenty here to interest contemporary-art lovers. There are several hundred **galleries** in the city, covering a wide range of aesthetics, cultural viewpoints, and styles; most of the prominent ones are in Soho and Chelsea. Even if you have no intention of buying, many of these high-profile galleries are well worth a visit, as are some of the alternative spaces, run on a nonprofit basis and less commercial than mainstream galleries.

Broadly speaking, Manhattan galleries fall into five main areas: the **Upper East Side** in the 60s and 70s for antiques and the occasional (minor) Old Master; **57th Street** between Sixth and Park avenues for important modern and contemporary names; **Soho** for established artists; **Chelsea** for the trendy and up-and-coming; and **Tribeca** for more experimental displays.

Some of the most vibrant gallery scenes in the city are to be found outside Manhattan, however, in Brooklyn's **DUMBO** and **Williamsburg** and the Queens neighborhood of **Long Island City**. Recently, Williamsburg has "done a Soho" and become almost as expensive as downtown Manhattan in terms of housing, pushing less-established artists farther out to Greenpoint and Bushwick. There are still lots of spaces, though, and a few worthwhile galleries are listed if you want to check out what's going on in the independent world of art in New York City.

Several of the city's more exclusive galleries are invitation-only, but most accept walk-ins (although sometimes with a bit of attitude). Pick up a copy of the *Gallery Guide* (Ⓦ www.galleryguide.org) – available upon request in the larger galleries

---

Art tours

One of the best ways to see the top galleries in the city is through an art tour. Here are a couple of your best bets:

Art Entrée 48–18 Purves St, Queens ⓣ718/391-0011, Ⓦ www.artentree.com. This excellent Long Island City–based company provides studio, gallery, museum, architecture, and public art tours throughout NYC.

New York Gallery Tours 526 W 26th St, Manhattan ⓣ212/946-1548. First-rate tours of Chelsea's galleries, including $15 Saturday visits to the neighborhood's "eight most fascinating shows," as well as $200 group tours for up to 10 people, available any day of the week.

– for listings of current shows and each gallery's specialty. The weekly *Time Out New York* offers broad listings of the major commercial galleries. Admission is almost always free; the galleries that do charge a fee are considered a bit tacky.

Listed below are some of the more interesting exhibition spaces in Manhattan and elsewhere. Opening times are roughly Tuesday through Saturday 10am to 6pm, but note that many galleries have truncated summer hours and are closed during August. The best time to gallery-hop is on weekday afternoons; the absolute worst time is on Saturday, when out-of-towners flood into the city's trendier areas to do just that. Openings – usually free and easily identified by crowds of people drinking wine from plastic cups – are excellent times to view work, eavesdrop on art-world gossip, and even eat free food. A list of openings appears, again, in the *Gallery Guide*.

Tribeca and Soho galleries

14 Sculptors Gallery 332 Bleecker St, Suite K35 ☎212/966-5790, ⊛www.14sculptors.com. Just as the name implies, an exhibition space formed by fourteen diverse sculptors to display noncommercial figurative and abstract contemporary art. Open by appointment only.

123 Watts 123 Watts St ☎212/219-1482, ⊛www.123watts.com. Trendy gallery known for its photography, along with other forms of contemporary art; has shown work by Robert Mapplethorpe, Arturo Cuenca, and Bruno Ulmer. Open by appointment only.

The Drawing Center 35 Wooster St ☎212/219-2166, ⊛www.drawingcenter.org. Presents shows of contemporary and historical works on paper, from emerging artists to the sketches of the Great Masters.

Louis Meisel 141 Prince St ☎212/677-1340, ⊛www.meiselgallery.com. Specializes in Photorealism – past shows have included Richard Estes and Chuck Close – as well as Abstract Illusionism (owner Meisel claims to have invented both terms). Also exhibits saucy American pin-ups.

O K Harris 383 W Broadway ☎212/431-3600, ⊛www.okharris.com. Named for a mythical traveling gambler, O K is the gallery of Ivan Karp, a cigar-munching champion of Super-Realism. One of the first Soho galleries and, although not as influential as it once was, still worth a look.

Chelsea galleries

The galleries listed below are housed in independent spaces, but there are also several large **warehouses** in this neighborhood that hold multiple galleries and are worth exploring as a group, if you have time.

303 Gallery 525 W 22nd St ☎212/255-1121, ⊛www.303gallery.com. 303 Gallery shows works in a comprehensive range of media by fairly well-established contemporary artists.

Allen Sheppard Gallery 530 W 25th St ☎212/989-9919. One of the most interesting painter galleries in the district, this space exhibits great stuff from the likes of David Konisberg, Willy Lenski, and Sonya Sklaroff.

Annina Nosei 530 W 22nd St ☎212/741-8695, ⊛www.anninanoseigallery.com. Global works, especially contemporary pieces by emerging Latin American and Middle Eastern artists.

Barbara Gladstone Gallery 515 W 24th St ☎212/206-9300, ⊛www.gladstonegallery .com. Paintings, sculpture, and photography by hot contemporary artists like Matthew Barney and Rosemarie Trockel.

Edward Thorp 210 Eleventh Ave, 6th floor ☎212/691-6565, ⊛www.edwardthorpgallery .com. Mainstream contemporary American, South American, and European painting and sculpture. Highlights of their roster include painter Matthew Blackwell and sculptor Deborah Butterfield.

Feature 530 W 25th St ☎212/675-7772, ⊛www.featureinc.com. This former Chicago gallery tends toward briefly exhibiting fairly cerebral modern artists (such as the controversial Richard Kern of "New York Girls" fame) rather than extensively highlighting a select few.

Gagosian Gallery 555 W 24th St ☎212/741-1111, ⊛www.gagosian.com. A stalwart fixture on the New York scene, the Gagosian features both modern and contemporary works, including pieces by artists like Damien Hirst, David Salle, Eric Fischl, Richard Serra, and photographer Alec Soth, who's made a big mark of late. There's also a branch uptown, at 980 Madison Ave.

Gavin Brown's Enterprise 620 Greenwich St ☎212/627-5258. An ultra-hip space featuring the young, cool, and fearless of the mixed-media art world.

Greene Naftali 526 W 26th St ☎212/463-7770, ⓦwww.greenenaftaligallery.com. A wide-open, airy gallery noted for its top-notch large group shows and conceptual installations. Very cool stuff.

Lehmann Maupin 540 W 26th St ☎212/255-2923, ⓦwww.lehmannmaupin.com. Shows a range of established international and American contemporary artists working in a wide range of media, among them Tracey Emin, Juergen Teller, and Gilbert & George. Also showcases diverse new talent.

▽ Installation at Lehmann Maupin Gallery

Mary Boone Gallery 541 W 24th St ☎212/752-2929, ⓦwww.maryboonegallery.com. An extension of Boone's uptown gallery (745 Fifth Ave; see p.406), this Chelsea space has facilities for large-scale works and installations by the up-and-coming darlings of the art world. At least a couple of the artists nurtured by Boone – David Salle and Julian Schnabel – have achieved superstar status.

Matthew Marks Gallery 522 W 22nd St ☎212/243-0200, ⓦwww.matthewmarks.com. The centerpiece of Chelsea's art scene, Matthew Marks shows pieces by such well-known minimalist and abstract artists as Cy Twombly and Ellsworth Kelly. They also have nearby branches at 523 W 24th St and 521 W 21st St.

Paula Cooper 534 W 21st St ☎212/255-1105. An influential gallery that shows a wide range of contemporary painting, sculpture, drawings, prints, and photographs, particularly minimalist and conceptual works, and even has a recording label, Dog w/a Bone.

Robert Miller 524 W 26th St ☎212/366-4774, ⓦwww.robertmillergallery.com. Exceptional shows of twentieth-century artists (Lee Krasner, Joan Nelson, and Bernar Venet, to name but a few). This is one of New York's true big-gun galleries.

Sonnabend 536 W 22nd St ☎212/627-1018, ⓦwww.sonnabendgallery.com. A top gallery featuring painting, photography, and video from contemporary American and European artists. Regular exhibitions from the likes of Robert Morris and Gilbert & George.

Sikkema Jenkins 530 W 22nd St ☎212/929-2262, ⓦwww.sikkemajenkins.com. This somewhat controversial space often features exhibits with a definite political slant. Recently they've been focusing on illustration.

Sperone Westwater 415 W 13th St ☎212/999-7337, ⓦwww.speronewestwater.com. High-quality European and American painting and works on paper. Artists have included Francesco Clemente, Frank Moore, and Susan Rothenberg.

Team Gallery 527 W 26th St ☎212/279-9219, ⓦwww.teamgal.com. Beautiful, voyeuristic, and cutting-edge work by artists such as Tracey Emin and Genesis P-Orridge is shown here.

Upper East Side galleries

Knoedler & Co 19 E 70th St ☎212/794-0550, ⓦwww.knoedlergallery.com. Renowned, nearly ancient gallery specializing in postwar and contemporary art, particularly the New York School. Shows some of the best-known names in twentieth-century art, such as Stella, Rauschenberg, and Fonseca.

Leo Castelli 18 E 77th St ☎212/249-4470, ⓦwww.castelligallery.com. One of the original dealer-collectors, Castelli was instrumental in aiding the careers of Rauschenberg and Warhol, and this gallery offers big contemporary names at high prices.

West 57th Street and around galleries

Gemini G.E.L. at Joni Moisant Weyl 58 W 58th St, 21B ☎212/308-0924, ⓦwww.joniweyl.com. Etchings and contemporary graphics, with some vintage prints; has shown works by Roy Lichtenstein and Robert Rauschenberg. By appointment only.

Marlborough New York 40 W 57th St ☎212/541-4900, ⓦwww.marlboroughgallery.com. Internationally renowned gallery showing top modern

(30)

and contemporary artists and graphic designers. Recent shows have included well-known sculptors Jacques Lipchitz and Tom Otterness. Has branches in Chelsea and abroad.

Mary Boone 745 Fifth Ave, at 57th St, 4th floor ☏ 212/752-2929, ⓦ www.maryboonegallery .com. Mary Boone was Leo Castelli's protégée, and her gallery specializes in installations, paintings, and works by up-and-coming European and American artists, as well as established artists already involved with the gallery. The Mary Boone now also has an interesting branch in Chelsea.

Pace Wildenstein 32 E 57th St ☏ 212/421-3292, ⓦ www.pacewildenstein.com. This celebrated gallery exhibits works by most of the great modern American and European artists, from Picasso to Calder to Noguchi and Rothko. Recent shows have included Diane Arbus and Agnes Martin. Also has a good collection of prints and African art. A Chelsea satellite located at 534 W 25th St (☏ 212/929-7000) specializes in edgier works and large installations.

DUMBO and Brooklyn Heights galleries

DUMBO Arts Center 30 Washington St, DUMBO ☏ 718/694-0831, ⓦ www.dumboartscenter .org. A huge warehouse space dedicated to showing innovative new group work in 5–6 shows yearly. The self-proclaimed origin and center of DUMBO's art scene.

The Rotunda Gallery 33 Clinton St, Brooklyn Heights ☏ 718/875-4047, ⓦ www.brooklynx .org/rotunda. This mixed-media, not-for-profit exhibition space features work by Brooklyn-based contemporary artists.

Smack Mellon Gallery 92 Plymouth St, DUMBO ☏ 718/834-8761, ⓦ www.smackmellon.org. An interesting space that displays multidisciplinary, high-tech work by artists who have for the most part flown under the radar of art critics and spectators.

UrbanGlass 647 Fulton St, DUMBO ☏ 718/625-3685, ⓦ www.urbanglass.org. Small but amazing glass gallery attached to the studio of the same name.

Williamsburg galleries

Flipside 84 Withers St ☏ 718/389-7108, ⓦ www.flipsideart.com. This Williamsburg gallery, which aims to facilitate an exchange of diverse ideas and methods, features experimental work and installations by

emerging and established artists.

Front Room 147 Roebling St ☏ 718/782-2556, ⓦ www.frontroom.org. One of the neighborhood's best galleries and also a popular performance-art space. Best place to get a good first sense of the local scene.

Pierogi 177 N 9th St ☏ 718/599-2144, ⓦ www .pierogi2000.com. This former workshop mounts fascinating installations of various kinds. It is noted in the art world for its traveling "flatfiles," a collection of folders containing the work of 600 or so artists, stored clinically and provocatively in metal, sliding cabinets.

WAH (Williamsburg Art and Historical Center) 135 Broadway ☏ 718/486-7372, ⓦ www .wahcenter.net. Beautiful, fascinating multimedia arts center, with a focus on painting and sculpture. See p.262.

Alternative spaces

The galleries listed above (at least those in Manhattan) are part of a system designed to channel artists' work through the gallery spaces and, eventually, into the hands of collectors. While initial acceptance by a major gallery is an important rite of passage for an up-and-coming artist, it shouldn't be forgotten that this system's philosophy is based on making money for gallery owners, who normally receive fifty percent of the sale price. For an artist's work to be noncommercial in these spaces is perhaps even more damning than being socially or politically unacceptable.

The galleries included below, often referred to as **alternative spaces**, provide a forum for the kind of risky and non-commercially viable art that many other galleries may not be able to afford to show. Those mentioned here are at the cutting edge of new art in the city.

Apex Art 291 Church St ☏ 212/431-5270, ⓦ www .apexart.org. A nonprofit exhibition space that invites dealers, artists, writers, critics, and international art-world bodies to act as curators and mount idea-based shows, along with lectures and associated events.

Art in General 79 Walker St ☏ 212/219-0473, ⓦ www.artingeneral.org. Experimental, nonprofit gallery with multimedia exhibits and performances, and an emphasis on multicultural themes.

Artists Space 38 Greene St, 3rd floor ☎212/226-3970, ⓦ www.artistsspace.org. One of the most respected alternative spaces, with frequently changing theme-based exhibits, film screenings, videos, installations, and events. In over thirty years of existence, Artists Space has presented the work of thousands of emerging artists.

Dia: Chelsea 548 W 22nd St ☎212/989-5566, ⓦ www.diachelsea.org. This eminent gallery is dedicated to large-scale, site-specific installations by contemporary artists. The owners also have several other exhibit spaces, including the New York Earth Room (see below), "The Broken Kilometer" exhibit at 393 W Broadway, and Dia: Beacon, a large, delightful museum about an hour upstate.

Exit Art 475 Tenth Ave ☎212/966-7745, ⓦ www .exitart.org. A hip crowd frequents this huge alternative gallery, now located in Hell's Kitchen. It favors big installations, up-and-coming, multimedia, and edgy cultural and political subjects. Nice café, too.

New York Earth Room 141 Wooster St ☎212/989-5566, ⓦ www.earthroom.org. An incredible permanent exhibit by Walter de Maria, featuring a room filled, as the name suggests, with masses of dirt.

PS122 Gallery 150 First Ave ☎212/228-4249, ⓦ www.ps122gallery.org. Nonprofit gallery, affiliated with a high-profile experimental performance space that highlights emerg-ing artists.

White Columns 320 W 13th St, enter on Horatio St ☎212/924-4212, ⓦ www.whitecolumns .org. White Columns focuses on emerging artists, and is considered very influential. Check out the fascinating, ever-changing group shows.

Shopping

R etail junkies beware: shops are one of New York's killer attractions. The city is the undisputed commercial capital of America, especially in fashion. There are flagship stores for every major brand, both ubiquitous (The Gap) and exclusive (Gucci), so you can stock up just as easily on a designer leather clutch as you can a pair of tennis socks. In between all the big names, you'll also find dozens of quirky local boutiques and bazaars worth seeking out. We've sifted through the best that the city has to offer and presented our pick of Manhattan's retail wonders below.

Practicalities

Opening hours in midtown Manhattan are roughly Monday through Saturday 9am to 6pm, with a later closing time (usually) on Thursday. Downtown shops (Soho, Tribeca, the East and West villages, the Lower East Side) tend to stay open later, at least until 8pm and sometimes until about midnight; bookstores especially are often open late. Chinatown's shops and stalls are open all day, every day, while the stores that serve workers in the Financial District stick to nine-to-five office hours, and are usually shuttered on Saturday and Sunday. Aside from the shops in this neighborhood, expect stores to be most crowded on weekends, especially in Soho and midtown.

Credit cards are widely accepted: even the smallest shops usually take American Express, MasterCard, or Visa. An 8.375 percent **sales tax** will be added to your bill for all purchases except clothing and footwear totaling under $110.

Finally, wherever you're shopping, **be careful**. Manhattan's crowded, frenzied stores are ripe territory for pickpockets and bag-snatchers.

The best places for browsing

If you'd rather browse than make a beeline for a specific store, listed below are the best areas in the city for a bit of ambling and window-shopping.
- The whole of Soho
- Lower East Side: Orchard and Ludlow streets
- NoLita: Mulberry, Mott, and Elizabeth streets just south of Houston Street
- East Village: 7th and 9th streets
- Meatpacking District: 14th Street between Eighth and Tenth avenues
- Lower Fifth: Fifth Avenue between 14th and 23rd streets
- Midtown: Fifth Avenue between 42nd and 60th streets
- Upper East Side: Madison Avenue between 60th and 80th streets

Shopping categories

Beauty and cosmetics	p.409	Fashion: shoes	p.421
Books	p.410	Flea markets and craft fairs	p.422
Department stores		Food and drink	p.423
and malls	p.413	Music	p.424
Electronics	p.414	Specialty stores	p.425
Fashion: accessories	p.415	Sporting goods	p.426
Fashion: clothing	p.415		

Beauty and cosmetics

All department stores stock the main brands of beauty products (as does Century 21, often at a deep discount – see p.419), but if you're looking for quirkier cosmetics, here are the best options.

Aveda 233 Spring St, between Sixth Ave and Varick St ☏212/807-1492. New-agey cosmetics company specializing in plant extract-based shampoos, conditioners, and skincare; some locations also have a spa where you can sign up for pricey treatments. Call for more locations.

C.O. Bigelow Apothecary 414 Sixth Ave, between 8th and 9th sts ☏212/473-7324. Established in 1882, C.O. Bigelow is the oldest apothecary in the country – and that's exactly how it looks, with the original Victorian shopfittings still in place. Specializing in lesser-known and European beauty brands, this is the place to come for beauty and cosmetic items that you can't find elsewhere in the city.

Kiehl's 109 Third Ave, between 13th and 14th sts ☏212/677-3171, ⓦwww.kiehls.com. Decorated with aviation and motorcycle memorabilia, this 150-year-old pharmacy sells its own range of natural-ingredient-based classic creams, oils, etc. Known for giving out plenty of samples to customers, whether you're buying or not. Lots of celebs swear by this stuff, especially the patented Crème de Corps body lotion.

Lush 2165 Broadway, at 76th St ☏212/787-5874, ⓦwww.lush.com. Cosmetics and beauty products made from fresh fruits, vegetables, and oils. Popular items include the water-soluble "bath bombs," chunks of specialty soap that the staff cuts for you from large bricks, and thick facial cleansers the consistency of mousse.

MAC 113 Spring St, between Greene and Mercer sts ☏212/334-4641; also 175 Fifth Ave, at 22nd St ⓦwww.maccosmetics.com. MAC is known for both its high-quality, non-animal-tested cosmetics and its HIV/AIDS fundraising (pick up a Viva Glam lipstick to donate). Quite popular with models and celebs.

Ray's Beauty Supply 721 Eighth Ave, at 45th St ☏212/757-0175, ⓦwww.raybeauty.com. This ramshackle store supplies most of the city's hairdressers with their potions and props. Something of a place for industry insiders, but the public is welcome. The low prices are worth a detour.

Ricky's 590 Broadway, between Houston and Prince sts ☏212/226-5590. New York's haven for the overdone, the brash, and the OTT (think drag-diva favorites and plenty of lurid wigs). Stocks cool brands like Urban Decay and Tony & Tina as well as a house line of products.

Sephora 555 Broadway, between Prince and Spring sts ☏212/625-1309; also 636 Fifth Ave, at 51st St ☏212/245-1633, ⓦwww.sephora.com. "Warehouse" of perfumes, make-up, and body-care products all lined up alphabetically rather than by producer, so everything's easy to find and you don't have to brave any sales people to browse.

Zitomer 969 Madison, at 76th ☏212/737-5561. A venerable pharmacy that has transformed itself into a full-blown mini-department store, Zitomer serves the beauty and cosmetic needs of the Fifth-Avenue gentry. Stocked to the gills with every brand and item imaginable.

Salons and spas

Antonio Prieto 127 W 20th St, between Sixth and Seventh aves ☏212/255-3741. One of the top hair salons in town, requiring reservations at

Beauty and cosmetics

SHOPPING

㉛

least a month in advance. Prieto himself is only in town part-time, but his trained stylists are equally outstanding.

Astor Place Hair Designers 2 Astor Place, at Broadway T 212/475-9854. If you're caught short in the city and need a cheap haircut, try this local institution, a unisex barbershop with dozens of haircutters sprawled across two floors. Trims $12 and up.

Bliss 568 Broadway, 2nd floor, between Houston and Prince sts T 212/219-8970, W www.blissworld.com. Top-notch spa with massage, facial, nail, and wax services. There's a bevy of beauty potions waiting for you to purchase as you depart, including the spa's own popular lotions and the full line of Crème de la Mer skin products.

John Frieda 30 E 76th St, at Madison Ave T 212/327-3400. An excellent hair salon that's also home to the city's top colorist, Clark Wood.

Jin Soon 56th E 4th St, between Second Ave and the Bowery T 212/473-2047. Small, soothing Japanese hand and foot spa. It's great for manicure/pedicures.

Ling 191 Prince St, at Sullivan St T 212/982-8833. The city's most prominent facial spa, located in the heart of Soho. Call for additional locations.

Sally Hersberger 425 W 14th St, between Ninth and Tenth aves T 212/206-8700. Stylist to stars like Sarah Jessica Parker, Sally Hersberger reigns supreme among New York's hair pros. She's in town about half the time, but her entire staff is trained in "the Hersberger method." Good spot for star gawking.

Soho Sanctuary 119 Mercer St, between Prince and Spring sts T 212/334-5550. One of the best spas in the city, with a steam room, a sauna, and a full range of services. Eminently relaxing, and women-only.

Stephen Knoll 625 Madison, at 59th St T 212/421-0100. Knoll made his name as Cindy Crawford's stylist in the 1990s and is still one of New York's very finest. He's in the salon year-round, so there's a decent chance you can book an appointment with him personally.

Books

New York is something of a literary mecca. All the major publishing houses have an office in the city, and there are more independent booksellers here than in most other parts of America. Dedicated bibliophiles will be in heaven, surrounded by shops that run the gamut from clever and focused (Partners & Crime, see p.412) to quirky and expansive (St Mark's Bookshop, see below). Quick literary fixes can be easily taken care of, too – superstores like Barnes & Noble are omnipresent in New York.

General interest and new books

Coliseum Books 11 W 42nd St, at Fifth Ave T 212/803-5890, W www.coliseumbooks.com. Well-stocked, long-standing New York bookstore. Good on academic books but with plenty of reading material for all tastes.

Corner Bookstore 1313 Madison Ave, at 93rd St T 212/831-3554, E cornerbook@aol.com. Upscale bookstore with an excellent literature selection and a chilled-out atmosphere.

Labyrinth Books 536 112th St, between Broadway and Amsterdam Ave T 212/865-1588. The largest independent bookstore in the city, Labyrinth boasts a fine selection of literary (especially international) fiction and academic texts for local Columbia students and faculty.

McNally Robinson 50 Prince St, at Mulberry St T 212/274-1160. This Canadian book

chain has gained a foothold in the heart of Manhattan with its prime Soho location. Great service – the staff here is friendly and actually knowledgeable about books.

St Mark's Bookshop 31 Third Ave, at 9th St T 212/260-7853, W www.stmarksbookshop .com. The best-known independent bookstore in the city, with a good selection of titles on contemporary art, politics, feminism, the environment, and literary criticism, as well as more obscure subjects. Good postcards, too, and stocked full of radical and art magazines. Open until midnight.

Shakespeare & Co 939 Lexington Ave, at 69th St T 212/570-0201; also 716 Broadway, at Washington Place T 212/529-1330; 137 E 23rd St, at Lexington Ave T 212/505-2021; and 1 Whitehall St, at Broadway T 212/742-7025; W www .shakeandco.com. New and used books, both

There are Manhattan branches of Barnes & Noble at:
- 4 Astor Place, at Broadway and Lafayette St ℡212/420-1322
- 396 Sixth Ave, at 8th St ℡212/674-8780
- 33 E 17th St, on Union Square ℡212/253-0810
- 105 Fifth Ave, at E 18th St ℡212/807-0099. This claims to be "The World's Largest Bookstore" and concentrates on college textbooks.
- 675 Sixth Ave, at W 22nd St ℡212/727-1227
- 600 Fifth Ave, at W 48th St ℡212/765-0592
- Citicorp Building, at E 54th St and Third Ave ℡212/750-8033
- 750 Third Ave, at 47th St ℡212/697-2251
- 2289 Broadway, at W 82nd St ℡212/362-8835
- 240 E 86th St, at Second Ave ℡212/794-1962
- 1280 Lexington Ave, at E 86th St ℡212/423-9900
- 1972 Broadway, across from Lincoln Center ℡212/595-6859

paper and hardcover. Great for fiction and psychology. There's also a branch at the Brooklyn Academy of Music (see p.246). **Three Lives & Co 154 W 10th St, at Waverly Place** ℡212/741-2069, Ⓦwww.threelives .com. Excellent literary bookstore that has an especially good selection of works by and for women, as well as general titles. There's an excellent reading series in the fall.

Second-hand books

Argosy Bookstore 116 E 59th St, at Park Ave ℡212/753-4455, Ⓦwww.argosybooks.com. Unbeatable for rare books, Argosy also sells clearance books and titles of all kinds, though the shop's reputation means you may find mainstream works cheaper elsewhere.

Housing Works Used Books Café 126 Crosby St, between Houston and Prince sts ℡212/334-3324, Ⓦwww.housingworkssubc.com. The Housing Works has a good selection of very cheap books. With a small espresso and snack bar and comfy chairs, it's a great place to spend an afternoon. They're fairly paranoid about shoplifting; check your purses and backpacks at the door. Proceeds benefit AIDS charity.

Ruby's Book Sale 119 Chambers St, between W Broadway and Church St ℡212/732-8676. City Hall Park's used bookstore, dealing especially in paperbacks and ancient dog-eared magazines.

Strand Bookstore 828 Broadway, at 12th St ℡212/473-1452; also an annex at 95 Fulton St, at Gold St ℡212/732-6070, Ⓦwww .strandbooks.com. Yes, it's hot and crowded,

Books

SHOPPING ㉛

△ Strand Bookstore

411

and the staff seems to resent working there, but with eight miles of books and a stock of more than 2.5 million titles, this is the largest discount book operation in the city – and one of few survivors in an area once rife with second-hand bookstores. There are recent review copies and new books for half price, stacked alphabetically by author in the basement; older books go for anything from 50¢ up.

West Sider Books 2246 Broadway, at 80th St ☎212/362-0706. Used and out-of-print books, especially art, illustrated, and antique children's titles. Watch out for overpriced works – there are a good few.

Special-interest bookstores

Art and architecture

Untitled 159 Prince St, between Thompson and W Broadway ☎212/982-2088, ⓦwww.fineart inprint.com. The premiere location for contemporary architecture and art books, including art criticism and cultural theory.
Urban Center Books 457 Madison Ave, at 50th St ☎212/935-3592, ⓦwww.urbancenterbooks .org. Architectural-book specialists with a very helpful staff.

Comics and sci-fi

Forbidden Planet 840 Broadway, at 13th St ☎212/473-1576, ⓦwww.forbiddenplanet .co.uk. Science fiction, fantasy, horror fiction, graphic novels, and comics. Great for its large backlist of indie and underground comix, they also hawk T-shirts and the latest sci-fi toys and collectibles.
St Mark's Comics 11 St Mark's Place, between Second and Third aves ☎212/598-9439. Tons of comic books, including some under-ground editions; well known for their large stock. Action figures, trading cards, and a whole room of back issues.
Village Comics 214 Sullivan St, at Bleecker St ☎212/777-2770, ⓦwww.villagecomics.com. Old and new comics and graphic novels, limited editions, trading cards, action figures, and occasional celebrity appearances.

Crime and mystery

Murder Ink 2486 Broadway, at 92nd St ☎212/362-8905, ⓦwww.murderink.com. In business since 1972, this was the first bookstore in the city to specialize in mystery and detective fiction. It's still the

best, stocking every murder, mystery, or suspense title in print, and plenty that have gone out, as well.
The Mysterious Bookshop 129 W 56th St, between Sixth and Seventh aves ☎212/765-0900, ⓦwww.mysteriousbookshop.com. The founder of this store started the Mysterious Press (now owned by Warner Books). The shop sells mysteries of every kind, from classic detectives to just-published titles.
Partners & Crime 44 Greenwich Ave, at Charles St ☎212/243-0440, ⓦwww.crimepays.com. Crime novels. Also home to the Cranston and Spade Theater Co, which performs classic 1940s radio scripts on the first Saturday night of every month (tickets $5).

Language and foreign

Kinokuniya Bookstore 10 W 49th St, at Fifth Ave ☎212/765-7766, ⓦwww.kinokuniya.com/ny. The largest Japanese bookstore in New York, with English books on Japan, too.
Librairie de France/Librería Hispánica/The Dictionary Store 610 Fifth Ave, in the Rockefel-ler Center Promenade ☎212/581-8810, ⓦwww .frencheuropean.com. Small space housing a wealth of French and Spanish books, a dictionary store with 8000 dictionaries of more than 100 languages, and a depart-ment of teach-yourself language books, records, and tapes.
Rizzoli 31 W 57th St, at Fifth Ave ☎212/759-2424. Manhattan branch of the prestigious Italian bookstore chain and publisher. They specialize in European publications, and have a good selection of foreign newspapers and magazines.

Miscellaneous

Biography Bookshop 400 Bleecker St, at 11th St ☎212/807-8655. Venerable Greenwich Village corner bookstore focusing exclusively on letters, diaries, memoirs, autobiographies, and, of course, biographies.
Bluestockings 172 Allen St, at Stanton St ☎212/777-6028. New and used titles, but only those authored by or related to women. Cozy, well-stocked collective-style store in what was once a dilapidated crack house; nice café, too.
Books of Wonder 16 W 18th St, at Fifth Ave ☎212/989-3270, ⓦwww.booksofwonder.com. A heavenly collection of literature for kids.
Center for Book Arts 28 W 27th St, at Sixth Ave, 3rd floor ☎212/481-0295, ⓦwww .centerforbookarts.org. Not so much a

bookstore as a space dedicated to the art of bookmaking. Hosts regular readings and workshops – fascinating stuff.

Cookbooks 488 Greenwich St, at Canal St ⓣ212/226-5731. Cozy Soho bookstore that specializes in out-of-print and antiquarian cookbooks.

Kitchen Arts & Letters 1435 Lexington Ave, at 94th St ⓣ212/876-5550. Cookbooks and books about food; run by a former cookbook editor.

Revolution Books 9 W 19th St, at Fifth Ave ⓣ212/691-3345. New York's major left-wing bookstore and contact point. A wide range of political and cultural books, pamphlets, and periodicals. Get their take on current human-rights and globalization controversies.

Cinema, music, and theater

Applause Theater & Cinema Books 211 W 71st St, at Broadway ⓣ212/496-7511. New and used titles focusing on theater, film, television, and screenplays. It's a good place to check for titles unavailable elsewhere.

Drama Bookshop 723 Seventh Ave, between 48th and 49th sts, 2nd floor ⓣ212/944-0595, ⓦwww.dramabookshop.com. Theater books, scripts, and publications on all manner of drama-related subjects.

Religion and spirituality

East West Books 78 Fifth Ave, at 13th St ⓣ212/243-5994. Bookstore with a mind, body, and spirit slant. Eastern religions, New Age, and health and healing.

J. Levine Judaica 5 W 30th St, at Fifth Ave ⓣ212/695-6888, ⓦwww.levinejudaica.com. The ultimate Jewish bookstore. Closed Sat.

Logos Bookstore 1575 York Ave, at 83rd St ⓣ212/517-7292. Christian books and gifts.

West Side Judaica 2412 Broadway, at 88th St ⓣ212/362-7846. Books about Judaism, with funky menorahs for sale on the side.

Department stores and malls

Barneys, Bergdorf Goodman, and Saks Fifth Avenue are among the world's most famous (and most beautiful) **department stores** – each of their buildings is a landmark in itself. In general, the status of department stores in America is not what it once was; the last decades of the twentieth century were particularly tough, as specialty outlets swallowed up business. The department stores that have survived this transition, especially those in New York, have tweaked their offerings to provide fewer essentials and more luxuries (Macy's is a rare exception).

Barneys New York 660 Madison Ave, at 61st St ⓣ212/826-8900, ⓦwww.barneys.com. Mon–Fri 10am–8pm, Sat 10am–7pm, Sun noon–6pm. Barneys has been considered the trendiest New York department store for over a decade now, and shows no sign of weakening, with exclusive rights to sell Balenciaga and other top lines. It's a temple to designer fashion, and the best place to find cutting-edge labels or next season's hot item. The Co-op section, focusing on younger styles, was such a hit that the powers that be opened a standalone Barneys Co-op store downtown (116 Wooster St, at Prince ⓣ212/965-9964).

🏃 **Bergdorf Goodman** 754 Fifth Ave, at 57th St ⓣ212/753-7300. Mon–Wed, Fri & Sat 10am–7pm, Thurs 10am–8pm, Sun noon–6pm. Make sure you come here, even if it's only to ogle the windows, which approach high art. With in-house tailoring, superb service, the most comprehensive cosmetics department known to humankind and superior hair, nail, and brow salons, Bergdorf's is the store of choice for many New Yorkers. It has exclusive rights to lines by Yves Saint Laurent and Chloe, among others. The men's store is across Fifth Avenue.

Bloomingdale's 1000 Third Ave, at 59th St ⓣ212/705-2000, ⓦwww.bloomingdales.com. Mon–Thurs 10am–8.30pm, Fri & Sat 9am–10pm, Sun 11am–7pm. When an Upper East Side matron dies, "Bloomies," not "Rosebud," is most likely the last word on her lips. Out-of-towners flock here for its famed "classiness," though local power-shoppers are more likely to view it as a bit of a frumpy has-been. It does still have the atmosphere of a large, bustling bazaar, packed with concessionaires offering perfumes and designer clothes.

Henri Bendel 712 Fifth Ave, between 55th and 56th sts ☎212/247-1100 or 1-888/423-6335. Mon–Wed, Fri & Sat 10am–7pm, Thurs 10am–8pm, Sun noon–6pm. More gentle in its approach than the biggies, this store's refinement is thanks in part to its classic reuse of the Coty perfume building, with windows by René Lalique. There's an array of top-shelf make-up at street level and gorgeous designer clothing, with price tags certain to send your blood pressure soaring, upstairs. The powder rooms appear designed for royalty.

Jeffrey 449 W 14th St, at Tenth Ave ☎212/206-3928. Opening in the 1990s, Jeffrey is a relative newcomer to New York's department-store scene. The all-white emporium is set squat in the middle of the city's cutting-edge Meatpacking District, and features offerings from trend-setting lines like Boudicca and Tess Giberson. The just-opened sheen has worn off in recent years (and the service has become much friendlier).

Macy's 151 W 34th St, on Broadway at Herald Square ☎212/695-4400 or 1-800/289-6229, ⓦwww.macys.com. Mon–Sat 9am–9pm, Sun 11am–7pm. With two buildings, two million square feet of floor space, and ten floors (four for women's garments alone), Macy's is, quite simply, the largest department store in the world. Given its size, it's not the hotbed of top fashion it ought to be: most merchandise is of mediocre quality (particularly the jewelry). The real reason to come here is The Cellar, the housewares department in the basement. It's arguably the best in the city.

Saks Fifth Avenue 611 Fifth Ave, at 50th St ☎212/753-4000, ⓦwww.saks.com. Mon–Wed, Fri & Sat 10am–6.30pm, Thurs 10am–8pm. Since 1924, the name Saks has been virtually synonymous with style. No less true today, the store has updated itself to carry the merchandise of all the big designers, while still retaining its reputation for quality. The ground floor can be a bit like Grand Central terminal as multiple salesgirls assault you with drive-by perfume sprays, but they stock top cosmetic lines (like Armani) that you can't find elsewhere in the city.

Takashimaya 693 Fifth Ave, between 54th and 55th sts ☎212/350-0100. This beautiful Japanese department store is a Manhattan mainstay, offering a scaled-down assortment of expensive merchandise simply displayed and exquisitely wrapped. The café, *The Tea Box*, on the lower level, has an assortment of teapots and loose teas.

Time Warner Center 10 Columbus Circle, at 60th St ☎212/823-6300, ⓦwww.shopsatcolumbus circle.com. Gleaming mega-mall that anchors

▽ Takashimaya

the city's massive Time Warner headquarters. It's known for its upscale eateries, large Whole Foods grocer, and branches of Sephora, J. Crew, Dean & Deluca, and Benetton. Also houses Lincoln Center's snazzy venue, Jazz at Lincoln Center.

Electronic and video equipment

The sole reason to buy **electronic and video equipment** in New York is if you are visiting from Europe, where such merchandise is more expensive. Tech-heads can brave the risky discount shopping on Sixth and Seventh avenues north of Times Square in the 50s for cameras, stereos, and MP3 players; there's another cluster of camera stores in midtown along Fifth and Sixth avenues between 30th and 50th streets. The motto here is *caveat emptor*: know what you want or expect a hard sell for more expensive equipment than you need. It's much easier to head for the meccas of B&H or J&R, where merchandise is not only cheap, but reliable as well.

B&H Photo Video 420 Ninth Ave, between 33rd and 34th sts ☎212/268-1594 or 1-800/606-6969. For film, cameras, and specialty equipment; knowledgeable sales staff will take the time to guide you through a buying decision. Excellent used-goods selection upstairs. Closed Sat.

Bang & Olufsen 952 Madison Ave, at 75th St ☎212/879-6161, ⊕www.bang-olufsen.com. Incredibly good, high-quality audio and some video equipment, all in sleek modern Danish design. Call for other locations.

CompUSA 420 Fifth Ave, at 38th St ☎212/627-0222; also 1775 Broadway, at W 57th St ☎212/262-9711. This superstore runs a computer camp for kids, offers training for adults, and carries the largest inventory in the city.

Harvey Electronics 2 W 45th St, at Fifth Ave ☎212/575-5000, ⊕www.harveyonline.com. Top-of-the-line electronics equipment, sold by experts.

J&R Music and Computer World 15–23 Park Row, between Beekman and Ann sts ☎212/238-9100. You'll find a good selection (for decent prices) of stereo and computer equipment at this store down by City Hall, as well as home appliances and CDs. If you can plug it in, they sell it here – and often at the cheapest prices in the city.

Fashion: accessories

Agent Provocateur 133 Mercer St, at Prince St ☎212/965-0229. New York outpost of the saucy, sexy, luxury lingerie line, co-owned by Joe Corre, son of avant-garde designer Vivienne Westwood. Think frills, bows, and lashings of lace.

Alain Mikli Optique 880 Madison Ave, between 71st and 72nd sts ☎212/472-6085. The French king of eyewear. This is the *only* place to go for high-end fashionable frames. Treat yourself – you won't regret it.

Kate Spade 454 Broome St, at Prince St ☎212/274-1991. Boxy, high-quality fabric bags that were all the rage in the late 1990s. Get yourself one now that they're out of vogue and you may be doing yourself a favor – the "retro" Kate Spade craze is only a matter of time.

Me & Ro 241 Elizabeth St, between Houston and Prince sts ☎917/237-9215, ⊕www.meandrojewelry.com. The hottest, most distinctive jeweler in Manhattan, with tasteful modernist designs worth going out of your way for. Some items are quite expensive, but you can get really nice earrings here for a reasonable price.

Robert Marc 551 Madison Ave, at 55th St ☎212/319-2000. Exclusive New York distributor of frames by the likes of Lunor and Kirei Titan; also sells Retrospecs, restored antique eyewear from the 1890s to the 1940s. Very expensive and very hot. Call for other locations.

Selima Optique 59 Wooster St, at Greene St ☎212/343-9490; also 899 Madison, at 72nd ☎988-6690. Owner Selima Selaun stocks her own line of girly, groovy specs, alongside favorites from well-known designers like Dior and Kata. Bond 07 by Selima, 7 Bond St, at Lafayette (☎212/677-8487), is her concept boutique, which stocks clothes as well as eyewear.

Fashion: clothing

New York is one of the five nerve centers of the global fashion industry, though the emphasis here is on sportswear rather than couture. In addition to hot local designers, you'll find boutiques for just about every major designer on the planet, with prices significantly lower than in European cities or Tokyo.

As such, **clothing shopping** here is a feast for any fashionista; if you are prepared to search the city with sufficient dedication you can find just about anything. We've divided this section into five categories: **boutiques and**

Women's dresses and skirts

American	4	6	8	10	12	14	16	18
British	8	10	12	14	16	18	20	22
Continental	38	40	42	44	46	48	50	52

Women's blouses and sweaters

American	6	8	10	12	14	16	18
British	30	32	34	36	38	40	42
Continental	40	42	44	46	48	50	52

Women's shoes

American	5	6	7	8	9	10	11
British	3	4	5	6	7	8	9
Continental	36	37	38	39	40	41	42

Men's suits

American	34	36	38	40	42	44	46	48
British	34	36	38	40	42	44	46	48
Continental	44	46	48	50	52	54	56	58

Men's shirts

American	14	15	15.5	16	16.5	17	17.5	18
British	14	15	15.5	16	16.5	17	17.5	18
Continental	36	38	39	41	42	43	44	45

Men's shoes

American	7	7.5	8	8.5	9.5	10	10.5	11	11.5
British	6	7	7.5	8	9	9.5	10	11	12
Continental	39	40	41	42	43	44	44	45	46

trendy labels, where you can pick up local big names or one-offs; **chain stores**, Manhattan flagships of well-known American retail names; **designer stores**; **discount stores**, like legendary low-priced designer palace Century 21, where you can pick up big names at deep discounts; and **vintage and thrift**, including the increasingly popular (and browse-worthy) resale or consignment stores, where owners sell off last season's barely worn outfits.

Boutiques and trendy labels

American Apparel 712 Broadway, at 8th St ☎ 646/383-2258, ⊛ www.americanapparel .net. Guaranteed sweatshop-free, 100% PC tees and other items from LA. Worth checking out as much for the endless colors, low prices, and sharp cut as for their ethics.

Bagutta 76 Greene St, at Spring St ☎ 212/925-5262. A smallish but well-chosen selection of top-name designers: favorites include Helmut Lang, Prada, Gaultier, Plein Sud, and Dolce & Gabbana.

Calypso St Barth's 407 Broome St, at Lafayette St ☎ 212/941-6100. Forget black; color is the name of the game here. Vibrant fashions imbued with a rich hippie aesthetic – think

string bikinis at $75 a pop. There are several other branches, specializing in jewelry and accessories, on the same block.

DDC Lab 427 W 14th St, at Ninth Ave ☎ 212/414-5801. The designer-denim label's flagship store, stocking finessed, highly finished jeans as well as experimental knitwear made from high-tech fabrics. There's also a smaller store at 180 Orchard St, at Houston St (☎ 212/375-1647).

Hotel Venus 382 W Broadway, between Broome and Spring sts ☎ 212/966-4066. Touted as the founder of Manhattan's most inventive clothing store, Pat Field was one of the first NYC vendors of "punk chic"; her recent renaissance came as the *tour de force* costumier behind Carrie Bradshaw's outfits in *Sex and the City*. This basement store has plenty of her wild designs at reasonable prices, as well as wacky accessories.

Intermix 1003 Madison Ave, at 77th St Ⓣ212/249-7858; also 125 Fifth Ave, at 19th St Ⓣ212/533-9720; and 98 Prince St, between Mercer and Greene sts Ⓣ212/966-5303. Trendy boutiques for the working-girl fashionista, and a flat-out fun place to shop. A wide assortment of brands both high and low, and an admittedly confusing merchandise layout – they're called "intermix" for a reason.

Kirna Zabête 96 Greene St, at Prince St Ⓣ212/941-9656. The best of the downtown shops, this is a concept store that stocks hand-picked highlights from capsule collections of Rick Owens, Proenza Schouler, Chloe, Ghesquiere, and other icons *du jour*. The great vibe and service here have kept the store in business for over 15 years.

Opening Ceremony 35 Howard St, at Broadway Ⓣ212/219-2688. Concept store that stocks foreign brands that you can't find elsewhere in the US, including London's Topshop. Plans are afoot to add lines from other unavailable designers from Milan and Tokyo.

Scoop 1275 Third Ave, at 73rd St Ⓣ212/535-5577. Every season is cruise season at this lively fashion outpost for youngish Upper East Side girls. There's a bit of a bubblegum, Paris Hilton vibe to the place, but it's well stocked with the latest designs from a dozen different labels.

Seize Sur Vingt 243 Elizabeth St, at Prince St Ⓣ212/343-0476. James and Gwendolyn Jurney offer exquisite old-school men's shirts at their store – and for $40 more will run up a bespoke version specially for you. They also have a small selection of suits and crisp boxer shorts.

TG-170 170 Ludlow St, at Stanton St Ⓣ212/995-8660. Small, unique store featuring emerging local designers. It's a good spot for very cool bargain-priced items from the up-and-coming. Highly recommended.

Triple 5 Soul 290 Lafayette St, between Houston and Prince sts Ⓣ212/431-2404. The city's top skategear shop also stocks a healthy supply of popular men's & ladies' hip-hop gear.

Unis 226 Elizabeth St, at Prince St Ⓣ212/431-5533, ⓦ www.unisnewyork.com. Designer Eunice Lee offers skinny T-shirts, slouchy jeans, and slimfit sweaters in muted colors that are part Britpop revival, part Tokyo teen.

Designer stores

We've listed all the outlets for the major **designer labels** – no big-name brand worth its cashmere would be without a Manhattan outpost, so the choice is enormous. As a general rule, internationally known design houses are concentrated uptown on Fifth Avenue in the 50s and on Madison Avenue in the 60s and 70s. The newer, younger designers are found downtown in Soho, NoLita, the East and West villages, and Tribeca.

agnès b 103 Greene St, at Prince St (women) Ⓣ212/431-0552; also 79 Greene St, at Prince St (men) Ⓣ212/548-9730; 13 E 16th St, at Fifth Ave (men) Ⓣ212/741-2585; and 1063 Madison Ave, between 80th and 81st sts (women) Ⓣ212/570-9333. Pared-down Parisian chic.

Alexander McQueen 417 W 14th St, at Ninth Ave Ⓣ212/645-1797. Theatrical but flattering and well-cut clothes for women. His stablemate at the Gucci group, Stella McCartney, has a store a few doors down.

Anna Sui 113 Greene St, at Prince St Ⓣ212/941-8406. Funky, thrift-store-inspired clothes for girly girls.

Balenciaga 542 W 22nd St, between 10th and 11th aves Ⓣ212/206-0872. The high-glamour designs of Nicolas Ghesquiere have brought this eminent Italian house back to the very top of high fashion, with prices to match. Unique fabrics and unparalleled attention to detail in each piece make this the designer of choice for those who can afford it.

Burberry's 131 Spring St, at Green St Ⓣ212/925-9300; also 9 E 57th St, at Fifth Ave Ⓣ212/355-6314. Their classic plaids and tweeds are still available, but these days they're on the back burner in favor of hot designer Christopher Bailey's more up-to-date offerings. Their women's coats are among the world's most sought-after.

Calvin Klein 654 Madison Ave, at 60th St Ⓣ212/292-9000. Sleek, minimalist sportswear from the master of classic American fashion.

Chloe 850 Madison Ave, at 70th St Ⓣ212/717-8220. Industry watchers predicted the demise of this line when Stella McCartney departed, but her former partner Phoebe Philo has this brand flying higher than ever with one stunning collection after

SHOPPING

③①

another, including the hottest bag to come out in years (the Paddington).

Christian Dior 21 E 57th St, at Madison Ave ℡212/931-2950. John Galliano amps up the glamour here with his show-stopping designs, though they still haven't given him the couture line he craves.

Comme des Garçons 520 W 22nd St, at Tenth Ave ℡212/604-9200. Japanese designer Rei Kawakubo's avant-garde line has a stunning showcase in this Chelsea store – worth stopping to see even if you don't plan to buy any clothes.

DKNY 655 Madison Ave, at 60th St ℡212/223-3569; also 420 W Broadway, at Spring St ℡646/613-1100. Donna Karan's younger, cheaper line has two concept-store locations in the city, selling accessories and homewares for the "DKNY lifestyle" alongside clothes.

Dolce & Gabbana 434 W Broadway, at Spring St; also 825 Madison Ave, at 68th St ℡212/965-8000. Both the diffusion and designer lines by this Italian duo offer studded, showy clothes – just make sure you're thin enough to slip into them.

Donna Karan 817 Madison Ave, at 69th St ℡1-866/240-4700. Subtle clothes in understated shades guaranteed to flatter any figure.

Giorgio Armani 760 Madison Ave, at 65th St ℡212/988-9191. Splash out on one of Armani's legendary deconstructed suits.

Gucci 685 Fifth Ave, at 54th St ℡212/826-2600; also 840 Madison Ave, at 70th St ℡212/717-2619. Tom Ford may be gone, but his revamping of this classic label has had a lasting effect. Cutting-edge leather accessories and retro-cool clothes for a new generation.

Helmut Lang 80 Greene St, at Spring St ℡212/625-4600. Look like a fashion editor in Lang's monochrome basics.

Hermes 691 Madison Ave, at 57th St ℡212/751-3181. More than just scarves for your mother and ties for your dad; check out the clothes designed by camera-shy Martin Margiela.

Issey Miyake 992 Madison Ave, at 77th St ℡212/439-7822. Come here for classic, arty separates – there's also a branch stocking his micro-pleated womenswear, Pleats Please, at 128 Wooster St, at Prince St (℡212/226-3600).

J. Lindeberg 126 Spring St, at Greene St ℡212/625-9403. The namesake line of the designer who launched Diesel, aimed at

anyone who wants to channel his inner rockstar. There's also a smallish womenswear selection.

John Varvatos 149 Mercer St, at Prince St ℡212/431-4490. Boxy, flattering casualwear and suits, plus his highly successful line of leather Converse sneakers.

Krizia 769 Madison Ave, at 66th St ℡212/879-1211. Pick up a lightweight linen suit or a floaty sundress or two here.

Marc Jacobs 163 Mercer St, between Houston and Prince sts ℡212/343-1490. Marc Jacobs rules the New York fashion world like a Cosmopolitan-sipping colossus. Women from all walks of life come here to blow the nest egg on his latest "it" bag or pair of boots. Check out his second line, Marc by Marc, at 403 Bleecker St, at 11th St (℡212/924-0026).

Marni 159 Mercer St, between Houston and Prince sts ℡212/343-3912. Get here before prices go completely through the roof – this relative newcomer from Milan has already been anointed "the new Prada" by fashion editors everywhere. The tops here are especially exquisite, with an emphasis on bright colors and unique patterns.

Miu Miu 100 Prince St, at Greene St ℡212/334-5156; also 831 Madison Ave, at 70th St ℡212/249-9660. Miuccia Prada's fun, often bizarre, diffusion line; note that both stores only stock the women's collection.

Nicole Farhi 10 E 60th St, at Fifth Ave ℡212/223-8811. Everything's understated and elegant here, though the knitwear is the standout. *Nicole's*, the café in the basement, is a favorite place for fashionistas to refuel on black coffee.

Paul Smith 108 Fifth Ave, at 16th St ℡212/229-2471. Excellent, sophisticated menswear, often employing eccentric, eye-catching color combinations.

Philosophy di Alberta Ferretti 452 W Broadway, at Prince St ℡212/460-5500. Summery clothes for that sun-soaked long lunch in the Tuscan hills.

Polo Ralph Lauren 867 Madison Ave ℡212/606-2100 and **Polo Sport Ralph Lauren** 888 Madison Ave ℡212/434-8000; both between 71st and 72nd sts. The master of all things preppy: buy a blazer here and make like you're landed gentry.

Prada 575 Broadway, at Prince St ℡212/334-8888. The jaw-dropping flagship store designed by Rem Koolhaas is as much

31

of a sight as Miuccia's deservedly famous clothes.

Stella McCartney 429 W 14th St, at Tenth Ave ⏚212/255-1556. More of the same stuff she produced at Chloe – uniform for It girls slumming downtown. Her fellow Gucci-group designer Alexander McQueen is close by (see p.417).

Valentino 747 Madison Ave, at 65th St ⏚212/772-6969. Wall-to-wall glamorous gowns.

Versace 647 Fifth Ave, at 52nd St ⏚212/317-0224; also 815 Madison Ave, at 68th St ⏚212/744-6868. Loud, brassy, red-carpet-worthy clothes for those who like to enter a room with an exclamation point.

Yohji Yamamoto 103 Grand St, at Mercer St ⏚212/966-9066. Huge boutique in south Soho selling fragrances, clothes, and shoes, all in Japanese avant-garde designs.

Yves Saint Laurent 855 Madison Ave, at 71st St ⏚212/988-3821. Sexy, oh-so-French separates for men and women.

Zero 225 Mott St, between Prince and Spring sts ⏚212/925-3849. Much-celebrated local designer Maria Cornejo's NoLita boutique features the best of her cutting-edge fashions, which tend toward a simple color palette and some unconventional cuts.

Discount stores

Aaron's 627 Fifth Ave at 17th St, Park Slope, Brooklyn ⏚718/768-5400. This 10,000-square-foot store carries discounted women's designer fashions ranging from Jones New York to Adrienne Vittadini at the beginning of each season, not the end. Prices are marked down about 25 percent.

Century 21 22 Cortlandt St, at Broadway ⏚212/227-9092, ⓦwww.c21store.com. The grandaddy of designer discount department stores, where all the showrooms send their samples to be sold at the end of the season, usually at 40 to 60 percent off retail prices – the richest pickings are in July and January. No dressing rooms, so buy what you want and return whatever doesn't fit.

Daffy's 1311 Broadway, at 34th St, Herald Square ⏚212/736-4477. Name-brand clothes at discount prices for men, women, and children. Specializes in Italian designers like Les Copian. Five other locations in Manhattan; call for details.

Loehmann's 101 Seventh Ave, between 16th and 17th sts ⏚212/352-0856, ⓦwww.loehmanns

.com. New York's best-known department store for designer clothes at knockdown prices, especially glamorous evening wear. No refunds and no exchanges, but there are individual dressing rooms.

Syms 42 Trinity Place, at Rector St ⏚212/797-1199; also 400 Park Ave, at 54th St ⏚212/317-8200. "Where the educated consumer is our best customer" – the stock's stuffier than elsewhere, so plan on picking up a suit for work or a classic white blouse.

Woodbury Common Premium Outlet Mall 498 Red Apple Court, Central Valley, New York State ⏚845/928-4000, ⓦwww.premiumoutlets.com. Dedicated bargain-hunters should hop on a bus from Port Authority Terminal (see p.23) for the 1hr ride north of the city to this designer-label discount-outlet mall. There are factory stores from Gucci, Chanel, Versace, and Dior – and that's just for starters – though you'll mostly find discards and leftovers from the previous season.

Vintage, second-hand, and thrift stores

Aside from the standout shops we've listed below, there's a heavy concentration of thrift and vintage stores in the Lower East Side, especially around Ludlow and Rivington streets. Don't be surprised to find a famous designer (or one of their minions) rifling through the racks in this area – they're probably searching about for inspiration for their next collection.

Amarcord 84 E 7th St, at First Ave ⏚212/614-7133. This place is a real find. The owners make regular trips through their home country of Italy in search of discarded Dior, Gucci, Yves Saint Laurent, and so forth from the 1940s onward. Things aren't too expensive, especially considering all the pieces are in mint condition.

Andy's Chee-pees 691 Broadway, at 3rd St ⏚212/420-5980. The place to go for those all-American bowling shirts, pump-attendant tees, and beat-up denimwear.

Cheap Jack's 841 Broadway, at 13th St ⏚212/995-0403. Not as cheap as it once was, but still a good and comprehensive source of used clothing and accessories.

Cherry 19 Eighth Ave, at Jane St ⏚212/924-1410. Everything from vintage Halston cocktail dresses to swing-era chiffon gowns, with an especially large selection of 60s

SHOPPING

③①

419

mod clothing. High-end, but cheaper than Resurrection (see below).

Domsey's 431 Kent Ave, Williamsburg, Brooklyn ☎718/384-6000. Discreetly embedded along the East River's decrepit warehouse district, this five-story thrift store sells everything from boutique pieces to boot-camp salvage . . . by the pound! Plan to rifle ruthlessly and expect good rewards as a result.

🏃 **Edith & Daha 104 Rivington St, at Ludlow St** ☎212/979-9992. Extremely popular with the trendy vintage set, this used-clothing emporium holds some amazing finds (particularly shoes) for those willing to sift through the massive stock.

Gabay's Outlet 225 First Ave, at E 14th St ☎212/254-3180. An East Village store crammed with remaindered merchandise (Marc Jacobs, YSL, and the like) from midtown's department stores.

Housing Works Thrift Shop 143 W 17th St, at Seventh Ave ☎212/366-0820; **also 306 Columbus Ave, at 75th St** ☎212/579-7566; **and 202 E 77th St, at Third Ave** ☎212/772-8461. Upscale thrift stores where you can find second-hand designer pieces in very good condition. All proceeds benefit Housing Works, an AIDS social-service organization.

🏃 **INA 101 Thompson St, at Prince St** ☎212/941-4757; **also 21 Prince St, at Elizabeth St** ☎212/334-9048; **and 208 E 73rd St, at Second Ave** ☎212/249-0014. Designer resale shop usually crammed with end-of-season, barely worn pieces by hot designers. Fair prices make it by far the best second-hand store in the city. The men's store is at 262 Mott St, at Prince St (☎212/334-2210).

Marmalade 172 Ludlow St, between Houston and Stanton sts ☎212/473-8070. Great spot for mid-range vintage fare, from funky T-shirts to Valentino pumps. Prices are reasonable and there are always some unique items.

Michael's: The Consignment Shop 1041 Madison Ave, at 79th St, 2nd floor ☎212/737-7273. Bridal wear as well as slightly used designer women's clothing from names like Ungaro, Armani, and Chanel.

Reminiscence 50 W 23rd St, between Fifth and Sixth aves ☎212/243-2292. Designed to evoke your memories of the 1980s everything-with-palm-trees phase (the store's logo is a palm tree). It also carries funky new and used clothes for men and women – expect plenty of Hawaiian shirts, tie-string overalls, and tube tops.

Resurrection 217 Mott St, at Spring St ☎212/625-1374, ⓦwww.resurrectionvintage .com. Hands down the best high-end place for vintage clothing in the city, with first-class Pucci and Halston classics from the 60s through to the 80s. The prices are very high, but it's still worth it just to check out the Pucci gowns and python Dior jackets.

Screaming Mimi's 382 Lafayette St, at Great Jones St ☎212/677-6464, ⓦwww .screamingmimis.com. One of the most well-established lower-end second-hand stores in Manhattan. Vintage clothes, including lingerie, bags, shoes, and housewares at reasonable prices.

Sample sales

At the beginning of each fashion season, designers' and manufacturers' showrooms are still full of leftover merchandise from the previous season. These pieces are removed via informal sample sales, which kick off in October and run through March, though there are usually a few in April and May. You'll always save at least fifty percent off the retail price, though you may not be able to try on the clothes and you can never return them. Always take plenty of cash with you; some sales will not accept credit cards. The best way to find out what sales are coming up is to check the current issues of *Time Out New York* (ⓦwww.timeoutny.com) and *New York* magazine (ⓦwww.newyorkmetro.com), or **Charlie Suisman's M.U.G.** (ⓦwww .manhattanusersguide.com). If you're really determined to hunt out a bargain or two, or just want to spend your entire time in New York sample-sale shopping, consider subscribing to the **S&B Report**, published monthly. For more info, visit ⓦwww .lazarshopping.com,
Clothing Line (ⓦwww.clothingline.com), or
Daily Candy (ⓦwww.dailycandy.com).

Tokio 7 64 E 7th St, between First and Second aves ☎212/353-8443. Attractive second-hand and vintage designer consignment items; known for its flashy, eccentric selection – think plenty of Gaultier, Moschino, and McQueen – rather than boring, basic black.

What Comes Around Goes Around 351 W Broadway, between Broome and Grand sts ☎212/343-9303, ⊛www.wcaga.com. Established and well-loved downtown vintage store. Popular with magazine stylists borrowing pieces for shoots.

Fashion: shoes

Most department stores carry two or more shoe salons – one for less expensive brands and one for finer shoes. **Barneys** and **Loehmann's** are both known for their selection of high-end footwear, while the greatest concentration of bargain shoe shops can be found in the Village on West 8th Street, between University Place and Sixth Avenue, and on Broadway below West 8th Street.

Shoes on Sale is the largest shoe sale open to the public, with more than 50,000 pairs of shoes. It is held each year around the second week in October, in a tent in Central Park, at Fifth Avenue and 60th Street. Check the newspaper for details.

Alife 161 Bowery, between Delancey and Broome sts ☎212/219-3505. Sneaker nirvana, with an entire wall filled with limited-edition Adidas, Pumas, and lesser-known brands.

Camper 125 Prince St, at Wooster St ☎212/358-1842. Cult Spanish footwear with springy soles; some are based on eccentric takes on the bowling shoe.

The Diamond District

The strip of 47th Street between Fifth and Sixth avenues is known as the **Diamond District**. Crammed into this one block are more than 100 shops: combined they sell more jewelry than any other area in the world. The industry has traditionally been run by Hasidic Jews, and you'll still see plenty of black-garbed men with *payess* (sidelocks) on this block.

At street level are dozens of retail shops and more than twenty "exchanges" – marts containing booths where many different dealers sell very specific merchandise. For example, 55 W 47th St is home to 115 independent jewelers and repair specialists. Less known is the Swiss Center, 608 Fifth Ave, at 49th St, which specializes in antique and estate jewelry and is housed in a historic Art Deco building.

There are different dealers for different gems, gold, and silver – even dealers who will string your beads for you, and "findings" stores where you can pick up the basic makings of do-it-yourself jewelry, like chains and earring posts. Some jewelers trade only among themselves; some sell retail; and others do business by appointment only. Most shops are open Monday through Saturday 10am to 5.30pm, though a few close on Friday afternoon and Saturday for religious reasons, and the standard vacation time is from the end of June to the second week in July.

It is very important that you go to the exchanges educated. Research what you are looking for and be as particular as possible. If possible, it's always better to go to someone who has been specifically recommended to you. Some good starting points are Andrew Cohen, Inc, at 579 Fifth Ave, 15th floor, for diamonds; Myron Toback, 25 W 47th St, a trusted dealer of silver findings; and Bracie Company, Inc, 608 Fifth Ave, Suite 806, a friendly business specializing in antique and estate jewelry. Once you buy, there's AA Pearls & Gems, 10 W 47th St, the industry's choice for pearl and gem stringing; and, if you want to get your gems graded, the Gemological Institute of America, is at 580 Fifth Ave, 2nd floor.

Charles Jourdan 152 W 57th St, between Sixth and Seventh aves ☎212/421-4250. Outstanding French designer of fine shoes, who strikes a delicate balance between traditional and contemporary looks.

Jimmy Choo 645 Fifth Ave, at 51st St ☎212/593-0800. Popular British designer has a huge Manhattan following for his high-heeled, high-priced, high-quality shoes.

John Fluevog 250 Mulberry St, at Prince St ☎212/431-4484. Innovative designs for a walk about town – most styles are casual but quirky, with buckles or brightly colored detailing.

Jutta Neumann 158 Allen St, between Stanton and Rivington sts ☎212/982-7048. Her custom-designed, super-comfy sandals are all the rage downtown, and she also sells popular leather handbags.

Kenneth Cole 610 Fifth Ave, at 49th St ☎212/373-5800. Classic and contemporary shoes and beautiful bags in excellent full-grain leather. Call for more locations.

Manolo Blahnik 31 W 54th St, at Fifth Ave ☎212/582-3007. World-famous strappy stilettos – good for height (of fashion), hell for feet. More popular than ever thanks to

Carrie Bradshaw and company in *Sex and the City*.

Nine West 675 Fifth Ave, at 53rd St ☎212/319-6893. Immensely popular designer look-alikes, often with good seasonal reductions. Call for other locations.

Otto Tootsi Plohound 413 W Broadway, at Spring St ☎212/925-8931; also 273 Lafayette St, at Prince St ☎212/431-7299; and 38 E 57th St, at Park Ave ☎212/231-3199. If you want to run with a trendy crowd, these shoes will help: the best place to browse a range of brands, from Prada loafers to DSquared sneakers.

🏃 **Sigerson Morrison** 28 Prince St, at Mott St ☎212/219-3893. Kari Sigerson and Miranda Morrison make timeless, simple, and elegant shoes for women. A required pilgrimmage for shoe worshippers. The location just round the corner, 242 Mott St, at Prince St (☎212/941-5404), stocks their popular line of handbags.

Steve Madden 45 W 34th St, at Sixth Ave ☎212/736-3283. Very popular copies of up-to-the-minute styles, well loved for their ability to take on New York's "shoe-killing" streets.

Flea markets and craft fairs

New York **flea markets** are outstanding for funky and old clothes, collectibles, lingerie, jewelry, and crafts; there's also any number of odd places – parking lots, playgrounds, or maybe just an extra-wide bit of sidewalk – where people set up to sell their wares, especially in spring and summer.

Annex Antiques Fair and Flea Market Sixth Ave, at 26th St. Sat & Sun 10am–6pm. Surrounded by antique shops, this is the fastest-growing fair in New York, with 600 vendors selling furniture, clothes, and bric-a-brac. Four other locations within two blocks. Admission $1.

Essex Street Covered Market Essex St, between Rivington and Delancey sts. Mon–Thurs & Sat 8am–6pm, Fri 8am–8pm. ☎212/388-0449. A kosher fish market, Latino grocers, and a Chinese greenmarket, all live under one roof, reflecting the diverse neighborhood. Also jewelry and clothes.

Green Flea I.S. 44 Flea Market Columbus Ave, at 77th St. Sun 10am–6pm. One of the best

and largest markets in the city: antiques and collectibles, new merchandise, and a farmers' market.

Malcolm Shabazz Harlem Market 52 W 116th St, at Fifth Ave. Daily 8am–9pm. Bazaar-like market, with an entrance marked by colorful fake minarets. A dazzling array of West African cloth, clothes, jewelry, masks, Ashanti dolls, and beads. Also sells leather bags, music, and Black Pride T-shirts.

Tower Market Broadway, at 4th St. Sat & Sun 10am–7pm. House music, jewelry, clothes, woven goods from South America, New Age paraphernalia, and the like.

Food and drink

Food is a New York obsession – hence the proliferation of **gourmet grocer-ies** and **specialty markets** across the city. For general snacking and late-night munchies, there's usually a 24-hour corner shop (known as a "bodega") within a few blocks' walk of anywhere.

Note that New York State's liquor-licensing laws mean that supermarkets and bodegas can only sell beer, and wine and spirits are only available in liquor stores. In either place, you'll need to be 21 to buy (and be able to prove it with a photo ID if asked). An added wrinkle is that the laws also preclude liquor-store owners from opening seven days a week, so most – though not all – are shut on Sundays.

Agata Valentina 1505 First Ave, at 79th St ⓣ212/452-0690. The top gourmet grocer in town, with fresh pastas made on the premises, an enviable deli and cheese counter, a variety of pricey delicacies, and an outstanding butcher.

Barney Greengrass 541 Amsterdam Ave, at 86th St ⓣ212/724-4707. "The Sturgeon King" – an Upper West Side smoked-fish institution since 1908 – also sells brunch makings to go.

Chelsea Market 75 Ninth Ave, at 15th St ⓣ212/243-6005, ⓦwww.chelseamarket.com. A complex of eighteen former industrial build-ings, among them the old Nabisco Cookie Factory. A true smorgasbord of stores, including Amy's Bread, Bowery Kitchen Supplies, the Chelsea Wholesale Flower Market, the Chelsea Wine Vault, Hale & Hearty Soups, the Lobster Place, and the Manhattan Fruit Exchange.

Dean & Deluca 560 Broadway, between Prince and Spring sts ⓣ212/226-6800. One of the original big neighborhood food emporia. Very chic, very Soho, and not at all cheap. They also have several other locations throughout the city.

Economy Candy 108 Rivington St, at Essex St ⓣ212/254-1832. A candy shop on the Lower East Side, selling tubs of sweets, nuts, and dried fruit at low prices.

Elk Candy Co 1628 Second Ave, between 84th and 85th sts ⓣ212/650-1177. This Yorkville candy store sells Yorkville-style candies (ie, rich and heavy on the marzipan).

Fairway 2127 Broadway, at 74th St ⓣ212/595-1888, ⓦwww.fairwaymarket.com. Long-established Upper West Side grocery store that many locals find a better value than the more famous Zabar's (see p.424). They have their own farm on Long Island, so the produce is always fresh, and the range in some items is enormous. Fantastic organic selection upstairs.

Li-Lac 120 Christopher St, at Hudson St ⓣ212/242-7374. Li-Lac's delicious choco-lates have been handmade on the premises since 1923. One of the city's best treats for those with a sweet tooth – try the fresh fudge or hand-molded Lady Liberties and Empire States.

Murray's Cheese Shop 257 Bleecker St, at Sixth Ave ⓣ212/243-3289. More than 300 fresh cheeses and excellent panini sandwiches, all served by a knowledgeable staff. Free tastings on Saturday afternoons.

Porto Rico Importing Company 201 Bleecker St, at Sixth Ave ⓣ212/477-5421. Best for coffee, and local rumor has it that the house blends are as good as many of the more expensive coffees.

Russ & Daughters 179 E Houston St, at Orchard St ⓣ212/475-4880. Technically, this store is known as an "appetizing" – the original Manhattan gourmet shop, set up around 1900 to sate the appetites of homesick immigrant Jews, selling smoked fish, pickled vegetables, cheese, and bagels. This is one of the oldest and best.

Sahadi 187 Atlantic Ave, between Clinton and Court sts, Brooklyn Heights ⓣ718/624-4550. Fully stocked Middle Eastern grocery store selling everything from Iranian pistachios to creamy home-made hummus.

Titan 25–56 31st St, between Astoria Blvd and 20th St, Queens ⓣ718/626-7771. Olympic-sized store for comestible Greek goods, including imported feta cheese, yogurt, and stuffed grape leaves.

Vintage New York 482 Broome St, at Wooster St ⓣ212/226-9463; also 2492 Broadway, at 93rd St ⓣ212/721-9999. This New York State–based winery is one place where you'll be able to pick up a bottle on Sundays. It's worth stopping by at other times to try the tasting bar, where you can sample different vintages for as low as $5.

Several days each week, long before sunrise, hundreds of farmers from Long Island, the Hudson Valley, and parts of Pennsylvania and New Jersey set out in trucks to transport their fresh-picked bounty to New York City, where they are joined by bakers, cheesemakers, and other artisans at **greenmarkets**. These are run by the city authorities, roughly one to four days a week, and are busiest from June through September. Usually you'll find apple cider, jams and preserves, flowers and plants, maple syrup, fresh meat and fish, pretzels, cakes and breads, herbs, honey – just about anything and everything produced in the rural regions around the city – not to mention occasional live-worm composts and baby dairy goats.

To find the greenmarket nearest to you, call ☎212/788-7476; the largest and most popular is held in Union Square, at E 17th St and Broadway, year-round on Mon, Wed, Fri & Sat from 8am to 6pm.

Warehouse Wines and Spirits 735 Broadway, between 8th St and Waverly Place ☎212/982-7770. The top place to get a buzz for your buck, with a wide selection and frequent reductions on popular lines.

Zabar's 2245 Broadway, at 80th St ☎212/787-2000, ⊛www.zabars.com. The apotheosis of New York food-fever, Zabar's is still the city's pre-eminent gourmet shop. Choose from an astonishing variety of cheeses, olives, cooked meats, salads, freshly baked breads and croissants, excellent bagels, and cooked dishes. Upstairs, shop for shiny kitchen and household implements to help you put it all together at home; there are often good bargains on electric items like fans and European coffeemakers.

▽ Zabar's

Music

While the top **music megastores** in New York are Tower Records and the Virgin Megastore, many excellent **independent record stores** are clustered in the East and West villages, with particularly cheap used bargains available around St Mark's Place. Especially popular are small stores dedicated to various permutations of electronica, and venerable jazz-record stores with great LP selections that have been around for decades.

The big names

J&R Music World 23 Park Row, at Beekman St ☎212/238-9000
Tower Records 692 Broadway, at 4th St ☎212/505-1500; also 1961 Broadway, at 66th St ☎212/799-2500; and 725 Fifth Ave, at 56th St in Trump Tower ☎212/838-8110
Virgin Megastore 1540 Broadway, at 45th St ☎212/921-1020; also 52 E 14th St, at Union Square ☎212/598-4666

Special interest and second-hand

Breakbeat Science 181 Orchard St, at Stanton St ☎212/995-2592, ⊛www.breakbeatscience.com. Breakbeat Science was the first drum'n'bass-only store to open in the US; it's still great for imports.
Dance Tracks 91 E 3rd St, at First Ave ☎212/260-8729, ⊛www.dancetracks.com. A gold mine for techno, house, and other forms of electronic music on vinyl – more

SHOPPING | Music

(31)

oldies from the 1970s and 1980s than from today's DJs.

Etherea 66 Ave A, at 5th St ☎212/358-1126, ⓦwww.ethereaonline.com. Specializing in indie rock and electronica, both domestic and import, on CD and vinyl, this is one of the best shops in the city. Good used selection and sweet, obsessive staff.

Fat Beats 406 Sixth Ave, at 8th St, 2nd floor ☎212/673-3883. The name says it all: it's *the* source for hip-hop on vinyl in New York City.

Footlight Records 113 E 12th St, at Third Ave ☎212/533-1572, ⓦwww.footlight .com. Your one-stop shop for show music, film soundtracks, and jazz. Everything from Broadway to Big Band, Sinatra to Merman. A must for record collectors.

Generation Records 210 Thompson St, at Bleecker St ☎212/254-1100. The focus here is on hardcore, metal, and punk with some indie. New CDs and vinyl upstairs, used goodies downstairs. It also gets many of the imports the others don't have, plus fine bootlegs. A ginger giant masquerades as the store cat.

Gryphon Record Shop 233 W 72nd St, at Broadway ☎212/874-1588. Specializes in rare LPs.

House of Oldies 35 Carmine St, at Bleecker St ☎212/243-0500, ⓦwww.houseofoldies.com. Just what the name says – oldies but goldies of all kinds. Vinyl only.

Jazz Record Center 236 W 26th St, between Seventh and Eighth aves ☎212/675-4480, ⓦwww.jazzrecordcenter.com. The place to come for rare or out-of-print jazz LPs from the dawn of recording through the bebop revolution, avant-jazz, and beyond. They

also have rare books, videos, and memorabilia.

Kim's 6 St Mark's Place, at Second Ave ☎212/598-9985; also 350 Bleecker St, at 10th St ☎212/675-8996. Extensive selection of new and used indie obscurities on CD and vinyl, some very cheap. Esoteric videos upstairs. Expect the staff to have a serious attitude problem.

Other Music 15 E 4th St, at Broadway ☎212/477-8150, ⓦwww.othermusic.org. Around the corner from Tower Records, this is an excellent spot for "alternative" CDs, both old and new, that can be hard to find. Stocking less indie on vinyl than it once did, and now leaning toward experimental and electronica, the store retains the same ever-friendly and knowledgeable staff.

Rocks In Your Head 157 Prince St, between Thompson St and W Broadway ☎212/475-6729, ⓦwww.rocksinyourhead.com. Friendly, well-stocked downtown store, specializing in indie rock and 1960s bands. Carries some Rough Guides music titles (so they must be good) and a wide selection of obscure music magazines. A fun place to browse.

Satellite 259 Bowery, between Houston and Stanton sts ☎212/995-1744. An encyclopedic palace of rave electronica of all stripes – from funky breaks to drum'n'bass to psytrance – with two dozen listening stations from which to sample the grooves.

Vinyl Mania 60 Carmine St, at Bedford St ☎212/924-7223. This is where DJs come for the newest, rarest releases, especially of dance music. Hard-to-find imports, too, as well as home-made dance tapes.

Specialty stores

The shops below are either offbeat and interesting to visit or sell useful items that are cheaper in New York than elsewhere.

ABC Carpet and Home 888 Broadway, at 19th St ☎212/473-3000. Six floors of antiques and country furniture, knick-knacks, linens, and, of course, carpets. The grandiose, museum-like setup is half the fun. Wander through to garner decorating ideas.

Dinosaur Designs 250 Mott St, at Prince St ☎212/680-3523. Chunky resin homewares and jewelry from Australia in a dazzling palette of bright reds, greens, blues, yellows, and violets. The bold bangles are best-sellers.

Enchanted Forest 85 Mercer St, at Spring St ☎212/925-6677. Truly lives up to its name: a veritable magic forest with a plank bridge and a whimsical collection of toys, books, gems, and folk art. Perfect for kids both big and little.

Exit 9 64 Ave A, at 4th St ☎212/228-0145, ⓦwww.shopexit9.com. Quirky, kooky emporium of kitsch, stocking soaps, bags, cards, and various other offbeat goodies – great for last-minute gifts.

(31)

Flight 001 96 Greenwich Ave, at 12th St ☎212/691-1001. The best place for bags in the city, from Mandarina Duck to Freitag, plus a stylish selection of travel accessories and books.

MoMA Design Store 81 Spring St, at Crosby ☎646/613-1367. The Museum of Modern Art's retail wing, this shop holds a host of super-stylish housewares, modish knick-knacks, and contemporary art books.

Moss 146 Greene St, at Prince St ☎212/226-2190. By far the premier shop for top-quality designer home accessories and furniture. Owner Murry Moss is a design guru, and his playland of a store offers everything from wacky but expensive furniture (think sofas made from corrugated cardboard) to more affordable but still super-stylish salt and pepper shakers.

Mxyplyzyk 125 Greenwich Ave, at 13th St ☎212/989-4300, ⊛www.mxyplyzyk.com. Don't let the weird name put you off (for the record, it's pronounced "Mixee-plizz-ik," and is taken from a character in a Superman comic); this is a homewares and gift shop, with sleek table-top and bath products as well as stationery, watches, and sundries.

New York Yankees Clubhouse Shop 8 Fulton St, at Front St, opposite the South Street Seaport ☎212/514-7182. In case you want that "NY" logo on all your clothing.

Village Chess Shop 230 Thompson St, at W 3rd St ☎212/475-8130. Every kind of chess set for every kind of pocketbook. Usually packed with people playing. Open until midnight.

Sporting goods

There are quite a number of sporting-goods outlets in the city – from cookie-cutter chain stores to mom–and–pop cycle shops to multistory sneaker pleasure domes. Use them for merchandise as well as for their wealth of information about sports in and around the city.

Bicycle Renaissance 430 Columbus Ave, at 81st St ☎212/724-2350, ⊛www.bicyclerenaissance.com. A classy place with competitive prices, custom-bike building, and usually, same-day service. Trek and Cannondale bikes and Campagnolo and Shimano frames in stock.

BLADES Board & Skate 120 W 72nd St, at Amsterdam Ave ☎212/787-3911; also 659 Broadway, at 2nd St ☎212/477-7074. Rent or buy rollerblades, snowboards, and the like. Handy for Central Park. Call for other locations.

Eastern Mountain Sports (EMS) 20 W 61st St, at Broadway ☎212/397-4860; also 591 Broadway, at Houston St ☎212/966-8730. Top-quality merchandise covering almost all outdoor sports, including skiing and kayaking.

Mason's Tennis Mart 56 E 53rd St, at Park Ave ☎212/755 5805. New York's last remaining tennis specialty store – they let you try out all rackets.

Nike iD Lab 255 Elizabeth St, between Houston and Prince sts ⊛www.nike.com. Design your own super-high-end sneakers at this appointment-only studio. To sign up for an appointment (at least a month beforehand), go to the website listed above and click "Nike iD Studios".

Niketown 6 E 57th St, at Fifth Ave ☎212/891-6453. You can enter this sneaker temple through Trump Tower; listen for the cheering crowds as you pass through the door. Every 30min, a screen descends the full five stories of the store and shows Nike commercials – most of the memorabilia relates to Michael Jordan. Oh, and you can also purchase Nike clothing and accessories at full price.

Paragon Sporting Goods 867 Broadway, at 18th St ☎212/255-8036. Family-owned, with three levels of general merchandise, stocking nearly everything you'll need for most sports. A fine store.

Reebok Store 160 Columbus Ave, at 66th St ☎212/595-1480. This is the flagship Reebok store, although there is an outlet at Chelsea Piers. Not as dazzling as Niketown, but it does house the Reebok Sports Club and features European Reebok lines not found anywhere else in the States.

Super Runners Shop 1337 Lexington Ave, at 89th St ☎212/369-6010; also 360 Amsterdam Ave, at 77th St ☎212/787-7665; and 1246 Third Ave, at 72nd St ☎212/249-2133. Experienced runners work at all three locations; co-owner Gary Muhrcke won the first NYC Marathon in 1970.

Sports and outdoor activities

I f measured by sheer number of teams and the coverage they are given, New York ranks as the number-one **sports** city in America. TV stations cover most regular-season games and all post-season games in the big four American team sports – **baseball**, **football**, **basketball**, and **ice hockey**. Baseball is a vital part of New York culture, and by far the most popular of the city's spectator sports; even tepid sports fans have some allegiance to either the Yankees or the Mets. Anyone wanting to see a game should understand that tickets can often be hard to find (some are impossible – it all depends on what team is in town) and most don't come cheap. Nothing compares to the chill of the arena, the smell of the grass, and the anxiety of pre-game introductions, but if you don't get a chance to see this slice of Americana in person, there are always **sports bars** – establishments with free-flowing beer, king-sized television screens, and their own special kind of rabid fans (see the box on p.433 for listings).

Many **participatory activities** in the city are either free or fairly affordable, and take place in all kinds of weather. New Yorkers are passionate about **jogging** – there are plenty of places to take a scenic run – and you can **swim** at local pools or borough beaches. Your first resources for any participatory activity should be the spectacular City of New York **Parks and Recreation Department** and the **Urban Park Rangers**, both of which offer any number of facilities and activities (T311, W www.nycgovparks.org). However, even with the help of the Parks Department it can be hard to find facilities for some sports (like tennis), especially if you are not a city resident. To this end, many New Yorkers spend between $40 and $100 (or more) a month to be members of private **health clubs**; you can usually get a free trial week at one of the major ones (the Ys, New York Sports Clubs, Crunch, Bally's, etc), particularly if you use the address where you are staying in New York.

Spectator sports

In this section, we've included details on the main **spectator sports** and the teams that represent New York.

Minor-league baseball

Attending a minor-league baseball game is great fun. Not only do you get the chance to see up-and-coming players compete with those hanging on for one last shot at The Show, but the crowds are smaller and the seats are better. Expect to see more "true" fans keeping score in the stands at these games than teenage girls scouting the next Derek Jeter.

1999 saw the birth of the first new baseball franchise in New York in several decades: the minor-league **Staten Island Yankees** (℡718/720-9265, ⒲www.siya-nks.com), who play in the Class A New York–Penn League. They can be seen at the Richmond County Bank Ballpark at St George, within walking distance of the Staten Island ferry terminal. In addition to being a fun place to see a game, the location provides a great view of Lower Manhattan and the Statue of Liberty.

After a 43-year absence, baseball returned to Brooklyn in 2001 in the form of the **Brooklyn Cyclones** (℡718/449-8497, ⒲www.brooklyncyclones.com). This team, a Class A New York–Penn League affiliate of the National League Mets, is sponsored by KeySpan Corporation, which provided major funding for the beautiful, oceanside stadium at the former Steeplechase Park in Coney Island.

Baseball

In the early 1840s, the New York Knickerbocker Club played "base ball" in the northeast part of Madison Square in Manhattan, before moving to Elysian Fields, across the Hudson River in Hoboken, New Jersey. There, on June 26, 1846, they laid down the basic rules (the "Knickerbocker Rules") of the game of **baseball**, as it is played to this day.

For half a century, New York was home to three Major League Baseball (MLB) teams: the New York Giants and the Brooklyn Dodgers, who represented the National League, and the **New York Yankees**, who represented the American League. Additionally, in the years before MLB was integrated, the Negro League had several notable teams based in the city, including the New York Lincoln Giants, the Royal Brooklyn Giants, and the New York Black Yankees.

The almost-decade between 1947 and 1956 was the golden age of baseball in New York, with the Yankees steamrolling their opponents and larger-than-life, heroic competitors like Mickey Mantle, Joe DiMaggio, and Jackie Robinson playing for the Dodgers. This period ended abruptly in 1957, when the Giants and Dodgers

bolted to California at the end of the season – though the city has mostly forgotten the Giants, many Brooklyn residents are still scarred by the loss of the Dodgers. New York was bereft of a National League franchise until the **Mets** arrived at the Polo Grounds in 1962, moving two years later to their current home, Shea Stadium in Flushing, Queens.

The MLB **season** lasts for the better part of the year: Spring Training exhibition games occur in March, the **regular season** runs from April to the end of September, and the post-season series takes place in October.

New York Yankees

Reciting the achievements of the **Yankees** (also known as "The Bronx Bombers") over the decades can get tedious. They are the team with the most World Series titles (through 2005, they boast 26), and they have been in the playoffs for 43 of the last 84 seasons: an almost unheard-of success rate for major-league sports.

If possible, try to catch a game when the Boston Red Sox are in town. The long-running rivalry between the teams' fans – originating in 1920, when former Red Sox star pitcher Babe Ruth was traded to the Yankees – makes for an exciting time. The

Yankee Stadium

Yankee Stadium, the Bronx home of the New York Yankees, has witnessed more than a few awe-inspiring moments since Babe Ruth christened it with a home run on opening day in 1923. Certain images from the stadium, recycled over and over, have become iconic in American sports history: Babe Ruth tiptoeing daintily around the bases after yet another majestic moonshot; Joe DiMaggio's phenomenal 56-game hitting streak and his effortless grace in centerfield; Mickey Mantle's awesome power; and the dying Lou Gehrig's farewell to the game on July 4, 1939, when he declared himself "the luckiest man on the face of the earth."

Though baseball is (justly) the stadium's most famous activity, other sports have seen their moment in the sun here as well. On June 22, 1938, black heavyweight champion Joe Louis knocked out Hitler's National Socialist hero Max Schmeling in the first round. In football, "the greatest game ever played" took place at Yankee Stadium in December 1958 between the New York Giants and the Baltimore Colts. The televised championship game went into a dramatic overtime period, indirectly helping popularize (American) football across the country.

After more than 83 years, though, Yankee Stadium is outdated, with limited amenities for players and fans alike, and plans for a new Yankee Stadium are currently in the works – it will be just north of the current location, between 161st and 164th streets. It's being designed as part of a larger Bronx redevelopment project that also includes a hotel, a conference center, and a school. Construction is scheduled to be finished for the beginning of the 2009 season.

other great games to try for are the "Subway Series," when the Bombers face their cross-town rivals, the Mets, in June interleague play. The players on both teams are seemingly unphased by the series, but it makes for high drama among their divided fans.

The powers-that-be have decided that the Yankees have outgrown their home, and construction on a new Yankee Stadium is slated to be complete for the 2009 season. The chance to cozy up with the spirits of bygone greatness, before the ballpark becomes a playground and parking lot, is more than enough reason to pony up for tickets. For more on the Bombers, see the box on p.279; for more on their stadium, see the box above.

Ticket prices: $12–115; for details on buying tickets, see p.434.

New York Mets

There was a time when the **Mets** were the ugly bridesmaids of the city, but they have been reborn with the 2006 season. A change in management has sparked a revival among the Amazin's, attracting the likes of future Hall of Fame pitcher (and former Boston Red Sox star) Pedro Martinez and former Yanks bench coach Willie Randolph. You can bet that ticket prices at Shea Stadium are going to rely heavily on the team's predicted future successes. For now, though, tickets are almost always easier to get for the Mets than the Yankees, and the atmosphere at Shea decidedly more mellow.

Ticket prices: $5–75; for details on Shea Stadium and buying tickets, see p.434.

Football

The **National Football League (NFL) regular season** stretches from September through the end of December. New York's teams are the **Jets** and the **Giants**; both play at **Giants Stadium**, part of the Meadowlands Sports Complex in New Jersey. Plans are supposedly afoot for a new Giants stadium on the west shore of Manhattan near Javits Convention Center in midtown, though each time the idea is proposed, it's blown apart by various neighborhood committees. Tickets for both teams are always sold out well in advance, but if you're willing to pay the price, you can often buy tickets outside the stadium before the game (from scalpers or extra-ticket holders). That said, proceed at your own risk: buying from scalpers is both frowned upon and illegal.

New York Giants

Due to the length of the waiting list for season tickets (incredibly long), the **Giants** (☎201/935-8222, ⓦwww .giants.com) actually encourage current ticket holders to sell their unused seats to people farther down on the list; you have to sign up through the team to have a shot at these tickets. Since 1925, the **Giants** have won four NFL and two Super Bowl championships (1987 and 1991). They also hold the record for the most championship losses ever, and are the only team to twice fail to make the playoffs in the season immediately following a Super Bowl victory.

  Ticket prices: $45 and $50; for details on Giants Stadium and buying tickets, see p.434.

New York Jets

Founded in 1960 as part of an upstart American Football League, the **Jets** (☎516/560-8200, ⓦwww .newyorkjets.com), originally known as the Titans, have yet to find a home of their own (currently, they are tenants of the New York Giants). The Jets' 16–7 Super Bowl III victory in 1969 (following the 1968 regular season) earned respect for the fledgling AFL and set the stage for the creation of the National Football League as it is today.

  Ticket prices: $40 and $50; for details on Giants Stadium and buying tickets, see p.434.

Professional basketball

The **National Basketball Association** (**NBA**) **regular season** begins in November and runs through the end of April. The two professional teams in the New York area are the **New York Knicks** (Knickerbockers), who play at Madison Square Garden, and the **New Jersey Nets**, whose current venue is the Continental Airlines Arena at the Meadowlands Sports Complex in New Jersey, though their new digs in Brooklyn are scheduled to open in 2008. There is also a women's professional team in New York, the WBNA **Liberty**. Tickets to see them play are fairly easy to come by, though the team is growing in popularity.

New York Knicks

It's not easy being a **Knicks** (ⓦwww .nba.com/knicks) fan. Madison Square Garden is one of the ugliest structures in North America; their last championship win was way back in 1973 (though the Knicks consistently make the playoffs); and after all that, tickets are expensive and impossible to come by. This partly explains the number of celebrities in the stands: spectators can usually count on the attendance of Spike Lee, Woody Allen, Sarah Jessica Parker, and a contingent of Baldwin brothers. Meanwhile, the vast majority of fans can only dream of attending a game in person.

  Ticket prices: $10–290; for details on Madison Square Garden and buying tickets, see p.434.

New Jersey Nets

The **Nets** (ⓦwww.nba.com/nets/) began life in 1967, as the New Jersey Americans. Led by the legendary Julius Irving (Dr J), they won two championships (1974 and 1976) while playing on Long Island before joining the NBA. In 2002 and 2003, the Nets, led by consummate point guard Jason Kidd, made valiant playoff runs only to lose in the NBA finals. Although

SPORTS AND OUTDOOR ACTIVITIES | Spectator sports

32

the Nets are more successful than the Knicks, tickets are easier to come by owing to the comparative difficulty of getting to their New Jersey arena. This will most likely change, though, when the Nets move to Brooklyn for the 2008 season.

Ticket prices: $35–95; for details on Continental Airlines Arena and buying tickets, see p.434.

New York Liberty

The Women's National Basketball Association (WNBA) season opens when the NBA season ends and runs through the summer to its playoffs in September. The league jumped off in 1997, with the New York team, the **Liberty**, finishing as runners-up for the title. Games are at Madison Square Garden, and prices low compared with those for the Knicks. You can usually get a ticket; call ☏1-877/WNBA-TIX, go to ⓦwww.wnba.com/liberty or pick some up at MSG.

Ticket prices: $10–65.

College basketball

The **college basketball** season begins in November and ends with "March Madness," in which conference tournaments are followed by a 65-team tournament to select a national champion. The national tournament may be the most exciting, eagerly anticipated sporting event in the US.

Madison Square Garden (☏212/465-6741, ⓦwww.thegarden.com and ⓦwww.bigeast.org) hosts pre-season

tournaments and the Big East Conference tournament. Metropolitan-area colleges pursuing hoop dreams include Long Island, Stony Brook, Columbia, Seton Hall, and St John's universities.

Ice hockey

There are two professional hockey teams in New York: the **Rangers**, who play at Madison Square Garden, and the **Islanders**, whose venue is the Nassau Coliseum on Long Island. In addition, the **New Jersey Devils** play out at Continental Airlines Arena. All three compete in the Atlantic Division of the Eastern Conference of the **National Hockey League** (**NHL**). The **regular season** lasts throughout the winter and into early spring, when the playoffs take place.

New York Rangers

One of the six original NHL teams, the **Rangers** (☏212/465-6000, ⓦwww.newyorkrangers.com) were founded in 1926 and won the Stanley Cup – awarded to the winner of the playoffs – three times in the next fifteen years. According to hockey lore, giddy from their 1940 playoff-finals victory over the Toronto Maple Leafs, the Madison Square Garden owners paid off their $3million mortgage and celebrated by burning the deed in Lord Stanley's cup – an act of desecration that provoked a curse upon the franchise and its fans. The Rangers finally ended their 54-year championship drought in 1994, but their mediocre

32

Street basketball

Free of the image-building and marketing that makes the NBA so superficial, and the by-the-books officiating of the NCAA, **street basketball** presents the game in its purest and, arguably, most attractive form. New York City is the capital of playground hoops, with a host of asphalt legends: Lew Alcindor (Kareem Abdul-Jabbar), Wilt Chamberlain, Julius Irving, and Stephon Marbury are a few who have made it to the pros. If you want to play yourself, *Hoops Nation* by Chris Ballard is an invaluable guide to basketball courts in the five boroughs (and across the nation) and a useful primer in the etiquette of pickup ball. Scout out the next NBA superstar – or look for current ones dropping by for an off-season tune-up.

performance since suggests that the hockey gods may be working on another malediction.

Ticket prices: $28–155; for details on Madison Square Garden and buying tickets, see p.434.

New York Islanders

Founded in 1972, the **Islanders** (℡ 1-800/882-ISLES, ⓦ www .newyorkislanders.com) were fortunate enough to string together their four Stanley Cups in consecutive years (1980–83) and thus qualify as a bona fide hockey dynasty. Since then, however, it's been mostly downhill, though they did have a brief spell of success in 2003–04, when they went 14 for 18.

Ticket prices: $25–140; for details on Nassau Coliseum and buying tickets, see p.434.

New Jersey Devils

The nomadic **New Jersey Devils** franchise (ⓦ www.newjerseydevils .com) was founded in 1974 as the Kansas City Scouts, and moved to New Jersey (after a brief stint as the Colorado Rockies in Denver) in 1982. A succession of mediocre seasons was interrupted when the Devils beat the heavily favored Detroit Red Wings in four straight games to win the 1995 Stanley Cup. They regained the Cup in 2003, but lost it to the Philadelphia Flyers in the first round of the 2004 playoffs. The Devils are reportedly going to move from the Continental to a new arena in Newark, though probably not for another few years.

Ticket prices: $30–75; for details on Continental Airlines Arena and buying tickets, see p.434.

Soccer

The game of **soccer** (European football) continues to grow in popularity in America. While there is a federation of major-league soccer teams that enjoy moderate success, the US national team has performed inconsistently in the last several World Cup tournaments. Though soccer coverage is not as extensive in the US as it is abroad, it's not too hard to catch on TV and in sports bars (see box, opposite). European teams will play at the Meadowlands occasionally during the summer.

The **New York/New Jersey Metrostars** (℡ 201/583-7000, ⓦ www .metrostars.com), who play at Giants Stadium, are the metropolitan area's Major League Soccer representatives. They won the Eastern Division title in 2000 and got as far as the playoff semifinals; their performance since has often been less stellar.

Ticket prices: $18–38; for details on Giants Stadium and buying tickets, see p.434.

Horse racing

The two busiest **horse-racing** tracks in the area are the **Aqueduct Race Track** and the **Belmont Race Track**, both with thoroughbred racing.

Aqueduct (℡ 718/641-4700, ⓦ www .nyra.com/aqueduct) in Howard Beach, Queens, has racing from October through December, and again from January through May. **Belmont** (℡ 516/488-6000, ⓦ www.nyra.com /belmont), in Elmont, Long Island, is home to the Belmont Stakes (June), one of the three races in which three-year-olds compete for the **Triple Crown**. Belmont is open May through July and September through October. Admission at both tracks ranges from $1 to $5 depending on where you park and sit. Valet parking costs $5 at Aqueduct and $6 at Belmont.

Off-Track Betting

To **place a bet** anywhere other than the track itself, find an **OTB (Off-Track Betting)** office. There are plenty around the city; call ℡ 212/221-5200 or check ⓦ www .nycotb.com for locations. You need an established account to place a

Sports bars

The Central Bar 109 E 9th St ☎212/529-5333, ⓦcentralbar.8m.com. Warm, friendly Irish bar showing European football alongside American games.

ESPN Zone 1472 Broadway, at W 42nd St ☎212/921-3776, ⓦespn.go.com/espn-inc/zone. ESPN-affiliated sports bar/restaurant, where you can catch the action from one of 278 screens (even in the bathroom), assuming you can get in.

Jimmy's Corner 140 W 44th St, between Broadway and Sixth Ave ☎212/221-9510. See p.372 for review.

Kinsdale Tavern 1672 Third Ave, at 93rd St ☎212/348-4370. Upper East Side Irish sports bar.

Mickey Mantle's 42 Central Park S, between Fifth and Sixth aves ☎212/688-7777. Perhaps the city's most famous sports bar, packed with memorabilia; it's hard to tell which is more bland, though, the food or the décor.

Ships of Fools 1590 Second Ave, between 82nd and 83rd sts ☎212/570-2651. No matter what the game, the amiable owner at this Upper East Side postgrad hangout will try to put it up for you on one of their sixteen TVs. The bar grub is better than expected.

Stitch 247 37th St, between Seventh and Eighth aves ☎212/852-4826, ⓦwww.stitchnyc.com. See p.372 for review.

phone bet: to set one up, call ☎1-800/OTB-8118.

To watch racing in comfort, try The Inside Track (run by OTB) at 991 Second Ave, at 53rd St (☎212/752-1940), or OTB's two other tele-theaters, the Winner's Circle, 515 Seventh Ave, at 38th St (☎212/730-4900) and the maritime-themed Yankee Clipper, 170 John St, at Water St (☎212/344-5959), with food, drink, schmoozing, and wagering on the premises.

Tennis

The **US Open Championships**, held each September at the National Tennis Center in Flushing Meadows–Corona Park, in Queens, is the top US tennis event of the year. In 1997,

the Flushing complex opened a new center court, the Arthur Ashe Stadium. Tickets go on sale the first week or two of June at the Tennis Center's box office (☎718/760-6200, ⓦwww.usta.com), open Monday through Friday 9am–5pm. Promenade-level seats at the stadium cost $22–69 (better seats can cost several hundred dollars), and seats are more expensive at night and closer to the finals. If they are sold out, keep trying up to the day of the event because corporate tickets are often returned. Tickets for the big matches are incredibly difficult to get – you can either take a chance with scalpers or try your luck at the Will Call window for people who don't show up.

(32)

Tickets and venues

Tickets for most sporting events can be booked ahead with a credit card through Ticketmaster (☎212/307-7171, ⓦwww.ticketmaster.com) and collected at the gate, though it's cheaper – and of course riskier for popular events – to try to pick up tickets on the night of the event. You can also call or go to the stadium's box office and buy advance tickets. If the box office has sold out, call one of the city's many ticketing agencies, which buy large quantities of tickets for resale. Expect to pay a little bit or substantially more, depending on the importance of the game and the seats – look in the *Yellow Pages* under "Tickets," in the back pages of the free city entertainment papers, or the *Village Voice*.

Scalping (reselling a ticket, usually on the day of the event outside the arena, at an inflated price) is illegal; but selling the ticket for face value is generally permitted. If all else fails, simply catch the action on the big screen in a sports bar.

Madison Square Garden Seventh Ave, between 31st and 33rd sts ☏212/465-6741, ⊛www .thegarden.com. Take #1, #2, #3, #A, #C, or #E to 34th St–Penn Station. Box-office hours vary.

Meadowlands Sports Complex containing both Giants Stadium and Continental Airlines Arena, off routes 3, 17, and New Jersey Turnpike exit 16W, East Rutherford, New Jersey ☏201/935-8500, ⊛www.meadowlands.com. Regular buses from Port Authority Bus Terminal on 42nd St and Eighth Ave. Box office open for all arenas Mon–Sat 11am–6pm.

Nassau Coliseum 1255 Hempstead Turnpike, Uniondale ☏516/794-9303, ⊛www .nassaucoliseum.com. Not very accessible other than by car. If you don't have your own transportation, take the Long Island Railroad to Hempstead, then bus #N70, #N71, or #N72 from Hempstead bus terminal, one block away. Another option, which may be safer at night, is to take the LIRR to West-bury and take a cab (5–10min ride) to the stadium. Box office daily 9.30am–4.45pm.

Shea Stadium 126th St, at Roosevelt Ave, Queens ☏718/507-8499, ⊛www.newyork .mets.mlb.com. Take #7 train, direct to Willets Point/Shea Stadium Station. Box office Mon–Fri 9am–6pm, Sat, Sun & holidays 9am–5pm. Dress warmly in early spring and fall: Shea is a windy icebox.

Yankee Stadium 161st St and River Ave, South Bronx ☏718/293-6000, ⊛www.newyork .yankees.mlb.com. Subway #C, #D, or #4 direct to 161st St Station. Box office Mon–Fri 9am–5pm. Get to the game early and visit Monument Park, where all the Yankee greats are memorialized.

Participatory activities

Beaches

New York's **beaches** aren't worth a trip to the city in and of themselves, but they can be a cool summer escape from Manhattan. Most are only a MetroCard ride away.

Brooklyn

Brighton Beach #B and #Q trains to Brighton Beach. Technically the same stretch as Coney Island Beach, but less crowded and popu-lated mainly by the local Russian community. Boardwalk vendors sell ethnic snacks.

Coney Island Beach at the end of half a dozen subway lines: fastest is the #D train to Stillwell Ave. After Rockaway (see below), this is NYC's most popular bathing spot, jam-packed on summer weekends. The Atlantic here is only moderately dirty and there's a good, reliable onshore breeze.

Queens

Jacob Riis Park #2 and #5 trains to Flatbush Ave, then #Q35 bus. Good sandy stretches and very pristine. Some parts are popular with gay men. Nude bathing, once popular here, is no longer permitted.

Rockaway Beach #A and #C trains to any stop along the beach. Forget California: this seven-mile strip is where hundreds of thousands of New Yorkers come to get the best surf around – surf so good that the Ramones even wrote a song about it. Best beaches are at 9th St, 23rd St, and 80–118th sts.

Staten Island

Great Kills Park bus #S103 from Staten Island ferry terminal. Quiet and used by locals.

South Beach bus #S52. Ball fields, rollerblad-ing areas, and low-key beaches.

Wolfe's Pond Park bus #S103 to Main St in Tottenville, at Hylan and Cornelia. Regularly packs in the crowds from New Jersey.

Bicycling

New York has over 100 miles of **cycle paths**; those in Central Park, Riverside Park, and the East River

Promenade are among the nicest. Two sources have done an excellent job of providing specific cycling routes and maps, laws and regulations, and other relevant info: the bike advocacy organization Transportation Alternatives (☎ 212/629-8080, ⓦ www.transalt .org), which has some good maps, and The New York City Department of City Planning (ⓦ www.ci.nyc.ny .us/html/dcp/html/bike/home.html), which has a wealth of information available as part of their BND (Bicycle Network Development) project. You'll find extensive (and download-able) bike maps for all five boroughs, in addition to information on how to use mass transit in planning your bike ride. By law, you must wear a helmet when riding your bike on the street. Most bike stores rent bicycles by the day or hour. (Refer to the *Yellow Pages* or call Loeb Boathouse in Central Park; see p.168.)

Here are some clubs and resources for cycling enthusiasts:

Bicycle Habitat 244 Lafayette St ☎ 212/431-3315, ⓦ bicyclehabitat.com. Known for an excellent repair service, they also offer rentals, tune-ups, and advice.

Critical Mass ⓦ www.critical-mass.org. A grassroots movement whose main agenda is to promote cycling as an alternate means of transportation. Group rides are organized on the last Friday of the month. Place and time decided last minute. Be sure to check the website.

Five Borough Bike Club ☎ 212/932-2300 ext 115, ⓦ www.5bbc.org. This club organizes rides throughout the year, including the Montauk Century, where riders can chose routes varying between 65 and140 miles from New York to Montauk, Long Island.

New York Cycle Club ☎ 212/828-5711, ⓦ www .nycc.org. This 1400-member club offers many rides.

Boating

Downtown Boathouse Hudson River Pier 26, Pier 66A and 72nd St ☎ 646/613-0740 or 613-0375, ⓦ www.downtownboathouse.org. Free kayaks and canoes available for rent May–Oct.

Loeb Boathouse East Side of Central Park, between 74th and 75th sts ☎ 212/517-2233, ⓦ www.centralparknyc.org/virtualpark/thegreat-lawn/loebboathouse. Rowboats for hire March–Oct, daily 10am–5pm. Rates are $10 for the first hour, $2.50 per additional 15 minutes, plus $30 deposit. Bikes and gondola rides, too.

Bowling

Bowlmor Lanes 110 University Place, between 12th and 13th sts ☎ 212/255-8188, ⓦ www .bowlmor.com. Long-established, large disco/bowling alley with a bar and shop. Open Mon, Fri & Sat 11am–4am, Tues, Wed & Sun 11am–1am, Thurs 11am–2am. $6.45 per game per person weekdays before 5pm, $8.45 evenings, weekends and holidays. $5 shoe rental.

Chelsea Piers Lanes W 23rd St and Hudson River ☎ 212/835-2695, ⓦ www.chelseapiers .com. AMF runs a 40-lane alley that occasionally morphs into a laser-lit, Day-Glo alternate universe called Extreme Bowling (nobody under 21 allowed without an adult, although unfortunately, kids are the ones who would most enjoy it). $7.50 per game per person; $8.25 during Extreme Bowling (Fri 9pm–closing, Sat 8pm–closing, Sun 10pm–closing). $4.50 shoe rental.

Fishing

Sometimes the amount of concrete in New York can make you forget that the city is actually surrounded by water, much of it teeming with fish. Call the New York State Department of Health's Center for Environmental Health Information line (☎ 1-800/458-1158) for the latest tips on clean water and if you should toss your catch in the frying pan or back in the current.

The East River consider the 69th Street Pier in Bay Ridge, Brooklyn, and Gantry Plaza State Park in Long Island City, Queens, as possible locations. No permit or license necessary to throw a line after striper, bluefish, weakfish, and flounder.

New York Harbor Sportfishing ☎ 201/451-1988, ⓦ captainjoeshastay.com. Reliable local charter with more than 1900 charters in 12 years. Rates range from $450–550 for a four-and-a-half-hour tour.

Golf

Manhattan has no **public golf courses**, though there is a four-level driving range at Chelsea Piers (T212/336-6400). Recommended among those in the outer boroughs are the following, all of which are subject to low but variable prices; information is available at Wwww .nycparks.org.

Dyker Beach Golf Course 86th St and 11th Ave, Dyker Heights, Brooklyn T718/836-9722. Often noted for its striking views of the Verrazano Narrows, Dyker is also convenient, right near the 86th Street stop on the #R train. Greens fees up to $20.

Split Rock Golf Course & Pelham Golf Course 870 North Shore Rd, Pelham T718/885-1258. Split Rock is considered the most challenging course in the city. Pelham, right next door, is somewhat easier. Greens fees $15–36.

Van Cortlandt Park Golf Course Van Cortlandt Park S and Bailey Ave, Bronx T718/543-4595. The oldest 18-hole public golf course in the country. Greens fees $20–49.

Health and fitness: pools, gyms, and baths

You can join one of the city's **recreation centers** (T212/447-2020, Wwww.nycparks.org) for $50–70 per year (ages 18–54), $10 (seniors), or free (under 18). All have gym facilities; some hold fitness and other classes, and most have an indoor and/or outdoor pool.

Riverbank State Park W 145th St and Riverside Drive T212/694-3600. Beautiful facility built on top of a waste refinery in Harlem. Despite the strange location, it has great tennis courts, an outdoor track, an ice-skating rink, and several indoor facilities including a skating rink and Olympic-sized pool. Park admission is free; pool is $2, seniors and ages 4–15 $1, physically challenged free.

Russian & Turkish Baths 268 E 10th St T212/473-8806 or 674-9250, Wwww .russianturkishbaths.com. A neighborhood landmark that's still going strong, with steam baths, sauna, and an ice-cold pool, as well as a massage parlor and a restaurant. Free soap, towel, robe, slip-

---

Central Park, Chelsea Piers, and the Hudson River Park Project

Central Park is, at 843 acres, the center of the city's recreational life, from croquet to chess to soccer to socializing to sunning to swimming. Joggers, in-line skaters, walkers, and cyclists have the roads to themselves on weekdays 10am–3pm and 7–10pm and all day on weekends and holidays. It is not recommended that you hang out in the park too long after the sun goes down; at any rate, it is closed during the wee hours. To find out what is going on where and when, call T212/310-6600 or look at Wwww.centralparknyc.org. You can also pick up a calendar of events or directory in the park. See Chapter 14, "Central Park," for more information.

Chelsea Piers W 23rd St and the Hudson River (between 17th and 23rd sts) T212/336-6666, Wwww.chelseapiers.com. It features Manhattan's only year-round outdoor golf course (really a driving range), a track, the largest rock-climbing wall in the northeast (as well as a smaller one for kids), basketball courts, a health club, indoor sand volleyball courts, and more. You can also join the crew of the *Adirondack*, a beautiful 78-foot wooden schooner, which sails from Pier 62. During the two-hour sail of lower New York Harbor, passengers can take the wheel, help hoist the sails, or just enjoy the surroundings. Boat operates May–Oct daily 1pm, 3.30pm, 6pm & 8pm; $40–50, includes drinks; T646/336-5270, Wwww.sail-nyc.com.

The **Hudson River Park Project** T212/533-7275, Wwww.hudsonriverpark.org. Twenty years in the planning, the Hudson River Project is a massive redevelopment of the west-side waterfront from Battery Park to 59th St. The project (slated to be completed in 2008) will modify 550 acres of river and shoreline and repair or reconstruct thirteen historic piers for recreational use. Fishing is possible, and any number of sports facilities have already opened or are in the works. A few highlights so far are the Children's Park on **Pier 25** and the Downtown Boathouse on **Pier 26** (for opening times T646/613-0740, Wwww.downtownboathouse.org).

pers, etc. Admission $25, additional fee for massages and other extras. Open Mon, Tues, Thurs & Fri 11am–10pm, Wed 9am–10pm, Sat & Sun 7.30am–10pm; men only Sun opening until 2pm; women only Wed opening until 2pm; co-ed otherwise (shorts are mandatory).

Hiking

For **hikes**, nature walks, and other ambulatory activities around the city, try the following organizations:

Appalachian Mountain Club ☎212/986-1430, Ⓦwww.amc-ny.org or www.outdoors.org. Helpful for getting off the beaten, urban track. You can sail around Fire Island, tour the historic neighborhoods of the five boroughs, or hike scenic Bear Mountain. Activities are good for all ages. National membership $25–50; 4-month chapter guest membership $15.

Shorewalkers ☎212/330-7686, Ⓦwww.shorewalkers.org. This group offers an extensive roster of hikes of different lengths. May's annual Great Saunter ($10) is a 32-mile jaunt around Manhattan. Contribution $3.

Horse riding

Claremont Riding Academy 175 W 89th St ☎212/724-5100. This place hires out ponies for riding on Central Park's 6-mile bridal path. Saddles are English-style; you must be an experienced rider. One hour is $55; lessons $65 per half-hour.

Jamaica Bay Riding Academy 7000 Shore Parkway, Brooklyn ☎718/531-8949, Ⓦwww.horsebackride.com/jbra.htm. Trail riding, both Western and English, around the eerie landscape of Jamaica Bay. $30 for a guided 45min ride; lessons $70 for one hour.

Ice-skating

New York's freezing winter weather makes for good **ice-skating**. The best rinks are in Central and Prospect parks; don't try skating on a lake, as the ice can be deceptively thin.

Lasker Rink 110th St, Central Park ☎212/534-7639, Ⓦwww.centralparknyc.org. This lesser-known ice rink is at the north end of the park, and used as a pool in summer. Much cheaper than the Wollman Rink, though less accessible. $4, under 12 $2.

▽ Skaters in Central Park

Rockefeller Center Ice Rink between 49th and 50th sts, off Fifth Ave ☎212/332-7654. It's a quintessential New York scene, lovely to look at but with long lines and high prices.

Sky Rink Pier 61 ☎212/336-6100, Ⓦwww.chelseapiers.com. Ice-skate year-round at this indoor rink at Chelsea Piers. Daily sessions start at noon, exact times vary. $11, youth and seniors $8.50. Rentals $6.

Wollman Rink 62nd St, Central Park ☎212/439-6900, Ⓦwww.wollmanskatingrink.com. Lovely rink, where you can skate to the marvelous, inspiring backdrop of the lower Central Park skyline – incredibly impressive at night. There's also a Wollman Rink in Prospect Park (Ⓦwww.prospectpark.org). $9.50–12, under 12 $4.75–5, seniors $4.75–8. Rentals $5.

Jogging and running

Jogging is still very much the number-one fitness pursuit in the city. The most popular venue is Central Park. A favorite circuit in the park is the 1.57 miles around the reservoir; just make sure you jog in the right direction – counterclockwise. For company on your runs, contact the New York Road Runners Club (☎212/860-4455, Ⓦwww.nyrrc.org), which sponsors many races and fun runs per year, including the Frostbite 10 Mile and the Brooklyn Half-Marathon, plus numerous other events for runners. The East River

㉜

New York City Marathon

Every year on the first Sunday in November 30,000 runners come to New York to run the **New York City Marathon**. Along with the competitors come the fans: on average, two million people turn out each year to watch the runners try to complete the 26.2-mile course, which starts in Staten Island, crosses the Verrazano Narrows Bridge and passes through all the other boroughs before ending at the *Tavern on the Green* in Central Park. The race is taken very, very seriously, although not with the solemnity usually awarded to home baseball games.

If you are a runner, you can try to take part, but beware: the competition is fierce before the race even starts. Not everyone who submits the necessary entry forms is chosen to participate; race veterans (who have run fifteen or more New York Marathons), qualified New York Road Runners Club (NYRRC) members, and those who have applied and been rejected for the last three NYC marathons receive guaranteed entry, which can also be (completely legitimately) procured for you by a travel agent in your home country. Many athletes with disabilities participate as well; the reigning wheelchair champion holds the time of 1:31:11. Obtain forms from ⓦ www.nycmara-thon.org or the NYRRC. Applications must be sent before May 1 for that year's race (US lottery applications June 1), and you must be at least 18 years old on race day.

Promenade and almost any other stretch of open space long enough to get up speed are also good places to jog.

Pool

Along with bars and nightclubs, a good option for an evening in Manhattan is to play **pool**, not only in dingy but serious halls but also in gleaming bars where well-heeled yuppies mix with the regulars. A number of sports, dive, and gay and lesbian bars have pool tables as well, though these are often much smaller than regulation size. Snooker fans will also find a few tables throughout the city.

Amsterdam Billiards 344 Amsterdam Ave, at 76th St ⓣ212/496-8180, ⓦ amsterdam billiardclub.com. Very popular uptown billiards club with 31 tables. They serve liquor and beer along with bar food.

Corner Billiards 85 Fourth Ave, at E 11th St ⓣ212/995-1314. A sexy but unpretentious 28-table hall popular with locals and students.

Slate 54 W 21st St, between Fifth and Sixth aves ⓣ212/989-0096, ⓦ www.slate-ny.com. Extremely gentrified two-story sports-bar-like Chelsea hall (over 30 tables) that serves better-than-average food and has well-kept facilities. Go during the day when it's less crowded.

Rock climbing

Manhattan's skyline is the Himalayas of cityscapes, and while many have tried (illegally) scaling the city's skyscrapers, the concrete jungle is also full of difficult (and sanctioned) climbing routes. Chelsea Piers has one of the nicest climbing walls in the city (and the largest); see p.436 for more information.

59th Street Rec Center 533 W 59th St, between 10th and 11th aves ⓣ212/397-3159. There are jazzier gyms in the city, but this is headquarters for the City Climbers Club and the yearly membership ($250) or daily passes ($14) are a fraction of what they cost elsewhere.

City Climbers Club ⓣ212/974-2250, ⓦ www .climbnyc.com. Their website has all the info you need on bouldering in Central Park, indoor rock gyms, and people looking for climbing buddies.

Extra Vertical Climbing Center 61 W 62nd St, at Broadway ⓣ212/586-5832, ⓦ www .extravertical.com. Al fresco rock-wall blocks away from Lincoln Center, designed for the "everyman" of the sport. One climb, two tries to the top, and gear for $9. $5 for each additional climb.

SCUBA diving

Sea Gypsies ⓦ www.seagypsies.com. Twenty-five-year-old dive club. Meets second

Wednesday of every month (except December) at various locations.

Village Divers 125 E 4th St, between First and Second aves ☎212/780-0879, ⓦwww.villagedivers.com. Reputable dive shop that specializes in certification classes, gear, and trips.

Tennis

There's not a great deal of court space in New York, so finding an affordable one can be tough. For information on all city courts, including those in Central Park (see below), go to ⓦwww.nyc.gov/parks.

Central Park Tennis Courts ☎212/360-8133. Their $100 permit, which runs from April through November, provides access to all municipal courts in the five boroughs.

Yoga

Still considered esoteric by many visitors, **yoga** has become a day-to-day part of New York's social and recreational life, so the city is a great place to try it for the first time. Classes are offered throughout the day at scores of locations. You'll find all difficulty levels and numerous styles (from traditional forms like *jivamukti* to aerobic hybrids like Yogalates). Yoga studios will also be able to tell you where to practice martial arts and Pilates. If you intend to take a number of sessions, you may want to purchase a New York Yoga PassBook, an excellent deal at $75 for a year of sessions at name workshops throughout the city and suburbs (☎212/808-0765, ⓦwww.health-fitness.org/ny.html). From spring through fall, many outdoor classes are free; check *Time Out New York* and contact major parks and gardens for more information.

Om Yoga 826 Broadway ☎212/254-9642, ⓦwww.omyoga.com. Many classes for beginners, plus more advanced workshops. Includes meditation. $16 per session, $25 two introductory classes, $1 mat rental.

Yoga Center of Brooklyn 474 Smith St, at 9th St ☎718/858-4554, ⓦwww.brooklynyoga.com. Carroll Gardens newbie offering strenuous classes at all levels and in different styles, informed by ideas of wellness and spirituality. $15 per session.

Participatory activities | **SPORTS AND OUTDOOR ACTIVITIES**

(32)

Parades and festivals

New York City takes its numerous **parades and festivals** extremely seriously. They are often political or religious in origin, but as in most of the world, whatever their official reason for existing, they are generally just an excuse for music, food, and dance. Almost every large ethnic group in the city holds an annual get-together, often using Fifth Avenue as the main drag. In general, it is a big mistake to drive, take a taxi, or ride the buses anywhere near these events.

Chances are, your stay will coincide with at least one festive happening. For more details and exact dates of the events listed below, phone ☎ 1-800/NYC-VISIT or go to ⓦ www.nycvisit.com. Also look at listings in the *Village Voice*'s "Voice Choices" and *Time Out New York*'s "Around Town" sections.

January

Jewish Film Festival (mid–late Jan ☎ 212/496-3809 or 875-5600, ⓦ www.filmlinc.com): Screenings of complex, provocative Jewish films with an international bent, as well as some rare oldies. Films are shown at Lincoln Center's Walter Reade Theater.

Lunar (Chinese) New Year (first full moon between Jan 21 and Feb 19 ⓦ www.explorechinatown.com): A noisy, joyful occasion celebrated for two weeks along and around Mott Street in Lower Manhattan, as

well as in Sunset Park, Brooklyn, and Flushing, Queens. The chances of getting a meal without a reservation anywhere in Manhattan's Chinatown during this time are slim.

Martin Luther King Jr Day Tributes (third Mon ☎ 718/636-4100, ⓦ www.bam.org): City-wide celebration honoring Dr King's contribution to civil rights and African-American heritage. The free talks and performances at the Brooklyn Academy of Music are the day's most notable occurences.

Outsider Art Fair (late Jan ☎ 212/777-5218, ⓦ www.sanfordsmith.com): Leading dealers of outsider, primitive, visionary, and intuitive art exhibit their collections at the Puck Building, 295–309 Lafayette St, at Houston St.

Restaurant Week (late Jan–early Feb ☎ 212/484-1200, ⓦ www.restaurantweek.com): For about ten weekdays, you can get prix-fixe three-course lunches at some of the city's finest establishments for $25, or three-course dinners for $35. This can be quite a savings at restaurants like *Aquavit* and *Nobu*, though the limited menus don't always show off the cuisine at its best, and you must make reservations months in advance for the most desirable places. Also in July.

▽ Chinese New Year Parade

Street fairs

In various sections of the city on weekend afternoons in the spring, summer, and fall, **street fairs** close a stretch of several blocks to traffic to offer pedestrians T-shirts, curios, and gut-busting snacks like sausage sandwiches and fried dough. Unfortunately, once you've seen one, you've seen them all, as the vendors are rarely neighborhood-specific. You'll find the most local flavor at the raucously tacky Feast of San Gennaro (see p.445), which could be called the prototypical street fair. Heading to the outer boroughs often yields more character too – you might happen across *lucha libre* (Mexican wrestling) along with the usual fare.

Street fairs are usually listed in *Time Out New York* and neighborhood newspapers. Smaller block parties, sponsored by community groups rather than business organizations, are more intimate affairs, generally with one sidestreet closed to cars, kids performing, politicos popping in to shake hands, and everyone taking part in a huge pot-luck meal. They're typically not advertised, however, so consider yourself lucky to stumble on one.

February

Westminster Kennel Club Dog Show (mid-Feb ☎212/213-3165, ⓦwww.westminster kennelclub.org): Second only to the Kentucky Derby as the oldest continuous sporting event in the country, this show at Madison Square Garden welcomes 2500 canines competing for best in breed, along with legions of fanatic dog-lovers.

March

New York Underground Film Festival (mid-March ☎212/614-2775, ⓦwww.nyuff.com): Experimental video, fringy political documentaries, animated shorts, and more at this catch-all, way-out-of-the-mainstream event at the Anthology Film Archives, 32 Second Ave, at 2nd St.
St Patrick's Day Parade (March 17 ☎212/484-1222, ⓦwww.saintpatricksdayparade.com): Based on an impromptu march through the Manhattan streets by Irish militiamen on St Patrick's Day in 1762, this parade is a draw for every Irish band and organization in the US and Ireland, and it's impressive for the sheer mobs of people – no cars or floats

are allowed. Gay and lesbian groups have long been prohibited from marching, but they have a vocal presence on the sidelines. Starting around 11am at St Patrick's Cathedral on Fifth Ave (following 8.30am Mass), it heads uptown to 86th St.
Greek Independence Day Parade (late March ☎718/204-6500, ⓦwww.greekparade.org): Not as long or as boozy as St Pat's, more a patriotic nod to the old country from floats of pseudo-classically dressed Hellenes. When Independence Day (March 25) falls in the Orthodox Lent, the parade is shifted to April or May. It usually kicks off from 60th St and Fifth Ave and runs up to 79th St.

April

Macy's Flower Show (early April ☎212/494-4495): Thirty thousand species of fragrant flowers, plants, and trees, plus lush landscapes and global gardens in Herald Square. The schedule coincides with Easter, so occasionally the show begins in March.

Easter Parade (Easter Sun ☎212/360-8111, ⓦwww.nycgovparks.org): Evoking the old fashion parade on the city's most stylish avenue, hundreds of people promenade up Fifth Ave in elaborate, flower-bedecked Easter bonnets. There's also usually an "Eggstravaganza," a free children's festival including an egg-rolling contest, on the Lower Forty Acres in Central Park.

New Directors, New Films (early April ⊙ 212/875-5638, ⊛ www.filmlinc.com): Lincoln Center and MoMA present this two-week series, one of the city's best, but rarely surrounded by hype. Films range from the next indie hits to obscure, never-to-be-seen-again works of genius, and the majority of the filmmakers are from other countries. Tickets go on sale several weeks before the beginning of the festival (which sometimes starts in late March), and films with a lot of buzz will sell out.

May

Sakura Matsuri: Cherry Blossom Festival (early May ⊙ 718/623-7200, ⊛ www.bbg.org/exp/cherrywatch):** Music, art, dance, traditional fashion, and sword-fighting demonstrations celebrate Japanese culture and the brief, sublime blossoming of the Brooklyn Botanic Garden's 200 cherry trees. Free with garden admission.

Five Boro Bike Tour (early May ⊙ 212/932-2453, ⊛ www.bikenewyork.org):** Cars are banished from the route of this 42-mile ride through all five boroughs, and some 30,000 cyclists take to the streets.

Ukrainian Festival (mid-May ⊙ 646/472-5388): East 7th St between Second and Third aves is filled with marvelous Ukrainian costumes,

Summer outdoor fun

Summer arts programs are nice treats for those who stay in the city through the muggiest months. As most of these shows are free or at least very cheap, they're swarmed with fun-seeking New Yorkers – plan on arriving very early to stake out a picnic spot on the grass, and book tickets ahead when possible.

Bryant Park Summer Film Festival (late June–Aug ⊙ 212/512-5700, ⊛ www.bryantpark.org): Each Monday night picnickers watch classic films like *Breakfast at Tiffany's* on the lush lawn of Bryant Park. Get there very early, and bring a lawn chair.

Celebrate Brooklyn (June–Aug ⊙ 718/855-7882, ⊛ www.celebratebrooklyn.org): One of New York's longest-running free music series, at the band shell in Prospect Park; great Latin performances, among others; $3 donation requested.

Midsummer Night Swing (mid-June–mid-July ⊙ 212/875-5766, ⊛ www.lincolncenter.org/programs/swing_home.asp): At Lincoln Center's Josie Robertson Plaza, 66th St at Broadway, every Tuesday through Saturday evening; learn a different dance en masse each night to the rhythm of live swing, mambo, merengue, samba, or country. Free lessons at 6.30pm, music and dancing ($15) at 7.30pm.

New York Philharmonic (June–Aug ⊙ 212/875-5656, ⊛ www.newyorkphilharmonic.org): Free summer events at the Great Lawn in Central Park; bring a picnic basket and blanket.

River to River Festival (June–Sept ⊙ 718/417-7362, ⊛ www.rivertorivernyc.com): Big-name performers in pop and world music and dance take the stage in Battery Park, Roosevelt Park, and elsewhere in Lower Manhattan; free.

Rooftop Films (June–Sept ⊙ 718/417-7362, ⊛ www.rooftopfilms.com): Set on factory roofs in Brooklyn, this movie series offers one of the niftiest backdrops for watching hip indie shorts; $8.

Shakespeare in the Park (June–Aug ⊙ 212/539-8500, ⊛ www.publictheater.org): Film and theater stars perform in the Bard's plays, plus other classics, at Central Park's Delacorte Theater. Some of the best-quality theater of the season, though you must queue for the free tickets, in what is one of the city's classic crowd frenzies.

SummerStage (June–Aug ⊙ 212/360-2756, ⊛ www.summerstage.org): Free concerts with an international bent, along with dance performances and storytelling in Central Park's Rumsey Playfield.

folk music and dance, plus foods and traditional crafts like egg-painting, during this weekend festival.

Salute to Israel Parade (late May ☎212/245-8200, ⓦwww.salutetoisrael.com): This celebration of Israeli independence attempts to display unity within New York's ideologically and religiously diverse Jewish community.

On Fifth Ave, between 57th and 79th sts, rain or shine.

Fleet Week (end of May ⓦwww.fleetweek .navy.mil): The boisterous annual welcome of sailors from the US, Canada, Mexico, and the UK, among others, with ceremonies at the Intrepid Sea, Air & Space Museum.

June

Museum Mile Festival (first Tues evening ☎212/606-2296, ⓦwww.museummilefestival .org): On Fifth Ave from 82nd to 105th sts. Museums, including the Museum of the City of New York, the Jewish Museum, the Guggenheim, the Met, and others are open free 6–9pm.

American Crafts Festival (early June ☎973/746-0091, ⓦwww.craftsatlincoln.org): Over two weekends in June, entertainment and food accompany the juried exhibits at Lincoln Center.

National Puerto Rican Day Parade (second Sun ☎718/401-0404, ⓦwww.national puertoricandayparade.org): The largest of several buoyant Puerto Rican celebrations in the city: seven hours of bands, flag-waving, and baton-twirling from 44th to 86th sts on Fifth Ave, with an estimated two million people in attendance.

Mermaid Parade (first Sat after June 21 ☎718/372-5159, ⓦwww.coneyislandusa .com): At this outstanding event, partici-

pants dress like mermaids, fish, and King Neptune, and saunter down the Coney Island boardwalk, led by assorted offbeat celebs like David Byrne and Queen Latifah. Don't miss it.

Dyke March (fourth Sat ☎212/479-8520, ⓦwww.nycdykemarch.org): This technically illegal march rallies a diverse group of lesbian and bisexual women, from youngsters to topless grannies, at Bryant Park to protest discrimination.

Pride Week (third or fourth week of June ☎212/807-7433, ⓦwww.hopinc.org): The world's biggest lesbian, gay, bisexual, and transgender Pride event kicks off with a rally and ends with a march down Fifth Ave, a street fair in Greenwich Village, and a huge last-night dance.

JVC Jazz Festival (mid-June ☎212/501-1390, ⓦwww.festivalproductions.net): The jazz world's top names appear at Carnegie Hall, the Beacon, and other venues around the city.

July

Washington Square Music Festival (mid-July– mid-Aug ☎212/252-3621, ⓦwww .washingtonsquaremusicfestival.org): Since 1953, a series of classical, jazz, and big-band concerts, every Tues night, at this outdoor venue.

Festa del Giglio (mid-July ☎718/384-0223, ⓦwww.olmcfeast.com): Havemeyer St between N 8th and N 11th sts in Williamsburg is taken over by this ten-day Catholic street festival, which centers around a procession of a giant wooden boat and a figure of St Paulinus on an 85-foot tower.

Mostly Mozart (late July–late Aug ☎212/875-5766, ⓦwww.lincolncenter.org): More than forty concerts and Mozart-themed events at

Lincoln Center, in the longest-running indoor summer festival in the US.

International African Arts Festival (first weekend ☎718/638-6700, ⓦwww.international africanartsfestival.com): Music and dance, both American and African, as well as a parade, talent contest, and children's programs, at Commodore Barry Park in Brooklyn.

Independence Day (July 4 ☎212/494-4495): The fireworks above the East River are visible from all over Manhattan, but the best places to view them are the South Street Seaport, the Esplanade in Brooklyn Heights, or the waterfront in Greenpoint or Williamsburg, starting at about 9pm. The

Antiques-lovers can find plenty of treasures in New York; these are only a few of the city's notable annual expos.

Winter Antiques Show (late Jan ☎718/292-7392, ⓦwww.winterantiquesshow.com): Foremost American antiques show, at the Seventh Regiment Armory, Park Ave and 67th St.

New York Antiquarian Book Fair (mid-April ☎212/944-8291, ⓦwww.abaa.org): Collection of rare books, letters, drawings, etc, held at the Seventh Regiment Armory. Get free appraisals of up to five items on "Discovery Day"; $15 admission per day.

WFMU Record Fair (early Nov ☎207/521-1416, ⓦwww.wfmu.org): Everything from ancient 78s to 1980s hip-hop is up for grabs in this celebration of vintage vinyl at the Metropolitan Pavilion, 125 W 18th St; $5 admission per day.

Park Avenue Antiques Show (Nov ☎212/288-3588): At Park Ave and 84th St, in St Ignatius Loyola Church, a small show with quality antiques at relatively affordable prices.

Triple Pier Expo (two weekends, mid-Nov ☎212/255-0020, ⓦwww.stellashows .com): Largest metropolitan antiques fair, including vintage clothing, on piers 88, 90, and 92, at 50th St on the west side. Also in late March.

---

crowds are unimaginable, especially on FDR Drive below 42nd St, which is closed to cars; if you do come here, know that there are no restrooms in the area, nor any kind of refreshment vendors.

New York City Tap Festival (early July ☎646/230-9564, ⓦwww.nyctapfestival.com): This week-long festival features hundreds of tap dancers who perform and give workshops.

Bastille Day (Sun closest to July 14 ☎212/355-6100, ⓦwww.fiaf.org): Celebrate with the Alliance Française and numerous notable

French restaurants on 60th St between Lexington and Fifth aves.

Asian American International Film Festival (mid-July ☎212/989-1422, ⓦwww.asiancinevision .org): New films from Asia and the Asian diaspora, held at the Walter Reade Theater.

Restaurant Week (mid-July): See p.440.

New York International Latino Film Festival (late July ☎212/726-2358 or 265-8452, ⓦwww .nylatinofilm.com): Mainstream and independent films by Latinos presented at several Midtown East locations.

August

Harlem Week (all month ☎212/862-8473, ⓦwww.harlemdiscover.com): What began as a week-long festival around Harlem Day on Aug 20 has stretched into a month of African, Caribbean, and Latin performances, lectures, and parties; some events in Sept and Oct too.

Hong Kong Dragon Boat Festival (first weekend in Aug ☎718/767-1776, ⓦwww.hkdbf-ny.org): Flushing Meadows is the site of this highly competitive race of 38-foot-long sculls, for which huge Chinese crowds turn out.

New York International Fringe Festival (mid–late Aug ☎212/279-4488, ⓦwww .fringenyc.org): With more than two hundred

companies performing at various downtown venues, this cutting-edge series is the biggest for performance art, theater, dance, puppetry, and more, offering the chance to see the hit shows before they move to bigger stages.

HOWL! Festival of East Village Arts (late Aug ☎212/505-2225, ⓦwww.howlfestival.com): Eight days devoted to the Beats and other neighborhood heroes, with an Allen Ginsberg Poetry Fest, a Charlie Parker jazz jam, and the great drag extravaganza Wigstock; in and around Tompkins Square Park.

September

West Indian–American Day Parade and Carnival (Labor Day ☎718/467-1797, ⓦwww.wiadca .com): Brooklyn's largest parade, modeled after the carnivals of Trinidad and Tobago, features music, food, dance, floats with enormous sound systems, and scores of steel-drum bands – not to mention more than a million attendees.

Broadway on Broadway (mid-Sept ☎212/768-1560, ⓦwww.broadwayonbroadway.com): Free performances featuring songs by casts of the major Broadway musicals, culminating in a shower of confetti; held in Times Square.

Feast of San Gennaro (ten days in mid-Sept ☎212/226-6427, ⓦwww.sangennaro.org): Since 1927, the festival has celebrated the patron saint of Naples along Mulberry St and its environs in Little Italy, with a cannoli-eating contest, midway games, and tasty things to eat. In three parades (the largest

is Sept 19, the saint's day), a San Gennaro statue is carried through the streets with donations pinned to his cloak.

African–American Day Parade (late Sept ☎212/862-7200): Drumlines, step-dancers, and other marchers parade through Harlem from 111th St and Adam Clayton Powell Blvd to 142nd St, then east toward Fifth Ave.

New York Film Festival (two weeks in late Sept ☎212/875-5600, ⓦwww.filmlinc.com): One of the world's leading film festivals unreels at Lincoln Center; tickets can be very hard to come by, as anticipated art hits get their debuts here.

Next Wave Festival (Oct–Nov ☎718/636-4100, ⓦwww.bam.org): Consistently excellent experimental arts festival at the Brooklyn Academy of Music, bringing the likes of Pina Bausch and Laurie Anderson to the stage in elaborate productions since 1981.

October

Pulaski Day Parade (early Oct ☎718/499-0026, ⓦwww.pulaskiparade.com): On Fifth Ave, for the celebration of Polish heritage.

Autumn Crafts on Columbus (first three weekends of Oct ☎212/866-2239): Crafts fair held on Columbus Ave behind the American Museum of Natural History.

Columbus Day Parade (second Mon ☎212/249-9923, ⓦwww.columbuscitizensfd.org): On Fifth Ave between 49th and 79th sts, one of the city's largest binges commemorates Italian-American heritage and the day America was put on the map. Parallel events celebrate the heritage of American Indians and other native peoples.

Open House New York (mid-Oct ☎212/626-6869, ⓦwww.ohny.org): For one weekend, take tours of more than 175 landmark buildings, eco-friendly structures, and other

remarkable architectural spaces in all five boroughs, most of which are usually closed to the public.

DUMBO Art Under the Bridge Festival (mid-Oct ☎718/624-3772, ⓦwww.dumboartscenter.org/ festival): More than 200 resident artists show their work in open studios, bands perform, and bizarre installations fill the streets in the stylish waterfront neighborhood in Brooklyn.

Affordable Art Fair (late Oct ☎212/255-2003, ⓦwww.aafnyc.com): A week of art sales for which everything is priced less than $5000, held at the Metropolitan Pavilion, 125 W 18th St.

Village Halloween Parade (Oct 31 ☎212/475-3333 ext 14044, ⓦwww.halloween-nyc.com): In America's largest Halloween celebration, starting at 7pm on Sixth Ave at Spring St and making its way up to 23rd, you'll

PARADES AND FESTIVALS

㉝

Macy's Parade Inflation Eve

See Mickey Mouse and the other characters being inflated the night before **Macy's Thanksgiving Day Parade**. It's not as crowded as on parade day, and you can experience something not broadcast to every home in America. The giant nylon balloons are set up on West 77th and 81st streets between Central Park West and Columbus Avenue at the American Museum of Natural History. Wander around the feet of these giants and watch them gradually take shape.

see spectacular costumes, giant puppets, bands, and any other bizarre stuff New Yorkers can muster. Get there early for a good viewing spot; marchers (anyone in costume is eligible) line up at 6pm. (A tamer children's parade usually takes place earlier that day in Washington Square Park.)

November

New York City Marathon (first Sun ☎212/423-2249, ⓦwww.ingnycmarathon.org): Some 30,000 runners from all over the world – from the Kenyan champs to regular folks in goofy costumes – assemble for this 26.2-mile run on city pavement through the five boroughs. One of the best places to watch is Central Park S, almost at the finish line.

Veterans Day Parade (Nov 11 ☎212/693-1476): The United War Veterans sponsor this annual event on Fifth Ave from 23rd to 59th sts. Ceremony at 10.15am, salute and parade at 11am.

Chocolate Show (mid-Nov ☎1-866/CHOC-NYC, ⓦwww.chocolateshow.com): A massive celebration of all things cocoa-based, held at the Metropolitan Pavilion, 125 W 18th St, includes vendors' booths, demonstrations, plenty of free samples, and even couture made of the sweet stuff.

Macy's Thanksgiving Day Parade (Thanksgiving Day ☎212/494-4495, ⓦwww.macysparade. com): A made-for-TV extravaganza, with big corporate floats, dozens of marching bands from around the country, and Santa Claus's first appearance of the season. Some two million spectators watch it along Central Park W from 77th St to Columbus Circle, and along Broadway down to Herald Square, 9am–noon.

Rockefeller Center Christmas Tree Lighting (late Nov ☎212/632-3975, ⓦwww.rockefellercenter .com): Switching on the lights on the enormous tree in front of the ice rink begins the holiday season, in a glowing moment sure to warm even the most Grinch-like heart. The crowds, however, can be oppressive.

African Diaspora Film Festival (late Nov–early Dec ☎212/864-1760, ⓦwww.nyadff.org): Films from throughout the world, by and about people of African descent, are shown at several Manhattan venues.

December

Holiday Windows (beginning around Dec 1): The windows on Fifth Ave, especially those of Lord & Taylor and Saks Fifth Avenue, are displays of fantasy and flair; Barneys, on Madison Ave, always does a tongue-in-cheek take on the tradition. Prepare for crowds, or go immediately after Christmas.

Out of the Darkness (early Dec ☎212/620-7310, ⓦwww.gaycenter.org): Several days of events in honor of World AIDS Day (Dec 1), including a large vigil, sponsored by the LGBT Community Center and others.

Dyker Heights Christmas Lights (early Dec–Jan 1): This Brooklyn neighborhood (between 79th and 86th sts and 11th and 13th aves) is renowned for its over-the-top approach to holiday home-decorating. Take the #R to 86th Street in Brooklyn and walk east.

Hanukkah Celebrations (usually mid-Dec): During the eight nights of this Jewish feast, a menorah-lighting ceremony takes place at Brooklyn's Grand Army Plaza (☎718/778-6000), and the world's largest menorah is illuminated on Fifth Ave near Central Park (☎212/736-8400).

Kwanzaa (mid-Dec ☎212/568-1645, ⓦwww .africanfolkheritagecircle.org): Celebrations city-wide, including a story-telling show by the African Folk Heritage Circle in Harlem.

New Year's Eve in Times Square (Dec 31 ☎212/768-1560, ⓦwww.timessquarebid.org): Several hundred thousand revelers party in the cold and well-guarded streets – a crowd-management nightmare, so take the subway and get where you're going early. Elsewhere in the city, you can choose from alcohol-free singles bashes, all-out clubbing, or calmer activities, like meditation marathons.

Kids' New York

I t may come as a bit of a surprise, but New York can be quite a wonderful place to bring **children**. Obvious attractions like museums, theaters, skyscrapers, ferry rides, and all the diversions of Central Park will certainly thrill them, but a visit with kids may also give you reason to appreciate the simpler pleasures of the city, from watching street entertainers to introducing your youngsters to strange foods and fascinating neighborhoods like Chinatown. The city is full of high-caliber free events aimed at children, especially in the summer; puppet shows, garden plantings, cultural celebrations in the city's parks, and storytelling hours at local libraries and bookstores are all excellent ways to entertain. Many museums and theaters also feature specific children's programs. Following are details on some attractions especially appealing to kids. Make sure to phone ahead for specific times, events, and availability to avoid any disappointment.

General advice

For a **listing** of what's available when you're in town, see the detailed NYCk-idsARTS Cultural Calendar (free; ⓦ www.nyckidsarts.org). *Time Out New York* (and the extra-specialized *TONY Kids*), the *Village Voice*, and websites such as ⓦ www.gocitykids.com are also valuable resources. A solid directory of family-oriented events all around the city is available through NYC & Co., the convention and visitors bureau, 810 Seventh Ave between 52nd and 53rd streets (Mon–Fri 8.30am–6pm, Sat & Sun 9am–5pm; ☏ 212/484-1222, ⓦ www .nycvisit.com).

Once in the city, your main problem won't be finding stuff to do with your kids, but transporting the younger ones and keeping your eyes on the older ones. Though some natives navigate the streets and subway stairs with strollers, most prefer to keep infants and even toddlers conveniently contained in a backpack or front carrier – ultimately a much better way of getting around with small children. Indeed, many attractions do not allow strollers, though some will store yours for you while you visit – call ahead for details. Most sights, restaurants, and stores, however, are at the very least quite tolerant of children.

Subways are the fastest way to get around and are perfectly safe – don't worry about taking your young ones on them; in fact, they will probably get a kick out of them, crowds, noise, and all. Buses are slower, but antsy or bored kids can stare through the large windows at the hustle and bustle outside. As a bonus, children under 44 inches (112cm) ride free on the subway and buses when accompanied by an adult.

The **Babysitters' Guild**, 60 E 42nd St (℡212/682-0227, ⓦwww.babysittersguild
.com), offers childcare services with carefully selected staff, most of whom have teaching and nursing backgrounds; sixteen foreign languages are spoken. Fees are $20 an
hour, four hours minimum, plus $4.50 to cover transportation ($7 after midnight). The
organization is fully licensed and bonded. Book as far in advance as you can.
Check ⓦwww.gocitykids.com for many more childcare options.

Finally, if all else fails, or if you want some quiet time to enjoy the city's more
mature offerings, just hire a **babysitter** (see box, above).

Museums

You could spend an entire holiday just checking out the city's many **museums**,
almost all of which contain something fascinating for kids. The following is a
brief overview of the ones that tend to evoke special enthusiasm. See the appropriate Guide chapters for more details on these and other museums.

American Museum of Natural History and the Rose Center for Earth and Space

Central Park W at 79th St ℡212/769-5100,
ⓦwww.amnh.org. Daily 10am–5.45pm, Rose
Center Fri until 8.45pm. IMAX shows 10.30am–
4.30pm, every hour on the half-hour Mon–Thurs,
Sat & Sun 10am–4.30pm, Fri 10am–7.30am.
Suggested donation $14, children $8, students/
seniors $10.50 (includes the Rose Center).
Special exhibits and IMAX additional charge;
combination packages available.
One of the best museums of its kind, this
enormous complex is filled with fossils,
gems, meteorites, and other natural objects
(more than 34 million in all). Your first stop
should be the **Fossil Halls**, where you'll
find towering dinosaur skeletons and interactive computer stations that are sure to
please all ages. Other halls are dedicated
to more contemporary beasts: a full-scale
herd of elephants dominates the **Akeley
Hall of African Mammals**, a 94-foot-long
blue whale hangs over the **Milstein Hall of
Ocean Life**, and the **Hall of Biodiversity**
offers video presentations about the world's
environment and a multimedia recreation of
a Central African rain forest. In the winter, the
Butterfly Conservatory is a sure hit with
younger children. Weekends bring special
events for families, including very young kids.
Just across from the Hall of Biodiversity lies
the **Rose Center for Earth and Space**,

which features the Space Theater, the Big
Bang Theater (in which the beginning of the
universe is recreated every half-hour), and
the lavish **Hayden Planetarium**, among
other awesome attractions.

American Museum of the Moving Image

35th Ave at 36th St, Astoria, Queens ℡718/784-
0077, ⓦwww.ammi.org. Wed & Thurs 11am–
5pm, Fri 11am–8pm, Sat & Sun 11am–6.30pm;
$10, students & seniors $7.50, children $5, free
Fri 4–8pm (museum admission includes film
screening on weekend afternoons).
This museum, attached to Kaufman Astoria Studios (see p.271), is dedicated to
all aspects of film, video, and TV production. Its exhibit halls are filled with historic
costumes, cameras, and props, including
a trove of *Seinfeld* paraphernalia. Kids can
see demos of movie special effects, mug
for do-it-yourself animated flipbooks, play
classic video games, and watch vintage
adventure serials in a lovely recreation of an
old-fashioned movie palace. Definitely worth
a visit, especially for kids 6 and older.

Brooklyn Children's Museum

145 Brooklyn Ave, at St Mark's Ave ℡718/735-
4400, ⓦwww.bchildmus.org. Summer Tues–Fri
1–6pm, Sat & Sun 11am–6pm; fall to spring
Wed–Fri 1–6pm, Sat & Sun 11am–6pm; open
most school holidays; suggested donation $4.
Founded in 1899, this was the world's first

museum designed specifically for children. It's full of authentic ethnological, historical, and technological artifacts with which kids can play, plus live animals, including a 17-foot-long Burmese python. The museum's space – it's largely underground – creates a cool atmosphere; a new street-level wing with an emphasis on "green" learning is scheduled to open in late 2007.

Children's Museum of Manhattan

212 W 83rd St, between Broadway and Amsterdam Ave ☎212/721-1234, ⓦwww.cmom.org. Wed–Sun 10am–5pm; $8, under age 1 free.
This terrific participatory museum, founded in 1937, has five floors full of imaginative displays that involve a lot of clambering around. Older children can produce their own television shows in the Media Center, and exhibits often have a hip edge – Andy Warhol's kid-friendly art, for instance. Highly recommended for children ages 1–12.

Children's Museum of the Arts

182 Lafayette St, between Broome and Grand sts ☎212/941-9198, ⓦwww.cmany.org. Wed–Sun noon–5pm, Thurs until 6pm; $8, pay what you wish Thurs 4–6pm; under 1 year free.
At this gallery, children are encouraged to look at different types of art and then create their own with paints, clay, plaster of paris, and other simple media. Holiday special events are particularly interesting – African mask-making for Kwanzaa, for example.

Admission includes various dance, movie, and music programs on weekends.

Intrepid Sea, Air & Space Museum

Pier 86, W 46th St at Twelfth Ave ☎212/245-0072, ⓦwww.intrepidmuseum.org. April–Sept Mon–Fri 10am–5pm, Sat & Sun 10am–6pm; Oct–March Tues–Sun 10am–5pm; $16.50, kids 6–17 $11.50, kids 2–5 $4.50.
Even non-military-minded kids will be impressed by the massive scale of this aircraft-carrier-cum-museum – not to mention the huge collection of airplanes and helicopters. Especially nifty: the close quarters of the *USS Growler* submarine, moored next to the *Intrepid* (entry limited to age 6 and up). Last admission is one hour before closing.

Museum of the City of New York

1220 Fifth Ave, at 103rd St ☎212/534-1672, ⓦwww.mcny.org. Tues–Sun 10am–5pm; suggested donation $7, students & seniors $5, families $15.
The "New York Toy Stories" exhibit showcases dollhouses, old-fashioned toys, and fantasy objects like Eloise's life-sized room at the *Plaza*. Kids will also have fun identifying the city's landmarks, depicted in paintings in the picture gallery.

New York City Fire Museum

278 Spring St, between Hudson and Varick sts ☎212/691-1303, ⓦwww.nycfiremuseum.org.

▽ New York City Fire Museum

(34)

Tues–Sat 10am–5pm, Sun 10am–4pm; suggested donation $5, students and seniors $2, under 12 $1.
A sure hit with the preschool crowd, this space pays pleasing homage to New York City's firefighters. On display are fire engines from yesteryear (hand-drawn, horse-drawn, and steam-powered), helmets, dog-eared photos, and a host of motley objects on three floors of a former fire station. A neat and appealing display, even though it's not full of interactive doodads.

New York Hall of Science

47-01 111th St, at 46th Ave, Flushing Meadows–Corona Park, Queens ⓣ718/699-0005, ⓦwww.nyhallsci.org. July & Aug Mon–Fri 9.30am–5pm, Sat & Sun 10am–6pm; Sept–June Tues–Thurs 9.30am–2pm, Fri 9.30am–5pm, Sat & Sun 10am–5pm; $11, students & children $8.
Housed in a glowing blue tower built for the 1964–65 World's Fair, this is one of the top science museums in the country. A highlight is the outdoor Science Playground (open March–Dec; an additional $3), where kids can clamber around as they learn about scientific principles. Located in Queens, the Hall of Science makes for a good day-trip combined with a visit to Shea Stadium, the Queens Zoo, or the Queens Museum of Art, all nearby.

New York Transit Museum

Old subway entrance at Schermerhorn St and Boerum Place, Brooklyn ⓣ718/694-1600, ⓦwww.mta.info/mta/museum. Tues–Fri 10am–4pm, Sat & Sun noon–5pm; $5, children & seniors $3. Also: Transit Museum Gallery and Store at Grand Central Terminal, open daily; free.
Housed in an abandoned 1930s subway station, this museum offers more than a hundred years of transportation memorabilia, including old subway cars and buses dating back to the turn of the nineteenth century. Frequent activities for kids include underground tours, workshops, and an annual bus festival – all best for younger school kids. It's a quick hop on the subway, but if you don't want to go to Brooklyn, at least stop in to the museum's annex, at Grand Central in Manhattan, which has its own rotating exhibits.

South Street Seaport Museum

207 Front St, at the east end of Fulton St at the East River ⓣ212/748-8758, ⓦwww.southstseaport.org. Nov–March daily 10am–5pm, April–Oct Tues–Sun 10am–6pm; $8, students & seniors $6, ages 5–12 $4.
South Street Seaport's dock is home to a small fleet of historic ships that kids are welcome to tour, including a nicely preserved 1893 fishing schooner, a merchant vessel with a towering mast, and a hard-working harbor tugboat. With some planning, you may even be able to go out on one of the crafts for a harbor tour (summers only). The museum building itself will seem staid in comparison to the boats.

Staten Island Children's Museum

Snug Harbor Cultural Center, 1000 Richmond Terrace, Staten Island ⓣ718/273-2060, ⓦwww.statenislandkids.org. Tues–Fri noon–5pm, Sat & Sun 10am–5pm; $5, grandparents free Wed.
This is a good way to round off a trip on the Staten Island ferry; the #S40 bus runs from the ferry terminal. Expect, among other things, giant chess sets, a small-scale playhouse complete with costumes, a great exhibit about bugs that includes a human-size anthill, and an outdoor play area on the water where kids can sail boats and learn about oysters.

Sights and entertainment

Again, this is just a small selection of the top attractions children will enjoy:

Brooklyn Botanic Garden

1000 Washington Ave ⓣ718/623-7200, ⓦwww.bbg.org. April–Sept Tues–Fri 8am–6pm, Sat, Sun & holidays 10am–6pm; Oct–March Tues–Fri 8am–4.30pm, Sat, Sun & holidays 10am–4.30pm; $5, students & seniors $3, free Tues, Sat before noon, Nov–Feb weekdays; seniors free Fri.
This gorgeous landscape behind the Brooklyn Museum of Art is very child-friendly, with giant carp in the ponds and ducks to chase around. Parents can drop in to the "Discovery Garden" program, Tues during

the summer starting at 2pm. Families crowd the place for special seasonal events like the Cherry Blossom Festival in late April.

Bronx Zoo

Bronx River Parkway at Fordham Rd ℡718/367-1010, Ⓦwww.bronxzoo.org. Nov–March daily 10am–4.30pm; $8, kids & seniors $6; April–Oct Mon–Fri 10am–5pm, Sat & Sun 10am–5.30pm; $11, kids & seniors $8, free Wed, parking $7.
The largest urban zoo in America, with thrilling permanent exhibits – check out Wild Asia (summer only), the lush rainforest of JungleWorld, and the Congo Gorilla Forest. Kids can watch penguins being fed, get up close with Siberian tigers, or ride a giant bug on an insect-themed carousel. Highly recommended for an all-day excursion, particularly in spring, when many baby animals are born, or summer. Be prepared for small additional fees once inside; check website for "bad weather bargains" and other specials.

Central Park

Central Park provides year-round, sure-fire entertainment for children. In the summer it becomes one giant playground, with activities ranging from storytelling to rollerblading to boating. Highlights include the nature exhibits at **Belvedere Castle**, in mid-park at 79th St; the surprisingly fast **Carousel**, at 64th St, a vintage model salvaged from Coney Island; **Central Park Wildlife Conservation Center**, Fifth Ave at 64th St, where youngsters will be delighted at the singing bronze animals on the musical clock at the entrance to the Children's Zoo; **Loeb Boathouse**, east side at 74th St, where you can rent rowboats; and iceskating at **Wollman Rink**, east side at 62nd St. For more detailed information on these and other sights, see Chapter 14, "Central Park."

New York Aquarium

Surf Ave at W 8th St, Coney Island, Brooklyn ℡718/265-3474, Ⓦwww.nyaquarium.com. Hours vary by season; $12, under 12 & seniors $8.
Despite being established in 1896, the aquarium has very modern-looking exhibits dedicated to jellyfish and sea horses, along with 8000 other underwater animals. Openair shows of sea lions, as well as shark, penguin, sea otter, and walrus feedings are held several times daily. This is also the site of the famous Coney Island boardwalk and amusement park – older children and teens will find it a good spot to people-watch.

New York Botanical Garden

Bronx River Parkway at Fordham Rd, Bronx (across from the Bronx Zoo) ℡718/817-8700, Ⓦwww.nybg.org. Tues–Sun & Mon holidays: April–Oct 10am–6pm; Nov–March 10am–5pm; $13, students & seniors $11, under 12 $5; free before noon Sat & Wed, parking $7.
One of America's foremost public gardens, with an enormous conservatory showcasing a rainforest and other climates, plus the 12-acre Everett Children's Adventure Garden, which includes several mazes. Prices above are for the entire complex; tickets to individual sections are available, in case you want to just take your baby in to a green spot for a discreet nap.

Sony Wonder Technology Lab

550 Madison Ave, at 56th St ℡212/833-8100, Ⓦwww.sonywondertechlab.com. Tues–Sat 10am–5pm, Sun noon–5pm; free.
Sony's gee-whiz exhibit space emphasizes the marvels of the digital age, and although it's a bit corporate-slick, tech-minded kids will enjoy creating their own video games and trying out TV editing, among other computer-driven activities. This is a hugely popular attraction, so make reservations (no fee) up to three months in advance; sameday tickets are sometimes available as well.

(34)

Shops: toys, books, and clothes

Bank Street Bookstore 610 W 112th St, at Broadway ℡212/678-1654, Ⓦwww.bankstreetbooks.com. The first floor of this

store – which is affiliated with Bank Street College of Education – is filled with children's books and games, while the second floor is devoted to nonfiction books and educational materials. Frequent special events and afternoon story hours with big names like E.L. Konigsburg and Hilary Knight, of *Eloise* fame.

Books of Wonder 18 W 18th St, between Fifth and Sixth aves ⓣ212/989-3270, ⓦwww .booksofwonder.com. Showpiece kids' bookstore, with a great Oz section, plus story hour on Sun at noon and author appearances Sat in the spring and fall.

Cozy's Cuts for Kids 1125 Madison Ave, at 84th St ⓣ212/744-1716; also 448 Amsterdam Ave, at 81st St ⓣ212/579-2600, and 1416 Second Ave, at 74th St ⓣ212/585-2699, ⓦwww.cozyscutsforkids.com. Children can get their hair cut while blowing bubbles, sitting in a play Jeep, or watching videos. The shop also sells its own shampoo, as well as distracting toys. It's not too expensive (about $30), and walk-ins are fine.

Dylan's Candy Bar 1011 Third Ave, at 60th St ⓣ646/735-0078. Kids will catch a sugar high just walking in the door of this stylish shop devoted to all things sweet. The selection is almost paralyzing, with everything from a rainbow of gummy candy to retro favorites like Charleston Chews.

F.A.O. Schwarz 767 Fifth Ave, at 58th St ⓣ212/644-9400, ⓦwww.fao.com. Back from bankruptcy by popular demand, this multi-

story toy emporium features an on-site ice-cream parlor, a whole wing dedicated to Legos, and the legendary danceable floor piano featured in the 1988 film *Big*. Very popular (and very expensive), but a less frenzied experience than the plasticky Toys 'R' Us in Times Square.

Metropolitan Museum Store 15 W 49th St ⓣ212/332-1360, ⓦwww.metmuseum.org/store. The second floor of the shop is devoted to artsy children's toys, many of which teach about pieces in the museum's collection.

Red Caboose 23 W 45th St, between Fifth and Sixth aves, lower level ⓣ212/575-0155. A unique shop specializing in models, particularly train sets and train sets.

Space Kiddets 46 E 21st St, between Park Ave and Broadway ⓣ212/420-9878, ⓦwww .spacekiddets.com. Show your baby's musical taste with a CBGB onesie or a David Bowie tee from this funky clothes shop that stocks infant through pre-teen sizes, along with vintage toys.

Tannen's Magic Studio 45 W 34th St, 6th floor, between 5th and 6th aves ⓣ212/929-4500, ⓦwww.tannens.com. Your kids will never forget a visit to the largest magic shop in the world, with nearly 8000 props, tricks, and magic sets. The staff is made up of magicians who perform free shows throughout the day.

Theater, circuses, and other entertainment

The following is a highly selective roundup of **cultural activities** that might be of interest to children. As always, find out more by checking the listings in the *New York Times* (which publishes its calendar of youth activities in the arts section on Fridays) and magazines such as *Time Out New York Kids*. Note too that the Brooklyn Museum and the Met, among other museums, often have events for children, as do many bookstores.

BAMfamily Brooklyn Academy of Music, 30 Lafayette Ave ⓣ718/636-4100, ⓦwww.bam .org/events/BAMfamily.aspx. This periodic series presents public performances for families on weekends, as well as the international BAMkids Film Festival each March.

Barnum & Bailey Circus Madison Square Garden ⓣ212/465-6741, ⓦwww.ringling.com. This large touring circus arrives in New York on a mile-long train in mid-March and stays for about three weeks. The real highlight is before the circus starts, when the elephants are escorted from the rail yards in Queens

to the west side of Manhattan – usually around midnight, but the sight is worth staying up for. Keep an eye on local papers for the precise date and route.

Big Apple Circus Lincoln Center ⓣ212/721-6500, ⓦwww.bigapplecircus.org. Small circus that performs in a tent in Damrosch Park next to the Met, from late Oct to early Jan. Tickets $38–76, or $18–30 for matinees.

Manhattan Children's Theatre 52 White St ⓣ212/226-4085, ⓦwww.manhattan childrenstheatre.org. $15, ages 2–16 $10. Classic plays, fairy tales, and musicals, plus some new works.

For many teenagers, the sights and sounds of New York (paired with a little well-placed down-time) will be fascinating enough, particularly if they have certain obsessions (movies, Buddhism, soccer, indie rock, pizza – anything, really) easily satisfied by the city. If your adolescent travel companions need something a little extra, try wandering around the East Village (particularly along St Mark's Place and in Tompkins Square Park, longtime punk hangouts that have softened enough not to alarm parents too terribly), or throw in some strategic shopping on the streets of Chinatown and on Broadway in neighboring Soho, especially in the inexpensive teen clothing stores – H&M and Yellow Rat Bastard, among others, plus numerous cut-rate sneaker and shoe stores. Independent record stores abound in the East and West villages, and crafty types can head to Knit New York (307 E 14th St, ☏212/387-0707, ⓦwww.knitnewyork.com), a friendly store-café that also offers knitting classes. Obscure theme restaurants such as *Ninja New York* (25 Hudson St ☏212/274-8500), *Jekyll and Hyde Club* (1409 Sixth Ave ☏212/989-7701), and the unbelievable rice-pudding shop Rice to Riches (37 Spring St ☏212/274-0008) should wow all but the most jaded teenage traveler, as will the Hip Hop Look at NY tours of the Bronx ($70; ☏212/714-3527, ⓦwww.hushtours.com), run by scene veterans.

Some teens will also get a kick out of walking around the NYU and Columbia campuses (see p.110 and p.218) and imagining themselves as students in a few years (older ones who are serious about applying can even arrange interviews). Teens can also get free makeovers at Sephora (1500 Broadway, in Times Square ☏212/944-6789, ⓦwww.sephora.com; plus eight other locations in Manhattan), Bloomingdale's, and other upscale make-up counters. They can watch skateboarding stunts in the city's skate parks (Chelsea Piers has the best; ⓦwww.skateboardparks.com for a full list) or enjoy the thrill of trapeze classes (see below). With a high-school ID, they're eligible for $5 tickets to hundreds of films, museums, and performances through High 5 Tickets (☏212/445-8587, ⓦwww.highfivetix.org).

New Victory Theater 209 W 42nd St, at Broadway ☏646/223-3020, ⓦwww.newvictory.org. The city's first theater for families, located in a grand old renovated Times Square space, shows a rich mix of theater, music, dance, storytelling, film, and puppetry, in addition to pre-performance workshops and post-performance participation. Affordable shows (most tickets $10–30) run 1–2hr. In keeping with the larger city cultural calendar, the theater is dark (no performances) during the summer.

Streb Laboratory for Action Mechanics 51 N 1st St, Williamsburg, Brooklyn ☏718/384-6491, ⓦwww.strebusa.org. MacArthur-grant-winning choreographer Elizabeth Streb has developed a dynamic, physical dance style she calls Pop Action – go for one of the company's inspiring performances in its raw Brooklyn warehouse, or sign kids up for one- or three-day classes, scaled for ages 18 months up to 12 years, that involve trampoline work, trapeze fun, and basic tumbling.

Trapeze School New York Hudson River Park at Canal St ☏917/797-1872, ⓦwww.trapezeschool.com. Two-hour classes on the flying trapeze, for ages 6 and up, start at $57 and include an amazing view over the Hudson River from high atop the rig. Parents must accompany children – but if this seems too daunting, you can just go sit in the park and watch the intrepid high-flyers practice their moves. Classes run year-round (a heated tent is set up in the winter); book well in advance.

Theater, circuses, and other entertainment | KIDS' NEW YORK | (34)

Directory

City information Dial ☎311 for all non-emergency queries or complaints. The operator will direct you to the appropriate government department.

Consulates Australia, 150 E 42nd St (☎212/351-6500, ⓦwww.australianyc.org); Canada, 1251 Sixth Ave, at 50th St (☎212/596-1628, ⓦwww.canada-ny.org); Denmark, Dag Hammarskjöld Plaza, 885 Second Ave, between 47th and 48th sts (☎212/223-4545, ⓦwww.denmark.org); France, 934 Fifth Ave, between 74th and 75th sts (☎212/606-3600, ⓦwww.consulfrance-newyork.org); Germany, 871 UN Plaza (☎212/610-9700, ⓦwww.germanconsulate.org/newyork); Ireland, 345 Park Ave, between 51st and 52nd sts (☎212/319-2555, ⓔcongenny@aol.com); Israel, 800 Second Ave, between 42nd and 43rd sts (☎212/499-5400, ⓦwww.israelfm.org); Italy, 690 Park Ave, between 68th and 69th sts (☎212/439-8600, ⓦwww.italconsulnyc.org); Netherlands, 1 Rockefeller Plaza (☎212/246-1429, ⓦwww.cgny.org); New Zealand, 222 E 41st St, between Second and Third aves (☎212/832-4038); South Africa, 333 E 38th St, between First and Second aves (☎212/213-4880, ⓦwww.southafrica-newyork.net/consulate); Sweden, Dag Hammarskjöld Plaza, 885 Second Ave, between 47th and 48th sts (☎212/583-2550, ⓦwww.webcom.com/sis); UK, 845 Third Ave, between 51st and 52nd sts (☎212/745-0200, ⓦwww.britainusa.com/ny).

Contraception Condoms are available in all pharmacies and delis. If you're on the pill, it's obviously best to bring a supply with you; should you run out, require emergency contraception or a pregnancy test, or need advice on other aspects of contraception, abortion, or sexuality, contact Planned Parenthood, 26 Bleecker St, at Mott St (☎212/965-7000, ⓦwww.ppnyc.org).

Emergencies For Police, Fire, or Ambulance dial ☎911. For non-emergency queries or complaints, dial ☎311.

Getting married If it's a quick holiday wedding you're after but Vegas doesn't suit you, consider New York. Get two money orders – one for the marriage license ($35) and one for the ceremony itself ($25). You'll both need passports (or US ID) and, if applicable, details concerning the dissolution of any previous marriages. Licenses may be purchased and ceremonies performed at any of the five borough halls (Manhattan's is listed below). After obtaining a license, a 24-hour waiting period is required before you can be married, giving you ample time to find the required witness. Domestic partnership (for same-sex and opposite-sex cohabiting couples) is not available to non-residents, unless one is an employee of the City of New York. City Hall, Municipal Building South Side, 2nd floor, 1 Centre St, Mon–Fri 8.30am–3.45pm; ☎212/669-2400, ⓦwww.nycmarriagebureau.com.

Hospitals Mount Sinai, 1190 Fifth Ave at 101st St (☎212/241-6500, ⓦwww.mountsinai.org); New York Methodist, 506 6th St, at Seventh Ave, Park Slope, Brooklyn (☎718/780-3000, ⓦwww.nym.org); St Vincent's, 170 W 12th St, at Seventh Ave (☎212/604-7000, ⓦwww.svcmc.org/manhattan).

ID Carry a photo ID at all times. Almost every bar and most restaurants (serving alcohol) in New York will ask for proof of age (21 and over).

Jaywalking This is how New Yorkers cross the streets – when and where they can, regardless of what color the light is.

Libraries The real heavyweight is the reference section of the New York Public Library, Fifth Ave at 42nd St (see p.132), though it's not a lending library. To borrow books, you must go to a branch (such as the one across Fifth Avenue; for a full list, see Ⓦwww.nypl.org), but only those who can show proof of residence in the city are eligible for a library card. Libraries provide free Internet access, though you usually have to reserve a time in advance.

Lost property For things lost on buses or the subway: NYC Transit Authority, at the 34th St/Eighth Ave Station (#A, #C, and #E), on the lower-level subway mezzanine (Mon–Wed & Fri 8am–noon, Thurs 11am–6.30pm; ℡212/712-4500). For anything lost on Amtrak: Penn Station upper level, near tracks 5 and 6E (Mon–Fri 7.30am–4pm; ℡212/630-7389). For items lost on Metro North: Grand Central Station lower level (Mon–Fri 7am–6pm, Sat 9am–5pm; ℡212/340-2555). For property left in a cab: Taxi & Limousine Commission Lost Property Dept (Mon–Fri 9am–5pm except national holidays; ℡212/227-0700); you can file a report online (Ⓦwww.nyc.gov/taxi) if you have the cab's medallion number (printed on your receipt).

Measurements and sizes The US has yet to go metric, so measurements of length are in inches, feet, yards, and miles, with weight measured in ounces, pounds, and tons. Liquid measures are slightly more confusing to visitors from abroad in that an imperial pint is 20 oz, so equivalent to 1.25 American pints, which measure only 16 oz. An American gallon is thus equal only to four-fifths of an imperial one, as is a pint of beer or ice cream. Only soft drinks are sold in liters. For disparities in clothing and shoe sizes between Britain and the US, see "Clothing and shoe sizes" box, p.416.

Notice boards For contacts, casual work, articles for sale, short-term rentals and sublets, and often bizarre personals ads, it's hard to beat the free listings on craigslist (Ⓦwww.newyork.craigslist.com). Otherwise there are numerous notice boards around Columbia University and NYU, and in the groovier coffee shops, health-food stores, and restaurants.

Passport and visa office The New York Passport Agency's main office is at 376 Hudson St, at Houston St (Mon–Fri 7.30am–3pm; ℡1-877/487-2778). The agency only handles urgent processing (between two weeks and one day before your date of travel), and will renew or issue passports the same day you apply; however, you absolutely must make an appointment. If you have failed to do this and need urgent service, call an expediting agency (see "Passport services" in the phone book) and be prepared to spend an additional $150. If you have more than two weeks, apply or renew passports through the post.

Religious services The following (and many, many others) conduct regular services and masses: Anglican (Episcopal): Cathedral of St John the Divine, 1047 Amsterdam Ave at 112th St (℡212/316-7490, Ⓦwww.stjohndivine.org); St Bartholomew's, Park Ave at 51st St (℡212/378-0200, Ⓦwww.stbarts.org). Catholic: St Patrick's Cathedral, Fifth Ave between 50th and 51st sts (℡212/753-2261, Ⓦwww.ny-archdiocese.org). Jewish (Reform): Temple Emanu-El, 1 E 65th St, at Fifth Ave (℡212/744-1400, Ⓦwww.emanuelnyc.org). Jewish (Conservative): Park Avenue Synagogue, 50 E 87th St, at Madison Ave (℡212/369-2600, Ⓦwww.pasyn.com). Muslim: Islamic Cultural Center of New York, 1711 Third Ave, at 96th St (℡212/722-5234). Unitarian: Church of All Souls, 1157 Lexington Ave, at 80th St (℡212/535-5530, Ⓦwww.allsoulsnyc.org).

Souvenirs Good things to take home include American-style gear (baseball caps, basketball shoes, and Levis). CDs are significantly cheaper than in many of parts of the US and Europe; the same is true of most photographic and electronic equipment (foreign visitors, see p.37 for info on America's electric current). See Chapter 31, "Shopping," for details.

Taxes There is an 8.375 percent sales tax on almost everything; groceries, and individual items of clothing and shoes less than $110 are exempt. Hotels are subject to sales tax, 5 percent hotel tax, a $3.50 per night "occupancy tax," and a $5.50 "hospitality tax."

Terminals and transit information Grand Central Station, 42nd St between Park and Lexington aves: Metro-North commuter trains (℡212/532-4900, Ⓦwww.mta.info). Pennsylvania Station, 33rd St and Seventh Ave: Amtrak (℡1-800/USA-RAIL, Ⓦwww.amtrak.com); New Jersey Transit (℡1-800/626-RIDE, Ⓦwww.njtransit.com); Long Island Rail Road (℡718/217-5477, Ⓦwww.mta.info); PATH trains (℡1-800/234-7284,

35

Ⓦwww.panynj.gov/path). Port Authority Bus Terminal, Eighth Ave between 40th and 42nd sts, and George Washington Bridge Bus Terminal, 4211 Broadway, between 178th and 179th sts (both ☎212/564-8484; Ⓦwww.panynj.gov/tbt/pabframe, and Ⓦwww.panynj.gov/tbt/gwbframe): New Jersey Transit (see above); Greyhound (☎1-800/231-2222, Ⓦwww.greyhound.com); Peter Pan (☎1-800/237-8747, Ⓦwww .peterpanbus.com).

Tipping In New York, you're expected to tip in restaurants, bars, taxicabs, hotels (both the bellboy and the cleaning staff), and even some posh restrooms. In restaurants in particular, it's unthinkable not to leave the minimum (15 percent of the bill) – even if you hated the service.

Contexts

Contexts

The historical framework 459

Books 471

New York on film 480

Glossary 491

The historical framework

To Europe she was America, to America she was the gateway of the earth. But to tell the story of New York would be to write a social history of the world.

H.G. Wells

Early days and colonial rule

Long before the arrival of European settlers, New York was inhabited by several Native American tribes; the **Algonquin** tribe was the largest and most populous in the area that is now New York City. Although descendants of the Algonquins and other tribes still live on Long Island's Shinnecock reservation, the appearance of Europeans in the sixteenth century essentially destroyed their settled existence, bringing an end to Native American life as it had existed here for several thousand years.

Giovanni da Verrazano was the first explorer to discover Manhattan in 1524. An Italian in the service of French King Francis I, Verrazano had set out to find the Pacific's legendary Northwest Passage, but like his countryman Christopher Columbus, had been blown off-course, landing instead at:

A very agreeable situation located within two small prominent hills, in the midst of which flowed to the sea a very great river, which was deep within the mouth; and from the sea to the hills, with the rising of the tide, which we found at eight feet, any laden ship might have passed.

Verrazano returned to France to woo the court with tales of fertile lands and friendly natives, "leaving the said land with much regret because of its commodiousness and beauty, thinking it was not without some properties of value." But even with these mellifluous descriptions, it was nearly a century before the powers of Europe were tempted to follow him.

In 1609 **Henry Hudson**, an Englishman employed by the **Dutch East India Company**, landed at Manhattan, sailing his ship, the *Half-Moone*, upriver as far as Albany. Hudson found that the route did not lead to the Northwest Passage, which he, too, had been commissioned to discover – but in charting its course for the first time he gave his name to the mighty river. "This is a very good land to fall with," noted the ship's mate, "and a pleasant land to see." It was on this voyage that Hudson's men gave the native people their first real taste of what to expect from future adventurers – several encounters left the native population decimated by Dutch firepower and foreign diseases. Returning home, Hudson was chastised by the British for exploring new territory for the Dutch, and was persuaded to embark on another expedition, this time under the British flag. He arrived in Hudson Bay in the dead of winter, the temperature below freezing and his mutinous crew doubting his ability as a navigator; he, his son, and several loyal sailors were set adrift in a small boat on the icy waters where, presumably, they froze to death.

British fears that they had lost the upper hand in the newly discovered land proved justified when the Dutch established a trading post at the most northerly point on the river that Hudson had reached, **Fort Nassau**, and quickly seized the commercial advantage. In 1624, four years after the Pilgrims had sailed to Massachusetts, thirty families left Holland to become New York's first European settlers, most sailing up to Fort Nassau. But a handful – eight families in all – stayed behind on a small island they called Nut Island because of the many walnut trees there: today's Governors Island. The community slowly grew as more settlers arrived, and the little island became crowded; the **settlement of Manhattan**, taken from the Algonquin Indian word *Manna-Hata* meaning "Island of the Hills," began when families from Governors Island moved across the water.

The Dutch gave this new outpost the name **New Amsterdam**, and in 1626 **Peter Minuit** was sent out to govern the small community. Among his first, and certainly more politically adroit, moves was to buy the whole of Manhattan Island from the Native Americans for trinkets worth sixty guilders (about $25 today); the other side of this anecdote is that the Native Americans Minuit bought the island from didn't even come from Manhattan.

As the colony slowly grew, a string of governors succeeded Minuit, the most famous of them **Peter Stuyvesant** – "Peg Leg Pete," a seasoned colonialist from the Dutch West Indies who'd lost his leg in a scrap with the Portuguese. Under his leadership New Amsterdam doubled in size, population, and fortifications, with an encircling wall (today's **Wall Street** follows its course) and a rough-hewn fort on what is now the site of the Customs House built to protect the settlement from the encroaching British. Stuyvesant also built himself a farm (a *bouwerij*, in Dutch) nearby, giving Manhattan's Bowery district its name.

Meanwhile, the **British** were steadily and stealthily building up their presence to the north. They asserted that all of America's East Coast, from New England to Virginia, was theirs, and in 1664 Colonel Richard Nicholls was sent to claim the lands around the Hudson for King Charles II. To reinforce his sovereignty, Charles sent along four warships and enough troops to land on Nut and Long islands. Angered by Stuyvesant's increasingly dictatorial leadership, especially the high taxation demanded by the nominal owners of the colony, the Dutch West India Company, the Dutch settlers refused to defend the colony against the British. Captain Nicholls' men took New Amsterdam, renamed it **New York** in honor of Charles II's brother, the Duke of York, and started what was to be a hundred-odd years of British rule, a period interrupted only briefly in 1673 when the Dutch once more gained, then lost, power in the region.

Not all was smooth sailing for the British in New York. When King James II was forced to abdicate and flee Britain in 1689, a German merchant named **James Leisler** led an unsuccessful revolt against the colonial government – he was later hanged for treason. By the eighteenth century, black slaves constituted a major part of New York's population, and though laws denied them weapons and the right of assembly, in 1712 a number of slaves set fire to a building near Maiden Lane, killing nine people. When soldiers arrived, six of the arsonists committed suicide and 21 others were captured and executed. In 1734, **John Peter Zenger**, publisher of the *New York Weekly Journal*, was accused of libeling the British government; his trial and subsequent acquittal set the precedent for freedom of press in America, laying the groundwork for the First Amendment to the Constitution.

Revolution

By the 1750s the city had reached a population of 16,000, spread roughly as far north as Chambers Street. As the community grew, it also operated increasingly independently of the British. The 1763 **Treaty of Paris**, the conclusion of the Seven Years' War, put a stop to all this, as sovereignty over most of explored North America was conceded to England, thereby consolidating British power. Within a year, discontent over this stronger British rule was evident, especially following the passage of the punitive **Sugar**, **Stamp**, and **Colonial Currency acts**, which allowed the British to collect taxes on everyday goods in order to finance their local army. Further resentment erupted over the **Quartering Act**, which permitted British troops to requisition private dwellings and inns, their rent to be paid by the colonies themselves. Ill feeling steadily mounted, and skirmishes between British soldiers and the insurrectionist **Sons of Liberty** culminated in January 1770 with the killing of a colonist. The **Boston Massacre**, in which British troops fired upon taunting protestors, occurred a few weeks later and helped foster revolutionary sentiment.

In a way, New York's role during the **War of Independence** was not crucial, for all the battles fought in and around the city were generally won by the side that lost the war. But New York – the borough of Brooklyn, to be exact – was the site of one of the first military engagements between British and American forces. The British, driven from Boston, resolved that New York should be the place where they would reassert their authority over the rebels; in summer 1776 some two hundred ships under the command of **Lord Howe** arrived in New York Harbor, and the troops made camp on Staten Island. He decided to make his assault on the city by land: on August 22, 1776, 15,000 men, mainly Hessian mercenaries, were set ashore on the southwest corner of Brooklyn. In the **Battle of Long Island**, Howe's men penetrated the American forward lines at a number of points, the most important engagement taking place at what is today Prospect Park.

American commander **George Washington** had consolidated his troops before the battle began. As the Americans fell back to their positions and the British made preparations to attack, Washington could see that his garrison would be easily defeated. On the night of August 29, under cover of rain and fog, he evacuated his men safely to Manhattan from the ferry slip beneath where the Brooklyn Bridge now stands, preserving the bulk of his forces. A few days later Howe's army set out in boats from Greenpoint and Newtown Creek in Brooklyn to land at what is now the 34th Street heliport site. The Americans again retreated north, and though they made a stand at Harlem Heights, were pushed back to eventual defeat at the **Battle of White Plains** in Westchester County (the Bronx), where Washington lost 1400 of his 4000 men. More tragic still was the defense of **Fort Washington**, perched on a rocky cliff 230 feet above the Hudson, near today's George Washington Bridge. Here, rather than evacuate the troops, the post commander made the decision to stand and fight. It was a fatal mistake: trapped by the Hudson, over 3000 men were killed or taken prisoner. Gathering what was left of the Continental forces, Washington left New York to the British.

On September 21, only days after the British had taken control of the city, a **fire** broke out near the southern tip of Manhattan, burning hundreds of buildings, including Trinity Church. Although the fire's origin remains unknown, many historians believe it was set by revolutionary sympathizers who didn't want to leave the city intact for the British. For the next seven years, the British occupied what was left of New York as a garrison town. During this period many of the remaining inhabitants and most of the prisoners taken by the British slowly starved to death.

Lord Cornwallis's **surrender** to the Americans in October 1783 marked the end of the Revolutionary War, and a month later New York was finally liberated. Washington was there to celebrate, riding in triumphal procession down

Canal Street and saying farewell to his officers at **Fraunces Tavern**, a building that still stands at the end of Pearl Street. It was a tearful occasion for men who had fought together for years: "I am not only retiring from all public employments," Washington declared, "but am retiring within myself." Not for long, though, were either New York or Washington out of the public eye: as one of the largest cities in the colonies, New York became the fledgling nation's capital, and Washington its first president. On April 30, 1789, he took the oath of president at the site of the **Federal Hall National Memorial** on Wall Street. The seat of the federal government was transferred to the District of Columbia a year later.

Immigration and civil war

In 1790 the first official census of Manhattan numbered the population around 33,000. Business and trade were steadily increasing, with the forerunner of the New York Stock Exchange created under a buttonwood tree on Wall Street. A few years later, in 1807, **Robert Fulton** launched the *Clermont*, a steamboat that managed to splutter its way up the Hudson River from New York to Albany, pioneering trade with upstate areas. A year before his death in 1814, Fulton also started a ferry service between Manhattan and Brooklyn. The Brooklyn dock at which it moored became a maritime center, taking its name from the inventor.

It was the opening of the **Erie Canal** in 1825 that really allowed New York to develop as a port. The canal opened the rest of the country to New York; goods manufactured in the city could be sent easily and cheaply to the American heartland. It was because of this transportation network, and the mass of **cheap labor** that flooded in throughout the nineteenth and early twentieth centuries, that New York – and to an extent the nation – became wealthy. The first waves of **immigrants**, mainly **German** and **Irish**, began to arrive in the mid-nineteenth century, the latter forced out by famine, the former by unsettled politics – a failed revolution in 1848–49 had left many German liberals, laborers, intellectuals, and businessmen dispossessed. The city could not handle the arrival of so many people all at once: epidemics of yellow fever and cholera were common, exacerbated by poor water supplies, unsanitary conditions, and the poverty of most of the newcomers. By the 1880s, the large-scale immigration of **Italians**, mainly peasants from southern Italy and Sicily, was in full swing, while at the same time refugees from **Eastern Europe** – many of them Jewish – had also begun. These two communities shared a home on the **Lower East Side**, which became one of the most notorious slum areas of its day. On the eve of the Civil War the majority of New York's population of 750,000 were immigrants.

While immigrants packed into downtown tenements, life for New York's well-off was fairly pleasant during this period. Despite a great fire in 1835 that destroyed most of the city's business district, trade boomed, and was celebrated in the opening of the **World's Fair** of 1835 at the Crystal Palace on the site of Bryant Park. In the same year work began on clearing the shantytowns in the center of the island to make way for a new, landscaped open space – a marvelous design by Frederick Law Olmsted and Calvert Vaux that became **Central Park**.

During the American **Civil War** (1860–65), New York sided with the Union (North) against the Confederates (South), but saw little of the hand-to-hand fighting that ravaged the rest of the country. It was, however, stomping ground for much of the liberal thinking that informed the war, particularly with **Abraham Lincoln**'s influential "Might makes Right" speech from the **Cooper Union Building** in 1860. In 1863 a **conscription law** was passed that allowed the rich to buy themselves out of military service. Not surprisingly, this was deeply unpopular, and impoverished New Yorkers (especially Irish immigrants) rioted, burning buildings, looting shops, and lynching African-Americans; more than a thousand people were killed in these **Draft Riots**. A sad addendum to the war was the assassination of Lincoln in 1865; when his body lay in state in New York's City Hall, 120,000 people filed past to pay last respects.

The late nineteenth century

The end of the Civil War saw much of the country devastated but New York intact, and it was fairly predictable that the city would soon become the wealthiest and most influential in the nation. Broadway developed into the main thoroughfare, with grand hotels, restaurants, and shops catering to the rich; newspaper editors **William Cullen Bryant** and **Horace Greeley** respectively founded the *Evening Post* and the *Tribune*; and the city became a magnet for intellectuals, with **Washington Irving** and **James Fenimore Cooper** among notable residents. By dint of its skilled immigrant workers, its distribution networks, and financial resources, New York was the greatest business, commercial, and manufacturing center in the country. **Cornelius Vanderbilt** controlled a vast shipping and railroad empire from here, and **J.P. Morgan**, the banking and investment wizard, was instrumental in organizing financial mergers, creating the nation's first major corporations.

The biggest character in New York at the time, though, was not a businessman or an intellectual, but a politician: **William Marcy "Boss" Tweed**. Tweed worked his way up the Democratic Party ladder, starting as an alderman at the age of 21 and eventually becoming chairman of the party's State Committee. Appointed Commissioner of Public Works in 1870, Tweed operated from now-infamous **Tammany Hall**. Surrounding himself with friends and associates, he took total control of the city's government and finances, and set out to make himself a fortune. Anyone in a position to challenge his illegal moneymaking schemes was bought off with cash extorted from contractors eager to carry out municipal services; in this way $160 million found its way into Tweed's and his friends' pockets. Tweed stayed in power by organizing the speedy naturalization of immigrants, who, as repayment, were expected to vote his way. As a contemporary observer remarked, "The government of the rich by the manipulation of the poor is a new phenomenon in the world." Tweed's scams grew in audacity until a determined campaign by cartoonist **Thomas Nast**, whose vicious portrayals of Tweed appeared in *Harper's Weekly*, and *New York Times* editor **George Jones**, brought him down. A committee was established to investigate corruption in City Hall and Tweed found himself on trial. He escaped to Spain, where he was recognized by an admirer of Nast's cartoons, and was returned to the US. Convicted, Tweed died in Ludlow Street Jail – ironically, a building he had commissioned while in office.

The latter part of the nineteenth century was in many ways the city's golden age: elevated railways (**Els**) sprang up to transport people quickly and cheaply around the city; **Thomas Edison** lit the streets with his new electric light-bulb, powered by the first electricity plant on Pearl Street; and in 1883, the

Brooklyn Bridge was unveiled. Brooklyn, Staten Island, Queens, and the part of Westchester known as the Bronx, along with Manhattan, were officially **incorporated** into New York City in 1898. All this commercial expansion stimulated the city's cultural growth; **Walt Whitman** eulogized the city in his poems and **Henry James** recorded its manners and mores in novels like *Washington Square*. Along Fifth Avenue, **Richard Morris Hunt** built palaces for the wealthy robber barons who had plundered Europe's collections of fine art – collections that would eventually find their way into the newly opened **Metropolitan Museum**. For the "Four Hundred," the wealthy elite that essentially owned the city, New York in the "gay nineties" was a constant string of lavish balls and dinners that vied with each other until opulence became obscenity. At one particularly lavish banquet the millionaire guests arrived on horseback and ate their meals in the saddle; afterwards the horses were fed gourmet-prepared fodder.

Turn-of-the-century development

During this period's explosion of robust capitalism, immigration to the city continued unabated, and the 1880s saw the first wave of refugees from Asia, who settled in what became known as **Chinatown**. As the Vanderbilts, Astors, and Rockefellers lorded it in their uptown mansions, overcrowded tenements led to terrible living standards for the poor. Police reporter and photographer **Jacob Riis**, whose book *How the Other Half Lives* detailed the long working hours, exploitation, and child labor that allowed the rich to get richer, was one of the first to expose these appalling conditions to the public.

In 1898 the population of New York topped three million for the first time – making it the largest city in the world. Pressure to limit immigration grew, but still people flooded in. **Ellis Island**, the depot that processed arrivals, handled two thousand people a day. By the turn of the century, around half of the city's people were foreign-born, and a quarter of the population was made up of German and Irish migrants, most of them living in slums. Jewish immigrants arrived to cram the Lower East Side; over 1.5 million settled here. With 640,000 people per square mile, the section of Manhattan bounded by the East River, East 14th Street, Third Avenue, the Bowery, and Catherine Street was one of the most densely populated areas on earth. Despite advances in public building, caused by the outcry that followed Jacob Riis's reports, the area could not keep up with the number of inhabitants, and the poverty and inhuman conditions continued to worsen.

Many immigrants worked in sweatshops for the city's growing garment industry. Notoriously exploitive, manufacturers charged women workers for their needles and the hire of lockers, and handed out stiff fines for spoilage of fabrics. Workers began to strike for better wages and working conditions, but it took disaster to rouse public and civic conscience. On March 25, 1911, just before the **Triangle Shirtwaist Factory** on Washington Place was about to close for the day, a fire broke out. The workers were trapped on the tenth floor: 146 of them died (125 were women), many by leaping from the blazing building. Within months the state passed 56 factory-reform measures, and unionization spread through the city.

The early 1900s saw some of the city's wealth going into adventurous new architecture. Soho utilized **cast iron** to mass-produce classical facades, and the **Flatiron Building** of 1902 announced the arrival of what was to become the city's trademark – the skyscraper. On the arts front, **Stephen Crane, Theodore Dreiser**, and **Edith Wharton** all wrote stories about the city, **George M. Cohan** was the Bright Young Man of Broadway, and in 1913 the **Armory Exhibition** of paintings by Picasso, Duchamp, and others caused a sensation. Skyscrapers pushed ever higher, and in 1913 a building that many consider the *ne plus ultra* of the genre, downtown's **Woolworth Building**, was completed. **Grand Central Terminal** also opened that year, celebrating New York as the gateway to the continent.

The war years and the Depression: 1914–45

With America's entry into World War I in 1917, New York benefited from wartime trade and commerce. Perhaps surprisingly, there was little conflict between the various European communities crammed into the city. Although Germans comprised roughly one-fifth of the city's population, there were few of the attacks on their lives or property that occurred elsewhere in the country.

The postwar years saw New York dominated by **Prohibition**, passed in 1920 in an attempt to sober up the nation, and **Jimmy Walker**, elected mayor in 1925. Walker led a far from sober lifestyle: "No civilized man," he said, "goes to bed the same day he wakes up" – it was during his career that the city entered the Jazz Age. Writers as diverse as **Damon Runyon**, **F. Scott Fitzgerald**, and **Ernest Hemingway** portrayed the excitement of the times, and musicians such as **George Gershwin** and **Benny Goodman** packed nightclubs with their new sound. Bootleg liquor ran freely in speakeasies all over town. The **Harlem Renaissance** soared to prominence with writers like **Langston Hughes** and **Zora Neale Hurston**, and music from **Duke Ellington**, **Cab Calloway**, and **Billie Holiday**.

The **Wall Street** crash of 1929, however, brought the party to an abrupt end. In the early days of stock trading, shares could be bought "on margin," which meant the buyer needed to pay only a small part of their total cost, borrowing the rest and using the shares as security. This worked fine as long as the market kept rising – as share dividends came in to pay off the loans, investors' money bought more shares. But it was, as Alistair Cooke put it, "a mountain of credit on a molehill of actual money," and only a small scare was needed to start the avalanche. When investors had to find more cash to service their debts and make up for the fall in value of their stocks, they sold off their shares cheaply. A panicked chain reaction ensued, and on October 24, known as "**Black Tuesday**," sixteen million shares were traded; five days later, the whole Exchange collapsed as $125 million was wiped off stock values. Fortunes disappeared overnight. Millions lost their savings; banks, businesses, and industries shut their doors; and unemployment spiraled.

This marked the beginning of the Great Depression, a slump that really didn't end until World War II. Mayor Walker was sent packing, along with a torrent of civic corruption that the changing times had uncovered. By 1932 approximately one in four New Yorkers was unemployed, and shantytowns, known as "Hoovervilles" (after then–President Hoover who was widely blamed for the Depression), had sprung up in Central Park to house the jobless and homeless. Despite the desperation of the Depression, during this period three of New York's most beautiful skyscrapers were built: the **Chrysler Building** in 1930, the **Empire State** in 1931 (though it stood near-empty for years), and in 1932 **Rockefeller Center**. This spate of construction was very impressive, but of little immediate help to those in Hooverville, Harlem, or other depressed parts of the city.

It fell to **Fiorello LaGuardia**, Jimmy Walker's successor, to run the crisis-strewn city. He did so with stringent taxation, anti-corruption, and social-spending programs that won him the approval of the city's citizens. Walker's good living had gotten New York into trouble, reasoned voters; hard-headed, straight-talking LaGuardia would undo the damage. Moreover, President Roosevelt's **New Deal** supplied funds for roads, housing, and parks, the latter undertaken by controversial Parks Commissioner **Robert Moses**. Under LaGuardia and Moses, the most extensive public-housing program in the country was undertaken; the Triborough, Whitestone, and Henry Hudson bridges were completed; fifty miles of new expressway and five thousand acres of new parks were designed and built; and, in 1939, Mayor LaGuardia opened the airport in Queens that still carries his name.

LaGuardia was in office for three terms (twelve years), taking the city into the **war years**. The country's entry into World War II in 1941 had a few direct effects on New York City: lights were blacked out at night in case of bomb attacks, two hundred Japanese were interned on Ellis Island, and guards were placed on bridges and tunnels. Most importantly, Columbia University hosted under-the-radar experiments crucial to the creation of the first atomic weapon – later named the **Manhattan Project**.

The postwar years

After World War II, New York regained its top pre-Depression status in the fields of finance, art, and communications, both in America and the world, its intellectual and creative community swollen by European refugees. The city was the obvious choice as the permanent home of the **United Nations Organization**: lured by Rockefeller-donated land on the east side of Manhattan, the UN started construction in 1947. The building of the UN complex, along with the boost in the economy that followed the war, brought about the rapid development of midtown Manhattan. First off in the race to fill the once-residential Park Avenue with offices was the **Lever House** of 1952, quickly followed by skyscrapers, like the **Seagram Building**, that give the area its distinctive look. Downtown on the East River, the **Stuyvesant Town** and **Peter Cooper Village** housing projects went ahead, along with many others all over the city.

Mayor LaGuardia was succeeded in 1945 by Brigadier General **William O'Dwyer**, previously a judge and Kings County District Attorney. Just after his mayoral re-election in 1949, O'Dwyer was challenged by allegations of police corruption; he stepped down in 1950, and was followed by a series of uneventful characters who did little to stop the city from self-destructing in the face of new population pressures and a rising poverty line. Immigrants from Puerto Rico and elsewhere in Latin America once more crammed East Harlem and the Lower East Side, as did blacks from poor rural areas. Both ethnic groups were forced into the ghetto area of Harlem, unable to get a slice of the city's wealth. Racial disturbances and riots started flaring up in what had for two hundred years been one of the more liberal of American cities. One response to the problem was a general exodus of the white middle classes – the **Great White Flight** as the media labeled it – out of New York. Between 1950 and 1970 more than a million families left the city. Things went from bad to worse during the 1960s with **race riots** in Harlem and Bedford-Stuyvesant in Brooklyn.

The **World's Fair** of 1964 was a white elephant to boost the city's international profile, but on the streets the call for civil liberties for blacks and protest against US involvement in Vietnam were, if anything, stronger than in most of the rest of the country. As the ugly civic mood continued, the city itself started looking worse for the wear, a trend attributed by most to planner Robert Moses, who had accrued so much power by this point that he operated as a sort of shadow mayor. What few new buildings went up during this period seemed willfully to destroy much of the best of earlier traditions: a new and uninspired **Madison Square Garden** was built on the site of the grand old Neoclassical **Pennsylvania Station**, and the **Singer Building** in the Financial District was demolished to be replaced by an ugly skyscraper. In Harlem municipal investment stopped altogether and the community stagnated.

The 1970s and 1980s

Manhattan reached **crisis point** in 1975. The city was spending billions more than it received in taxes. Companies closed their headquarters in the city when offered lucrative relocation deals elsewhere, and their white-collar employees were usually glad to go with them, thus eroding the city's tax base even more than the White Flight. Even after municipal securities were sold, New York ran up a debt of millions of dollars. Essential services, long shaky due to underfunding, were ready to collapse. Ironically, the mayor who oversaw this fiasco, **Abraham Beame**, was an accountant.

Three things saved the city: the **Municipal Assistance Corporation**, which was formed to borrow the money the city could no longer get its hands on; the election of **Edward I. Koch** as mayor in 1978; and, in a roundabout way, the plummeting of the dollar on the world currency market following the rise of oil prices in the 1970s. This last factor, combined with cheap transatlantic airfares, brought European tourists into the city en masse for the first time: with them came money for the city's hotels and service industries. Tough-talking Koch helped reassure jumpy corporations that staying in New York was all right for business, and while his brash opinions and indifferent swagger offended liberal groups, it won him the critical electoral support of wealthy Upper East Siders, and the more conservative outer-borough white ethnic groups.

The city's slow reversal of fortunes coincided with the completion of two face-saving building projects: the former **World Trade Center** was a gesture of confidence by the Port Authority of New York and New Jersey which financed it (though, like the Empire State Building, it long remained half empty); and the 1977 construction of the **Citicorp Center** added modernity and prestige to its environs on Lexington Avenue. Despite the fact that the city was no longer facing bankruptcy, it was still suffering from the same massive recession as the rest of the country. New York turned to its nightlife for relief: starting in the mid-1970s, singles bars sprang up all over the city, gay bars proliferated in the Village, and disco was king. The impossible-to-get-into **Studio 54** was an internationally known hotspot, where drugs and illicit sex were the main events off the dance floor.

The real-estate and stock markets boomed during the 1980s, ushering in another era of Big Money; fortunes were made and lost overnight and big Wall Street names, like **Michael Milken**, were thrown in jail for insider trading. A spate of construction gave the city more eye-catching, though not necessarily well-loved, architecture, notably **Battery Park City**, and master builder **Donald Trump** provided glitzy housing for the super-wealthy. Nevertheless, the welfare rolls in the city, and throughout the country, swelled and the number of homeless people was staggering.

The stock market dip in 1987 started yet another downturn – a relatively negligible one, though, compared to the devastation wrought in 1929 – and Koch's popularity waned. Many middle-class constituents considered Koch to have only rich property-owners' and developers' interests at heart; he also alienated a number of minorities – particularly blacks – with ill-advised off-the-cuff statements. And although he was not directly implicated, a number of high-profile scandals in his administration took their political toll.

In 1989, Koch lost the Democratic mayoral nomination to **David Dinkins**, a 61-year-old black ex-marine who went on to beat Republican Rudolph Giuliani, a hard-nosed US attorney (whose role as leader of the prosecution in a police corruption case was made into the film *Prince of the City*) in a hard-fought election. Even before the votes were counted, though, pundits forecast that the city was beyond any mayoral healing.

New York slipped, hard and fast, into a **massive recession**: in 1989 the city's budget deficit ran at $500 million. Of the 92 companies that had made the city their base in 1980, only 53 remained, the others having moved to cheaper pastures; and one in four New Yorkers was officially classed as poor – a figure unequaled since the Depression. Union leaders went on the offensive when it was learned the city intended to lay off 15,000 workers, and crime – especially related to the sale of crack cocaine – escalated. Dinkins oversaw his first year as mayor reasonably well, quelling racial unrest and skillfully ushering a complex budget through the Council. His popularity fell swiftly in the summer of 1990, though, after a poorly considered response to a subway tourist murder, and became known as the man "to whom everything sticks but praise." By the end of the year, the city's budget deficit had reached $1.5 billion; creditors were less than amused.

The 1990s: the Giuliani years

Throughout 1991 the effects of these financial problems on the city's ordinary people became more and more apparent: homelessness increased as city aid was cut back; some public schools became no-go zones with armed police and metal detectors at the gates (fewer than half of high-school kids in the city graduated, the smallest proportion in the country); and a garbage-workers' strike left piles of rubbish rotting on the streets. Worse yet, a number of serious racial incidents and riots throughout his term contradicted Dinkins' pet phrase "gorgeous mosaic" for describing the city's multicultural make-up. Despite all this, Dinkins narrowly lost a rematch with **Rudolph Giuliani** in 1993. New York, traditionally a Democratic city, wanted a change and saw it in Giuliani – the city's first Republican mayor in 28 years.

The voters were rewarded: Giuliani's first term ushered in a dramatic upswing in New York's prosperity. A *New York Times* article described 1995 as "the best year in recent memory for New York City." The pope even came to town and called New York "the capital of the world." The city's reputation flourished, with remarkable decreases in crime and a revitalized economy that helped spur the tourism industry to some of its best years ever.

Giuliani emerged as a very proactive mayor, and one quite happy to take credit for reducing crime – making the city streets and its subways safe – and the bloated city bureaucracy. Giuliani made political friends and enemies in equal measure – and with equal energy. In 1996, Giuliani's constant battles with Police Commissioner **William Bratton**, whose policies of community policing and crackdowns on petty as well as major crime were widely considered responsible for the lower crime rates, forced the popular "Top Cop" into resigning. Many said that the notoriously egotistical Giuliani simply didn't like Bratton sharing the spotlight.

A bitter fight over **rent control** (it was salvaged, but with vacancy clauses that allow for rent increases) in 1997, along with a seriously overcrowded public-school system and cutbacks in health and welfare programs, seemed to be the end of the mayor. Nonetheless, Giuliani was handily re-elected to a second term in 1997. The city's economy continued to grow, and a series of civic improvements, including the cleaning up of Times Square, the renovation of Grand Central Terminal, and the influx of chain stores into Harlem, ensued. Tourism, and the city's coffers, felt the positive effects – if sometimes seemingly at the expense of local business and local workers.

Several high-profile incidents involving shocking allegations of **police brutality** marred Giuliani's second term and led to charges of indifference to minority rights at the top. His astounding popularity began to diminish – though it was never that high anyway with blacks and Hispanics – as reports on the practice of racial profiling and other "wide net" techniques used in catching criminals were published. These became major issues in the mayoral campaign in 2001, though they would all be superseded by events that would shock the city – and cause the locals to lean on Giuliani once more.

2000 and beyond

As if the dot-com bust in the spring of 2001 wasn't hobbling enough, New York City was hit by the worst terrorist attack of the modern era on **September 11, 2001**. The story is now horribly familiar: two hijacked planes crashed into the Twin Towers of the World Trade Center, and, as the flaming fuel melted their steel frames, the towers collapsed. Just under 3000 people are believed to have died on that day, though the remains of many were never found. The debris damaged several other nearby buildings, some of which – like the glass-roofed Winter Garden to the west – were restored, while others were condemned. The disaster's impact was more than just emotional or physical: when the towers collapsed, Manhattan lost office space equal to the whole of that in downtown Atlanta. Many large companies, and the taxes they paid, fled to New Jersey, throwing the economy into a tailspin.

Although recovery seemed unthinkable at the time, New York rebounded, as it always does. **Michael Bloomberg** replaced Rudy Giuliani as mayor immediately after the attacks: a bachelor billionaire businessman Republican in name but much more socially liberal than Giuliani, he's a radically different figure from his predecessor. Most of Bloomberg's successes have been fiscal, as he's used his corporate know-how to shore up the city's shaky finances – acts that have rarely been sexy enough to grab headlines. Soft-spoken and matter of fact, Bloomberg may lack Giuliani's common touch but he also polarizes locals far less. The mayor's most controversial act to date has been to follow California's lead and **ban smoking** in bars, clubs, and restaurants in March 2003. There was both fierce approval and pounding criticism of his decision at the time, though the mayor held firm and New Yorkers seem to have become accustomed to the idea surprisingly quickly.

Bloomberg backed away from another potentially difficult topic – the **rebuilding at Ground Zero**. From insurance claims to memorial demands, the entire process has been tricky. Renowned architect **Daniel Libeskind**, whose plan won the contest to create a new design for the site, threatened to walk away from the project several times owing to interference from special-interest groups. Officials and relatives of the dead continue to squabble over the future of the site. An agreement on the site's usage was finally reached in early 2006 between the site's owner, Larry Silverstein, and the Port Authority of New York and New Jersey, and construction of Libeskind's plan, which includes a park and memorial on and around the footprint of the Twin Towers, as well as the massive **Freedom Tower**, to the north, finally began in April 2006. The work is expected to be finished in 2012.

Bloomberg was re-elected for a second term in 2005, and in most parts of New York things are moving onward and upward. The economy is holding steady, and the city may even prove the launching pad for a future president: with Hillary Clinton a New York senator, there is a buzz among political observers about if and when she'll launch a run to take over Bill's old job.

△ The Brooklyn Bridge.

Books

Since the number of books about or set in New York is so vast, what follows is necessarily selective – use it as a place to begin further sleuthing.

Essays, memoirs, and narrative nonfiction

Ron Alexander *Metropolitan Diary: The Best Selections from the New York Times Column*. Indulge your eavesdropping fantasies with these observations, anecdotes, and quotes overheard in buses, restaurants, bars, elevators, and movie lines, to name just a few of the places where New Yorkers listen to each other's conversations.

Djuna Barnes *New York*. This collection of newspaper stories – from 1913 to 1919 – looks mostly at out-of-the-way characters and places. Highly evocative of the times – a period of great flux in New York, and the world over. See especially the piece on the "floating hotel for girls."

Anatole Broyard *Kafka was the Rage: A Greenwich Village Memoir*. Readable, if somewhat slight, account of "bohemian" 1940s Greenwich Village life; occasionally misogynistic and somewhat self-congratulatory, but Broyard's style and his descriptions of City College's radical/intellectual scene are gripping.

Jerome Charyn *Metropolis*. A native of the Bronx, Charyn dives into 1980s New York from every angle and comes up with a book that still reads as sharp, sensitive, and refreshingly real.

Josh Alan Friedman *Tales of Times Square*. Chronicles activities on and around the square between 1978 and 1984, pornography's golden age. Its no-nonsense style of narration documents a culture under siege of impresarios, pimps, and 25-cent thrills.

Phillip Lopate (ed) *Writing New York*. A massive literary anthology of both fiction and nonfiction writings on the city, with selections by authors from Washington Irving to Tom Wolfe.

Federico García Lorca *Poet in New York*. The Andalusian poet and dramatist spent nine months in the city around the time of the 1929 Wall Street Crash. This collection of over thirty poems reveals his feelings on loneliness, greed, corruption, racism, and mistreatment of the poor.

Frank McCourt *'Tis*. In the follow-up memoir to the phenomenon *Angela's Ashes*, McCourt relates life in NYC – concentrating on his time teaching in the public-school system – once he's left Ireland behind.

Joseph Mitchell *Up in the Old Hotel*. Mitchell's collected *New Yorker* essays (he calls them stories) are works of sober, if manipulative, genius. Mitchell depicts characters and situations with a reporter's precision and near-perfect style – he is the definitive chronicler of NYC streetlife.

Jan Morris *Manhattan '45*. Morris's best piece of writing on Manhattan, reconstructing New York as it greeted returning GIs in 1945. Effortlessly written, fascinatingly anecdotal, and marvelously warm about the city.

Willie Morris *New York Days*. The literary socialite and great editor of *Harper's* tells his story of moving from Mississippi to NYC – and his rise through the journalism ranks.

Georges Perec and Robert Bober *Ellis Island*. A brilliant, moving, original account of the "island of tears": part history, part meditation, and part interviews. Some of the stories are heartbreaking (between 1892 and 1924 there were 3000 suicides on the island), and the pictures are even more so.

Guy Trebay *In the Place to Be: Guy Trebay's New York*. Collected columns by one of the more notable *Village Voice* writers celebrating populations on society's margins which, as the warm columns show, are the very fabric and spirit of the city – and hence not "marginal" at all.

History, politics, and society

Tyler Anbinder *Five Points*. A fine companion to Asbury's seminal, if dated and somewhat fanciful, work (see below), this account of the Five Points neighborhood is a meticulously researched history of brutality and corruption in Manhattan during the second half of the nineteenth century.

Herbert Asbury *The Gangs of New York*. First published in 1928, this fascinating telling of the seamier side of New York is essential reading. Full of historical detail, anecdotes, and character sketches of crooks, the book describes New York mischief in all its incarnations and locales.

Edwin G. Burrows and Mike Wallace *Gotham: A History of New York City to 1898*. Enormous and encyclopedic in its detail, this is a serious history of the development of New York, with chapters on everything from its role in the Revolution to reform movements to its racial make-up in the 1820s.

Vincent Cannato *The Ungovernable City: John Lindsay and His Struggle to Save New York*. A not overly sympathetic portrait of New York's mayor during the volatile late 1960s and early 1970s, revealing for its depth on issues and city politics.

Robert A. Caro *The Power Broker: Robert Moses and the Fall of New York*. Despite its imposing length, this brilliant and searing critique of New York City's most powerful twentieth-century figure is one of the most important books ever written about the city and its environs. Caro's book brings to light the megalomania and manipulation responsible for the creation of the nation's largest urban infrastructure.

George Chauncey *Gay New York: The Making of the Gay Male World 1890–1940*. Definitive, revealing account of the city's gay subculture.

Anne Douglas *Terrible Honesty: Mongrel Manhattan in the 1920s*. The media and artistic culture of the Roaring Twenties, a fluke that was a casualty of the Depression.

Sanna Feirstein *Naming New York*. Read this and you'll never have to wonder any more about how the city streets, neighborhoods, and parks got their names.

Kenneth T. Jackson (ed) *The Enyclopedia of New York*. Massive, engrossing, and utterly comprehensive guide to just about everything in the city. Much dry detail, but packed with incidental wonders: did you know, for example, that there are more (dead) people in Calvary Cemetery, Queens, than there are (living) people in the whole borough? Or that Truman Capote's real name was Streckford Persons?

Roger Kahn *The Boys of Summer*. This account of the 1950s Brooklyn Dodgers by a beat writer who covered them is considered one of the classic baseball reads.

John A. Kouwenhoven *Columbia Historical Portrait of New York*. Interpreting the evolution of the city in visual terms (with illuminating captions accompanying the illustrations), this opus is monumental, fascinating, and definitive.

George J. Lankevich *American Metropolis*. Written in a direct, readable style, this is the concise alternative to *Gotham* (see opposite).

David Levering Lewis *When Harlem Was in Vogue*. Much needed account of the Harlem Renaissance, a brief flowering of the arts in the 1920s and 1930s that was suffocated by the dual forces of depression and racism. Lewis also edited the anthology *Portable Harlem Renaissance Reader*.

Legs McNeil and Gillian McCain *Please Kill Me*. An oral history of punk music in New York, artfully constructed by juxtaposing snippets of interviews as if the various protagonists (artists, financiers, impresarios) were in a conversation. Sometimes hilarious, often quite bleak.

Luc Sante *Low Life: Lures and Snares of Old New York*. This chronicle of the city's seamy side between 1840 and 1919 is a pioneering work. Full of outrageous details usually left out of conventional history, it reconstructs the day-to-day life of the urban poor, criminals, and prostitutes with shocking clarity. Sante's prose is poetic and nuanced, his evocations of the seedier neighborhoods, their dives and pleasure palaces, quite vivid.

James B. Stewart *Den of Thieves*. An account by a *Wall Street Journal* reporter about the wheeler-dealers of the takeover 1980s that gave Wall Street such a bad name, focusing on four major culprits – Ivan Boesky, Dennis Levine, Michael Milken, and Martin Siegel.

Gay Talese *Fame and Obscurity*. Talese deftly presents interviews with New York City's famous (Sinatra, DiMaggio, etc) and its obscure (bums, chauffeurs, etc) offering not only a window into the heart of NYC, but that of human existence.

Jennifer Toth *Mole People*. A creepy sociological study of the people who live below NYC streets, in the dark reaches of the subway tunnel system. You may never again ride the subway without your face plastered to the window looking for signs of human life.

Lloyd Ultan and Barbara Unger *Bronx Accent: A Literary and Pictorial History of the Borough*. The authors, two local university professors, use historical and contemporary personalities to tell the Bronx's past in text and photos. A must-read if you plan on spending time in the city's northernmost borough.

Art, architecture, and photography

Lorraine Diehl *The Late Great Pennsylvania Station*. The anatomy of a travesty. How could a railroad palace, modeled after the Baths of Caracalla in Rome, stand for only fifty years before being destroyed? The pictures alone warrant the price.

Horst Hamann *New York Vertical*. This beautiful book pays homage to the New York skyscraper, and is filled with dazzling black-and-white vertical shots of Manhattan, accompanied by witty quotes from famous and obscure folk.

Jane Jacobs *The Death and Life of Great American Cities*. Landmark 1961 screed that rails against over-planning in cities and uses Greenwich Village as an example of a model urban neighborhood. Author Jacobs lived for years at 555 Hudson St in the Village and was Robert Moses' nemesis.

H. Klotz (ed) *New York Architecture 1970–1990*. Extremely well-illustrated account of the shift from Modernism to postmodernism and beyond.

David McCullough *Great Bridge: The Epic Story of the Building of the Brooklyn Bridge*. The story of the father and son Roebling team who fought the laws of gravity, sharp-toothed competitors, and corrupt politicians to build a bridge that has withstood the test of time and become one of NYC's most noted landmarks.

Francis Morrone *An Architectural Guidebook to Brooklyn*. Delves deeply into the various architectural styles and standouts of this huge and historic borough.

Museum of the City of New York *Our Town: Images and Stories from the Museum of the City of New York*. A lovely collection of paintings, photographs, artifacts, and prints from the museum's collection which explore the city from early days to contemporary times, with essays by Oscar Hijuelos and Louis Auchincloss, among others.

Jacob Riis *How the Other Half Lives*. Photojournalism reporting on life in the Lower East Side at the end of the nineteenth century. Its original publication in 1890 awakened many to the plight of New York's poor.

Stern, Gilmartin and Mellins/ Stern and Gilmartin, Massengale/Stern and Mellins, Fishman *New York 1900/1930/1960*. These three exhaustive tomes, subtitled "Metropolitan Architecture and Urbanism," contain all you'll ever want or need to know about architecture and the organization of the city. The facts are dazzling and numbing, the photos nostalgia-inducing.

N. White and E. Willensky (eds) *AIA Guide to New York*. The definitive contemporary guide to the city's architecture, far more interesting than it sounds, and useful as an on-site reference.

Gerard R. Wolfe *New York: A Guide to the Metropolis*. Set up as a walking tour, this is a little more academic – and less opinionated – than others, but it does include some good stuff on the outer boroughs, as well as informed historical background.

Other guides

Richard Alleman *The Movie Lover's Guide to New York*. More than two hundred listings of corners of the city with cinematic associations. Interestingly written, painstakingly researched, and indispensable to anyone with even a remote interest in either New York or film history.

Raymond Alvin *Get a Grip New York: The 55 Things You Need to Know to Survive in New York*. Chatty, no-nonsense guide to the tricks of everyday life – from how to haggle with street vendors for the best price to "7 things to do in New York when you ain't got no money."

Joann Biondi and James Kaskins *Hippocrene USA Guide to Black New York*. Borough-by-borough gazetteer of historic sites, cultural spots, music, and food of special African-American interest. Somewhat out-of-date but the only one of its kind.

William Corbett *New York Literary Lights*. An informative introduction to New York's literary history, with thumbnail profiles of writers, publishers, and other figures of the literary scene, along with descriptions of their hangouts, neighborhoods, and favorite publications.

Judi Culbertson and Tom Randall *Permanent New Yorkers*. This unique guide to the cemeteries of New York includes the final resting places of such notables as Herman Melville, Duke Ellington, Billie Holiday, Horace Greeley, Mae West, Judy Garland, and 350 others.

Federal Writers' Project *The WPA Guide to New York City*. Originally written in 1939 and recently reissued, this detailed guide offers a fascinating look at life in New York City when the Dodgers played at Ebbets Field, a trolley ride cost five cents, and a room at the *Plaza* was $7.50. A surprising amount of description remains apt.

Alfred Gingold and Helen Rogan *The Cool Parents' Guide to All of New York*. A terrific resource for people traveling with kids, it covers everything from museums and kid-oriented theater to parks, sports, festivals, and other special events, all in a down-to-earth conversational style (it's obviously written by cool parents).

Rob Grader *The Cheap Bastard's Guide to New York City*. If the title doesn't immediately turn you off, this is the book for you.

Daniel Hurewitz *Stepping Out: 9 Walks through New York City's Gay and Lesbian Past*. An inspiring and avowedly trashy book, full of fascinating tidbits of gay lore. It takes you on walking tours through every corner of the city, pointing out the signs and highlights of gay life and gay culture in a conversational, anecdotal style.

Jim Leff *The Eclectic Gourmet Guide to Greater New York City*. An offbeat guide to the smaller, lesser-known, foreign food vendors in all five boroughs, where the decor may not be something to savor but the flavors are straight from their home countries.

Ed Levine *New York Eats*. Covering all five boroughs – with a small section on that trendiest of Manhattan "suburbs," the Hamptons – each chapter covers a different type of food. From smoked fish to spices, from pizza to pastries, Levine tells you where to find the best of each, arranged by neighborhood and covering the top butchers, bakeries, gourmet takeouts, greengrocers, delis, and restaurants in the city.

Andrew Roth *Infamous Manhattan*. A vivid and engrossing history of New York crime, revealing the sites of Mafia hits, celebrity murders, nineteenth-century brothels, and other wicked spots, including a particularly fascinating guide to restaurants with dubious, infamous, or gory pasts.

Fiction

Julia Alvarez *How the Garcia Girls Lost Their Accents*. Four Latina sisters are uprooted from their privileged life in the Dominican Republic to the Bronx in this compelling look at the modern immigrant experience.

Paul Auster *The New York Trilogy: City of Glass, Ghosts and The Locked Room*. Three Borgesian investigations into the mystery, madness, and murders of contemporary NYC. Using the conventions of the crime thriller, Auster unfolds a disturbed and disturbing picture of the city.

Kevin Baker *Dreamland*. A sprawling and dazzling novel, set in the late nineteenth century, which stitches together historical events and people like the Triangle Shirtwaist Fire and Sigmund Freud as the hero skittles around Brooklyn and Lower Manhattan.

James Baldwin *Another Country*. Baldwin's best-known novel, tracking the feverish search for meaningful relationships among a group of 1960s New York bohemians. The so-called liberated era in the city has never been more vividly documented.

Jennifer Belle *Going Down*. First novel that chronicles the "descent" of an NYU student into working as a call girl. Full of surprising turns of phrase and some deadpan black humor.

Lawrence Block *When the Sacred Ginmill Closes*. Tough to choose between Block's hard-hitting Matthew Scudder suspense novels, all set in the city; this might be the most compelling, with Hell's Kitchen, downtown Manhattan, and far-flung parts of Brooklyn expertly woven into a dark mystery. Try also *Small Town*, a non-Scudder thriller that paints as vivid a post-9/11 picture of New York as you'll find.

Claude Brown *Manchild in the Promised Land*. Gripping autobiographical fiction set on the hard streets of Harlem and published in the mid-1960s; not as famous as *Invisible Man*, but still worth your time.

Truman Capote *Breakfast at Tiffany's*. Far sadder and racier than the movie, this novel is a rhapsody to New York in the early 1940s, tracking the dissolute youthful residents of an uptown apartment building and their movements about town.

Caleb Carr *The Alienist*. This 1896-set thriller evokes old New York to perfection. The heavy-handed psychobabble grates at times, but the story line (the pursuit of one of the first serial killers) is still involving. Best for its descriptions of New York as well as saliva-inducing details of meals at long-gone restaurants.

Jerome Charyn *War Cries over Avenue C*. Alphabet City in the 1980s is the derelict backdrop for this suspenseful, offbeat tale of conspiracy and gang warfare among the Vietnam-crazed coke barons of New York. A later work, *Paradise Man*, is the violent story of a New York hit man.

Stephen Crane *Maggie: A Girl of the Streets*. 1893 melodrama about a girl growing up in a Lower East Side slum. Although luridly overdescribed, *Red Badge of Courage* author Crane was deservedly acclaimed for his ground-breaking naturalism; the fictional counterpart to Riis's work.

Don DeLillo *Underworld*. Following the fate of the baseball hit out of the park to win the 1951 pennant for the New York Giants, DeLillo's sprawling novel offers a counterhistory of twentieth-century America. Occasionally slow, but worthwhile.

E.L. Doctorow *Ragtime*. Doctorow cleverly weaves together fact and fiction in WWI-era New York to create a biting indictment of racism. See also *World's Fair*, a beautiful evocation of a Bronx boyhood in the 1930s.

Ralph Ellison *Invisible Man*. The definitive, if sometimes long-winded, novel of what it's like to be black and American, using

Harlem and the 1950s race riots as a backdrop.

Jack Finney *Time and Again*. Equal parts love story, mystery, and fantasy, this is really a glowing tribute to the city itself. Part of a secret government experiment in time travel, Simon Morley is transported back to 1880s New York and finds himself falling in love and being torn between his past and present lives. Rich details of old New York.

Paula Fox *Desperate Characters*. A clinical, unflinching portrait of a fracturing marriage set against the backdrop of the gentrification of an unnamed Brooklyn neighborhood.

Oscar Hijuelos *Our House in the Last World*. A warmly evocative novel of a Cuban immigrant's life in New York from before the war to the present day.

Chester Himes *The Crazy Kill*. Himes wrote violent, fast-moving, and funny thrillers set in Harlem; this and *Cotton Goes to Harlem* are among the best.

Andrew Holleran *Dancer from the Dance*. Enjoyable account of the embryonic gay disco scene of the early 1970s. Interesting location detail of Manhattan haunts and Fire Island, but suffers from over-exaltation of the central character.

Henry James *Washington Square*. Skillful and engrossing examination of the mores and strict social expectations of genteel New York society in the late nineteenth century.

Joyce Johnson *Minor Characters*. Women were never prominent members of the Beat generation; its literature examined a male world through strictly male eyes. This book, written by the woman who lived for a short time with Jack Kerouac, redresses the balance superbly; there's no better novel on the Beats in New York.

Sue Kaufman *Diary of a Mad Housewife*. Recently reissued, this is a classic dissection of 1960s New York, satirically chronicling the antics of a group of social climbers along with the disintegration of a marriage.

Joseph Koenig *Little Odessa*. An ingenious, twisting thriller set between Manhattan and Brooklyn's Brighton Beach. A readable, exciting novel and a good contemporary view of New York City.

Jonathan Lethem *Motherless Brooklyn*. Brooklyn author sets this quirky suspense novel in Cobble Hill and its environs, where a Tourette's sufferer tries to track down his boss's killer. See also his subsequent *The Fortress of Solitude*, which treats childhood and gentrification with great wit and sensitivity.

Mary McCarthy *The Group*. Eight Vassar graduates making their way in the New York of the Thirties. Sad, funny, and satirical.

Alice McDermott *Charming Billy*. Billy is a poetry-loving drunkard from Queens, looking to bring his Irish love over to New York City. National Book Award winner.

Jay McInerney *Bright Lights, Big City*. A trendy, "voice of a generation" book when it came out in the 1980s, it made first-time novelist McInerney a household name. The story follows a struggling New York writer in his job as a fact-checker at an important literary magazine (a thinly disguised *New Yorker*), and from one cocaine-sozzled nightclub to another. Amusing now, as it vividly captures the times.

Emma McLaughlin and Nicola Kraus *The Nanny Diaries: A Novel*. A delicious and nimble comic novel, culled from the authors' own experiences nannying to the wealthy families of the Upper East Side.

Steven Millhauser *Martin Dressler: Tale of an American Dreamer*. Masterful rags-to-riches tale of a mogul whose burgeoning fantasies reflect his ever-expanding ambition.

Dorothy Parker *Complete Stories*. Parker's stories are, at times, surprisingly moving, depicting New York in all its glories, excesses, and pretensions with perfect, searing wit.

Ann Petry *The Street*. The story of a black woman's struggle to rise from the slums of Harlem in the 1940s. Convincingly bleak.

Judith Rossner *Looking for Mr Goodbar*. A disquieting book, tracing the life – and eventual demise – of a female teacher in search of love in volatile and permissive 1970s New York.

Henry Roth *Call It Sleep*. Roth's novel traces the awakening of a small immigrant child to the realities of life among the slums of the Jewish Lower East Side. Read more for the evocations of childhood than the social comment.

Paul Rudnick *Social Disease*. Hilarious, often incredible send-up of Manhattan night owls. Very New York, very funny.

J.D. Salinger *The Catcher in the Rye*. Salinger's gripping novel of adolescence, following Holden Caulfield's sardonic journey of discovery through the streets of New York. A classic.

David Schickler *Kissing in Manhattan*. Schickler's series of interconnected stories about the residents of an Upper West Side apartment complex is engaging, if slight. The collection's highlight is the creepy and bizarre *The Smoker*, which was first published to gushing acclaim in *The New Yorker*.

Sarah Schulman *The Sophie Horowitz Story*; *After Delores*. Lesbian detective stories: dry, downbeat, and very funny. See also *Girls, Visions and Everything*, a stylish and humorous study of the lives of Lower East Side lesbians.

Hubert Selby, Jr *Last Exit to Brooklyn*. When first published in Britain in 1966, this novel was tried on charges of obscenity. Even now it's a disturbing read, evoking the sex, immorality, drugs, and violence of Brooklyn in the 1960s with fearsome clarity.

Betty Smith *A Tree Grows in Brooklyn*. A classic, and rightly so – a courageous Irish girl learns about family, life, and sex against a vivid prewar Brooklyn backdrop. Totally absorbing.

Kyle Smith *Love Monkey*. Scabrous media satire about a misanthropic journalist who works for a *New York Post*–like tabloid.

Rex Stout *The Doorbell Rang*. Stout's Nero Wolfe is perhaps the most intrinsically "New York" of all the literary detectives based in the city, a larger-than-life character who, with the help of his dashing assistant, Archie Goodwin, solves crimes from the comfort of his sumptuous midtown brownstone. Wonderfully evocative of the city in the 1940s and 1950s.

Plum Sykes *Bergdorf Blondes*. Utterly shallow beach-read that nevertheless serves as a spot-on sociological guide to the city's barely employed and disgustingly wealthy.

Kay Thompson *Eloise*. Renowned children's book that works just as well for adults. It details a day in the life of our heroine Eloise, who lives at the *Plaza* with her nanny.

Edward Lewis Wallant *The Tenants of Moonbloom*. Quirky, picaresque novel about a dreamer forced to work as rent collector for his slumlord brother.

Lauren Weisberger *The Devil Wears Prada*. A satirical snapshot of New York's cutthroat magazine world, this *roman à clef* from *Vogue* editor Anna Wintour's former assistant is pleasant enough, if blander than its dishy subject matter might suggest.

Edith Wharton *Old New York*. A collection of short novels on the manners and mores of New York in the mid-nineteenth century, written with Jamesian clarity and precision. See also her *Hudson River Bracketed* and *The Mother's Recompense*, both of which center around the lives of women in nineteenth-century New York.

Tom Wolfe *Bonfire of the Vanities*. Set all around New York City, this sprawling novel skewers 1980s status-mongers to great effect.

New York on film

With its skyline and rugged facades, its mean streets and swanky avenues, its electric energy and edgy attitude, New York City is a natural-born movie star. From the silent era's cautionary tales of young lovers ground down by the metropolis, through the smoky location-shot *noirs* of the 1940s, right through to the Lower East Side indies of the past twenty years, New York has probably been the most filmed city on earth. The city's visual pizzazz is matched by the vitality of its filmmaking, fostered by a tough, eccentric, and independent spirit that has created mavericks like John Cassavetes, Jim Jarmusch, Shirley Clarke, Spike Lee, and Martin Scorsese, as well as directors like Woody Allen and Sidney Lumet who hate to film anywhere else (and pretty much don't).

What follows is a selection not just of the best New York movies but the most New York of New York movies – movies that capture the city's atmosphere, pulse, and style; movies that celebrate its diversity or revel in its misfortunes; and movies that, if nothing else, give you a pretty good idea of what you're going to get before you get there.

Ten great New York movies

Breakfast at Tiffany's (*Blake Edwards, 1961*). The most charming and cherished of New York movie romances, starring Audrey Hepburn as party girl Holly Golightly. Hepburn and George Peppard run up and down each other's fire escapes and skip along Fifth Avenue, taking in the New York Public Library and that jewelry store.

Do the Right Thing (*Spike Lee, 1989*). Set over 24 hours on the hottest day of the year in Brooklyn's Bed-Stuy – a day on which the melting pot reaches boiling point – Spike Lee's colorful, stylish masterpiece moves from comedy to tragedy to compose an epic song of New York. It just looks better every time you see it.

King Kong (*Merian C. Cooper and Ernest B. Schoedsack, 1933*). Though half of it takes place on the tropical island, *King Kong* paints a vivid picture of Depression-era Manhattan, and gives us the city's most indelible movie image: King Kong straddling the Empire State Building and swatting at passing planes.

Manhattan (*Woody Allen, 1979*). This black-and-white masterpiece, one of the truly great eulogies to the city, details the self-absorptions, lifestyles, and romances of middle-class intellectuals, to the tune of a Gershwin soundtrack.

On the Town (*Gene Kelly and Stanley Donen, 1949*). Three sailors get 24 hours' shore leave in NYC and fight over whether to see the sights or chase the girls. Starring Gene Kelly, Frank Sinatra, and Ann Miller flashing her gams in the Museum of Natural History, this was the first musical taken out of the studios and onto the streets. Smart, cynical, and satirical with a bunch of terrific numbers.

On the Waterfront (*Elia Kazan, 1954*). Few images of New York are as unforgettable as Marlon Brando's rooftop pigeon coop at dawn and those misty views of the New York Harbor (actually shot just over the river in Hoboken), in this unforgettable story of long-suffering longshoremen and union racketeering.

Shadows (*John Cassavetes, 1960*). Cassavetes' debut film is a New York movie *par excellence*: a New Wave melody about jazz musicians, young love, and racial prejudice, shot with bebop verve and jazzy passion in Central Park, Greenwich Village, and even the MoMA sculpture garden.

The Sweet Smell of Success (*Alexander Mackendrick, 1957*). Broadway as a nest of vipers. Gossip columnist Burt Lancaster and sleazy press agent Tony Curtis eat each other's tails in this snappy, cynical study of showbiz corruption. Shot on location and mostly at night, in steely black and white, Times Square and the Great White Way never looked so alluring.

Taxi Driver (*Martin Scorsese, 1976*). A long night's journey into day by the great chronicler of the city's dark side. Scorsese's New York is hallucinatorily seductive and thoroughly repellent in this superbly unsettling study of obsessive outsider Travis Bickle (Robert De Niro).

West Side Story (*Robert Wise and Jerome Robbins, 1961*). Sex, singing, and Shakespeare in a hypercinematic Oscar-winning musical (via Broadway) about rival street gangs. Lincoln Center now stands where the Sharks and the Jets once rumbled and interracial romance ended in tragedy.

Modern New York

The 25th Hour (*Spike Lee, 2002*). Lee stacks his film (based on an excellent first novel by David Benioff) with an impressive cast, headed by Ed Norton and including the likes of Philip Seymour Hoffman and Anna Paquin. The story's about a drug dealer (played by Norton) and his last day before he goes to prison, ricocheting round between friends and lovers. Bleak, but gripping.

All Over Me (*Alex Sichel, 1997*). A beautifully acted coming-of-age tale about a heavyset teenager who is patently but unspokenly in love with her baby-doll best friend. Set during a humid Hell's Kitchen summer, this doomed romance is played out in cramped tenement bedrooms and sweltering neighborhood bars, and set to a pounding riot grrrl score.

Bad Lieutenant (*Abel Ferrara, 1992*). Nearly every movie by Ferrara, from *Driller Killer* to *The Funeral*, deserves a place in a list of great New York movies, but this, above all, seems his own personal *Manhattan*: a journey through the circles of Hell with Harvey Keitel as a depraved Dante.

The Cruise (*Bennett Miller, 1998*). A documentary portrait of a true New York eccentric, Timothy "Speed" Levitch, a Dostoyevskian character with a baroque flair for language and an encyclopedic knowledge of local history, who takes puzzled tourists on guided "cruises" around the city, on which he rails against the tyranny of the grid plan and rhapsodizes about "the lascivious voyeurism of the tour bus."

The Daytrippers (*Greg Mottola, 1996*). This sleeper hit follows a hilariously dysfunctional Long Island family on a Manhattan odyssey in search of their eldest daughter's errant husband, taking them from Park Avenue publishing houses to a startling denouement at a rooftop Soho party.

In America (*Jim Sheridan, 2003*). Sheridan and his two daughters wrote this autobiographical tale of an immigrant Irish family arriving in New York in the 1980s, and even in its bleakest moments, the tenderness and intimacy of the story is enchanting. Anachronisms aside (camcorders anyone?) he also establishes a fierce sense of 1980s Manhattan.

Kids (*Larry Clark, 1995*). The best New York summer movie since *Do the Right Thing*, and just as controversial. An overhyped but affecting portrait of a group of amoral, though supposedly typical, teenagers hanging out on the Upper East Side, in Washington Square Park, and in the Carmine Street swimming pool on one muggy, mad day.

Little Odessa (*James Gray, 1995*). Tim Roth plays the prodigal son returning to Brooklyn in this somber, beautifully shot story of the Russian mafia in Brighton Beach and Coney Island. One of a spate of New York ethnic gangster films made in the 1990s which, among others, portrayed Irish mobsters (*State of Grace*), Jewish hoodlums (*Amongst Friends*), and African-American gang-bangers (*New Jack City*). Gray's star-studded and superior, though overlooked, *The Yards* (2000) gives a similarly piercing look at corruption in the rail yards of Queens.

Metropolitan (*Whit Stillman, 1990*). Away from all the racism, crime, and homelessness, a group of debutantes and rich young men socialize on the Upper East Side one Christmas, tackling head-on such pressing issues as where to buy a good tuxedo, and behaving as if the 1980s, or the 1880s for that matter, had never ended.

Night Falls on Manhattan (*Sidney Lumet, 1996*). Gotham's great cinematic chronicler of police corruption delivers another swinging blow in the Giuliani era in this underrated drama about Harlem drug dealers, bent cops, and the District Attorney's office. Stars Andy Garcia as an idealistic D.A. and Ian Holm as his veteran cop pop.

Party Monster (*Fenton Bailey and Randy Barbato, 2003*). Hit-and-miss film version of a seemingly can't-fail story ripped from the headlines – the grisly clubland murder of a drug dealer by wunderkind promoter Michael Alig. The creepiest thing about the movie is Macaulay Culkin's highly convincing performance.

A Price Above Rubies (*Boaz Yakin, 1998*). Set among the ultra-orthodox Hasidic community of Brooklyn's Borough Park, this film offers tantalizing glimpses of a little-seen world, but its risible story of the rebellion of one young wife (Renee Zellweger) against patriarchal oppression offers little in the way of enlightenment.

Ransom (*Ron Howard, 1996*). The haves and the have-nots battle it out on the Upper East Side in this ludicrous Mel Gibson thriller about a millionaire airline magnate whose son is kidnapped by underworld thugs at the Bethesda Fountain in Central Park.

The Saint of Fort Washington (*Tim Hunter, 1992*). Nearly invisible on film, the plight of the city's homeless is portrayed in this heartfelt and sentimental tale of a schizophrenic (Matt Dillon) and a Vietnam vet (Danny Glover) who meet at the Fort Washington shelter in Washington Heights.

Six Degrees of Separation (*Fred Schepisi, 1993*). Brilliant, enthralling adaptation of John Guare's acclaimed play uses the story – a young black man (Will Smith) turns up at a rich Upper East Side apartment claiming to be the son of Sidney Poitier – a springboard for an examination of the great social and racial divides of the city.

Smoke (*Wayne Wang, 1995*). A clever, beguiling film scripted by novelist Paul Auster, which connects a handful of stories revolving around Harvey Keitel's Brooklyn cigar store.

C

Deals with the "beautiful mosaic" in a somewhat self-satisfied way, but, as a fairy tale about how we might all be able to get along, it's just fine. A companion film, *Blue in the Face*, has a looser, more improvised feel.

The Thomas Crown Affair (*John McTiernan, 1999*). Remake of the 1968 caper film, this time with Pierce Brosnan as the wealthy Mr Crown, Rene Russo as the insurance investigator, and the Metropolitan

Museum of Art playing host to a daring heist and its bookend scene.

Unmade Beds (*Nicholas Barker, 1998*). This poignant, occasionally hilarious, and beautifully stylized documentary about four single New Yorkers looking for love in the personal columns, visualizes the city as one endless Edward Hopper painting, full of lonely souls biding time in rented rooms.

New York past

The Age of Innocence (*Martin Scorsese, 1993*). The upper echelons of New York society in the 1870s brought gloriously to life. Though Scorsese restricts most of the action to drawing rooms and ballrooms, look out for the breathtaking matte shot of a then-undeveloped Upper East Side.

Basquiat (*Julian Schnabel, 1996*). Haunting portrait of the artist as a young (doomed) man, rising from spray-painting graffiti and living in a box in a Lower East Side park to taking the New York art world by storm in the early 1980s. David Bowie plays a sensitive Andy Warhol.

A Bronx Tale (*Robert De Niro, 1993*). An overlooked film with depth and heart. In a 1960s Bronx, Calogero witnesses a traffic accident and its aftermath at the hands of a local gangster, Sonny (Chazz Palminteri). Over the next several years, his loyalties to his bus-driver father (De Niro) are tested as he is seduced by Sonny's glamorous world. Great soundtrack.

Carlito's Way (*Brian De Palma, 1993*). Sumptuously filmed story of a Puerto Rican gangster (Al Pacino) trying to go straight – it plays somewhat by the numbers, but is notable

for its unfashionably tragic story arc and lively evocation of the 1970s disco- and salsa-club scenes.

The Crowd (*King Vidor, 1928*). "You've got to be good in that town if you want to beat the crowd." A young couple try to make it in the big city but are swallowed up and spat out by the capitalist machine. A bleak vision of New York in the 1920s, and one of the great silent films.

The Docks of New York (*Josef von Sternberg, 1928*). Opening with dramatic shots of New York's shoreline during its heyday, this story of a couple of sailors' shore leave in waterfront flophouses and gin-soaked bars is a far cry from *On the Town*; an ugly world beautifully filmed.

Gangs of New York (*Martin Scorsese, 2002*). Sprawling, overlong, but impressive historical yarn, detailing the bitter immigrant rivalries and gang warfare which dogged early Manhattan settlement. Cameron Diaz is out of her depth as the pickpocket with a heart, but both Leonardo DiCaprio and Daniel Day Lewis shine.

The Godfather Part II (*Francis Ford Coppola, 1974*). Flashing back to the early life of Vito Corleone, Coppola's great sequel recreated the Italian immigrant experience at the turn of the century, portraying Corleone quarantined at Ellis Island and growing up tough on the meticulously recreated streets of Little Italy.

Hallelujah, I'm a Bum (*Lewis Milestone, 1933*). Set during the Depression, this eccentric musical comedy (written in rhyming dialogue) imagines Central Park as a benign haven for the homeless. Die-hard hobo Al Jolson travels north to spend the summer *en plein air* in New York, but when he falls in love with a girl he meets in the park, he has to take a job on Wall Street.

Hester Street (*Joan Micklin Silver, 1975*). Young, tradition-bound Russian-Jewish immigrant joins her husband in turn-of-the-century Lower East Side to find he's cast off old-world ways. Simple but appealing tale with splendid period feeling. The tenements and markets of 1896 Hester Street were convincingly recreated on the quaint backstreets of the West Village.

The Last Days of Disco (*Whit Stillman, 1998*). About the most unlikely setting for Stillman's brand of square WASPy talkfests would be the bombastic glittery bacchanals that were *Studio 54* in its late-1970s heyday, which is what makes this far more enjoyable than the same season's overly literal and melodramatic *54* (*Mark Christopher, 1998*).

Little Fugitive (*Morris Engel and Ruth Orkin, 1953*). A Brooklyn 7-year-old, tricked into believing he has killed his older brother, takes flight to Coney Island where he spends a day and a night indulging in all its previously forbidden pleasures. This beautifully photographed time capsule of 1950s Brooklyn influenced both the American indie scene and the French New Wave.

Lonesome (*Paul Fejos, 1928*). This recently rediscovered silent classic follows two lonely working-class New Yorkers through one eventful summer Saturday, culminating in an ebullient afternoon at a breathtakingly crowded Coney Island.

Pollock (*Ed Harris, 2000*). From a cramped Manhattan apartment to the barren nature of the Hamptons, abstract artist Jackson Pollock drips on canvases and battles his wife (Oscar-winner Marcia Gay Harden), fame, and drink. Harris is powerful in the title role.

Radio Days (*Woody Allen, 1987*). Woody contrasts reminiscences of his loud, vulgar family in 1940s Rockaway with reveries of the golden days of radio and the glamour of Times Square. He used the same kind of cynical nostalgia in *Bullets Over Broadway* (1994), a yarn about gangsters and theater folk in the 1920s, and in the trials of show-biz manager/former comic *Broadway Danny Rose* (1984), which begins and ends at the *Carnegie Deli*.

Speedy (*Ted Wilde, 1928*). This silent Harold Lloyd comedy shot on location in the city is a priceless portrait of New York in the 1920s, featuring a horse-drawn trolley chase through the Lower East Side, a visit to Yankee Stadium, and an unforgettably exuberant trip to Coney Island.

Summer of Sam (*Spike Lee, 1999*). The dark summer of 1977 – the summer of the "Son of Sam" killings, a blistering heatwave, power blackouts, looting, arson, and the birth of punk – provides the perfect backdrop for Lee's sprawling tale of paranoia and betrayal in an Italian-American enclave of the Bronx.

Yankee Doodle Dandy (*Michael Curtiz, 1932*). James Cagney's Oscar-winning performance as showbiz renaissance man George M. Cohan is a big-spirited biopic with music.

New York comedy and romance

An Affair to Remember (*Leo McCarey, 1957*). After a romance at sea, Cary Grant and Deborah Kerr dock in New York and plan to meet six months hence at the top of the Empire State Building if they can free themselves from prior engagements, and if playboy Grant can make it as a painter in Greenwich Village. Quite weepy, it inspired the Tom Hanks/Meg Ryan collaboration, *Sleepless in Seattle* (1993), a modern romantic classic.

Annie Hall (*Woody Allen, 1977*). Oscar-winning autobiographical comic romance, which flits from reminiscences of Alvy Singer's childhood living beneath the Coney Island Cyclone, to life and love in uptown Manhattan (enlivened by endless cocktail parties and trips to see *The Sorrow and the Pity* at the Thalia), is a valentine both to ex-lover co-star Diane Keaton and to the city. Simultaneously clever, bourgeois, and very winning.

Big (*Penny Marshall, 1988*). Feeling underappreciated as the big brother to a new baby, one night Tom Hanks wishes he could be a grown-up. Grow he does, waking as a young man. The movie watches him move from New Jersey to the Big City – hired as a computer clerk at a Madison Avenue toy firm, he impresses his boss with his unbridled enthusiasm for F.A.O. Schwarz, and relocates from a Times Square dive to a to-die-for Soho loft, all while he tries to reverse his premature aging. The basic premise was remade in the gender-switched, still Manhattan-set comedy *13 Going on 30* (2004).

Crossing Delancey (*Joan Micklin Silver, 1989*). Lovely story of a Jewish woman (Amy Irving) who lives uptown but visits her grandmother south of Delancey each week. The grandmother and the local *yenta*

hitch her up with a nice, young pickle vendor when all she wants is a nasty famous novelist. An engaging view of contemporary life in the Jewish Lower East Side and the yuppie Upper West.

Desperately Seeking Susan (*Susan Seidelman, 1985*). Bored New Jersey housewife Rosanna Arquette arrives in Manhattan on a mission: to find Madonna, or rather Susan, the mysterious subject of a number of cryptic personal ads. Infected with East Village *élan*, Arquette is transformed into a grungy Madonna clone and finds happiness in this charming paean to the joys of downtown.

Men in Black (*Barry Sonnenfeld, 1997*). One of the most wittily imaginative Manhattan movies portrays the city as a haven for a brave new wave of immigration, with Tommy Lee Jones and Will Smith keeping watch for extraterrestrials and the future of the universe hanging in the balance in a MacDougal Street jewelry store.

Miracle on 34th Street (*George Seaton, 1947*). The perfect antidote to all the nightmares and mean streets of New York films, *Miracle* opens during Macy's annual Christmas parade, where a kindly old gentleman with a white beard offers to replace the store's inebriated Santa.

Moonstruck (*Norman Jewison, 1988*). Plenty of nostalgic New York backdrops in this middling romance, in which an Italian woman with "no luck" (an Oscar-winning role for Cher) reluctantly falls for her fiancé's estranged brother (Nicolas Cage). Heavy on the tomato sauce, opera, and accents.

Quick Change (*Howard Franklin and Bill Murray, 1990*). The "change" is cash stolen from a bank. The "quick" of the title is ironic: though the robbery was easy, it's fleeing the city that proves difficult, as Bill Murray and his cohorts are delayed by cops, other crooks, and regular, eccentric New Yorkers. One of Murray's best efforts.

The Seven Year Itch (*Billy Wilder, 1955*). When his wife and kid vacate humid Manhattan, Mitty-like pulp editor Tom Ewell is left guiltily leching over the innocent TV-toothpaste temptress upstairs – Marilyn Monroe, at her most wistfully comic. The sight of her pushing down her billowing skirt as she stands on a subway grating (at Lexington Ave and 52nd St) is one of the era's and the city's most resonant movie images.

So This is New York (*Richard Fleischer, 1948*). A bomb on its initial release, this rarely shown but edgy and innovative comedy plants three Midwesterners amongst the sharpies and operators of 1930s New York. The voiceover by star Henry Morgan (an Indiana salesman thoroughly unimpressed by the big city) is sublimely sarcastic.

Stranger than Paradise (*Jim Jarmusch, 1984*). Only the first third of this, the original slacker indie, is set in New York, but its portrayal of Lower East Side lethargy is hilariously spot-on and permeates the rest of the film in which a couple of hipster fish venture out of water in Ohio and Florida. The film's downtown credentials – John Lurie is a jazz saxophonist with the Lounge Lizards, Richard Edson used to drum for Sonic Youth, and Jarmusch himself is an East Village celebrity – are impeccable.

Tootsie (*Sidney Pollack, 1982*). Tired of being rejected in audition after audition, a struggling actor (comic turn for Dustin Hoffman) dons a wig and woman's attire to win a prize role on an afternoon soap. Great script, with a memorable scene set in the *Russian Tea Room*.

Unfaithful (*Adrian Lyne, 2002*). Diane Lane is the title character in this movie about marital infidelity: though she and husband Richard Gere live in the suburbs, her French lover, Olivier Martinez, has a crashpad in Soho and some of Lane's most impressive scenes take place on its windswept streets.

Working Girl (*Mike Nichols, 1988*). Fun fluff about a secretary (Melanie Griffith) who dreams of breaking away from her drab Staten Island existence. Her chance comes when her boss (Sigourney Weaver) breaks a leg on a ski trip; taking over her job, Griffiths discovers Weaver was planning to steal one of her ideas. Comedy and romance (with Harrison Ford) ensue.

New York nightmares

The Addiction (*Abel Ferrara, 1995*). A simple trip home from the college library turns into a living nightmare for Lili Taylor when she's bitten by a vampiric streetwalker on Bleecker Street and transformed into a blood junkie cruising the East Village for fresh kill.

After Hours (*Martin Scorsese, 1985*). Yuppie computer programmer, Griffin Dunne, inadvertently ends up on a nightlong odyssey into the Hades of downtown New York, a journey that goes from bad to worse to awful as he encounters every kook south of 14th Street.

American Psycho (*Mary Harron, 2000*). This stylized adaptation of the Bret Easton Ellis novel succeeds largely due to Christian Bale, pulling off some blacker-than-black comedy in his role as a securities trader consumed by designer labels, the ladder of success, and Huey Lewis lyrics.

Escape from New York (*John Carpenter, 1981*). In the then-not-too-distant future (1997, in fact), society has given up trying to solve the problems of Manhattan and has walled it up as a lawless maximum-security prison from which Kurt Russell has to rescue the hijacked US president. Ludicrous but great fun.

Gravesend (*Salvatore Stabile, 1996*). Low-rent literally (shot for $5000) and figuratively, this wannabe gangster movie relates one crazy, violent night in the lives of its do-nothing protagonists in deepest Brooklyn.

In the Cut (*Jane Campion, 2003*). Meg Ryan plays against type as the dowdy, sexually frustrated brunette Frannie in this claustrophobic, bleak thriller. The plot's full of holes, but Jennifer Jason Leigh's grimy performance as Ryan's sister is a standout, as is the movie's sensitive sense of place – Campion filmed extensively on location in and around the East Village and Alphabet City, and it shows.

Jacob's Ladder (*Adrian Lyne, 1990*). Tim Robbins gets off the subway in Brooklyn but discovers himself locked inside a deserted station . . . and then his troubles really begin as his Vietnam-induced hallucinations turn the city into one hell of a house of horrors.

The Lost Weekend (*Billy Wilder, 1945*). Alcoholic Ray Milland is left alone in the city with no money and a desperate thirst. The film's most famous scene is his long trek up Third Avenue (shot on location) trying to hawk his typewriter to buy booze, only to find all the pawn shops closed for Yom Kippur.

Marathon Man (*John Schlesinger, 1976*). Innocent, bookish Dustin Hoffman runs for his life all over Manhattan after he's dragged into a conspiracy involving old Nazis and tortured with dental instruments. ("Is it safe?") Shot memorably around the Central Park Reservoir and Zoo, Columbia University, the Diamond District, and Spanish Harlem.

The Out-of-Towners (*Arthur Hiller, 1969*). If you have any problems getting into town from the airport take solace from the fact that they can be nothing compared to those endured by Jack Lemmon and Sandy Dennis – for whom everything that can go wrong does go wrong – in Neil Simon's frantic comedy. Remade with Steve Martin and Goldie Hawn (but stick with the original).

Requiem for a Dream (*Darren Aronofsky, 2000*). A jagged and harrowing adaptation of Hubert Selby's novel about a band of junkies' descent into insanity amidst their cold, gray Coney Island surroundings.

Rosemary's Baby (*Roman Polanski, 1968*). Mia Farrow and John Cassavetes move into their dream New York apartment in the Dakota Building (72nd and Central Park West, where John Lennon lived and died) and think they have problems with nosy neighbors and thin walls – but that's just until Farrow gets pregnant and hell, literally, breaks loose. Arguably the most terrifying film ever set in the city.

The Siege (*Edward Zwick, 1998*). Zwick's controversial film speculates on what would happen if a series of major terrorist attacks by Arab militants in New York City were to lead to the declaration of martial law and the sealing off of Brooklyn. The results are muddle-headed but the images of troops marching over the Brooklyn Bridge are indelible.

The Taking of Pelham One Two Three (*Joseph Sargent, 1974*). Just when you thought it was safe to get back on the subway. A gang of mercenary hoods hijacks a train on its way through midtown and threatens to start killing one passenger per minute if their million-dollar ransom is not paid within the hour.

The Warriors (*Walter Hill, 1979*). The Coney Island Warriors ride to the Bronx for a meeting with all of New York's gangs; when the organizer is killed, the Warriors are unjustly blamed and have to navigate their way back to their home turf. Old-school subway graffiti, distinctive gang costumes, and a pervading sense of nighttime paranoia all contribute to this original cult film.

Wolfen (*Michael Wadleigh, 1981*). The sins of New York's founding fathers and venal property developers return to haunt the city in the form of vicious wolves in this beautiful and serious horror movie from the director (oddly enough) of *Woodstock*, one of the very few films that touch on the city's Native American history and one of the first to use the Steadicam to intelligent effect.

The mean streets

The Cool World (*Shirley Clarke, 1964*). A 1960s *Boyz'n'the Hood*, this radical, documentary-type study of a Harlem teenager who longs to be a gun-toting gang member proved Clarke to be the political conscience of New York's streets.

Cruising (*William Friedkin, 1980*). The Greenwich Village scene of the late 1970s plays a supporting character in this crime flick, in which cop Al Pacino delves into the underworld of gay S&M clubs to nab a serial killer. As one might expect, it was loudly protested by just about everyone on its release.

Dead End (*William Wyler, 1937*). Highly entertaining, stage-derived tragedy of the Lower East Side's teeming poor, starring Humphrey Bogart as a mother-obsessed small-time gangster, and a pack of lippy adolescents who earned their own movie series as The Dead End Kids.

Fort Apache, The Bronx (*Daniel Petrie, 1981*). A film to confirm people's worst fears about the Bronx. Paul Newman stars as a veteran cop based in the city's most crime-infested and corrupt precinct. Tense, entertaining, and totally unbelievable.

The French Connection (*William Friedkin, 1971*). Plenty of heady Brooklyn atmosphere in this sensational Oscar-winning cop thriller starring Gene Hackman, whose classic car-and-subway chase takes place under the Bensonhurst Elevated Railroad.

Goodfellas (*Martin Scorsese, 1990*). Vibrant and nuanced tale, based on the true story of a mob turncoat; another in a fine series of Scorsese New York stories. Seduced by the allure of the Mafia from a young age, Brooklyn native Henry Hill (a fine Ray Liotta) recounts 25 years of crime, his rise through the ranks, and decision to turn on his brethren.

King of New York (*Abel Ferrara, 1990*). Glossy pre-Giuliani saga in which Christopher Walken (having entirely too much fun) plays a crime boss trying to take over the entire city. The closest thing to a mainstream success by the frequently muddled Ferrara, it sports an incredible supporting cast, including Wesley Snipes, Giancarlo Esposito, Paul Calderon, and a psychotic, pre-*Matrix* Laurence Fishburne.

Kiss of Death (*Henry Hathaway, 1947; Barbet Schroeder, 1995*). The 1947 *Kiss*, with squealing ex-con Victor Mature battling giggling psycho Richard Widmark, was one of the very first films to be shot entirely on real New York locations. Schroeder's remake retells the story in the brighter, tackier Queens of the 1990s, with squealing ex-con David Caruso battling dumb ox Nicolas Cage.

Madigan (*Don Siegel, 1968*). A vivid study of the inevitability of police corruption that opens with a jazzy montage of Manhattan skyscrapers and affluent avenues before plunging rogue cop Richard Widmark into the mean streets of Spanish Harlem.

Mean Streets (*Martin Scorsese, 1973*). Scorsese's brilliant break-through film breathlessly follows small-time hood Harvey Keitel and his volatile, harum-scarum buddy Robert De Niro around a vividly portrayed Little Italy before reaching its violent climax.

Midnight Cowboy (*John Schlesinger, 1969*). The odd love story between Jon Voight's bumpkin hustler and Dustin Hoffman's touching urban creep Ratso Rizzo plays out against both the seediest and swankiest of New York locations. The only X-rated film to receive an Oscar for Best Picture (it also won for Direc-tor and Adapted Screenplay), it looks considerably tamer today.

Naked City (*Jules Dassin, 1948*). A crime story that views the city with a documentarist's eye. Shot on actual locations, it follows a police manhunt for a ruthless killer all over town toward an unforgettable chase through the Lower East Side and a shoot-out on the Williamsburg Bridge.

Prince of the City (*Sidney Lumet, 1981*). Lumet is a die-hard New York director, and his crime films, including *Serpico*, *Dog Day Afternoon*, *Q&A*, and *Twelve Angry Men* are all superb New York movies, but this is his New York epic. A corrupt narcot-ics detective turns federal informer to assuage his guilt, and Lumet takes us from drug busts in Harlem to the cops' suburban homes on Long Island, to federal agents' swanky pads overlooking Central Park.

State of Grace (*Phil Joanou, 1990*). Terry Noonan (Sean Penn) returns to Hell's Kitchen after ten years and promptly falls in with the same thugs he outgrew (Gary Oldman, Ed Harris), while falling for their sister. The pull of the neighborhood is everywhere, from the shadow of the *Intrepid* to the slo-mo St Patrick's Day Parade footage intercut with the bloody finale.

Superfly (*Gordon Parks Jr, 1972*). Propelled by its ecstatic Curtis Mayfield score, this blaxploitation classic about one smooth-looking drug dealer's ultimate score is best seen today for its mind-boggling fashion excess and almost documen-tary-like look at the Harlem bars, streets, clubs, and diners of thirty-odd years ago.

New York song and dance

42nd Street (*Lloyd Bacon, 1933*). One of the best films ever made about Broadway – though the film rarely ventures outside the theater. Starring Ruby Keeler as the young chorus girl who has to replace the ailing leading lady: she goes on stage an unknown and, well, you know the rest.

Fame (*Alan Parker, 1980*). Set in Manhattan's High School for the Performing Arts, the film may be a

CONTEXTS

C

gawky musical, but in its haphazard, sentimental, ungainly way it still manages to capture some of the city's agony and ecstasy.

A Great Day in Harlem (*Jean Bach, 1994*). A unique jazz documentary that spins many tales around the famous Art Kane photograph for which the cream of New York's jazz world assemble on the steps of a Harlem brownstone one August morning in 1958. Using home-movie footage of the event and present-day interviews, Bach creates a wonderful portrait of a golden age.

Guys and Dolls (*Joseph L. Mankiewicz, 1955*). The great Broadway musical shot entirely on soundstages and giving as unlikely a picture of Times Square hoodlums (all colorfully suited sweetie-pies) as was ever seen. And a singing and dancing Marlon Brando to boot.

Hair (*Milos Forman, 1979*). Film version of the counterculture musical turns Central Park into a hippie paradise for the hirsute, charismatic (and very young) Treat Williams and his fellow Aquarians. Laced with humor, it's got a spectacular opening sequence, with choreography (including dancing police horses) by Twyla Tharp.

New York, New York (*Martin Scorsese, 1977*). Scorsese's homage to the grand musicals of postwar Hollywood, reimagined for the post-Vietnam era. His grand folly opens on V-J day in Times Square with sax player Robert de Niro picking up Liza Minnelli in a dance hall, and follows their career and romance together through the Big Band era. Unusually for Scorsese, but befitting the film, the eponymous city was stylishly recreated on studio soundstages.

Saturday Night Fever (*John Badham, 1977*). What everybody remembers is the tacky glamour of flared white pantsuits and mirror-balled discos, but *Saturday Night Fever* is actually a touching and believable portrayal of working-class youth in the 1970s (Travolta works in a paint store when he's not strutting the dance floor), Italian-American Brooklyn, and the road to Manhattan.

Sweet Charity (*Bob Fosse, 1969*). Shirley MacLaine's lovable prostitute Charity hoofs around Manhattan getting the short end of the stick at every turn. Mugged in Central Park *by her boyfriend*, Charity blithely wanders the city dancing on rooftops and in swank uptown clubs, and ends up back in the park rescued by a merry band of escapees from *Hair*.

Glossary

New York people

ALLEN Woody Writer, director, comedian. Many people's clichéd idea of the neurotic Jewish Manhattanite. His clever, crafted films comment on, and have become part of, the New York myth. Allen suffered a major fall from grace in 1993, when he was accused of child abuse by Mia Farrow for moving in with, and later marrying, the adopted child they'd raised as their daughter.

ASTOR John Jacob (1822–90) Robber baron, slum landlord and, when he died, the richest man in the world. Astor made his packet from exacting exorbitant rents from those living in abject squalor in his many tenement buildings. By all accounts, a real bastard.

BEECHER Henry Ward (1813–87) Revivalist preacher famed for his support of women's suffrage, the abolition of slavery – and as the victim of a scandalous accusation of adultery that rocked nineteenth-century New York. His sister, Harriet Beecher Stowe, wrote the best-selling novel *Uncle Tom's Cabin*, which contributed greatly to the anti-slavery cause.

BLOOMBERG Michael Billionaire businessman-turned-politician, whose corporate mayoral style directly contrasts with predecessor Rudy Giuliani's autocratic manner. Bloomberg quietly dragged the city out of the financial mess caused by the Twin Towers disaster and dot-com bust.

BRESLIN Jimmy Bitter, often brilliant columnist for *New York Newsday*. Once ran for mayor on a Secessionist ticket (declaring New York City

independent from the State) with Norman Mailer as running mate.

BRYANT William Cullen (1794–1878) Poet, newspaper editor, and main proponent of Central Park and the Metropolitan Museum. The small park that bears his name at 42nd Street and Fifth Avenue has been expertly cleaned up and is now a fitting memorial to this nineteenth-century hero.

BURR Aaron (1756–1836) Fascinating politician whose action-packed career included a stint as vice-president, a trial and acquittal for treason, and, most famously, the murder of Alexander Hamilton in a duel. His house, the Morris–Jumel Mansion, still stands.

CARNEGIE Andrew (1835–1919) Émigré Scottish industrialist who spent most of his life amassing a vast fortune and his final years giving it all away. Unlike most of his wealthy contemporaries he was not an ostentatious man, as his house, now the Cooper-Hewitt Museum, shows.

CHISHOLM Shirley In 1968 she became the first black woman elected to Congress, from her home district in Brooklyn.

DINKINS David First black mayor of New York City, elected in 1989 after a hard, mud-slinging mayoral battle against Republican Rudolph Giuliani. His term in office left him seeming ineffectual and weak: "Everything sticks to him but praise," said a pundit.

FRICK Henry Clay (1849–1919) One of the robber barons, Frick's single contribution to civilization was to use his inestimable wealth to collect some of the finest art treasures of Europe, now on show at his home on Fifth Avenue.

GARVEY Marcus (1887–1940) Activist and demagogue who did much to raise the consciousness of blacks in the early part of the twentieth century (and is now a Rasta myth). When he started to become a political threat to the white government he was thrown in prison for fraud; pardoned but deported, he spent his last years in London.

GIULIANI Rudolph Former US district attorney who carried his bulldog ways of prosecuting crimes to the mayor's office. He presided over two terms of relative prosperity and reduced crime, though was occasionally criticized for his arrogant tactics and for giving too much power to the police; but his leadership of the city during the September 11 crisis was praised by critics and fans alike.

GOULD Jay (1836–92) Robber baron extraordinaire. Gould made his fortune with a telegraph network during the Civil War, and went on to manipulate the stock market and make millions more. His most spectacular swindle cornered the gold market, netted him $11 million in a fortnight, and provoked the "Black Friday" crash of 1869.

GREELEY Horace (1811–72) Campaigning founder-editor of the *Tribune* newspaper who coined the phrase, "Go West, young man!," but never did himself. An advocate of women's rights, union rights, the abolition of slavery, and other worthy, liberal causes.

HAMILTON Alexander (1755–1804) Brilliant Revolutionary propagandist, soldier, political thinker (drafted sections of the Constitution), and statesman (first Secretary to the Treasury). Shot and killed in a duel by Aaron Burr. His house, Hamilton Grange, is preserved at the edge of Harlem.

HARING Keith (1958–90) Big-name artist who used crude animal forms for decoration and art. His early death of AIDS prematurely removed one of America's most promising artists and designers.

HELMSLEY Harry (1904–97) Property-owning tycoon who, like Donald Trump, had a penchant for slapping his name on all that fell into his grasp – hence many old hotels are now Helmsley Hotels. His surgically age-defying wife, Leona – known as the "Queen of Mean" for her penny-pinching ways – continues to helm the empire.

IRVING Washington (1783–1859) Satirist, biographer, short-story writer (*The Legend of Sleepy Hollow*, *Rip Van Winkle*), and diplomat. His house, just outside the city near Tarrytown, New Jersey, is worth a visit.

JOHNSON Philip Architect. Disciple of Ludwig Mies van der Rohe and high priest of the International Style glass-box skyscraper, he designed the Seagram Building on Park Avenue, the AT&T Building on Third Avenue, and the Federal Reserve Plaza on Liberty Street, among others.

KOCH Ed Still-popular former mayor, elected by a slender majority in 1978, who gained popularity with his straight-talking approach. After three terms in office, he lost the Democratic nomination in 1989 to David Dinkins following scandals involving other city officials and his insensitive handling of black issues.

LAGUARDIA Fiorello (1882–1947) NYC mayor who replaced Jimmy Walker and who gained great popularity with his honest and down-to-earth administration, focusing on anti-corruption programs and social spending for the poor. One of the city's airports is named in his honor.

LEE Spike Outspoken director Lee is Woody Allen's African-American counterpart, documenting a distinctly New York vision of Black America. In recent years as his films' success has dwindled, Lee's become as famous for his mouthy media presence as his movie-making.

MORGAN J. Pierpont (1837–1913) Top industrialist and financier who used a little of his spare cash to build the Morgan Library on Madison Avenue. He created a financial empire that was bigger than the Gettys' and enabled him to buy out both Andrew Carnegie and Henry Frick.

MOSES Robert (1889–1981) Responsible for the way the city looks today. Holder of all the key planning and building posts from the 1930s to the 1960s, his philosophy of urban development was to tear down whatever was old, build anew, and create ordered public spaces with a lot of concrete.

OLMSTED Frederick Law (1822–1903) Landscape designer and writer. Central Park, Riverside Park, and many others were the fruits of his partnership with architect Calvert Vaux.

ONASSIS Jacqueline Kennedy (1929–94). The former First Lady spent most of her later years in the city, working as an editor for Doubleday. Long a byword in style and grace, by the time of her death she had regained much of the public favor lost after her unpopular marriage to a Greek shipping magnate.

O'NEILL Eugene (1888–1953) NYC's (and America's) most influential playwright. Many of the characters from plays like *Mourning Becomes Electra*, *The Iceman Cometh*, and *Long Day's Journey into Night* are based on his drinking companions in *The Golden Swan* bar.

PARKER Dorothy (1893–1967) Playwright, essayist, and acid wit. A founding member of the Round Table group at the *Algonquin Hotel*, she was one of the few respected women in the New York literary world.

POWELL JR Adam Clayton (1908–1972) A reverend (at Harlem's Abyssinian Baptist Church) and longtime Representative (the first black Congressman from New York), tireless civil-rights crusader Powell was a force to be reckoned with. His later career, however, was somewhat tarnished by scandal and he spent the last two years of his life in Miami.

ROCKEFELLER JR John D. (1874–1960) Unlike his tightfisted dad (founder of the fortune), Rockefeller Junior gave away tidy sums for philanthropic ventures in New York. The Cloisters Museum, The Museum of Modern Art, Lincoln Center, Riverside Church, and, most famously, Rockefeller Center were mostly his doing.

ROCKEFELLER Nelson (1908–79) Politician son of John D. Jr. Elected governor of New York State in 1958, he held on to the post until 1974, when he turned to greater things and sought the Republican Party presidential nomination. He didn't get it, but before his death served briefly as vice-president under Gerald Ford.

SHARPTON JR Al (The Reverend) Ordained minister, political activist, and perennial candidate for office, Sharpton is regularly accused of chasing controversial publicity by wading into any incident involving police corruption or racial bias. Best known for his shrill support for teenager Tawana Brawley's gang-rape

C

claims against half a dozen white police officers in 1987 – which later turned out to be spurious.

STEINBRENNER George Controversial baseball-team owner/ entrepreneur. Known as "The Boss," Steinbrenner runs the beloved New York Yankees, often with an iron fist, though generous pockets.

TRUMP Donald Property tycoon whose creations include the glammed-out Trump Tower on Fifth Avenue and Trump Plaza near Bloomingdale's. Reinvented as a reality TV-show star, "The Donald," as he was nicknamed by ex-wife Ivana, is an arrogant but loveable *nouveau riche* caricature.

TWEED William Marcy "Boss" (1823–78) Head of the NY Democratic Party machine whose corrupt practices netted him city funds to the tune of $200 million and gave Democratic Party headquarters Tammany Hall its bad name.

WARHOL Andy (1926–87) Artist and media hound. Instigator of Pop Art, the Velvet Underground, The Factory, *Interview* magazine, and *Empire* – a 24-hour movie of the Empire State Building (no commentary, no gorillas, nothing but the building). Died, oddly enough, after a routine gallstone operation.

WHITE Stanford (1853–1906) Partner of the architectural firm McKim, Mead and White, which designed such Neoclassical landmarks as the General Post Office, Washington Square Arch, the Municipal Building, and parts of Columbia University. He was famously murdered by his lover's husband, shot in the face while attending a show on the roof of Madison Square Garden, a building he designed.

C

Travel store

Travel Specials
First-Time Around the World
First-Time Asia
First-Time Europe
First-Time Latin America
Travel Online
Travel Health
Travel Survival
Walks in London & SE England
Women Travel

Maps
Algarve
Amsterdam
Andalucia & Costa del Sol
Argentina
Athens
Australia
Barcelona
Berlin
Boston
Brittany
Brussels
California
Chicago
Corsica
Costa Rica & Panama
Crete
Croatia
Cuba
Cyprus
Czech Republic
Dominican Republic
Dubai & UAE
Dublin
Egypt
Florence & Siena
Florida
France
Frankfurt
Germany
Greece
Guatemala & Belize
Hong Kong
Iceland
Ireland
Kenya & Northern Tanzania
Lisbon
London

Los Angeles
Madrid
Mallorca
Malaysia
Marrakesh
Mexico
Miami & Key West
Morocco
New England
New York City
New Zealand
Northern Spain
Paris
Peru
Portugal
Prague
The Pyrenees
Rome
San Francisco
Sicily
South Africa
South India
Spain & Portugal
Sri Lanka
Tenerife
Thailand
Toronto
Trinidad & Tobago
Tuscany
Venice
Vietnam, Laos & Cambodia
Washington DC
Yucatán Peninsula

Dictionary Phrasebooks
Croatian
Czech
Dutch
Egyptian Arabic
French
German
Greek
Hindi & Urdu
Italian
Japanese
Latin American Spanish
Mandarin Chinese
Mexican Spanish
Polish
Portuguese
Russian
Spanish

Swahili
Thai
Turkish
Vietnamese

Computers
Blogging
iPods, iTunes & music online
The Internet
Macs & OS X
PCs and Windows
PlayStation Portable
Website Directory

Film & TV
American Independent Film
British Cult Comedy
Chick Flicks
Comedy Movies
Cult Movies
Gangster Movies
Horror Movies
Kids' Movies
Sci-Fi Movies
Westerns

Lifestyle
Babies
eBay
Ethical Shopping
Pregnancy & Birth

Music Guides
The Beatles
Bob Dylan
Classical Music
Elvis
Frank Sinatra
Heavy Metal
Hip-Hop
Jazz
Book of Playlists
Opera
Pink Floyd
Punk
Reggae
Rock
The Rolling Stones
Soul and R&B
World Music (2 vols)

Popular Culture
Books for Teenagers
Children's Books, 5-11
Conspiracy Theories
Cult Fiction
The Da Vinci Code
Lord of the Rings
Shakespeare
Superheroes
Unexplained Phenomena

Sport
Arsenal 11s
Celtic 11s
Chelsea 11s
Liverpool 11s
Man United 11s
Newcastle 11s
Rangers 11s
Tottenham 11s
Poker

Science
Climate Change
The Universe
Weather

Visit us online
www.roughguides.com
Information on over 25,000 destinations around the world

- **Read** Rough Guides' trusted travel info
- **Access** exclusive articles from Rough Guides authors
- **Update** yourself on new books, maps, CDs and other products
- **Enter** our competitions and win travel prizes
- **Share** ideas, journals, photos & travel advice with other users
- **Earn** points every time you contribute to the Rough Guide community and get rewards

BROADEN YOUR HORIZONS

THE ROUGH GUIDE TO

weste

The story • The songs • The solo years

HE ROUGH GUIDE TO

he **Beatles**

Chris Ingha

THE BOOK
THE MOVIE
THE TRUTH

E **ROUGH GUIDE** to

HE **DA VINCI**
CODE

ALLY UNAUTHORISED

Michael Haag and Veronica Haag

THE ROUGH GUID

Unex

Phenom

The filth • the fury • the fa

The songs • the singers • the stories • the soul

ROUGH GUIDE to

Punk

THE **ROUGH GUIDE** to

Soul and R&B

THE ROUGH GUIDE to

The **Rolling Stones**

Sean Egan

THE ROUC

Bl

Avoid Guilt Trips

Buy fair trade coffee + bananas ✓

Save energy – use low energy bulbs ✓

– don't leave tv on standby ✓

Offset carbon emissions from flight to Madrid ✓

Send goat to Africa ✓

Join Tourism Concern today ✓

Slowly, the world is changing.
Together we can, and will, make a difference.

Tourism Concern is the only UK registered charity fighting exploitation in one of the largest industries on earth: people forced from their homes in order that holiday resorts can be built, sweatshop labour conditions in hotels and destruction of the environment are just some of the issues that we tackle.

Sending people on a guilt trip is not something we do. We know as well as anyone that holidays are precious. But you can help us to ensure that tourism always benefits the local communities involved.

Call 020 7133 3330
or visit **tourismconcern.org.uk** to find out how.

A year's membership of Tourism Concern costs just £20 (£12 unwaged)
- that's 38 pence a week, less than the cost of a pint of milk, organic of course.

NOTES

Small print and

Index

A Rough Guide to Rough Guides

Published in 1982, the first Rough Guide – to Greece – was a student scheme that became a publishing phenomenon. Mark Ellingham, a recent graduate in English from Bristol University, had been travelling in Greece the previous summer and couldn't find the right guidebook. With a small group of friends he wrote his own guide, combining a highly contemporary, journalistic style with a thoroughly practical approach to travellers' needs.

The immediate success of the book spawned a series that rapidly covered dozens of destinations. And, in addition to impecunious backpackers, Rough Guides soon acquired a much broader and older readership that relished the guides' wit and inquisitiveness as much as their enthusiastic, critical approach, and value-for-money ethos.

These days, Rough Guides include recommendations from shoestring to luxury and cover more than 200 destinations around the globe, including almost every country in the Americas and Europe, more than half of Africa, and most of Asia and Australasia. Our ever-growing team of authors and photographers is spread all over the world, particularly in Europe, the USA, and Australia.

In the early 1990s, Rough Guides branched out of travel, with the publication of Rough Guides to World Music, Classical Music, and the Internet. All three have become benchmark titles in their fields, spearheading the publication of a wide range of books under the Rough Guide name.

Including the travel series, Rough Guides now number more than 350 titles, covering: phrasebooks, waterproof maps, music guides from Opera to Heavy Metal, reference works as diverse as Conspiracy Theories and Shakespeare, and popular culture books from iPods to Poker. Rough Guides also produce a series of more than 120 World Music CDs in partnership with World Music Network.

Visit www.roughguides.com to see our latest publications.

Rough Guide travel images are available for commercial licensing at www.roughguidespictures.com

SMALL PRINT

Rough Guide credits

Text editor: Ella Steim
Layout: Sachin Tanwar
Cartography: Maxine Repath
Picture editor: Jj Luck
Production: Aimee Hampson
Proofreader: Diane Margolis
Cover design: Chloë Roberts
Photographer: Angus Oborn
Editorial: **London** Kate Berens, Claire Saunders, Geoff Howard, Ruth Blackmore, Polly Thomas, Richard Lim, Alison Murchie, Karoline Densley, Andy Turner, Keith Drew, Edward Aves, Nikki Birrell, Helen Marsden, Alice Park, Sarah Eno, Joe Staines, Duncan Clark, Peter Buckley, Matthew Milton, Tracy Hopkins, David Paul, Lucy White, Ruth Tidball; **New York** Andrew Rosenberg, Steven Horak, April Isaacs, AnneLise Sorensen, Amy Hegarty, Sean Mahoney
Design & Pictures: **London** Simon Bracken, Dan May, Diana Jarvis, Mark Thomas, Harriet Mills; **Delhi** Umesh Aggarwal, Ajay Verma, Jessica Subramanian, Ankur Guha, Pradeep Thapliyal, Anita Singh

Production: Sophie Hewat, Katherine Owers
Cartography: **London** Ed Wright, Katie Lloyd-Jones; **Delhi** Jai Prakash Mishra, Rajesh Chhibber, Ashutosh Bharti, Rajesh Mishra, Animesh Pathak, Jasbir Sandhu, Karobi Gogoi, Amod Singh, Alakananda Bhattacharya
Online: **New York** Jennifer Gold, Kristin Mingrone; **Delhi** Manik Chauhan, Narender Kumar, Shekhar Jha, Rakesh Kumar, Amit Verma, Amit Kumar, Rahul Kumar
Marketing & Publicity: **London** Richard Trillo, Niki Hanmer, Louise Maher, Jess Carter; **New York** Geoff Colquitt, Megan Kennedy, Katy Ball; **Delhi** Reem Khokhar
Custom publishing and foreign rights: Philippa Hopkins
Manager India: Punita Singh
Series editor: Mark Ellingham
Reference Director: Andrew Lockett
PA to Managing and Publishing Directors: Megan McIntyre
Publishing Director: Martin Dunford

Publishing information

This tenth edition published January 2007 by
Rough Guides Ltd,
80 Strand, London WC2R 0RL
345 Hudson St, 4th Floor,
New York, NY 10014, USA
14 Local Shopping Centre, Panchsheel Park,
New Delhi 110017, India
Distributed by the Penguin Group
Penguin Books Ltd,
80 Strand, London WC2R 0RL
Penguin Putnam, Inc.
375 Hudson Street, NY 10014, USA
Penguin Group (Australia)
250 Camberwell Road, Camberwell,
Victoria 3124, Australia
Penguin Books Canada Ltd,
10 Alcorn Avenue, Toronto, Ontario,
Canada M4V 1E4
Penguin Group (NZ)
67 Apollo Drive, Mairangi Bay, Auckland 1310,
New Zealand
Cover concept by Peter Dyer.

Typeset in Bembo and Helvetica to an original design by Henry Iles.

Printed and bound in China

© Martin Dunford 2007

528pp includes index

A catalogue record for this book is available from the British Library

ISBN 1-84353-692-7

ISBN 13 978-1-84353-692-5

1   3   5   7   9   8   6   4   2

Help us update

We've gone to a lot of effort to ensure that the tenth edition of **The Rough Guide to New York City** is accurate and up to date. However, things change – places get "discovered", opening hours are notoriously fickle, restaurants and rooms raise prices or lower standards. If you feel we've got it wrong or left something out, we'd like to know, and if you can remember the address, the price, the time, the phone number, so much the better. We'll credit all contributions, and send a copy of the next edition (or any other Rough Guide if you

prefer) for the best letters. Everyone who writes to us and isn't already a subscriber will receive a copy of our full-colour thrice-yearly newsletter. Please mark letters: "**Rough Guide to New York City Update**" and send to: Rough Guides, 80 Strand, London WC2R 0RL, or Rough Guides, 4th Floor, 345 Hudson St, New York, NY 10014. Or send an email to **mail@roughguides.com** Have your questions answered and tell others about your trip at
www.roughguides.atinfopop.com

Acknowledgements

Martin Dunford would like to thank Ella Steim for being such a patient and meticulous editor.

Ken Derry would like to thank his parents, Douglass and Martha, for their unyielding support and encouragement. Also, Rough Guides editors Ella Steim and Andrew Rosenberg.

Zora O'Neill would like to thank Livia Alexander, David Feige, David Prince and Ariel Borow, Tal Rachleff, and John Roleke.

The editor would like to thank Martin Dunford, as well as Ken Derry, Sean Harvey, Zora O'Neill, Sachin Tanwar, Maxine Repath, Jj Luck, Diane Margolis, Stephen Keeling, Umesh Aggarwal, AnneLise Sorensen, Steve Horak, and Andrew Rosenberg.

Readers' letters

Thanks to all the readers who have taken the time to write in with comments and suggestions (and apologies if we've inadvertently omitted anyone's name):

David Authers, Cristina de Avila, Elaine Harris, Peter Heller, Paddy Hughes, Tina Humphrey, Colin Lees, Mariana Leeves, Saskia van Loenen, Anne Marley, Anne O'Connor, Caroline Porter, Noel Richardson, Owen Smith, Heidi van Spaandonk, Helen Thomas, Ulrich Weisenseel

SMALL PRINT

ROUGH GUIDES

Photo credits

Index

Map entries are in color.

1 Chase Manhattan
    Plaza.............................54
21 Club, the..................136
42nd Street...133, 152, 156
57th Street....152, 162, 405
116th Street..................226
125th Street..........220, 223

A

ABC No Rio.....................96
Abyssinian Baptist
    Church...............222, 229
accommodation... 297–313
accommodation.... 298–299
Adam Clayton Powell, Jr
    Boulevard 220, 222,
    223, 228
Adam Clayton Powell, Jr
    State Office Building... 223
African Burial Ground.....71
airlines
    in Australia and
        New Zealand 22
    in the UK and Ireland......... 22
    in the US and Canada 20
airports 134,
    305, 369
Algonquin Hotel...........134,
    305, 369
Algonquin tribe..............459
Alice Austen House......290
Alice Tully Hall 209, 387
Alleva Dairy.....................91
Alphabet City.................105
American Merchant
    Mariners' Memorial......60
**American Museum of
    Natural History**........211,
    213, 448
American Museum of
    the Moving Image.....271,
    393, 448
Ansonia Hotel...............210
antique fairs..................444
apartments 38
apartment swapping 309
Apollo Theater..............223
Apthorp
    Apartments.................210
Aquarium 259, 451

architecture...........*see New
    York Architecture* color
    section
area codes......................39
arrival..............................23
Asia Society..................199
Asser Levy Recreation
    Center........................126
Astor, John Jacob 101,
    102, 233, 491
Astor Place 101
Astoria 265, 270
    & *Ethnic New York* color
    section
Astoria...........................268
Atlantic Avenue 240, 246
Atlantic Yards 245
Audubon Ballroom 233
Audubon, James..........212,
    233
Audubon Terrace..........232
Avenue of the
    Americas...................160
Avenues A, B, C,
    D........................104–106
Avery Fisher Hall 209,
    388
AXA Financial Center ...161

B

babysitters....................448
bagels............................317
BAM *see* Brooklyn
    Academy of Music
banks...............................39
Barnard College 219
bars 363–375
    Brooklyn 373
    Bronx................................. 375
    Chelsea 370
    Chinatown, Little Italy, and
        NoLita 366
    East Village 367
    Financial District 365
    gay and lesbian.........399–401
    happy hour........................ 363
    Harlem............................... 373
    hotel 369
    karaoke 367
    Lower East Side............... 366
    Midtown East.................... 371

Midtown West..................372
    prices 363
    Queens............................. 374
    smoking ban in 364, 470
    sports 433
    Tribeca and Soho............. 365
    Union Square, Gramercy Park,
        and the Flatiron District
        370
    Upper East Side............... 372
    Upper West Side.............. 372
    West Village...............368–370
Barrow Street 113
Bartow-Pell Mansion
    Museum......................286
baseball 428
basketball 430
Battery Park 59
Battery Park City 60, 468
Bay Ridge.............237, 256
beaches........................434
bed and breakfasts
   311–313
Bedford Street..............113
Bedford-Stuyvesant 237,
    254
Beecher, Henry Ward
    ....243, 491
Beekman Place 145
Belmont 281, 361
    & *Ethnic New York* color
    section
Bergdorf Goodman 137,
    413
Berlin, Irving 87, 120,
    134, 284
bicycling 27, 165,
    257, 434
Big Apple Greeter....34, 36,
    239
bike rental.......27, 165, 434
Bleecker Street.....111, 113
Bloomberg, Michael 203,
    245, 469, 470, 491
Bloomingdale's......33, 143,
    200, 413
Blumstein's...................223
boat tours.................34, 63,
    64
boating 168, 169, 435
Boerum Hill...................247
books 471–479
Borough Hall (Brooklyn)....33,
    240, 244

Bowery 96, 460
Bowery Savings Bank
  (Chinatown) 89
Bowery Savings Bank
  (Midtown East) 141
bowling 156, 435
Bowling Green 58
Bowne House 275
breakfast 322
Brighton Beach 237, 259
  & *Ethnic New York* color
  section
Broadway 57, 78, 101,
  121, 156, 204, 210
Broken Kilometer 81
Bronx, the 277–286
  & *Ethnic New York* color
  section
Bronx, the 278
  bars 375
  cafés 328
  Central Bronx 281–284
  North Bronx 284–286
  restaurants 361
  South Bronx 277, 278–281
Bronx Cultural Card 277
Bronx Museum of the
  Arts 279
Bronx Zoo 277, 282, 451
Brooklyn 33, 237–264
  & *Ethnic New York* color
  section
Brooklyn 238
  bars 373
  cafés 326
  Central Brooklyn 254–256
  Coastal Brooklyn 256–260
  Downtown Brooklyn .. 240–246
  Downtown Brooklyn 241
  Northern Brooklyn ... 260–264
  Northern Brooklyn 261
  Prospect Park 249–254
  Prospect Park 250
  restaurants 356–359
  South Brooklyn 247–249
Brooklyn Academy of
  Music 246, 385, 388,
  389, 392, 452
Brooklyn Botanic Garden
  .... 253, 442, 450
Brooklyn Brewery ... 262, 373
Brooklyn Bridge 64, 65,
  71, 239, 240, 464 & *New
  York Architecture* color
  section
Brooklyn Children's
  Museum 256, 448
Brooklyn Cyclones 259,
  428
Brooklyn Heights 237,
  242–244

Brooklyn Historical
  Society 242, 244
Brooklyn Museum
  251–253
Brooklyn Navy Yard 263
Brooklyn Public Library 250
brunch 346
Bryant Park 38,
  133, 389
Bryant, William Cullen
  .... 133, 163, 463, 491
buggy rides 165
Burr, Aaron 232, 233, 491
bus tours 33
buses
  to and from the airport 23
  in the city 26
  to and from New York City
  .... 19, 24

C

cabarets 390
cafés and light meals
  314–328
  breakfast 322
  Bronx 328
  Brooklyn 326
  Chelsea 320
  Chinatown, Little Italy, and
    NoLita 315
  East Village 317
  Financial District 314
  Harlem and above 325
  Lower East Side 316
  Midtown East 321
  Midtown West 322
  pizza by the slice 323
  Queens 327
  Staten Island 328
  Tribeca and Soho 314
  Union Square, Gramercy Park,
    and the Flatiron District ... 321
  Upper East Side 323
  Upper West Side 324
  West Village 318
Café Le Figaro 111, 319
Café Wha? 111
Canal Street 77, 81,
  82, 87, 89, 97
Cantor Roof Garden 181
Carnegie, Andrew 162,
  195, 250, 491
Carnegie Hall 162, 388
Carroll Gardens 237, 247,
  248
cast-iron architecture
  .... 77, 80 & *New York
  Architecture* color section
Castle Clinton 59

Cathedral Church of St
  John the Divine 204,
  217, 388
CBGB 102
CBS Building 162
cell phones *see* mobile
  phones
Central Park 163–172,
  389, 436, 451
Central Park 164
Central Park Carousel
  167
Central Park
  Reservoir 165, 171
Central Park Visitor
  Centers 163
Central Park West 204,
  211–213
Central Park Zoo 167
Central Synagogue 144
Chambers Street 75
Charles Scribner's Sons
  bookstore 135
Charlie Parker's House
  104
Charlotte Gardens 280
Chatham Square 87
Chelsea 115–120
Chelsea 116
  bars 370
  cafés 320
  galleries 115, 116, 118, 404
  restaurants 343
Chelsea Antiques Market
  120
Chelsea Flower Market
  120
Chelsea Historic District
  117
Chelsea Hotel 115,
  119, 303
Chelsea Market 116
Chelsea Piers 116,
  118, 436
Children's Museum of
  Manhattan 210, 449
Children's Museum of the
  Arts 449
Chinatown 82–90,
  464 & *Ethnic New York*
  color section
Chinatown 83
  bars 366
  cafés and teahouses 316
  Chinese New Year 89, 440
  history 84–86
  restaurants 82, 335
  shopping 82, 89
Chisholm, Shirley 491
Christopher Street 113

517

Chrysler Building ....129, 143, 466 & *New York Architecture* color section
Chumley's 113
Church of the Ascension 112
Church of the Holy Trinity 202
Church of the Most Precious Blood 91
Church of St Paul the Apostle 207
Church of the Transfiguration (Chinatown) 86
Church of the Transfiguration (Flatiron District) 127
Circle Line ferry 34, 43
circuses 452
Citicorp Center .....143, 467 & *New York Architecture* color section
City College 230
City Hall 65, 66
City Hall Park 33, 65–72
City Hall Park 66
City Island 285
city transportation ...25–28
classical music and opera 387–389
climate change 21
Clinton Street 96
Cloisters Museum 220, 234–236
CNN 206
Cobble Hill 237, 247
Colonnade Row............101
Columbia University 204, 218
Columbus Circle............206
Columbus Park 86
comedy clubs................390
community gardens 105
Coney Island 237, 256, 257–259
Coney Island Museum 259
Conference House 293
Confucius Plaza 87
Conservatory Garden (Central Park).............172
contraception 454
Convent Avenue 230
Cooper Square 103, 107
Cooper Union 103
Cooper–Hewitt National Design Museum 195

Corinthian Baptist Church 227
Corona 272
costs 36
crime 28–30
Criminal Courts Building 71
Crown Heights ......250, 255 & *Ethnic New York* color section
Cunard Building..............57

D

Dahesh Museum of Art 139
Daily News Building 144
Dakota Building 168, 206, 211, 212
dance 389
Dante Park....................210
Deitch Projects 80
Delancey Street 96
Delmonico's 51, 57, 331
Diamond Row 134, 161, 421
Dinkins, David 468, 491
directory 454–456
disabled travelers 36
diving 438
Dodge, Mabel 109
drinking 363–375
driving 24, 27
drugs 381
Duane Park 75
DUMBO 237, 242
Dyckman Farmhouse Museum 236
Dylan, Bob............113, 119

E

East Broadway 97
East Coast Memorial 60
East River 237, 240
East Village ....99–106 & *Ethnic New York* color section
East Village 100
  bars 105, 367
  cafés 317
  restaurants.......105, 338-340
Easter Parade...............441
Eastern States Buddhist Temple 87

eating *see* cafés and light meals & restaurants
Ed Sullivan Theater 159
Eighth Avenue 116
El Barrio ....199, 220 & *Ethnic New York* color section
Eldridge Street Synagogue 97
electricity 37
Ellington, Duke 120, 162, 172, 217, 222, 284
Ellis Island 43, 45–48, 60, 464
Ellis Island Museum of Immigration............ 46–48
email 37
emergencies 454
Empire State Building ....129–131, 466 & *New York Architecture* color section
entry requirements 37
Essex Street 96, 98
Essex Street Market.......96

F

Federal Hall 52, 462
Federal Reserve Bank 53
Federal Reserve Plaza....53
ferries.......................34, 43, 287, 288
Festa di San Gennaro ...91, 445
Fifth Avenue 112, 129–138, 188–196
film 392–394
  festivals 75, 393, 440-446
  first-run 392
  industry 75
  New York on.............480–484
  revivals 392–394
Financial District 50–64
Financial District............51
  bars 365
  cafés 314
  restaurants 330
Fire Museum.................449
First Avenue 145
First Presbyterian Church 112
First Unitarian Church (Brooklyn)...................244
Fisher Landau Art Center 269
fishing 435
Five Points 70, 84

Flatbush Avenue...........237
Flatiron Building 127,
465 & *New York
Architecture* color section
Flatiron District..........121,
126–128
Flatiron District 122
flights
  booking online 20
  from Australia and New
    Zealand..........................20
  from North America 19
  from the UK and Ireland 20
Flushing 265,
275 & *Ethnic New York*
color section
**Flushing Meadows–
Corona Park**............266,
273–275
Foley Square 70
Forbes Galleries 112
Ford Foundation Building
......................................145
Fordham University 281
Fort Greene...237, 240, 245
Fort Greene Park..........246
Fort Wadsworth............291
Fraunces Tavern 62, 462
Free Synagogue of
Flushing 276
Freedom Tower 55, 470
Freedomland 286
Fresh Kills Landfill 289
Frick Collection 188, 191
Frick, Henry Clay.........191,
491
Friends Meeting House
......................................275
Fuller Building...............139
Fulton Ferry District.....237,
240
Fulton Fish Market 63
Fulton, Robert 53, 63, 240,
462
Fulton Street (Brooklyn)
....................244, 245, 254

G

Gainsborough Studios
......................................159
galleries 403–407
  57th Street 405
  alternative 406
  Chelsea 404
  DUMBO and Brooklyn
    Heights 406
  tours.................................403
  Tribeca and Soho.............404

Upper East Side...............405
Williamsburg 406
Ganesh Temple 276
Garment District
............................152–156
Garvey, Marcus 224, 491
gay and lesbian New York
...........114, 116, 396–402
  accommodation 397
  arts and culture...............398
  bars 399–401
  cafés 399
  clubs 401
  media 397, 398, 401
  neighborhoods.................396
  Pride Parade 397, 443
  religion.............................402
  resources 397
  restaurants 399
  safety 396
  sex....................................401
  shopping 402
General Electric Building
......................................142
General Post Office 156
& *New York Architecture*
color section
General Theological
Seminary....................117
George Washington Bridge
......................................233
Ginsberg, Allen 99, 104,
111, 219
Giuliani, Rudy 56, 122,
202, 252, 468, 491
glossary 491
golf................................436
gospel music 229
Governors Island 43, 48
Gowanus Canal....247, 248
Grace Church 102
Gracie Mansion 202
Gramercy Park...........121,
123–126
Gramercy Park..............122
  bars 370
  cafés 321
  restaurants 344–346
Grand Army Plaza
(Manhattan)...........137, 190
Grand Army Plaza
(Brooklyn)...................250
Grand Central
Terminal 19, 23, 24,
129, 140, 465 & *New
York Architecture* color section
Grand Concourse 277,
279
Grand Concourse 280
Grand Street.............89, 98
Grant's Tomb 219
Great Kills Park.............291

Great Lawn (Central Park)
......................................170
Greeley Square.............154
Greene Street 80
Greenpoint....238, 260, 263
& *Ethnic New York* color
section
Green–Wood Cemetery
......................................254
Grey Art Gallery............110
Ground Zero 55, 68, 470
& *New York Architecture*
color section
Guggenheim Museum
....................190, 193–195
gyms.............................436

H

Hale, Nathan...................65
Hall of Fame for Great
Americans..................284
Halloween Parade 445
Hamilton, Alexander......52,
53, 230, 232, 492
Hamilton Grange 230
Hamilton Heights..........220,
230–232
Hamilton Heights.........231
Harbor Defense Museum
......................................257
Harbor Islands 43–49
Harbor Islands 44
Harlem 33, 220–236
& *Ethnic New York* color
section
Harlem...........................221
  bars 373
  cafés 325
  restaurants 355
Harlem Meer.................172
Harlem Renaissance 221,
222, 465
Harvard Club 133
Haughwout Building.......79
& *New York Architecture*
color section
Hayden Planetarium.....215
health............................37, 436
Hearst World Headquarters
......................................159
helicopter tours 34
Hell's Kitchen........152, 159
Helmsley Building.........141
Henderson Place..........202
Herald Square 154
Hispanic Society of
America 233

Historic Richmond Town 292
horse racing 432
horse riding 437
hospitals 454
hostels 310
Hotel des Artistes.........211
hotels 300–310
   airport...............................309
   booking services..............301
   prices 297, 300
   taxes and fees 300
Houston Street 94, 107
Hudson River.....60, 63, 75, 76, 107, 204, 215, 285
Hudson River Park 76
Hudson Street 114
Hudson Waterfront Museum....................249
Hunters Point 267
Hunts Point..................280

I

IBM Building.................139
ice cream.....................325
ice hockey 431
ice-skating...................437
Iglesia San Isidiro y San Leandro 105
Indian Row 103
information..............33–35
insurance 37
International Center of Photography 161
Internet 37
Intrepid Sea, Air & Space Museum....................152, 160, 449
Inwood..................220, 236
Irving Place...................123

J

Jackson Heights..........265, 272 & *Ethnic New York* color section
Jacob Riis Park 276
Jacques Marchais Museum of Tibetan Art.............291
Jamaica Bay.........266, 276
jazz venues...................379
Jefferson Market Courthouse................112
Jewish Children's Museum 256

Jewish Museum 196
JFK Airport 19, 23
jogging.........................437
Johnson, Philip....136, 139, 142, 147, 203, 210, 492
Joyce Kilmer Park 279
Juilliard School of Music 210, 377, 380
July 4 fireworks 443

K

Katz's Deli...............95, 337
Kaufman Astoria Studios 271
Kenilworth Apartments 212
kids' New York.... 447–453
Kingsland Homestead...275
Koch, Ed.......467, 468, 492
Koons, Jeff 81, 99, 151

L

LaGuardia Airport 19, 24
LaGuardia, Fiorello 466
Lafayette Street 77, 101
Landmarks Preservation Law 155
laundry............................38
Lazarus, Emma...............44
Lee, Spike 245, 480, 481, 492
Lefferts Historic House 251
Leisler, James................460
Lenape Indians........... 238
Lennon, John 68, 211, 212
Lenox Avenue.......220, 224
Letterman, David....31, 159
Lever House ....142, 466 & *New York Architecture* color section
Lexington Avenue 142–144, 188, 200
Liberty Island.................43
Libeskind, Daniel....56, 470
Lincoln Center 204, 208–210, 368, 375, 377–378, 380, 384
Little Brazil Street 161
Little India (Manhattan) 128
Little India (Queens) 272

Little Italy............. 82, 90 & *Ethnic New York* color section
Little Italy 83
   bars 366
   cafés 315
   restaurants 90, 335, 336
Little Senegal................227
Little Singer Building 78
London Terrace Apartments 117
Long Island City ... 267–270
Long Island City 268
lost property 455
Louis Armstrong House 272
Lower East Side .... 93–98, 462 & *Ethnic New York* color section
Lower East Side 94
   bars 95, 366
   cafés 316
   restaurants 94
Lower East Side Tenement Museum........................95
Ludlow Street 95

M

MacDougal Street 111
Macy's 131, 152, 154, 414
   Flower Show 441
   Thanksgiving Day Parade 154, 445
Madison Avenue 129, 138, 188, 196–199
Madison Square Garden 127, 128, 152, 155, 377, 434, 467
Madison Square Park...127
Mahayana Buddhist Temple 89
mail 38
Maine Monument 207
Majestic 211
Malcolm Shabazz Harlem Market...........226
Malcolm X 223, 226, 233
Manhattan Bridge 89, 237, 239
Manhattan Project........466
maps 33
marathon 439, 446
Marcus Garvey Park 224
Marine Midland Bank Building 55

Masjid Malcolm Shabazz mosque 226
McCarren Park 264
McKim, Mead and White 68, 128, 155, 156, 173, 251, 493
Meatpacking District 114
media 30–32
Melville, Herman.....61, 284
Merchant's House Museum 102
Met Life Building 141
MetroCard 25, 26
Metropolitan Museum of Art 170, 173–187, 464
Metropolitan Museum of Art...............................175
Metropolitan Opera House 209
Midtown East 129–146
Midtown East...............130
    bars 371
    cafés 321
    restaurants 346–348
Midtown West 152–162
Midtown West..............153
    bars 372
    cafés 322
    restaurants 348–351
mobile phones...............39
money 39
Montague Street 244
Moore, Clement Clarke 115, 117, 233
Morgan, JP 125, 126, 138, 183, 190, 463, 492
Morgan Guaranty Trust Building........................53
Morgan Library 138
Morningside Heights 204, 217–219
Morningside Heights...205
Morris–Jumel Mansion 233
Moses, Robert 78, 109, 166, 208, 216, 284, 466, 472, 492
Mott Haven...................280
Mott Street 86, 87
Mount Morris Park Historic District 224
Mount Vernon Hotel Museum and Garden.......................200
Mulberry Street 90
Municipal Building 65, 68, 75
Murray Hill 138
Museo del Barrio 228

Museum Mile................188
Museum of American Finance.........................57
Museum of American Folk Art 137
Museum of American Illustration 200
Museum of Arts & Design 137, 207
Museum of the American Indian 58
Museum of Chinese in the Americas 86
Museum of the City of New York...................196, 449
Museum of Comic and Cartoon Art.................78
Museum of Jewish Heritage 60
Museum of Modern Art 147–151, 394
Museum of Modern Art 148
Museum of Television and Radio 136
music stores 424
music venues, live 377–379
    jazz......................................379
    rock, pop, and eclectic 376–379

N

Nathan's (Coney Island) 258, 327
National Academy of Design 195
National Tennis Center 273
NBC Studios 135
Neue Galerie................192
New Jersey Devils 431, 432
New Jersey Nets 430
New York Airport Service 23, 24
New York Aquarium see Aquarium
New York Botanical Garden 277, 282, 451
New York Buddhist Church 216, 217
New York Chinese Scholar's Garden.......290
New York County Courthouse 70

New York Earth Room 80
New York Giants ...429, 430
New York Hall of Science 273, 450
New York Harbor 43, 48, 59
New–York Historical Society 212
New York Islanders 431, 432
New York Liberty 431
New York Jets 429, 430
New York Knicks ...155, 430
New York Mets ...273, 428, 429
New York/New Jersey Metrostars 432
New York Public Library ....38,132, 455 & New York Architecture color section
New York Racquet & Tennis Club 140
New York Rangers 155, 431
New York Society for Ethical Culture 207
New York State Theater 208
New York Stock Exchange 50, 52
New York Times.......30, 67, 68, 134, 157, 383
New York Transit Museum 245, 450
New York Unearthed 61
New York Yacht Club ...134
New York Yankees.......279, 428, 429, 493
Newark Airport 19, 24
newspapers 30–32
nightclubs............ 380–382
nightlife................ 376–382
Ninth Avenue........116, 159
NoLita..........................82, 92
NoLita...........................83
Noguchi, Isamu 55, 269
Noguchi Museum 269
Nuyorican Poets Café...394
NYU 99, 110

O

O'Neill, Eugene....110, 113, 492
Old Police Headquarters 91

Old Stone House..........253
Olmsted, Frederick Law
..........164, 167, 173, 216,
234, 250, 251, 292
opening hours 39
Orchard Beach 277, 286
Orchard Street...............95

P

Paine, Thomas 113
Panorama of the City of
New York 274
parades and festivals
.............440–446 & *Ethnic
New York* color section
Paris Café...............63, 331
Park Avenue......................
129, 140–142, 188, 199
Park Row..................65, 67
Park Row Building..........67
& *New York Architecture*
color section
Park Slope...........237, 253
Park Slope 250
Parker, Charlie 104
Parker, Dorothy....134, 305,
478, 493
Pearl Street.....................62
Pelham Bay Park..........286
Penn Station......19, 23, 24,
152, 155, 467
performing arts... 383–391
Pete's Tavern........123, 371
Peter Cooper Village 125,
466
pharmacies.............37, 112
Philip Morris Building
..............................141
phones...........................39
Pier 17 64
Plaza Hotel 137, 190
Plymouth Church of
Pilgrims......................243
Poe Cottage 283
Poe, Edgar Allan...........283
police......................29, 469
Police Headquarters.......70
Police Museum..............62
pool (billiards) 438
Port Authority Bus Terminal
.................20, 23, 24, 156
Powell, Reverend Adam
Clayton, Jr 223, 228,
229, 493
Promenade (Brooklyn
Heights) 244

Prospect Park 237, 249,
251
Prospect Park...............250
Prospect Park Zoo 251
PS1 Contemporary Arts
Center........................267
public holidays 39
Public Theater 102
Puerto Rican Day Parade
...................................443

Q

Queens ....265–276 &
Ethnic New York color
section
Queens.........................266
Astoria.............................. 270
Astoria.............................. 268
bars 374
cafés 327
Corona 272–275
Flushing........................... 275
Jamaica Bay and the
Rockaways 276
Long Island City........267–270
Long Island City 268
restaurants 360
Sunnyside, Woodside, and
Jackson Heights........... 271
Queens Museum of Art
...................................274
Queens Zoo.................273
Queensborough Bridge
...........................200, 202

R

radio 32
Radio City Music Hall
...................135, 161, 377
Ramble, the (Central Park)
...................................168
readings and literary events
...................................394
Red Hook 237, 247, 248
restaurants 329–362
Bronx............................... 361
Brooklyn 356–359
brunch 346
burgers 331
Chelsea 343
Chinatown, Little Italy, and
NoLita 335–337
East Village 338–340
Financial District and City Hall
.... 330
Harlem and above 355

Lower East Side.............. 337
Midtown East............346–348
Midtown West...........348–351
pizza by the pie................ 353
Queens............................. 360
quintessential New York
.... 343
Soho................................. 333
Staten Island 362
sushi................................. 332
Tribeca 331–333
Union Square, Gramercy Park,
and the Flatiron District
...................................344–346
Upper East Side........351–353
Upper West Side.......353–355
vegetarian 334
West Village...............340–343
Restaurant Row............159
Riis, Jacob.......70, 93, 276,
464, 474
Riverdale.......................285
Riverside Church..........219
Riverside Drive 204, 216,
219
Riverside Park 215
Robert F. Wagner Jr. Park
...................................60
rock climbing................438
Rockaways 266, 276
Rockefeller Center.......135,
466 & *New York
Architecture* color section
Rockefeller, John
D., Jr.................135, 145,
147, 234, 493
Roerich Museum 211
Roosevelt, Eleanor 111,
215
Roosevelt Island....188, 202
Roosevelt, Theodore
(Teddy) 63, 67, 125,
126, 213, 285
Rose Center for Earth and
Space 215, 448
Round Table, the 134
running 437
Russian Orthodox Church
of the Transfiguration
...................................264

S

safety ...25, 27, 28–30, 165
Sahadi's.........................246
St Ann's Warehouse 242,
386
St Bartholomew's Church
...................................142

St Clement's Episcopal Church 159
St George 289
St George's Church 275
St James' Church 197
St Mark's Place 103
St Mark's Church–in–the–Bowery 103
St Patrick's Cathedral 136
St Patrick's Day Parade 441
St Patrick's Old Cathedral 91
St Paul's Chapel 57
St Peter's Lutheran Church 144
St Philip's Church 227
Saks Fifth Avenue 136, 414
San Remo Apartments 211
Sarah Delano Roosevelt Memorial House 191
Schomburg Center for Research in Black Culture 225
Scorsese, Martin 70, 91
SculptureCenter 269
Seagram Building ....129, 142, 466 & *New York Architecture* color section
Second Avenue 103, 144
September 11, 2001 ....53, 55, 56, 60,61, 75, 86, 122, 469
Seventh Regiment Armory 199
Shakespeare in the Park 171
Shea Stadium 266, 273
Sharpton, Al 493
Sheep Meadow (Central Park) 168
Sheepshead Bay 260
Sheridan Square ...113, 114
shopping 408–426
  beauty and cosmetics 409
  books 410–413
  children 451
  clothing 415–421
  department stores and malls 413
  electronics........................ 414
  fashion accessories 415
  flea markets 422
  food and drink.................. 423
  music................................ 424
  sample sales 154, 420
  shoes................................ 421
  specialty 425

sporting goods 426
Shrine of St Elizabeth Seton 61
Sixth Avenue 112, 113, 116, 119, 152, 160–162
Skyscraper Museum 60
Snug Harbor Cultural Center 290
soccer...........................432
Socrates Sculpture Garden 269
Soho 73, 76–81
Soho 74
  architecture 77–81
  bars 81, 365
  cafés 314
  galleries 73, 76, 80, 81
  restaurants 81, 333
SoHo House 114
Sony Building ....139 & *New York Architecture* color section
Sony Wonder Technology Lab...............................451
Sotheby's......................201
South Beach..................291
South Bronx 277, 278–281
South Street Seaport 50, 62–64, 450
South Street Seaport Museum 61, 63, 450
Spanish Harlem 227
sports and outdoor activities 427–439
  baseball............................ 428
  basketball........................ 430
  bars 433
  beaches 434
  bicycling 434
  boating 435
  bowling............................. 435
  diving................................ 438
  fishing............................... 435
  football............................. 429
  golf 436
  health and fitness............. 436
  hiking................................ 437
  horse racing 432
  horse riding 437
  ice hockey........................ 431
  ice-skating 437
  jogging 437
  participatory sports...434–439
  pool (billiards).................. 438
  rock climbing 438
  soccer 432
  spectator sports........427–434
  tennis 433, 439
  tickets and venues........... 433
  yoga 439
Staten Island 287–293
Staten Island 288

Staten Island Botanical Garden 290
Staten Island Children's Museum.............290, 450
Staten Island Ferry 34, 43, 287, 288
Staten Island Greenbelt 292
Staten Island Institute of Arts & Sciences 289
Staten Island Yankees 289, 428
State Street 61
Statue of Liberty 44, 59
Stonewall Riots 109, 114
Strand, the...........103, 411
Strauss Park 211
Strawberry Fields (Central Park) 168, 212
street fairs.....................441
Strivers' Row 230
Studio 54 467
Studio Museum in Harlem 224
Stuyvesant Heights Historic District 255
Stuyvesant Square 125
Stuyvesant Town ...125, 466
Stuyvesant, Peter 99, 103, 126, 460
subways 23, 25, 447
summer concerts and events, free 389, 442
Sunnyside...... 271 & *Ethnic New York* color section
Sunset Park 254
Sutton Place..................145
swimming pools 436
Sylvan Terrace 233
Symphony Space 210, 388, 395

T

Tammany Hall 122, 463
Tavern on the Green....168, 354
taxis 23, 26
television 31, 32
Temple Emanu–El 190
teenagers......................453
tennis 433, 439
Tenth Avenue................118
Tenth Street Russian and Turkish Baths.....103, 436
Thanksgiving Day Parade 446

theater 384–387
Theater District 152, 156, 158
theft 29, 408
Theodore Roosevelt's birth-place 126
Theresa Towers 223
Third Avenue 144
Tiffany & Co. 79, 137
time.................................. 40
Time & Life Building 161
Time Warner Center .... 206, 414 & *New York Architecture* color section
Times Square 33, 152, 156–159, 446
Times Tower 157
tipping 456
Tin Pan Alley................. 120
TKTS..................... 158, 384
Tompkins Square Park 99, 104
tour companies 21, 34
tourist offices ... 33, 266, 277
tours......................... 33–35
trains
to and from the airport....... 23
to and from New York City 19, 24
transit information ... 23, 455
travel agents................... 21
travel insurance 37
Triangle Shirtwaist Fire 111, 464
Tribeca 73–76
Tribeca 74
bars 365
cafés 314
restaurants 331–333
TriBeCa Bridge 76
TriBeCa Cinemas............ 76
TriBeCa Film Center 75
Tribeca Film Festival....... 75
Trinity Church (Financial District) 53
Trinity Church Cemetery (Washington Heights) 233
Trump City 216
Trump, Donald..... 137, 207, 468, 493
Trump International Hotel 207
Trump Tower................. 137
Tudor City 145
Turtle Bay 144
Tweed Courthouse 65, 68
Tweed, William Marcy "Boss" 68, 254, 463, 493

U

Ukrainian Museum 103
Union Square 121–123
Union Square 122
bars 370
cafés 321
Farmers' Market....... 121, 123
restaurants 344–346
United Nations .... 129, 145, 466 & *New York Architecture* color section
Upper East Side 188–203
Upper East Side.............. 189
bars 372
cafés 323
restaurants 351–353
Upper West Side ....204–217 & *Ethnic New York* color section
Upper West Side 205
bars 372
cafés 324
restaurants 353–355
US Army Garrison Fort Hamilton 257
US Customs House........ 58 & *New York Architecture* color section
US Steel Building 57

V

Valentine-Varian House 283
Van Cortlandt House Museum.................... 284
Van Cortlandt Park 284
Vanderbilt, Cornelius ... 102, 129, 140, 190, 463
Vaux, Calvert 86, 164, 173, 213, 216, 250, 251
Varick Street 76
Verdi Square 210
Verrazano Narrows Bridge.................... 257, 287
Vietnam Veterans' Memorial 62
Village Vanguard........... 113
Village Voice 30, 107, 383
visas 37
visitors bureaus 33
Vivian Beaumont Theater 209, 385

W

Waldorf-Astoria Hotel... 131, 142
Walker, Jimmy 113, 465
walking 28, 165, 437
walking tours 34, 65, 239
Wall Street 50–52, 465
Warhol, Andy 99, 119, 123, 150, 151, 186, 198, 199, 493
Washington, George...... 52, 57, 62, 66, 109, 121, 232, 233, 238, 285, 461, 462
Washington Heights .... 220, 232–234, & *Ethnic New York* color section
Washington Heights 231
Washington Market Park 75
Washington Mews........ 111
Washington Square 101, 107, 109–112, 378
Water Street 62
Water Taxi Beach 267
Wave Hill............... 277, 285
Weather Underground, the 112
Weeksville...................... 255
West Broadway 80
West Indian-American Day Parade .... 256, 445 & *Ethnic New York* color section
West Village......... 107–114
West Village 108
bars 368–370
cafés 318–320
restaurants 340–343
Wharton, Edith 120
White Horse Tavern...... 114
Whitman, Walt 96, 97, 241, 464
Whitney at Philip Morris 141
Whitney Museum of American Art............. 141, 197–199
Wildlife Refuge, Jamaica Bay 276
Williamsburg .... 237, 260–263 & *Ethnic New York* color section
Williamsburg Bridge 96, 239, 260
Williamsburg Savings Bank 245
Winter Garden 61

Wollman Memorial Rink
.... 166
women travelers 29, 40
Woodlawn Cemetery 284
Woodside 265,
271 & *Ethnic New York*
color section
Woolworth Building 65,
67, 75, 465 & *New York
Architecture* color section
work visas 38
working 38

World Financial Center ... 61
World Trade Center 50,
55, 56, 75, 467, 469

Y

Yankee Stadium 277,
279, 429, 434
Yankee Stadium 280
YMCAs 311

yoga 439
Yonah Schimmel's ... 95, 316
Yorkville 201

Z

Zabar's 210, 325
Zenger, John Peter 52,
460

Map symbols

Interstate		▲	Peak
US highway		✈	Airport
State highway		Ⓜ	Subway station
Railway		⊞	Hospital
Ferry route		♠	Buddhist temple
Coastline/river		✡	Synagogue
Chapter division boundary		⸸	Cemetery
State boundary		ⓘ	Information center
Borough/county boundary		⊠	Post office
Tunnel			Building
Point of Interest			Church
Fountain			Park/wildlife refuge
Lighthouse			Beach

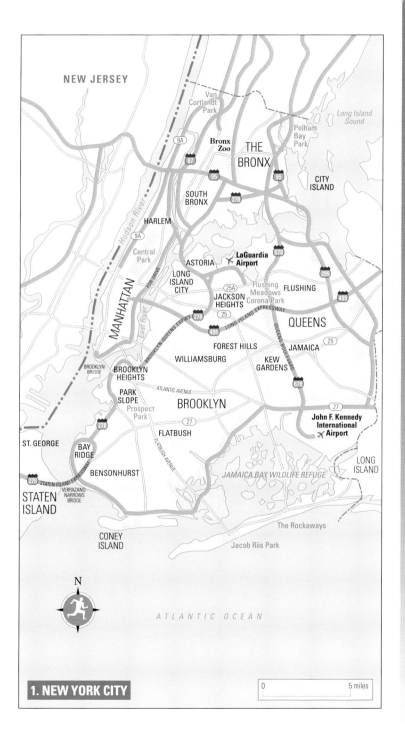

1. NEW YORK CITY

0   5 miles

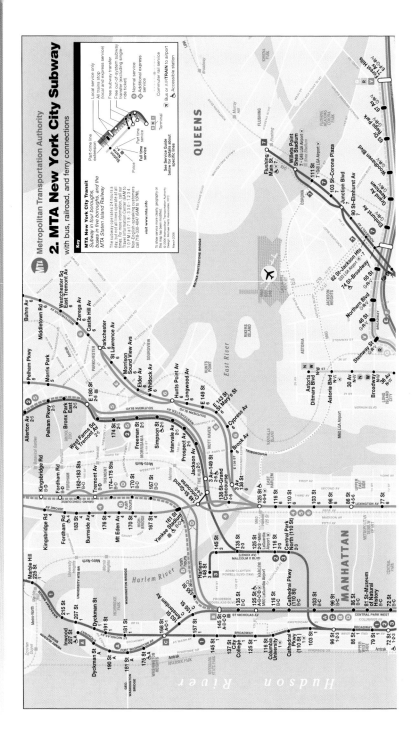

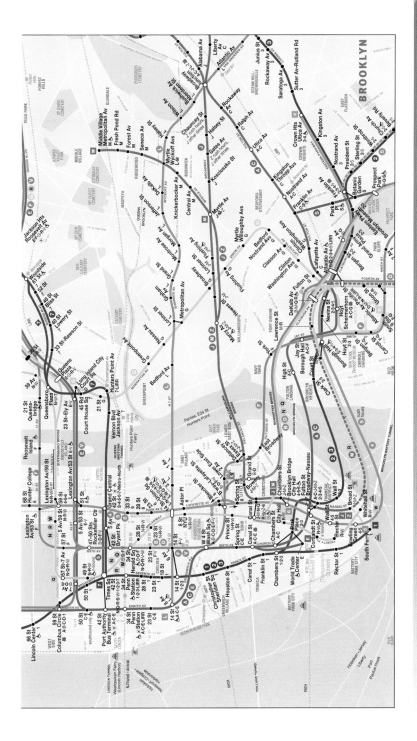

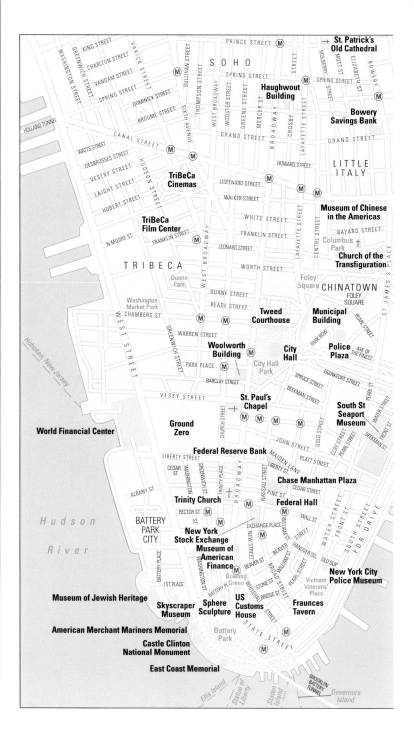

KING STREET
CHARLTON STREET
VANDAM STREET
SPRING STREET
DOMINICK STREET
BROOME STREET

WASHINGTON STREET
GREENWICH STREET

VARICK STREET

SULLIVAN STREET
THOMPSON STREET
WEST BROADWAY
WOOSTER STREET
GREENE STREET
MERCER ST
BROADWAY
CROSBY
LAFAYETTE STREET

PRINCE STREET Ⓜ

→ St. Patrick's
Old Cathedral

S O H O

SPRING STREET

SPRING STREET Ⓜ

Haughwout
Building

MULBERRY STREET
MOTT ST
ELIZABETH ST
BOWERY

Ⓜ

Ⓜ

Bowery
Savings Bank

HOLLAND TUNNEL

CANAL STREET

SIXTH AVENUE

GRAND STREET

GRAND STREET

WATTS STREET
DESBROSSES STREET
VESTRY STREET
LAIGHT STREET
HUBERT STREET

HUDSON STREET

Ⓜ

Ⓜ

TriBeCa
Cinemas

HOWARD STREET

LISPENARD STREET Ⓜ

WALKER STREET

LITTLE
ITALY

N MOORE ST

TriBeCa
Film Center

FRANKLIN STREET

BROADWAY

WHITE STREET

FRANKLIN STREET

LEONARD STREET

Ⓜ

Ⓜ

Ⓜ

Museum of Chinese
in the Americas

LAFAYETTE STREET
CENTRE STREET

BAYARD STREET

Columbus
Park

Church of the
Transfiguration

T R I B E C A

WEST BROADWAY

WORTH STREET

Duane
Park

Foley
Square CHINATOWN

FOLEY
SQUARE

ST JAMES PLACE

Washington
Market Park

WEST STREET

DUANE STREET

READE STREET

CHAMBERS ST Ⓜ

WARREN STREET

Ⓜ

Tweed
Courthouse

Municipal
Building

PEARL STREET

Hoboken, New Jersey

GREENWICH STREET

Woolworth
Building Ⓜ

PARK PLACE Ⓜ

City
Hall

City Hall
Park

PARK ROW

Police
Plaza

AVE OF
THE FINEST

BARCLAY STREET

FRANKFORT STREET

SPRUCE STREET

PEARL STREET

VESEY STREET

St. Paul's
Chapel

CHURCH STREET

Ⓜ Ⓜ

BEEKMAN STREET

South St
Seaport
Museum

WATER STREET
FRONT STREET
BEEKMAN ST

World Financial Center

Ground
Zero

Federal Reserve Bank

LIBERTY STREET

CEDAR
ST

WASHINGTON ST

GREENWICH ST

TRINITY PLACE

BROADWAY

NASSAU STREET

MAIDEN LANE

LIBERTY ST

PLATT STREET

JOHN STREET

GOLD STREET
CLIFF STREET
PEARL STREET

Chase Manhattan Plaza

ALBANY ST

Trinity Church

RECTOR ST Ⓜ

CEDAR ST

PINE ST

Federal Hall

WALL ST

WATER STREET
FRONT ST
SOUTH STREET
FDR DRIVE

H u d s o n

BATTERY
PARK
CITY

New York
Stock Exchange

EXCHANGE PLACE

Ⓜ

NEW STREET

BEAVER ST

WILLIAM STREET
HANOVER SQ
OLD SLIP

R i v e r

BATTERY PLACE

Museum of
American
Finance Ⓜ

WASHINGTON ST

BEAVER ST

BROAD STREET

STONE ST

PEARL STREET

New York City
Police Museum

Museum of Jewish Heritage

1ST PLACE

BATTERY PL

Bowling
Green Ⓜ

Skyscraper
Museum

Sphere
Sculpture

US
Customs
House

WHITEHALL ST
BRIDGE ST

Vietnam
Veterans'
Plaza

Fraunces
Tavern

American Merchant Mariners Memorial

STATE STREET

Battery
Park Ⓜ

Castle Clinton
National Monument

East Coast Memorial

Ellis Island

Statue of
Liberty

Staten Island

BROOKLYN
BATTERY
TUNNEL

Governors
Island

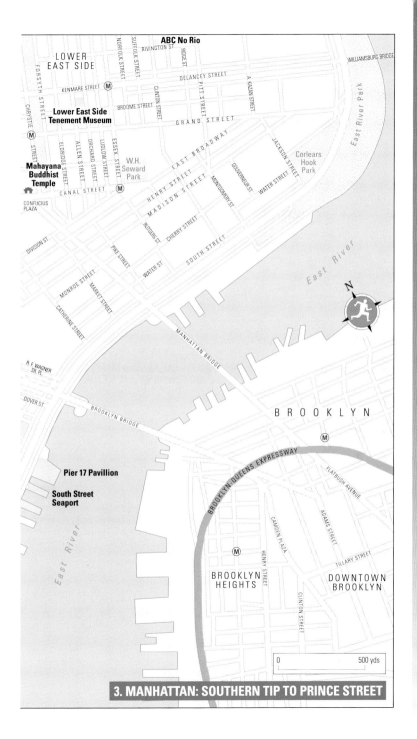

ABC No Rio

LOWER EAST SIDE

WILLIAMSBURG BRIDGE

RIVINGTON ST

NORFOLK STREET
SUFFOLK STREET
RIDGE ST

FORSYTH STREET

DELANCEY STREET

KENMARE STREET (M)

CLINTON STREET
PITT STREET
A KAZAN STREET

BROOME STREET

Lower East Side
Tenement Museum

GRAND STREET

CHRYSTIE STREET

(M)

EAST BROADWAY

JACKSON STREET
GOUVERNEUR ST
WATER STREET

Corlears
Hook
Park

ELDRIDGE STREET
ALLEN STREET
ORCHARD STREET
LUDLOW STREET
ESSEX STREET

W.H.
Seward
Park

East River Park

Mahayana
Buddhist
Temple

CANAL STREET

(M)

HENRY STREET
MADISON STREET
MONTGOMERY ST

CONFUCIUS
PLAZA

RUTGERS ST

CHERRY STREET

DIVISION ST

PIKE STREET

SOUTH STREET

WATER ST

East River

MONROE STREET
MARKET STREET

CATHERINE STREET

N

R. F. WAGNER
SR. PL.

DOVER ST

MANHATTAN BRIDGE

BROOKLYN BRIDGE

BROOKLYN

(M)

Pier 17 Pavillion

BROOKLYN-QUEENS EXPRESSWAY

FLATBUSH AVENUE

South Street
Seaport

East River

CAMDEN PLAZA

ADAMS STREET

(M)

HENRY STREET

TILLARY STREET

BROOKLYN
HEIGHTS

DOWNTOWN
BROOKLYN

CLINTON STREET

0   500 yds

3. MANHATTAN: SOUTHERN TIP TO PRINCE STREET

Intrepid Sea, Air & Space Museum

Circle Line Ferry

LINCOLN TUNNEL

TO N.J.

N.J.

Algonquin Hotel

International Center of Photography

W 47TH ST
W 46TH ST
W 45TH ST
W 44TH ST
W 43RD ST
W 42ND ST
W 41ST ST
W 40TH ST
W 39TH ST

ELEVENTH AVENUE
TENTH AVENUE
NINTH AVENUE
EIGHTH AVENUE
SEVENTH AVENUE
SIXTH AVENUE
FIFTH AVE

WEST SIDE HIGHWAY

TIMES SQUARE

BROADWAY

Bryant Park

New York Public Library

Port Authority Bus Terminal

Jacob Javits Convention Center

W 38TH ST
W 37TH ST
W 36TH ST
W 35TH ST
W 34TH ST
W 33RD ST

GARMENT

DISTRICT **Macy's** HERALD SQUARE

Empire State Building

Pennsylvania Station GREELEY SQUARE

General Post Office ✉

Madison Square Garden

W 32ND ST

Church of the Transfiguration †

W 31ST ST
W 30TH ST
W 29TH ST
W 28TH ST Chelsea Park
W 26TH ST
W 25TH ST
W 24TH ST

London Terrace Apartments

FIFTH AVENUE

Madison Square Park

W 23RD ST
W 22ND ST
W 21ST ST
W 20TH ST
W 19TH ST
W 18TH ST
W 17TH ST
W 16TH ST
W 15TH ST

C H E L S E A

Flatiron Building

BROADWAY

Chelsea Hotel

Chelsea Piers

Chelsea Market

W 14TH ST

Forbes Galleries

W 13TH ST
LITTLE W 12TH ST
GANSEVOORT ST
HORATIO ST
JANE ST
GREENWICH

GREENWICH AVENUE

First Presbyterian Church →

W 11TH ST

Church of the Ascension →

W 10TH ST
W 9TH ST
W 8TH ST

MEATPACKING DISTRICT

ABINGDON SQUARE

W 12TH ST
BETHUNE ST
GREENWICH ST
HUDSON ST
BLEECKER STREET
W 4TH ST
BANK ST

Jefferson Market Courthouse WAVERLEY PL

WASHINGTON SQ N
Washington Square Park
WASHINGTON SQ S

W E S T
V I L L A G E

SHERIDAN SQUARE W WASHINGTON PL

JONES ST
CORNELIA ST

WEST SIDE HIGHWAY

CHRISTOPHER STREET
GROVE ST
BARROW ST
MORTON ST
LEROY ST
CLARKSON ST
CHARLTON STREET

BEDFORD STREET
CARMINE STREET
DOWNING ST
WEST

BARROW ST

SEVENTH AVENUE

SIXTH AVENUE

HOUSTON STREET

MACDOUGAL ST
BLEECKER ST

SULLIVAN ST
THOMPSON ST
WOOSTER ST

KING STREET

S O H O

Hudson River

N

0   500 yds

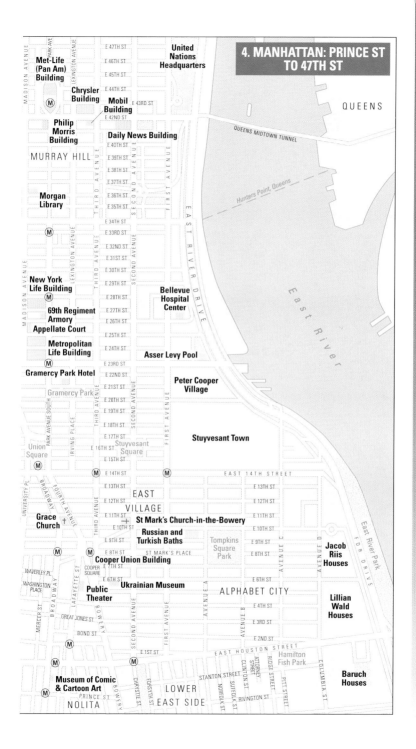

QUEENS

Met-Life (Pan Am) Building

Chrysler Building

Mobil Building

Philip Morris Building

Daily News Building

MURRAY HILL

Morgan Library

New York Life Building

69th Regiment Armory

Appellate Court

Metropolitan Life Building

Gramercy Park Hotel

Gramercy Park

Union Square

United Nations Headquarters

QUEENS MIDTOWN TUNNEL

Hunters Point, Queens

East River

Bellevue Hospital Center

Asser Levy Pool

Peter Cooper Village

Stuyvesant Town

Stuyvesant Square

EAST VILLAGE

St Mark's Church-in-the-Bowery

Russian and Turkish Baths

Tompkins Square Park

East River Park

FDR DRIVE

Jacob Riis Houses

Grace Church

Cooper Union Building

Ukrainian Museum

Public Theater

ALPHABET CITY

Lillian Wald Houses

Museum of Comic & Cartoon Art

NOLITA

LOWER EAST SIDE

Hamilton Fish Park

Baruch Houses

MADISON AVENUE

PARK AVE

LEXINGTON AVENUE

E 47TH ST

E 46TH ST

E 45TH ST

E 44TH ST

E 43RD ST

E 42ND ST

E 40TH ST

E 39TH ST

E 38TH ST

E 37TH ST

E 36TH ST

E 35TH ST

E 34TH ST

E 33RD ST

E 32ND ST

E 31ST ST

E 30TH ST

E 29TH ST

E 28TH ST

E 27TH ST

E 26TH ST

E 25TH ST

E 24TH ST

E 23RD ST

E 22ND ST

E 21ST ST

E 20TH ST

E 19TH ST

E 18TH ST

E 17TH ST

E 16TH ST

E 15TH ST

E 14TH ST

EAST 14TH STREET

E 13TH ST

E 12TH ST

E 11TH ST

E 10TH ST

E 9TH ST

ST MARK'S PLACE

E 8TH ST

E 7TH ST

E 6TH ST

E 5TH ST

E 4TH ST

E 3RD ST

E 2ND ST

EAST HOUSTON STREET

STANTON STREET

RIVINGTON ST

E 1ST ST

PRINCE ST

THIRD AVENUE

SECOND AVENUE

FIRST AVENUE

MADISON AVENUE

LEXINGTON AVENUE

THIRD AVENUE

SECOND AVENUE

FIRST AVENUE

PARK AVENUE SOUTH

IRVING PLACE

THIRD AVENUE

SECOND AVENUE

FIRST AVENUE

AVENUE A

AVENUE B

AVENUE C

AVENUE D

UNIVERSITY PL

BROADWAY

FOURTH AVENUE

LAFAYETTE ST

COOPER SQUARE

WAVERLEY PL

WASHINGTON PLACE

MERCER ST

BROADWAY

GREAT JONES ST

BOND ST

BOWERY

CHRYSTIE ST

FORSYTH ST

CHRISTIE ST

STANTON STREET

CLINTON ST

ATTORNEY STREET

RIDGE STREET

SUFFOLK ST

NORFOLK ST

PITT STREET

COLUMBIA ST

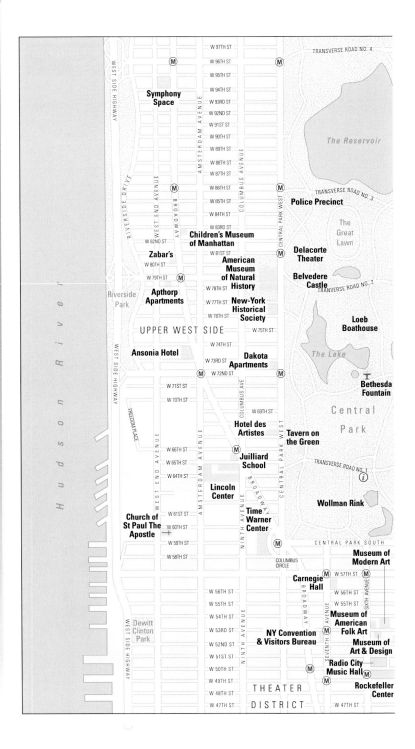

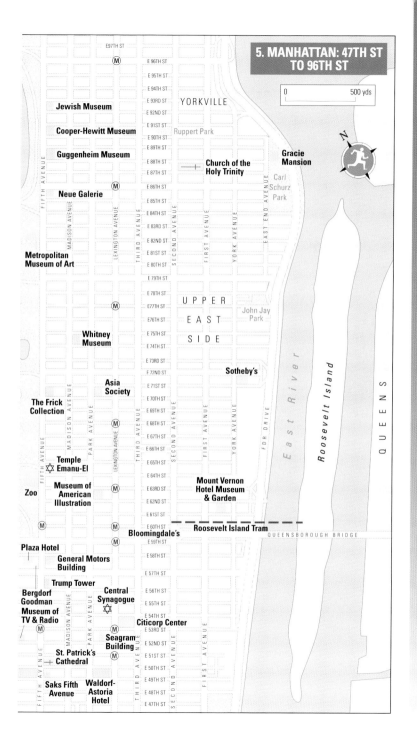

0   500 yds

E 97TH ST

E 96TH ST

E 95TH ST

E 94TH ST

E 93RD ST   YORKVILLE

Jewish Museum   E 92ND ST

E 91ST ST

Cooper-Hewitt Museum   Ruppert Park

E 90TH ST

E 89TH ST   Gracie
Mansion
Guggenheim Museum   E 88TH ST   Church of the
Holy Trinity   Carl
E 87TH ST   Schurz
E 86TH ST   Park

Neue Galerie   E 85TH ST

E 84TH ST

FIFTH AVENUE

MADISON AVENUE

LEXINGTON AVENUE

THIRD AVENUE

SECOND AVENUE

FIRST AVENUE

YORK AVENUE

EAST END AVENUE

E 83RD ST

E 82ND ST

E 81ST ST

Metropolitan
Museum of Art   E 80TH ST

E 79TH ST

E 78TH ST

E 77TH ST   U P P E R

E 76TH ST   E A S T   John Jay
Park
Whitney   E 75TH ST
Museum   S I D E
E 74TH ST

E 73RD ST

E 72ND ST

Asia   Sotheby's
Society   E 71ST ST

E 70TH ST

The Frick
Collection   E 69TH ST

E 68TH ST

MADISON AVENUE

PARK AVENUE

LEXINGTON AVENUE

THIRD AVENUE

SECOND AVENUE

FIRST AVENUE

YORK AVENUE

FDR DRIVE

East River

Roosevelt Island

QUEENS

E 67TH ST

E 66TH ST

Temple   E 65TH ST
Emanu-El

FIFTH AVENUE

E 64TH ST

Museum of   E 63RD ST
American   Mount Vernon
Zoo   Illustration   Hotel Museum
E 62ND ST   & Garden

E 61ST ST

E 60TH ST

Bloomingdale's   Roosevelt Island Tram

E 59TH ST   QUEENSBOROUGH BRIDGE

Plaza Hotel

E 58TH ST
General Motors
Building   E 57TH ST

Trump Tower   E 56TH ST
Central
Bergdorf   Synagogue   E 55TH ST
Goodman
Museum of   E 54TH ST
TV & Radio   Citicorp Center
E 53RD ST

MADISON AVENUE

PARK AVENUE

Seagram   E 52ND ST
Building
St. Patrick's   E 51ST ST

FIRST AVENUE

SECOND AVENUE

THIRD AVENUE

Cathedral   E 50TH ST

E 49TH ST

Saks Fifth   Waldorf-
Avenue   Astoria   E 48TH ST
Hotel   E 47TH ST

FIFTH AVENUE

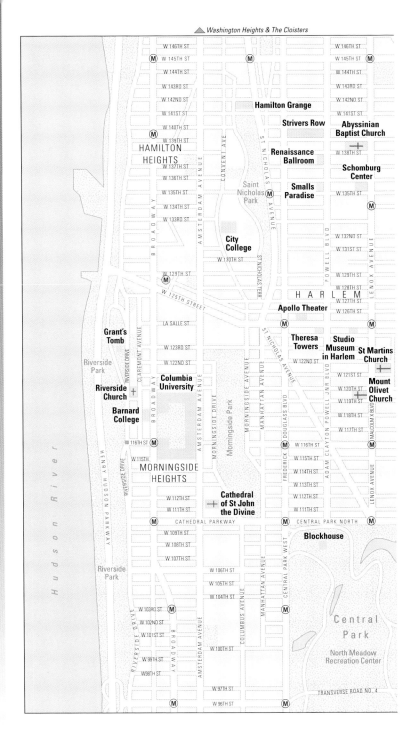

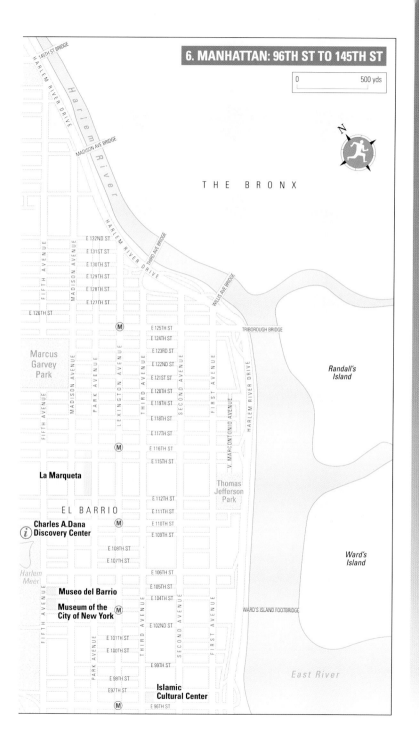

6. MANHATTAN: 96TH ST TO 145TH ST

0   500 yds

N

THE BRONX

145TH ST BRIDGE

HARLEM RIVER DRIVE

MADISON AVE BRIDGE

Harlem River

HARLEM RIVER DRIVE

THIRD AVE BRIDGE

WILLIS AVE BRIDGE

E 132ND ST
E 131ST ST
E 130TH ST
E 129TH ST
E 128TH ST
E 127TH ST

E 126TH ST

FIFTH AVENUE

MADISON AVENUE

TRIBOROUGH BRIDGE

Randall's Island

Ⓜ

E 125TH ST
E 124TH ST
E 123RD ST
E 122ND ST
E 121ST ST
E 120TH ST
E 119TH ST
E 118TH ST
E 117TH ST

Marcus Garvey Park

MADISON AVENUE

PARK AVENUE

LEXINGTON AVENUE

THIRD AVENUE

SECOND AVENUE

FIRST AVENUE

V. MARCANTONIO AVENUE

HARLEM RIVER DRIVE

FIFTH AVENUE

Ⓜ

E 116TH ST
E 115TH ST

La Marqueta

E 112TH ST
E 111TH ST
E 110TH ST
E 109TH ST

EL BARRIO

Ⓜ

ⓘ **Charles A. Dana Discovery Center**

E 108TH ST
E 107TH ST

Thomas Jefferson Park

Ward's Island

E 106TH ST
E 105TH ST

Harlem Meer

Museo del Barrio

E 104TH ST

Museum of the City of New York Ⓜ

FIFTH AVENUE

PARK AVENUE

THIRD AVENUE

SECOND AVENUE

FIRST AVENUE

WARD'S ISLAND FOOTBRIDGE

E 102ND ST
E 101TH ST
E 100TH ST
E 99TH ST
E 98TH ST
E 97TH ST

Islamic Cultural Center

Ⓜ

E 96TH ST

East River

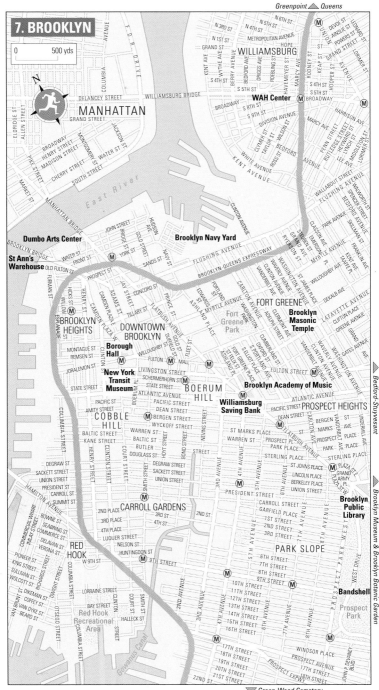

Greenpoint ▲ Queens

7. BROOKLYN

0   500 yds

N 6TH ST
N 5TH ST
N 3RD ST   N 4TH ST
N 1ST ST
METROPOLITAN AVENUE
GRAND AVE
HOPE
WILLIAMSBURG

DELANCEY STREET
WILLIAMSBURG BRIDGE

MANHATTAN
GRAND STREET

BROADWAY

WAH Center Ⓜ BROADWAY

DIVISION AVENUE

East River

KENT AVENUE

WHITE AVENUE

Dumbo Arts Center

Brooklyn Navy Yard

St Ann's Warehouse

FLUSHING AVENUE

BROOKLYN-QUEENS EXPRESSWAY

BROOKLYN HEIGHTS

DOWNTOWN BROOKLYN

FORT GREENE

Fort Greene Park

Brooklyn Masonic Temple

Borough Hall

New York Transit Museum

BOERUM HILL

Brooklyn Academy of Music

Williamsburg Saving Bank

PROSPECT HEIGHTS

ATLANTIC AVENUE

COBBLE HILL

CARROLL GARDENS

PARK SLOPE

RED HOOK

Red Hook Recreational Area

Gowanus Canal

Brooklyn Public Library

Bandshell

Prospect Park

Bedford-Stuyvesant ▶

Brooklyn Museum & Brooklyn Botanic Garden ▶

▼ Green-Wood Cemetery